HANA HIGHWAY (left) Maui's most famous road, the Hana Highway, is a destination in itself, not just the route to one. Hugging the windy, rocky coastline, this 50-mile road traverses awe-inspiring seascapes, tumbling waterfalls, and lush rainforests.

Thousands of cars take this wiggle of a road every day. Too many of them rush to "get there," not realizing there is no "there"—the road is the "there." Take your time, stop to smell the ginger, jump in a freshwater pool, and watch the clouds float by.

MOLOKINI (above) Like a crescent moon fallen from the sky, the remains of the crater of Molokini, about halfway between Maui and the uninhabited island of Kahoolawe, is a dream destination for snorkel and dive enthusiasts. Tilted so that only the thin rim of its southern side shows above water in a perfect semicircle, Molokini stands like a scoop against the tide, and serves, on its concave side, as a natural sanctuary for tropical fish.

SILVERSWORD (left) The silversword, a rare plant, grows high on the slopes of 10,000ft. Haleakala and blooms only once a year (between July and September). A relative of the sunflower family, the silversword looks like a pine cone with a fountain of red-petaled, daisy-like flowers that turn silver soon after blooming.

PROTEA (below) Originally from South Africa, and looking more like something from outer space, proteas come in more than 40 different varieties, ranging from pincushions (pictured) to something resembling a bouquet of feathers. Grown on the slopes of Haleakala, proteas are a long-lasting cut flower, and will last up to a year if dried.

KAHAKULOA (above) Nestled in a crevice between two steep hills, along the very narrow Kahekili Highway, is the picturesque village of Kahakuloa, composed of a few weather-worn houses, a church with a red-tile roof, and vivid green taro patches. The village gets its name from the 636ft. high "Kahakuloa" (or tall lord) Head rising at the edge of the bay.

LEIS (right) Nothing says Hawaii like a lei. The tropical beauty of the delicate garland, the delicious sweet fragrance of the blossoms, the sensual way the flowers curl softly around your neck—getting lei'd in Hawaii is a sensuous experience.

WINDSURFING AT HOOKIPA (left) With constant wind and endless waves, Hookipa Beach Park, on Maui's windward side, attracts top windsurfers from around the globe. The best place to watch these athletes leap over the waves is on the grassy cliffs above the beach. They take to the water after noon (board surfers claim the waves in the morning).

IAO NEEDLE (below) Jetting up at an impressive 2,250ft., the Iao Needle is actually the eroded remnant of a basaltic core that sits in the volcanic caldera of the West Maui Mountains. Before Westerners came to Maui, the Needle was a sacred place where Hawaiians came to honor their gods. They named the valley where the Needle stands Iao, or "supreme light."

© Clay M. Rogers/Alamy

© Adina Tovy Amsel/Lonely Planet Images

HUMPBACK WHALE (above) Visitors to Maui come in all sizes. Maui's largest visitors—the humpback whales—are also its most faithful, arriving every year around December and staying until April. Humpbacks migrate from Alaska to the Hawaiian Islands to mate and calve. As big as a city bus and weighing several tons each, these frolicking leviathans are easy to spot from shore, off the coasts of Maui, Molokai and Lanai.

SURFING PEAHI (right) The massive waves at Peahi, which the local residents call Jaws (because the waves can eat you up), have always been there—but for years, they were too far off shore, too big, coming in too fast for surfers to catch and ride them. About a decade ago, surfers like Laird Hamilton started experimenting, using jet boats to tow a surfer far offshore and bring him up to speed, before whipping him into the path of these giants (some waves as high as 60ft.). Jaws has been conquered.

ONELOA BEACH (left) The Hawaiians called this white-sand beach "Oneloa," which means long sand. The local residents know it as "Big Beach," and at 3,300ft. long and 100ft. wide it is one of Maui's most popular. When the water is calm, this picture-perfect beach is great for swimming, fishing, and surfing. Snorkeling is great at the north end, around Puu Olai, a 360ft. cinder cone. But when a storm rolls in, the waves can lash the shore with a strong rip current around the steep drop-off, making it dangerous for inexperienced open-ocean swimmers.

HALEAKALA (above) Driving, hiking, or biking through the otherworldly landscape of Haleakala (House of the Sun) National Park is an experience not to be missed. Here you can hike above the clouds and peer down into Haleakala crater, which, at 7.5 miles long by 2.5 miles wide by 3,000ft. deep, is big enough to swallow Manhattan. To the Hawaiians, 10,000ft. Haleakala, a dormant volcano, was a spiritual place where kahuna (priests) performed rituals. Today it's home to two of Hawaii's most endangered species: nene (Hawaiian geese) and silversword plants.

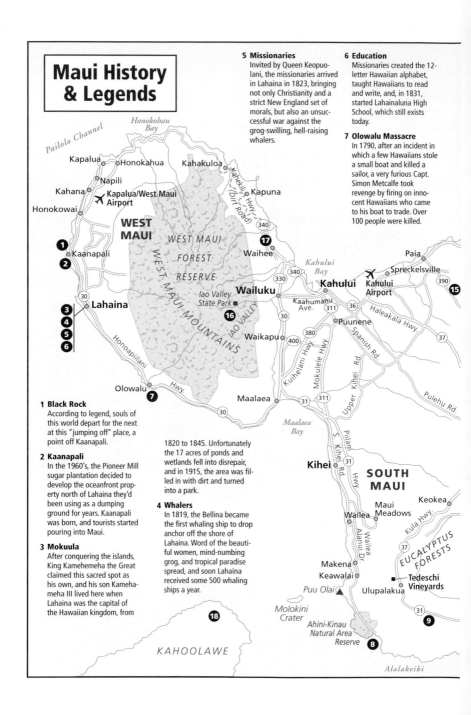

Maui History & Legends

5 Missionaries
Invited by Queen Keopuo-
lani, the missionaries arrived
in Lahaina in 1823, bringing
not only Christianity and a
strict New England set of
morals, but also an unsuccessful war against the
grog-swilling, hell-raising
whalers.

6 Education
Missionaries created the 12-
letter Hawaiian alphabet,
taught Hawaiians to read
and write, and, in 1831,
started Lahainaluna High
School, which still exists
today.

7 Olowalu Massacre
In 1790, after an incident in
which a few Hawaiians stole
a small boat and killed a
sailor, a very furious Capt.
Simon Metcalfe took
revenge by firing on inno-
cent Hawaiians who came
to his boat to trade. Over
100 people were killed.

1 Black Rock
According to legend, souls of
this world depart for the next
at this "jumping off" place, a
point off Kaanapali.

2 Kaanapali
In the 1960's, the Pioneer Mill
sugar plantation decided to
develop the oceanfront property north of Lahaina they'd
been using as a dumping
ground for years. Kaanapali
was born, and tourists started
pouring into Maui.

3 Mokuula
After conquering the islands,
King Kamehemeha the Great
claimed this sacred spot as
his own, and his son Kamehameha III lived here when
Lahaina was the capital of
the Hawaiian kingdom, from

1820 to 1845. Unfortunately
the 17 acres of ponds and
wetlands fell into disrepair,
and in 1915, the area was filled in with dirt and turned
into a park.

4 Whalers
In 1819, the Bellina became
the first whaling ship to drop
anchor off the shore of
Lahaina. Word of the beautiful women, mind-numbing
grog, and tropical paradise
spread, and soon Lahaina
received some 500 whaling
ships a year.

8 La Perouse
The first European explorer to set foot on Maui was Admiral Comte de la Perouse, in 1786. He didn't like the "burning climate" of Kihei and sailed off.

9 Cape Kinau
Overlooking La Perouse Bay is the site of the last lava flow on Maui, estimated to have occurred in the 1790's.

10 Haleakala
Maui, the demi-god whom the island is named after, is said to have stood atop Haleakala and lassoed the sun to slow down its daily path across the sky.

11 Sugar
The first successful sugar plantation, once the largest industry on Maui, was started by George Wilfong in 1849, along the Hana coast.

12 Kuiki Hill
Kaahumanu, born in a cave in this prominent point on Hana Bay in 1768, had a huge impact on Hawaiian culture despite such humble beginnings. After the death of her husband Kamehameha in 1820, she helped end Hawaii's *kapu* (taboo) system by sitting down and eating with men—a major *kapu* at the time.

13 Piilanihale Heiau
This *heiau* (temple), the largest in the state was named for one of Maui's greatest chiefs, Piilani, who united the island of Maui in the 15th century.

14 1946 Tsunami
In 1946, an earthquake in the Aleutian Islands caused a tsunami that slammed into the Hana coastline, devastating the village of Hamoa and sweeping clean most of the buildings on the Keanae Peninsula.

15 Haiku Ditch
Claus Spreckels changed the face of Maui when he built the 30-mile Haiku Ditch in 1878. The ditch brought 50 million gallons of water a day from rain-rich Haiku to arid, dry Puunene to irrigate his sugar fields.

16 Kepaniwai
In 1790, in his effort to gain control of all the Hawaiian islands, Kamehameha and his men fought and won a bloody battle in Iao Valley that left the Iao Stream blocked with fallen bodies, giving the area the name Kepaniwai, or "damming of the waters."

17 Halekii-Pihana Heiau
These two *heiau*, built in 1240, sit on a hill with a commanding view of central Maui and Haleakala. Kahekili, the last chief of Maui, lived here.

18 Kahoolawe
The U.S. military took over this island, a sacred site to Hawaiians, during World War II and used it as a bombing target until 1993, when it was returned to the state.

The Road to Hana

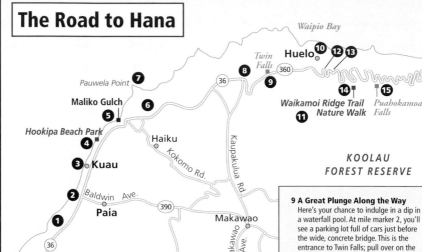

Waipio Bay

Huelo ⑩ ⑫ ⑬

Twin Falls 360

⑧ ⑨

36

⑭ ⑮

Pauwela Point ⑦

Waikamoi Ridge Trail *Puahokamoa*
Nature Walk *Falls*
⑪

Maliko Gulch ⑥

⑤

Hookipa Beach Park

④

Haiku

③ **Kuau**

Kokomo Rd.

Kaupakulua Rd.

**KOOLAU
FOREST RESERVE**

② *Baldwin* Ave.

Paia

390

Makawao

Makawao Ave.

①

36

Halaeakala Hwy.

Airport   To Kahului

37

1 Before You Start
Fill up your gas tank before you get to Paia. Gas in Paia is very expensive, and it's the last place for gas until you get to Hana.

2 Paia
The former plantation village of Paia was once a thriving sugar-mill town. Today, chic eateries and trendy shops stand next door to mom-and-pop establishments.

3 Kuau
After you leave Paia you'll pass the Kuau Mart on your left. The road then bends into an S-turn; in the middle of the S is the entrance to Mama's Fish House and an adjacent small sandy cove. Ocean access is treacherous, but the beach is a great place to sit and soak up some sun.

4 Hookipa Beach Park
A mile from Mama's, just before mile marker 9, is a place known around the world as one of the greatest windsurfing spots on the planet: Hookipa Beach Park.

5 Maliko Gulch
At mile marker 10, look for the road on your right, which goes under the bridge and past a rodeo arena, and on to the rocky beach at Maliko Bay. The 1946 tidal wave wiped out the once-thriving community at the mouth of the bay. If the surf is up, it's a great place to watch the waves.

6 Haiku
Around mile marker 11, you'll pass through the rural area of Haiku, with banana patches, cane grass blowing in the wind, and forests of guava trees, avocados, and kukui trees. This was once a thriving pineapple area, but lately million-dollar homes have become the new crop.

7 Jaws
If it's winter and the waves are up, stop here to watch expert surfers battle the mammoth waves off Pauwela Point at an area known as Jaws (as in, the waves can chew you up). To get there, turn left off the Hana Highway at Hahana Road, between mile markers 13 and 14. Park where the paved road ends, and hike about a mile and a half along the private dirt road (Maui Land and Pine property) to the ocean. Practice aloha-don't park in the pineapple fields, and hands off the pineapples.

8 Change in Miles
At mile marker 16, the curves begin, one right after another. Slow down and enjoy the view of bucolic rolling hills, mango trees, and vibrant ferns. After mile marker 16, the road is still called the Hana Highway, but the number changes from Highway 36 to Highway 360, and the mile markers go back to 0.

9 A Great Plunge Along the Way
Here's your chance to indulge in a dip in a waterfall pool. At mile marker 2, you'll see a parking lot full of cars just before the wide, concrete bridge. This is the entrance to Twin Falls; pull over on the mountain side and park. Be aware that this is private property and trespassing is illegal in Hawaii. If you decide that you want to "risk it," from the gate you have a 3 to 5 minute walk to the first waterfall and pool, then you can continue on another 10 to 15 minutes to the second, larger waterfall and pool (don't go in if it has been raining).

10 Hidden Huelo
Just before mile marker 4 on a blind curve, look for a double row of mailboxes on the left-hand side by the pay phone. Down the road lies a hidden Hawaii, where ocean waves pummel soaring lava cliffs and serenity prevails. Only a few hundred people live among the scattered homes on this windswept land. The lone tourist attraction in Huelo is the historic 1853 Kaulanapueo Church.

11 Koolau Forest Reserve
After Huelo, you'll reach the edge of the lush Koolau Forest Reserve. The coastline here gets about 60 to 80 inches of rain a year, and farther up the mountain, the rainfall is 200 to 300 inches a year. Here you will see 20- to 30-foot-tall guava trees, mangos, java plums, and avocados the size of softballs.

12 Dangerous Curves
About a half mile after mile marker 6, there's a sharp U-curve in the road, going uphill. The road is practically one lane here, so sound your horn at the start of the U-curve to let approaching cars know you are coming. Take this curve, as well as those coming up in the next several miles, very slowly.

Map showing locations along the Hana Highway including Keanae, Wailua, Nahiku, Hana, Waianapanapa State Park, Kaumahina State Wayside Park, Keanae Arboretum, Puaa Kaa State Wayside Park, and numbered points of interest 16-25.

13 Kaaiea Bridge
Just before mile marker 7 is a forest of waving bamboo. For the best view, pull over at the Kaaiea Bridge, just after mile marker 7, and look back.

14 Family Hike
At mile marker 9, there's a small state wayside area with restrooms, a pavilion, picnic tables, and a barbecue area. The well-marked Waikamoi Ridge Trail is an easy three-quarter-mile loop that meanders through eucalyptus, ferns, and hala trees.

15 Warning-Use Caution
As you approach the 11 mile marker, the highway becomes a congested one-lane road due to all the cars parked along it (they're stopping for Puohokamoa Falls, which I no longer recommend because it's overrun with tourists), so drive slowly and safely through this area.

16 Photo Op
Just past mile marker 12 is the Kaumahina (Moonrise) State Wayside Park. Not only is this a good pit stop (restrooms are available here) and a wonderful place to have a picnic (tables and barbecue area), but the view of the rugged coastline makes an excellent photo-you can see all the way down to the jutting Keanae Peninsula.

17 Honomanu Bay Beach Park
Turn left just after mile marker 14; the rutted dirt-and-cinder road takes you down to the rocky black-sand beach of Honomanu. There are no facilities here, but it's a popular site among surfers and net fishermen. There are strong rip currents offshore, so swimming is best in the stream inland from the ocean. Stand on the beach and turn to look back on the steep cliffs covered with vegetation.

18 Keanae Arboretum
Between mile markers 16 and 17 you'll see a cluster of bunkhouses belonging to the YMCA Camp Keanae. A quarter-mile down is the Keanae Arboretum. You can visit the arboretum, swim in the pools of Piinaau Stream, or press on along a mile-long trail into Keanae Valley and a lovely tropical rainforest.

19 Keanae Peninsula
The old Hawaiian village of Keanae stands out against the Pacific like a place time forgot. The native Hawaiians who live here still grow taro and pound it into poi, pluck opihi (limpet) from tide pools along the jagged coast, and cast throw-nets at schools of fish.

20 Yet Another Photo Op
Just past mile marker 17 is a wide spot on the ocean side of the road where you can see the entire Keanae Peninsula's checkerboard pattern of green taro fields and its ocean boundary etched in black lava.

21 Wailua
After the Keanae School, around mile marker 18, look for the Wailua Road on the left. This will take you through the hamlet of homes and churches of Wailua, including the blue and white Coral Miracle Church, home of the Our Lady of Fatima Shrine. According to legend, in 1860, the men of this village were building a church by diving for coral to make the stone; an arduous project. A freak storm hit the area and deposited the coral from the deep on a nearby beach. If you look back at Haleakala from here, on your left you can see the spectacular Waikani Falls.

22 Panoramic View
Back on the Hana Highway, just before mile marker 19, is the Wailua Valley State Wayside Park, on the right side of the road. Climb up the stairs for a view of the Keanae Valley, waterfalls, and Wailua Peninsula. For a better view of the Wailua Peninsula, continue down the road about a quarter-mile, to the pull-off area on the ocean side.

23 Nakihu
Just after mile marker 25 is a narrow 3-mile road leading to the remains of the old Hawaiian community of Nahiku. This once was a thriving village of thousands; today, the beautiful, remote area is home to fewer than a hundred-mostly wealthy mainland residents visiting their luxurious vacation homes. At the turn of the 20th century, this site saw brief commercial activity as home of the Nahiku Rubber Co.

24 Piilanihale Heiau
Turn toward the ocean on Ulaino Road, by mile marker 31. Drive down the paved road (which turns into a dirt road) to the first stream (about 1[bf]1/2 miles). If the stream is flooded, go back. If you can forge the stream, cross it and park on the right side of the road by the huge breadfruit trees. The Piilanihale Heiau, believed to be the largest in the state, measures 340 feet by 415 feet, and it was built in a unique terrace design. Historians believe that Piilani's two sons and his grandson built the mammoth temple sometime in the 1500s.

25 Waianapanapa State Park
At mile marker 32, just on the outskirts of Hana, shiny black-sand Waianapanapa Beach appears like a vivid dream, with bright-green jungle foliage on three sides and cobalt-blue water lapping at its feet. The 120-acre park includes sea cliffs, lava tubes, arches, camping, picnic pavilions, restrooms, showers, drinking water, and hiking trails.

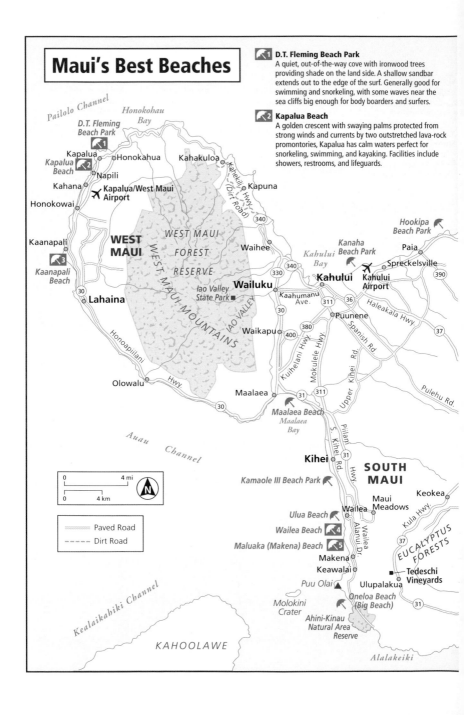

Maui's Best Beaches

D.T. Fleming Beach Park
A quiet, out-of-the-way cove with ironwood trees providing shade on the land side. A shallow sandbar extends out to the edge of the surf. Generally good for swimming and snorkeling, with some waves near the sea cliffs big enough for body boarders and surfers.

Kapalua Beach
A golden crescent with swaying palms protected from strong winds and currents by two outstretched lava-rock promontories, Kapalua has calm waters perfect for snorkeling, swimming, and kayaking. Facilities include showers, restrooms, and lifeguards.

Pailolo Channel

Honokohau Bay

D.T. Fleming Beach Park

Kapalua
Kapalua Beach
Napili
Kahana
Honokowai

Honokahua

Kahakuloa

Kapuna

Kapalua/West Maui Airport

Kaanapali

Kaanapali Beach

WEST MAUI

WEST MAUI FOREST RESERVE

WEST MAUI MOUNTAINS

Waihee

Kahului Bay

Kanaha Beach Park

Hookipa Beach Park

Paia

Spreckelsville

340

330

Wailuku

Kahului

Kahului Airport

390

Lahaina

Iao Valley State Park

IAO VALLEY

Kaahumanu Ave.

311

36

Haleakala Hwy.

30

Puunene

37

Waikapu

380

400

Honoapiilani Hwy.

Kuihelani Hwy.

Mokulele Hwy.

Spanish Rd.

Upper Kihei Rd.

Olowalu

30

Maalaea

31

311

Maalaea Beach
Maalaea Bay

Pulehu Rd.

Auau Channel

Kihei

S. Kihei Rd.

Piilani Hwy.

SOUTH MAUI

0   4 mi
0   4 km

N

Kamaole III Beach Park

Maui Meadows

Keokea

Wailea

Kula Hwy.

Paved Road
Dirt Road

Ulua Beach

Wailea Beach

Maluaka (Makena) Beach

Makena

Keawalai

Puu Olai

Wailea Alanui Dr.

37

EUCALYPTUS FORESTS

Tedeschi Vineyards

Ulupalakua

31

Molokini Crater

Oneloa Beach (Big Beach)

Ahini-Kinau Natural Area Reserve

Kealaikahiki Channel

KAHOOLAWE

Alalakeiki

3 Kaanapali Beach

Four-mile-long Kaanapali boasts grainy gold sand as far as the eye can see. A paved beach walk links hotels and condos, open-air restaurants, and the Whalers Village shopping center. Summertime swimming is excellent, and snorkeling is great around Black Rock, in front of the Sheraton.

4 Wailea Beach

This gold-sand, crescent-shaped beach is big, wide, and protected on both sides by black-lava points. From the beach, the view out to sea is magnificent, framed by neighboring Kahoolawe and Lanai and the tiny crescent of Molokini; you can often spot whales from shore here in season (Dec-Apr), and catch unreal sunsets nightly. The clear waters tumble to shore in waves just the right size for gentle riding, with or without a board.

5 Maluaka Beach (Makena Beach)

This wide, palm-fringed crescent of golden sand is set between two black-lava points and bounded by big sand dunes topped by a grassy knoll. Makena offers great swimming when it's flat and placid, excellent bodysurfing when the waves come rolling in, and lovely vistas of Molokini Crater and Kahoolawe off in the distance.

6 Hamoa Beach

This half-moon-shaped, gray-sand beach (a mix of coral and lava) in a truly tropical setting sits below 30-foot black-lava sea cliffs. An unprotected beach open to the ocean, Hamoa is often swept by powerful rip currents. Surf breaks offshore and rolls ashore, making it a popular surfing and bodysurfing area. The calm left side is best for snorkeling in the summer.

7 Waianapanapa State Park

This state park is perhaps best known for its black-sand beach (actually small black pebbles). Swimming is generally unsafe due to strong waves and rip currents, but it's a great spot for picnicking, hiking along the shore, and simply sitting and relaxing.

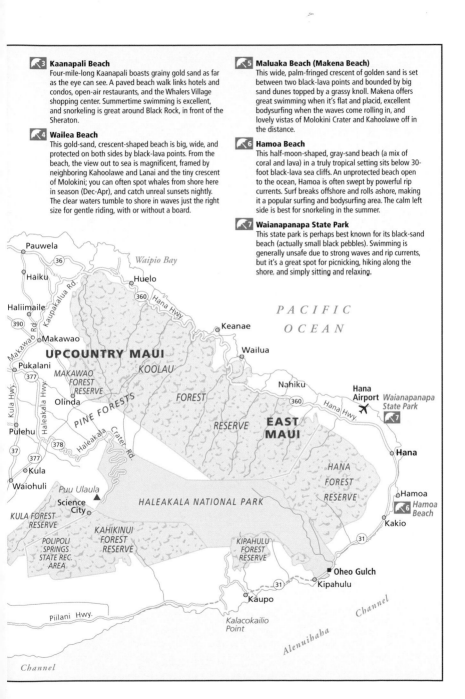

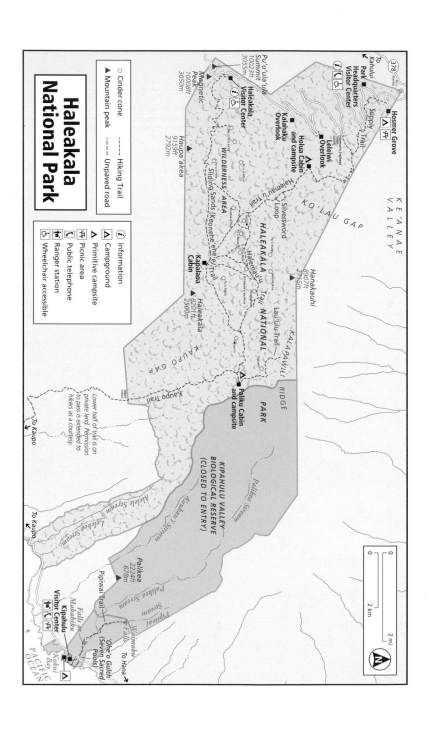

Haleakala National Park

○ Cinder cone   ----- Hiking Trail
▲ Mountain peak   ---- Unpaved road

(i) Information
△ Campground
▲ Primitive campsite
⛽ Picnic area
📞 Public telephone
🏠 Ranger station
♿ Wheelchair accessible

Frommer's®

Maui

2006

by Jeanette Foster

Here's what the critics say about Frommer's:

"Amazingly easy to use. Very portable, very complete."

—*Booklist*

"Detailed, accurate, and easy-to-read information for all price ranges."

—*Glamour Magazine*

"Hotel information is close to encyclopedic."

—*Des Moines Sunday Register*

"Frommer's Guides have a way of giving you a real feel for a place."

—*Knight Ridder Newspapers*

Wiley Publishing, Inc.

About the Author

A resident of the Big Island, **Jeanette Foster** has skied the slopes of Mauna Kea—during a Fourth of July ski meet, no less—and gone scuba diving with manta rays off the Kona Coast. A prolific writer widely published in travel, sports, and adventure magazines, she's also a contributing editor to *Hawaii* magazine and the editor of *Zagat's Survey to Hawaii's Top Restaurants*. In addition to this guide, Jeanette is the author of *Frommer's Hawaii, Frommer's Hawaii from $80 a Day, Frommer's Honolulu, Waikiki & Oahu,* and *Frommer's Hawaii with Kids.*

Published by:

Wiley Publishing, Inc.

111 River St.
Hoboken, NJ 07030-5774

ISBN-13: 978-0-7645-8902-7
ISBN-10: 0-7645-8902-4

Editor: Christine Ryan
Production Editor: Ian Skinnari
Cartographer: Roberta Stockwell
Photo Editor: Richard Fox
Production by Wiley Indianapolis Composition Services

For information on our other products and services or to obtain technical support, please contact our Customer Care Department within the U.S. at 800/762-2974, outside the U.S. at 317/572-3993 or fax 317/572-4002.

Wiley also publishes its books in a variety of electronic formats. Some content that appears in print may not be available in electronic formats.

Manufactured in the United States of America

5 4 3 2

Contents

8 Seeing the Sights 192

9 Shops & Galleries 229

10 Maui After Dark 243

11 Molokai: The Most Hawaiian Isle 251

12 Lanai: A Different Kind of Paradise   286

Appendix: Maui in Depth   309

Index   326

List of Maps

An Invitation to the Reader

In researching this book, we discovered many wonderful places—hotels, restaurants, shops, and more. We're sure you'll find others. Please tell us about them, so we can share the information with your fellow travelers in upcoming editions. If you were disappointed with a recommendation, we'd love to know that, too. Please write to:

Frommer's Maui 2006
Wiley Publishing, Inc. • 111 River St. • Hoboken, NJ 07030-5774

An Additional Note

Please be advised that travel information is subject to change at any time—and this is especially true of prices. We therefore suggest that you write or call ahead for confirmation when making your travel plans. The authors, editors, and publisher cannot be held responsible for the experiences of readers while traveling. Your safety is important to us, however, so we encourage you to stay alert and be aware of your surroundings. Keep a close eye on cameras, purses, and wallets, all favorite targets of thieves and pickpockets.

Other Great Guides for Your Trip:

Frommer's Hawaii
Frommer's Hawaii from $80 a Day
Frommer's Honolulu, Waikiki & Oahu
Frommer's Portable Big Island
Frommer's Portable Maui
The Unofficial Guide to Hawaii
Maui For Dummies

Frommer's Star Ratings, Icons & Abbreviations

Every hotel, restaurant, and attraction listing in this guide has been ranked for quality, value, service, amenities, and special features using a **star-rating system.** In country, state, and regional guides, we also rate towns and regions to help you narrow down your choices and budget your time accordingly. Hotels and restaurants are rated on a scale of zero (recommended) to three stars (exceptional). Attractions, shopping, nightlife, towns, and regions are rated according to the following scale: zero stars (recommended), one star (highly recommended), two stars (very highly recommended), and three stars (must-see).

In addition to the star-rating system, we also use **seven feature icons** that point you to the great deals, in-the-know advice, and unique experiences that separate travelers from tourists. Throughout the book, look for:

Finds	Special finds—those places only insiders know about
Fun Fact	Fun facts—details that make travelers more informed and their trips more fun
Kids	Best bets for kids, and advice for the whole family
Moments	Special moments—those experiences that memories are made of
Overrated	Places or experiences not worth your time or money
Tips	Insider tips—great ways to save time and money
Value	Great values—where to get the best deals

The following **abbreviations** are used for credit cards:

AE	American Express	DISC	Discover	V	Visa
DC	Diners Club	MC	MasterCard		

Frommers.com

Now that you have the guidebook to a great trip, visit our website at **www.frommers.com** for travel information on more than 3,000 destinations. With features updated regularly, we give you instant access to the most current trip-planning information available. At Frommers.com, you'll also find the best prices on airfares, accommodations, and car rentals—and you can even book travel online through our travel booking partners. At Frommers.com, you'll also find the following:

- Online updates to our most popular guidebooks
- Vacation sweepstakes and contest giveaways
- Newsletter highlighting the hottest travel trends
- Online travel message boards with featured travel discussions

What's New in Maui

One of the reasons that Maui has been so successful in attracting visitor attention for more than a decade and a half is its ability to reinvent itself.

First Maui was the getaway vacation. Then it became "the" place to go for your wedding or honeymoon, followed by the "in spot" for families. Last year it was the "happening" place for health and wellness, and this year the Maui Visitors Bureau has an all-out campaign to focus on Maui's cultural and agricultural resources.

Dubbed "*Malama* Maui" (preserve Maui), the emphasis is on Maui's new farm tours, some of which I feature in this book: **Chef James McDonald's** (I'o and Pacific'o Restaurants) tour of his 8-acre farm (p. 143); the **Surfing Goat Dairy Farm** tour (p. 220); the tour of **Alii Kula Lavender** farm (p. 215); and the **Tedeschi Winery** tour (p. 215).

Malama Maui also refers to Hawaii's history, culture, arts, and music. Inside this book are the best dates to come to Maui if you are interested in cultural festivals (see chapter 2); the most authentic luau (see chapter 10); the best cultural experiences (see chapter 8); and the best places to find Hawaiian art (see chapter 9).

WHERE TO STAY I've tracked down some great new places for this edition of the guide. For inexpensive accommodations in the otherwise expensive town of Lahaina, try the **Makai Inn** (© 808/662-3200; www.makaiinn.net; p. 96) or **The Spinnaker** condominium (© 808/662-3200; www.makaiinn.net; p. 97).

In Kihei the just-opened **Pineapple Inn** (© 877/212-MAUI [6284] or 808/298-4403; www.pineappleinnmaui.com; p. 115) has rooms starting at $99 a night—it's one of the best buys on Maui. The just-renovated **Wailana Kai** (© 800/541-3060 or 808/879-3328; www.bellomaui.com; p. 115) has rates starting at $85 for one-bedroom units and $110 for two-bedroom units.

Also in Kihei the condo **Hale Pau Hana Resort** (© 800/367-6036 or 808/879-2715; www.hphresort.com) has some wallet-pleasing prices (one bedroom from $173, two bedrooms from $270) considering its location—right on the beach. See my review on p. 108.

Although it's expensive (but worth every penny), the **Aloha Cottage** (© 888/328-3330 or 808/573-8555; www.aloha cottage.com) in Olinda has two exquisitely decorated bungalows in the rolling hills, perfect for honeymoon couples, starting at $245 (the full review is on p. 120).

One of my favorite hotels, **Kapalua Bay–A Renaissance Resort** (© 800/367-8000 or 808/669-5656; www. kapaluabayhotel.com), is closing in the spring of 2006, to be torn down and replaced with a new resort (see the review on p. 106).

The **Hotel Hana-Maui** (© 800/321-HANA or 808/248-8211; www.hotel hanamaui.com) is better than ever. This slice of paradise in the quaint old Hawaiian town of Hana is expensive (though you can find surprisingly reasonable deals on the Internet), but the renovated cottages, the excellent spa, and the elegant cuisine coming out of the kitchen make it well worth a splurge. For a complete review, see p. 127.

WHERE TO DINE   The new chef at **The Banyan Tree Restaurant** (℃ 808/ 669-6200), at the Ritz-Carlton, is one of the hottest new chefs to hit Maui in a long time. His incredible "Australian cuisine" has earned one rave review after another. See p. 147 for a review.

Another new opening is chef and owner Pris Nabavi's **Cilantro: Fresh Mexican Grill** (℃ 808/667-5444). The creator of Maui's Pizza Paradiso Italian Kitchen, Nabavi has taken his talent to Lahaina and is serving fresh (even healthy), fast Mexican cuisine, made "the old-fashioned way." See my review on p. 141.

Another healthy restaurant is a tiny hole in the wall in Kihei, **Joy's Place** (℃ 808/879-9258), where you can get unbelievably delicious food to take to the beach. For details, see p. 151.

I've liked every single restaurant that has been at 2051 Main St. in Wailuku (Who's the Boss restaurant, before that Iao Café, and before that the Café O Lei), including the latest reincarnation, the **Main Street Bistro** (℃ 808/244-6816). For my review, see p. 135.

In the category of great restaurants that are getting even better, chef and restaurateur D. K. Kodama, owner of Sansei Seafood in both Kapalua and Kihei, has renamed his just-opened restaurant in the former Kapalua Village Course Clubhouse. Now called **Vino Italian Tapas & Wine Bar** (℃ 808/661-VINO), Kodama's new venture signals the new trend toward tapas, or small dishes. This dining style lets you try several different culinary masterpieces at one go. See p. 148 for a full review.

FUN ON & OFF THE BEACH   Join the celebrities who have learned to surf from **Rivers to the Sea** surf school (℃ 808/280-8795 or 808/280-6236; www.riverstothesea.com). Clients include Academy Award winner Adrien Brody *(The Pianist),* Sundance Film Festival Director's Award Winner Catherine Hardwicke *(Thirteen),* and *X-Men 2* costar Kelly Hu. See p. 176 for details.

SHOPPING   For those looking for an upscale shopping experience, check out Maui's two designer stores, **Maggie Coulombe** (℃ 808/662-0696; www.maggie coulombe.com) in Lahaina, reviewed on p. 234, and **Paul Ropp** (℃ 808/661-8000; p. 236), in the Whalers Village in Kaanapali.

Even **Maui's farmers markets** have gone upscale with the opening of the **Aloha Friday Farmers Market,** which takes place on Friday at the Maui Community College. You'll find gourmet vendors like Surfing Goat Dairy, Waipoli Hydroponic Greens/Pacific Produce, Alii Lavender, and terrific baked goods from the MCC culinary-art students. See the review on p 34.

The recently opened **Maui County Store** (℃ 808/877-6669; www.maui countystore.com), in the Maui Mall in Kahului, features logo wear from the Maui police and fire departments and the University of Hawaii, and it's run by students from Maui Community College studying retail sales. See p. 230.

MAUI AFTER DARK   Two new Hawaiian cultural programs are presented by the Ritz-Carlton Kapalua: **Masters of Hawaiian Slack Key Guitar Series** (℃ 808/669-3858; www.slackkey.com) and *The Legend of Kaulula'au* (℃ 888/ 808-1055).

The Hawaiian Slack Key Guitar Series, held every week in the indoor amphitheater, presents a side of Hawaii that few visitors ever get to see. Host George Kahumoku, Jr., introduces a new slack-key master every week. Not only is there incredible Hawaiian music and singing, but George and his guest "talk story" about old Hawaii, music, and Hawaiian culture. Not to be missed. See p. 243.

In old Hawaii, legends and family history would be passed down from generation to generation orally. *Mo'olelo,* or the art of storytelling, would captivate the listeners, and the best storytellers would receive the same attention a movie star gets today. In *The Legend of Kaulula'au,* Hawaiian actor Moses Goods puts on a one-man play with agility and a spellbinding performance as he acts out the legend of Kaulula'au, a mischievous child who was banished to the island of Lanai.

According to the legend, Lanai was inhabited by ghosts. Kaulula'au not only defeats the ghosts but he goes on to become the chief of Lanai and Maui.

Out in Hana, a place not particularly known for nightlife but well known for practicing the Hawaiian culture, the **Hotel Hana-Maui** (© **800/321-HANA** or 808/248-8211; www.hotelhanamaui. com) now features Hawaiian music in the Paniolo Lounge, Thursday through Sunday from 6:30 to 9:30pm, and has a hula show every Thursday and Sunday from 7:30 to 8:15pm in the Main Dining Room.

1

The Best of Maui

Maui, also called the Valley Isle, is just a small dot in the vast Pacific Ocean, but it has the potential to offer visitors unforgettable experiences: floating weightless through rainbows of tropical fish, standing atop a 10,000-foot volcano watching the sunrise color the sky, and listening to the raindrops in a bamboo forest.

Whether you want to experience the "real" Hawaii, go on a heart-pounding adventure, or simply relax on the beach, this book is designed to help you create the vacation of your dreams.

It can be bewildering to plan your trip with so many options vying for your attention; to make your task easier, this chapter highlights what I consider the very best that Maui has to offer.

1 The Best Beaches

- **D. T. Fleming Beach Park:** This quiet, out-of-the-way beach cove, located north of the Ritz-Carlton Hotel, starts at the 16th hole of the Kapalua golf course (Makaluapuna Point) and rolls around to the sea cliffs on the other side. Ironwood trees provide shade on the land side. Offshore, a shallow sandbar extends out to the edge of the surf. Generally, the waters are good for swimming and snorkeling, but sometimes, off near the sea cliffs, the waves are big enough to suit body boarders and surfers. See p. 162.

- **Kapalua Beach:** On an island of many great beaches, this one takes the prize. A golden crescent with swaying palms protected from strong winds and currents by two outstretched lava-rock promontories, Kapalua has calm waters that are perfect for snorkeling, swimming, and kayaking. Even though it borders the Kapalua Bay hotel, the beach is long enough for everyone to enjoy. Facilities include showers, restrooms, and lifeguards. See p. 163.

- **Kaanapali Beach:** Four-mile-long Kaanapali stands out as one of Maui's best beaches, with grainy gold sand as far as the eye can see. Most of the beach parallels the sea channel, and a paved beach walk links hotels and condos, open-air restaurants, and the Whalers Village shopping center. Summertime swimming is excellent. The best snorkeling is around Black Rock, in front of the Sheraton; the water is clear, calm, and populated with brilliant tropical fish. See p. 163.

- **Wailea Beach:** This is the best goldsand, crescent-shaped beach on Maui's sunbaked southwestern coast. One of five beaches within Wailea Resort, Wailea is big, wide, and protected on both sides by black-lava points. It serves as the front yard for the Four Seasons Wailea, Maui's most elegant hotel, and the Grand Wailea Resort

Hotel & Spa, its most outrageous. From the beach, the view out to sea is magnificent, framed by neighboring Kahoolawe and Lanai and the tiny crescent of Molokini. The clear waters tumble to shore in waves just the right size for gentle riding, with or without a board. While all the beaches on the west and south coasts are great for spotting whales and watching sunsets, Wailea, with its fairly flat sandy beach that gently slopes down to the ocean, provides exceptionally good whale-watching from shore in season (Dec–Apr), as well as unreal sunsets nightly. See p. 166.

- **Maluaka Beach (Makena Beach):** On the southern end of Maui's resort coast, development falls off dramatically, leaving a wild, dry countryside punctuated by green kiawe trees. The wide, palm-fringed crescent of golden sand is set between two black-lava points and bounded by big sand dunes topped by a grassy knoll. Makena can be perfect for swimming when it's flat and placid, but it can also offer excellent bodysurfing when the waves come rolling in. Vistas of Molokini Crater and Kahoolawe can be seen off in the distance. See p. 166.
- **Waianapanapa State Park:** In east Maui, a few miles from Hana, the 120 acres of this state park offer 12 cabins, a caretaker's residence, a picnic area, a shoreline hiking trail, and, best of all, a black-sand beach (actually small black pebbles). Swimming is generally unsafe, though, due to strong waves breaking offshore, which roll into the beach unchecked, and strong rip currents. But it's a great spot for picnicking, hiking along the shore, and simply sitting and relaxing. See p. 168.
- **Hamoa Beach:** This half-moon-shaped, gray-sand beach (a mix of coral and lava) in a truly tropical setting is a favorite among sunbathers, snorkelers, and bodysurfers in Hana. The 100-foot-wide beach is three football fields long and sits below 30-foot black-lava sea cliffs. An unprotected beach open to the ocean, Hamoa is often swept by powerful rip currents. Surf breaks offshore and rolls ashore, making it a popular surfing and bodysurfing area. The calm left side is best for snorkeling in the summer. See p. 168.
- **Hulopoe Beach (Lanai):** This golden, palm-fringed beach off the south coast of Lanai gently slopes down to the azure waters of a Marine Life Conservation District, where clouds of tropical fish flourish and spinner dolphins come to play. A tide pool in the lava rocks defines one side of the bay, while the other is lorded over by the Manele Bay Hotel, which sits prominently on the hill above. Offshore, you'll find good swimming, snorkeling, and diving; onshore, there's a full complement of beach facilities, from restrooms to camping areas. See p. 170.

2 The Best Maui Experiences

- **Taking the Plunge:** Don mask, fins, and snorkel, and explore the magical world beneath the surface of the ocean, where kaleidoscopic clouds of tropical fish flutter by exotic corals; a sea turtle might even come over to check you out. Molokini is everyone's favorite snorkeling destination, but the shores of Maui are lined with magical spots as well. Can't swim? No problem: Hop on the **Atlantis Submarines** (© 800/548-6262) for a plunge beneath the waves without getting wet. See "Watersports" in

Maui

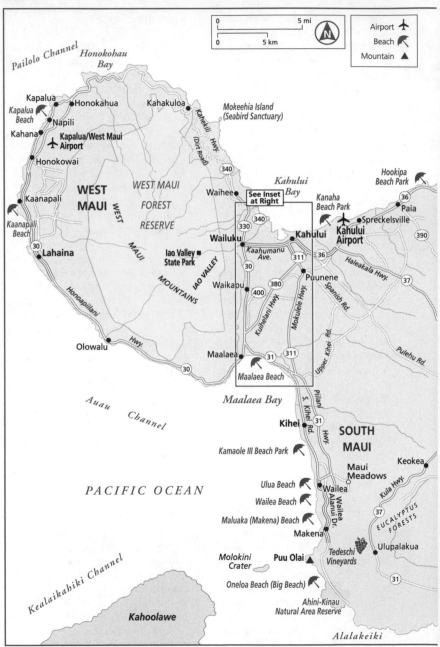

Pailolo Channel

Honokohau Bay

0   5 mi
0   5 km

N

Airport ✈
Beach 🏖
Mountain ▲

Kapalua
Kapalua Beach
Kahana
Napili
Kahakuloa
Honokahua

Kapalua/West Maui Airport ✈

Honokowai

Mokeehia Island (Seabird Sanctuary)

Hookipa Beach Park

Kaanapali

WEST MAUI

WEST MAUI FOREST RESERVE

Waihee

Kahului Bay

See Inset at Right

Kanaha Beach Park

Kaanapali Beach

340

WEST

330   340

Kahului

Spreckelsville
Paia

36

390

Lahaina

30

MAUI

MOUNTAINS

Iao Valley State Park

Wailuku

Kaahumanu Ave.

311   36

Kahului Airport ✈

Haleakala Hwy.

37

IAO VALLEY

Waikapu

30

Puunene

380

Olowalu

Honoapiilani

Hwy.

400

Kuihelani Hwy.

Mokulele Hwy.

Spanish Rd.

Pulehu Rd.

30

Maalaea

Maalaea Beach

31   311

Upper Kihei Rd.

Auau Channel

Maalaea Bay

Piilani Hwy.

S. Kihei Rd.

31

Kihei

SOUTH MAUI

Keokea

PACIFIC OCEAN

Kamaole III Beach Park

Ulua Beach
Wailea Beach
Maluaka (Makena) Beach

Wailea

Maui Meadows

Wailea Alanui Dr.

Kula Hwy.

37

EUCALYPTUS FORESTS

Makena

Tedeschi Vineyards

Ulupalakua

Kealaikahiki Channel

Molokini Crater

Puu Olai ▲

Oneloa Beach (Big Beach)

31

Ahini-Kinau Natural Area Reserve

Kahoolawe

Alalakeiki

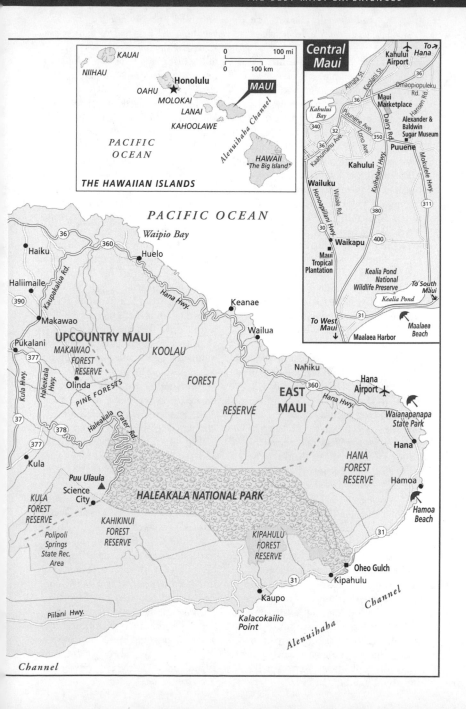

THE HAWAIIAN ISLANDS

KAUAI

NIIHAU

OAHU

Honolulu

MOLOKAI

LANAI

KAHOOLAWE

MAUI

PACIFIC
OCEAN

Alenuihaha Channel

HAWAII
"The Big Island"

0   100 mi
0   100 km

Central
Maui

To Hana

Kahului
Airport

Amala St.

Keolani St.

Omaopiopuleku Rd.

36

Hansen Rd.

Maui
Marketplace

36

Kahului
Bay

340

Puunene Ave.

Lono Ave.

Dairy Rd.

Alexander &
Baldwin
Sugar Museum

32

350

Puuene

36

Kaahumanu Ave.

Kuihelani Hwy.

Mokulele Hwy.

Kahului

Wailuku

Honoapiilani Hwy.

Waiale Rd.

Waiale Rd.

380

311

30

Waikapu

400

Maui
Tropical
Plantation

Kealia Pond
National
Wildlife Preserve

To South
Maui

To West
Maui

31

Kealia Pond

Maalaea
Beach

Maalaea Harbor

PACIFIC OCEAN

Waipio Bay

36

360

Huelo

Haiku

Haliimaile

Kaupakalua Rd.

Hana Hwy.

Keanae

390

Makawao

Wailua

Pukalani

UPCOUNTRY MAUI

MAKAWAO
FOREST
RESERVE

KOOLAU

Nahiku

377

Haleakala Hwy.

Olinda

PINE FORESTS

FOREST

Hana
Airport

360

Hana Hwy.

EAST
MAUI

Waianapanapa
State Park

37

Kula Hwy.

378

Haleakala

Crater Rd.

RESERVE

Hana

377

Hamoa

Kula

Puu Ulaula

Science
City

HALEAKALA NATIONAL PARK

HANA
FOREST
RESERVE

Hamoa

Hamoa
Beach

KULA
FOREST
RESERVE

KAHIKINUI
FOREST
RESERVE

KIPAHULU
FOREST
RESERVE

31

Polipoli
Springs
State Rec.
Area

Oheo Gulch

31

Kipahulu

Kaupo

Piilani Hwy.

Kalacokailio
Point

Alenuihaha

Channel

Channel

chapter 7 and "By Air, Land & Sea: Guided Island Adventures" in chapter 8.

- **Hunting for Whales on Land:** No need to shell out megabucks to go out to sea in search of humpback whales—you can watch these majestic mammals breach and spy hop from shore. I recommend scenic McGregor Point, at mile marker 9 along Honoapiilani Highway, just outside Maalaea in South Maui. The humpbacks arrive as early as November, but the majority travel through Maui's waters from mid-December to mid-April. See "Watersports" in chapter 7.

- **Watching the Windsurfers:** Sit on a grassy bluff or stretch out on the sandy beach at Hookipa, on the north shore, and watch the world's top-ranked windsurfers twirling and dancing on the wind and waves like colorful butterflies. World-championship contests are held at Hookipa, one of the greatest windsurfing spots on the planet. See "Watersports" in chapter 7 and "Driving the Road to Hana" in chapter 8.

- **Experiencing Maui's History:** Wander the historic streets of the old whaling town of Lahaina, where the 1800s are alive and well thanks to the efforts of the Lahaina Restoration Society. Drive the scenic Kahekili Highway, where the preserved village of Kahakuloa looks much as it did a century ago. Stand in awe at Piilanihale, Hawaii's largest *heiau* (temple), located just outside Hana. See "Lahaina & West Maui" in chapter 8.

- **Greeting the Rising Sun from Haleakala's Summit:** Bundle up in warm clothing, fill a thermos full of hot java, and drive up to the summit to watch the sky turn from inky black to muted charcoal as a small sliver of orange forms on the horizon. Standing at 10,000 feet,

breathing in the rarefied air, and watching the first rays of light streak across the sky is a mystical experience of the first magnitude. See "House of the Sun: Haleakala National Park" in chapter 8.

- **Exploring a Different Hawaii—Upcountry Maui:** On the slopes of Haleakala, cowboys, farmers, ranchers, and other country people make their homes in serene, neighborly communities like Makawao, Kula, and Ulupalakua—worlds away from the bustling beach resorts. Acres of onions, lettuce, tomatoes, carrots, cabbage, and flowers cover the hillsides. Maui's only winery is located here, offering the perfect place for a picnic. See "More in Upcountry Maui" in chapter 8.

- **Driving Through a Tropical Rainforest:** The Hana Highway is not just a "drive" but an adventure: Stop along the way to plunge into icy mountain ponds filled by cascading waterfalls; gaze upon vistas of waves pummeling soaring ocean cliffs; inhale the sweet aroma of blooming ginger; and take a walk back in time, catching a glimpse of what Hawaii looked like before concrete condos and fast-food joints washed ashore. See "Driving the Road to Hana" in chapter 8.

- **Taking a Day Trip to Lanai:** From Lahaina, join **Trilogy Lanai Ocean Sports' snorkel cruise** to Lanai (© **800/874-2666**), or take the Expeditions Lahaina/Lanai Passenger Ferry over and rent a four-wheel-drive jeep on your own. It's a two-for-one island experience: Board in Lahaina Harbor and admire Maui from offshore, then get off at Lanai and go snorkeling in the clear waters, tour the tiny former plantation island, and catch the last ferry home. See chapter 12.

3 The Best Adventures

Branch out while you're in Maui; do something you wouldn't normally do—after all, you're on vacation. Below is a list of adventures I highly recommend. Some are a bit pricey, but these splurges are worth every penny.

- **Scuba Diving:** You're in love with snorkeling and the chance to view the underwater world, but it's just not enough—you want to get closer and see even more. Take an introductory scuba dive; after a brief lesson on how to use the diving equipment, you'll plunge into the deep to swim with the tropical fish and go eyeball to eyeball with other marine critters. See "Watersports" in chapter 7.

- **Skimming over the Ocean in a Kayak:** Glide silently over the water, hearing only the sound of your paddle dipping beneath the surface. This is the way the early Hawaiians traveled along the coastline. You'll be eye level and up close and personal with the ocean and the coastline, exploring areas you can't get to any other way. Venture out on your own or go with an experienced guide—either way, you won't be sorry. See "Watersports" in chapter 7.

- **Exploring a Lava Tube:** Most people come to Maui to get outdoors and soak up some Hawaiian sunshine, but don't miss the opportunity to see firsthand how volcanic islands were formed. With **Maui Cave Adventures** (© **808/248-7308**), you can hike into the subterranean passages of a huge, extinct lava tube with 40-foot ceilings—an offbeat adventure and a geology lesson you won't soon forget. See "Biking, Horseback Riding & Other Outdoor Activities" in chapter 7.

- **Seeing the Stars from Inside a Volcanic Crater:** Driving up to see the sunrise is a trip you'll never forget, but to *really* experience Haleakala, plan to hike in and spend the night. To get a feel for why the ancient Hawaiians considered this one of the most sacred places on the island, you simply have to wander into the heart of the dormant volcano, where you'll find some 27 miles of hiking trails, two camping sites, and three cabins. See "Hiking & Camping" in chapter 7 and "House of the Sun: Haleakala National Park" in chapter 8.

- **Hiking to a Waterfall:** There are waterfalls, and there are waterfalls; the magnificent 400-foot Waimoku Falls, in Oheo Gulch outside of Hana, are worth the long drive and the uphill hike you have to take to get there. The falls are surrounded by lush green ferns and wild orchids, and you can even stop to take a dip in the pool at the top of Makahiku Falls on the way. See "Hiking & Camping" in chapter 7.

- **Flying over the Remote West Maui Mountains:** Your helicopter streaks low over razor-thin cliffs, then flutters past sparkling waterfalls and down into the canyons and valleys of the inaccessible West Maui Mountains. There's so much beauty to absorb that it all goes by in a rush. You'll never want to stop flying over this spectacular, surreal landscape—and it's the only way to see the dazzling beauty of the prehistoric area of Maui. See "By Air, Land & Sea: Guided Island Adventures" in chapter 8.

- **Taking a Drive on the Wild Side:** Mother Nature's wild side, that is—on the Kahekili Highway on Maui's northeast coast. This back-to-nature experience will take you past ancient Hawaiian *heiau* (temples); along steep ravines; and by rolling pastures, tumbling waterfalls, exploding blowholes, crashing surf, and jagged lava coastlines. You'll wander through the tiny Hawaiian village of Kahakuloa and around the "head" of Maui to the Marine Life Conservation Area of Honolua-Mokuleia and on to the resort of Kapalua. You'll remember this adventure for years. See "Lahaina & West Maui" in chapter 8.

- **Riding a Mule to Kalaupapa:** Even if you have only 1 day to spend on Molokai, spend it on a mule. The

Molokai Mule Ride ⚓ (© 800/567-7550) trek from "topside" Molokai to the Kalaupapa National Historic Park (Father Damien's world-famous leper colony) is a once-in-a-lifetime adventure. The cliffs are taller than 300-story skyscrapers, and the narrow 3-mile trail includes 26 dizzying switchbacks, but Buzzy Sproat has never lost one of his trustworthy mules (or any riders) on the difficult trail. The mules make the trek daily, rain or shine. See "Seeing the Sights" in chapter 11.

4 The Best of Underwater Maui

An entirely different Maui greets anyone with a face mask, snorkel, and fins. Under the sea you'll find schools of brilliant tropical fish, green sea turtles, quick-moving game fish, slack-jawed moray eels, and prehistoric-looking coral. It's a kaleidoscope of color and wonder.

- **Black Rock:** This spot, located on the Kaanapali Beach just off the Sheraton Maui Resort, is excellent for beginner snorkelers during the day and for scuba divers at night. Schools of fish congregate at the base of the rock and are so used to snorkelers that they go about their business as if no one were around. If you take the time to look closely at the crannies of the rock, you'll find lion fish in fairly shallow water. At night (when a few outfitters run night dives here), lobsters, Spanish dancers, and eels come out. See "Kaanapali Beach" under "Beaches" in chapter 7.

- **Olowalu:** When the wind is blowing and the waves are crashing everywhere else, Olowalu, the small area 5 miles south of Lahaina, can be a scene of total calm—perfect for snorkeling and diving. You'll find a good snorkeling area around mile marker 14. You might have to swim about 50 to 75

feet; when you get to the large field of finger coral in 10 to 15 feet of water, you're there. You'll see a turtle-cleaning station here, where turtles line up to have small cleaner wrasses pick off small parasites. This is also a good spot to see crown-of-thorns starfish, puffer fish, and lots of juvenile fish. See "Watersports" in chapter 7 and "Lahaina & West Maui" in chapter 8.

- **Hawaiian Reef:** Scuba divers love this area off the Kihei-Wailea coast because it has a good cross section of topography and marine life typical of Hawaiian waters. Diving to depths of 85 feet, you'll see everything from lava formations and coral reef to sand and rubble, plus a diverse range of both shallow- and deep-water creatures. See the box "An Expert Shares His Secrets: Maui's Best Dives" in chapter 7.

- **Third Tank:** Scuba divers looking for a photo opportunity will find it at this artificial reef, located off Makena Beach at 80 feet. This World War II tank acts like a fish magnet—because it's the only large solid object in the area, any fish or invertebrate looking for a safe home comes here. Surrounding the tank is a cloak of schooling snappers and goatfish just waiting for a photographer with a wide-angle lens. It's small, but Third Tank is loaded with more marine life per square inch than any site off Maui. See the box "An Expert Shares His Secrets: Maui's Best Dives" in chapter 7.

- **Molokini:** Shaped like a crescent moon, this islet's shallow concave side serves as a sheltering backstop against sea currents for tiny tropical fish; on its opposite side is a deep-water cliff inhabited by spiny lobsters, moray eels, and white-tipped sharks. Neophyte snorkelers report to the concave side, experienced scuba divers, the cliff side. Either way, the clear water and abundant marine life make this islet off the Makena coast one of Hawaii's most popular dive spots. See "Watersports" in chapter 7.

- **Ahihi-Kinau Natural Preserve:** Fishing is strictly *kapu* (forbidden) in Ahihi Bay (at the end of the road in South Maui), and the fish seem to know it; they're everywhere in this series of rocky coves and black-lava tide pools. The black, barren, lunarlike land stands in stark contrast to the green-blue water, which is home to a sparkling mosaic of tropical fish. Scuba divers might want to check out **La Pérouse Pinnacle** in the middle of La Pérouse Bay; clouds of damselfish and triggerfish will greet you on the surface. See "Watersports" in chapter 7.

5 The Best Golf Courses

- **Kaanapali Courses** (✆ 808/661-3691): All golfers, from high handicappers to near-pros, will love these two challenging courses. The North Course is a true Robert Trent Jones, Jr., design: an abundance of wide bunkers; several long, stretched-out tees; and the largest, most contoured greens on Maui. The South Course is an Arthur Jack Snyder design; although shorter than the North Course, it does require more accuracy on the narrow, hilly fairways. Just like its sibling course, it has a water hazard on its final hole, so don't tally up your score card until you sink your final putt. See p. 187.

- **Kapalua Resort Courses** (✆ 877/527-2582): Kapalua is probably the best nationally known golf resort in Hawaii, due to the PGA Kapalua Mercedes played here each January. The Bay Course and the Village Course are vintage Arnold Palmer designs; the new Plantation Course is a strong entry from Ben Crenshaw and Bill Coore. All sit on Maui's windswept northwestern shore, at the rolling foothills of Puu Kukui, the summit of the West Maui Mountains. See p. 187.

- **Wailea Courses** (✆ 888/328-MAUI): On the sunbaked south shore of Maui stands Wailea Resort, *the* hot spot for golf in the islands. You'll find great golf at these three resort courses: The Blue course is an Arthur Jack Snyder design, and the Emerald and Gold courses are both by Robert Trent Jones, Jr. All boast outstanding views of the Pacific and the mid–Hawaiian Islands. See p. 188.

- **Makena Courses** (✆ 808/879-3344): Here you'll find 36 holes by "Mr. Hawaii Golf"—Robert Trent Jones, Jr.—at his best. Add to that spectacular views: Molokini islet looms in the background, humpback whales gambol offshore in winter, and the tropical sunsets are spectacular. The South Course has magnificent views (bring your camera) and is kinder to golfers who haven't played for a while. The North Course is more difficult but also more stunning. The 13th hole, located partway up the mountain, has a view that makes most golfers stop and stare. The next hole is even more memorable: a 200-foot drop between tee and green. See p. 188.

• **The Lanai Courses:** For quality and seclusion, nothing in Hawaii can touch Lanai's two golf-resort offerings. **The Experience at Koele** (✆ 800/321-4666), designed by

Ted Robinson and Greg Norman, and **The Challenge at Manele** (✆ 800/321-4666), a wonderful Jack Nicklaus course with ocean views from every hole, both rate among Hawaii's best courses. Both are tremendous fun to play, with The Experience featuring the par-4 8th hole, which drops some 150 yards from tee to fairway, and The Challenge boasting the par-3 12th, which plays from one cliff side to another over a Pacific inlet—one of the most stunning holes in Hawaii. See p. 301.

6 The Best Luxury Hotels & Resorts

• **Ritz-Carlton Kapalua** (✆ 800/262-8440 or 808/669-6200; www.ritz carlton.com): With its great location, style, and loads of hospitality, this is the best Ritz anywhere. Situated on the coast below the picturesque West Maui Mountains, this grand, breezy hotel overlooks the Pacific and Molokai across the channel. The natural setting, on an old coastal pineapple plantation, is the picture of tranquillity. The service is legendary, the golf courses are daunting, and the nearby beaches are perfect for snorkeling, diving, and just relaxing. See p. 106.

• **Sheraton Maui** (✆ 800/782-9488 or 808/661-0031; www.sheraton-maui.com): Offering the best location on Kaanapali Beach, recent renovations, and a great "hassle-free" experience, the Sheraton is my pick of Kaanapali hotels. This is the place for travelers who just want to arrive, have everything ready for them, and get on with their vacation. (Sheraton has a "no-hassle" check-in: The valet takes you and your luggage straight to your room, which means no time wasted standing in line at registration.) See p. 98.

• **Kaanapali Alii** (✆ 800/642-6284 or 808/661-3330; www.kaanapali-alii.com): The height of luxury, these oceanfront condominium units (right on Kaanapali Beach) combine all the amenities of a luxury hotel (including a 24-hr. front desk) with the convenience of a condominium. One-bedroom units (1,500 sq. ft.) start at $360 for four people. The beachside recreation area includes a swimming pool, plus a separate children's pool, whirlpool, gas barbecue grills and picnic areas, exercise rooms, saunas, and tennis courts. See p. 98.

• **Hyatt Regency Maui Resort and Spa** (✆ 800/233-1234 or 808/661-1234; www.maui.hyatt.com): Spa goers will love Hawaii's only oceanfront spa. The 806 rooms of this fantasy resort have undergone $19 million in renovations. Spread out among three towers, the rooms have very comfortable separate sitting areas and private lanais with eye-popping views. This huge place covers some 40 acres; even if you don't stay here, you might want to walk through the expansive tree-filled atrium and the parklike grounds. See p. 97.

- **Four Seasons Resort Maui at Wailea** (© 800/334-MAUI [6284] or 808/874-8000; www.fshr.com): This is the ultimate beach hotel for latter-day royals, offering excellent cuisine, spacious rooms, gracious service, and Wailea Beach—one of Maui's best gold-sand beaches—right outside the front door. Every room has at least a partial ocean view from a private lanai. The luxury suites are as big as some Honolulu condos and full of marble and deluxe appointments. See p. 117.
- **Grand Wailea Resort Hotel & Spa** (© 800/888-6100 or 808/875-1234; www.grandwailea.com): There's nothing subtle or understated about it, but many travelers adore this over-the-top fantasy resort. It has 10,000 tropical plants in the lobby; a fabulous pool with slides, waterfalls, and rapids; Hawaii's largest spa; plush oceanview rooms; and a superb location on a gorgeous stretch of beach. See p. 117.
- **The Fairmont Kea Lani Maui** (© 800/659-4100 or 808/875-4100; www.kealani.com): This all-suite luxury hotel in Wailea has 840-square-foot suites featuring kitchenettes with microwaves and coffeemakers; living rooms with high-tech media centers and pullout sofa beds (great if you have the kids in tow); marble wet bars; and spacious bedrooms. The oversize marble bathrooms have separate showers big enough for a party. Large lanais off the bedrooms and living rooms overlook the pools and lawns, with views that sweep right down to the white-sand beach. See p. 116.
- **Hotel Hana-Maui** (© 800/321-HANA or 808/248-8211; www.hotelhanamaui.com): Picture Shangri-La, Hawaiian-style: 66 acres rolling down to the sea in a remote Hawaiian village, with two pools and access to one of the best beaches in Hana. This is the atmosphere, the landscape, and the culture of old Hawaii set in the latest accommodations of the 21st century. A white-sand beach just a 5-minute shuttle away, top-notch wellness center, and numerous activities (horseback riding, mountain bicycles, tennis, pitch-and-putt golf) all add up to make this one of the top resorts in the state. See p. 127.
- **The Lodge at Koele** (Lanai; © 800/321-4666; www.lanai-resorts.com): The Lodge, as folks here call it, stands in a 21-acre grove of Norfolk Island pines at 1,700 feet above sea level, 8 miles inland from any beach. The 102-room resort resembles a grand English country estate. Inside, heavy timbers, beamed ceilings, and the two huge stone fireplaces of the Great Hall complete the look. The guest rooms continue the English theme with four-poster beds, sitting areas (complete with window seats), flowery wallpaper, formal writing desks, and luxury bathrooms with oversize tubs. There are plenty of activities here and at the sister resort down the hill, on the ocean, the Manele Bay Hotel. See p. 291.

7 The Best Moderately Priced Accommodations

- **Kahana Sunset** (© 800/669-1488 or 808/669-8011; www.kahanasunset.com): This is a great choice for families, featuring a series of wooden condo units stair-stepping down the side of a hill to a postcard-perfect white-sand beach. The units feature full kitchens, washers/dryers, large lanais with terrific views, and sleeper sofas (starting at $140 for up to four people). See p. 102.

- **Lahaina Inn** (✆ 800/669-3444 or 808/661-0577; www.lahainainn. com): If the romance of historic Lahaina catches your fancy, a stay here will really complete the experience. Built in 1938 as a general store, it has been restored as a charming, Victorian antiques–filled inn right in the heart of town, with room rates as low as $125. Downstairs you'll find one of Hawaii's most popular storefront bistros, David Paul's Lahaina Grill. See p. 92.
- **The Plantation Inn** (✆ 800/ 433-6815 or 808/667-9225; www. theplantationinn.com): Attention romantic couples: You need look no further. This charming Lahaina hotel looks like it's been here 100 years or more, but looks can be deceiving. The Victorian-style inn is actually of 1990s vintage—an artful deception. The rooms are romantic to the max, tastefully done with period furniture, hardwood floors, stained glass, ceiling fans, and four-poster canopy beds. The rooms wrap around the large pool and deck; also on-site are a spa and an elegant pavilion lounge, where breakfast is served, all starting at $160 double. See p. 95.
- **Punahoa Beach Apartments** (✆ 800/564-4380 or 808/879-2720; www.punahoa.com): This small oceanside Kihei condo complex is hidden on a quiet side street; the grassy lawn out front rolls about 50 feet down to the beach. You'll find great snorkeling just offshore and a popular surfing spot next door, with shopping and restaurants all within walking distance. Every well-decorated unit features a lanai with fabulous ocean views, from $94 off season. See p. 111.
- **Paniolo Hale** (Molokai; ✆ 800/ 367-2984 or 808/552-2731; www. molokai-vacation-rental.com): This is far and away Molokai's most charming lodging and probably its best value. The two-story old-Hawaii ranch-house design is airy and homey, with oak floors and walls of folding-glass doors that open to huge screened verandas. The whole place overlooks the Kaluakoi Golf Course, a green barrier that separates these condos (which start at $105 for two) from the rest of Kaluakoi Resort. See p. 260.
- **Hotel Lanai** (Lanai; ✆ 800/795-7211 or 808/565-7211; www.hotel lanai.com): This simple, down-home, plantation-era relic has recently been Laura Ashley–ized. The Hotel Lanai is homey, funky, and fun—and, best of all, a real bargain (starting at $105 for two) compared to its ritzy neighbors. See p. 292.

8 The Best Bed & Breakfasts

- **Old Wailuku Inn at Ulupono** (✆ 800/305-4899 or 808/244-5897; www.mauiinn.com): Located in historic Wailuku, the most charming town in central Maui, this restored 1924 former plantation manager's home is the place to stay if you're looking for a night in the old Hawaii of the 1920s. The guest rooms are wide and spacious, with exotic ohia-wood floors and traditional Hawaiian quilts. Rates start at $125. The morning meal is a full gourmet breakfast served on the enclosed back lanai or on a tray delivered to your room if you prefer. See p. 91.
- **Guest House** (✆ 800/621-8942 or 808/661-8085; www.mauiguest house.com): This is one of the great

bed-and-breakfast deals in Lahaina: a charming inn offering more amenities than the expensive Kaanapali hotels just down the road. The spacious home features floor-to-ceiling windows, parquet floors, and a large swimming pool. Guest rooms have quiet lanais and romantic hot tubs. Breakfasts are a gourmet affair. All units are $129 double. See p. 96.

- **Pineapple Inn Maui** (© 877/212-MAUI or 808/298-4403; www.pineappleinnmaui.com): Just opened at the end of 2004, this charming inn (only four rooms, plus a darling two-bedroom cottage) is not only an exquisite find, but the prices are terrific (starting at $99 a night). Located in the residential Maui Meadows area, with panoramic ocean views, this two-story inn features a giant saltwater pool and Jacuzzi overlooking the ocean. Each of the sound-proof rooms is expertly decorated with a small kitchenette, comfy bed, free wireless Internet access, TV/VCR, and an incredible view off your own private lanai. See p. 115.
- **Two Mermaids on the Sunnyside of Maui B&B** (© 800/262-9912 or 808/985-7488; www.bestbnb.com): Two avid scuba divers are the hosts at this very friendly Kihei B&B, professionally decorated in brilliant, tropical colors, complete with hand-painted art of the island (above and below the water) in a quiet neighborhood just a short 10-minute walk from the beach. Comfy rooms from $120 with breakfast. See p. 115.
- **What a Wonderful World B&B** (© 800/943-5804 or 808/879-9103; www.amauibedandbreakfast.com): Another one of Kihei's best B&Bs offers a great central location in town—just ½ mile to Kamaole II Beach Park, 5 minutes from Wailea golf courses, and convenient to

shopping and restaurants. All rooms boast cooking facilities and private entrances, bathrooms, and phones. A family-style breakfast (eggs Benedict, Alaskan waffles, skillet eggs with mushroom sauce, fruit blintzes) is served on the lanai, which has views of white-sand beaches, the West Maui Mountains, and Haleakala. From $75 double. See p. 115.

- **Nona Lani Cottages** (© 800/733-2688 or 808/879-2497; www.nonalanicottages.com): Picture this: a grassy expanse dotted with eight cottages tucked among palm, fruit, and sweet-smelling flower trees, right across the street from a white-sand beach. This is one of the great hidden deals in Kihei. The cottages are tiny but contain everything you'll need. At $90 a night, this is a deal. See p. 114.
- **Wild Ginger Falls** (© 808/573-1173; www.wildgingerfalls.com): This cozy, romantic, intimate cottage, hidden in Miliko Gulch, just outside of Haliimaile, overlooks a stream with a waterfall, bamboo, sweet-smelling ginger, and banana trees. It's perfect for honeymooners, lovers, and fans of Hawaiian art. You will be delighted at the carefully placed memorabilia throughout this 400-square-foot artistically decorated Hawaiian cottage (with additional 156-sq.-ft. screened deck). Priced at $125 double. See p. 125.
- **Olinda Country Cottages & Inn** (© 800/932-3435 or 808/572-1453; www.mauibnbcottages.com): Breathe the crisp, clean air of Olinda at this charming B&B, located on an 8½-acre protea farm on the slopes of Haleakala and surrounded by 35,000 acres of ranch lands (with miles of great hiking). The 5,000-square-foot Tudor mansion, refurbished and outfitted with priceless antiques, has

large windows with incredible panoramic views of all of Maui. In addition to the guest rooms in the country house, two cozy cottages and a romantic country suite are also available. From $140 with breakfast. See p. 120.

- **Malu Manu** (© **888/878-6161** or 808/878-6111; www.maui.net/~alive): Tucked into the side of Haleakala Volcano at 4,000 feet, in the Kula region, is this old Hawaiian estate. It offers a single-room cabin with a full kitchen, fireplace, and antiques for just $150. Built as a writer's retreat in the early 1900s, it's one of the most romantic places to stay on Maui, with a panoramic view of the entire island from the front door. See p. 122.

- **Kili's Cottage** (© **800/262-9912** or 808/985-7488; www.bestbnb.com): If you're looking for a quiet getaway in the cool upcountry elevation of Kula, this sweet three-bedroom cottage with a large lanai, situated on 2 acres, is the perfect place. The price is right (just $115), and the numerous amenities make this a great place for families: full kitchen, gas barbecue, washer/dryer, even toys for the kids. See p. 123.

- **Ekena** (© **808/248-7047**; www.ekenamaui.com): Situated on 8½ acres in the hills above Hana, this Hawaiian-style wooden pole house, with 360-degree views of the coastline, the ocean, and Hana's verdant rainforest, is perfect for those in search of a quiet, peaceful vacation. Inside, the elegantly furnished home features floor-to-ceiling sliding-glass doors and a fully equipped kitchen (starting at $185 for two); outside,

hiking trails into the rainforest start right on the property. Beaches, waterfalls, and pools are mere minutes away. See p. 128.

- **Hamoa Bay Bungalow** (© **808/248-7884**; www.hamoabay.com): This enchanting retreat sits on 4 verdant acres within walking distance of Hamoa Beach, just outside Hana. The romantic, 600-square-foot, Balinese-style cottage has a full kitchen and hot tub. This very private place is perfect for honeymooners. The price? Just $195. See p. 128.

- **Heavenly Hana Inn** (© **808/248-8442**; www.heavenlyhanainn.com): Just a stone's throw from the center of Hana is this tiny Japanese-style inn, where no attention to detail has been spared. Flowers are everywhere, ceiling fans keep the rooms cool, and the delicious gourmet breakfast is served in a setting filled with art. The 2 acres of grounds are impeccable, with tiny bridges over a meandering stream and Japanese gardens. Rooms start at $200. See p. 129.

- **Aloha Beach House** (© **888/828-1008** or 808/828-1100; www.molokaivacation.com): Nestled on the lush East End of Molokai lies this Hawaiian-style beach house sitting right on the white-sand beach of Waialua. Perfect for families, this impeccably decorated two-bedroom, 1,600-square-foot beach house has a huge open living/dining/kitchen area that opens out to an old-fashioned porch for meals or just sitting in the comfy chairs and watching the clouds roll by. Just $220 for up to five people. See p. 261.

9 The Best Resort Spas

- **Spa Grande at the Grand Wailea Resort** (© **800/888-6100** or 808/875-1234; www.grandwailea.com):

This is Hawaii's biggest spa, at 50,000 square feet and with 40 treatment rooms. The spa incorporates

(Moments Pampering in Paradise

Hawaii's spas have raised the art of relaxation and healing to a new level. The traditional Greco-Roman-style spas, with lots of marble and big tubs in closed rooms, have evolved into airy, open facilities that embrace the tropics. Spa goers in Hawaii are looking for a sense of place, seeped in the culture. They want to hear the sound of the ocean, smell the salt air, and feel the caress of the warm breeze. They want to experience Hawaiian products and traditional treatments they can get only in the islands.

The spas of Hawaii, once nearly exclusively patronized by women, are now attracting more male clients. There are special massages for children and pregnant women, and some spas have created programs to nurture and relax brides on their big day.

Today's spas offer a wide diversity of treatments. There is no longer plain, ordinary massage, but Hawaiian lomilomi, Swedish, aromatherapy (with sweet-smelling oils), craniosacral (massaging the head), shiatsu (no oil, just deep thumb pressure on acupuncture points), Thai (another oil-less massage involving stretching), and hot stone (with heated, and sometimes cold, rocks). There are even side-by-side massages for couples. The truly decadent might even try a duo massage—not one, but *two* massage therapists working on you at once.

Massages are just the beginning. Body treatments, for the entire body or for just the face, involve a variety of herbal wraps, masks, or scrubs using a range of ingredients from seaweed to salt to mud, with or without accompanying aromatherapy, lights, and music.

After you have been rubbed and scrubbed, most spas offer an array of water treatments—a sort of hydromassage in a tub with jets and an assortment of colored crystals, oils, and scents.

Those are just the traditional treatments. Most spas also offer a range of alternative healthcare like acupuncture, chiropractic, and other exotic treatments like ayurvedic and siddha from India or reiki from Japan. Many places offer specialized, cutting-edge treatments, like the Grand Wailea Resort's full-spectrum color-light therapy pod (based on NASA's work with astronauts).

Once your body has been pampered, spas also offer a range of fitness facilities (weight-training equipment, racquetball, tennis, golf, and so on) and classes (yoga, aerobics, step, spinning, stretch, tai chi, kickboxing, aquacize, and so on). Several even offer adventure fitness packages (from bicycling to snorkeling). For the nonadventurous, most spas have salons dedicated to hair and nail care and make-up.

If all this sounds a bit overwhelming, not to worry: All the spas in Hawaii have individual consultants who will help you design an appropriate treatment program to fit your individual needs.

Of course, all this pampering doesn't come cheap. Massages are generally $95 to $130 for 50 minutes and $145 to $180 for 80 minutes; body treatments are in the $120-to-$165 range; and alternative healthcare treatments can be as high as $150 to $220. But you may think it's worth the expense to banish your tension and stress.

the best of the Old World (romantic ceiling murals, larger-than-life Roman-style sculptures, mammoth Greek columns, huge European tubs), the finest Eastern traditions (a full Japanese-style traditional bath and various exotic treatments from India), and the lure of the islands (tropical foliage, ancient Hawaiian treatments, and island products). This spa has everything from a top fitness center to a menu of classes and is constantly on the cutting edge of the latest trends. See p. 117.

- **Spa Kea Lani at The Fairmont Kea Lani Maui** (© 800/659-4100 or 808/875-4100; www.kealani.com): This intimate, Art Deco boutique spa (just a little over 5,000 sq. ft., with nine treatment rooms), which opened in 1999, is the place for personal and private attention. The fitness center next door is open 24 hours (a rarity in Hawaiian resorts) with a personal trainer on duty some 14 hours a day. See p. 116.

- **Spa Moana at the Hyatt Regency Maui Resort and Spa** (© 800/233-1234 or 808/661-1234; www.maui.hyatt.com): The island's first oceanfront spa, a 9,000-square-foot facility,

opened recently with a $3.5-million price tag. The new spa offers an open-air exercise lanai, wet-treatment rooms, massage rooms, a relaxation lounge, sauna and steam rooms, a Roman pool illuminated by overhead skylights, and a duet treatment suite for couples. See p. 97.

- **Spa at Ritz-Carlton Kapalua** (© 800/262-8440 or 808/669-6200; www.ritzcarlton.com): Book a massage on the beach. The spa itself is welcoming and wonderful, but there is nothing like smelling the salt in the air and feeling the gentle caressing of the wind in your hair while experiencing a true Hawaiian massage. See p. 106.

- **The Health Centre at the Four Seasons Resort Maui** (© 800/334-MAUI [6284] or 808/874-8000; www.fshr.com): Imagine the sounds of the waves rolling on Wailea Beach as you are soothingly massaged in the privacy of your cabana, tucked into the beachside foliage. This is the place to come to be absolutely spoiled. Yes, there's an excellent workout area and tons of great classes, but their specialty is hedonistic indulgence. See p. 117.

10 The Best Restaurants

- **The Banyan Tree Restaurant** (© 808/669-6200): Fasten your seat belts food fans: This is one of the hottest, most creative chefs to come to Hawaii in decades. Australian Chef Antony Scholtmeyer, operating out of the Ritz-Carlton Kapalua, is dishing out a blend of flavors and textures like crispy-skin moi (the Hawaiian fish of royalty) or honey-roasted duck breast. See p. 147.

- **Mañana Garage** (© 808/873-0220): It's great fun dining here, and the food is fantastic, too. Tuck into fabulous

arepas (cornmeal-cheese griddle cakes with smoked salmon), fried green tomatoes, excellent ceviche, and a host of new flavors in an ambience of spirited color and industrial edge. You'll dine among vertical garage doors, hubcap table bases, cobalt walls, and chrome accents, with *Buena Vista Social Club* on the sound system and very hip servers who will bring you the best desserts in this neck of the woods—Kahului, of all places! The chef, Tom Lelli, came here from Haliimaile General Store. See p. 132.

- **A Saigon Cafe** (© 808/243-9560): Jennifer Nguyen's unmarked dining room in an odd corner of Wailuku is always packed, a tribute to her clean, crisp Vietnamese cuisine—and the Maui grapevine. Grab a round of rice paper and wrap your own Vietnamese "burrito" of tofu, noodles, and vegetables. See p. 135.
- **AK's Café** (808/244-8774; www. akscafe.com): Chef Elaine Rothermel has a winner with this tiny cafe in the industrial district of Wailuku. It may be slightly off the tourist path, and the decor isn't much to look at, but it is well worth the effort to find this delicious eatery, with creative cuisine coming out of the kitchen—most of it healthy. Prices are so eye-poppingly cheap, you might find yourself wandering back here again during your vacation. See p. 135.
- **Café O'Lei** (© 808/661-9491): The delicious, creative cuisine of Dana Pastula, who managed fancy restaurants on Lanai and in Wailea before opening her own, has two restaurants serving her fresh, healthy cuisine: Café O'Lei Lahaina (p. 139) and the Ma'alaea Grill (p. 150). For reasonably priced, interesting, and memorable meals, don't miss the chance to eat at the O'Leis.
- **David Paul's Lahaina Grill** (© 808/ 667-5117): Tirelessly popular and universally appreciated for its high quality, David Paul's is still most folks' favorite Maui eatery—even without David Paul. No one seems to tire of the Kalua duck he turned into a Maui institution, or the Kona coffee–roasted rack of lamb, or the much-imitated tequila shrimp. The menu changes often, but thank goodness the room doesn't; its pressed-tin ceilings and 1890s decor continue to intrigue. See p. 138.
- **Old Lahaina Luau** (© 800/248-5828 or 808/667-1998): It's not exactly a restaurant, but it's certainly an unforgettable dining experience. Maui's best luau serves top-quality food that's as much Pacific Rim as authentically Hawaiian, served from an open-air thatched structure. It's one-third entertainment, one-third good food, and one-third ambience. See p. 138.
- **Gerard's** (© 808/661-8939): Proving that French is fabulous, particularly in the land of sushi and sashimi, Gerard Reversade is the Gallic gastronome who delivers ecstasy with every bite. From the rack of lamb to the spinach salad and oyster mushrooms in puff pastry, every meal is memorable. The fairy lights on the veranda in the balmy outdoor Lahaina setting are the icing on the gâteau. See p. 138.
- **Swan Court** (© 808/661-1234): For a romantic setting with candlelight, a Japanese garden, and swans gliding by serenely, this is the ticket. It isn't often that I find a fine dining experience in a hotel that is terrific, but this is the exception to the rule. In addition to excellent seafood, impeccable service, and a dreamy ocean view, Swan Court is a wonderful change of pace, a year-round Valentine dinner where you can dress up and impress your date. See p. 142.
- **Roy's Kahana Bar & Grill** (© 808/ 669-6999; www.roysrestaurant.com): This restaurant bustles with young, hip servers impeccably trained to deliver blackened ahi or perfectly seared lemon grass *shutome* (broadbill swordfish) hot to your table, in rooms that sizzle with cross-cultural tastings. See p. 145.
- **Vino Italian Tapas & Wine Bar** (© 808/661-VINO): Probably the

best Italian food on Maui is served at this exquisite restaurant, overlooking the rolling hills of the Kapalua Golf Course. The surprise is that it's run by two Japanese guys—D. K. Kodama, chef and owner of Sansei Seafood Restaurant and Sushi Bar (p. 148), and master sommelier Chuck Furuya. The two teamed up to create this culinary adventure for foodies. Every dish is perfectly paired with wine (the wine list alone features more than 150 selections, many of them estate wines exclusive to Vino). The menu changes constantly but always has homemade pastas and seafood masterpieces. See p. 148.

- **Sansei Seafood Restaurant** (© **808/ 669-6286** in Kapalua and **808/879- 0004** in Kihei): Relentlessly popular, Sansei serves sushi and then some: hand rolls warm and cold, udon and ramen, and the signature Asian rockshrimp cake with the oh-so-complex lime chili butter and cilantro pesto. This Kapalua choice is flavor central—simplicity is not the strong suit, so be prepared for some busy tasting. Another branch has opened in Kihei. See p. 148.

- **Plantation House Restaurant** (© **808/669-6299**): At Plantation House, there are teak tables, a fireplace, open sides, mountain and ocean views, and chef Alex Stanislaw's love for Mediterranean flavors and preparations. It's a friendly, comfortable restaurant with great food from a breakfast of sublime eggs Mediterranean to polenta, crab cakes, several preparations of fish, pork tenderloin, filet mignon, and other delights at dinner. The ambience is superb. See p. 147.

- **Joe's Bar & Grill** (© **808/875- 7767;** www.joesbarandgrill.com): The impressive view spans the Wailea golf course, tennis courts, ocean, and

Haleakala—a worthy setting for Beverly Gannon's style of American home cooking with a regional twist (also see "Haliimaile General Store," below). The hearty staples include excellent mashed potatoes, lobster, fresh fish, and filet mignon, but the meatloaf (a whole loaf, like Mom used to make) seems to upstage them all. See p. 152.

- **Moana Bakery & Cafe** (© **808/ 579-9999**): In the unlikely location of Paia, the Moana gets high marks for its stylish concrete floors, high ceilings, booths and cafe tables, and fabulous food. Don Ritchey, formerly a chef at Haliimaile General Store, has created the perfect Paia eatery, a casual bakery-cafe that highlights his stellar skills. It may not look like much from the outside, but don't be fooled. This innovative eatery serves breakfast, lunch, and dinner and offers live entertainment at night. See p. 158.

- **Haliimaile General Store** (© **808/ 572-2666**): More than a decade later, Bev Gannon, one of the 12 original Hawaii Regional Cuisine chefs, is still going strong at her foodie haven in the pineapple fields. You'll dine at tables set on old wood floors under high ceilings. The food, a blend of eclectic American with ethnic touches, bridges Hawaii with Gannon's Texas roots and puts an innovative spin on Hawaii Regional Cuisine. Examples include sashimi napoleon and the house salad—island greens with mandarin oranges, onions, toasted walnuts, and blue-cheese crumble. See p. 154.

- **Casanova Italian Restaurant** (© **808/572-0220**): Yes, I still love Casanova in upcountry Makawao, and for more than one reason: garlic spinach topped with Parmesan and pine nuts, polenta with radicchio, tiramisu, and the spaghetti fradiavolo.

This is pasta heaven and the center of nightlife on this half of the island. See p. 154.

- **Henry Clay's Rotisserie** (Hotel Lanai, Lanai City; ℂ **808/565-7211**): Henry Clay Richardson, a New Orleans native, has made some welcome changes to Lanai's dining landscape with his rustic inn in the middle of Lanai City. The menu focuses on French country fare: fresh meats, seafood, and local produce in assertive preparations. The decor consists of plates on the pine-paneled walls, chintz curtains, peach tablecloths and hunter-green napkins, and a roaring fireplace. See p. 294.

- **Pele's Other Garden** (ℂ **808/565-9628**): You do not have to spend a fortune at the high-priced eateries at the two resorts on Lanai; this charming bistro in the heart of Lanai City has a full-scale New York deli (yummy pizzas), and you can also get box lunches and picnic baskets to go. Dinner is now served on china on cloth-covered tables—a real dining room! See p. 296.

11 The Best Shops & Galleries

- **Summerhouse** (ℂ **808/871-1320**): Bright and sassy tropical wear and the jewelry and accessories to go with it are a cut above at Kahului's Summerhouse. T-shirts are tailored and in day-to-evening colors, while dresses are good for either the office or a night out. See p. 231.

- **Bailey House Gift Shop** (ℂ **808/244-3326**): You can travel Hawaii and peruse its past with the assemblage of made-in-Hawaii items at this museum gift shop in Wailuku. Tropical preserves, Hawaiian music, pareus, prints by esteemed Hawaiian artists, cookbooks, hatbands, and magnificent wood bowls reflect a discerning standard of selection. Unequaled for Hawaiian treasures on Maui. See p. 231.

- **Brown-Kobayashi** (ℂ **808/242-0804**): At this quiet, tasteful, and elegant Asian shop in Wailuku, the selection of antiques and collectibles changes constantly but reflects an unwavering sense of gracious living. There are old and new European and Hawaiian objects, from koa furniture (which disappears fast) to lacquerware, Bakelite jewelry, Peking glass beads, and a few priceless pieces of antique ivory. See p. 232.

- **Sig Zane Designs** (ℂ **808/249-8997**): This Hilo icon didn't skip a beat in winning the hearts of Maui residents when he moved to Wailuku. Located on Wailuku's Market Street, his new shop of aloha wear and Hawaiian lifestyle treasures is a boon to historic Wailuku. (At press time, Zane was considering moving the store to Kahului; call before you go.) See p. 232.

- **Hui No'eau Visual Arts Center** (ℂ **808/572-6560**): Half the experience is the center itself, one of Maui's historic treasures: a strikingly designed 1917 *kamaaina* (native-born or old-timer) estate on 9 acres in Makawao; two of Maui's largest hybrid Cook and Norfolk pines; and an art center with classes, exhibitions, and demonstrations. The gift shop is as memorable as the rest of it. You'll find one-of-a-kind works by local artists, from prints to jewelry and pottery. See "Upcountry Maui" in chapter 9.

- **Village Galleries** (ℂ **808/661-4402** in Lahaina or **808/669-1800** in Kapalua): Maui's oldest galleries have maintained high standards and the respect of a public that is increasingly impatient with clichéd island art. On exhibit are the finest contemporary

Maui artists in all media, with a discerning selection of handcrafted jewelry. In Lahaina the new contemporary gallery has a larger selection of jewelry, ceramics, glass, and gift items, as well as paintings and prints. See p. 235 and p. 237.

- **Viewpoints Gallery** (© **808/572-5979**): I love this airy, well-designed Makawao gallery and its helpful staff, which complement the fine Maui art: paintings, sculpture, jewelry, prints, woods, and glass. This is Maui's only fine-arts cooperative, showcasing the work of dozens of local artists. See p. 240.

- **Hana Coast Gallery** (© **808/248-8636**): This gallery is a good reason to go to Hana: It's an esthetic and cultural experience that informs as it enlightens. Tucked away in the posh hideaway hotel, the gallery is known for its high level of curatorship and commitment to the cultural art of Hawaii. The 3,000-square-foot gallery is devoted entirely to Hawaiian artists. Dozens of well-established local artists display their sculptures, paintings, prints, feather work, stonework, and carvings in displays that are so natural they could well exist in someone's home. See p. 242.

- **Dis 'N Dat** (Lanai; © **866-DIS-NDAT** or 808/565-9170): This is my favorite shop on Lanai, where Barry (Dis) and Susie (Dat) have collected the unusual, the bizarre, and the hilariously funny. You'll find everything from finely crafted teak and exotic wood sculptures and carvings to mobiles and wind chimes (the more outrageous, the better), plus an impressive line of handmade jewelry, stained glass, and more. See p. 305.

- **The Local Gentry** (© **808/565-9130**): This wonderful boutique, on the island of Lanai, features clothing and accessories that are not the standard resort-shop fare. You'll find fabulous silk aloha shirts by Iolani; Putumayo separates (perfect for Hawaii) in easy-care fabrics; a fabulous line of silk aloha shirts by Tiki; top-quality hemp-linen camp shirts; inexpensive sarongs; fabulous socks; and the Tommy Bahama line for men and women. There are also great T-shirts, swimwear, jewelry, bath products, picture frames, jeans, chic sunglasses, and offbeat sandals. The most recent additions are wonderful children's clothes. See p. 307.

2

Planning Your Trip to Maui

Maui has so many places to explore, things to do, and sights to see that it's hard to know where to start—that's where I come in. In the pages that follow, I've compiled everything you need to know to plan your ideal trip to Maui: information on airlines, seasons, a calendar of events, how to make camping reservations, and much more (even how to tie the knot).

1 The Island in Brief

CENTRAL MAUI

This flat, often windy corridor between Maui's two volcanoes is where you'll most likely arrive—it's the site of the main airport. It's also home to the majority of the island's population, the heart of the business community, and the local government (courts, cops, and county/state government agencies). You'll find good shopping and dining bargains here but very little in the way of accommodations.

KAHULUI This is "Dream City," home to thousands of former sugar-cane workers who dreamed of owning their own homes away from the plantations. A couple of small hotels near the airport are convenient for 1-night stays if you have a late arrival or early departure, but this is not a place to spend your vacation.

WAILUKU With its faded wooden storefronts, old plantation homes, and shops straight out of the 1940s, Wailuku is like a time capsule. Although most people race through on their way to see the natural beauty of **Iao Valley** 𝒜, this quaint little town is worth a brief visit, if only to see a real place where real people actually appear to be working at something other than a tan. Beaches surrounding Wailuku are not great for swimming,

but the old town has a spectacular view of Haleakala, a couple of hostels and an excellent historic B&B, great budget restaurants, some interesting bungalow architecture, a Frank Lloyd Wright building on the outskirts of town, and the always-endearing Bailey House Museum.

WEST MAUI

This is the fabled Maui you see on postcards. Jagged peaks, green valleys, a wilderness full of native species—the majestic West Maui Mountains are the epitome of earthly paradise. The beaches here are some of the islands' best. And it's no secret: This stretch of coastline along Maui's "forehead," from Kapalua to the historic port of Lahaina, is the island's most bustling resort area (with South Maui close behind). Expect a few mainland-style traffic jams.

If you want to book into a resort or condo on this coast, first consider which community you'd like to make your base. The coastal communities are listed from south to north below.

LAHAINA 𝒜 This old whaling seaport teems with restaurants, T-shirt shops, and a gallery on nearly every block, but there's still lots of real history to be found amid the tourist development. This vintage village is a tame version of its former self, when whalers swaggered ashore in search of women and grog. The town is a great base for visitors: A few old hotels (like the restored 1901 Pioneer Inn on the harbor), quaint B&Bs, and a handful of oceanfront condos offer a variety of choices. This is the place to stay if you want to be in the center of things—restaurants, shops, and nightlife—but parking can be a problem.

KAANAPALI 🐦🐦 Farther north along the West Maui coast is Hawaii's first master-planned resort. Pricey midrise hotels, which line nearly 3 miles of lovely gold-sand beach, are linked by a land-scaped parkway and separated by a jungle of plants. Golf greens wrap around the slope between beachfront and hillside properties. **Whalers Village** (a seaside mall with pricey shops like Tiffany and Louis Vuitton, plus a great little whale museum) and restaurants are easy to reach on foot along the waterfront walkway or via the resort shuttle, which also serves the small West Maui airport to the north. Shuttles also go to Lahaina, 3 miles to the south, for shopping, dining, entertainment, and boat tours. Kaanapali is popular with convention groups and families.

FROM HONOKOWAI TO NAPILI In the building binge of the 1970s, condominiums sprouted along this gorgeous coastline like mushrooms after a rain. Today these older oceanside units offer excellent bargains for astute travelers. The great location—along sandy beaches, within minutes of both the Kapalua and the Kaanapali resort areas, and close to the goings-on in Lahaina town—makes this area a great place to stay for value-conscious travelers. It feels more peaceful and residential than either Kaanapali or Lahaina.

In **Honokowai** and **Mahinahina** you'll find mostly older units that tend to be cheaper. There's not much shopping here aside from convenience stores, but you'll have easy access to the shops and restaurants of Kaanapali.

Kahana is a little more upscale than Honokowai and Mahinahina. Most of the condos here are big high-rise types, built more recently than those immediately to the south. You'll find a nice selection of shops and restaurants in the area, and Kapalua–West Maui Airport is nearby.

Napili is a much-sought-after area for condo seekers: It's quiet; has great beaches, restaurants, and shops; and is close to Kapalua. Units are generally more expensive here (although I've found a few affordable gems; see the Napili Bay entry on p. 105).

KAPALUA 🐦 North beyond Kaanapali and the shopping centers of Napili and Kahana, the road starts to climb, and the vista opens up to fields of silver-green pineapple and manicured golf fairways. Turn down the country lane of Pacific pines toward the sea, and you could only be in Kapalua. It's the very exclusive domain of two gracious and expensive hotels, set on one of Hawaii's best gold-sand beaches, next to two bays that are marine-life preserves (with fabulous surfing in winter).

However, one of the hotels, the Kapalua Bay Resort, is scheduled to be torn down in 2006 and then a new resort will be built in its place.

Even if you don't stay here, you're welcome to come and enjoy Kapalua. Both of the fancy hotels provide public parking and beach access. The resort champions innovative environmental programs and also has an art school, a golf school, three golf courses, historic features, a collection of swanky condos and homes (many available for vacation rental at astronomical prices), and wide-open spaces that include a rainforest preserve—all open to the general public. Kapalua is a great place to stay put. However, if you plan to "tour" Maui, know that it's a long drive from here to get to many of the island's highlights. You might want to consider a more central place to stay because even Lahaina is a 15-minute drive away.

SOUTH MAUI

This is the hottest, sunniest, driest coastline on Maui—Arizona by the sea. Rain rarely falls, and temperatures stick around 85°F (29°C) year-round. On former scrubland from Maalaea to Makena, where cacti once grew wild and cows grazed, are now four distinct areas— Maalaea, Kihei, Wailea, and Makena— and a surprising amount of traffic.

MAALAEA   If the western part of Maui were a head, Maalaea would be just under the chin. This windy oceanfront village centers around the small boat harbor (with a general store, a couple of restaurants, and a huge new mall) and the **Maui Ocean Center** ⟨⟩, an aquarium/ ocean complex. This quaint region offers several condominium units to choose from, but visitors staying here should be aware that it is almost always very windy.

KIHEI   Kihei is less a proper town than a nearly continuous series of condos and minimalls lining South Kihei Road. This is Maui's best vacation bargain: Budget travelers flock to the eight sandy beaches along this scalloped, condo-packed, 7-mile stretch of coast. Kihei is neither charming nor quaint, but it does offer sunshine, affordability, and convenience. If you want a latte in the morning, fine beaches in the afternoon, and Hawaii Regional Cuisine in the evening, all at budget prices, head to Kihei.

WAILEA ⟨⟩   Only 3 decades ago, this was wall-to-wall scrub kiawe trees, but now Wailea is a manicured oasis of multi-million-dollar resort hotels strung along 2 miles of palm-fringed gold coast. It's like Beverly Hills by the sea, except California never had it so good: warm, clear water full of tropical fish; year-round sunshine and clear blue skies; and hedonistic pleasure palaces on 1,500 acres of black-lava shore. It's amazing what a billion dollars can do.

This is the playground of the stretch-limo set. The planned resort development—practically a well-heeled town—has an upscale shopping village, three prized golf courses of its own and three more in close range, and a tennis complex. A growing number of large homes sprawls over the upper hillside (some offering excellent bed-and-breakfast units at reasonable prices).

Appealing natural features include the coastal trail, a 3-mile round-trip path along the oceanfront with pleasing views everywhere you look—out to sea and to the neighboring islands, or inland to the broad lawns and gardens of the hotels. The trail's south end borders an extensive garden of native coastal plants, as well as ancient lava-rock house ruins juxtaposed with elegant oceanfront condos. But the chief attractions, of course, are those five outstanding beaches (the best is Wailea).

MAKENA ⟨⟩   After passing through well-groomed Wailea, suddenly the road enters raw wilderness. After Wailea's overmanicured development, the thorny landscape is a welcome relief. Although beautiful, this is an end-of-the-road kind of place: It's a long drive from Makena to anywhere on Maui. If you want to tour a lot of the island, you might want to book somewhere else. But if you crave a quiet, relaxing respite, where the biggest trip of the day is from your bed to the gorgeous, pristine beach, Makena is your place.

Beyond Makena you'll discover Haleakala's last lava flow, which ran to the sea in 1790; the bay named for French explorer La Perouse; and a chunky lava trail known as the King's Highway, which leads around Maui's empty south shore past ruins and fish camps. Puu Olai stands like Maui's Diamond Head on the shore, where a sunken crater shelters tropical fish, and empty golden-sand beaches stand at the end of dirt roads.

UPCOUNTRY MAUI

After a few days at the beach, you'll probably take notice of the 10,000-foot mountain in the middle of Maui. The slopes of Haleakala ("House of the Sun") are home to cowboys, farmers, and other country people who wave back as you drive by. They're all up here enjoying the crisp air, emerald pastures, eucalyptus, and flower farms of this tropical Olympus—there's even a misty California redwood grove. You can see 1,000 tropical sunsets reflected in the windows of houses old and new, strung along a road that runs like a loose hound from Makawao, an old *paniolo* (cowboy)-turned–New Age village, to Kula, where the road leads up to the crater and **Haleakala National Park** *AAA*. The rumpled, two-lane blacktop of Highway 37 narrows on the other side of Tedeschi Winery, where wine grapes and wild elk flourish on the Ulupalakua Ranch, the biggest on Maui. A stay upcountry is usually affordable, a chance to commune with nature, and a nice contrast to the sizzling beaches and busy resorts below.

MAKAWAO *A*   Until recently, this small, two-street upcountry town consisted of little more than a post office, gas station, feed store, bakery, and restaurant/bar serving the cowboys and farmers living in the surrounding community; the hitching posts outside storefronts were really used to tie up horses. As the population of Maui started expanding in the 1970s, a health-food store popped up, followed by boutiques and a host of health-conscious restaurants. The result is an eclectic amalgam of old *paniolo* Hawaii and the baby-boomer trends of transplanted mainlanders. **Hui No'eau Visual Arts Center,** Hawaii's premier arts collective, is definitely worth a peek. The

only accommodations here are reasonably priced bed-and-breakfasts, perfect for those who enjoy great views and don't mind slightly chilly nights.

KULA *A*   A feeling of pastoral remoteness prevails in this upcountry community of old flower farms, humble cottages, and new suburban ranch houses with million-dollar views that take in the ocean, isthmus, West Maui Mountains, Lanai, and Kahoolawe off in the distance. At night the lights run along the gold coast like a string of pearls, from Maalaea to Puu Olai. Kula sits at a cool 3,000 feet, just below the cloud line, and from here a winding road snakes its way up to Haleakala National Park. Everyone here grows something—Maui onions, carnations, orchids, and proteas, those strange-looking blossoms that look like *Star Trek* props. The local B&Bs cater to guests seeking cool tropical nights, panoramic views, and a rural upland escape. Here you'll find the true peace and quiet that only rural farming country can offer—yet you're still just 30 to 40 minutes away from the beach and an hour's drive from Lahaina.

EAST MAUI

THE ROAD TO HANA *AA*   When old sugar towns die, they usually fade away in rust and red dirt. Not **Paia.** The tangle of electrical, phone, and cable wires hanging overhead symbolizes the town's ability to adapt to the times. Here, trendy restaurants, eclectic boutiques, and high-tech windsurf shops stand next door to the ma-and-pa grocery, fish market, and storefronts that have been serving customers since the plantation days. Hippies took over in the 1970s, and although their macrobiotic restaurants and old-style artists' co-op have made way for Hawaii Regional Cuisine and galleries featuring the works of renowned international artists, Paia still manages to maintain a pleasant vibe of hippiedom. The town's main attraction, though, is **Hookipa Beach Park,** where the wind that roars through the isthmus of Maui brings windsurfers from around the world.

Ten minutes down the road from Paia and up the hill from the Hana Highway—the connector road to the entire east side of Maui—sits **Haiku.** Once a pineapple-plantation village, complete with cannery (today a shopping complex), Haiku offers vacation rentals and B&Bs in a quiet, pastoral setting: the perfect base for those who want to get off the beaten path and experience a quieter side of Maui but don't want to feel too removed (the beach is only 10 min. away).

About 15 to 20 minutes past Haiku is the largely unknown community of **Huelo.** Every day thousands of cars whiz by on the road to Hana. But if you take the time to stop, you'll discover a hidden Hawaii, where Mother Nature is still sensual and wild, where ocean waves pummel soaring lava cliffs, and where serenity prevails. Huelo is not for everyone, but if you want the magic of a place still largely untouched by "progress," check in to a B&B or vacation rental here.

HANA 𝒜𝒜 Set between an emerald rainforest and the blue Pacific is a village probably best defined by what it lacks: golf courses, shopping malls, and McDonald's. Except for two gas stations and a bank with an ATM, you'll find little of what passes for progress here. Instead, you'll discover fragrant tropical flowers, the sweet taste of backyard bananas and papayas, and the easy calm and unabashed small-town aloha spirit of old Hawaii. What saved "Heavenly" Hana from the inevitable march of progress? The 52-mile **Hana Highway,** which winds around 600 curves and crosses more than 50 one-lane bridges on its way from Kahului. You can go to Hana for the day—it's a 3-hour drive (and a half-century away)—but 3 days are better. The tiny town has one hotel, a handful of great B&Bs, and some spectacular vacation rentals.

2 Visitor Information

For advance information on traveling in Maui, contact the **Maui Visitors Bureau,** 1727 Wili Pa Loop, Wailuku, Maui, HI 96793 (✆ **800/525-MAUI** or 808/244-3530; fax 808/244-1337; www.visitmaui. com).

The **Kaanapali Beach Resort Association** is at 2530 Kekaa Dr., Suite 1-B, Lahaina, HI 96761 (✆ **800/245-9229** or 808/661-3271; fax 808/661-9431; www. maui.net/~kbra).

The state agency responsible for tourism is the **Hawaii Visitors and Convention Bureau (HVCB),** Suite 801, Waikiki Business Plaza, 2270 Kalakaua Ave., Honolulu, HI 96815 (✆ **800/ GO-HAWAII** or 808/923-1811; www. gohawaii.com).

If you want information about working and living in Maui, contact **Maui Chamber of Commerce,** 250 Alamaha St., Unit N-16A, Kahului, HI 96732 (✆ **808/871-7711;** www.mauichamber. com).

INFORMATION ON MAUI'S PARKS

NATIONAL PARKS Both Maui and Molokai have one national park each: **Haleakala National Park,** P.O. Box 369, Makawao, HI 96768 (✆ **808/572-4400;** www.nps.gov/hale); and **Kalaupapa National Historical Park,** P.O. Box 2222, Kalaupapa, HI 96742 (✆ **808/ 567-6802;** www.nps.gov/kala). For more information, see "Hiking & Camping" in chapters 7 and 11.

STATE PARKS To find out more about state parks on Maui and Molokai, contact the **Hawaii State Department**

of Land and Natural Resources, 54 S High St., Wailuku, HI 96793 (© **808/ 984-8109;** www.hawaii.gov), which provides information on hiking and camping and will send you free topographic trail maps on request.

COUNTY PARKS   For information on Maui County Parks, contact **Maui County Parks and Recreation,** 1580-C Kaahumanu Ave., Wailuku, HI 96793 (© **808/270-7230;** www.co.maui.hi.us/ departments/Parks/Recware).

3 Money

ATMS

Hawaii pioneered the use of **ATMs** more than 2 decades ago, and now they're everywhere. You'll find them at most banks, in supermarkets, at Long's Drugs, and in most resorts and shopping centers. **Cirrus** (© **800/424-7787;** www.mastercard. com) and **PLUS** (© **800/843-7587;** www.visa.com) are the two most popular networks; check the back of your ATM card to see which network your bank belongs to (most banks belong to both these days).

TRAVELER'S CHECKS

Traveler's checks are something of an anachronism from the days before the ATM made cash accessible at any time. Traveler's checks used to be the only sound alternative to traveling with dangerously large amounts of cash. They were as reliable as currency, but, unlike cash, could be replaced if lost or stolen.

These days traveler's checks are less necessary because most cities have 24-hour ATMs that allow you to withdraw small amounts of cash as needed. However, keep in mind that you will likely be charged an ATM withdrawal fee if the bank is not your own, so if you're withdrawing money every day, you might be better off with traveler's checks—

provided that you don't mind showing identification every time you want to cash one.

You can get traveler's checks at almost any bank. **American Express** offers denominations of $20, $50, $100, $500, and (for cardholders only) $1,000. You'll pay a service charge ranging from 1% to 4%. You can also get American Express traveler's checks over the phone by calling © **800/221-7282;** Amex gold- and platinum-card holders who use this number are exempt from the 1% fee.

Visa offers traveler's checks at Citibank locations nationwide, as well as at several other banks. The service charge ranges between 1.5% and 2%; checks come in denominations of $20, $50, $100, $500, and $1,000. Call © **800/732-1322** for information. AAA members can obtain Visa checks for a $9.95 fee (for checks up to $1,500) at most AAA offices or by calling © **866/339-3378. MasterCard** also offers traveler's checks. Call © **800/223-9920** for a location near you.

If you choose to carry traveler's checks, be sure to keep a record of their serial numbers separate from your checks in the event that they are stolen or lost. You'll get a refund faster if you know the numbers.

Tips **Dear Visa: I'm Off to Kapalua, Kaanapali & Kahakuloa!**

Some credit card companies recommend that you notify them of any impending trip so that they don't become suspicious when the card is used numerous times in an exotic destination and block your charges.

CREDIT CARDS

Credit cards are accepted all over the island. They're a safe way to carry money and they provide a convenient record of all your expenses. You can also withdraw cash advances from your credit cards at banks or ATMs, provided you know your PIN. If you don't know yours, call the number on the back of your credit card and ask the bank to send it to you. It usually takes 5 to 7 business days, though some banks will provide the number over the phone if you tell them your mother's maiden name or some other personal information. Still, be sure to keep some cash on hand for that rare occasion when a restaurant or small shop doesn't take plastic.

4 When to Go

Most visitors don't come to Maui when the weather's best in the islands; rather, they come when it's at its worst everywhere else. Thus, the **high season**—when prices are up and resorts are booked to capacity—generally runs from mid-December through March or mid-April. The last 2 weeks of December in particular are the prime time for travel to Maui. If you're planning a holiday trip, make your reservations as early as possible, count on holiday crowds, and expect to pay top dollar for accommodations, car rentals, and airfare. Whale-watching season begins in January and continues through the rest of winter, sometimes lasting into May.

The **off seasons,** when the best bargain rates are available, are spring (mid-Apr to mid-June) and fall (Sept to mid-Dec)—a paradox, since these are the best seasons in terms of reliably great weather. If you're looking to save money, or if you just want to avoid the crowds, this is the time to visit. Hotel rates tend to be significantly lower during these off seasons. Airfares also tend to be lower—again, sometimes substantially—and good packages and special deals are often available.

Note: If you plan to come to Maui between the last week in April and the first week in May, be sure to book your accommodations, interisland air reservations, and car rental in advance. In Japan the last week of April is called **Golden Week,** because three Japanese holidays take place one after the other. The islands are especially busy with Japanese tourists during this time.

Due to the large number of families traveling in **summer** (June–Aug), you won't get the fantastic bargains of spring and fall. However, you'll still do much better on packages, airfare, and accommodations than you will in the winter months.

THE WEATHER

Because Maui lies at the edge of the tropical zone, it technically has only two seasons, both of them warm. The dry season corresponds to summer, and the rainy season generally runs during the winter from November to March. It rains every day somewhere in the islands at any time of the year, but the rainy season can cause "gray" weather and spoil your tanning opportunities. Fortunately, it seldom rains for more than 3 days straight, and rainy days often just consist of a mix of clouds and sun, with very brief showers.

The **year-round temperature** usually varies no more than 15°F (9°C), but it depends on where you are. Maui's **leeward** sides (the west and south) are usually hot and dry, whereas the **windward** sides (east and north) are generally cooler and moist. If you want arid, sunbaked, desertlike weather, go leeward. If you want lush, often wet, junglelike weather, go windward. Your best bets for total year-round sun are the Kihei-Wailea and Lahaina-Kapalua coasts.

Maui is also full of **microclimates,** thanks to its interior valleys, coastal plains, and mountain peaks. If you travel into the mountains, it can change from summer to winter in a matter of hours, because it's cooler the higher up you go. In other words, if the weather doesn't suit you, go to the other side of the island—or head into the hills.

HOLIDAYS

When Hawaii observes holidays, especially those over a long weekend, travel between the islands increases, interisland airline seats are fully booked, rental cars are at a premium, and hotels and restaurants are busier than usual.

Federal, state, and county government offices are closed on all federal holidays: January 1 (New Year's Day); third Monday in January (Martin Luther King Day); third Monday in February (Presidents' Day, Washington's Birthday); last Monday in May (Memorial Day); July 4th (Independence Day); first Monday in September (Labor Day); second Monday in October (Columbus Day); November 11 (Veterans' Day); fourth Thursday in November (Thanksgiving Day); and December 25 (Christmas).

State and county offices also are closed on local holidays, including Prince Kuhio Day (Mar 26), honoring the birthday of Hawaii's first delegate to the U.S. Congress; King Kamehameha Day (June 11), a statewide holiday commemorating Kamehameha the Great, who united the islands and ruled from 1795 to 1819; and Admission Day (third Fri in Aug), which honors Hawaii's admission as the 50th state in the United States on August 21, 1959.

Other special days celebrated by many people in Hawaii but that do not involve the closing of federal, state, or county offices are Chinese New Year (in Jan or Feb), Girls' Day (Mar 3), Buddha's Birthday (Apr 8), Father Damien's Day (Apr 15), Boys' Day (May 5), Samoan Flag Day (in Aug), Aloha Festivals (in Sept or Oct), and Pearl Harbor Day (Dec 7).

MAUI, MOLOKAI & LANAI CALENDAR OF EVENTS

As with any schedule of upcoming events, the following information is subject to change; always confirm the details before you plan your schedule around an event. For a complete and up-to-date list of events throughout Maui, Molokai, and Lanai, point your browser to **www.visitmaui.com, www.molokai-hawaii. com,** or **www.visitlanai.net.**

January

PGA Kapalua Mercedes Championship, Kapalua Resort. Top PGA golfers compete for $1 million. Call 𝄫 **808/669-2440** or visit www. kapaluamaui.com. January 2 to January 8, 2006.

Ka Molokai Makahiki, Kaunakakai Town Baseball Park, Mitchell Pauole Center, Kaunakakai, Molokai. Makahiki, a traditional time of peace in ancient Hawaii, is re-created with performances by Hawaiian music groups and hula halau, ancient Hawaiian games, a sporting competition, and Hawaiian crafts and food. It's a wonderful chance to experience the Hawaii of yesteryear. Call 𝄫 **800/800-6367** or 808/553-3876; www.molokai-hawaii. com. Late January.

Hula Bowl Football All-Star Classic, War Memorial Stadium. An annual all-star football classic featuring America's top college players. Call 𝄫 **808/ 874-9500** or visit www.hulabowlmaui. com; ticket orders are processed beginning April 1 for the next year's game.

Chinese New Year. Lahaina town rolls out the red carpet for this important event with a traditional lion dance at the historic Wo Hing Temple on Front Street, accompanied by fireworks, food booths, and a host of activities. Call

© **888/310-1117** or 808/667-9175. Also on Market Street in Wailuku; call © **808/270-7414.** January 29, 2006.

February

Wendy's Champions Skins Game at Wailea, Wailea Golf Courses. Longtime golfing greats participate in this four-man tournament for $600,000 in prize money. Call © **800/332-1614;** www.seniorskinswailea.com. Early February.

Whale Day Celebration, Kalama Park, Kihei. A daylong celebration in the park with a parade of whales, entertainment, a crafts fair, games, and food. Call © **808/249-8811** or visit www.visitmaui.com. February 18, 2006.

March

Ocean Arts Festival, Lahaina. The entire town of Lahaina celebrates the annual migration of Pacific humpback whales with an Ocean Arts Festival in Banyan Tree Park. Artists display their best ocean-themed art for sale, and Hawaiian musicians and hula troupes entertain. Enjoy marine-related activities, games, and a Creature Feature touch-pool exhibit for children. Call © **888/310-1117** or 808/667-9194; www.visitlahaina.com. Mid-March.

Run to the Sun, Paia to Haleakala. The world's top ultramarathoners make the journey from sea level to the top of 10,000-foot Haleakala, some 37 miles. Call © **808/891-2516** or visit www.virr.com. March 27, 2006.

East Maui Taro Festival, Hana. Here's your chance to taste taro in many different forms, from poi to chips. Also on hand are Hawaiian exhibits, demonstrations, and food booths. Call © **808/248-8972;** www.calendarmaui.com. Generally the end of March or early April.

Molokai Hawaiian Paniolo Heritage Rodeo, Molokai Rodeo Arena, Maunaloa, Molokai. A celebration of Hawaii's *paniolo* (cowboy) heritage. Call © **808/552-2791.**

April

Buddha Day, Lahaina Jodo Mission, Lahaina. Each year this historic mission holds a flower festival pageant honoring the birth of Buddha. Call © **808/661-4303;** www.calendarmaui.com. April 1, 2006.

Maui Polo Spring Season Begins. For a complete list of all the polo matches in the cool, upcountry area of Maui, call © **808/877-7744.**

Annual Ritz-Carlton Kapalua Celebration of the Arts, Ritz-Carlton Kapalua. Contemporary and traditional artists give free hands-on lessons. Call © **808/669-6200;** www.celebrationofthearts.org. The 4-day festival begins the Thursday before Easter. April 13 to April 16, 2006.

David Malo Day, Lahaina. Lahainaluna High School celebrates its famous Hawaiian scholar with a luau and hula performances. Call © **808/662-4000;** www.visitmaui.com. Usually mid- to late April.

Banyan Tree Birthday Party, Lahaina. Come celebrate the 133rd birthday of Lahaina's famous Banyan Tree with a weekend of activities. Call © **888/310-1117** or 808/667-9194; www.visitlahaina.com. April 22 and 23, 2006.

Earth Day, Kahului and Maalaea. Maui Nui Botanical Gardens in Kahului (© **808/249-2798**) and the Harbor Shops in Maalaea (© **808/249-8811**) host Earth Day celebrations. April 22 and 23, 2006.

That Ulupalakua Thing! Maui County Agricultural Trade Show and Sampling, Ulupalakua Ranch and Tedeschi Winery, Ulupalakua. The name may be long and cumbersome, but this event is hot, hot, hot. It features local-product exhibits, food booths, and live entertainment. Call © **808/878-2839;** www.ulupalakua thing.com. April 29, 2006.

May

Outrigger Canoe Season, all islands. From May to September nearly every weekend, canoe paddlers across the state participate in outrigger canoe races. Call © **808/261-6615,** or go to www.y2kanu.com for this year's schedule of events.

Annual Lei Day Celebration, Fairmont Kea Lani, Wailea. May Day is Lei Day in Hawaii, celebrated with lei-making contests, pageantry, arts and crafts, and concerts throughout the islands. Call © **808/875-4100;** www. visitmaui.com. May 1.

Kapalua Jr. Vet/Sr. Tennis Championships, Kapalua. Men and women ages 35 and over compete in singles and doubles championship tournaments. Call © **808/669-5677.** May 5 to May 7, 2006.

International Festival of Canoes, West Maui. Celebration of the Pacific islands' seafaring heritage. Events include canoe paddling and sailing regattas, a luau feast, cultural arts demonstrations, canoe-building exhibits, and music. Call © **888/310-1117;** www. calendarmaui.com. May 13 to May 27, 2006.

Molokai Ka Hula Piko, Papohaku Beach Park, Kaluakoi, Molokai. This daylong celebration of the hula takes place on the island where it was born. It features performances by hula schools, musicians, and singers from across Hawaii, as well as local food and Hawaiian crafts, including quilting, woodworking, feather work, and deer-horn scrimshaw. Call © **800/800-6367** or 808/553-3876; www.molokai-hawaii.com. Third Saturday in May.

He Makana Aloha, Molokai. The fourth annual Hawaiian performing-arts competition with workshops, lectures, and a Hawaiian luau. Call © **808/630-5861.** May 23 and 24, 2006.

June

Neil Pryde Slalom, Kahului. Annual windsurfing slalom race at Kanaha Beach Park. Call © **808/877-2111.** Early June.

King Kamehameha Celebration, statewide. It's a state holiday with a massive floral parade, *hoolaulea* (party), and much more. Call © **888/310-1117** or 808/667-9194 or visit www.visitlahaina.com for Maui events; © **808/567-6361** for Molokai events. June 10 and 11, 2006.

Maui Film Festival, Wailea Resort. Five days and nights of screenings of premieres and special films, along with traditional Hawaiian storytelling, chants, hula, and contemporary music. Call © **808/579-9996;** mauifilm festival.com. The second or third week in June.

Hawaiian Slack-Key Guitar Festival, Maui Arts and Cultural Center, Kahului. Great music performed by the best musicians in Hawaii. It's 5 hours long and absolutely free. Call © **808/239-4336;** www.hawaiianslackkeyguitar festivals.com. Late June.

Kapalua Clambake Pro-Am Golf Tournament, Kapalua Resort. This 20th annual Pro-Am tournament ends with a giant clam bake on the beach. Call © **808/669-8802.** June 23 to June 25, 2006.

Makana Aloha Performing Arts Competition, Molokai. Free competition featuring Hawaiian song and dance, with Hawaiian food, arts and crafts, and games for kids. Call © **808/552-2800;** www.molokaievents.com. Last Saturday in June (June 24, 2006).

July

Polo Season, Olinda Polo Field, Makawao, Maui. Polo matches featuring Hawaii's top players, often joined by famous international players. Call ℂ **808/572-7326.** Held every Sunday at 1pm throughout the summer.

Pineapple Festival, Lanai City, Lanai. Celebrates Lanai's history of pineapple plantation and ranching and includes a pineapple-eating contest, pineapple-cooking contest, entertainment, arts and crafts, food, and fireworks. Call ℂ **808/565-7600;** www.visitlanai.net. First Saturday in July (July 1, 2006).

Fourth of July. Lahaina holds an old-fashioned Independence Day celebration with fireworks lighting the night sky over Lahaina's roadstead. Call ℂ **888/310-1117** or 808/667-9194 (www.visitlahaina.com). Kaanapali puts on a grand old celebration with live music, children's activities, and fireworks. Call ℂ **808/661-3271.**

Makawao Parade and Rodeo, Makawao, Maui. The annual parade and rodeo event have been taking place in this upcountry cowboy town for generations. Call ℂ **800/525-MAUI** or 808/572-9565. July 4, 2006.

Kapalua Wine and Food Festival, Kapalua. Famous wine and food experts and oenophiles gather at the Ritz-Carlton and Kapalua Bay hotels for formal tastings, panel discussions, and samplings of new releases. Call ℂ **800/KAPALUA;** www.kapalua resort.com.

Bon Dance and Lantern Ceremony, Lahaina. This colorful Buddhist ceremony honors the souls of the dead. Call ℂ **808/661-4304.** Usually early July.

August

Maui Onion Festival, Whalers Village, Kaanapali, Maui. Everything you ever wanted to know about the sweetest onions in the world. Food, entertainment, tasting, and the Maui Onion Cook-Off. Call ℂ **808/661-4567;** www.whalersvillage.com. August 5 and 6, 2006.

Hawaii State Windsurf Championship, Kanaha Beach Park, Kahului. Top windsurfers compete. Call ℂ **808/ 877-2111.** August 5, 2006.

Tahiti Fete, Wailuku. Annual Tahitian dance competition, arts and crafts, and food, held in the War Memorial Gym, Wailuku. Call ℂ **808/244-5831.** August 12 and 13, 2006.

September

Aloha Festivals, various locations. Parades and other events celebrate Hawaiian culture. Call ℂ **800/852-7690** or 808/545-1771 or visit www.alohafestivals.com for a schedule of events.

LifeFest Kapalua, Kapalua Resort. A 3-day health-and-wellness event featuring lectures and panel presentations by leaders in the health and wellness field, plus ocean sporting events, fitness activities, a health and wellness expo, and sumptuous gala dinners. Wailea resorts and condominiums offer special package rates. For more information, call ℂ **866/669-2440** or 808/669-2440 (www.lifefestmaui.com). September 8 to September 10, 2006.

Maui Writer's Conference, Marriott Wailea, an Outrigger Resort. Workshops, lectures, and panel discussions with writers, agents, and publishers. Call ℂ **888/974-8373** or 808/879-0061; www.mauiwriters.com. Labor Day weekend.

A Taste of Lahaina, Lahaina Civic Center, Maui. Some 30,000 people show up to sample 40 signature entrees of Maui's premier chefs during this weekend festival, which includes

Ongoing Events

Every Friday night from 7 to 10pm, as part of **Friday Night Is Art Night** in Lahaina, the town's galleries open their doors for special shows, demonstrations, and refreshments. There are even strolling musicians wandering the streets.

On the first and third weekends of the month, Hawaiian artists sell and share culture, arts, and crafts under the famous landmark **Banyan Tree** in Lahaina. On the other weekends the Lahaina Arts Society has an exhibit and sale of various works of art in the same place.

Every Wednesday at 4:30 and 7:30pm, outstanding contemporary and art films are shown at the Maui Arts & Culture Center in Kahului as part of the **Maui Film Festival** (© 808/242-SHOW; www.mauifilmfestival.com).

You don't have to spend a good chunk of change and order two drinks to experience the Hawaiian art of hula. There are **free hula performances** every week. In **Lahaina:** every Saturday and Sunday at 1pm and Tuesday and Thursday at 7pm in the Lahaina Cannery Mall; and every Wednesday at 2pm and every Friday at 2 and 6pm at the Lahaina Center. In **Kaanapali:** every Monday, Wednesday, and Friday at 7pm at the Whalers Village. In **Kapalua:** every Thursday at 10am at the Kapalua Shops.

It's also fun to check out Maui's **outdoor markets,** where you can find good deals on gifts to bring home, try the local produce, and meet the locals. Every Saturday from 7am to 1pm, the **Maui Swap Meet** is held next to the post office on Puunene Avenue in Kahului. This is Maui's largest outdoor market, filled with everything from produce to Hawaiian art. For upscale culinary items, stop by the **Aloha Friday Farmers Market,** held every Friday from 7am to 1pm at Maui Community College in Kahului. Here you'll find gourmet vendors like Surfing Goat Dairy, Waipoli Hydroponic Greens/Pacific Produce, Alii Lavender, and terrific baked goods from the MCC culinary art students. If you want to sleep in, you can always go to the **Kaahumanu Shopping Center,** Kaahumanu Avenue, Kahului, where the parking lot is filled with bargains every Friday from 9am to 5pm. The **Hana Farmer's and Crafter's Market,** Hasegawa Service Station, Hana Highway, Hana, is a chance to meet local artists and farmers every Thursday from 9:30am to 3:30pm. At the **Kahului Shopping Center,** also on Kaahumanu Avenue in Kahului, you'll get great deals on produce every Wednesday morning from 7am to noon. Arrive early to get the best bargains at the **Suda Store,** on Kihei Road in Kihei, which hosts an outdoor market every Monday, Wednesday, and Friday from 1:30 to 5:30pm. On Lower Honoapiilani Road in **Honokowai,** you'll find a great farmers market and other items for sale every Monday, Wednesday, and Friday from 7 to 11am.

cooking demonstrations, wine tastings, and live entertainment. The event begins Friday night with Maui Chefs Present, a themed dinner/cocktail party featuring about a dozen of Maui's best chefs. Call © **888/310-1117** or 808/667-9194; www.visitlahaina.com. Early September.

Hana Relays, Hana Highway. Hundreds of runners, in relay teams, crowd the Hana Highway from Kahalui to Hana (you might want to avoid the road this day). Call ℭ **808/871-6441;** www.virr.com. September 9, 2006.

Maui Marathon, Kahului to Kaanapali, Maui. Runners line up at the Maui Mall before daybreak and head off for Kaanapali. Call ℭ **808/871-6441;** www.virr.com. Sunday, September 17, 2006.

Maui County Fair, War Memorial Complex, Wailuku. The oldest county fair in Hawaii features a parade, amusement rides, live entertainment, and exhibits. Call ℭ **800/525-MAUI** or 808/244-3530; www.calendarmaui. com. September 28 to October 1, 2006.

October

Aloha Classic World Wavesailing Championship, Hookipa Beach, Maui. The top windsurfers in the world gather for this final event in the Pro Boardsailing World Tour. If you're on Maui, don't miss it—it's spectacular to watch. Call ℭ **808/575-9151.** Depending on the waves and the wind, the championship could be held in October or November.

Aloha Festivals Ho'olaule'a, Lahaina. This all-day cultural festival, which culminates the end of Maui island's Aloha Festivals Week, is held at Banyan Tree Park and features Hawaiian food, music, and dance, along with arts and crafts on display and for sale. Call ℭ **888/310-1117** or 808/667-9194 (www.visitlahaina.com). Either in September or October.

Molokai Hoe, Molokai to Oahu. This men's 40-mile outrigger contest starts in Molokai and finishes at Fort DeRussy Beach in Waikiki. Call ℭ **808/261-6615** or visit www.molokai-hawaii. com. Mid-October.

Halloween in Lahaina, Maui. There's Carnival in Rio, Mardi Gras in New Orleans, and Halloween in Lahaina. Come to this giant costume party (some 20,000 people show up) on the streets of Lahaina; Front Street is closed off for the party. Call ℭ **888/310-1117** or 808/667-9194 or visit www.visitlahaina.com. October 31, 2006.

November

Hawaii International Film Festival, various locations on Maui. A cinema festival with a cross-cultural spin, featuring filmmakers from Asia, the Pacific Islands, and the United States. Call ℭ **800/752-8193** or 808/528-FILM or visit www.hiff.org. Mid-November.

Maui Invitational Basketball Tournament, Lahaina Civic Center, Maui. Top college teams vie in this annual preseason tournament. Call ℭ **312/755-3504.** Usually held around Thanksgiving.

December

Hui Noeau Christmas House, Makawao. The festivities in the beautifully decorated Hui mansion include shopping, workshops and art demonstrations, children's activities and visits with Santa, holiday music, fresh-baked goods, and local foods. Call ℭ **808/572-6560;** www. huinoeau.com. Late November and early December.

Festival of Lights, island-wide. Festivities include parades and tree-lighting ceremonies. Call ℭ **808/667-9175** on Maui or 808/567-6361 on Molokai. Early December.

Na Mele O Maui, Student Song and Art Competition, Maui Marriott Ballroom. Students from kindergarten to 12th grade perform traditional Hawaiian songs in a scholarship fundraiser. Call ℭ **808/667-1200.** December 1, 2006.

Tips What to Pack

Maui is very informal: You'll get by with shorts, T-shirts, and sneakers at most attractions and restaurants; a casual sundress or a polo shirt and khakis is fine even in the most expensive places. Dinner jackets for men are required only at very few resorts, such as the Lodge at Koele on Lanai, and they'll cordially provide a jacket if you don't bring your own. Don't forget a long-sleeved cover-up (to throw on at the beach when you've had enough sun for the day), rubber water shoes or flip-flops, and hiking shoes and several pairs of good socks if you plan to do any hiking. You might also want to bring binoculars for whale-watching.

Be sure to bring **sun protection:** sunglasses, strong sunscreen, a light hat (like a baseball cap or a sun visor), and a canteen or water bottle if you'll be hiking—you'll easily dehydrate on the trail in the tropic heat. Campers should bring water purification tablets or devices. Also see "Health & Safety" below.

Don't bother overstuffing your suitcase with 2 whole weeks' worth of shorts and T-shirts: Maui has **laundry facilities** everywhere. If your accommodations don't have a washer and dryer or laundry service (most do), there will most likely be a laundry nearby. The only exception to this is Hana. The tiny town has no laundromat, so either check with the place you're staying beforehand, or do a load of laundry before you arrive.

One last thing: **It really can get cold on Maui.** If you plan to see the sunrise from the top of Haleakala, bring a warm jacket; even in summer—when it's 80°F (27°C) at the beach, 40°F (4°C) upcountry temperatures are not uncommon. It's always a good idea to bring long pants and a windbreaker, sweater, or light jacket. And be sure to bring along rain gear if you'll be in Maui from November to March.

Festival of Trees, Lahaina Cannery Mall. Look for decorated trees, along with entertainment. Call ℰ **808/661-5304.** December 2, 2006.

Lightening of the Banyan Tree, Lahaina, Maui. At 6:30pm Lahaina's historic Banyan Tree is lit up with thousands of Christmas lights for the entire holiday season. Santa Claus makes an appearance and choirs sing Christmas carols accompanied by hula. Kids can join a cookie workshop. Banyan Tree Park on Front Street. Call ℰ **888/310-1117** or 808/667-9194 or go to www.visitlahaina.com. December 2 and 3, 2006.

Tree Lighting Ceremony, Ritz-Carlton Kapalua. With the flick of a switch, more than 250,000 sparkling lights will illuminate the 25-foot holiday tree and dozens of pine and palm trees around the courtyards of the Ritz-Carlton Kapalua and throughout the resort. Call ℰ **808/669-6200** or visit www.kapaluaresort.com. December 3, 2006.

Annual Christmas Light Parade, Kaunakakai, Molokai. A light parade with music and holiday arts and crafts. Call ℰ **808/567-6180** or visit www.visitmaui.com. Mid-December.

First Light 2006, Maui Arts and Cultural Center, Maui. The Academy of Motion Pictures holds major screenings of top films. Not to be missed.

Call © **808/579-9996;** www.maui filmfestival.com. December 26 to December 31, 2006.

5 Travel Insurance

Check your existing insurance policies and credit card coverage before you buy travel insurance. You may already be covered for lost luggage, canceled tickets, or medical expenses. The cost of travel insurance varies widely, but expect to pay between 5% and 8% of the total cost of your vacation.

TRIP-CANCELLATION INSURANCE Trip-cancellation insurance helps you get your money back if you have to back out of a trip, if you have to go home early, or if your travel supplier goes bankrupt. Allowed reasons for cancellation can range from sickness to natural disasters to the State Department declaring your destination unsafe for travel. (Insurers usually won't cover vague fears, though, as many travelers discovered who tried to cancel their trips in Oct 2001 because they were wary of flying.) In this unstable world, trip-cancellation insurance is a good buy if you're getting tickets well in advance—who knows what the state of the world, or of your airline, will be in 9 months? Insurance policy details vary, so read the fine print—and especially make sure that your airline or cruise line is on the list of carriers covered in case of bankruptcy. A good resource is **"Travel Guard Alerts,"** a list of companies considered high-risk by Travel Guard International (see website below). Protect yourself further by paying for the insurance with a credit card—by law, consumers can get their money back on goods and services not received if they report the loss within 60 days after the charge is listed on their credit card statement.

For more information, contact one of the following recommended insurers:

Access America (© 800/284-8300; www. accessamerica.com); **Travel Guard International** (© 800/826-1300; www. travelguard.com); **Travel Insured International** (© 800/243-3174; www.travel insured.com); or **Travelex Insurance Services** (© 800/228-9792; www. travelex-insurance.com).

MEDICAL INSURANCE Most health insurance policies cover you if you get sick away from home—but check, particularly if you're insured by an HMO. If you require additional medical insurance, try **MEDEX Assistance** (© 410/ 453-6300; www.medexassist.com) or **Travel Assistance International** (© 800/ 821-2828; www.travelassistance.com); for general information on services, call the company's Worldwide Assistance Services, Inc., at © **800/777-8710.**

LOST-LUGGAGE INSURANCE On domestic flights checked baggage is covered up to $2,800 per ticketed passenger. On international flights (including U.S. portions of international trips), baggage coverage is limited to approximately $9.07 per pound, up to approximately $635 per checked bag. If you plan to check items more valuable than the standard liability, see if your valuables are covered by your homeowner's policy. You may also get baggage coverage as part of your comprehensive travel-insurance package or you can buy Travel Guard's "BagTrak" product. Don't buy insurance at the airport, as it's usually overpriced. Be sure to take any valuables or irreplaceable items with you in your carry-on luggage, as many valuables (including books, money, and electronics) aren't covered by airline policies.

If your luggage is lost, immediately file a lost-luggage claim at the airport, detailing the luggage contents. For most airlines, you must report delayed, damaged, or lost baggage within 4 hours of arrival (if you've flown with multiple airlines, file the claim with the last airline you flew). The airlines are required to deliver luggage, once found, directly to your house or destination free of charge. The lost-luggage claims desk loves to tell people: "Oh, your bag will be in on the next flight." Smile, and politely ask them if they have proof that the bag is in the system and booked on that flight. If they can't guarantee it, you might want to proceed to your destination rather than wait around the airport in hopes that the suitcase might be on the next flight.

Some tips for getting your bag back quickly: Make sure you have your destination information (not just your home address, but the address of your hotel/condo in Hawaii, with a contact phone number) on the outside and inside of your luggage. And before you leave the airport, be sure to get the following: a copy of your lost-luggage claim form, the phone number to call to check on your luggage, an estimate on when they will have more information on when your bag will arrive, and what you should do if your bag does not arrive.

6 Health & Safety

ON LAND

Like any tropical climate, Hawaii is home to lots of bugs. Most of them won't harm you. However, watch out for mosquitoes, centipedes, and scorpions, which do sting and may cause anything from mild annoyance to severe swelling and pain.

MOSQUITOES These pesky insects are not native to Hawaii but arrived as larvae stowed away in water barrels on the ship *Wellington* in 1826, when it anchored in Lahaina. There's not a whole lot you can do about them, except to apply commercial repellent, which you can pick up at any drugstore.

CENTIPEDES These segmented bugs with a jillion legs come in two varieties: 6- to 8-inch-long brown ones and 2- to 3-inch-long blue guys. Both can really pack a wallop with their stings. Centipedes are generally found in damp, wet places, such as under wood piles or compost heaps. Wearing closed-toe shoes can help prevent stings. If you're stung, apply ice at once to prevent swelling. See a doctor if you experience extreme pain, swelling, nausea, or any other severe reaction.

SCORPIONS Rarely seen, scorpions are found in arid, warm regions, and their stings can be serious. Campers in dry

---

Tips A Few Words of Warning About Crime

Although Hawaii is generally a safe tourist destination, visitors have been crime victims, so stay alert. The most common crime against tourists is rental-car break-ins. Never leave any valuables in your car, not even in your trunk: Thieves can be in and out of your trunk faster than you can open it with your own keys. Be especially leery of high-risk areas, such as beaches, resorts, scenic lookouts, and other visitor attractions. Also, never carry large amounts of cash. Stay in well-lighted areas after dark.

Tips Don't Get Burned: Smart Tanning Tips

Hawaii's Caucasian population has the highest incidence of malignant melanoma (deadly skin cancer) in the world. And nobody is completely safe from the sun's harmful rays: All skin types and races can burn. To ensure that your vacation won't be ruined by a painful sunburn, here are some helpful tips:

- **Wear a strong sunscreen at all times.** Use a sunscreen with an SPF of 15 or higher; people with light complexions should use SPF 30. Apply it liberally, and reapply every 2 hours.
- **Wrinkle prevention:** Wrinkles, sagging skin, and other signs of premature aging can be caused by ultraviolet A (UVA) rays. Some sunscreens only block out ultraviolet B (UVB) rays. Look for a sunscreen that blocks both. Zinc oxide, benzophenone, oxybenzone, sulisobenzone, titanium dioxide, or avobenzone (also known as Parsol 1789) all protect against UVA rays.
- **Wear a hat and sunglasses.** The hat should have a brim all the way around, to cover not only your face but also the sensitive back of your neck. Make sure your sunglasses have UV filters.
- **Protect children from the sun.** Infants under 6 months should not be in the sun at all. Older babies need zinc oxide to protect their fragile skin, and all children should be slathered with sunscreen frequently.
- **If it's too late.** The best remedy for a sunburn is to stay out of the sun until all the redness is gone. Aloe vera, cool compresses, cold baths, and anesthetic benzocaine also help with the pain of sunburn.

areas should always check their boots before putting them on, and shake out sleeping bags and bed rolls. Symptoms of a scorpion sting include shortness of breath, hives, swelling, and nausea. In the unlikely event that you're stung, apply diluted household ammonia and cold compresses to the area of the sting and seek medical help immediately.

HIKING SAFETY

In addition to taking the appropriate precautions regarding Hawaii's bug population, hikers should always let someone know where they're heading, when they're going, and when they plan to return. Too many hikers get lost in Hawaii because they don't let others know their basic plans.

Always check weather conditions with the **National Weather Service** (☎ 808/973-4381 on Oahu; see individual island chapters for local weather information) before you go. Hike with a pal, never alone. Wear hiking boots, a sun hat, clothes to protect you from the sun and from getting scratches, and high-SPF sunscreen on all exposed areas of skin. Take water. Stay on the trail. Watch your step. It's easy to slip off precipitous trails and into steep canyons. Many experienced hikers and boaters today pack a cellphone in case of emergency; just dial ☎ **911.**

VOG

The volcanic haze dubbed *vog* is caused by gases released when molten lava—from the continuous eruption of Kilauea volcano on the Big Island—pours into the ocean. Some people claim that long-term exposure to the hazy, smoglike air has caused bronchial ailments, but it's highly unlikely to cause you any harm in the course of your visit.

There actually is a vog season in Hawaii: the fall and winter months, when the trade winds that blow the fumes out to sea die down. The vog is felt not only on the Big Island but also as far away as Maui and Oahu.

OCEAN SAFETY

Because most people coming to Hawaii are unfamiliar with the ocean environment, they're often unaware of the natural hazards it holds. With just a few precautions, your ocean experience can be a safe and happy one. An excellent book is *All Stings Considered: First Aid and Medical Treatment of Hawaii's Marine Injuries* (University of Hawaii Press, 1997) by Craig Thomas and Susan Scott.

Note that sharks are not a big problem in Hawaii. In fact, they appear so infrequently that locals look forward to seeing them. Since records have been kept, starting in 1779, there have been only about 100 shark attacks in Hawaii, of which 40% have been fatal. Most attacks occurred after someone fell into the ocean from the shore or from a boat. In these cases, the sharks probably attacked after the person was dead. But general rules for avoiding sharks are: Don't swim at sunrise, sunset, or where the water is murky due to stream runoff—sharks may mistake you for one of their usual meals. And don't swim where there are bloody fish in the water, as sharks become aggressive around blood.

SEASICKNESS   The waters in Hawaii can range from calm as glass (off the Kona Coast on the Big Island) to down-right frightening (in storm conditions), and they usually fall somewhere in between. In general, expect rougher conditions in winter than in summer. Some 90% of the population tends toward seasickness. If you've never been out on a boat, or if you've been seasick in the past, you might want to heed the following suggestions:

- The day before you go out on the boat, avoid alcohol, caffeine, citrus and other acidic juices, and greasy, spicy, or hard-to-digest foods.
- Get a good night's sleep the night before.
- Take or use whatever seasickness prevention works best for you—medication, an acupressure wrist-band, gingerroot tea or capsules, or any combination. But do it *before you board*—once you set sail, it's generally too late.
- While you're on the boat, stay as low and as near the center of the boat as possible. Avoid the fumes (especially if it's a diesel boat); stay out in the fresh air and watch the horizon. Do not read.
- If you start to feel queasy, drink clear fluids like water, and eat something bland, such as a soda cracker.

Everything You've Always Wanted to Know About Sharks

The Hawaii State Department of Land and Natural Resources has launched a website with more information than you probably want to know about sharks: www.hawaiisharks.com. The site covers the biology, history, and culture of these carnivores, and provides information on safety and data on shark bites in Hawaii.

STINGS The most common stings in Hawaii come from jellyfish, particularly Portuguese man-of-war and box jellyfish. Since the poisons they inject are very different, you need to treat each sting differently.

A bluish-purple floating bubble with a long tail, the **Portuguese man-of-war** causes some 6,500 stings a year on Oahu alone. These stings, although painful and a nuisance, are rarely harmful; fewer than 1 in 1,000 requires medical treatment. The best prevention is to watch for these floating bubbles as you snorkel (look for the hanging tentacles below the surface). Get out of the water if anyone near you spots these jellyfish.

Reactions to stings range from mild burning and reddening to severe welts and blisters. *All Stings Considered* (see above) recommends the following treatment: First, pick off any visible tentacles with a gloved hand, a stick, or anything handy; then rinse the sting with salt- or freshwater, and apply ice to prevent swelling and to help control pain. Avoid folk remedies like vinegar, baking soda, or urinating on the wound, which may actually cause further damage. Most Portuguese man-of-war stings will disappear by themselves within 15 to 20 minutes if you do nothing at all to treat them. Still, be sure to see a doctor if pain persists or a rash or other symptoms develop.

Transparent, square-shaped **box jellyfish** are nearly impossible to see in the water. Fortunately, they seem to follow a monthly cycle: 8 to 10 days after the full moon, they appear in the waters on the leeward side of each island and hang around for about 3 days. Also, they seem to sting more in the morning hours, when they're on or near the surface.

The stings can cause anything from no visible marks to red, hivelike welts, blisters, and pain lasting from 10 minutes to 8 hours. *All Stings Considered* recommends the following treatment: First, pour regular household vinegar on the sting; this will stop additional burning. Do not rub the area. Pick off any vinegar-soaked tentacles with a stick. For pain, apply an ice pack. Seek additional medical treatment if you experience shortness of breath, weakness, palpitations, muscle cramps, or any other severe symptoms. Most box-jellyfish stings disappear by themselves without any treatment.

PUNCTURES Most sea-related punctures come from stepping on or brushing against the needlelike spines of sea urchins (known locally as *wana*). Be careful when you're in the water; don't put your foot down (even if you have booties or fins on) if you can't clearly see the bottom. Waves can push you into *wana* in a surge zone in shallow water. The spines can even puncture a wet suit.

A sea-urchin puncture can result in burning, aching, swelling, and discoloration (black or purple) around the area where the spines entered your skin. The best thing to do is to pull any protruding spines out. The body will absorb the spines within 24 hours to 3 weeks, or the remainder of the spines will work themselves out. Again, contrary to popular wisdom, do not urinate or pour vinegar on the embedded spines—this will not help.

CUTS All cuts obtained in the marine environment must be taken seriously, because the high level of bacteria present in the water can quickly cause the cut to become infected. The best way to prevent cuts is to wear a wet suit, gloves, and reef shoes. Never touch coral: Not only can you get cut, but you can also damage a living organism that took decades to grow.

The symptoms of a coral cut can range from a slight scratch to severe welts and blisters. *All Stings Considered* recommends gently pulling the edges of the skin open and removing any embedded coral or grains of sand with tweezers. Next, scrub the cut well with freshwater.

Tips Enjoying the Ocean & Avoiding Mishaps

The Pacific Whale Foundation has a free brochure called *Enjoying Maui's Unique Ocean Environment* that introduces visitors to Hawaii's ocean, beaches, tide pools, and reefs. It includes maps showing Maui's beaches and is a great resource on how to stay safe around the ocean, with hints on how to assess weather before you jump into the water and the best ways to view the marine wildlife. To get the brochure, contact the Pacific Whale Foundation at © 808/ 244-8390 or visit www.pacificwhale.org.

If pressing a clean cloth against the wound doesn't stop the bleeding, or the edges of the injury are jagged or gaping, seek medical treatment.

WHAT TO DO IF YOU GET SICK AWAY FROM HOME

In most cases your existing health plan will provide the coverage you need. But double-check—you may want to buy **travel medical insurance** instead. (See the section on insurance, earlier in this chapter.) Bring your insurance ID card with you when you travel.

If you suffer from a chronic illness, consult your doctor before your departure. For conditions like epilepsy, diabetes, or heart problems, wear a **MedicAlert identification tag** (© 888/633-4298; www.medicalert.org), which will immediately alert doctors to your condition and give

them access to your records through MedicAlert's 24-hour hot line.

Pack **prescription medications** in your carry-on luggage, and carry prescription medications in their original containers, with pharmacy labels—otherwise they won't make it through airport security. Also bring along copies of your prescriptions in case you lose your pills or run out. Don't forget an extra pair of contact lenses or prescription glasses.

If you get sick, consider asking your hotel concierge to recommend a local doctor—even his or her own. You can also try the emergency room at a local hospital; many have walk-in clinics for emergency cases that are not life-threatening. You may not get immediate attention, but you won't pay the high price of an emergency-room visit.

7 Specialized Travel Resources

FOR TRAVELERS WITH DISABILITIES

Travelers with disabilities are made to feel very welcome in Maui. Hotels are usually equipped with wheelchair-accessible rooms, and tour companies provide many special services. The **Hawaii Center for Independent Living,** 414 Kauwili St., Suite 102, Honolulu, HI 96817 (© 808/ 522-5400; fax 808/586-8129), can provide information.

The only travel agency in Hawaii specializing in needs for travelers with

disabilities is **Access Aloha Travel** (© 800/480-1143; www.accessaloha travel.com), which can book anything, including rental vans, accommodations, tours, cruises, airfare, and just about anything else you can think of.

The following travel agencies don't specialize in Hawaiian travel, but they offer customized tours and itineraries for travelers with disabilities. **Flying Wheels Travel** (© 507/451-5005; www.flying wheelstravel.com) offers escorted tours and cruises that emphasize sports and private tours in minivans with lifts. **Access-Able Travel Source** (℗ 303/ 232-2979; www.access-able.com) offers extensive access information and advice for traveling around the world with disabilities. **Accessible Journeys** (℗ 800/ 846-4537 or 610/521-0339; www. disabilitytravel.com) caters specifically to slow walkers and wheelchair travelers and their families and friends.

For travelers with disabilities who wish to do their own driving, hand-controlled cars can be rented from **Avis** (℗ 800/ 331-1212; www.avis.com) and **Hertz** (℗ 800/654-3131; www.hertz.com). The number of hand-controlled cars in Hawaii is limited, so be sure to book well in advance. For wheelchair-accessible vans, contact **Accessible Vans of Hawaii,** 186 Mehani Circle, Kihei (℗ 800/303-3750 or 808/879-5521; fax 808/879-0640; www.accessiblevans.com). Maui recognizes other states' windshield placards indicating that the driver of the car is disabled, so be sure to bring yours with you.

Vision-impaired travelers who use a Seeing Eye dog can now come to Hawaii without the hassle of quarantine. A recent court decision ruled that visitors with Seeing Eye dogs only need to present documentation that the dog is a trained Seeing Eye dog and has had rabies shots. For more information, contact the Animal Quarantine Facility (℗ 808/483-7171; www.hawaii.gov).

Organizations that offer assistance to travelers with disabilities include **Moss-Rehab** (www.mossresourcenet.org), which provides a library of accessible-travel resources online; **SATH** (Society for Accessible Travel & Hospitality) (℗ 212/ 447-7284; www.sath.org; annual membership fees: $45 adults, $30 seniors and students), which offers a wealth of travel resources for all types of disabilities and informed recommendations on destinations, access guides, travel agents, tour operators, vehicle rentals, and companion services; and the **American Foundation for the Blind (AFB)** (℗ 800/232-5463; www.afb.org), a referral resource for the blind or visually impaired that includes information on traveling with Seeing Eye dogs.

For more information specifically targeted to travelers with disabilities, the community website **iCan** (www.ican online.net/channels/travel/index.cfm) has destination guides and several regular columns on accessible travel. Also check out the quarterly magazine *Emerging Horizons* ($14.95 per year, $19.95 outside the U.S.; www.emerginghorizons. com) and *Open World* magazine, published by SATH (see above; subscription: $13 per year, $21 outside the U.S.).

FOR GAY & LESBIAN TRAVELERS

Known for its acceptance of all groups, Hawaii welcomes gays and lesbians just as it does anybody else.

For the latest information on the gay marriage issue, contact the **Hawaii Marriage Project** (℗ 808/532-9000).

Pacific Ocean Holidays, P.O. Box 88245, Honolulu, HI 96830 (℗ 800/ 735-6600 or 808/923-2400; www.gay hawaii.com), offers vacation packages that feature gay-owned and gay-friendly lodgings. It also publishes the *Pocket Guide to Hawaii: A Guide for Gay Visitors & Kamaaina,* a list of gay-owned and gay-friendly businesses throughout the islands. Send $5 for a copy (mail order only; no phone orders, please), or access the online version on the website.

The International Gay and Lesbian Travel Association (IGLTA) (℗ 800/ 448-8550 or 954/776-2626; www.iglta. org) is the trade association for the gay and lesbian travel industry and offers an online directory of gay- and lesbian-friendly travel businesses; go to their website and click on "Members."

FOR SENIORS

Discounts for seniors are available at almost all of Maui's major attractions, and occasionally at hotels and restaurants. Always inquire when making hotel reservations, and especially when you're buying your airline ticket—most major domestic airlines offer senior discounts. Members of **AARP** (© 800/424-3410 or 202/434-2277; www.aarp.org) are usually eligible for such discounts. AARP also puts together organized-tour packages at moderate rates.

Some great, low-cost trips to Hawaii are offered to people 55 and older through **Elderhostel,** 75 Federal St., Boston, MA 02110 (© 617/426-8056; www.elderhostel.org), a nonprofit group that arranges travel and study programs around the world. You can obtain a complete catalog of offerings by writing to Elderhostel, P.O. Box 1959, Wakefield, MA 01880-5959.

If you're planning to visit Haleakala National Park, you can save sightseeing dollars if you're 62 or older by picking up a **Golden Age Passport** from any national park, recreation area, or monument. This lifetime pass has a one-time fee of $10 and provides free admission to all of the parks in the system, plus a 50% savings on camping and recreation fees. You can pick one up at any park entrance. Be sure to have proof of your age with you.

FOR FAMILIES

Maui is paradise for children: beaches to frolic on, water to splash in, unusual sights to see, and a host of new foods to taste. Be sure to look for the "Kids" icon throughout the book, and see the box "Especially for Kids" in chapter 8.

The larger hotels and resorts have supervised programs for children and can refer you to qualified babysitters. You can also contact **People Attentive to Children (PATCH;** © 808/242-9232; www.patchhawaii.org), which will refer you to individuals who have taken their training courses on child care. If you are traveling to Molokai or Lanai, call © 800/498-4145; or visit www.patchhawaii.org.

Baby's Away (© 800/942-9030 or 808/875-9093; www.babysaway.com) rents cribs, strollers, highchairs, playpens, infant seats, and the like, to make your baby's vacation (and yours) much more enjoyable.

Remember that Maui's sun is probably much stronger than what you're used to at home, so it's important to protect your kids, and keep infants out of the sun altogether. Infants under 6 months should not be in the sun at all. Older babies need zinc oxide to protect their fragile skin, and children should be slathered with sunscreen every hour.

Condo rentals are a great option for families; the convenience of having your own kitchen is great for mom and dad. See "Types of Accommodations" later in this chapter. My favorite condo complexes are reviewed throughout that chapter.

Recommended family travel Internet sites include **Family Travel Forum** (www.familytravelforum.com), a comprehensive site that offers customized trip planning; **Family Travel Network** (www.familytravelnetwork.com), an award-winning site that offers travel features, deals, and tips; **Traveling Internationally with Your Kids** (www.travelwithyourkids.com), a comprehensive site offering sound advice for long-distance and international travel with children; and **Family Travel Files** (www.thefamilytravelfiles.com), which offers an online magazine and a directory of off-the-beaten-path tours and tour operators for families.

Also look for the just-released, first edition of *Frommer's Hawaii with Kids* (Wiley Publishing, Inc.).

8 Getting Married on Maui

Maui is a great place for a wedding. Not only does the entire island exude romance and natural beauty, but after the ceremony, you're only a few steps away from the perfect honeymoon.

More than 20,000 marriages are performed each year on the islands, and nearly half of the couples married here are from somewhere else. This booming business has spawned dozens of companies that can help you organize a long-distance event and stage an unforgettable wedding.

The easiest way to plan your wedding is to let someone else handle it at the resort or hotel where you'll be staying. Most Maui resorts and hotels have wedding coordinators who can plan everything from a simple (relatively) low-cost wedding to an extravaganza that people will talk about for years. Remember that resorts can be pricey—be frank with your wedding coordinator if you want to keep costs down. You don't have to use a coordinator: You can also plan your own island wedding, even from afar, and not spend a fortune doing it.

THE PAPERWORK

To obtain a marriage license, contact the **Marriage License Office,** State Department of Health Building, 54 S. High St., Wailuku, HI 96793 (© **808/984-8210;** www.state.hi.us/doh/records/vr_marri. html), open Monday through Friday from 8am to 4pm. The staff will mail you a brochure called *Getting Married* and direct you to the marriage-licensing agent closest to where you'll be staying on Maui.

Once on Maui the prospective bride and groom must go together to the marriage-licensing agent to get a license. A license costs $60 and is good for 30 days. The only requirements for a marriage license are that both parties are 15 years

of age or older (couples 15–17 years old must have proof of age, written consent of both parents, and the written approval of the judge of the family court) and are not more closely related than first cousins.

After a protracted legal battle and much discussion in the state legislature, in late 1999 the Hawaii Supreme Court ruled that the state won't issue a marriage license to a couple of the same sex. For the latest information on this issue, contact the **Hawaii Marriage Project** (© **808/532-9000**).

PLANNING THE WEDDING

DOING IT YOURSELF   The marriage-licensing agents, which range from the governor's satellite office to private individuals, are usually friendly, helpful people who can steer you to a nondenominational minister or someone who's licensed by the state of Hawaii to perform the ceremony. These marriage performers are great sources of information for budget weddings. They usually know great places to have the ceremony for free or for a nominal fee.

If you don't want to use a wedding planner (see below) but want to make arrangements before you arrive on Maui, my best advice is to get a copy of the daily newspaper the *Maui News,* P.O. Box 550, Wailuku, HI 96793 (© **808/244-7691;** www.mauinews.com). People willing and qualified to conduct weddings advertise in the classifieds. They're great sources of information and can recommend locations, caterers, florists, and everything else you'll need.

USING A WEDDING PLANNER
Wedding planners can arrange everything for you, and charge anywhere from $150 to a small fortune—it all depends on what you want.

Planners on Maui include **First Class Weddings** (℡ **800/262-8433** or 808/877-1411; www.firstclassweddings.com); **A Dream Wedding: Maui Style** (℡ **800/743-2777** or 808/661-1777; fax 808/667-2042; www.maui.net/~dreamwed/dream.html); **A Romantic Maui Wedding** (℡ **800/808-4144** or 808/874-6444; fax 808/879-5525; www.justmauied.com);

Dolphin Dream Weddings (℡ **800/793-2-WED** or 808/661-8535; www.dolphindreamweddings.com); and **Simply Married** (℡ **800/291-0110** or 808/572-7898; fax 800/368-6933 or 808/572-1240; www.maui.net/~married). For a more complete list, contact the Maui Visitors Bureau, www.visitmaui.com.

9 Getting There

If possible, fly directly to Maui. Doing so can save you a 2-hour layover in Honolulu and another plane ride. If you're headed for Molokai or Lanai, you'll have to connect through Honolulu.

If you think of the island of Maui as the shape of a head and shoulders of a person, you'll probably arrive on its neck, at **Kahului Airport.**

At press time six airlines fly directly from the U.S. mainland to Kahului: **United Airlines** (℡ 800/241-6522; www.ual.com) offers daily nonstop flights from San Francisco and Los Angeles; **Aloha Airlines** (℡ 800/367-5250; www.alohaair.com) has nonstop service from Sacramento, Oakland, Orange County, and San Diego, all in California. **Hawaiian Airlines** (℡ 800/367-5320; www.hawaiianair.com) has direct flights from Portland and Seattle; **American Airlines** (℡ 800/433-7300; www.aa.com) flies direct from Los Angeles and San Jose; **Delta Airlines** (℡ 800/221-1212; www.delta.com) offers direct flights from San Francisco and Los Angeles; and **American Trans Air** (℡ 800/435-9282; www.ata.com) has direct flights from Los Angeles, San Francisco, and Phoenix.

The other carriers—including **Continental** (℡ 800/525-0280; www.continental.com) and **Northwest Airlines** (℡ 800/225-2525; www.nwa.com)—fly to Honolulu, where you'll have to pick up an interisland flight to Maui. (The airlines listed in the paragraph above also offer many more flights to Honolulu from additional cities on the mainland.) Both **Aloha Airlines** and **Hawaiian Airlines** offer jet service from Honolulu. See "Interisland Flights" below.

For information on airlines serving Hawaii from places other than the U.S. mainland, see chapter 3, "For International Visitors."

FLY FOR LESS: TIPS FOR GETTING THE BEST AIRFARES

- Keep your eye out for periodic **sales.** It's rare to find a sale during the peak winter vacation months, but during the rest of the year, you can find deals. *Note:* The lowest-priced fares are often nonrefundable, require advance purchase of 1 to 3 weeks and a certain length of stay, and carry penalties for itinerary changes.
- If your schedule is flexible, you can almost always get a cheaper fare by **staying over a Saturday night** or by **flying midweek.**
- **Consolidators,** also known as bucket shops, are a good place to find low fares, often below even the airlines' discounted rates. There's nothing shady about the reliable ones—basically, they're just big travel agents that get discounts for buying in bulk and pass some of the savings on to you. But be aware that consolidator tickets are usually nonrefundable or come with stiff cancellation penalties.

Reliable consolidators include **Cheap Tickets** 𝄞 (© 800/377-1000; www.cheaptickets.com); **Lowestfare.com** (© 888/278-8830; www.lowestfare.com); **Cheap Seats** (© 800/451-7200; www.cheapseats travel.com); and **1-800-FLY-CHEAP** (www.flycheap.com).

- **Search the Internet for cheap fares,** though it's still best to compare your findings with the research of a dedicated travel agent, if you're lucky enough to have one, especially when you're booking more than just a flight. Three of the best-respected virtual travel agents are **Expedia** (www. expedia.com), **Travelocity** (www. travelocity.com), and **Yahoo! Travel** (http://travel.yahoo.com).
- Join **frequent-flier clubs.** Accrue enough miles and you'll be rewarded with free flights and elite status. It's free. You don't need to fly to build frequent-flier miles—**frequent-flier credit cards** can provide thousands of miles for doing your everyday shopping.

LONG-HAUL FLIGHTS: HOW TO STAY COMFORTABLE

Long flights can be trying; stuffy air and cramped seats can make you feel as if you're being sent parcel post in a small box. But with a little advance planning, you can make an otherwise unpleasant experience almost bearable.

- Your choice of airline and airplane will definitely affect your legroom. Find more details at www.seatguru. com, which has extensive details about almost every seat on six major U.S. airlines. For international airlines, check www.airlinequality.com.
- Emergency-exit seats and bulkhead seats typically have the most legroom. Emergency-exit seats are usually held back to be assigned the day of a flight; it's worth getting to the ticket counter early to snag one of these

spots for a long flight. Many passengers find that bulkhead seating (the row facing the wall at the front of the cabin) offers more legroom, but families with infants and small children are often seated here as well.

- If you're traveling with a companion, book an aisle and a window seat. Middle seats are usually booked last, so chances are good you'll end up with three seats to yourselves. If someone is assigned the middle seat, he or she will probably be happy to trade for a window or an aisle.
- To sleep, avoid the last row of any section or a row in front of an emergency exit, as these seats are the least likely to recline. Avoid seats near highly trafficked toilet areas. You also may want to reserve a window seat so that you can rest your head and avoid being bumped in the aisle.
- Get up, walk around, and stretch every 60 to 90 minutes to keep your blood flowing. This helps avoid **deep vein thrombosis,** or "economy-class syndrome," a potentially deadly condition that can be caused by sitting in cramped conditions for too long. Staying hydrated (see next bullet) helps too.
- Drink water before, during, and after your flight to combat the lack of humidity in airplane cabins. Bring a bottle of water onboard. Avoid alcohol, which will dehydrate you.
- If you're flying with kids, don't forget to carry on toys, books, pacifiers, and chewing gum to help them relieve ear pressure buildup during ascent and descent. Let each child pack his or her own backpack with favorite toys.

GETTING THROUGH THE AIRPORT

With the federalization of airport security, security procedures at U.S. airports are more stable and consistent than ever. When you leave Maui, get to the airport

90 minutes before your flight's schedule departure. The airport was not designed or built with the new security measures in mind, and you have to stand in four different lines before you get to your gate (agricultural inspection, ticket line, baggage inspection, and security), where you will stand in line for your flight. Believe me, it will take you at least 90 minutes to get through all these lines. Your airline carrier will tell you when to show up for your flight to Hawaii from your departing city.

Bring a **current, government-issued photo ID** such as a driver's license or passport, and if you've got an e-ticket, print out the **official confirmation page;** you'll need to show your confirmation at the security checkpoint, and your ID at the ticket counter or the gate. (Children under 18 do not need photo IDs for domestic flights, but the adults checking in with them do.)

If you want to speed up security, **do not wear metal objects** such as big belt buckles or clanky earrings. Most boots and many shoes have a steel shaft in them that will set off metal detectors. Save yourself some trouble by taking them off and running them through the X-ray machines along with your carry-on luggage. If you've got metallic body parts, a note from your doctor can prevent a long chat with the security screeners.

Federalization has standardized **what you can carry on** and **what you can't.** The general rule is that sharp things are out, nail clippers are okay, and food and beverages must be passed through the X-ray machine—but that security screeners can't make you drink from your coffee cup. Bring food in your carry-on rather than checking it, as explosive-detection machines used on checked luggage have been known to mistake food (especially chocolate, for some reason) for bombs. Travelers in the U.S. are allowed one carry-on bag, plus a "personal item" such as a purse, briefcase, or laptop bag. The

Transportation Security Administration (TSA) has issued a list of restricted items; check its website (www.tsa.gov/public/index.jsp) for details.

Passengers with e-tickets and without checked bags can still beat the ticket-counter lines by using **electronic kiosks** or even **online check-in.** Ask your airline which alternatives are available. If you're checking bags, you will still be able to use most airlines' kiosks; again, call your airline for up-to-date information. **Curbside check-in** is also a good way to avoid lines, although a few airlines still ban curbside check-in entirely; call before you go.

Airport screeners may decide that your checked luggage needs to be searched by hand. You can now purchase luggage locks that allow screeners to open and relock a checked bag if hand-searching is necessary. Look for Travel Sentry certified locks at luggage or travel shops and Brookstone stores (www.brookstone.com). These locks, approved by the TSA, can be opened by luggage inspectors with a special code or key. For more information on the locks, visit www.travelsentry.org. If you use something other than TSA-approved locks, your lock will be cut off your suitcase if a TSA agent needs to hand-search your luggage.

LANDING AT KAHULUI AIRPORT

If there's a long wait at baggage claim, step over to the state-operated **Visitor Information Center,** where you can pick up brochures and the latest issue of *This Week Maui,* which features great regional maps of the islands, and ask about island activities. After collecting your bags from the poky, automated carousels, step out, take a deep breath, proceed to the curbside rental-car pickup area, and wait for the appropriate rental-agency shuttle van to take you ½ mile away to the rental-car checkout desk. (All major rental companies have branches at Kahului; see "Getting Around" later in this chapter.)

⟨ Moments ⟩   The Welcoming Lei

Nothing makes you feel more welcome than a lei. The tropical beauty of the delicate garland, the deliciously sweet fragrance of the blossoms, the sensual way the flowers curl softly around your neck—there's no doubt about it: Getting lei'd in Hawaii is a sensuous experience.

Leis are much more than just a decorative necklace of flowers—they're also one of the nicest ways to say hello, goodbye, congratulations, I salute you, my sympathies are with you, or I love you.

During ancient times, leis given to *alii* (royalty) were accompanied by a bow, since it was *kapu* (forbidden) for a commoner to raise his arms higher than the king's head. The presentation of a kiss with a lei didn't come about until World War II; it's generally attributed to an entertainer who kissed an officer on a dare, then quickly presented him with her lei, saying it was an old Hawaiian custom. It wasn't then, but it sure caught on fast.

Lei making is a tropical art form. All leis are fashioned by hand in a variety of traditional patterns; some are sewn of hundreds of tiny blooms or shells or bits of ferns and leaves. Some are twisted, some braided, some strung. Every island has its own special flower lei. Maui likes the *lokelani,* a small rose. Leis are available at the Kahului Airport, from florists, and even at supermarkets.

Leis are the perfect symbol for Hawaii: They're given in the moment, their fragrance and beauty are enjoyed in the moment, but when they fade, their spirit of aloha lives on. Welcome to the islands!

If you're not renting a car, the cheapest way to get to your hotel is **SpeediShuttle** (© **808/875-8070;** www.speedishuttle. com), which can take you between Kahului Airport and all the major resorts between 5am and 11pm daily. Rates vary, but figure on $30 for one to Wailea (one-way), $41 one-way to Kaanapali, and $57 one-way to Kapalua. Be sure to call before your flight to arrange pickup.

You'll see taxis outside the airport terminal, but note that they are quite expensive—expect to spend around $60 to $75 for a ride from Kahului to Kaanapali and $50 from the airport to Wailea.

If possible, avoid landing on Maui between 3 and 6pm, when the working stiffs on Maui are "pau work" (finished with work) and a major traffic jam occurs at the first intersection.

AVOIDING KAHULUI If you're planning to stay at any of the hotels in Kapalua or at the Kaanapali resorts, you might consider flying **Island Air** (© **800/ 323-3345;** www.islandair.com) from Honolulu to **Kapalua–West Maui Airport.** From this airport, it's only a 10- to 15-minute drive to most hotels in West Maui, as opposed to an hour from Kahului. **Pacific Wings** (© **888/873-0877** or 808/575-4546; fax 808/873-7920; www. pacificwings.com) flies eight-passenger, twin-engine Cessna 402C aircraft into tiny **Hana Airport** and also flies into Kahului.

INTERISLAND FLIGHTS

Don't expect to jump a ferry between any of the Hawaiian islands. Today everyone island-hops by plane. Since September 11, 2001, the two interisland carriers have

Tips Coping with Jet Lag

Hawaii is two time zones from the West Coast (three time zones during daylight saving time). When you travel across so many time zones, your body becomes thoroughly confused about what time it is, and everything from your digestion to your brain gets knocked for a loop.

Here are some tips for combating jet lag:

• **Reset your watch** to Hawaii time when you board the plane.
• **Drink lots of water** and avoid alcohol.
• **Exercise and sleep well** for a few days before your trip.
• If you have trouble sleeping on planes, **fly eastward on morning flights.**
• **Daylight** is the key to resetting your body clock. At the website for **Outside In** (www.bodyclock.com), you can get a customized plan of when to seek and avoid light.
• If you need help getting to sleep earlier than you usually would, see your doctor about a prescription for the hormone **melatonin** or the sleeping pill **Ambien.**

cut way, way, way back on the number of interisland flights. The airlines warn you to show up at least 90 minutes before your flight and believe me, with all the security inspections, you will need all 90 minutes to catch your flight. Also, be sure to book your interisland connection from Honolulu to Maui in advance.

Aloha Airlines (✆ **800/367-5250** or 808/244-9071; www.alohaair.com) is the state's largest provider of interisland air transport service. It offers 15 regularly scheduled daily jet flights a day from Honolulu to Maui on their all-jet fleet of Boeing 737 aircraft. Aloha's sibling company, **Island Air** (✆ **800/323-3345** or 808/484-2222; www.islandair.com), operates deHavilland DASH-8 and DASH-6 turboprop aircraft and serves Hawaii's small interisland airports on Maui, Molokai, and Lanai, with flights connecting them to Oahu.

Hawaiian Airlines (✆ **800/367-5320** or 808/871-6132; www.hawaiianair.com) is Hawaii's other interisland airline featuring jet planes.

Kahului-based **Pacific Wings** (✆ **888/873-0877** or 808/575-4546; www.pacificwings.com) flies eight-passenger, twin-engine Cessna 402C aircraft. It currently offers flights between Kahului and Hana, Molokai, Lanai, and Honolulu.

Just as we went to press, a new start-up airline was announced, which, if it can raise enough capital and get the necessary FAA certification, plans to be in operation in 2006 with flights from Honolulu to Maui. **FlyHawaii Airlines** was still in the planning stages but proposes to use three 68-seat ATR-72 turboprop aircraft. For more information, call ✆ **808/599-5588;** www.flyhi.com.

10 Money-Saving Package Deals

Booking an all-inclusive travel package that includes some combination of airfare, accommodations, rental car, meals, airport and baggage transfers, and sightseeing can be the most cost-effective way to travel to Maui. Package tours are not the same as escorted tours. They are simply a way to buy airfare and accommodations (and sometimes extras like sightseeing tours and rental cars) at the same time. When you're visiting Hawaii, a package can be a smart way to go. You can sometimes save so much money by buying all the pieces of your trip through a packager that your transpacific airfare ends up, in effect, being free. That's because packages are sold in bulk to tour operators, who then resell them to the public at a cost that drastically undercuts standard rates.

Packages, however, vary widely. Some offer a better class of hotels than others. Some offer the same hotels for lower prices. With some packagers, your choice of accommodations and travel days may be limited. Which package is right for you depends entirely on what you want.

Start out by **reading this guide.** Do a little homework, and read up on Maui so that you can be a smart consumer. Compare the rack rates in this guide to the discounted rates being offered by the packagers to see what kinds of deals they're offering—find out whether you're actually being offered a substantial savings or they've just gussied up the rack rates to make their offer *sound* like a deal. If you're being offered a stay in a hotel I haven't recommended, do more research to learn about it, especially if it isn't a reliable franchise. It's not a deal if you end up at a dump.

Be sure to **read the fine print.** Make sure you know *exactly* what's included in the price you're being quoted and what's not. Are hotel taxes and airport transfers included or will you have to pay extra? Before you commit to a package, make sure you know how much flexibility you have, say, if your kid gets sick or your boss suddenly asks you to adjust your vacation schedule. Some packagers require iron-clad commitments, while others will go with the flow, charging only minimal fees for changes or cancellations.

The best place to start looking for a package deal is in the travel section of your local Sunday newspaper. Also check the ads in the back of such national travel magazines as *Arthur Frommer's Budget Travel* and *Travel Holiday.* **Liberty Travel** (© 888/271-1584; www.libertytravel. com), for instance, one of the biggest packagers in the Northeast, usually boasts a full-page ad in Sunday papers. **American Express Travel** (© 800/AXP-6898; www.americanexpress.com/travel) can also book you a well-priced Hawaiian vacation; it also advertises in many Sunday travel sections.

Excellent deals, like a rental car and 7 nights in a Maui condo starting at $480 per person (based on double occupancy), can be found at **More Hawaii for Less** (© 800/967-6687; www.hawaii4less. com), a California-based company that specializes in air-condominium packages at unbelievable prices.

Other reliable packagers include the airlines themselves, which often package their flights with accommodations.

Tips **Package-Buying Tip**

For one-stop shopping on the Web, go to **Pleasant Hawaiian Holidays** (© 800/ 2-HAWAII or 800/242-9244; www.pleasantholidays.com), the biggest and most comprehensive packager to Hawaii. It offers an extensive, high-quality collection of 50 condos and hotels in every price range. As we went to press, they had a package deal that included airfare from Los Angeles or San Francisco to Maui, 6 nights in Lahaina (based on double occupancy), and 6 days' car rental starting at $1,595 for two.

Among the airlines offering good-value package deals to Hawaii are **American Airlines FlyAway Vacations** (℡ 800/321-2121; www.aa.com), **Continental Airlines Vacations** (℡ 800/634-5555 or 800/301-3800; www.coolvacations.com), **Delta Dream Vacations** (℡ 800/872-7786; www.deltavacations.com), and **United Vacations** (℡ 800/328-6877; www.unitedvacations.com). If you're traveling to the islands from Canada, ask your travel agent about package deals through **Air Canada Vacations** (℡ 800/776-3000; www.aircanada.ca).

Hawaii's **top hotel chains** offer package deals and special rates as well. Packages may be available for families, seniors, honeymooners, and golfers, and some offer discounts on rental cars or multi-night stays. Check with **Outrigger's** "Ohana" (Hawaiian for "family") Hotels (℡ **800/462-6262;** www.ohanahotels.com) and the more upscale "Outrigger" resorts and condominiums (℡ **800/OUTRIGGER;** www.outrigger.com); and the **Aston** chain (℡ **800/92-ASTON;** www.aston-hotels.com), which, in addition to packages galore, has a wonderful Island Hopper deal that allows you to travel from island to island and get 25% off on 7 nights or more at Aston properties.

11 Planning Your Trip Online

SURFING FOR AIRFARES

The "big three" online travel agencies, **Expedia.com, Travelocity.com,** and **Orbitz.com** sell most of the air tickets bought on the Internet. (Canadian travelers should try Expedia.ca and Travelocity.ca; U.K. residents can go to Expedia.co.uk and Opodo.co.uk.) Each has different business deals with the airlines and may offer different fares on the same flights, so it's wise to shop around. Expedia and Travelocity will also send you **e-mail notification** when a cheap fare becomes available to your favorite destination.

Also remember to check **airline websites.** You can often shave a few bucks from a fare by booking directly through the airline and avoiding a travel agency's transaction fee. But you'll get these discounts only by **booking online:** Most airlines now offer online-only fares that even their phone agents know nothing about. For the websites of airlines that fly to and from your destination, go to "Getting There" earlier in this chapter.

Great **last-minute deals** are available through free weekly e-mail services provided directly by the airlines. Most of these are announced on Tuesday or Wednesday and must be purchased online. Most are only valid for travel that weekend, but some can be booked in advance. Sign up for weekly e-mail alerts at airline websites or check megasites that compile comprehensive lists of last-minute specials, such as **Smarter Travel** (smartertravel.com). For last-minute trips, **site59.com** and **lastminutetravel.com** often have good air-and-hotel package deals. A website listing numerous bargain sites and airlines around the world is **www.itravelnet.com.**

If you're willing to give up some control over your flight details, use what is called an "**opaque" fare service** like **Priceline** (www.priceline.com; www.priceline.co.uk for Europeans) or its smaller competitor **Hotwire** (www.hotwire.com). Both offer rock-bottom prices in exchange for travel on a "mystery airline" at a mysterious time of day. The mystery airlines are all major, well-known carriers—and the possibility of being sent from Philadelphia to Chicago via Tampa is remote; the airlines' routing computers have gotten a lot better than they used to be. But your chances of getting a 6am or 11pm flight are pretty high. Hotwire tells you flight prices before you buy; Priceline usually has better deals than Hotwire, but you have to play their "name our price" game. If you're new at this, the helpful folks at **BiddingForTravel** (www.biddingfor travel.com) do a good job of demystifying Priceline's prices and strategies. Priceline and Hotwire are great for flights within North America and between the U.S. and Europe. But for flights to other parts of the world, consolidators will almost always beat their fares. *Note:* In 2004 Priceline added nonopaque service to its roster. You now have the option to pick exact flights, times, and airlines from a list of offers.

For much more about airfares and savvy air-travel tips and advice, pick up a copy of *Frommer's Fly Safe, Fly Smart* (Wiley Publishing, Inc.).

SURFING FOR HOTELS

You can shop online for hotels by booking through the hotel's own website or through an independent booking agency (or a fare-service agency like Priceline; see below). These Internet hotel agencies have multiplied in mind-boggling numbers of late, and prices can vary considerably from site to site. Keep in mind that hotels at the top of a site's listing may be there for no other reason than that they paid money to get the placement.

Of the "big three" sites, **Expedia** offers a long list of special deals and "virtual tours" or photos of available rooms so you can see what you're paying for (a feature that helps counter the claims that the best rooms are often held back from bargain-booking websites). **Travelocity** posts unvarnished customer reviews and ranks its properties according to the AAA rating system. Also reliable are **Hotels.com** and **Quikbook.com.** An excellent free program, **TravelAxe** (www.travelaxe.net) can help you search multiple hotel sites at once and conveniently lists the total price of the room, including the taxes and service charges. Another booking site, **Travelweb** (www.travelweb.com), is partly owned by

the hotels it represents (including the Hilton, Hyatt, and Starwood chains) and is therefore plugged directly into the hotels' reservations systems—unlike independent online agencies, which have to fax or e-mail reservation requests to the hotel, some of which get misplaced in the shuffle. To be fair, many of the major sites are undergoing improvements in service and ease of use, and Expedia will soon be able to plug directly into the reservations systems of many hotel chains. In the meantime it's a good idea to **get a confirmation number** and **make a printout** of any online booking transaction.

In the opaque-website category, **Priceline** and **Hotwire** are even better for hotels than for airfares. With both, you're allowed to pick the neighborhood and quality level of your hotel before offering up your money. Priceline's hotel product even covers Europe and Asia, though it's much better at getting five-star lodging for three-star prices than at finding anything at the bottom of the scale. On the downside many hotels stick Priceline guests in their least desirable rooms. Go to BiddingForTravel.com before bidding on a hotel room on Priceline; it features a fairly up-to-date list of hotels that Priceline uses in major cities. For both Priceline and Hotwire, you pay upfront, and the fee is nonrefundable. *Note:* Some hotels do not provide loyalty-program credits or points or other frequent-stay amenities when you book a room through opaque online services.

SURFING FOR RENTAL CARS

For booking rental cars online, the best deals are usually found at rental-car company websites, although all the major online travel agencies also offer rental-car reservations services. Priceline and Hotwire work well for rental cars too. The only "mystery" is which major rental company you get, and for most travelers the difference between Hertz, Avis, and Budget is negligible.

Frommers.com: The Complete Travel Resource

For an excellent travel-planning resource, we highly recommend **Frommers. com** (www.frommers.com). We're a little biased, of course, but we guarantee that you'll find the travel tips, reviews, monthly vacation giveaways, and online-booking capabilities thoroughly indispensable. Among the special features are our popular **Message Boards,** where Frommer's readers post queries and share advice (sometimes even our authors show up to answer questions); **Frommers.com Newsletter,** for the latest travel bargains and inside travel secrets; and Frommer's **Destinations Section,** where you'll get expert travel tips, hotel and dining recommendations, and advice on the sights to see for more than 2,500 destinations around the globe. When your research is done, the **Online Reservation System** (www.frommers.com/ book_a_trip) takes you to Frommer's favorite sites for booking your vacation at affordable prices.

HAWAII ON THE WEB

Below are some of the best Hawaii-specific websites for planning your trip.

- **Maui Visitors Bureau (www.visit maui.com):** An excellent, all-around guide to travel tips, Hawaiian culture, activities, tours, lodging, family vacations and events, weddings, and honeymoons. Info on Molokai and Lanai are also listed. But keep in mind that only members of the MVB are listed.
- **Planet Hawaii (www.planet-hawaii. com):** An island-by-island guide to activities, lodging, shopping, culture, the surf report, weather, and more. Mostly, you'll find short listings with links to companies' own websites.
- **Internet Hawaii Radio (www. hotspots.hawaii.com):** This eclectic site features great Hawaiian music, with opportunities to order a CD or cassette. You can also purchase Hawaiian historical and cultural books.
- **Maui Island Currents (www.island currents.com):** Specializing in arts and culture, Island Currents gives the most detailed lowdown on current exhibitions and performance art.

Gallery listings are organized by town, while in-depth articles highlight local artists. Consult restaurant reviews from the *Maui News* "Best of Maui" poll for suggestions and prices.

- **Maui Net (www.maui.net):** The clients of this Internet service provider are featured in this extensive directory of links to accommodations, activities, and shopping. The activities section has links to golf, hiking, airborne activities, and ocean adventures, such as scuba and snorkeling. These links lead to outfitters' sites, where you can learn more and set up excursions before you arrive in paradise.
- **Molokai: The Most Hawaiian Island (www.molokai-hawaii.com):** This is a very complete site for activities, events, nightlife, accommodations, and family vacations. Enjoy the landscape by viewing a virtual photo tour, get driving times between various points, and learn about local history.
- **The Hawaiian Language Website (www.geocities.com/~olelo):** This fabulous site not only has easy lessons

on learning the Hawaiian language but also a great cultural calendar, links to other Hawaii websites, a section on the hula, and lyrics (and translations) to Hawaiian songs.

• **Visit Lanai (www.visitlanai.net):** Everything you wanted to know about the island of Lanai from activities and accommodations to maps, a calendar of events, and even romance.

12 The 21st-Century Traveler

INTERNET ACCESS AWAY FROM HOME

Travelers have any number of ways to check their e-mail and access the Internet on the road. Of course, using your own laptop—or even a PDA or electronic organizer with a modem—gives you the most flexibility. But even if you don't have a computer, you can still access your e-mail and even your office computer from cybercafes.

WITHOUT YOUR OWN COMPUTER

It's hard nowadays to find a city that *doesn't* have a few cybercafes, and Maui is no exception. Although there's no definitive directory for cybercafes, some good places to start are **www.cybercaptive.com**, **www.netcafeguide.com**, and **www.cyber cafe.com**.

In Kihei you can get Internet access at the **Hale Imua Internet Café,** in the Kamaole Center (© **808/891-9219**). In Lahaina drop by **Buns of Maui,** Old Lahaina Shopping Center, 878 Front St. (© **808/661-5407**).

Aside from formal cybercafes, all **public libraries** on Maui offer free access if you have a library card, which you can purchase for a $10 fee. All hotels on Maui have **in-room dataports** and **business centers,** but the charges can be exorbitant.

To retrieve your e-mail, ask your **Internet service provider (ISP)** if it has a Web-based interface tied to your existing e-mail account. If your ISP doesn't have such an interface, you can use the free **mail2web** service (www.mail2web.com) to view and reply to your home e-mail.

For more flexibility, you may want to open a free, Web-based e-mail account with **Yahoo! Mail** (mail.yahoo.com). (Microsoft's Hotmail is another popular option, but Hotmail has severe spam problems.) Your home ISP may be able to forward your e-mail to the Web-based account automatically.

WITH YOUR OWN COMPUTER

Wi-Fi (wireless fidelity) is the buzzword in computer access, and more and more hotels, cafes, and retailers are signing on. You can get a Wi-Fi connection one of several ways. Many laptops sold in the last year have built-in Wi-Fi capability (an 802.11b wireless Ethernet connection). Mac owners have their own networking technology called Apple AirPort. For those with older computers, an 802.11b/**Wi-Fi card** (around $50) can be plugged into your laptop. You sign up for wireless access service much as you do cellphone service, through a plan offered by one of several commercial companies that have made wireless service available in airports, hotel lobbies, and coffee shops, primarily in the U.S. (followed by the U.K. and Japan). **T-Mobile Hotspot** (www.t-mobile.com/hotspot) serves up wireless connections at more than 1,000 Starbucks coffee shops nationwide. **Boingo** (www.boingo.com) and **Wayport** (www.wayport.com) have set up networks in airports and high-class hotel lobbies. iPass providers (see below) also give you access to a few hundred wireless hotel-lobby setups. Best of all, you don't need to be staying at the Four Seasons to use the hotel's network; just set yourself up on a nice couch in the lobby.

There are also places that provide **free wireless networks** in cities around the world. To locate these free hotspots, go to **www.personaltelco.net/index.cgi/ WirelessCommunities**.

If Wi-Fi is not available at your destination, most business-class hotels throughout the world offer dataports for laptop modems, and a few thousand hotels in the U.S. and Europe now offer free high-speed Internet access using an Ethernet network cable. You can bring your own cables, but most hotels rent them for around $10. **Call your hotel in advance** to see what your options are.

In addition, major Internet service providers (ISPs) have **local access numbers** around the world, allowing you to go online by simply placing a local call. Check your ISP's website or call its toll-free number and ask how you can use your current account away from home and how much it will cost.

If you're traveling outside the reach of your ISP, the **iPass** network has dial-up numbers in most countries around the world. You'll have to sign up with an iPass provider, who will then tell you how to set up your computer for your destination(s). For a list of iPass providers, go to www.ipass.com and click on "Individuals Buy Now." One solid provider is **i2roam** (www.i2roam.com; ℂ **866/811-6209** or 920/235-0475).

USING A CELLPHONE

Just because your cellphone works at home doesn't mean it'll work in Hawaii (thanks to our fragmented cellphone system). Take a look at your wireless company's coverage map on its website before heading out. If you need to stay in touch at a destination where you know your phone won't work, **rent** a phone that does from **InTouch USA** (ℂ **800/872-7626; www.intouchglobal.com**) or a car-rental location, but be aware that you'll pay $1 a minute or more for airtime.

If you're not from the U.S., you'll be appalled at the poor reach of our **GSM (Global System for Mobiles) wireless network,** which is used by much of the rest of the world. To see where GSM phones work in the U.S., check out www.t-mobile.com/coverage/national_popup.asp).

13 Getting Around

The only way to really see Maui is by rental car. There's no real island-wide public transit.

Maui has only a handful of major roads: One follows the coastline around the two volcanoes that form the island, Haleakala and Puu Kukui; one goes up to Haleakala's summit; one goes to Hana; one goes to Wailea; and one goes to Lahaina. It sounds simple, but the names of the few roads change en route. Study the foldout map included with this book before you set out. Also, you should expect to encounter a traffic jam or two in the major resort areas.

The best and most detailed road maps are published by *This Week* magazine, a free visitor publication available on Maui.

Most rental-car maps are pretty good, too.

CAR RENTALS

Maui has one of the least expensive car-rental rates in the country—about $44 a day (including all state tax and fees); the national average is about $54. Cars are usually plentiful on Maui, except on holiday weekends, which in Hawaii also means King Kamehameha Day, Prince Kuhio Day, and Admission Day (see "When to Go" earlier in this chapter). Rental cars are usually at a premium on Molokai and Lanai, so book well ahead.

All the major car-rental agencies have offices on Maui, usually at both Kahului and West Maui airports. They include:

(*Tips* Traffic Advisory

The road from central Maui to Kihei and Wailea, **Mokulele Highway (Hwy. 311)**, is a dangerous strip that's often the scene of head-on crashes involving intoxicated and speeding drivers. Be careful. Also be alert on the **Honoapiilani Highway (Hwy. 30)** en route to Lahaina because drivers who spot whales in the channel between Maui and Lanai often slam on the brakes and cause major tie-ups and accidents.

All highways on Maui are jampacked, bumper-to-bumper, between 7 and 9am and 4 and 6pm, so plan accordingly.

If you get into trouble on Maui's highways, look for the flashing blue strobe lights on 12-foot poles; at the base are emergency, solar-powered call boxes (programmed to dial *℡* 911 as soon as you pick up the handset). There are 29 emergency call boxes on the island's busiest highways and remote areas, including along the Hana and Haleakala highways and on the north end of the island in the remote community of Kahakuloa.

Another traffic note: Buckle up your seat belt—Hawaii has stiff fines for non-compliance.

Alamo (*℡* 800/327-9633; www.go alamo.com), **Avis** (*℡* 800/321-3712; www.avis.com), **Budget** (*℡* 800/572-0700; www.budget.com), **Dollar** (*℡* 800/800-4000; www.dollarcar.com), **Hertz** (*℡* 800/654-3011; www.hertz. com), and **National** (*℡* 800/227-7368; www.nationalcar.com).

There are also a few frugal car-rental agencies offering older cars at discount prices. **Word of Mouth Rent-a-Used-Car** *ℝ*, in Kahului (*℡* 800/533-5929 or 808/877-2436; www.mauirentacar.com), offers an older, four-door compact without air-conditioning for $120 a week, plus tax; with air-conditioning, it's $140 a week, plus tax. **Maui Cruisers,** in Wailuku (*℡* 877/749-7889 or 808/ 249-2319; www.mauicruisers.net), with free airport pickup and return, rents used Nissan Sentras and Toyota Tercels, 8 to 12 years old but in good running condition, for $31 a day or $154 a week (including tax and insurance).

To rent a car in Hawaii, you must be at least 25 years old and have a valid driver's license and a credit card.

INSURANCE Hawaii is a no-fault state, which means that if you don't have collision-damage insurance, you are required to pay for all damages before you leave the state, whether or not the accident was your fault. Your personal car insurance back home may provide rental-car coverage; read your policy or call your insurer before you leave home. Bring your insurance identification card if you decline the optional insurance, which usually costs from $12 to $20 a day. Obtain the name of your company's local claim representative before you go. Some credit card companies also provide collision-damage insurance for their customers; check with yours before you rent.

EASY RIDING AROUND MAUI

Don black denim and motorcycle boots and ride around Maui on a hog, available for $99 for 6 hours and $149 a day at **Island Riders,** 126 Hinau St. (by Pizza Hut), Lahaina (*℡* **800/529-2925** or 808/ 661-9966; www.islandriders.com), and in Kihei at 1975 S. Kihei Rd. (*℡* **808/874-0311**). Forget the greasy Hell's Angels image; latter-day Wild Ones are buttoned-down corporate types or California Highway Patrol officers on holiday. Whether you blast up Haleakala's grand corniche or haul ass to Hana, it's the most fun you can have on two wheels. This toy store for big boys and girls also rents exotic cars (Dodge Vipers, Prowlers, and Corvettes), which start at about $169 for 5 hours and $249 a day. Island Riders offers free pickup from most Maui hotels—convenient if you're throwing caution to the wind for just a day. They also have 4×4 Jeeps starting at $69 for 8 hours and $79 for 24 hours.

MOPEDS

Mopeds are available for rent from **Toy Cars,** 640 Front St., #5, Lahaina (*(C)* **888/628-4227** or 808/661-1212; www.maui.net/~toystore/bike10.htm). Mopeds, which start at $35 for 4 hours and $50 for all day (8am–4:30pm), are little more than motorized bicycles that get up to around 35 mph (with a good wind at your back), so I suggest using them only locally (to get to the beach or to go shopping). Don't take them out on the highway because they can't keep up with the traffic. Toy Cars also rents motorcycles and dune buggies.

OTHER TRANSPORTATION OPTIONS

TAXIS   For island-wide 24-hour service, call **Alii Cab Co.** (*(C)* 808/661-3688 or 808/667-2605). You can also try **Kihei Taxi** (*(C)* 808/879-3000), **Wailea Taxi** (*(C)* 808/874-5000), or **Maui Central Cab** (*(C)* 808/244-7278) if you need a ride.

SHUTTLES   SpeediShuttle (*(C)* **808/ 875-8070;** www.speedishuttle.com) can take you between Kahului Airport and all the major resorts from 5am to 11pm daily (for details, see "Landing at Kahului Airport" under "Getting There," earlier in this chapter).

Holo Ka'a Public Transit (*(C)* 808/879-2828; www.akinatours.com) is a public/private partnership that has convenient, economical, and air-conditioned shuttle buses. The costs range from free shuttle vans within the resort areas, like Wailea, to just $1 for the bus from Kaanapali to Lahaina.

14 Tips on Accommodations

Maui offers a tremendous variety of accommodations, from ritzy resorts to simple bed-and-breakfasts. Read this section before booking a room to find out what each option typically has to offer. I've also included some tips on how to get the best rates.

TYPES OF ACCOMMODATIONS

HOTELS   In Hawaii the term *hotel* can indicate a wide range of options, from few or no on-site amenities to enough extras to qualify as a resort. Generally, a hotel offers daily maid service and has a restaurant, on-site laundry facilities, a pool, and a sundries/convenience-type shop (as opposed to the shopping arcades that most resorts have). Top hotels also provide activities desks, concierge service,

business centers, a bar and/or lounge, and perhaps a few more shops. The advantages of staying in a hotel are privacy and convenience; the disadvantage is generally noise—either thin walls between rooms or loud music from a lobby lounge late into the night.

RESORTS   In Hawaii a resort offers everything a hotel does—and more. You can expect direct beach access, with beach cabanas and lounge chairs; pools and a Jacuzzi; a spa and fitness center; restaurants, bars, and lounges; a 24-hour front desk; concierge, valet, and bellhop services; room service (often around the clock); an activities desk; tennis and golf; ocean activities; a business center; kids' programs; and more.

The advantages of a resort are that you have everything you could possibly want in the way of services and things to do; the disadvantage is that the price generally reflects this. And don't be misled by a name—just because a place is called "ABC Resort" doesn't mean it actually *is* a resort. Make sure you're getting what you pay for.

CONDOS   The roominess and convenience of a condo—which is usually a fully equipped, multiple-bedroom apartment—makes this a great choice for families. Condominium properties in Hawaii generally consist of several apartments set in either a single high-rise or a cluster of low-rise units. Condos usually have amenities such as some maid service (ranging from daily to weekly; it may or may not be included in your rate), a pool, and an on-site front desk or a live-in property manager. Condos tend to be clustered in resort areas. There are some very high-end condos, but most are quite affordable, especially if you're traveling in a group.

The advantages of a condo are privacy, space, and conveniences—which usually include a full kitchen, a washer and dryer, a private phone, and more. The downsides are the standard lack of an on-site restaurant and the density of the units (versus the privacy of a single-unit vacation rental).

BED & BREAKFASTS   Hawaii has a wide range of places that call themselves B&Bs: everything from a traditional B&B—several bedrooms in a home, with breakfast served in the morning—to what is essentially a vacation rental on an owner's property that comes with fixings for you to make your own breakfast. Make sure that the B&B you're booking matches your own mental picture. Note that laundry facilities and private phones are not always available. I've reviewed lots of wonderful B&Bs in the island chapters that follow. If you have to share a bathroom, I've spelled it out in the listings; otherwise, you can assume that you will have your own.

The advantages of a traditional B&B are its individual style and congenial atmosphere, with a host who's often happy to act as your own private concierge. In addition, they're usually an affordable way to go. The disadvantages are lack of privacy, usually a set time for

---

What If Your Dream Hotel Becomes a Nightmare?

To avoid any unpleasant surprises, find out when you make your reservation exactly what the accommodations are offering you: cost, minimum stay, included amenities. Ask if there's any penalty for leaving early. Discuss what the cancellation policy is if the accommodations fail to meet your expectations—and get this policy in writing.

If you're not satisfied with your room, notify the front desk or booking agency immediately. Approach the management in a calm, reasonable manner, and suggest a solution (like moving to another unit). Be willing to compromise. Do not leave; if you do, you may not get your deposit back.

If all else fails, when you get home, write to any association the establishment may be a member of (such as the Hawaii Visitors and Convention Bureau or a resort association). Describe your complaint and why the issue was not resolved to your satisfaction. And be sure to let us know if you have a problem with a place recommended in this book!

breakfast, few amenities, and generally no maid service. Also, B&B owners usually require a minimum stay of 2 or 3 nights, and it's often a drive to the beach.

VACATION RENTALS This is another great choice for families and for long-term stays. "Vacation rental" usually means that there will be no one on the property where you're staying. The actual accommodations can range from an apartment to an entire fully equipped house. Generally, vacation rentals allow you to settle in and make yourself at home for a while. They have kitchen facilities (at least a kitchenette), on-site laundry facilities, and phones; some also come with such extras as a TV, VCR, and stereo.

The advantages of a vacation rental are complete privacy, your own kitchen (which can save you money on meals), and lots of conveniences. The disadvantages are a lack of an on-site property manager and generally no maid service. Often, a minimum stay is required (sometimes as much as a week). If you book a vacation rental, be sure that you have a 24-hour contact to call if the toilet won't flush or you can't figure out how to turn on the air-conditioning.

BARGAINING ON PRICES

Rates can sometimes be bargained down, but it depends on the place. The best bargaining can be had at **hotels** and **resorts.** If business is slow and you book directly, some places may give you at least part of the commission they'd normally pay a travel agent. Most hotels and resorts also have local rates for islanders, which they may extend to visitors during slow periods. It never hurts to ask about discounted or local rates; a host of special rates are available for the military, seniors, members of the travel industry, families, corporate travelers, and long-term stays. Also ask about **package deals,** which might include a car rental or free breakfast for the same price as a room by itself. Hotels and resorts offer packages for everyone: golfers, tennis players, families, honeymooners, and more (see "Money-Saving Package Deals" earlier in this chapter). I've found that it's worth the extra few cents to make a local call to the hotel; sometimes the local reservations person knows about package deals that the toll-free operators are unaware of. If all else fails, try to get the hotel or resort to upgrade you to a better room for the same price as a budget room or waive the parking fee or extra fees for children. Persistence and polite inquiries can pay off.

It's harder to bargain at **bed-and-breakfasts.** You may be able to negotiate down the minimum stay or get a discount if you're staying a week or longer. But generally a B&B owner has only a few rooms and has already priced the property at a competitive rate; expect to pay what's asked.

You have somewhat more leeway to negotiate at **vacation rentals** and **condos.** In addition to asking for a discount on a multinight stay, also ask if they can

---

Nickel-and-Dime Charges at High-Priced Hotels

Several upscale resorts in Hawaii have begun a practice that I find distasteful and dishonest: charging a so-called "resort fee." This daily fee is added on to your bill for such "complimentary" items as a daily newspaper, local phone calls, and use of the fitness facilities—amenities that the resort has been happily providing free to its guests for years. In most cases you do not have an option to decline the resort fee—in other words, this is a sneaky way to increase the nightly rate without telling you.

Tips **B&B Etiquette**

In Hawaii it is traditional and customary to remove your shoes before entering anyone's home. The same is true for most bed-and-breakfast facilities. If this custom is unpleasant to you, a B&B may not be for you.

Hotels, resorts, condos, and vacation rentals generally allow smoking in the guest rooms (most also have nonsmoking rooms available), but the majority of bed-and-breakfast units forbid smoking in the rooms. Be sure to check the policy of your accommodations before you book.

---

throw in a rental car to sweeten the deal; believe it or not, they often will.

USING A BOOKING AGENCY VERSUS DOING IT YOURSELF

If you don't have the time to call several places yourself to make sure they offer the amenities you'd like, you might consider a booking agency.

The top reservations service in the state is **Hawaii's Best Bed & Breakfasts** (© 800/262-9912 or 808/985-7488; fax 808/967-8610; www.bestbnb.com). This service charges $20. The owners personally select the traditional home stays, cottages, and inns based on each one's

hospitality and charm. They also book vacation rentals, hotels, and resorts.

Other great statewide booking agents are **Bed & Breakfast Hawaii** (© 800/733-1632 or 808/822-7771; fax 808/822-2723; www.bandb-hawaii.com), offering a range of accommodations from vacation homes to B&Bs, starting at $65 a night. For vacation rentals, contact **Hawaii Beachfront Vacation Homes** (© 808/247-3637; fax 808/235-2644). **Hawaii Condo Exchange** (© 800/442-0404; http://hawaiicondoexchange.com) acts as a consolidator for condo and vacation-rental properties.

15 The Active Vacation Planner

If you want nothing more on your vacation than a fabulous beach and a perfectly mixed mai tai, you're in luck—Maui has some of the most spectacular beaches (not to mention the best mai tais) in the world. But Maui's wealth of natural wonders is hard to resist: The year-round tropical climate and spectacular scenery tend to inspire even the most committed desk jockeys and couch potatoes to get outside and explore.

If you have your own snorkel gear or other watersports equipment, bring it if you can. If not, don't fret: Everything you'll need is available for rent. I've listed all kinds of places to rent or buy gear in chapter 7, "Fun on & off the Beach."

SETTING OUT ON YOUR OWN VS. USING AN OUTFITTER

There are two ways to go: Plan all the details before you go and schlep your gear 2,500 miles across the Pacific, or go with an outfitter or a guide and let them worry about the details.

Experienced outdoors enthusiasts can follow their noses to coastal campgrounds or even trek into the rainforest on their own, but it's often preferable to go with a local guide who is familiar with the conditions at both sea level and the summit, knows the land and its flora and fauna in detail, and has all the gear you'll need. It's also good to go with a guide if time is an issue. If you really want to see native

---

⸤Tips⸥ Safety Tips

Be sure to see "Travel Insurance," earlier in this chapter, before setting out on any adventure—it includes useful information on hiking, camping, and ocean safety. Even if you just plan to lie on the beach, check out the box called "Don't Get Burned: Smart Tanning Tips," earlier in this chapter, to learn how to protect yourself against the sun's harmful rays.

When planning sunset activities, be aware that Hawaii, like other places close to the equator, has a very short (5–10 min.) twilight period after the sun sets. After that, it's dark. If you hike out to watch the sunset, be sure you can make it back quickly, or take a flashlight.

---

birds, for instance, an experienced guide will take you directly to the best areas for sightings. And many forests and valleys in the interior of the islands are accessible only on guided tours. If you go with a guide, plan on spending at least $100 a day per person; I recommend the best local outfitters and tour-guide operators in chapter 7.

But if you have the time, already own the gear, and love doing the research and planning, try exploring on your own. Chapter 7 discusses the best spots to set out on your own, from the best offshore snorkel and dive spots to great daylong hikes, as well as the federal, state, and county agencies that can help you with hikes on public property. I also list references for spotting birds, plants, and sea life. I recommend that you always use the resources available and inquire about weather, trail or surf conditions, water availability, and other conditions before you take off on your adventure.

For hikers, a great alternative to hiring a private guide is taking one of the guided hikes offered by the **Nature Conservancy of Hawaii,** 1116 Smith St., Honolulu, HI 96817 (© **808/573-4147** on Maui, 808/553-5236 on Oahu, or 808/524-0779 on Molokai), and the **Hawaii Chapter of the Sierra Club,** P.O. Box 2577, Honolulu, HI 96803 (© **808/573-4147** on Maui; www.hi.sierraclub.org). Both organizations offer guided

hikes, as well as 1- to 7-day work trips to restore habitats and trails and root out invasive plants. It might not sound like a dream vacation to everyone, but it's a chance to see the "real" Maui—including wilderness areas that are usually off-limits.

All Nature Conservancy hikes are free. However, you must reserve a spot, and a deposit is required for guided hikes to ensure that you'll show up; your deposit is refunded once you do. The hikes are generally offered once a month on Maui, Molokai, and Lanai (call the Oahu office for reservations). There's also no charge for the trips to restore habitats. Write for a schedule of guided hikes and other programs.

The Sierra Club offers weekly hikes on Maui. Hikes are led by certified Sierra Club volunteers and are classified as easy, moderate, or strenuous. These half-day or all-day affairs cost $1 for Sierra Club members, $3 for nonmembers (bring exact change). For a copy of the newsletter, which lists all outings and trail repair work, send $2 to the address above.

USING ACTIVITIES DESKS TO BOOK YOUR ISLAND FUN

If you're interested in an activity that requires an outfitter or a guide, you might want to consider booking through a discount activities center or activities desk. These agents—who act as a clearinghouse for activities—can often get you a better price than you'd get by booking an activity directly with the outfitter yourself.

Discount activities centers will, in effect, split their commission with you, giving themselves a smaller commission to get your business—and passing, on average, a 10% discount on to you. Good activities centers should also be able to help you find, say, the snorkel cruise that's right for you, or the luau that's most suitable for both you *and* the kids.

But it's in the activity agent's best interest to sign you up with outfitters from which they earn the most commission. If an agent tries to push a particular outfitter or activity too hard, be skeptical. Conversely, they may try to steer you away from outfitters that don't offer big commissions. For example, Trilogy, the company that offers Maui's most popular snorkel cruises to Lanai (and the only one with rights to land at Lanai's Hulupoe Beach), offers only minimal commissions to agents and does not allow agents to offer any discounts at all; as a result, most activities desks on Maui will automatically try to steer you away from Trilogy.

Another important word of warning: Be careful to avoid those activities centers offering discounts as fronts for timeshare-sales presentations. Using a free snorkel cruise or luau tickets as bait, they'll suck you into a 90-minute presentation—and try to get you to buy into a Maui timeshare in the process. Not only will they give you the hard sell, they also won't be as interested, or as knowledgeable, about which activities might be right for you. These shady deals seem to be particularly rampant on Maui.

On Maui I recommend **Tom Barefoot's Cashback Tours** ✿, 834 Front St., Lahaina (✆ **888/222-3601** or 808/661-8889; www.barefoothawaii.com). Tom

---

⌒Value Fun for Less: Don't Leave Home Without a Gold Card

Almost any activity you can think of, from submarine rides to Polynesian luaus, can be purchased at a discount by using the **Activities and Attractions Association of Hawaii Gold Card,** 355 Hukilike St., No. 202, Kahului, HI 96732 (✆ **800/398-9698** or 808/871-7947; fax 808/877-3104; www.hawaiifun.org). The Gold Card, accepted by members on all the Hawaiian islands, offers a discount of 10% to 25% off activities and meals for up to four people; it's good for a year and costs $30.

You can save big bucks with the Gold Card. For example, if you have your heart set on taking a helicopter ride that goes for $149, you'll pay only $119 with your Gold Card, saving you $30 per person—that's $120 in savings for a family of four. With just one activity alone, you've gotten the cost of the card back in savings. And there are hundreds of activities to choose from: air tours, attractions, bicycling tours, dinner cruises, fishing, guided tours, helicopter tours, horseback riding, kayaking, luaus, snorkeling, rafting, sailing, scuba diving, submarine rides, and more. It also gets you discounts on rental cars, restaurants, and golf.

You can get a card from the Activities and Attractions Association (see above). You contact the activity vendor directly, give them your Gold Card number, and get discounts ranging from 10% to 25%.

offers a 10% discount on all tours, activities, and adventures when you pay in cash or with traveler's checks. If you pay with a credit card or personal check, he'll give you a 7% discount. The two showrooms are loaded with pictures and maps of all the activities the company books.

OUTDOOR ETIQUETTE

Carry out what you carry in. Find a trash container for all your litter (including cigarette butts). Litterbugs anger the gods.

Observe *kapu* (taboo) and NO TRESPASSING signs. Don't climb on ancient Hawaiian *heiau* (temple) walls or carry home rocks, all of which belong to the Hawaiian volcano goddess, Pele. Some say it's just a silly superstition, but each year the national and state park services get boxes of lava rocks in the mail, sent back to Hawaii by visitors who have experienced unusually bad luck.

16 Recommended Reading

In addition to the books discussed below, those planning an extended trip to other islands in Hawaii should check out *Frommer's Hawaii 2006* (Wiley Publishing, Inc.), *Frommer's Hawaii from $80 a Day* (Wiley Publishing, Inc.), *Frommer's Kauai* (Wiley Publishing, Inc.), *Frommer's Honolulu, Waikiki & Oahu* (Wiley Publishing, Inc.), and *Hawaii with Kids* (Wiley Publishing, Inc.).

FICTION

The first book people think about is James A. Michener's *Hawaii* (Fawcett Crest, 1974). This epic novel manages to put the island's history into chronological order, but remember: It is still fiction, and very sanitized fiction at that. For a more contemporary look at life in Hawaii today, one of the best novels is *Shark Dialogue,* by Kiana Davenport (Plume, 1995). The novel tells the story of Pono, the larger-than-life matriarch, and her four daughters of mixed races. Davenport skillfully weaves legends and myths of Hawaii into the "real life" reality that Pono and her family face in the complex Hawaii of today. Lois-Ann Yamanaka uses a very "local" voice and stark depictions of life in the islands in her fabulous novels *Wild Meat and the Bully Burgers* (Farrar, Straus and Giroux, 1996), *Blu's Hanging* (Avon, 1997), and *Heads by Harry* (Avon, 1999).

NONFICTION

Mark Twain's writing on Hawaii in the 1860s offers a wonderful introduction to Hawaii's history. One of his best books is *Mark Twain in Hawaii: Roughing It in the Sandwich Islands* (Mutual Publishing, 1990). Another great depiction of Hawaii in 1889 is *Travels in Hawaii* (University of Hawaii Press, 1973), by Robert Louis Stevenson. For contemporary voices on Hawaii's unique culture, one of the best books to get is *Voices of Wisdom: Hawaiian Elders Speak,* by M. J. Harden (Aka Press, 1999). Some 24 different *kahuna* (experts) in their fields were interviewed about their talent, skill, or artistic practice. These living treasures talk about how Hawaiians of yesteryear viewed nature, spirituality, preservation and history, dance and music, arts and crafts, canoes, and the next generation.

Native Planters in Old Hawaii: Their Life, Lore and Environment (Bishop Museum Press, Honolulu, 2004), was originally published in 1972 but still is one of the most important ethnographic works on traditional Hawaiian culture, portraying the lives of the common folk and their relationship with the land before the arrival of Westerners.

FLORA & FAUNA

Because Hawaii is so lush with nature and blessed with plants, animals, and reef fish seen nowhere else on the planet, a few reference books can help you identify what you're looking at and make your trip more interesting. In the botanical world, Angela Kay Kepler's *Hawaiian Heritage Plants* (A Latitude 20 Book, University of Hawaii Press, 1998) is the standard for plant reference. In a series of essays, Kepler weaves culture, history, geography, botany, and even spirituality into her vivid descriptions of plants. Great color photos and drawings help you sort thorough the myriad species. Another great plant book is *Tropicals* (Timber Press, 1988), by Gordon Courtright, which is filled with color photos identifying everything from hibiscus to palms. Courtright calls it "a visual plant dictionary."

Snorkelers should check out John E. Randall's *Shore Fishes of Hawaii* (University of Hawaii Press, 1998). Randall is the expert on everything that swims underwater, and his book is one of the best. Two other books on reef-fish identification, with easy-to-use spiral bindings, are *Hawaiian Reef Fish—The Identification Book* (Blue Kirio Publishing, 1993), by Casey Mahaney, and *Hawaiian Reef Fish* (Island Heritage, 1998), by Astrid Witte and Casey Mahaney.

H. Douglas Pratt's *A Pocket Guide to Hawaii's Birds* (Mutual Publishing, 1996) gives birders everything they need to identify Hawaii's birds.

HISTORY

David E. Eyre's *By Wind, By Wave: An Introduction to Hawaii's Natural History* (Bess Press, 2000) vividly chronicles the formation of the Hawaiian islands, as well as the complex interrelationships among the plants, animals, ocean, and people. Eyre points out that Hawaii has become the "extinction capital of the world," then urges readers to do something about it and spells out how.

For history of "precontact" Hawaii (before Westerners arrived), David Malo's *Hawaiian Antiquities* (Bishop Museum Press, 1976) is the preeminent source. Malo was born around 1793 and wrote about the Hawaiian religion and lifestyle at that time. It's an excellent reference book. For more readable books on old Hawaii, try *Stories of Old Hawaii* (Bess Press, 1997), by Roy Kakulu Alameide, on myths and legends; *Hawaiian Folk Tales* (Mutual Publishing, 1998) by Thomas G. Thrum; and *The Legends and Myths of Hawaii* (Charles E. Tuttle Company, 1992) by His Hawaiian Majesty King David Kalakaua.

The best book on the 1893 overthrow of the Hawaiian monarchy is told by Queen Liliuokalani in her book *Hawaii's Story by Hawaii's Queen Liliuokalani* (Mutual Publishing, 1990). When it was written, it was an international plea for justice for her people, but it is a poignant read even today. It's also a "must-read" for people interested in current events and the recent rally in the 50th state for sovereignty. Two contemporary books on the question of Hawaii's sovereignty are Tom Coffman's *Nation Within—The Story of America's Annexation of the Nation of Hawaii* (Epicenter, 1998) and *Hawaiian Sovereignty: Do the Facts Matter?* (Goodale, 2000), by Thurston Twigg-Smith, which explores the opposite view. Twigg-Smith, former publisher of the statewide newspaper the *Honolulu Advertiser,* is the grandson of Lorrin A. Thurston, one of the architects of the 1893 overthrow of the monarchy. His "politically incorrect" views present a different look on this hotly debated topic.

For more recent history, Lawrence H. Fuchs's *Hawaii Pono* (Bess Press, 1991) is a carefully researched tome on the contributions of each of Hawaii's main immigrant communities (Chinese, Japanese, and Filipino) between 1893 and 1959.

FAST FACTS: Maui

American Express For 24-hour traveler's check refunds and purchase information, call © **800/221-7282.** Local offices are located in South Maui at the **Grand Wailea Resort** (© **808/875-4526**) and the **Westin Maui** at Kaanapali Beach (© **808/661-7155**).

Area Code All of the islands are in the **808** area code. Note that if you're calling one island from another, you must dial 1-808 first, and you'll be billed at long-distance rates (often more expensive than calling the mainland).

Business Hours Most offices are open from 8am to 5pm. Bank hours are Monday through Thursday from 8:30am to 3pm, Friday from 8:30am to 6pm; some banks are open on Saturday. Shopping centers are open Monday through Friday from 10am to 9pm, Saturday from 10am to 5:30pm, and Sunday from 10am to 5 or 6pm.

Dentists Emergency dental care is available at **Kihei Dental Center,** 1847 S. Kihei Rd., Kihei (© **808/874-8401**), or in Lahaina at the **Aloha Lahaina Dentists,** 134 Luakini St. (in the Maui Medical Group Building), Lahaina (© **808/661-4005**).

Doctors No appointment is necessary at **West Maui Healthcare Center,** Whalers Village, 2435 Kaanapali Pkwy., Suite H-7 (near Leilani's Restaurant), Kaanapali (© **808/667-9721**), which is open 365 days a year nightly until 10pm. In Kihei call **Urgent Care,** 1325 S. Kihei Rd., Suite 103 (at Lipoa St., across from Star Market; © **808/879-7781**), open daily from 6am to midnight; doctors are on call 24 hours a day.

Emergencies Dial © **911** for the police, an ambulance, and the fire department. District stations are located in Lahaina (© **808/661-4441**) and in Hana (© **808/248-8311**). For the **Poison Control Center,** call © **800/362-3585.**

Hospitals For medical attention, go to **Maui Memorial Hospital,** in Central Maui at 221 Mahalani, Wailuku (© **808/244-9056**), or East Maui's **Hana Medical Center,** on Hana Highway (© **808/248-8924**).

Liquor Laws The legal drinking age in Hawaii is 21. Beer, wine, and liquor are sold in grocery and convenience stores 7 days a week. It's illegal (though rarely prosecuted) to have an open container on the beach.

Post Offices To find the nearest post office, call © **800/ASK-USPS.** In Lahaina there are branches at the Lahaina Civic Center, 1760 Honoapiilani Hwy.; in Kahului there's a branch at 138 S. Puunene Ave.; and in Kihei there's one at 1254 S. Kihei Rd.

Safety Although Hawaii is generally a safe tourist destination, visitors have been crime victims, so stay alert. The most common crime against tourists is rental-car break-ins. Never leave any valuables in your car, not even in your trunk. Be especially careful at high-risk areas such as beaches and resorts. Never carry large amounts of cash with you. Stay in well-lighted areas after dark. Don't hike on deserted trails alone. See also section 6 of this chapter, "Health & Safety," for other safety tips.

Smoking It's against the law to smoke in public buildings, including restaurants. Hotels have nonsmoking rooms available and car-rental agencies have smoke-free cars. Most bed-and-breakfasts prohibit smoking indoors.

Taxes Hawaii's sales tax is 4%. Hotel occupancy tax is 7.25%, and hoteliers are allowed by the state to tack on an additional .001666% excise tax. Thus, expect taxes of about 11.42% to be added to every hotel bill.

Time Hawaii Standard Time is in effect year-round. Hawaii is 2 hours behind Pacific Standard Time and 5 hours behind Eastern Standard Time. In other words, when it's noon in Hawaii, it's 2pm in California and 5pm in New York during standard time on the mainland. There's no daylight saving time here, so when daylight saving time is in effect on the mainland, Hawaii is 3 hours behind the West Coast and 6 hours behind the East Coast.

Hawaii is east of the international date line, putting it in the same day as the U.S. mainland and Canada.

Weather For the current weather, call © **808/871-5111**; for recreational activities, call © **808/871-5054**; for Haleakala National Park weather, call © **808/ 871-5111**; for marine weather and surf and wave conditions, call © **808/877-3477**.

3

For International Visitors

Whether it's your first visit or your 10th, a trip to the United States may require additional planning. The pervasiveness of American culture around the world may make the United States feel like familiar territory to foreign visitors, but leaving your own country for the States—especially the unique island of Maui—still requires some arrangements before you leave home. This chapter will provide you with essential information, helpful tips, and advice for the more common problems that some international visitors encounter.

1 Preparing for Your Trip

ENTRY REQUIREMENTS

Check at any U.S. embassy or consulate for current information and requirements. You can also obtain a visa application and other information online at the **U.S. State Department**'s website at **http://travel.state.gov**.

VISAS The U.S. State Department has a **Visa Waiver Program** allowing citizens of certain countries to enter the United States without a visa for stays of up to 90 days. At press time these included Andorra, Australia, Austria, Belgium, Brunei, Denmark, Finland, France, Germany, Iceland, Ireland, Italy, Japan, Liechtenstein, Luxembourg, Monaco, the Netherlands, New Zealand, Norway, Portugal, San Marino, Singapore, Slovenia, Spain, Sweden, Switzerland, and the United Kingdom. Citizens of these countries need only a valid passport and a round-trip air or cruise ticket in their possession upon arrival. If they first enter the United States, they may also visit Mexico, Canada, Bermuda, and/or the Caribbean islands and return to the United States without a visa. Further information is available from any U.S. embassy or consulate. Canadian citizens may enter the United States without visas; they need only proof of residence.

Citizens of all other countries must have (1) a valid passport that expires at least 6 months later than the scheduled end of their visit to the United States, and (2) a tourist visa, which may be obtained without charge from any U.S. consulate.

To obtain a visa, the traveler must submit a completed application form (either in person or by mail) with a 1½-inch-square photo and must demonstrate binding ties to a residence abroad. Usually you can obtain a visa at once or within 24 hours, but it may take longer during the summer rush from June through August. If you cannot go in person, contact the nearest U.S. embassy or consulate for directions on applying by mail. Your travel agent or airline office may also be able to provide you with visa applications and instructions. The U.S. consulate or embassy that issues your visa will determine whether you will be issued a multiple- or single-entry visa and any restrictions regarding the length of your stay.

British subjects can obtain up-to-date visa information by calling the

U.S. Embassy Visa Information Line (© **0891/200-290**) or by visiting the "Visa Services" section of the American Embassy in London's website at www.usembassy.org.uk.

Irish citizens can obtain up-to-date visa information through the **Embassy of the USA Dublin,** 42 Elgin Rd., Dublin 4, Ireland (© **353/1-668-8777;** or by checking the "Visa Services" section of the website at http://dublin.usembassy.gov.

Australian citizens can obtain up-to-date visa information by contacting the **U.S. Embassy Canberra,** Moonah Place, Yarralumla, ACT 2600 (© **02/6214-5600**), or by checking the U.S. Diplomatic Mission's website at http://usembassy-australia.state.gov/consular.

Citizens of **New Zealand** can obtain up-to-date visa information by contacting the **U.S. Embassy New Zealand,** 29 Fitzherbert Terr., Thorndon, Wellington (© **644/472-2068**), or get the information directly from the "Services to New Zealanders" section of the website at http://usembassy.org.nz.

MEDICAL REQUIREMENTS Unless you're arriving from an area known to be suffering from an epidemic (particularly cholera or yellow fever), inoculations or vaccinations are not required for entry into the United States. If you have a medical condition that requires **syringe-administered medications,** carry a valid signed prescription from your physician—the Federal Aviation Administration (FAA) no longer allows airline passengers to pack syringes in their carry-on baggage without documented proof of medical need. If you have a disease that requires treatment with **narcotics,** you should also carry documented proof with you—smuggling narcotics aboard a plane is a serious offense that carries severe penalties in the U.S.

For **HIV-positive visitors,** requirements for entering the United States are somewhat vague and change frequently.

According to the latest publication of *HIV and Immigrants: A Manual for AIDS Service Providers,* the Immigration and Naturalization Service (INS) doesn't require a medical exam for entry into the United States, but INS officials may stop individuals because they look sick or because they are carrying AIDS/HIV medicine.

If an HIV-positive noncitizen applies for a nonimmigrant visa, the question on the application regarding communicable diseases is tricky no matter which way it's answered. If the applicant checks "no," INS may deny the visa on the grounds that the applicant committed fraud. If the applicant checks "yes" or if INS suspects the person is HIV-positive, it will deny the visa unless the applicant asks for a special waiver for visitors. This waiver is for people visiting the United States for a short time, to attend a conference, for instance, to visit close relatives, or to receive medical treatment. It can be a confusing situation. For up-to-the-minute information, contact **AIDSinfo** (© **800/448-0440,** or 301/519-6616 outside the U.S.; www.aidsinfo.nih.gov) or the **Gay Men's Health Crisis** (© **212/367-1000;** www.gmhc.org).

DRIVER'S LICENSES Foreign driver's licenses are mostly recognized in the U.S., although you may want to get an international driver's license if your home license is not written in English.

PASSPORT INFORMATION

Safeguard your passport in an inconspicuous, inaccessible place like a money belt. Make a copy of the critical pages, including the passport number, and store it in a safe place, separate from the passport itself. If you lose your passport, visit the nearest consulate of your native country as soon as possible for a replacement. Passport applications are downloadable from the websites listed below.

Note: The International Civil Aviation Organization has recommended a policy requiring that *every* individual who travels by air have a passport. In response, many countries are now requiring that children must be issued their own passport to travel internationally, where before those under 16 or so may have been allowed to travel on a parent's or guardian's passport.

FOR RESIDENTS OF CANADA

You can pick up a passport application at one of 28 regional passport offices or most travel agencies. Canadian children who travel must have their own passport. However, if you hold a valid Canadian passport issued before December 11, 2001, that bears the name of your child, the passport remains valid for you and your child until it expires. Passports cost C$85 for those 16 years and older (valid 5 years), C$35 for children 3 to 15 (valid 5 years), and C$20 for children under 3 (valid 3 years). Applications, which must be accompanied by two identical passport-size photographs and proof of Canadian citizenship, are available at travel agencies throughout Canada or from the central **Passport Office,** Department of Foreign Affairs and International Trade, Ottawa, ON K1A 0G3 (© 800/567-6868; www.dfait-maeci.gc.ca/passport). Processing takes 5 to 10 days if you apply in person, or about 3 weeks by mail.

FOR RESIDENTS OF THE UNITED KINGDOM

As a member of the European Union, you need only an identity card, not a passport, to travel to other E.U. countries. However, if you already possess a passport, it's always useful to carry it. To pick up an application for a standard 10-year passport (5-year passport for children under 16), visit the nearest Passport Office, major post office, or travel agency. You can also contact the **United Kingdom Passport Service** at © 0870/571-0410 or visit its website at www.passport.gov.uk. Passports are £33 for adults and

£19 for children under 16, with another £30 fee if you apply in person at a Passport Office. Processing takes about 2 weeks (1 week if you apply at the Passport Office).

FOR RESIDENTS OF IRELAND

You can apply for a 10-year passport, costing €57, at the **Passport Office,** Setanta Centre, Molesworth Street, Dublin 2 (© 01/671-1633; www.irlgov.ie/iveagh). Those under age 18 and over 65 must apply for a €12 3-year passport. You can also apply at 1A South Mall, Cork (© 021/272-525) or over the counter at most main post offices.

FOR RESIDENTS OF AUSTRALIA

You can get an application from your local post office or any branch of Passports Australia, but you must schedule an interview at the passport office to present your application materials. Call the **Australian Passport Information Service** at © 131-232, or visit the government website at www.passports.gov.au. Passports for adults are A$144 and for those under 18, A$72.

FOR RESIDENTS OF NEW ZEALAND

You can pick up a passport application at any New Zealand Passports Office or download it from their website. Contact the **Passports Office** at © 0800/225-050 in New Zealand, or 04/474-8100, or log on to www.passports.govt.nz. Passports for adults are NZ$80 and for children under 16 NZ$40.

CUSTOMS
WHAT YOU CAN BRING IN

Every visitor more than 21 years of age may bring in, free of duty, the following: (1) 1 liter of wine or hard liquor; (2) 200 cigarettes, 100 cigars (but not from Cuba), or 3 pounds of smoking tobacco; and (3) $100 worth of gifts. These exemptions are offered to travelers who spend at least 72 hours in the United States and who have not claimed them within the preceding 6 months. It is altogether forbidden to bring into the country foodstuffs (particularly fruit, cooked meats, and canned goods) and plants (vegetables, seeds, tropical plants, and the like). Foreign tourists may bring in or take out up to $10,000 in U.S. or foreign currency with no formalities; larger sums must be declared to U.S. Customs on entering or leaving, which includes filing form CM 4790. For more specific information regarding U.S. Customs and Border Protection, contact your nearest U.S. embassy or consulate or the **U.S. Customs** office (𝄢 202/927-1770; www.customs.ustreas.gov).

WHAT YOU CAN TAKE HOME

U.K. citizens returning from a non-E.U. country have a Customs allowance of: 200 cigarettes; 50 cigars; 250 grams of smoking tobacco; 2 liters of still table wine; 1 liter of spirits or strong liqueurs (over 22% volume); 2 liters of fortified wine, sparkling wine, or other liqueurs; 60 cubic centimeters (ml) perfume; 250 cubic centimeters (ml) of toilet water; and £145 worth of all other goods, including gifts and souvenirs. People under 17 cannot have the tobacco or alcohol allowance. For more information, contact **HM Customs & Excise** at 𝄢 **0845/010-9000** (from outside the U.K., 020/8929-0152) or consult their website at www.hmce.gov.uk.

For a clear summary of **Canadian** rules, request the booklet *I Declare,* issued by the **Canada Customs and Revenue Agency** (𝄢 **800/461-9999** in Canada, or 204/983-3500; www.ccra-adrc.gc.ca). Canada allows its citizens a C$750 exemption, and you're allowed to bring back duty-free one carton of cigarettes, one can of tobacco, 40 imperial ounces of liquor, and 50 cigars. In addition, you're allowed to mail gifts to Canada valued at less than C$60 a day, provided they're unsolicited and don't contain alcohol or tobacco (write on the package "Unsolicited gift, under C$60 value"). All valuables should be declared on the Y-38 form before departure from Canada, including serial numbers of valuables you already own, such as expensive foreign cameras. *Note:* The C$750 exemption can only be used once a year and only after an absence of 7 days.

The duty-free allowance in **Australia** is A$400 or, for those under 18, A$200. Citizens ages 18 and over can bring in 250 cigarettes or 250 grams of loose tobacco, and 1,125 milliliters of alcohol. If you're returning with valuables you already own, such as foreign-made cameras, you should file form B263. A helpful brochure available from Australian consulates or Customs offices is *Know Before You Go.* For more information, call the **Australian Customs Service** at 𝄢 **1300/363-263** or log on to www. customs.gov.au.

The duty-free allowance for **New Zealand** is NZ$700. Citizens over 17 can bring in 200 cigarettes, 50 cigars, or 250 grams of tobacco (or a mixture of all three if their combined weight doesn't exceed 250g); plus 4.5 liters of wine and beer or 1.125 liters of liquor. New Zealand currency does not carry import or export restrictions. Fill out a certificate of export, listing the valuables you are taking out of the country; that way, you can bring them back without paying duty. Most questions are answered in a free pamphlet available at New Zealand consulates and Customs offices: *New Zealand Customs Guide for Travellers, Notice no. 4.* For more information, contact **New Zealand Customs,** The Customhouse, 17–21 Whitmore St., Box 2218, Wellington (𝄢 **0800/428-786** or 04/473-6099; www.customs.govt.nz).

HEALTH INSURANCE

Although it's not required of travelers, health insurance is highly recommended. Unlike many European countries, the United States does not usually offer free or low-cost medical care to its citizens or visitors. Doctors and hospitals are expensive and in most cases will require advance payment or proof of coverage before they render their services. Policies can cover everything from the loss or theft of your baggage and trip cancellation to the guarantee of bail in case you're arrested. Good policies will also cover the costs of an accident, repatriation, or death. See "Travel Insurance" in chapter 2 for more information. Packages such as **Europ Assistance's "Worldwide Healthcare Plan"** are sold by European automobile clubs and travel agencies at attractive rates. **Worldwide Assistance Services Inc.** (© **800/821-2828;** www.world wideassistance.com) is the agent for Europ Assistance in the United States.

Though lack of health insurance may prevent you from being admitted to a hospital in nonemergencies, don't worry about being left on a street corner to die: The American way is to fix you now and bill the living daylights out of you later.

INSURANCE FOR BRITISH TRAVELERS   Most big travel agents offer their own insurance and will probably try to sell you their package when you book a holiday. Think before you sign. **Britain's Consumers' Association** recommends that you insist on seeing the policy and reading the fine print before buying travel insurance. **The Association of British Insurers** (© **020/7600-3333;** www.abi.org.uk) gives advice by phone and publishes *Holiday Insurance,* a free guide to policy provisions and prices. You might also shop around for better deals: Try **Columbus Direct** (© **020/7375-0011;** www.columbusdirect.net).

INSURANCE FOR CANADIAN TRAVELERS   Canadians should check with their provincial health plan offices or call **Health Canada** (© **613/957-2991;** www.hc-sc.gc.ca) to find out the extent of their coverage and what documentation and receipts they must take home in case they are treated in the United States.

MONEY

CURRENCY   The U.S. monetary system is very simple: The most common **bills** are the $1 (colloquially, a "buck"), $5, $10, and $20 denominations. There are also $2 bills (seldom encountered), $50 bills, and $100 bills (the last two are usually not welcome as payment for small purchases). All the paper money was recently redesigned, making the famous faces adorning them disproportionately large. The old-style bills are still legal tender.

There are seven denominations of coins: 1¢ (1 cent, or a penny); 5¢ (5 cents, or a nickel); 10¢ (10 cents, or a dime); 25¢ (25 cents, or a quarter); 50¢ (50 cents, or a half dollar); the gold-colored "Sacagawea" coin worth $1; and, prized by collectors, the rare, older silver dollar.

EXCHANGING CURRENCY   Exchanging foreign currency for U.S. dollars is not as easy on Maui as it is on Oahu. There also are currency services at **Honolulu International Airport.** Most of the major hotels offer currency-exchange services, but generally the rate of exchange is not as good as what you'll get at a bank. There are no currency-exchange facilities on Maui. You'll need to either go to a bank (call first to see if currency exchange is available) or use your hotel.

TRAVELER'S CHECKS   Though traveler's checks are widely accepted, make sure that they're denominated in U.S. dollars, as foreign-currency checks are often difficult to exchange. The three traveler's checks that are most widely recognized—and least likely to be denied—are **Visa, American Express,** and **Thomas**

Cook. Be sure to record the numbers of the checks, and keep that information in a separate place in case they get lost or stolen. Most businesses are pretty good about taking traveler's checks, but you're better off cashing them in at a bank (in small amounts, of course) and paying in cash. *Remember:* You'll need identification, such as a driver's license or passport, to change a traveler's check.

CREDIT CARDS Credit cards are widely used in Hawaii. You can save yourself trouble by using plastic rather than cash or traveler's checks in most hotels, restaurants, retail stores, and a growing number of food and liquor stores. You must have a credit card to rent a car in Hawaii.

SAFETY

GENERAL SAFETY Although tourist areas are generally safe, visitors should always stay alert. It's wise to ask the island tourist office if you're in doubt about which neighborhoods are safe. Avoid deserted areas, especially at night. Generally speaking, you can feel safe in areas where there are many people and open establishments.

Avoid carrying valuables with you on the street, and don't display expensive cameras or electronic equipment. Hold on to your pocketbook, and place your billfold in an inside pocket. In theaters, restaurants, and other public places, keep your possessions in sight.

Remember also that hotels are open to the public and that, in a large hotel, security may not be able to screen everyone entering. Always lock your room door—don't assume that once inside your hotel, you're automatically safe.

DRIVING SAFETY Safety while driving is particularly important. Ask your rental agency about personal safety, or request a brochure of traveler-safety tips when you pick up your car. Get written directions or a map with your route clearly marked in red showing you how to get to your destination.

Recently, crime has involved more burglary of tourist rental cars in hotel parking structures and at beach parking lots. Park in well-lighted and well-traveled areas if possible. Never leave any packages or valuables visible in the car. If someone attempts to rob you or steal your car, do not try to resist the thief or carjacker—report the incident to the police department immediately.

For more information on driving rules and getting around by car in Maui, see "Getting Around" in chapter 2.

2 Getting to & Around the United States

The only airline with direct flights from foreign cities to Maui is **Air Canada** (© 800/776-3000; www.aircanada.ca). Because of Maui's short runway, most international visitors will have to fly to Honolulu first to clear Customs, then get an interisland flight to Maui.

Airlines serving Hawaii from places other than the U.S. mainland include **Air Canada** (© 800/776-3000; www.air canada.ca); **Air New Zealand** (© 0800/ 737-000 in Auckland, 64-3/379-5200 in Christchurch, or 800/926-7255 in the U.S.; www.airnewzealand.com), which flies between Auckland and Hawaii; **Qantas** (© 008/177-767 in Australia, or 800/227-4500 in the U.S.; www. qantas.com.au), which flies between Sydney and Honolulu; **Japan Air Lines** (© 03/5489-1111 in Tokyo, or 800/525-3663 in the U.S.; www.japanair.com); **All Nippon Airways (ANA)** (© 03/5489-1212 in Tokyo, or 800/235-9262 in the U.S.; www.fly-ana.com); **China Airlines** (© 02/715-1212 in Taipei, or 800/227-5118 in the U.S.; www.china-airlines. com); **Air Pacific,** serving Fiji, Australia, New Zealand, and the South Pacific

(© 800/227-4446; www.airpacific.com); **Korean Airlines** (© 02/656-2000 in Seoul, 800/223-1155 on the East Coast, 800/421-8200 on the West Coast, or 800/438-5000 from Hawaii; www.koreanair.com); and **Philippine Airlines** (© 631/816-6691 in Manila, or 800/435-9725 in the U.S.; www.philippineair.com).

Locally, **Hawaiian Airlines** (© 800/367-5320; www.hawaiianair.com) flies nonstop to Sydney, Tahiti, and American Samoa. If you're traveling in the United States beyond Hawaii, some large American airlines—such as **American, Delta, Northwest, TWA,** and **United**—offer travelers on transatlantic or transpacific flights special discount tickets under the name **Visit USA,** allowing travel between any U.S. destinations at reduced rates. These tickets must be purchased before you leave your foreign point of departure.

This system is the best, easiest, and fastest way to see the United States at low cost. You should obtain information well in advance from your travel agent or the office of the airline concerned.

Visitors arriving by air should cultivate patience and resignation before setting foot on U.S. soil. Getting through immigration control may take as long as 2 hours on some days, especially summer weekends. Add the time it takes to clear Customs, and you'll see that you should make a very generous allowance for delay in planning connections between international and domestic flights—an average of 2 to 3 hours at least.

After you have cleared Customs in Honolulu, hop a short, 20-minute interisland flight to Maui. For further information about travel to Hawaii, see "Getting There" and "Getting Around" in chapter 2.

FAST FACTS: For International Visitors

Automobile Organizations Auto clubs will supply maps, suggested routes, guidebooks, accident and bail-bond insurance, and emergency road service. The major auto club in the United States, with 955 offices nationwide, is the **American Automobile Association (AAA;** often called "Triple A"), however there are no offices on Maui, Molokai, or Lanai. Members of some foreign auto clubs have reciprocal arrangements with AAA and enjoy its services at no charge. If you belong to an auto club, inquire about AAA reciprocity before you leave. AAA can also provide you with an **International Driving Permit** validating your foreign license. You may be able to join AAA even if you are not a member of a reciprocal club. To inquire, call © **800/736-2886** or visit www.aaa.com.

Some car-rental agencies now provide automobile club–type services, so inquire about their availability when you rent your car.

Automobile Rentals To rent a car in the United States, you need a valid driver's license, a passport, and a major credit card. The minimum age is usually 25, but some companies will rent to younger people and add a surcharge. It's a good idea to buy maximum insurance coverage unless you're positive your own auto or credit card insurance is sufficient.

Business Hours See "Fast Facts: Maui" in chapter 2.

Climate See "When to Go" in chapter 2.

Drinking Laws The legal age for purchase and consumption of alcoholic beverages is 21; proof of age is required and often requested at bars, nightclubs, and restaurants, so it's always a good idea to bring ID when you go out. Beer and wine often can be purchased in supermarkets.

Do not carry open containers of alcohol in your car or any public area. The police can fine you on the spot. And nothing will ruin your trip faster than getting a citation for DUI ("driving under the influence"), so don't even think about driving while intoxicated.

Electricity Hawaii, like the U.S. mainland and Canada, uses 110–120 volts (60 cycles), compared to the 220–240 volts (50 cycles) used in most of Europe and in other areas of the world, including Australia and New Zealand. Small appliances of non-American manufacture, such as hair dryers or shavers, will require a plug adapter with two flat, parallel pins; larger ones will require a 100-volt transformer.

Embassies & Consulates All embassies are in Washington, D.C. Some countries have consulates general in major U.S. cities, and most have a mission to the United Nations in New York City. If your country isn't listed below, call for directory information in Washington, D.C. (© **202/555-1212**), or visit **www. embassy.org/embassies**.

The embassy of **Australia** is at 1601 Massachusetts Ave. NW, Washington, D.C. 20036 (© **202/797-3000**; www.austemb.org). There is also an Australian consulate in Hawaii at 1000 Bishop St., Penthouse Suite, Honolulu, HI 96813 (© 808/524-5050).

The embassy of **Canada** is at 501 Pennsylvania Ave. NW, Washington, D.C. 20001 (© **202/682-1740**; www.canadianembassy.org). Canadian consulates are also at 1251 Ave. of the Americas, New York, NY 10020 (© 212/596-1628), and at 550 South Hope St., Ninth floor, Los Angeles, CA 90071 (© 213/346-2700).

The embassy of **Japan** is at 2520 Massachusetts Ave. NW, Washington, D.C. 20008 (© **202/238-6700**; www.embjapan.org). The consulate general of Japan is located at 1742 Nuuanu Ave., Honolulu, HI 96817 (© 808/543-3111).

The embassy of **New Zealand** is at 37 Observatory Circle NW, Washington, D.C. 20008 (© **202/328-4800**; www.nzemb.org). The only New Zealand consulate in the United States is at 780 Third Ave., New York, NY 10017 (© 202/ 328-4800).

The embassy of the **Republic of Ireland** is at 2234 Massachusetts Ave. NW, Washington, D.C. 20008 (© **202/462-3939**; www.irelandemb.org). There's a consulate office in San Francisco at 44 Montgomery St., Suite 3830, San Francisco, CA 94104 (© 415/392-4214).

The embassy of the **United Kingdom** is at 3100 Massachusetts Ave. NW, Washington, D.C. 20008 (© **202/588-6640**; www.fco.gov.uk/directory). British consulates are at 845 Third Ave., New York, NY 10022 (© 212/745-0200), and 11766 Wilshire Blvd., Suite 400, Los Angeles, CA 90025 (© 310/477-3322).

Emergencies Call © **911** to report a fire, call the police, or get an ambulance.

Gasoline (Petrol) One U.S. gallon equals 3.8 liters, while 1.2 U.S. gallons equal 1 imperial gallon. You'll notice there are several grades (and price levels) of gasoline available at most gas stations. You'll also notice that their names change from company to company. The ones with the highest octane are the most expensive, but most rental cars take the least expensive "regular" gas, with an octane rating of 87.

Holidays See "When to Go" in chapter 2.

Legal Aid The ordinary tourist will probably never become involved with the American legal system. If you're pulled over for a minor infraction (for example, driving faster than the speed limit), never attempt to pay the fine directly to a police officer; you may wind up arrested on the much more serious charge of attempted bribery. Pay fines by mail or directly into the hands of the clerk of the court. If accused of a more serious offense, it's wise to say and do nothing before consulting a lawyer (under the U.S. Constitution, you have the rights both to remain silent and to consult an attorney). Under U.S. law, an arrested person is allowed one telephone call to a party of his or her choice; call your embassy or consulate.

Mail Mailboxes, which are generally found at intersections, are blue with a blue-and-white eagle logo and carry the inscription u.s. POSTAL SERVICE.

At press time, domestic postage rates were 23¢ for a postcard and 37¢ for a letter. For international mail, a first-class letter of up to 1 ounce costs 80¢ (60¢ to Canada and Mexico); a first-class postcard costs 70¢ (50¢ to Canada and Mexico); and a preprinted postal aerogramme costs 70¢. Point your Web browser to **www.usps.com** for complete U.S. postal information, or call ℭ **800/275-8777** for information on the nearest post office. Most branches are open Monday through Friday from 8am to 5 or 6pm, and Saturday from 9am to noon or 3pm.

Taxes The United States has no VAT (value-added tax) or other indirect taxes at a national level. Every state, and every city in it, has the right to levy its own local tax on all purchases, including hotel and restaurant checks, airline tickets, and so on. In Hawaii sales tax is 4%; there's also a 7.25% hotel-room tax and a small excise tax, so the total tax on your hotel bill will be 11.42%.

Telephone & Fax The telephone system in the United States is run by private corporations, so rates, particularly for long-distance service and operator-assisted calls, can vary widely—especially on calls made from public telephones. Local calls—that is, calls to other locations on the island you're on—made from public phones in Hawaii cost 50¢.

Generally, hotel surcharges on long-distance and local calls are astronomical. You are usually better off using a **public pay telephone,** which you will find clearly marked in most public buildings and private establishments as well as on the street. Many convenience stores and newsstands sell **prepaid calling cards** in denominations up to $50.

Most **long-distance** and **international calls** can be dialed directly from any phone. **For calls within the United States and to Canada,** dial 1 followed by the area code and the seven-digit number. **For other international calls,** dial 011 followed by the country code, city code, and the telephone number of the person you are calling. Some country codes are as follows: **Australia** 61, **Ireland** 353, **New Zealand** 64, **United Kingdom** 44.

In Hawaii interisland phone calls are considered long-distance and are often as costly as calling the U.S. mainland. The international country code for Hawaii is 1, just as it is for the rest of the United States and Canada.

Note that all phone numbers with the area code 800, 888, 866, and 877 are toll-free.

For **local directory assistance** ("information"), dial 🕿 411. For **long-distance information**, dial 1, then the appropriate area code and 555-1212; for **directory assistance for another island,** dial 1, then 808, then 555-1212.

Fax facilities are widely available and can be found in most hotels and many other establishments. Try **The UPS Store, FedEx Kinko's** (check the local Yellow Pages), or any photocopying shop.

Telephone Directories There are two kinds of telephone directories in the United States. The general directory, the so-called White Pages, lists private and business subscribers in alphabetical order. The inside front cover lists the emergency numbers for police, fire, and ambulance, along with other vital numbers. The first few pages are devoted to community-service numbers, including a guide to long-distance and international calling, complete with country codes and area codes.

The second directory, printed on yellow paper (hence its name, Yellow Pages), lists all local services, businesses, and industries by type of activity, with an index at the front. The Yellow Pages also include detailed maps, postal zip codes, and a calendar of events.

Time Zone See "Fast Facts: Maui" in chapter 2.

Tipping It's part of the American way of life to tip. Many service employees receive little direct salary and must depend on tips for their income. The following are some general rules:

In **hotels** tip bellhops at least $1 per piece of luggage ($2–$3 if you have a lot of luggage), and tip the housekeeping staff $1 per person per day. Tip the doorman or concierge only if he or she has provided you with some specific service (for example, obtaining difficult-to-get theater tickets). Tip the valet-parking attendant $1 to $2 every time you get your car.

In **restaurants, bars,** and **nightclubs,** tip service staff 15% to 20% of the check, tip bartenders 10% to 15%, and tip valet-parking attendants $1 to $2 per vehicle. Tipping is not expected in cafeterias and fast-food restaurants.

Tip **cab drivers** 15% of the fare.

Toilets Visitors can usually find a toilet in a bar, fast-food outlet, restaurant, hotel, museum, or department store—and it will probably be clean. (The cleanliness of toilets at service stations, parks, and beaches is more open to question.) Some restaurants and bars display a notice that toilets are for the use of patrons only. Paying for a cup of coffee or soft drink will qualify you as a patron.

4

Suggested Maui Itineraries

Your vacation time is precious—you only have so many days and you don't want to waste one of them. That's where I come in. Below are several suggestions for what to do and how to spend your time on Maui. I've included ideas if you have 1 week or 2, are traveling with kids, or want a more active vacation. I've also included the best things to see and do on the islands of Molokai and Lanai.

The number-one thing I would suggest is this: Don't max out your days. This is Hawaii—allow some time to do nothing but relax. Remember that you most likely will arrive jet-lagged, so it's a good idea to ease into your vacation. In fact, exposure to sunlight can help reset your internal clock, so I include time at the beach on day 1 of most of these itineraries.

Finally, think of your first trip to Maui as a "scouting" trip. Maui is too beautiful, too sensual, too enticing to see just once in a lifetime. You'll be back. You don't need to see and do everything on this trip.

One last thing—you will need a car to get around the islands. But also plan to get out of the car as much as possible. Hawaii is not a place to "view" from your car window. You have to get out to smell the sweet perfume of plumerias, to hear the sound of the wind through a bamboo forest, and to plunge into the gentle waters of the Pacific.

The following itineraries are designed to appeal to a wide range of travelers. If you are a golf fan or a scuba diver, check out the best golf courses and dive spots in chapter 1 to plan your trip around your passion.

1 A Week on Maui

I've outlined the highlights of Maui for those who just have 7 days and want to see everything. Two things I suggest: First, spend 2 nights in Hana, a decision you will not regret, and second, take the Trilogy boat trip to Lanai for the day. I've designed this itinerary assuming you'll stay in West Maui for 5 days. If you are staying elsewhere (like Wailea or Kihei), allow extra driving time.

Day ❶: Arrival & Kapalua Beach ★★★

Check in to your hotel, then head for **Kapalua Beach** (p. 163). Don't overdo the sun on your first day. After an hour or two at the beach, drive to **Lahaina** (p. 196) and spend a couple of hours walking the historic old town. To really feel like you are in Hawaii, go to the **Old Lahaina Luau** (p. 245) at sunset to immerse yourself in Hawaiian culture.

Day ❷: Up a 10,000-Foot Dormant Volcano & Down Again ★★★

You'll likely wake up early on your first day in Hawaii, so take advantage of it and

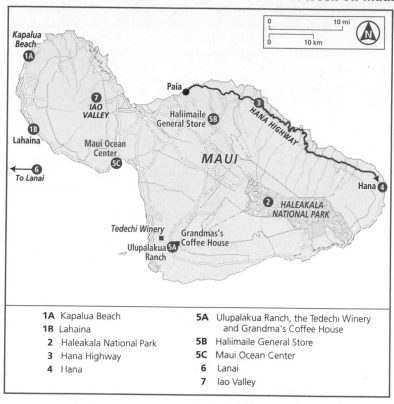

1A	Kapalua Beach	**5A**	Ulupalakua Ranch, the Tedechi Winery and Grandma's Coffee House
1B	Lahaina		
2	Haleakala National Park	**5B**	Haliimaile General Store
3	Hana Highway	**5C**	Maui Ocean Center
4	Hana	**6**	Lanai
		7	Iao Valley

head up to the 10,000-foot (dormant) volcano, **Haleakala.** You can **hike in the crater** (p. 180), **speed down the mountain on a bicycle** (p. 189), or just wander about **Haleakala National Park.** You don't have to be at the top for sunrise, but I have to tell you—it is a near-religious experience you'll never forget. On your way back down, stop and tour **Upcountry Maui** (p. 188), particularly the communities of **Kula, Makawao,** and **Paia.** Plan for a sunset dinner in **Paia** or **Kuau.**

Day ❸: Hana Highway ✦✦✦

Pack a lunch and spend the entire day driving the scenic **Hana Highway** (p. 216). Pull over often, get out to take photos, smell the flowers, and jump in

the mountain-stream pools. Wave to everyone, move off the road for those speeding by, and breathe in Hawaii. Plan to spend at least 2 nights in Hana (hotel recommendations start on p. 127).

Day ❹: A Day in Heavenly Hana ✦✦✦

An entire day in paradise, so many things to do. Take an early-morning hike along the black sands of **Waianapanapa State Park** (p. 168), then explore the tiny town of **Hana,** especially seeing the **Hana Cultural Center and Museum** (p. 224), **Hasegawa General Store** (p. 242), and **Hana Coast Gallery** (p. 242). Get a picnic lunch and drive out to the **Kipihulu end of the Haleakala National Park** at

Oheo Gulch (p. 182). Hike to the water-falls, swim in the pools, take lots of photos. Splurge on dinner and eat at the dining room at the **Hotel Hana Maui**. Spend another night in Hana.

Day ❺: Wine, Food & (Hawaiian) Song

Continue driving around the island, past **Kaupo** and up to the **Ulupalakua Ranch** (p. 215) and the **Tedeschi Winery** (p. 215). Stop at **Grandma's Coffee House** (p. 157) for a cup of java and head down the mountain, with a stop for lunch at **Haliimaile General Store** (p. 154). Spend the afternoon at the **Maui Ocean Center** in Maalaea (p. 208) checking out the marine life, especially the sharks. Have dinner in Lahaina and see the drama/dance/music show **Ulalena** (p. 246).

Day ❻: Sailing to Lanai 𝄇𝄇𝄇

Trilogy (p. 170) is the best sailing/snorkeling trip in Hawaii, so don't miss it. You'll spend the day (breakfast and lunch included) sailing to the island of Lanai, snorkeling, touring the island, and sailing back to Lahaina. Plus you still have the afternoon to go shopping for souvenirs or take a nap.

Day ❼: Relaxing & Shopping

Depending on how much time you have on your final day, you can choose from relaxing on the beach, being pampered in a spa, or shopping. Spa goers have a range of terrific **spas** to choose from and **shopping** aficionados should check out some of my favorite stores (recommendations start on p. 229). If you have a late flight, you might want to check out **Iao Valley** (p. 195).

2 Two Weeks on Maui

Lucky travelers will get 2 weeks to totally relax on the Valley Isle. I'd suggest adding lots of naps, vegging out on the beach, and stopping to smell all the exotic flowers to the 1-week itinerary above. Below are suggestions for your second week on Maui.

Days ❶ through ❼: Follow itineraries as outlined above

Day ❽: Fly or Ferry over to Molokai for the Mule Ride 𝄇𝄇𝄇

If you have a spare day or two, head over to the "Friendly Isle" to experience the **Mule Ride** down into the **Kalaupapa Peninsula** (p. 278). This is an all-day experience that you will remember the rest of your life. You can either take the ferry over (p. 278) or fly (p. 278); either way, don't miss this opportunity.

Day ❾: Snorkeling in an old Volcanic Crater 𝄇𝄇𝄇

Take a day to see the fish inside the **Molokini Crater.** Go in the morning before the wind comes up. If it's whale season and you're lucky, you may spot whales on the way over or back. You'll

have to go as part of a tour—my recommendations start on p. 172.

Day ❿: Glide over the Water in a Kayak 𝄇𝄇𝄇

Kayaking is so easy that you will be paddling away within a few minutes of lessons. One of the best kayak places is in **Makena**—it's calm, the water is so clear you can see the fish, and you are protected from the wind. See "Ocean Kayaking" under "Watersports" in chapter 7 for more suggestions. After a couple of hours of kayaking and snorkeling, stop for a picnic lunch at **Makena Landing,** then explore this area. If you still have some energy to spare, hike over to **La Pérouse Monument,** along the rugged shoreline. See "Makena" under "South Maui" in chapter 8 for more information.

Two Weeks on Maui

0 — 10 mi
0 — 10 km

N

Kapalua Beach 1A
Kahakuloa 13C
13D
Whale Center of the Pacific 13B
Lahaina 13A
1B
7 **IAO VALLEY**
Wailuku 12
Paia
3 **HANA HIGHWAY**
Haliimaile General Store 5B
Maui Ocean Center 5C
MAUI
6 **To Lanai**
8 **To Molokai**
Kula 11
Hana 4
2 **HALEAKALA NATIONAL PARK**
Makena **Tedechi Winery** 10
Molokini Crater **Ulupalakua Ranch** 5A **Grandmas's Coffee House**
9

Day ⓫: Take a Tour ★

Plan at least one off-the-beaten-path tour while you're on Maui. If you love good food, book the farm tour of **Chef James McDonald** (p. 143), which includes a tour of his 8-acre farm and lunch. Cheese aficionados will love the **Surfing Goat Dairy** tour (p. 220) and the sampling of their cheeses. For a really exotic tour, take the **Garden and Culinary Tour of the Alii Kula Lavender** farm (p. 215), which includes a tour of the farm and lunch made with lavender products.

Day ⓬: See Maui from Above in a Helicopter ★★★

The feeling of suddenly lifting off straight up in the air and then floating over the island of Maui in a helicopter is a memory

that will stay with you forever. Of all the helicopter companies, I would recommend booking with **Blue Hawaiian Helicopter** (p. 192) for the most comfortable, informative, and fun tour in the air. After the tour take some time to explore old **Wailuku town**, wander through the shops (p. 231), stop at the **Bailey House** (p. 195), and then take in **Waikapu** (p. 195), **Kahului** (p. 194), and **Puunene** (p. 194).

Day ⓭: Walk Back in History— Spend a Day in Lahaina ★★

Plan to arrive in this historic town early, before the crowds. Eat a big breakfast, then put on your walking shoes and take the self-guided **historic walking tour** of the old town on p. 201. Plan to do some browsing in the **quaint stores** (recommendations start on p. 233), watch the surfers skim the waves in front of the library, and pop over to Kaanapali to the **Whale Center of the Pacific** (p. 206). Then drive around the head of the island on the **Kahekili Highway** (p. 207), stopping to see the ancient Hawaiian village of **Kahakuloa** and the **Halekii** and **Pihanakalani Heiau** on the Wailuku side.

Day ⑭: Your Last Day

After 13 days of exploring Maui, spend your last day doing what you loved best: beachcombing, snorkeling, hiking, shopping, or whatever your favorite Maui activity is. Pick up a lei before you go to the airport so you will have a little bit of Maui with you as you say aloha.

3 Maui with Kids

Your itinerary is going to depend on the ages of your kids. The number-one rule is *don't plan too much,* especially with young children, who will be fighting jet lag, trying to get adjusted to a new bed (and most likely new food), and might be very hyped up and excited to the point of exhaustion. The 7-day itinerary below is a guide to the various family-friendly activities available on Maui. Pick and choose the ones everyone in your family will enjoy.

Day ❶: Arrival & Pool Time 🌟🌟

If you have young kids who are not used to the waves, you might consider taking them to the swimming pool at your hotel. They'll be happy playing in the water, and you won't have to introduce them to ocean safety after that long plane ride. Plan an early dinner, with food your kids are used to. If you're in Lahaina, go to Cheeseburger in Paradise (p. 141); if you're in Kihei, consider either Shaka Sandwiches and Pizza (p. 151) or Stella Blues Cafe (p. 150). Get to bed early.

Day ❷: Up a 10,000-Foot Dormant Volcano & Down Again 🌟🌟🌟

Your family will likely be up early, so take advantage of it and head up to the 10,000-foot (dormant) volcano **Haleakala.** Depending on the age of your children, you can either **hike in the crater** (p. 179), **speed down the mountain on a bicycle** (p. 189), or just wander about the park. On your way back down, stop and tour the upcountry communities of **Kula, Makawao,** and **Paia.** Plan to tour the **Surfing Goat Dairy** (p. 220), stop and look at the strange flowers at the **Kula Botanical Garden** (p. 215), or take the

40-minute narrated tram tour of **Maui Tropical Plantation** (p. 195). Get an early dinner—try **AK's Café** in Wailuku (p. 135) or book at table at the **Mañana Garage** (p. 132) in Kahului.

Day ❸: Sharks, Stingrays & Starfish without Getting Wet 🌟🌟🌟

After a lazy breakfast, wander over to the **Maui Ocean Center** (p. 208) in Maalaea so your kids can see the fabulous underwater world without having to get wet. Plan to spend the morning immersed in the 5-acre oceanarium. Eat something fishy for lunch. Then head out to **Lahaina,** where you can take the kids under water in a Jules Vern–type submarine at **Atlantis Submarine** (p. 193), or if they are too small, hop aboard the **Lahaina-Kaanapali Sugar Cane Train** (p. 193), or rent some snorkel equipment and hit one of the **terrific beaches on West Maui** (recommendations start on p. 162). Book ahead for the **Old Lahaina Luau** (p. 138) in the evening.

Day ❹: Sailing to Lanai 🌟🌟🌟

Now that the kids have seen the underwater world, take them sailing to Lanai.

Maui with Kids

1A Lahaina	**4** Lanai
1B Kihei	**5** Hana Highway
2A Haleakala National Park.	**6** Hana
2B Surfing Goat Dairy	**7A** Ulupalakua Ranch and the Tedechi Winery
2C Kula Botanical Garden	**7B** Grandma's Coffee House
2D Maui Tropical Plantation	**7C** Haliimaile General Store
3A Maui Ocean Center	**7D** Maui Nature Center
3B Lahaina	and the Iao Valley State Park

Trilogy (p. 170) is the best sailing/snorkeling trip in Hawaii, so don't miss it. In the afternoon, wander around Lahaina and see the giant **banyan tree** (p. 198), the **Old Lahaina Courthouse** (p. 202), and the **old Prison** (p. 205).

Day ❺: Hana Highway: World's Most Scenic Tropical Road ☆☆☆

Pack a lunch and spend the entire day driving the **Hana Highway** (p. 216) for an unforgettable experience. Pull over often, get out to take photos, smell the flowers, and jump in the mountain-stream pools. Wave to everyone, move off the road for those speeding by, and breathe in Hawaii. Plan to spend at least 2 nights in Hana (hotel recommendations start on p. 127).

Day ❻: A Day in Heavenly Hana ☆☆☆

An entire day in paradise, so many things to do. Take an early-morning hike along the black sands of **Waianapanapa State Park** (p. 185), then explore the tiny town of **Hana.** Make sure you see the **Hana Cultural Center and Museum** (p. 224), **Hasegawa General Store** (p. 225), and **Hana Coast Gallery** (p. 242). Get a picnic lunch and drive out to the **Kipihulu end of the Haleakala National Park** at Oheo Gulch (p. 182). Hike to the waterfalls, swim in the pools, take lots of photos. Splurge on dinner and eat at the dining room at the **Hotel Hana-Maui** (p. 127). Spend another night in Hana.

Day ❼: See the World from a Dragonfly's Point of View 🐝🐝

Begin the journey back by continue driving around the island, past **Kaupo** and up to the **Ulupalakua Ranch** (p. 215) and the **Tedeschi Winery** (p. 210). Stop at **Grandma's Coffee House** (p. 157) for a cup of java and head down the mountain, with a stop for lunch at **Haliimaile General Store** (p. 154). Spend the afternoon at the **Maui Nature Center** (p. 196) and the **Iao Valley State Park** (p. 196) next door.

4 Maui for the Adventurous

If you can't stand the thought of just lazing around the beach all day, and your idea of the perfect vacation is to be up, active, and trying new adventures, then Maui is the place for you. This itinerary covers all the basics of what to see on Maui, with added adventures that active people like you will love.

Day ❶: Arrive in Maui & Head for the Beach 🐝🐝

Your first stop after you get off the plane should be Snorkel Bob's (p. 168) to pick up snorkel gear (they'll even show you how to use it). Check in to your hotel and then head for the beach. Great snorkeling spots in West Maui include **D.T. Flemming Beach, Black Rock on Kaanapali Beach, Kapalua Beach,** and **Wahikuli County Wayside Park.** In South Maui wonderful snorkeling beaches include the north end of **Oneloa (Big) Beach** in Makena (by the cinder cone), **Ulua** and **Wailea Beach** in Wailea, and **Kamaole III Beach** in Kihei. See "Beaches" in chapter 7 for descriptions. Don't overdo the sun on your first day. If you just can't get enough of the underwater world, take a trip on **Atlantis Submarine** (p. 176).

Day ❷: Up a 10,000-Foot Dormant Volcano & Down Again 🐝🐝🐝

You'll wake up early on your first day in Hawaii, so take advantage of it and head up to the 10,000-foot (dormant) volcano, **Haleakala.** Plan to either **hike in the crater** (p. 179), **speed down the mountain on a bicycle** (p. 189), see the crater on horseback with **Pony Express Tours** (p. 190), or just wander about **Haleakala National Park.** You don't have to be at the top for sunrise, but I have to tell you—watching the sky slowly light up is a near-religious experience you'll never forget. On your way back down, stop and take the **Skyline Eco-Adventure Zipline Haleakala Tour** (p. 180)—not for the faint of heart.

Day ❸: Hana Highway 🐝🐝🐝

Pack a lunch and spend the entire day driving the scenic **Hana Highway** (p. 216). Pull over often, get out to take photos, smell the flowers, and jump in the mountain-stream pools. Wave to everyone, move off the road for those speeding by, and breathe in Hawaii. Plan to spend at least 2 nights in Hana (hotel recommendations start on p. 127).

Day ❹: A Day in Heavenly Hana 🐝🐝🐝

An entire day in paradise, so many things to do. Take an early-morning hike along the black sands of **Waianapanapa State Park** (p. 222) and explore the **Piilanihale Heiau** in the **Kahanu Garden** (p. 227). Call **Hana-Maui Sea Sports** and go kayaking with them (p. 226). Or set up a spelunking tour with **Maui Cave Adventures** (p. 190). Get a picnic lunch and drive out to the **Kipahulu end of the Haleakala National Park** at Oheo Gulch (p. 182). Hike to the waterfalls, swim in the pools, take lots of photos. While you're out there, book a horseback tour with **Maui Stables** (p. 190).

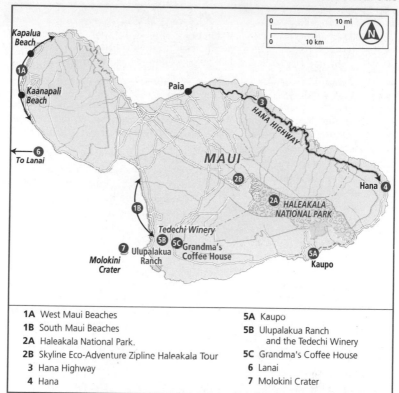

1A	West Maui Beaches	**5A**	Kaupo
1B	South Maui Beaches	**5B**	Ulupalakua Ranch and the Tedechi Winery
2A	Haleakala National Park.		
2B	Skyline Eco-Adventure Zipline Haleakala Tour	**5C**	Grandma's Coffee House
3	Hana Highway	**6**	Lanai
4	Hana	**7**	Molokini Crater

Day ⑤: Try Something New & Exciting

Get up early and continue driving around the island, past **Kaupo** and up to the **Ulupalakua Ranch** (p. 215) and the **Tedeschi Winery** (p. 215). Stop at **Grandma's Coffee House** (p. 157) for a cup of java and head down the mountain. Plan to do something you have never tried before like **learning how to surf** with **Rivers to the Sea** (p. 176), **ocean rafting with Capt. Steve's Rafting Excursions** (p. 174), or **windsurfing** (p. 178).

Day ⑥: Sailing to Lanai ⑂⑂⑂

Trilogy (p. 170) runs the best sailing/ snorkeling trip in Hawaii, so don't miss it. You'll spend the day (breakfast and lunch included) sailing to the island of Lanai, snorkeling, touring the island, and sailing back to Lahaina. The really adventurous can try **scuba diving.**

Day ⑦: Your Last Chance at Adventure

It's your last chance to do something out of the ordinary. My first pick would be to book a **helicopter ride** on Blue Hawaiian Helicopters (p. 192) to discover what Maui looks like from above. Or if you are an underwater fan, sign up for a **sailing/snorkel tour of Molokini** (p. 169). Even a **guided hike into Maui's rainforest** (p. 227) will remain etched in your memory.

5 A Week on Molokai

The island of Molokai is for people trying to get away from everything or those looking for adventure. There are no direct flights from the mainland to Molokai so you will have to fly into Honolulu and then take a commuter plane to Molokai.

Day ❶: Arrival & Kaunakakai

If you are staying in a condo or a vacation rental, head into **Kaunakakai** and stock up on groceries and supplies. While you're there wander around the old two-street town and check out the stores. Be sure to stop at the **Kapuaiwa Coconut Grove in Kiowea Park** (p. 275) and watch the sunset.

Day ❷: Ride a Mule to Kalaupapa ⚑⚑⚑

Your internal clock will still be set to mainland time, so you should have no problem getting up early and getting out to the **Molokai Mule Ride** (p. 278). This adventure will take you through 26 switchbacks on a 1,600-foot cliff and give you a chance to tour the **Kalaupapa Peninsula,** where people suffering from leprosy have lived for decades.

Day ❸: Head for the Beach

Molokai not only has terrific beaches, but on weekdays they generally are empty! Depending on the time of year and the weather, great beaches for snorkeling are **Murphy (Kumimi) Beach** and **Sandy Beach** (p. 267) on the East End, and **Kapukahehu (Dixie Maru) Beach** (p. 269) on the West End. Pack a picnic lunch or stop by **Outpost Natural Foods** or the **Sundown Deli** in Kaunakakai (p. 265). Stay all day. Relax.

Day ❹: Hike in a Tropical Valley & Venture into Paradise ⚑

After a day at the beach, you'll be ready for a hike into the tropical jungle of **Halawa Valley.** Book with **The Lodge at Molokai Ranch** (p. 259) before you head out, as you cannot venture into the valley on your own without trespassing. Bring a picnic lunch for after the hike, then spend the rest of the day on the beach at Halawa. Stop to see the **fishponds** (p. 280) before you leave the East End.

Day ❺: Outdoor Adventure ⚑

Spend a day kayaking, bicycling, or hiking on this Hawaiian oasis. **Molokai Outdoors Activities** (p. 271) can set you up with whatever equipment you need: kayaks, mountain bikes, or maps for hiking. My choice would be kayaking along the shallow water of the East End. Mountain bikers should know the best off-road bicycle trails in the state are on the **Molokai Ranch** (p. 252), and hikers should check out **Pepeopae Trail** (p. 270) or the **Kamakou Preserve** (p. 280).

Day ❻: Touring the West End ⚑⚑

Since you've already seen the East End, spend a day touring the rest of the island. Start out with a tour of the central part of the island by driving out to **Palaau State Park** (p. 271), which overlooks the Kalaupapa Peninsula, then stop off at the **Molokai Museum and Cultural Center** (p. 276) and take a coffee break at **Coffees of Hawaii** (p. 283). Next head for 3-mile-long, white-sand **Papohaku Beach** (p. 266). After an hour or so at the beach, drive up to the cool air in **Maunaloa** town to see the best store on the island: the **Big Wind Kite Factory & the Plantation Gallery** (p. 284).

Day ❼: Moomomi Dunes: Archaeology Heaven

Before you catch your plane back, stop by the **Moomomi Dunes** (p. 279), located close to the Hoolehua Airport. This wild, sand-covered coast is a treasure trove for archaeologists. Buried in the mounds are

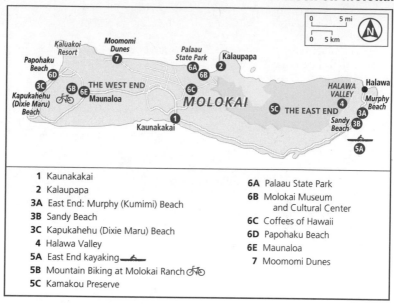

1 Kaunakakai

2 Kalaupapa

3A East End: Murphy (Kumimi) Beach

3B Sandy Beach

3C Kapukahehu (Dixie Maru) Beach

4 Halawa Valley

5A East End kayaking

5B Mountain Biking at Molokai Ranch

5C Kamakou Preserve

6A Palaau State Park

6B Molokai Museum and Cultural Center

6C Coffees of Hawaii

6D Papohaku Beach

6E Maunaloa

7 Moomomi Dunes

ancient Hawaiian burial sites, fossils, Hawaiian artifacts, and even the bones of prehistoric birds. If you have enough time, take the 20-minute easy walk west to **Kawaaloa Bay,** the perfect place to say aloha to Molokai.

6 A Week on Lanai

The smallest of all the Hawaiian islands, Lanai was once a big pineapple plantation and now is home to two exclusive resorts, hundreds of years of history, and just one small town with some of the friendliest people you will ever meet. Like the island of Molokai, there are no direct flights from the mainland to Lanai. You will have to fly into Honolulu and then take a commuter plane to Lanai.

Day ❶: Arrival & Hulopoe Bay

After you settle in to your hotel, head for the beach. The best beach on the island is the marine preserve at **Hulopoe Bay** (p. 297). It's generally safe for swimming, and because it's a marine preserve, no one can take the fish, which means snorkeling is terrific and the fish are so friendly that you practically have to shoo them away. On the way back, take advantage of the late-afternoon light and stop at the **Luahiwa Petroglyph Fields** (p. 303).

Day ❷: Tour the Island in a Four-Wheel-Drive Vehicle

Lanai is a fantastic place to go four-wheeling. Generally you will not need a car if you are staying at one of the two resorts or at the Hotel Lanai (they provide shuttle bus service). So splurge and rent a four-wheel-drive vehicle for 2 or 3 days. Get a picnic lunch from **Pele's Other Garden** (p. 296) and head out of Lanai City to the **Kanepuu Preserve** (p. 304), a 590-acre dry-land forest. Next

A Week on Lanai

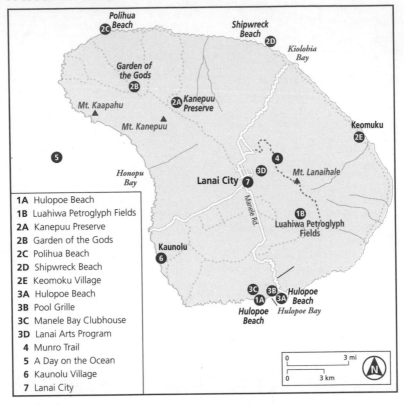

1A Hulopoe Beach
1B Luahiwa Petroglyph Fields
2A Kanepuu Preserve
2B Garden of the Gods
2C Polihua Beach
2D Shipwreck Beach
2E Keomoku Village
3A Hulopoe Beach
3B Pool Grille
3C Manele Bay Clubhouse
3D Lanai Arts Program
 4 Munro Trail
 5 A Day on the Ocean
 6 Kaunolu Village
 7 Lanai City

stop is **Garden of the Gods** (p. 302) and a picnic lunch at **Polihua Beach** (p. 248), Lanai's largest white-sand beach. The beach generally is not safe for swimming and it can be windy here, but it most likely will be deserted and you'll have a great view of Molokai in the distance. After lunch, reverse directions and head to **Shipwreck Beach** (p. 298) and then on to **Keomoku Village** (p. 305).

Day ❸: A Day at the Beach
Plan a lazy day at Hulopoe Beach (p. 297). Get a good book, watch the kids play in the surf, or take a long slow walk around the crescent-shaped bay. Wander over to the **Manele Bay Hotel** for lunch poolside at the **Pool Grille** (p. 295) or over to the **Manele Bay Clubhouse**

(p. 295). Plan a nap for the afternoon or try your hand at some island crafts at the **Lanai Arts Program** (p. 304).

Day ❹: Hike (or Drive) the Munro Trail
If it has not been raining and the ground is dry, do a little exploring. The adventurous will spend the day (plan on at least 7 hr.) climbing to the top of Lanai at Lanaihale on the **Munro Trail** (p. 300). The not-so-adventurous will take a four-wheel-drive vehicle. Pencil in a soak in a hot tub on your return.

Day ❺: A Day on the Ocean 🐟🐟
Ring up **Trilogy Lanai Ocean Sports** (p. 299) and book a sailing/snorkeling, whale-watching, or scuba trip.

Day ⑥: Kayaking or Horseback Riding, followed by a Trip Back in Time

If you can't get enough time on the ocean, plan a kayaking tour in the morning by calling **Trilogy Lanai Ocean Sports** (p. 298). A picnic lunch is included. Horse lovers should instead arrange a tour of Lanai through the **Stables at Koele** (p. 301). In the afternoon take a four-wheel-drive vehicle to the historic ruins of the old **Kaunolu Village** (p. 304), on the southwestern side of the island.

Day ⑦: Biking & Shopping

The best way to get around the tiny village of Lanai City is via bicycle. Rent one from **The Lodge at Koele** (p. 291) and ride (downhill) into town. Lanai City has some terrific boutique shops that you'll find nowhere else (descriptions of my favorites start on p. 305).

5

Where to Stay

Maui has accommodations to fit every taste and budget, from luxury oceanfront suites and historic bed-and-breakfasts to reasonably priced condos that will sleep a family of four.

The high season, during which rooms are always booked and rates are at the top end, runs from mid-December to March. A second high season, when rates are high but reservations are somewhat easier to get, is summer (late June to early Sept). The off seasons, with fewer tourists and cheaper rates, are April to early June and late September to mid-December.

Remember to add Hawaii's 11.42% accommodations tax to your final bill. Parking is free unless otherwise noted.

Important note: Before you book, be sure to read "The Island in Brief" in chapter 2, which will help you choose your ideal location, as well as "Tips on Accommodations," also in chapter 2. Also check out the accommodations categories in chapter 1, "The Best of Maui," for a quick look at my favorites.

1 Central Maui

KAHULUI

If you're arriving late at night or you have an early morning flight out, the best choice near Kahului Airport is the **Maui Beach Hotel,** 170 Kaahumanu Ave. (© **888/649-3222** or 808/877-0051; fax 808/871-5797; http://castleresorts.com/MBH). The nondescript, motel-like rooms (the standard room is so small, you can barely walk around the queen-size bed) start at $120 ($105 if you book on the Internet) and include free airport shuttle service (6am–9pm only). It's okay for a night, but it's not a place to spend your entire vacation.

WAILUKU
Moderate

Old Wailuku Inn at Ulupono ⋒⋒ (Finds This 1924 former plantation manager's home, lovingly restored by innkeepers Janice and Thomas Fairbanks, offers a genuine old Hawaii experience. The theme is Hawaii of the 1920s and 1930s, with decor, design, and landscaping to match. The spacious rooms are gorgeously outfitted with exotic ohia-wood floors, high ceilings, and traditional Hawaiian quilts. The mammoth bathrooms (some with claw-foot tubs, others with Jacuzzis) have plush towels and earth-friendly toiletries on hand. Recently, the Fairbanks added an additional building, the "Vagabond House," a modern three-room complex in the inn's lavishly landscaped back yard. The rooms are decorated in island-designer Sig Zane's floral prints, with rare framed prints of indigenous Hawaiian flowers plus all the modern amenities you can imagine (including an ultraluxurious multihead shower). A full

gourmet breakfast is served on the enclosed back lanai. You'll feel right at home loung-
ing on the generous-size living-room sofa or watching the world go by from an old
wicker chair on the lanai. The inn is located in the old historic area of Wailuku, just
a few minutes' walk from the Maui County Seat Government Building, the courthouse, and a wonderful stretch of antiques shops.

2199 Kahookele St. (at High St., across from the Wailuku School), Wailuku, HI 96732. © 800/305-4899 or 808/244-
5897. Fax 808/242-9600. www.mauiinn.com. 10 units. $125–$180 double. Rates include full breakfast. Extra person
$20. 2-night minimum. MC, V. **Amenities:** Jacuzzi; laundry service; dry cleaning. *In room:* A/C, TV/VCR, dataport,
coffeemaker, DSL.

Inexpensive

Backpackers should head to **Banana Bungalow Maui,** a funky Happy Valley hostel
at 310 N. Market St., Wailuku, HI 96793 (© **800/846-7835** or 808/244-5090;
www.mauihostel.com), with $20 dorm rooms and some private rooms ($40 single,
$50 double). They provide many amenities not often found in hostel-type accommo-
dations, such as free tours of Maui, free Internet access, free airport pickup, and a
Jacuzzi out back. Dorm-style accommodations ($20) and private rooms ($40 single,
$50 double) are also available at the **Northshore Hostel** in old Wailuku, at 2080
Vineyard St., Wailuku, HI 96793 (© **800/9HOSTEL** or ©/fax 808/242-1448; www.
northshorehostel.com). Note, however, that women traveling alone might not feel safe
here after dark.

Happy Valley Hale Maui *(Value*   The Kong family, owners of Nona Lani Cottages
in Kihei (p. 114), have taken the same loving care of this old plantation home and created a tiny oasis in the midst of this economically challenged area. Keep in mind these
are frugal, budget accommodations—really an alternative to a youth hostel. However,
it's immaculately clean, and the Kongs have done extensive renovations to this plantation home. There are four bedrooms (each with twin beds, a small refrigerator, dresser,
and closet) and two shared bathrooms. It's like staying in a family home, with a shared
kitchen (no stove, but microwave, griddle, coffeemaker, and so on) and a shared common room with television and comfy sofas. There are coin-operated laundry facilities
on-site. The front yard sports a barbecue and picnic area. The only drawback is that
Happy Valley is not exactly a resort area—public housing is just across the street. But
for those on extremely tight budgets, this could mean a few extra days on Maui.

332 Alahe'e Dr. Wailuku, HI 96793. © 800/733-2688 or 808/357-3737. www.nonalanicottages.com. 4 units. $25–$30
per bed shared room; $45–$50 per unit private room. Extra person $10–$15. 3-night minimum. No credit cards.
Amenities: Shared kitchen; coin-op laundry. *In room:* Small fridge, no phone.

2 West Maui

LAHAINA

VERY EXPENSIVE

Puunoa Beach Estates *★★* *(Kids*   If money is no problem and you are taking a
family to Maui, consider these 10 gorgeous town houses in an exclusive 3-acre enclave
on a white-sand beach. The individually owned and decorated units (1,700 sq. ft.
and larger), all with private beachfront lanais, boast hardwood floors, marble bathrooms, and the most up-to-date kitchens. Prices are high, but the amenity list has
everything you should want for a first-class vacation rental in a dream location. It's
within walking distance of the center of Lahaina, but the residential location makes
you feel miles away.

45 Kai Pali Place, Lahaina, HI 96761. Managed by Classic Resorts. © **800/642-6284** or 808/661-3339. Fax 808/667-1145. www.puunoabeachestates.com. 10 units. $650 2-bedroom (4 people); $875 3-bedroom with loft (8 people). 3-night minimum. AE, MC, V. **Amenities:** Outdoor pool; whirlpool; sauna; fitness center; concierge; dry-cleaning service; barbecues; daily maid service; free Internet access; complimentary snorkeling equipment, newspaper, video library, fax service. *In room:* A/C, TV/VCR, dataport, full kitchen, fridge, coffeemaker, hair dryer, iron, safe, master bedroom with whirlpool, washer and dryer.

MODERATE

If you dream of an oceanfront condo but your budget is on the slim side, consider **Lahaina Roads,** 1403 Front St. (a block north of the Lahaina Cannery Shopping Center). Reservations can be made c/o Klahani Travel, Lahaina Cannery Mall, 1221 Honoapiilani Hwy., Lahaina, HI 96761 (© **800/669-MAUI** or 808/667-2712; fax 808/661-5875; www.klahani.com). The 17 units here go for $125 for a one-bedroom unit (for up to four). A 3-night minimum stay is required.

In addition to the following choices, you may want to consider the oceanfront condos at **Lahaina Shores Beach Resort,** 475 Front St. (© **800/628-6699** or 808/661-4835; www.lahainashores.com); studio and one-bedroom units go for $185 to $225.

Best Western Pioneer Inn   This once-rowdy home away from home for sailors now seems respectable—even charming. The hotel is a two-story, plantation-style structure with big verandas that overlook the streets of Lahaina and the harbor, a short distance away. All rooms have been totally remodeled, with vintage bathrooms and new curtains and carpets. The quietest rooms face either the garden courtyard—devoted to refined outdoor dining accompanied by live (but quiet) music—or the square-block-size banyan tree next door. I recommend room no. 31, over the banyan court, with a view of the ocean and the harbor. If you want to watch all the Front Street action, book no. 49 or 36.

658 Wharf St. (in front of Lahaina Pier), Lahaina, HI 96761. © **800/457-5457** or 808/661-3636. Fax 808/667-5708. www.pioneerinnmaui.com. 34 units. $145–$180 double. Extra person $15 (12 or older). AE, DC, DISC, MC, V. Parking included in room rate. **Amenities:** Restaurant (good for breakfast); bar with live music; outdoor pool; big shopping arcade; laundry service. *In room:* A/C, TV, fridge, coffeemaker, hair dryer, iron.

House of Fountains Bed & Breakfast *Finds*   This 7,000-square-foot contemporary home, in a quiet residential subdivision at the north end of town, is popular with visitors from around the world. This place is immaculate (hostess Daniela Atay provides daily maid service). The oversize rooms are fresh and quiet, with white ceramic-tile floors, handmade koa furniture, Hawaiian quilt bedspreads, and a Hawaiiana theme. In 2002 Daniela won the prestigious "Most Hawaiian Accommodation" award from the Hawaii Visitors and Convention Bureau. The four downstairs rooms all open onto flower-filled private patios. Guests share the fully equipped guest kitchen and barbecue area and can curl up on the living-room sofa facing the fireplace (not really needed in Lahaina) with a book from the library. The nearest beach is about a 5-minute drive away, and tennis courts are nearby. Around the pool is a Hawaiian hale, an imu pit, and an area that's perfect for Hawaiian weddings (arrangements available).

1579 Lokia St. (off Fleming Rd., north of Lahaina town), Lahaina, HI 96761. © **800/789-6865** or 808/667-2121. Fax 808/667-2120. www.alohahouse.com. 6 units (shower only). $105–$160 double (2 people per room). Rates include full breakfast. AE, MC, V (additional 5% charge if using credit card). From Hwy. 30, take the Fleming Rd. exit; turn left on Ainakea; after 2 blocks, turn right on Malanai St.; go 3 blocks and turn left onto Lokia St. **Amenities:** Outdoor pool; Jacuzzi; washer/dryers. *In room:* A/C, TV/VCR, fridge, hair dryer, phone.

Lahaina Inn *K*   If you like old hotels that have genuine historic touches, you'll love this place. As in many old hotels, some of these Victorian antique–stuffed rooms are

Where to Stay in Lahaina & Kaanapali

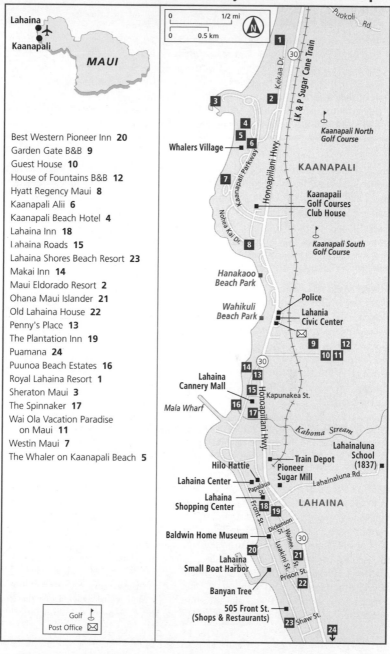

Best Western Pioneer Inn **20**
Garden Gate B&B **9**
Guest House **10**
House of Fountains B&B **12**
Hyatt Regency Maui **8**
Kaanapali Alii **6**
Kaanapali Beach Hotel **4**
Lahaina Inn **18**
Lahaina Roads **15**
Lahaina Shores Beach Resort **23**
Makai Inn **14**
Maui Eldorado Resort **2**
Ohana Maui Islander **21**
Old Lahaina House **22**
Penny's Place **13**
The Plantation Inn **19**
Puamana **24**
Puunoa Beach Estates **16**
Royal Lahaina Resort **1**
Sheraton Maui **3**
The Spinnaker **17**
Wai Ola Vacation Paradise on Maui **11**
Westin Maui **7**
The Whaler on Kaanapali Beach **5**

Tips B&B Etiquette

In Hawaii it is traditional and customary to remove your shoes before entering anyone's home. The same is true for most bed-and-breakfast facilities. Most hosts post signs or will politely ask you to remove your shoes before entering the B&B. If this custom is unpleasant to you, a B&B may not be for you.

Hotels, resorts, condos, and vacation rentals generally allow smoking in the guest rooms (most also have nonsmoking rooms available), but the majority of bed-and-breakfast units forbid smoking in the rooms.

---

small; if that's a problem for you, ask for a larger unit. All come with private bathrooms and lanais. The best room in the house is no. 7, which overlooks the beach, the town, and the island of Lanai; you can watch the action below or close the door and ignore it. There's an excellent, though unaffiliated, restaurant in the same building (David Paul's Lahaina Grill, p. 136), with a bar downstairs.

127 Lahainaluna Rd. (near Front St.), Lahaina, HI 96761. ℂ 800/669-3444 or 808/661-0577. Fax 808/667-9480. www.lahainainn.com. 12 units (most with shower only). $125–$175 double. AE, MC, V. Next-door parking $7/day. **Amenities:** Bar; concierge; activities desk. *In room:* A/C, hair dryer, iron.

Ohana Maui Islander 🌟 (*Value*) This wooden complex's units, especially those with kitchenettes, offer great value. The larger ones work well for families on a budget. The property sits on a quiet side street (a rarity in Lahaina) within walking distance of restaurants, shops, attractions, and the beach (just 3 blocks away). All of the good-size rooms, decorated in tropical-island style, are comfortable and quiet. The entire complex is spread across 10 landscaped acres and includes a sun deck, a barbecue, and a picnic area. The aloha-friendly staff will take the time to answer all of your questions. *Budget tip:* When booking, ask about "SimpleSaver Rates"; you can save a bundle off the rack rates.

660 Wainee St. (between Dickenson and Prison sts.), Lahaina, HI 96761. ℂ 800/462-6262 or 808/667-9766. Fax 808/661-3733. www.ohanahotels.com. 360 units. $159 double; $179 studio with kitchenette; $209 1-bedroom with kitchen (sleeps up to 4); $299 2-bedroom with kitchen (sleeps 6). Extra rollaway bed $18, cribs free. AE, DC, DISC, MC, V. Parking $5. **Amenities:** Outdoor pool; tennis courts (lit for night play until 10pm); activities desk; coin-op washer/dryers. *In room:* A/C, TV, kitchenette (in some units), fridge, coffeemaker, hair dryer, iron, safe.

Penny's Place in Paradise This Victorian-style bed-and-breakfast sits just 50 feet from the water, with a fabulous view of Molokai and Lanai from the front porch. Each of the four rooms is uniquely decorated, with themes ranging from contemporary Hawaii (with a canopy bed and a traditional island quilt) to formal Victorian (with a four-poster cherry bed and an antique gentleman's night chest). Guests are welcome to use the balcony kitchenette (fridge, microwave, toaster, coffeemaker, and ice machine). Only the location is a problem—Penny's is located in a small island bounded by Honoapiilani Highway on one side and busy Front Street on the other. The house is soundproof, and air-conditioning in each room drowns out the noise inside. Recently Penny enclosed the outside lanai area so you can enjoy your breakfast without the highway noise.

1440 Front St., Lahaina, HI 96761. ℂ 877/431-1235 or 808/661-1068. Fax 808/667-7102. www.pennysplace.net. 4 units. $88–$124 double. Rates include continental breakfast Mon–Sat. 3-night minimum. AE, DISC, MC, V. *In room:* A/C, TV, free wireless Internet, iron.

The Plantation Inn ⭐⭐ *Finds*   Attention, romance-seeking couples: Look no further. This charming Victorian-style inn, located a couple of blocks from the water, looks like it's been here 100 years or more, but it's actually of 1990s vintage—an artful deception. The rooms are romantic to the max, tastefully done with period furniture, hardwood floors, stained glass, and ceiling fans. There are four-poster canopy beds and armoires in some rooms, brass beds and wicker in others. All units are soundproof (a plus in Lahaina) and come with a private lanai; the suites have kitchenettes. The rooms wrap around the large pool and deck. Also on the property are a pavilion lounge and Gerard's, an outstanding French restaurant (hotel guests get a discount on dinner; p. 138). Breakfast is served around the pool and in the elegant pavilion lounge.

174 Lahainaluna Rd. (between Wainee and Luakini sts., 1 block from Hwy. 30), Lahaina, HI 96761. ⓒ 800/433-6815 or 808/667-9225. Fax 808/667-9293. www.theplantationinn.com. 19 units (some with shower only). $160–$265 double. (Check the Internet for great package deals.) Rates include full breakfast. Extra person $25. AE, DC, DISC, MC, V. **Amenities:** Acclaimed restaurant and bar; large outdoor pool; Jacuzzi; concierge; activities desk; coin-op washer/dryers. *In room:* A/C, TV/VCR, kitchenette (in suites), fridge, hair dryer, iron, safe.

Puamana   These 28 acres of town houses set right on the water are ideal for those who want to be able to retreat from the crowds and cacophony of downtown Lahaina into the serene quiet of an elegant neighborhood. Private and peaceful are apt descriptions for this complex: Each unit is a privately owned individual home, with no neighbors above or below. Most are exquisitely decorated, and all come with full kitchen, lanai, barbecue, and at least two bathrooms. Puamana was once a private estate in the 1920s, part of the sugar plantations that dominated Lahaina. The plantation manager's house has been converted into a clubhouse with an oceanfront lanai, library, card room, sauna, table-tennis tables, and office. I've found the best rates by booking through Klahani Travel (contact information below), but their office is not on-site, which has caused some problems with guests getting assistance. If you'd rather book directly with the Puamana association office, contact Puamana Community Association, 34 Puailima Place, Lahaina, HI 96761 (ⓒ **808/661-3423;** fax 808/667-0398; info@Puamana.info).

Front St. (at the extreme southern end of Lahaina, ½ mile from downtown). Reservations: c/o Klahani Travel, Lahaina Cannery Mall, 1221 Honoapiilani Hwy., Lahaina, HI 96761. ⓒ 800/669-6284 or 808/667-2712. Fax 808/661-5875. www.klahani.com. 40 units. $125–$200 1-bedroom unit; $150–$275 2-bedroom; $300–$500 3-bedroom. 3-night minimum. AE, DC, DISC, MC, V. **Amenities:** 3 pools (1 for adults only); tennis court; Jacuzzi; game room; activities desk; on-site laundry. *In room:* TV, kitchen, fridge, coffeemaker, hair dryer, iron, washer/dryer (in some units).

Wai Ola Vacation Paradise on Maui ⭐   Just 2 blocks from the beach, in a quiet, residential development behind a tall concrete wall, lies this lovely retreat, with shade trees, sitting areas, gardens, a pool, an ocean mural, and a range of accommodations (a small studio, a couple of suites inside the home, a separate honeymoon cottage, a one-bedroom apartment, or the entire 5,000-sq.-ft. house). Kim and Jim Wicker recently took over this vacation paradise and are more than willing to provide any information you need to make your vacation fabulous. Every unit has a welcome fruit basket when you arrive, plus coffee beans for the coffeemaker. Kim loves to bake, and sometimes surprises her guests with "a little something" from her kitchen. You'll also find a deck, barbecue facilities, and an outdoor wet bar on the property. There's a great beach just a 3-minute drive away and tennis courts are nearby.

1565 Kuuipo St. (P.O. Box 12580), Lahaina, HI 96761. ⓒ **800/492-4652** or 808/661-7901. Fax 808/661-1119. www. waiola.com. 5 units. Double rates $95 studio; $135 suite; $150 1-bedroom apt; $175 honeymoon cottage; entire house $725–$900. Extra person $15. AE, DISC, MC, V. **Amenities:** Outdoor pool; Jacuzzi; complimentary use of water-sports equipment; free high-speed Internet; free self-service washer/dryers. *In room:* A/C, TV/DVD/VCR, dataport, kitchenette, fridge, coffeemaker, hair dryer, iron.

INEXPENSIVE

In addition to the following choices, also consider value-priced **Old Lahaina House** (© **800/847-0761** or 808/667-4663; fax 808/669-9199; www.oldlahaina.com), which features comfy twin- and king-bedded doubles for just $79 to $129, plus a one-bedroom apartment across the street for $140 to $160; it's about a 2-minute walk to the water just across Front Street.

Garden Gate Bed and Breakfast   This oasis of a B&B, located on a quiet residential street just outside of Lahaina town, is just 5 minutes from the beach by car. The six units all have private entrances and a garden or ocean view; the deluxe suites have a deck and a separate pullout sofa for kids. Continental breakfast is served in the garden (Mon–Fri), and hosts Jamie and Bill Mosley are available to answer any questions about things to do or places to eat. Bicycles, boogie boards, beach chairs, and mats are available at no charge. The barbecue area and adjacent laundry facilities are available for guests' use.

67 Kaniau Rd., Lahaina, HI 96761. © **800/939-3217** or 808/661-8800. Fax 808/661-0209. 6 units. $89–$159. 3 nights minimum. Extra person $15. Rates include continental breakfast. AE, DC, DISC, MC, V. *In room:* A/C, TV, VCR (available on request), fridge, coffeemaker, hair dryer, iron, microwave.

Guest House 𝕽𝕽 ℱinds   This is one of Lahaina's great bed-and-breakfast deals: a charming house with more amenities than the expensive Kaanapali hotels just down the road. The roomy home features parquet floors and floor-to-ceiling windows; its swimming pool—surrounded by a deck and comfortable lounge chairs—is larger than some at high-priced condos. Every guest room has a quiet lanai and a romantic hot tub. Guests share the large, well-equipped kitchen and computers with high-speed Internet access. The Guest House also operates Trinity Tours and offers discounts on car rentals and many island activities. Tennis courts are nearby, and the nearest beach is about a block away. Scuba divers are welcome here, and are provided with places to store their gear.

1620 Ainakea Rd. (off Fleming Rd., north of Lahaina town), Lahaina, HI 96761. © **800/621-8942** or 808/661-8085. Fax 808/661-1896. www.mauiguesthouse.com. 4 units. $129 double; $115 single. Rates include full breakfast. MC, V. Take Fleming Rd. off Hwy. 30; turn left on Ainakea; it's 2 blocks down. **Amenities:** Huge outdoor pool; free water-sports equipment; concierge; activities desk; car-rental desk; self-service washer/dryers. *In room:* A/C, TV/VCR/DVD, fridge, free high-speed wireless Internet, Jacuzzi.

Makai Inn 𝒱alue   Budget travelers take note: Here's a small apartment complex located right on the water (no white-sand beach out front, but what do you want at these eye-popping prices?). You can take a 10-minute stroll to the closest white-sand beach or a 20-minute walk to the center of Lahaina town. The units are small (400 sq. ft.) but clean and filled with everything you should need for your vacation: full kitchens, views of the ocean (in most units), and separate bedrooms, all in a quiet neighborhood. There's a public phone by the office (none in the rooms, and no TVs either). In the middle of the complex is a tropical garden. I recommend the Ginger Hideaway unit with windows on two sides overlooking the ocean for just $130. Families will like the Pineapple Suite, the only two-bedroom unit (800 sq. ft.) for just $130.

1415 Front St., Lahaina, HI 96761. © **808/662-3200.** Fax 808/661-9027. www.makaiinn.net. 18 units. $75–$130 double. Extra person $10. MC, V. **Amenities:** Coin-op washer/dryer. *In room:* Kitchen, no phone.

The Spinnaker *(Value*   Run by the same people as the Makai Inn (see above), The Spinnaker comprises seven units in a residential complex on a side street in Lahaina town. Extremely affordable one- and two-bedroom budget apartments are offered only by the week, but at great prices. All units have full kitchens and all the comforts of home. There's no maid service, but at these prices, you might not mind cleaning up on your own.

760 Wainae St., Lahaina, HI 96761. ℂ 808/662-3200. Fax 808/661-9027. www.makaiinn.net. 7 units. $500/week 1-bedroom; $600/week 2-bedroom. 7-night minimum. MC, V. **Amenities:** Outdoor pool; whirlpool; barbecue area; coin-op laundry facilities. *In room:* A/C, TV, kitchen, iron.

KAANAPALI

Another option to consider, in addition to those below, is the **Royal Lahaina Resort** (ℂ **800/44-ROYAL** or 808/661-3611; fax 808/661-6150; www.hawaiianhotelsand resorts.com). But skip the overpriced hotel rooms; only stay here if you can get one of the 132 cottages tucked among the well-manicured grounds. *Tip:* Book on the Internet, where rates are $195 to $375; rack rates are double that price.

VERY EXPENSIVE

Hyatt Regency Maui Resort and Spa *(Kids*   Spa goers will love this resort. Hawaii's first oceanfront spa, the Spa Moana, opened here in 2000 with some 9,000 square feet of facilities, including an exercise floor with an ocean view, 11 treatment rooms, sauna and steam rooms, and a huge menu of massages, body treatments, and therapies. Book your treatment before you leave home—this place is popular.

The management has poured some $19 million in renovations into rooms in this fantasy resort, the southernmost of the Kaanapali beachfront properties. It certainly has lots of imaginative touches: a collection of exotic species (pink flamingos, unhappy-looking penguins, and an assortment of loud parrots and macaws in the lobby), nine waterfalls, and an eclectic Asian and Pacific art collection. The resort covers some 40 acres; even if you don't stay here, you might want to walk through the expansive tree-filled atrium and the parklike grounds. The ½-acre outdoor pool features a 150-foot lava tube slide, a cocktail bar under the falls, a "honeymooner's cave," and a swinging rope bridge. There's even a children-only pool with its own beach, tidal pools, and fountains, and a "Camp Hyatt" children's program.

The rooms, spread out among three towers, are pleasantly outfitted with an array of amenities and have very comfortable separate sitting areas and private lanais with eye-popping views. The latest, most comfortable bedding is now standard in every room (including fluffy feather beds). The very romantic Swan Court (p. 142) is not to be missed for a special dinner. Two Regency Club floors have a private concierge, complimentary breakfast, sunset cocktails, and snacks.

200 Nohea Kai Dr., Lahaina, HI 96761. ℂ 800/233-1234 or 808/661-1234. Fax 808/667-4714. www.maui.hyatt. com. 806 units. $345–$660 double; $530–$695 Regency Club; from $850 suite. All rooms are charged a mandatory $15 resort fee for access to new Moana Athletic Club, daily local newspaper, local and toll-free phone calls, in-room coffee and tea, in-room safe, and 1 hr. tennis-court time per day. Extra person $35 ($50 in Regency Club rooms). Children 18 and under stay free in parent's room using existing bedding. Packages available. AE, DC, DISC, MC, V. Valet parking $10, free self-parking. **Amenities:** 5 restaurants; 2 bars; a ½-acre outdoor pool; 36-hole golf course; 6 tennis courts; health club with weight room; brand-new, state-of-the-art spa; Jacuzzi; watersports equipment rentals; bike rentals; Camp Hyatt kids' program, offering supervised activities for 5- to 12-year-olds; game room; concierge; activities desk; car-rental desk; business center; big shopping arcade; salon; room service; in-room or spa massage; babysitting; coin-op washer/dryers; laundry service; dry cleaning; concierge-level rooms. *In room:* A/C, TV, dataport, minibar, fridge (on request), coffeemaker, hair dryer, iron, safe.

Kaanapali Alii ★★ *Kids*   The height of luxury, these oceanfront condominium units sit on 8 landscaped acres right on Kaanapali Beach. Kaanapali Alii combines all the amenities of a luxury hotel (including a 24-hr. front desk) with the convenience of a condominium to make a stay memorable. Each of the one-bedroom (1,500 sq. ft.) and two-bedroom (1,900 sq. ft.) units is impeccably decorated and comes with all the comforts of home (fully equipped kitchen, washer/dryer, lanai, two full bathrooms) and then some (room service, daily maid service, complimentary local newspaper). The beachside recreation area includes a swimming pool, plus a separate children's pool, whirlpool, gas barbecue grills and picnic areas, exercise rooms, saunas, and tennis courts. There's even a yoga class on Monday, Wednesday, and Friday on the lawn.

50 Nohea Kai Dr., Lahaina, HI 96761. ⓒ 800/642-6284 or 808/661-3330. Fax 808/667-1145. www.kaanapali alii.com. 264 units. $360–$540 1-bedroom for 4; $490–$760 2-bedroom for 6. AE, DC, DISC, MC, V. Free parking. **Amenities:** Poolside cafe; 2 outdoor pools; 36-hole golf course; 3 lighted tennis courts; fitness center; Jacuzzi; watersports equipment rentals; children's program; game room; concierge; activities desk; room service; in-room massage; babysitting; same-day dry cleaning. *In room:* A/C, TV, dataport, kitchen, fridge, coffeemaker, hair dryer, iron, safe, washer/dryers.

Sheraton Maui ★★ *Kids*   Terrific facilities for families and fitness buffs and a premier beach location make this beautiful resort an all-around great place to stay. The grande dame of Kaanapali Beach is built into the side of a cliff on the curving, white-sand cove next to Black Rock (a lava formation that rises 80 ft. above the beach), where there's excellent snorkeling. After its recent renovation, the resort is virtually new, with six buildings of six stories or less set in well-established tropical gardens. The lobby has been elevated to take advantage of panoramic views, while a new lagoonlike pool features lava-rock waterways, wooden bridges, and an open-air whirlpool. But not everything has changed, thankfully. Cliff divers still swan-dive off the torch-lit lava-rock headland in a traditional sunset ceremony—a sight to see. And the views of Kaanapali Beach, with Lanai and Molokai in the distance, are some of the best around.

The new emphasis is on family appeal, with a class of rooms dedicated to those traveling with kids. These "family suites" have three beds, a sitting room with full-size couch, and two TVs, both equipped with Nintendo. In addition, there's the Keiki Aloha program, with fun activities ranging from Hawaiian games to visits to nearby attractions. Children 12 and younger eat free when dining with one adult. Every unit is outfitted with amenities galore, right down to toothbrushes and toothpaste. Other pluses include a "no-hassle" check-in policy: The valet takes you and your luggage straight to your room—no time wasted standing in line at registration.

The Seaside Salon and Day Spa is a tiny boutique spa offering quite an array of services. I recommend the "Beauty in a Blanket" treatment, which gives you a massage, facial, wrap, and a scrub.

2605 Kaanapali Pkwy., Lahaina, HI 96761. ⓒ 800/782-9488 or 808/661-0031. Fax 808/661-0458. www.sheraton. com/maui. 510 units. $360–$680 double; from $800 suite. Extra person $55. Children 17 and under stay free in parent's room using existing bedding. "Resort fee" of $14 for self-parking, "free" local calls and credit card calls, in-room safe, daily coffee and newspaper, and use of fitness center. AE, DC, DISC, MC, V. Valet parking $5. **Amenities:** 3 restaurants; 2 bars (1 poolside); lagoon-style pool; 36-hole golf course; 3 tennis courts; fitness center; boutique spa; Jacuzzi; watersports equipment rentals; children's program; concierge; activities desk; car-rental desk; business center; salon; room service; babysitting; same-day laundry service and dry cleaning; coin-op washer/dryers. *In room:* A/C, TV, dataport, fridge, coffeemaker, hair dryer, iron, safe.

Westin Maui ★ *Kids*   The 758-room Westin Maui recently built a $5-million spa and gym. To further add to the healthy environment, smoking is no longer allowed in guest rooms (it is allowed in some public areas). I love the fabulous custom-designed, pillow-top "heavenly beds," which come with a choice of five different pillows. If that doesn't give you sweet dreams, nothing will. Once you get up, head to the "aquatic playground"—an 87,000-square-foot pool area with five free-form heated pools joined by swim-through grottoes, waterfalls, and a 128-foot-long water slide. This is the Disney World of water-park resorts, and your kids will be in water-hog heaven. The fantasy theme extends from the estatelike grounds into the interior's public spaces, which are filled with the shrieks of tropical birds and the splash of waterfalls. The oversize architecture and $2-million art collection make a pleasing backdrop for all the action. Most of the rooms in the two 11-story towers overlook the aquatic playground, the ocean, and the island of Lanai in the distance.

2365 Kaanapali Pkwy., Lahaina, HI 96761. (C) **888/625-4949** or 808/667-2525. Fax 808/661-5764. www.westin maui.com. 758 units. $360–$700 double; from $1,000 suite. Extra person $60. "Resort fee" of $18 for "free" local calls, use of fitness center and spa, coffee and tea, a souvenir shopping bag, shuttle services to golf and tennis facilities, in-room high-speed Internet access, parking, and local paper. AE, DC, DISC, MC, V. Valet parking $10. **Amenities:** 5 restaurants; 3 bars; 5 free-form outdoor pools; 36-hole golf course; tennis courts; health club and spa with aerobics, steam baths, sauna, massage, and body treatments; Jacuzzi; watersports equipment rentals; bike rental; children's program; game room; concierge; activities desk; car-rental desk; business center; shopping arcade; salon; room service; in-room and spa massage; babysitting; same-day laundry service and dry cleaning. In room: A/C, TV, dataport, minibar, fridge, coffeemaker, hair dryer, iron, safe.

EXPENSIVE

Maui Eldorado Resort (Kids) These spacious condominium units—each with full kitchen, washer/dryer, and daily maid service—were built at a time when land in Kaanapali was cheap, contractors took pride in their work, and visitors expected large, spacious units with views from every window. You'll find it hard to believe that this was one of Kaanapali's first properties in the late 1960s; this first-class choice still looks like new. The Outrigger chain has managed to keep prices down to reasonable levels, especially in spring and fall. This is a great choice for families, with big units, grassy areas that are perfect for running off excess energy, and a beachfront (with beach cabanas and a barbecue area) that's usually safe for swimming. Tennis courts are nearby.

2661 Kekaa Dr., Lahaina, HI 96761. (C) **800/688-7444** or 808/661-0021. Fax 808/667-7039. www.outrigger.com. 204 units. $205–$240 studio double; $255–$295 1-bedroom (rates for up to 4); $355–$480 2-bedroom (rates for up to 6). Numerous packages available, including 5th night free, rental-car packages, senior rates, and more. AE, DC, DISC, MC, V. **Amenities:** 3 outdoor pools; 36-hole golf course; concierge/activities desk; car-rental desk; some business services; washer/dryers. In room: A/C, TV, dataport, kitchen, fridge, coffeemaker, hair dryer, iron, safe, washer/dryer.

The Whaler on Kaanapali Beach In the heart of Kaanapali, right on the world-famous beach, lies this oasis of elegance, privacy, and luxury. The relaxing atmosphere strikes you as soon as you enter the open-air lobby, where light reflects off the dazzling koi in the meditative lily pond. No expense has been spared on these gorgeous accommodations; each unit has a full kitchen, washer/dryer, marble bathroom, 10-foot beamed ceilings, and blue-tiled lanai. Every unit boasts spectacular views of Kaanapali's gentle waves or the humpback peaks of the West Maui Mountains. Next door is Whalers Village, with numerous restaurants, bars, and shops. Kaanapali Golf Club's 36 holes are across the street.

2481 Kaanapali Pkwy. (next to Whalers Village), Lahaina, HI 96761. Aston Hotels (C) **800/922-7866** or 808/ 661-4861. Fax 808/661-8315. www.astonhotels.com. 360 units. High season $245–$290 studio double; $280–$500 1-bedroom (rate for up to 4 people); $470–$730 2-bedroom (up to 6). Off season $215–$260 studio; $280–$440 1-bedroom; $380–$600 2-bedroom. Check Internet for specials. Extra person $20. Parking $7/day. AE, DC, DISC, MC, V.

Amenities: Outdoor pool; 5 tennis courts; refurbished fitness room; Hinamana Salon & Spa (which offers massage, pedicure, and manicures); Jacuzzi; concierge desk; activities desk; coin-op washer/dryers; dry cleaning; BBQ area. *In room:* A/C, TV/VHS/DVD, dataport, kitchen, fridge, coffeemaker, hair dryer, iron, safe, free dial-up Internet access (wireless access additional fee), washer/dryer.

MODERATE

Kaanapali Beach Hotel 🍴 *Value*   It's older and less high-tech than its upscale neighbors, but the Kaanapali has an irresistible local style and a real Hawaiian warmth that's missing from many other Maui hotels. Three low-rise wings, bordering a fabulous stretch of beach, are set around a wide, grassy lawn with coco palms and a whale-shaped pool. The spacious, spotless motel-like rooms are done in wicker and rattan, with Hawaiian-style bedspreads and a lanai that looks toward the courtyard and the beach. The beachfront rooms are separated from the water only by Kaanapali's landscaped walking trail.

Old Hawaii values and customs are always close at hand, and the service is some of the friendliest around. Tiki torches, hula, and Hawaiian music create a festive atmosphere in the expansive open courtyard every night. As part of the hotel's extensive Hawaiiana program, you can learn to cut pineapple, weave lauhala, even dance the *real* hula. The children's program is complimentary. There's also an arts-and-crafts fair 4 days a week, a morning welcome reception Monday through Saturday, and a farewell lei ceremony when you depart.

2525 Kaanapali Pkwy., Lahaina, HI 96761. 📞 **800/262-8450** or 808/661-0011. Fax 808/667-5978. www.kbhmaui. com. 430 units. $169–$295 double; from $260 suite. Extra person $25. Car, golf, bed-and-breakfast, and romance packages available, as well as senior discounts. AE, DC, DISC, MC, V. Valet parking $8, self-parking $6. **Amenities:** 2 restaurants (plus a dinner show Tues–Sat); bar; outdoor pool; 36-hole golf course nearby; access to tennis courts; watersports equipment rentals; children's program; concierge/guest services; activities desk; convenience shops; salon; babysitting; coin-op washer/dryers. *In room:* A/C, TV, fridge, coffeemaker, iron, safe.

HONOKOWAI, KAHANA & NAPILI

EXPENSIVE

Also consider **Sands of Kahana** (📞 **800/326-9874** or 808/669-0423; www.sands-of-kahana.com), an eight-story condo/timeshare complex that's great for families. The one- to three-bedroom units have small kitchens and washer/dryers. The property is loaded with kid-friendly extras, including a large children's pool, a playground, and a stretch of beach that's safe for swimming. Rates range from $150 to $265 for one bedroom, $265 to $375 for two bedrooms, and $325 to $435 for three bedrooms (7-night minimum).

Napili Kai Beach Resort 🍴🍴 *Finds*   Just south of the Bay Club restaurant in Kapalua lies this comfortable oceanfront complex. The one- and two-story units with double-hipped Hawaii-style roofs face their very own gold-sand beach, which is safe for swimming. Many units have a view of the Pacific, with Molokai and Lanai in the distance. Those who prefer air-conditioning should book into the Honolua Building, where you'll get a fully air-conditioned room set back from the shore around a grassy, parklike lawn and pool. Most (but not all) units have a fully stocked kitchenette with full-size fridge, cooktop, microwave, toaster oven, washer/dryer, and coffeemaker; some have dishwashers as well. On-site pluses include daily maid service, even in the condo units; two shuffleboard courts; barbecue areas; complimentary morning coffee and afternoon tea; weekly lei making, hula lessons, and horticultural tours; and a free weekly mai tai party. There are three nearby championship golf courses and excellent tennis courts at next-door Kapalua Resort.

Where to Stay & Dine from Honokowai to Kapalua

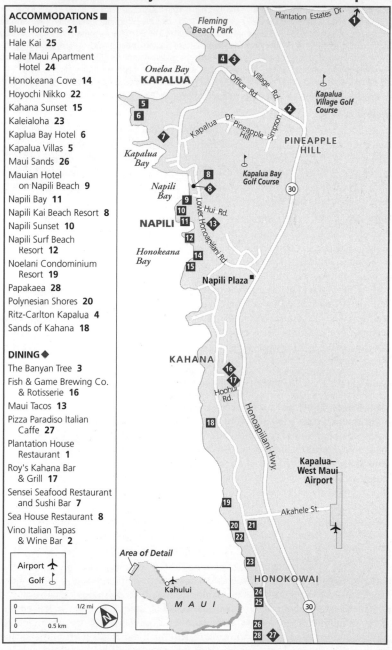

ACCOMMODATIONS ■

Blue Horizons **21**

Hale Kai **25**

Hale Maui Apartment
Hotel **24**

Honokeana Cove **14**

Hoyochi Nikko **22**

Kahana Sunset **15**

Kaleialoha **23**

Kaplua Bay Hotel **6**

Kapalua Villas **5**

Maui Sands **26**

Mauian Hotel
on Napili Beach **9**

Napili Bay **11**

Napili Kai Beach Resort **8**

Napili Sunset **10**

Napili Surf Beach
Resort **12**

Noelani Condominium
Resort **19**

Papakaea **28**

Polynesian Shores **20**

Ritz-Carlton Kapalua **4**

Sands of Kahana **18**

DINING ◆

The Banyan Tree **3**

Fish & Game Brewing Co.
& Rotisserie **16**

Maui Tacos **13**

Pizza Paradiso Italian
Caffe **27**

Plantation House
Restaurant **1**

Roy's Kahana Bar
& Grill **17**

Sensei Seafood Restaurant
and Sushi Bar **7**

Sea House Restaurant **8**

Vino Italian Tapas
& Wine Bar **2**

Airport ✈

Golf ⛳

0 _____ 1/2 mi

0 _____ 0.5 km

Area of Detail

Kahului

M A U I

Fleming
Beach Park

Oneloa Bay
KAPALUA

Plantation Estates Dr.

Village Rd.

Office Rd.

Kapalua
Village Golf
Course

Kapalua Dr.

Pineapple
Hill

Simpson

**PINEAPPLE
HILL**

*Kapalua
Bay*

*Napili
Bay*

NAPILI

Kapalua Bay
Golf Course

30

Hui Rd.

Lower Honoapiilani Rd.

*Honokeana
Bay*

Napili Plaza ■

KAHANA

Hoohui
Rd.

Honoapiilani Hwy.

**Kapalua–
West Maui
Airport**

Akahele St.

HONOKOWAI

30

5900 Honoapiilani Rd. (at the extreme north end of Napili, next to Kapalua), Lahaina, HI 96761. ℂ **800/367-5030** or 808/669-6271. Fax 808/669-0086. www.napilikai.com. 162 units. $200–$240 hotel room double; $250–$325 studio double (sleeps 3–4); $385–$405 1-bedroom suite (sleeps up to 5); $555–$700 2-bedroom (sleeps up to 7). Packages available. AE, DISC, MC, V. **Amenities:** Well-recommended restaurant; bar; 4 outdoor pools; 2 18-hole putting greens (with free golf putters for guest use); complimentary use of tennis racquets; good-size fitness room filled with the latest equipment; Jacuzzi; complimentary watersports equipment; free children's activities at Easter, June 15–Aug 31, and at Christmas; concierge; activities desk; babysitting; laundry service; dry cleaning; coin-op washer/dryers. *In room:* A/C (in most units), TV, kitchenette, fridge, coffeemaker, hair dryer, iron, safe.

MODERATE

In addition to the choices below, consider **Polynesian Shores,** 3975 Lower Honoapiilani Rd. (near Kahana and just 2 min. from the Kapalua–West Maui Airport), Lahaina, HI 96761 (ℂ **800/433-6284** or 808/669-6065; fax 808/669-0909; www.mauicondos rentals.com). Every unit (one to three bedrooms, $135–$245) has floor-to-ceiling sliding-glass doors that open onto a private lanai with an ocean view. There's great snorkeling off the beach out front.

Hale Kai 🌟 *Kids*   This small, two-story condo complex is ideally located, right on the beach and next door to a county park, which is great for those traveling with kids. Shops, restaurants, and ocean activities are all within a 6-mile radius. The units are older but in excellent shape, and come with well-equipped kitchens (with dishwasher, disposal, microwave, and even a blender), and louvered windows that open to the trade winds. Lots of guests clamor for the oceanfront pool units, but I find the park-view units cooler, and they still have ocean views (upstairs units also have cathedral ceilings). This place fills up fast, so book early; repeat guests make up most of the clientele.

3691 Lower Honoapiilani Rd. (in Honokowai), Lahaina, HI 96761. ℂ **800/446-7307** or 808/669-6333. Fax 808/669-7474. www.halekai.com. 25 units. $115–$130 1-bedroom double; $150–$170 2-bedroom (rates for up to 4); $225 3-bedroom (up to 6). Extra person $15. 5-night minimum. MC, V. **Amenities:** Outdoor pool; concierge; car-rental desk; coin-op washer/dryers. *In room:* TV/VCR, kitchen, fridge, coffeemaker, hair dryer, iron.

Honokeana Cove *Value*   These large, secluded units—cozily set around a pool in a lush tropical setting—have fabulous views of Honokeana Cove. The beach here isn't sandy (it's composed of smooth round rocks), but the water just offshore is excellent for snorkeling (turtles have been spotted here) and for whale-watching in winter. The units are well-appointed and all come with full kitchens and lanais. Amenities include laundry, barbecues, and deck chairs. The management holds weekly pupu-parties so you can meet the other guests. All in all, a well-priced option in an expensive neighborhood.

5255 Lower Honoapiilani Rd. (in Napili), Lahaina, HI 96761. ℂ **800/237-4948** or 808/669-6441. Fax 808/669-8777. www.honokeana-cove.com. 33 units. $156–$169 1-bedroom; $180–$261 2-bedroom (sleeps up to 4). 3-night minimum. Extra person $10–$15. MC, V. **Amenities:** Outdoor pool; concierge; coin-op washer/dryers. *In room:* TV/VCR, kitchen, fridge, coffeemaker, iron.

Kahana Sunset 🌟🌟 *Kids*   Lying in the crook of a sharp horseshoe curve on Lower Honoapiilani Road is this series of wooden condo units, stair-stepping down the side of a hill to a postcard-perfect white-sand beach. The unique location, nestled between the coastline and the road above, makes this a very private place to stay. In the midst of the buildings sits a grassy lawn with a small pool and Jacuzzi; down by the sandy beach are gazebos and picnic areas. The units feature full kitchens (complete with dishwashers), washer/dryers, large lanais with terrific views, and sleeper sofas. This is a great complex for families: The beach is safe for swimming, the grassy area is away from traffic, and the units are roomy. The two-bedroom units have parking just outside, making carrying luggage and groceries that much easier.

4909 Lower Honoapiilani Hwy. (at the northern end of Kahana, almost in Napili). Rentals c/o Premier Properties, P.O. Box 10219, Lahaina, HI 96761. ✆ 800/669-1488 or 808/669-8011 or c/o Sullivan Properties, ✆ 800/326-9874 or 808/669-0423. Fax 808/669-9170. www.kahanasunset.com. 79 units. $135–$265 1-bedroom (sleeps up to 4); $150–$410 2-bedroom (sleeps 6). AE, MC, V. From Hwy. 30, turn *makai* (toward the ocean) at the Napili Plaza (Napilihau St.), then left on Lower Honoapiilani Rd. **Amenities:** 2 outdoor pools (1 just for children); concierge; barbecue area. *In room:* TV/VCR/DVD, kitchen, coffeemaker, iron, safe (in some units), washer/dryer.

Mauian Hotel on Napili Beach ✿

The Mauian is perched above a beautiful ½-mile-long white-sand beach with great swimming and snorkeling; there's a pool with chaise longues, umbrellas, and tables on the sun deck, and the verdant grounds are bursting with tropical color. The rooms feature hardwood floors, Indonesian-style furniture, and big lanais with great views. Thoughtful little touches include fresh flowers, plus chilled champagne for guests celebrating a special occasion. There are no phones or TVs in the rooms, but the large *ohana* (family) room does have a TV with a VCR and an extensive library for those who can't bear the solitude. There's complimentary coffee, and phones and fax service are available in the business center. Great restaurants are just a 5-minute walk away, and Kapalua Resort is up the street. The nightly sunsets off the beach are spectacular.

5441 Lower Honoapiilani Rd. (in Napili), Lahaina, HI 96761. ✆ 800/367-5034 or 808/669-6205. Fax 808/669-0129. www.mauian.com. 44 units. $150–$195 double (sleeps up to 4). Rates include continental breakfast. Extra person $10. Children under 5 stay free in parent's room. AE, DISC, MC, V. **Amenities:** Outdoor pool; golf course nearby; tennis courts nearby; activities desk; barbecues; coin-op washer/dryer; shuffleboard court. *In room:* Kitchen, fridge, coffeemaker, no phone.

Maui Sands

The Maui Sands was built back when property wasn't as expensive and developers took the extra time and money to surround their condos with lush landscaping. It's hard to get a unit with a bad view: All face either the ocean (with views of Lanai and Molokai) or tropical gardens blooming with brilliant heliconia, flowering hibiscus, and sweet-smelling ginger. Each roomy unit has a big lanai and a full kitchen. With two big bedrooms, plus space in the living room for a fifth person (or even a sixth), the larger units are good deals for families. There's a narrow beach out front.

Maui Resort Management, 3600 Lower Honoapiilani Rd. (in Honokowai), Lahaina, HI 96761. ✆ 800/367-5037 or 808/669-1902. Fax 808/669-8790. www.mauigetaway.com. 76 units. $105–$155 1-bedroom (sleeps up to 3); $180–$220 2-bedroom (sleeps 5). Extra person $10. 7-night minimum. MC, V. **Amenities:** Outdoor pool; coin-op washer/dryer. *In room:* A/C, TV, kitchen, fridge, coffeemaker.

Napili Surf Beach Resort ✿ *Finds*

This well-maintained, superbly landscaped condo complex has a great location on Napili Beach. Facilities include two pools, three shuffleboard courts, and three gas barbecue grills. The well-furnished units (all with full kitchens) were renovated in 2004 with new carpet, new beds, and some units even have all-new kitchens. Free daily maid service, a rarity in condo properties, keeps the units clean. Management encourages socializing: In addition to weekly mai tai parties and coffee socials, the resort hosts annual shuffleboard and golf tournaments, as well as get-togethers on July 4th, Thanksgiving, Christmas, and New Year's.

50 Napili Place (off Lower Honoapiilani Rd., in Napili), Lahaina, HI 96761. ✆ 800/541-0638 or 808/669-8002. Fax 808/669-8004. www.napilisurf.com. 53 units (some with shower only). $140–$200 studio (sleeps up to 3); $215–$290 1-bedroom (sleeps up to 4). Extra person $15. No credit cards. **Amenities:** 2 outdoor pools; shuffleboard; barbecue grills; coin-op washer/dryers. *In room:* TV/VCR, full kitchen, fridge, coffeemaker, iron, safe.

Noelani Condominium Resort ⭐⭐ *(Kids)*   This oceanfront condo is a great value, whether you stay in a studio or a three-bedroom unit (ideal for large families). Everything is first class, from the furnishings to the oceanfront location. Though it's on the water, there's no sandy beach here (despite the photos posted on their website)—but next door is a sandy cove at the county park, just opened in 2001. There's good snorkeling off the cove, which is frequented by spinner dolphins and turtles in summer and humpback whales in winter. All units feature complete kitchens, entertainment centers, and spectacular views (all except the studio units also have their own washer/dryers and dishwashers). My favorites are in the Anthurium Building, where the condos have oceanfront lanais just 20 feet from the water. Frugal travelers will love the deluxe studios in the Orchid Building, with great ocean views for just $119. Guests are invited to a continental breakfast orientation on their first day and mai tai parties at night. There are also oceanfront barbecue grills for guest use.

4095 Lower Honoapiilani Rd. (in Kahana), Lahaina, HI 96761. © 800/367-6030 or 808/669-8374. Fax 808/669-7904. www.noelani-condo-resort.com. 50 units. $107–$150 studio double; $157–$180 1-bedroom (sleeps up to 4); $237–$257 2-bedroom (sleeps up to 6); $297–$317 3-bedroom (sleeps up to 8). Rates include continental breakfast on 1st morning. Extra person $10. Children under 18 stay free in parent's room. Packages for honeymooners, seniors, and AAA members available. 3-night minimum. AE, MC, V. **Amenities:** 2 freshwater swimming pools (1 heated for night swimming); access to nearby health club; oceanfront Jacuzzi; concierge; activities desk; car-rental desk; coin-op washer/dryers. *In room:* TV/VCR, kitchen, fridge, coffeemaker, hair dryer, iron, safe, washer/dryer (in larger units).

INEXPENSIVE

Another option is **Hoyochi Nikko,** 3901 Lower Honoapiilani Rd. (in Honokowai), Lahaina, HI 96761 (© **800/487-6002** or 808/669-8343; fax 808/669-3937; www.mauilodging.com), which has 17 older (but well maintained) one- and two-bedroom units sharing 180 feet of oceanfront ($115–$170 double for one bedroom).

In addition to the choices below, consider **Hale Maui Apartment Hotel** (© **808/669-6312;** fax 808/669-1302; www.maui.net/~halemaui), a wonderful tiny place run by Hans and Eva Zimmerman, whose spirit is 100% aloha. The one-bedroom suites, which run from $85 to $105 for a double, come with ceiling fans, private lanais, and complete kitchens. There's no pool, but a private path leads to a great swimming beach.

Blue Horizons *(Finds)*   This is the only bed-and-breakfast on this stretch of West Maui, about a 10-minute drive to Lahaina and about a 5-minute walk to sandy beaches. The four units, in a custom-built home in a subdivision, range from compact to spacious suites with separate bedrooms and a living-room area with sofa bed. Three units have kitchenettes, and all four are air-conditioned, which helps not only with the heat but also with the noise of the subdivision. A lavish breakfast is served in the screened dining area, where the ocean view may distract you from the banana pancakes. Amenities on-site include a tile lap pool, washer/dryer, gas barbecue, and video library.

3894 Mahinahina St. (in Kahana, 1 block from Honoapiilani Hwy.), Lahaina, HI 96761. © 800/669-1948 or 808/669-1965. Fax 808/665-1615. www.bluehorizonsmaui.com. 4 units. $99–$139 double. 2-night minimum. Rates include breakfast Mon–Sat. Extra person $15. AE, MC, V. **Amenities:** Small outdoor pool; free use of washer/dryers. *In room:* A/C, TV/VCR, kitchenette (in 3 rooms), fridge, coffeemaker (in some rooms).

Kaleialoha   This condo complex for the budget-minded has recently been upgraded with new paint, bedspreads, and drapes in each apartment. The one-bedroom units each have a sofa bed in the living room, which allows you to comfortably sleep four. All of the island-style units feature fully equipped kitchens, with everything from dishwashers to washer/dryers (the only thing not supplied is beach towels; bring your own). There's great ocean swimming just off the rock wall (no sandy beach); a protective reef mows waves down and allows even timid swimmers to relax.

3785 Lower Honoapiilani Rd. (in Honokowai), Lahaina, HI 96761. © 800/222-8688 or 808/669-8197. Fax 808/669-2502. www.mauicondosoceanfront.com. 21 units. $125–$135 1-bedroom double. Extra person $10. Children 3 and under stay free. 3-night minimum. $70 cleaning fee for less than 7-night stay. MC, V. **Amenities:** Outdoor pool; concierge; activities desk; coin-op washer/dryers. In room: TV, kitchen, fridge, coffeemaker, washer/dryer.

Napili Bay ⟨k⟩ ⟨Finds⟩ One of Maui's best secret bargains is this small, two-story complex right on Napili's beautiful ½-mile white-sand beach. It's perfect for a romantic getaway: The atmosphere is comfortable and relaxing, the ocean lulls you to sleep at night, and birdsong wakes you in the morning. The beach here is one of the best on the coast, with great swimming and snorkeling—in fact, it's so beautiful that people staying at much more expensive resorts down the road frequently haul all their beach paraphernalia here for the day. The studio apartments are definitely small, but they pack in everything you need to feel at home, from a full kitchen to a comfortable queen-size bed, and a roomy lanai that's great for watching the sun set over the Pacific. There's no air-conditioning, but louvered windows and ceiling fans keep the units fairly cool during the day. There are lots of restaurants and a convenience store within walking distance, and you're about 10 to 15 minutes away from Lahaina and some great golf courses.

33 Hui Dr. (off Lower Honoapiilani Hwy., in Napili), c/o Aloha Condos Hawaii, P.O. Box 396681, Keauhou, Hi 96740. © 877/782-5642. www.alohacondos.com. 33 units. $95–$225 studio for 2. 5-night minimum. MC, V. **Amenities:** Coin-op washer/dryers. In room: TV, kitchen, fridge, coffeemaker.

Napili Sunset ⟨Value⟩ Housed in three buildings (two on the ocean and one across the street) and located just down the street from Napili Bay (see above), these clean, older, well-maintained units offer good value. At first glance the plain two-story structures don't look like much, but the location, the bargain prices, and the friendly staff are the real hidden treasures here. In addition to daily maid service, the units all have full kitchens (with dishwashers), ceiling fans (no air-conditioning), sofa beds, small dining rooms, and small bedrooms. The beach—one of Maui's best—can get a little crowded because the public beach access is through this property (and everyone on Maui seems to want to come here). The studio units are all located in the building off the beach and a few steps up a slight hill; they're a good size, with a full kitchen and either a sofa bed or a Murphy bed, and they overlook the small pool and garden. The one- and two-bedroom units are all on the beach (the downstairs units have lanais that lead right to the sand). The staff makes sure each unit has the basics—paper towels, dishwasher soap, coffee filters, condiments—to get your stay off to a good start. There are restaurants within walking distance.

46 Hui Rd. (in Napili), Lahaina, HI 96761. © 800/447-9229 or 808/669-8083. Fax 808/669-2730. www.napili sunset.com. 42 units. High season $120 studio double; $245 1-bedroom double; $340 2-bedroom (sleeps up to 4). Off season $105 studio; $225 1-bedroom; $290 2-bedroom. Extra person $12. Children under 3 stay free in parent's room. 3-night minimum. MC, V. **Amenities:** Small outdoor pool; coin-op washer/dryers (free detergent supplied). In room: TV, kitchen, fridge, coffeemaker.

Papakea ⟨Value⟩ Just a mile down the beach from Kaanapali lie these low-rise buildings, surrounded by manicured, landscaped grounds and ocean views galore. Palm trees and tropical plants dot the property, a putting green wraps around two kidney-shaped pools, and a footbridge arches over a lily pond brimming with carp. Each pool has its own private cabana with sauna, Jacuzzi, and barbecue grills; a poolside shop rents snorkel gear for exploring the offshore reefs. All units have dishwashers and big lanais, and some units have their own washer/dryers. The studios have pull-down beds to save space during the day. Definitely a good value.

Maui Resort Management, 3600 Lower Honoapiilani Rd. (in Honokowai), Lahaina, HI 96761. © **800/367-5037** or 808/669-1902. Fax 808/669-8790. www.mauigetaway.com. 364 units. $115–$135 studio double; $150–$210 1-bedroom (sleeps up to 4); $190–$220 2-bedroom (sleeps up to 6). 7-night minimum. MC, V. **Amenities:** 2 outdoor pools; 3 tennis courts; 2 Jacuzzis; watersports equipment rental, washer/dryer. *In room:* A/C, TV/VCR, kitchen, fridge, coffeemaker, washer/dryer.

KAPALUA
VERY EXPENSIVE

Kapalua Bay–A Renaissance Resort 🌟🌟 *(Kids)*   Just as we went to press, the owners of this 30-year-old resort announced that it would be closed in the spring of 2006, then would be torn down to make room for a bigger resort. It's a shame, because few Hawaiian resorts have so much open space. We recommend you book the Kapalua Bay before it closes, so you can experience the 23,000 acres of green fields lined with spiky Norfolk pine windbreaks. The 1970s-style rectilinear building, down by the often-windy shore, is full of angles that frame stunning views of the ocean, mountains, and blue sky. The tastefully designed maze of oversize rooms fronts a palm-fringed gold-sand beach that's one of the best in Hawaii, and there's an excellent Ben Crenshaw golf course. Each guest room has a sitting area with sofa, a king-size or two double beds, and an entertainment center. Plantation-style shutter doors open onto private lanais with views of Molokai across the channel. The renovated bathrooms feature two granite vanities, a large soaking tub, and a glass-enclosed shower.

1 Bay Dr., Kapalua, HI 96761. © **800/367-8000** or 808/669-5656. Fax 808/669-4694. www.kapaluabayhotel.com. 210 units. $390–$525 double; from $1,250 suite; $540 1-bedroom villa; $820 2-bedroom villa. Resort fee of $15 per day for welcome lei, local and toll-free phone calls, complimentary sunset appetizer, "Kids Eat Free Dinner," use of fitness center, lobby coffee and tea, in-room safe, incoming faxes, resort shuttle, West Maui airport shuttle, valet or self-parking, and daily newspaper. Extra person $75. Children 17 and under stay free in parent's room using existing bedding. AE, DC, DISC, MC, V. **Amenities:** 3 restaurants; 3 bars; 2 outdoor pools; access to the Kapalua Resort's acclaimed trio of golf courses (each with its own pro shop); 10 Plexipave tennis courts for day and night play; 24-hr. fitness facilities; small spa; Jacuzzi; watersports equipment rentals; children's program; concierge; activities desk; car-rental desk; business center; shopping arcade; salon; room service; in-room and spa massage; babysitting; same-day laundry service and dry cleaning; concierge-level rooms. *In room:* A/C, TV, dataport, minibar, fridge, coffeemaker, hair dryer, iron, safe.

Ritz-Carlton Kapalua 🌟🌟 *(Kids)*   Hospitality, the hallmark of Ritz-Carltons around the world, was not up to the usual standard when I last visited the Ritz in Kapalua. First, we were not taken to our room by the bell staff, and the front desk gave us the wrong directions on how to get to our room. The next morning the service in the breakfast dining room was nonexistent. Guests had to hunt down the coffee pot and serve themselves.

I hope management can correct these flaws, because this Ritz is a complete universe, one of those resorts where you can happily sit by the ocean with a book for 2 whole weeks and never leave the grounds. It rises proudly on a knoll, in a singularly spectacular setting between the rainforest and the sea. During construction, the burial sites of hundreds of ancient Hawaiians were discovered in the sand, so the hotel was moved inland to avoid disrupting the graves. This setback worked to the hotel's advantage, giving it a commanding view of Molokai.

The style is fancy plantation, elegant but not imposing. The public spaces are open, airy, and graceful, with plenty of tropical foliage and landscapes by artist Sarah Supplee that recall the not-so-long-ago agrarian past. Rooms are up to the usual Ritz standard, outfitted with marble bathrooms, private lanais, and in-room fax capability. If you can

Nickel-&-Dime Charges at High-Priced Hotels

Several upscale resorts in Hawaii have begun a practice that I find distasteful, dishonest, and downright discouraging: charging a so-called "resort fee." This daily fee (generally $15 a day) is added on to your bill for such "complimentary" items as a daily newspaper, local phone calls, use of the fitness facilities, and so on. Amenities that the resort has been happily providing its guests for years are now tacked on to your bill under the guise of a "fee." In most cases, you do not have an option to decline the resort fee—in other words, this is a sneaky way to further increase the prices without telling you. I oppose this practice and urge you to voice your complaints to the resort management. Otherwise, what'll be next—a charge for using the tiny bars of soap or miniature shampoo bottles?

afford it, stay on the **Club Floor** ★★★—it offers the best amenities in the state, including French-roast coffee in the morning, a buffet at lunch, cookies in the afternoon, and pupus and drinks at sunset. The Ritz Kids program offers a variety of educational activities and sports.

The excellent The Banyan Tree Restaurant (p. 147) has a new chef, and the relaxing spa has just undergone extensive renovation and has a new menu of Hawaiian-influenced treatments. The resort's Hawaiian cultural program is one of Maui's best, with twice weekly movies and "talk story," along with other events.

1 Ritz-Carlton Dr., Kapalua, HI 96761. (℧ **800/262-8440** or 808/669-6200. Fax 808/669-1566. www.ritzcarlton.com. 548 units. $365–$675 double; from $405 suite; from $900 Club Floor suites. Extra person $50 ($100 in Club Floor rooms). "Resort fee" of $15 for "complimentary" use of fitness center, preferred tee times, Aloha Friday festivities, cultural history tours, self-parking, access to toll-free phone calls, resort shuttle service, tennis, morning coffee at the Lobby Lounge, use of the 9-hole putting green, and games of bocce ball on the lawn. Wedding/honeymoon, golf, and other packages available. AE, DC, DISC, MC, V. Valet parking $15; free self-parking. **Amenities:** 4 restaurants; 4 bars (including 1 serving drinks and light fare next to the beach); outdoor pool; access to the Kapalua Resort's 3 championship golf courses (each with its own pro shop) and its deluxe tennis complex; fitness room; spa; 2 outdoor hot tubs; watersports equipment rentals; bike rentals; children's program; game room; concierge; activities desk; car-rental desk; business center; shopping arcade; salon; room service; in-room and spa massage; babysitting; same-day laundry and dry cleaning; concierge-level rooms (some of Hawaii's best, with top-drawer service and amenities). *In room:* A/C, TV, dataport, minibar, coffeemaker, hair dryer, iron, safe, high-speed Internet access.

EXPENSIVE

If you're interested in a luxurious condo or town house, consider **Kapalua Villas** (℧ **800/545-0018** or 808/669-8088; www.kapaluavillas.com). The palatial units dotting the oceanfront cliffs and fairways of this idyllic coast are a (relative) bargain, especially if you're traveling with a group. The one-bedroom condos go for $209 to $369, two bedrooms for $309 to $579, three bedrooms for $435 to $585. There are numerous package deals (which include golf, tennis, honeymoon amenities, and car) to save even more money.

3 South Maui

MAALAEA

I recommend two booking agencies that rent a host of condominiums and unique vacation homes in the Kihei/Wailea/Maalaea area: **Kihei Maui Vacation** (℧ **800/ 541-6284** or 808/879-7581; www.kmvmaui.com) and **Condominium Rentals Hawaii** (℧ **800/367-5242** or 808/879-2778; www.crhmaui.com).

KIHEI
EXPENSIVE

In addition to the choices below, also consider the **Aston at the Maui Banyan** (© 800/ 92-ASTON or 808/875-0004; www.aston-hotels.com), a condo property across the street from Kamaole Beach Park II. The large one- to three-bedroom units are very nicely done and feature full kitchens, air-conditioning, and washer/dryers. Rates range from $200 for hotel rooms, $260 to $285 for one-bedroom units, $345 to $385 for two-bedroom units, and $510 for three-bedroom units; be sure to ask about packages.

Hale Pau Hana Resort ⚘ *Kids*   Located on the sandy shores of Kamaole Beach Park but separated from the white-sand beach by a velvet green manicured lawn, this is a great condo resort for families. Each of the large units has a private lanai, terrific ocean view, and complete kitchens. The management goes above and beyond, personally greeting each guest and acting as your own concierge service. Guests can mingle at the free coffee hour every morning, or at the pupu parties with local Hawaiian entertainment held twice a week at sunset. The location is in the heart of Kihei, close to shopping, restaurants, and activities.

2480 S. Kiehi Rd., Kihei 96753. © 800/367-6036 or 808/879-2715. Fax 808/875-0238. www.hphresort.com. 79 units. $173–$280 1-bedroom; $270–$335 2-bedroom. MC, V. **Amenities:** Pool; concierge; barbecue; coin-op laundry. *In room:* A/C in bedrooms, TV, full kitchens, fridge, coffeemaker, hair dryer, iron, safe.

Maalaea Surf Resort ⚘   This is the place for people who want a quiet, relaxing vacation on a well-landscaped property, with a beautiful white-sand beach right outside. Located at the quiet end of Kihei Road, this two-story complex sprawls across 5 acres of lush tropical gardens. The luxury town houses all have ocean views, big kitchens (with dishwashers), cable TV, and VCRs. Amenities include maid service (Mon–Sat), shuffleboard, barbecue grills, and discounts on tee times at nearby golf courses. Restaurants and shops are within a 5-minute drive.

12 S. Kihei Rd. (at S. Kihei Rd. and Hwy. 350), Kihei, HI 96753. © 800/423-7953 or 808/879-1267. Fax 808/ 874-2884. www.maalaeasurfresort.com. 34 units. $250–$285 1-bedroom unit (sleeps up to 4 people); $330–$390 2-bedroom (sleeps up to 6). MC, V. **Amenities:** 2 outdoor pools; 2 tennis courts; concierge; activities desk; car-rental desk; coin-op washer/dryers. *In room:* A/C, TV/VCR/DVD, kitchen, fridge, coffeemaker, hair dryer, iron, safe.

Maui Coast Hotel ⚘⚘   This place stands out as one of the only moderately priced hotels in Kihei (which is largely full of affordable condo complexes rather than traditional hotels or resorts). Ask about the room/car packages: The Maui Coast's Extra Value package gives you a rental car for just a few dollars more than the regular room rate. It's a great location, about a block from Kamaole Beach Park I, with plenty of bars, restaurants, and shopping within walking distance and a golf course nearby. The rooms offer extras such as sitting areas, whirlpool tubs, ceiling fans, and private lanais.

2259 S. Kihei Rd. (1 block from Kamaole Beach Park I), Kihei, HI 96753. © 800/895-6284 or 808/874-6284. Fax 808/875-4731. www.mauicoasthotel.com. 265 units. $195 double; $225 suite; $255 1-bedroom (sleeps up to 4). Children 17 and under stay free in parent's room using existing bedding. Rollaway bed $20. Packages including rental car available. AE, DC, DISC, MC, V. **Amenities:** Restaurant; pool bar with nightly entertainment; outdoor pool (plus children's wading pool); 2 night-lit tennis courts; fitness room; concierge; activities desk; room service; laundry service; dry cleaning; free use of self-serve washer/dryers. *In room:* A/C, TV, fridge, coffeemaker, hair dryer, iron, safe.

Maui Hill ⚘   If you can't decide between the privacy of a condo and the conveniences of a hotel, try this place. Managed by the respected Aston chain, Maui Hill gives you the best of both worlds. Located on a hill above the heat of Kihei town, this large, Spanish-style resort (with stucco buildings, red-tile roofs, and arched entries)

Where to Stay in South Maui

Aloha Journeys **23**
Aston at the Maui Banyan **16**
Dreams Come True **23**
Eva Villa **23**
Fairmont Kea Lani Maui **28**
Four Seasons Resort Maui
  at Wailea **27**
Grand Wailea Resort Hotel & Spa **26**
Hale Kumulani **23**
Hale Pau Hana Resort **17**
Kamanole Nalu Resort **15**
Kealia Resort **1**
Kihei Beach Resort **4**
Kihei Kai **2**
Koa Resort **10**
Leinaala **12**
Luanna Kai Resort **11**
Maalaea Surf Resort **3**
Mana Kai Maui Resort **21**
Maui Coast Hotel **14**
Maui Hill **22**
Maui Kamaole **20**
Maui Prince Hotel **29**
Menehune Shores **9**
Nona Lani Cottages **5**
Pineapple Inn **23**
Puahoa Beach Apts. **13**
Renaissance Wailea Beach Resort **24**
Sunseeker Resort **6**
Two Mermaids on the Sunnyside
  of Maui B&B **18**
Wailana Inn **7**
Wailana Kai **8**
Wailea Marriott,
  An Outrigger Resort **25**
What a Wonderful World B&B **19**

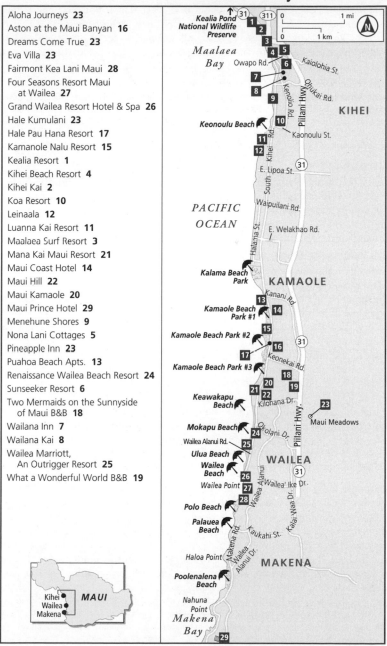

combines all the amenities and activities of a hotel—pool, hot tub, tennis courts, Hawaiiana classes, maid service, and more—with large luxury condos that have full kitchens and plenty of privacy. Nearly all units have ocean views, dishwashers, washer/dryers, queen-size sofa beds, and big lanais. Beaches, restaurants, and shops are within easy walking distance, and a golf course is nearby. Management goes out of its way to make sure your stay is perfect.

2881 S. Kihei Rd. (across from Kamaole Park III, between Keonekai St. and Kilohana Dr.), Kihei, HI 96753. ✆ 800/92-ASTON or 808/879-6321. Fax 808/879-8945. www.aston-hotels.com. 140 units. High season $215–$310 1-bedroom apt; $265–$350 2-bedroom; $305–$390 3-bedroom. AE, DC, DISC, MC, V. Amenities: Outdoor pool; putting green; tennis courts; Jacuzzi; concierge; activities desk; car-rental desk; laundry service; dry cleaning; barbecue grills; coin-op washer/dryers. In room: A/C, TV/VCR, kitchen, fridge, coffeemaker, hair dryer, iron, safe, washer/dryer.

MODERATE

The **Kihei Beach Resort,** 36 S. Kihei Rd., Kihei, HI 96753 (✆ **800/367-6034** or 808/879-2744; fax 808/875-0306; www.kiheibeachresort.com), has spacious condos right on the beach. The downside is the constant traffic noise from Kihei Road. Rates are $130 to $185 for a one-bedroom unit (two people), $180 to $250 for a two-bedroom (four people); there's a 4-night minimum and a $10 charge per extra person.

Eva Villa on the Slopes of Haleakala 𝒦𝒦 (Finds) True to its name, this three-unit bed-and-breakfast is located on ½-acre of lushly landscaped property at the top of the Maui Meadows subdivision. From the rooftop lanai, guests have a spectacular view of the sunset behind Kahoolawe and Lanai and of the West Maui Mountains. Hosts Rick and Dale Pounds have done everything to make this one of Maui's classiest vacation rentals. From the continental breakfast stocked in the unit's kitchen (fresh island fruit, juice, bread, muffins, jam, and coffee/tea) to the decor of the suites to the heated pool, Jacuzzi, and individual barbecue facilities, this is a great place to stay. The location couldn't be better—just a few minutes' drive to Kihei's sunny beaches, golf courses, tennis, and shopping, and restaurants in Kihei and Wailea. Each unit is a roomy 600 square feet. The separate cottage has a living room, full kitchen, and separate bedroom; the poolside studio is a one-room unit with a huge kitchen; and the poolside suite has two bedrooms and a kitchenette. You can't go wrong here.

815 Kumulani Dr., Kihei, HI 96753. ✆ **800/824-6409** or 808/874-6407. Fax 808/874-6407. www.mauibnb.com. 3 units. $125–$145. Extra person $15. No credit cards. Amenities: Heated outdoor pool; Jacuzzi; individual barbecue facilities. In room: TV/VCR, kitchen or kitchenette, coffeemaker, fridge, washer/dryer in cottage.

Kamaole Nalu Resort This six-story condominium complex is located between two beach parks, Kamaole I and Kamaole II, and right across the street from a shopping complex. Units have fabulous ocean views, large living rooms, and private lanais; the kitchens are a bit small but come fully equipped. I recommend no. 306 for its wonderful bird's-eye view. The property also has an oceanside pool and great barbecue facilities. Restaurants, bars, a golf course, and tennis courts are nearby; shopping is across the street. **Warning:** Because the building is right on Kihei Road, it can be noisy.

2450 S. Kihei Rd. (between Kanani and Keonekai roads, next to Kamaole Beach Park II), Kihei, HI 96753. ✆ 800/767-1497 or 808/879-1006. Fax 808/879-8693. www.kamaolenalu.com. 36 units. High season $155–$215 double. Off season $135–$195 double. Extra person $15. 5-night minimum. MC, V. Amenities: Outdoor pool; activities desk; car-rental desk. In room: TV, kitchen, fridge, coffeemaker, hair dryer, iron, safe, washer/dryer.

Kealia Resort (Value) This oceanfront property at the northern end of Kihei is well maintained and nicely furnished—and the price is excellent. But as tempting as the

$80 studio units may sound, don't give in: They face noisy Kihei Road and are near a major junction, so you'll be listening to big trucks downshifting all night. Instead, go for one of the oceanview units, which all have full kitchens and private lanais. The grounds face a 5-mile stretch of white-sand beach. Social gatherings include free coffee-and-doughnut get-togethers every Friday morning and pupu parties on Wednesday.

191 N. Kihei Rd. (north of Hwy. 31, at the Maalaea end of Kihei), Kihei, HI 96753. ✆ 800/265-0686 or 808/879-0952. Fax 808/875-1540. www.kealiaresort.com. 51 units. $80–$100 studio; $120–$170 1-bedroom double; $185–$220 2-bedroom (sleeps up to 4). Extra person $10. Children 12 and under stay free in parent's room. 4-night minimum. MC, V. **Amenities:** Recently retiled outdoor pool. *In room:* TV, kitchen, fridge, coffeemaker, hair dryer, iron, washer/dryer.

Leinaala ✪ *(Value)*   From Kihei Road, you can't see Leinaala amid the jumble of buildings, but this oceanfront boutique condo offers excellent accommodations at 1980s prices. The building is set back from the water, with a county park—an oasis of green grass and tennis courts—in between. A golf course lies nearby. The units are compact but filled with everything you need: a full kitchen, sofa bed, and oceanview lanai. (Hideaway beds are available if you need one.)

998 S. Kihei Rd., Kihei, HI 96753. ✆ 800/822-4409 or 808/879-2235. Fax 808/874-6144. www.mauicondo.com. 24 units. $145 1-bedroom double; $190 2-bedroom (sleeps up to 4). 4-night minimum. No credit cards. **Amenities:** Outdoor pool; coin-op washer/dryers. *In room:* A/C, TV, kitchen, fridge, coffeemaker.

Mana Kai Maui Resort ✪ *(Kids)*   This eight-story complex, situated on a beautiful white-sand cove, is an unusual combination of hotel and condominium. The hotel rooms, which account for half of the total number of units, are small but nicely furnished. The condo units are great for families and feature full kitchens and open living rooms with sliding-glass doors that lead to small lanais overlooking the sandy beach and ocean. Some units are beginning to show their age (the building is more than 30 years old), but they're all clean and comfortable. One of the best snorkeling beaches on the coast is just steps away; a golf course and tennis courts are nearby.

2960 S. Kihei Rd. (between Kilohana and Keonekai roads, at the Wailea end of Kihei), Kihei, HI 96753. ✆ 800/367-5242 or 808/879-2778. Fax 808/879-7825. www.crhmaui.com. 105 units. $130 hotel room double; $180–$255 1-bedroom (sleeps up to 4); $230–$310 2-bedroom (up to 6). AE, MC, V. **Amenities:** Restaurant (Five Palms, p. 150); bar; outdoor pool; concierge; coin-op washer/dryers. *In room:* A/C (in hotel rooms only), TV, kitchen (in condo units), fridge, coffeemaker, safe.

Maui Kamaole   You'll find this condo complex right across the street from the Kihei Public Boat Ramp and beautiful Kamaole Beach Park III, which is great for swimming, snorkeling, and beachcombing. Each roomy, fully furnished unit comes with a private lanai, two bathrooms (even in the one-bedroom units), and an all-electric kitchen. The one-bedroom units—which can comfortably accommodate four—are quite a deal, especially if you're traveling in the off season. The grounds are nicely landscaped and offer barbecues. Restaurants and bars are within walking distance; a golf course and tennis courts are also nearby.

2777 S. Kihei Rd. (between Keonekai and Kilohana roads, at the Wailea end of Kihei), Kihei, HI 96753. ✆ 800/822-4409 or 808/874-8467. Fax 808/875-9117. www.mauikamaole.com. 62 of the 210 units are in the rental pool. $170–$185 1-bedroom double (sleeps up to 4); $225–$240 2-bedroom (rates for 4, sleeps up to 6). AE, MC, V. **Amenities:** 2 outdoor pools; tennis courts, Jacuzzi. *In room:* A/C, TV, kitchen, fridge, coffeemaker, iron, safe (in some units), washer/dryer.

Punahoa Beach Apartments ✪ *(Value)*   Book this place! I can't put it any more simply than that. The location—off noisy, traffic-ridden Kihei Road, on a quiet side street with ocean frontage—is fabulous. A grassy lawn rolls about 50 feet down to the beach, where there's great snorkeling just offshore and a popular surfing spot next door; shopping and restaurants are all within walking distance. All of the beautifully decorated units in this small, four-story building have fully equipped kitchens and lanais with great ocean views. Rooms go quickly in winter, so reserve early.

2142 Iliili Rd. (off S. Kihei Rd., 300 ft. from Kamaole Beach I), Kihei, HI 96753. (℄ **800/564-4380** or 808/879-2720. Fax 808/875-9147. www.punahoabeach.com. 13 units. High season $130 studio double; $185–$198 1-bedroom double; $220 2-bedroom double. Off season $94 studio; $130–$145 1-bedroom; $160 2-bedroom. Extra person $15. 5-night minimum. AE, MC, V. **Amenities:** Coin-op washer/dryer. *In room:* TV, kitchen, fridge, coffeemaker, iron.

Sunseeker Resort *(Finds)*   This former budget property, located just across the street from a terrific white-sand beach, has been recently sold and the new management team has spiffed up the studio and one-bedroom units with custom furniture and added air-conditioning and other amenities not usually seen at small properties, like high-speed Internet access and concierge services. The redone units have been tastefully decorated. Studios offer terrific wallet-pleasing prices. The one-bedrooms, which have a pull-out sofa in the living room and new appliances in the kitchen, are a good deal in the off season at $160 but definitely not a deal during the high season at $200. All units have private lanais with ocean views and the beach just a few steps away.

551 S. Kihei Rd., P.O. Box 276, Kihei, HI 96753. (℄ **800/532-MAUI** or 808/879-1261. Fax 808/874-3877. www.mauisunseeker.com. 4 units. $85–$125 studio; $160–$200 1-bedroom. 3-night minimum. Extra person $15. AE, DISC, MC, V. **Amenities:** Hot tub; concierge; same-day laundry service; coin-op washer/dryer; gas barbecue. *In room:* A/C, TV/VCR, full kitchen (in 1-bedroom) or kitchenette (studio), coffeemaker, hair dryer, high-speed Internet.

Wailana Inn   The new owners of Sunseeker Resort (see above) just purchased this tiny, 12-unit one-bedroom-apartment complex as we went to press. They revamped everything and put in slate in the bathroom, new tile on the floor, bought new furniture, and repainted. The units are small, but the lanais are large and the price is right. The result is a terrific moderate property, with the beach just across the street. An unusual amenity they offer is a secluded "clothing-optional" rooftop with great ocean views, where you can sunbathe or sit in the hot tub.

Wailana Place, Kihei, 96753. (℄ **800/399-3885** or 808/874-3131. www.wailanainn.com. 12 units. $80–$120 standard room double; $100–$140 studio double; $140–$180 junior suite. Extra person $15. AE, DISC, MC. V. **Amenities:** Hot tub; concierge; same-day laundry service; coin-op washer/dryer; gas barbecue. *In room:* A/C, TV/VCR, full kitchen, coffeemaker, hair dryer, answering machine, high-speed Internet access.

INEXPENSIVE

In addition to the choices below, also check out **Luana Kai Resort,** 940 S. Kihei Rd., Kihei, HI 96753 (℄ **800/669-1127** or 808/879-1268; fax 808/879-1455; www.luanakai.com). This older condo complex has 113 units ($99–$179 one-bedroom; $119–$199 two-bedroom; $219–$269 three-bedroom; 4-night minimum).

Kihei Kai Resort, 61 N. Kihei Rd., Kihei, HI 96753 (℄ **888/778-7717** or 808/879-2357; fax 808/891-9403; www.kiheirentals.com), has one-bedroom apartments ($100–$140 double; 4-night minimum in off season, 7-night minimum in high season) that are ideal for families ($10 per extra person).

Aloha Journeys *(Finds)*   Tucked into the residential neighborhood of Maui Meadows (and a 5-min. drive from the nearest good beach) is an oasis of fruit trees, a flower garden, and a sun deck with picnic table, chairs, and a hot tub overlooking the ocean. Both rental cottages have their own washer/dryers. The two-bedroom Ginger Cottage is best for families, with full kitchen, two separate bedrooms, and an enclosed lanai.

The one-bedroom Palm Cottage makes a cozy honeymoon cottage (it also has a sofa bed). Guests can gather fresh fruits for their breakfast. Other great amenities for guests include beach toys and snorkel gear. Occasionally owner/hostess Karen will waive the 5-night minimum for last-minute bookings. They also rent a three-bedroom, million-dollar vacation home for just $265 double; and a another three-bedroom (one bathroom) house for $140 double.

490 Mikioi Place (Maui Meadows), Kihei, HI 96753. © 800/871-5032 or 808/875-4840. Fax 808/879-3998. www. alohajourneys.com. 2 units. Apr 16–Dec 14 $95 double (plus $50 cleaning fee), extra person $15; Dec 15–Apr 15 $115 double (plus $50 cleaning fee), extra person $20. 5-night minimum. MC, V. **Amenities:** Jacuzzi; laundry facilities. *In room:* A/C, TV/VCR/DVD, kitchen, fridge, coffeemaker, hair dryer.

Dreams Come True on Maui *(Value* This bed-and-breakfast was the dream come true for hosts Tom Croly and Denise McKinnon, who after several years of vacationing on Maui, opened this three-unit property in 2002. They're centrally located in the Maui Meadows subdivision, just a few minutes' drive to golf courses, tennis courts, white-sand beaches, shopping, and restaurants in Kihei and Wailea. They offer a one-bedroom, oceanview cottage (great for long stays) with its own (high-speed) Internet-connected computer, a gourmet kitchen, two TV sets, washer/dryer, and wraparound decks (6-night minimum). They also offer two rooms in the houses (one with king-size bed, one with queen-size bed) with TV, private entrance, kitchenettes (plus outdoor cooking area with barbecue grill, sink, and microwave), use of washer/dryer, and lots of other amenities not usually found in B&Bs (3- to 4-night minimum). Every guest is greeted and given personal concierge treatment, from the low-down on good snorkeling to a tour of the property. Guests are invited to use the centrally located oceanview deck and the living room in the house with its computer (with high-speed Internet connection). In the evenings Tom shows movies on the 8-foot-wide movie screen and frequently helps guests transfer digital photos to a CD. They recently acquired a two-bedroom/two-bathroom condo, across the street from beach, which they rent for $109 for two and $149 for three or more (6-night minimum).

3259 Akala Dr., Kihei, HI 96753. © 877/782-9628 or 808/879-7099. Fax 808/879-7099. www.dreamscometrueon maui.com. 3 units. $75–$99 units in house (3- to 4-night minimum); $105–$125 cottage (6-night minimum). MC, V. **Amenities:** Concierge service; washer/dryer. *In room:* A/C, TV/VCR, kitchen or kitchenette, fridge, coffeemaker, hair dryer, CD player.

Hale Kumulani *(Finds* At the top of Maui Meadows subdivision, right on the Wailea border and about a 5-minute drive to the beach, lies this ½-acre property, surrounded by a 40,000-acre wilderness area with two quaint units. The first is a darling one-room cottage with full kitchen, wood flooring, high beam ceilings, living-room area (with full-size guest sofa/futon), large deck, and outdoor shower. Underneath the main house, but with a private entrance and complete privacy, is the waterfall suite. It has a kitchenette and a giant outdoor patio with an overhang that provides shade, and it's landscaped with a waterfall plus banana and papaya trees. Both units have access to the organic vegetable garden, numerous fruit trees, and beach equipment. Hosts Ron and Merry couldn't be more gracious in helping you navigate around the island. They also have a full-size crib, stroller, and junior beds available for kids.

874 Kumulani Dr., Maui Meadows, Kihei, HI 96753. © 808/891-0425. Fax 808/891-0269. www.cottagemaui.com. 2 units. $125 double suite; $145 cottage double. 4-night minimum. MC, V. **Amenities:** 6 championship golf courses within 5 miles; aquatic center with 3 pools nearby (a 7-min. drive). *In room:* TV/VCR, kitchen (in cottage), kitchenette (in suite), fridge, coffeemaker, hair dryer, iron, washer/dryer.

Koa Resort 🄰 *(Kids)*   Located just across the street from the ocean, Koa Resort consists of five two-story wooden buildings on more than 5½ acres of landscaped grounds. The spacious, privately owned one-, two-, and three-bedroom units are decorated with care and come fully equipped, right down to the dishwasher and disposal in the kitchens. There's plenty of room for families, who can enjoy the tennis courts, pool, and putting green. The larger condos have both showers and tubs; the smaller units have showers only. All feature large lanais, ceiling fans, and washer/dryers. For maximum peace and quiet, ask for a unit far from Kihei Road. Bars, restaurants, and a golf course are nearby.

811 S. Kihei Rd. (between Kulanihakoi St. and Namauu Place). c/o Bello Realty, P.O. Box 1776, Kihei, HI 96753. ℂ 800/541-3060 or 808/879-3328. Fax 808/875-1483. www.bellomaui.com. 54 units (some with shower only). High season $85–$110 1-bedroom; $100–$130 2-bedroom; $160–$180 3-bedroom. MC, V. **Amenities:** Outdoor pool; 18-hole putting green; 2 tennis courts; Jacuzzi. *In room:* TV, kitchen, fridge, coffeemaker, iron, safe, washer/dryer.

Menehune Shores *(Value)*   If you plan to stay on Maui for a week, you might want to look into the car/condo packages here; they're a real deal, especially for families on a budget. The six-story Menehune Shores is more than 30 years old and is showing its age in some places, but all units are well maintained and have ocean views and lanais. The design is straight out of the 1970s, but the view is timeless. The kitchens are fully equipped, all units have washer/dryers, and the oceanfront location guarantees a steady breeze that keeps the rooms cool (there's no air-conditioning). The building sits in front of the ancient Hawaiian fish ponds of Kalepolepo. Some Hawaiians still fish them using traditional throw nets, but generally the pond serves as protection from the ocean waves, making it safe for children (and those unsure of their ability) to swim in the relatively calm waters. There's also a heated pool, shuffleboard courts, and a whale-watching platform on the roof garden.

760 S. Kihei Rd. (between Kaonoulu and Hoonani sts.), P.O. Box 1327, Kihei, HI 96753. ℂ 800/558-9117 or 808/879-3428. Fax 808/879-5218. www.menehunereservations.com. 70 units. $115–$145 1-bedroom double ($939/week with car); $140–$190 2-bedroom double ($1,099–$1,289/week with car); $185–$240 3-bedroom for up to 6 ($1,589/week with car). 3-night minimum. Extra person $7.50. No credit cards. **Amenities:** Restaurant; bar; outdoor pool. *In room:* TV/VCR, kitchen, fridge, coffeemaker, washer/dryers.

Nona Lani Cottages 🄰 *(Finds)*   Picture this: a grassy expanse dotted with eight cottages tucked among palm, fruit, and sweet-smelling flower trees, right across the street from a white-sand beach. This is one of the great hidden deals in Kihei. The cottages are tiny but contain everything you'll need: a small but complete kitchen, twin beds that double as couches in the living room, a separate bedroom with a queen-size bed, and a lanai with table and chairs. The cottages were renovated in 2002 with new ceramic flooring. The real attraction, however, is the garden setting next to the beach. There are no phones in the cabins, but there's a public one by the registration/check-in area.

If the cabins are booked, or if you want a bit more luxury, you might opt for one of the private guest rooms. These beautiful units feature plush carpet, koa bed frames, air-conditioning, lanais, and private entrances. The industrious Kong family, hosts here, also run Happy Valley Hale Maui, hostel accommodations on the other side of the island in Happy Valley, next to Wailuku.

455 S. Kihei Rd. (just south of Hwy. 31), P.O. Box 655, Kihei, HI 96753. ℂ 800/733-2688 or 808/879-2497. www.nonalanicottages.com. 11 units. $75–$95 double; $90–$105 cottage. Extra person $12–$15. 3-night minimum for rooms, 4-night minimum for cottages. No credit cards. **Amenities:** Coin-op washer/dryers. *In room:* A/C, TV, kitchen (in cottages), fridge, coffeemaker, no phone.

Pineapple Inn Maui ⍟⍟ *Finds*   Just opened at the end of 2004, this charming inn (only four rooms, plus a darling two-bedroom cottage) is an exquisite find, with terrific prices. Located in the residential Maui Meadows area, with panoramic ocean views, this two-story inn (one side of the building is the owner's home) boasts gorgeous landscaping, with tropical flowers and plants and a lily pond in the front and a giant saltwater pool and Jacuzzi overlooking the ocean. Each of the rooms is soundproof and expertly decorated, with a small kitchenette stocked with juice, pastries, and drinks on your arrival. There's also an incredible view off your own private lanai. If you need more room, they also offer a darling two-bedroom, one-bathroom cottage (wood floors, beautiful artwork) with a full kitchen (even a dishwasher), separate bedrooms, and a private lanai. The cottage is landscaped for maximum privacy.

3170 Akala Dr., Kihei, HI 96753 ℂ 877/212-MAUI (6284) or 808/298-4403. www.pineappleinnmaui.com. 4 units, 1 2-bedroom cottage. $99–$119 double; $165 cottage for 4. 3-night minimum for rooms, 6-night minimum for cottage. No credit cards. **Amenities:** Large saltwater pool; Jacuzzi; complimentary laundry facilities; barbecue area. *In room:* A/C,TV/VCR, kitchenette (in rooms), full kitchen (in cottage), fridge, coffeemaker, hair dryer, no phone in rooms, phone/answering machine in cottage, wireless Internet access.

Two Mermaids on the Sunnyside of Maui B&B ⍟
The two mermaids, Juddee and Miranda, both avid scuba divers, have friendly accommodations, professionally decorated in brilliant, tropical colors, complete with hand-painted art of the island (above and below the water) in a quiet neighborhood just a 10-minute walk from the beach. My favorite is the Ocean Ohana, a large one-bedroom (with option of a second connecting bedroom) apartment, complete with kitchenette, huge private deck, private entryway, and your own giant hot tub. Equally cute is the Poolside Suite, with private entry next to the outdoor pool. This studio (with the option of a separate connecting bedroom) is a living room during the day; at night it converts to a bedroom with a pull-down hide-a-bed. Continental breakfast, with some of the best homemade bread on the island, is placed on your doorstep every morning. Amenities include guitars in every unit, a range of complimentary beach equipment, microwave popcorn, a barbecue area, and a swimming pool. Juddee is also a licensed minister and performs weddings and vow renewal.

2840 Umalu Place, Kihei, 96753. ℂ 800/598-9550 or 808/874-8687. Fax 808/875-1833. www.twomermaids.com. 2 units. $120 studio double; $165 studio plus connecting bedroom double; $145 1-bedroom apt; $185 with connecting 2nd bedroom. Rates include continental breakfast. 3-night minimum stay. No credit cards. **Amenities:** Outdoor pool; golf nearby; tennis courts nearby; child care available; massage available; barbecue. *In room:* TV, VCR/DVD on request, kitchen, fridge, coffeemaker, iron, hair dryer, free local phone calls, private lanai and barbecue.

Wailana Kai ⍟ *Value*
Bello Realty has added this renovated, two-story, 10-unit, one- and two-bedroom apartment complex to its collection. As of this writing, one-bedroom units start at $85, but this is a deal that will not last long. Once they get a reputation, the prices most likely will go up. Located at the end of a cul-de-sac and just a 1-minute walk to the beach, the property was totally renovated in 2004 with two types of units: standard (perfectly acceptable, clean, with new paint, furniture, and more) and deluxe (the ones I recommend, for only a few dollars more). All units have full kitchens and soundproof concrete walls, and the second floor has ocean views.

34 Wailana Place. c/o Bello Realty, P.O. Box 1776, Kihei, HI 96753. ℂ 800/541-3060 or 808/879-3328. Fax 808/875-1483. www.bellomaui.com. 10 units. $85–$100 1-bedroom; $110–$125 2-bedroom. MC, V. **Amenities:** Outdoor pool; barbecue area, coin-op washer/dryer. *In room:* TV/VCR, kitchen, fridge, coffeemaker, iron.

What a Wonderful World B&B ⍟ *Value*
I couldn't believe what I'd discovered here: an impeccably done B&B with a great location, excellent rates, and thought and care

put into every room. Then I met hostess Eva Tantillo, who has not only a full-service travel agency, but also a master's degree—along with several years of experience—in hotel management. The result? One of Maui's finest bed-and-breakfasts, centrally located in Kihei (½ mile to Kamaole II Beach Park, 5 min. from Wailea golf courses, and convenient to shopping and restaurants). Choose from one of four units: the master suite (with small fridge, coffeemaker, and barbecue grill on the lanai); studio apartment (with fully equipped kitchen); or two one-bedroom apartments (also with full kitchens). You're also welcome to use the communal barbecue. Eva serves a gourmet family-style breakfast (eggs Benedict, Alaskan waffles, skillet eggs with mushroom sauce, fruit blintzes, and more) on her lanai, which boasts views of white-sand beaches, the West Maui Mountains, and Haleakala.

2828 Umalu Place (off Keonakai St., near Hwy. 31), Kihei, HI 96753. © **800/943-5804** or 808/879-9103. Fax 808/874-9352. www.amauibedandbreakfast.com. 4 units. $75 double; $89 studio double; $99 1-bedroom apt. 5% discount for paying in cash. Rates include full breakfast. Children 11 and under stay free in parent's room. AE, MC, V. **Amenities:** Hot tub; laundry facilities. *In room:* TV, kitchenette, fridge, coffeemaker, hair dryer, iron.

WAILEA

For a complete selection of condo units throughout Wailea and Makena, contact **Destination Resorts Hawaii** (© **800/367-5246** or 808/879-1595; fax 808/874-3554; www.drhmaui.com). Its luxury units include studio doubles starting at $200, one-bedroom doubles from $205, two bedrooms from $245, and three bedrooms from $345. Children under 12 stay free; minimum stays vary by property.

VERY EXPENSIVE

The Fairmont Kea Lani Maui ✶✶✶   At first glance this blinding-white complex of arches and turrets may look a bit out of place in tropical Hawaii (it's actually a close architectural cousin of Las Hadas, the Arabian Nights fantasy resort in Manzanillo, Mexico). But once you enter the flower-filled lobby and see the big blue Pacific outside, there's no doubt you're in Hawaii.

This is the place to get your money's worth. For the price of a hotel room, you get an entire suite—plus a few extras. Each unit in this all-suite luxury hotel has a kitchenette, a living room with entertainment center and sofa bed, a marble wet bar, an oversize marble bathroom with separate shower big enough for a party, a spacious bedroom, and a large lanai that overlooks the pools, lawns, and white-sand beach.

A real plus is the small boutique spa offering the very latest in body work in intimate, relaxing surroundings. Even if you are not staying on the property, try this spa.

The villas are definitely out of a fantasy. The rich and famous stay in these 2,000-square-foot two- and three-bedroom beach bungalows, each with its own plunge pool and gourmet kitchen.

4100 Wailea Alanui Dr., Wailea, HI 96753. © **800/659-4100** or 808/875-4100. Fax 808/875-1200. www.fairmont. com/kealani. 450 units. $345–$785 suite (sleeps up to 4); from $1,400 villa. AE, DC, DISC, MC, V. **Amenities:** 4 restaurants (including Nick's Fishmarket Maui, p. 153); 3 bars (with sunset cocktails and nightly entertainment at the Caffé Ciao restaurant, p. 153); 2 large swimming "lagoons" connected by a 140-ft. water slide and swim-up bar, plus an adult pool; use of Wailea Golf Club's 3 18-hole championship golf courses, as well as the nearby Makena and Elleair golf courses; use of Wailea Tennis Center's 11 courts (3 lit for night play, and a pro shop); fine 24-hr. fitness center; excellent full-service spa offering the latest in body treatments, facials, and massage; Jacuzzi; watersports equipment rentals; bike rentals; children's program; game room; concierge; activities desk; car-rental desk; business center; shopping arcade; salon; room service; in-room and spa massage; babysitting; same-day laundry service and dry cleaning. *In room:* A/C, TV, dataport, kitchenette, minibar, fridge, coffeemaker, hair dryer, iron, safe, high-speed Internet access (additional fee), microwave.

Four Seasons Resort Maui at Wailea ⭐⭐⭐ *Kids*   If money's no object, this is the place to spend it. It's hard to beat this modern version of a Hawaiian palace by the sea, with a relaxing, casual atmosphere. Although it sits on a glorious beach between two other hotels, you won't feel like you're on chockablock resort row: The Four Seasons inhabits its own separate world, thanks to an open courtyard of pools and gardens. Amenities are first-rate here, including outstanding restaurants, an excellent spa, and a wonderful activities program for kids (complimentary, of course). In fact, this may be the most kid-friendly hotel on Maui, with cookies and milk on arrival, children's menus in all restaurants, and complimentary baby gear (cribs, strollers, and even toilet-seat locks). You can even prepurchase necessities like diapers and baby food; the hotel will have them waiting for you when you arrive.

The spacious (about 600 sq. ft.) rooms feature furnished lanais (nearly all with ocean views) that are great for watching whales in winter and sunsets year-round. The grand bathrooms contain deep marble tubs, showers for two, and lighted French makeup mirrors.

Service is attentive but not cloying. At the pool, guests lounge in Casbah-like tents, pampered with special touches like iced Evian and chilled towels. And you'll never see a housekeeping cart in the hall: The cleaning staff works in teams, so they're as unobtrusive as possible and in and out of your room in minutes.

Wolfgang Puck's Spago restaurant (p. 152) features a fusion of Hawaiian and California cuisine in a dreamy open-air setting. Ferraro's at Seaside restaurant (p. 152) offers a casual atmosphere overlooking the Pacific by day; by night, it's transformed into a romantic atmosphere featuring authentic Italian *cucina rustica* with great sunset views and dining under the stars. The poolside Pacific Grill offers lavish breakfast buffets and dinners featuring Pacific Rim cuisine.

The ritzy neighborhood surrounding the hotel is home to great restaurants and shopping, the Wailea Tennis Center (known as Wimbledon West), and six golf courses—not to mention that great beach, with gentle waves and islands framing the view on either side.

3900 Wailea Alanui Dr., Wailea, HI 96753. ℂ 800/334-MAUI (6284) or 808/874-8000. Fax 808/874-2222. www.four seasons.com/maui. 380 units. $365–$705 double; $815 Club Floor double; from $660 suite. Packages available. Extra person $100 ($170 in Club Floor rooms). Children under 18 stay free in parent's room. AE, DC, MC, V. **Amenities:** 3 restaurants (including Spago, p. 152 and Ferraro's at Seaside, p. 152); 3 bars (with nightly entertainment); 3 fabulous outdoor pools; putting green; use of Wailea Golf Club's 3 18-hole championship golf courses, as well as the nearby Makena and Elleair golf courses; 2 on-site tennis courts (lit for night play); use of Wailea Tennis Center's 11 courts (3 lit for night play, and a pro shop); health club featuring outdoor cardiovascular equipment (with individual TV/video players); excellent spa (offering a variety of treatments in the spa, in-room, and oceanside); 2 whirlpools (1 for adults only); beach pavilion with watersports gear rentals and 1 hr. free use of snorkel equipment; complimentary use of bicycles; fabulous year-round kids' program, plus a teen recreation center and a children's video library and toys; game room (with shuffleboard, pool tables, jukebox, big-screen TV, and video games); one of Maui's best concierge desks; activities desk; car-rental desk; business center; shopping arcade; salon; room service; in-room, spa, or oceanside massage; babysitting; same-day laundry service and dry cleaning; concierge-level rooms. *In room:* A/C, TV, dataport, minibar, fridge, coffeemaker, hair dryer, iron, safe, high-speed Internet (additional fee).

Grand Wailea Resort Hotel & Spa ⭐⭐   Here's where grand becomes grandiose. The pinnacle of Hawaii's brief fling with fantasy megaresorts, this monument to excess is extremely popular with families, incentive groups, and conventions; it's the grand prize in Hawaii vacation contests and the dream of many honeymooners. It has a Japanese restaurant decorated with real rocks hewn from the slopes of Mount Fuji; 10,000 tropical plants in the lobby; an intricate pool system with slides, waterfalls, rapids, and a water-powered elevator to take you up to the top; Hawaii's most elaborate spa; a restaurant in a man-made tide pool; a floating New England–style wedding chapel; and nothing but oceanview rooms, outfitted with every amenity you could ask for. And it's all crowned with a $30-million collection of original art, much of it created expressly for the hotel by Hawaii artists and sculptors. Though minimalists may be put off, there's no denying that the Grand Wailea is plush, professional, and pampering, with all the diversions you could imagine. Oh, and did I mention the fantastic beach out front?

All the rooms and suites are nonsmoking. All the former smoking rooms have undergone a thorough cleaning and deodorization. Smoking is limited to the private lanais outside the rooms.

3850 Wailea Alanui Dr., Wailea, HI 96753. ℂ **800/888-6100** or 808/875-1234. Fax 808/874-2442. www.grand wailea.com. 780 units. $485–$905 double; from $1,700 suite. Concierge (Na Pua) tower from $875. Resort fee $18 for "complimentary" lei greeting on arrival, welcome drink, local calls, coffee in room, use of spa, admission to scuba-diving clinics and water aerobics, art and garden tours, nightly turndown service, high-speed Internet access, self-parking, and shuttle service to Wailea area. Extra person $50 ($100 in Na Pua Tower). AE, DC, DISC, MC, V. **Amenities:** 6 restaurants; 7 bars (including a nightclub with laser-light shows and a hydraulic dance floor); 2,000-ft.-long Action Pool, featuring a swim/ride through mountains and grottoes; use of Wailea Golf Club's 3 18-hole championship golf courses, as well as the nearby Makena and Elleair golf courses; use of Wailea Tennis Center's 11 courts (3 lit for night play, and a pro shop); complete fitness center; Hawaii's largest spa, the 50,000-sq.-ft. Spa Grande, with a blend of European-, Eastern-, and Hawaiian-style techniques; Jacuzzi; watersports equipment rentals; complimentary dive and windsurf lessons; bike rentals; children's program; game room; concierge; activities desk; car-rental desk; business center; shopping arcade; salon; room service; in-room and spa massage; babysitting; same-day laundry service and dry cleaning; concierge-level rooms. *In room:* A/C, TV, dataport, kitchenette, minibar, fridge ($25 per stay fee), coffeemaker, hair dryer, iron, safe.

EXPENSIVE

Renaissance Wailea Beach Resort ⭐⭐   This is the place for visitors in search of Wailea-style luxury but in a smaller, more intimate setting. Located on 15 acres of rolling lawn and tropical gardens, the Renaissance Wailea has the air of a small boutique hotel. Perhaps it's the resort's U-shaped design, the series of small coves and beaches, or the spaciousness of the rooms—whatever the reason, you just don't feel crowded here.

Each room has a sitting area, a large lanai, and three phones. The bathrooms include such extras as double vanities (one with lighted makeup mirror) and *hapi* coats (Japanese-style cotton robes). Rooms in the Mokapu Beach Club, an exclusive two-story building just steps from a crescent-shaped beach, feature such extras as private check-in, in-room continental breakfast, and access to a private pool and beach cabanas.

3550 Wailea Alanui Dr., Wailea, HI 96753. ℂ **800/9-WAILEA** or 808/879-4900. Fax 808/891-7086. www.renaissance hotels.com. 345 units. $430–$705 double; from $1,050 suite. Extra person $40. Children 18 and under stay free in parent's room using existing bedding. Package rates available. AE, DC, DISC, MC, V. Parking $10. **Amenities:** 3 restaurants; 2 bars; 2 freshwater outdoor pools; use of Wailea Golf Club's 3 18-hole championship golf courses, as well as the nearby Makena and Elleair golf courses; use of Wailea Tennis Center's 11 courts (3 lit for night play, and a pro shop); fitness center; small spa; 2 Jacuzzis; watersports equipment rentals; children's program; concierge; activities desk; car-rental desk; business center; shopping arcade; salon; room service; massage; babysitting; laundry service; dry cleaning. *In room:* A/C, TV/VCR, dataport, fridge, coffeemaker, hair dryer, iron, safe.

Wailea Marriott, an Outrigger Resort ⭐⭐   This classic open-air, 1970s-style hotel in a tropical garden by the sea gives you a sense of what Maui was like before the big resort boom. It was the first resort built in Wailea (in 1976), and it remains the most Hawaiian of them all. Airy and comfortable, with touches of Hawaiian art throughout and a terrific aquarium that stretches forever behind the front desk, it just feels right.

My, what an inefficient way to fish.

Ring toss, good. Horseshoes, bad.

Faster! Faster! Faster!

We take care of the fiddly bits, from providing over 43,000 customer reviews of hotels, to helping you find our best fares, to giving you 24/7 customer service. So you can focus on the only thing that matters. Goofing off.

travelocity®
You'll never roam alone.™

The hotel manages to fit into its environment without overwhelming it. Eight buildings, all low-rise except for an eight-story tower, are spread along 22 gracious acres of lawns and gardens spiked by coco palms, with lots of open space and a ½ mile of oceanfront property on a point between Wailea and Ulua beaches. The vast, park-like expanses are a luxury on this now-crowded coast.

In 2000 the resort went through a $25-million renovation that expanded the entrance into an open-air courtyard with a waterfall and carp pond, transformed the south pool into a water-activities area complete with two water slides, and refurbished and upgraded the guest rooms.

Recently they have added the small Mandara Spa with a large list of treatments from relaxing massages to aroma wraps to rejuvenating facials in a very Zen atmosphere. The only critique I have is that they do not (at this time) have a shower facility, so if you aren't staying at the hotel, bring a wash cloth to wipe down with afterwards.

3700 Wailea Alanui Dr., Wailea, HI 96753. © **800/367-2960** or 808/879-1922. Fax 808/874-8331. www.marriott hawaii.com. 524 units. $355–$525 double; from $650 suite. Extra person $40. Packages available. AE, DC, DISC, MC, V. **Amenities:** 2 restaurants; 2 bars; 3 outdoor pools; use of Wailea Golf Club's 3 18-hole championship golf courses; use of Wailea Tennis Center's 11 courts (3 lit for night play, and a pro shop); fitness room; Mandara Spa; Jacuzzi; water-sports equipment rentals; children's program (plus kids-only pool and recreation center); concierge; activities desk; business center; shopping arcade; salon; room service; in-room and spa massage; babysitting; same-day laundry serv-ice and dry cleaning; coin-op washer/dryers. In room: A/C, TV, dataport, fridge, coffeemaker, hair dryer, iron, safe.

MAKENA
EXPENSIVE

Maui Prince Hotel ⭐⭐   If you're looking for a vacation in a beautiful, tranquil spot with a golden-sand beach, here's your place. But if you plan to tour Maui, you might try another hotel. The Maui Prince is at the end of the road, far, far away from any-thing else on the island, so sightseeing in other areas would require a lot of driving.

When you first see the stark-white hotel, it looks like a high-rise motel stuck in the woods—but only from the outside. Inside, you'll discover an atrium garden with a koi-filled waterfall stream, an ocean view from every room, and a simple, clutter-free decor. Rooms are small but come with private lanais with great views.

5400 Makena Alanui, Makena, HI 96753. © **800/321-6284** or 808/874-1111. Fax 808/879-8763. www.mauiprince hotel.com. 310 units. $335–$525 double; from $700 suite. Extra person $40. Packages available. AE, DC, MC, V. **Amenities:** 4 restaurants (including the excellent Prince Court, p. 154); 2 bars with local Hawaiian music nightly; 2 outdoor pools (adults' and children's); 36 holes of golf (designed by Robert Trent Jones, Jr.); 6 Plexipave tennis courts (2 lit for night play); fitness room; Jacuzzi; watersports equipment rentals; children's program; concierge; activi-ties desk; shopping arcade; salon; room service; in-room massage; babysitting; same-day laundry service and dry cleaning. In room: A/C, TV, dataport, fridge, hair dryer, iron, safe.

4 Upcountry Maui
MAKAWAO, OLINDA & HALIIMAILE

When you stay in the cooler upcountry climate of Makawao, Olinda, and Haliimaile, on the slopes of Maui's 10,000-foot Haleakala volcano, you'll be (relatively) close to Haleakala National Park. Makawao and Olinda are approximately 90 minutes from the entrance to the park at the 7,000-foot level (you still have 3,000 ft. and another 30–45 min. to get to the top). Haliimaile, which is about 10 to 15 minutes driving time from Makawao, adds additional time to your drive up to the summit. Accom-modations in Kula are the only other options that will get you closer to the summit so you can make the sunrise.

EXPENSIVE

Aloha Cottage 👶👶 *Finds*   This could be one of the most romantic spots on Maui. Hidden in the secluded rolling hills of Olinda on a 5-acre parcel of manicured, landscaped tropical foliage are two separate cottages, both designed and decorated by the hosts, Ron and Ranjana Serle. The Thai Treehouse ($245 a night) resembles an upscale Thai home with high beam, vaulted ceilings, teak floors, and a king-size cherrywood bed in the center of the room. The private deck and private soaking tub make this a very romantic lodging. As fabulous as the Thai Tree House is, the Bali Bungalow ($275) is even better. Up a private driveway through a bamboo archway, the Balinese cottage features an octagonal design with multifaceted skylights, a large marble shower built for two, hand-carved teak cabinets in the kitchen area, and Oriental carpets on the hardwood floors. Out on the private deck is a soaking tub for two. Ranjana can arrange weddings, prepare a private dinner, set up personal massages, and even organize a private yoga session for two.

1879 Olinda Rd., Makawao, HI 96765. © 888/328-3330 or 808/573-8555. Fax 808/573-2551. www.alohacottage. com. 2 cottages. $245–$275 double. 3-night minimum. MC, V. *In room:* TV/VCR/CD, kitchen, fridge, coffeemaker, hair dryer, iron, safe, private soaking tub.

MODERATE

Olinda Country Cottages & Inn 👶👶 *Finds*   This charming B&B is set on the slopes of Haleakala in the crisp, clean air of Olinda, on an 8½-acre farm dotted with protea plants and surrounded by 35,000 acres of ranch lands (with miles of great hiking trails). The 5,000-square-foot country home, outfitted with a professional eye to detail, has large windows with incredible panoramic views of all of Maui. Upstairs are two guest rooms with country furnishings, private full bathrooms, and separate entryways. Connected to the main house but with its own private entrance, the Pineapple Sweet has a full kitchen, an antiques-filled living room, and a marble-tiled full bathroom. A separate 1,000-square-foot cottage is the epitome of cozy country luxury, with a fireplace, a bedroom with queen-size bed, cushioned window seats (with great sunset views), and cathedral ceilings. The 950-square-foot Hidden Cottage (located in a truly secluded spot surrounded by protea flowers) features three decks, 8-foot French glass doors, a full kitchen, a washer/dryer, and a private tub for two on the deck.

Restaurants are a 15-minute drive away in Makawao, and beaches are another 15 minutes beyond that. Once ensconced, however, you may never want to leave this enchanting inn.

2660 Olinda Rd. (near the top of Olinda Rd., a 15-min. drive from Makawao), Makawao, HI 96768. © 800/932-3435 or 808/572-1453. Fax 808/573-5326. www.mauibnbcottages.com. 5 units. $140 double; $140 suite double; $195–$245 cottage for 2 (sleeps up to 5). Extra person $25. 2-night minimum for rooms and suite, 3-night minimum for cottages. No credit cards. *In room:* TV, kitchen (in cottages), fridge, coffeemaker, washer/dryer (cottages only).

INEXPENSIVE

If you'd like your own private cottage, consider **Peace of Maui,** 1290 Haliimaile Rd. (just outside Haliimaile town), Haliimaile, HI 96768 (© **888/475-5045** or 808/572-5045; www.peaceofmaui.com), which has a full kitchen, two bedrooms, a day bed, and a large deck. The cottage goes for $120, and children are welcome. The owners also have rooms in the main house (with shared bathroom and kitchen facilities) from $50 single and $55 for two.

Banyan Tree House 👶 *Finds*   Huge monkeypod trees (complete with swing and hammock) extend their branches over this 2½-acre property like a giant green canopy.

Where to Stay in Upcountry & East Maui

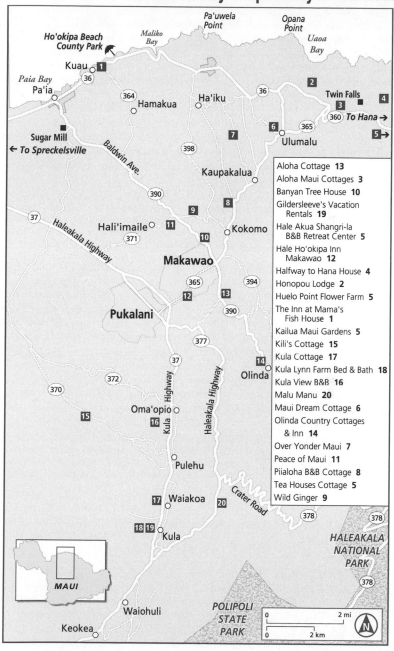

Aloha Cottage **13**
Aloha Maui Cottages **3**
Banyan Tree House **10**
Gildersleeve's Vacation
  Rentals **19**
Hale Akua Shangri-la
  B&B Retreat Center **5**
Hale Ho'okipa Inn
  Makawao **12**
Halfway to Hana House **4**
Honopou Lodge **2**
Huelo Point Flower Farm **5**
The Inn at Mama's
  Fish House **1**
Kailua Maui Gardens **5**
Kili's Cottage **15**
Kula Cottage **17**
Kula Lynn Farm Bed & Bath **18**
Kula View B&B **16**
Malu Manu **20**
Maui Dream Cottage **6**
Olinda Country Cottages
  & Inn **14**
Over Yonder Maui **7**
Peace of Maui **11**
Piialoha B&B Cottage **8**
Tea Houses Cottage **5**
Wild Ginger **9**

The restored 1920s plantation manager's house is decorated with Hawaiian furniture from the 1930s. The house can accommodate a big family or a group of friends; it has three spacious bedrooms with big, comfortable beds and three marble-tiled bathrooms. A fireplace stands at one end of the huge living room, a large lanai runs the entire length of the house, and the hardwood floors shine throughout. The four smaller guest cottages have been totally renovated and also feature hardwood floors and marble bathrooms.

New additions to this grand property include a full-size swimming pool and Jacuzzi. The quiet neighborhood and old Hawaii ambience give this place a comfortable, easygoing atmosphere. Restaurants and shops are just minutes away in Makawao, and the beach is a 15-minute drive away—but this place is so relaxing that you may find yourself wanting to do nothing more than lie in the hammock and watch the clouds float by.

3265 Baldwin Ave. (next to Veteran's Cemetery, less than a mile below Makawao), Makawao, HI 96768. © 808/572-9021. Fax 808/573-5072. www.hawaii-maurirentals.com. 1 house, 4 cottages. $85–$115 cottage for 2; $350 3-bedroom house (sleeps up to 9). Extra person $20. Children 12 and under stay for $10 in parent's room. 3-night minimum for house. No credit cards. **Amenities:** Outdoor pool; Jacuzzi; babysitting; small charge for self-serve washer/dryer. *In room:* Kitchen or kitchenette, fridge, coffeemaker.

Hale Ho'okipa Inn Makawao ⭐ *Finds* Step back in time at this 1924 plantation-style home, rescued by owner Cherie Attix in 1996 and restored to its original charm (on the State and National Historic Registers). Cherie lovingly refurbished the old wooden floors, filled the rooms with furniture from the 1920s, and hung works by local artists on the walls. The result is a charming, serene place to stay, just a 5-minute walk from the shops and restaurants of Makawao, 15 minutes from beaches, and an hour's drive from the top of Haleakala. The guest rooms have separate outside entrances and private bathrooms. The house's front and back porches are both wonderful for sipping tea and watching the sunset. The Kona Wing is a two-bedroom suite with private bathroom and use of the kitchen. Cherie recently added a separate cottage next door with one bed and bathroom, plus a sleeping loft with a half bathroom upstairs for $145 double.

32 Pakani Place, Makawao, HI 96768. © 877/572-6698 or 808/572-6698. Fax 808/573-2580. www.maui-bed-and-breakfast.com. 4 units (2 with shower only). $95–$125 double; $145–$165 suite with full kitchen. Cottage is $145 double. Rates include continental breakfast. Extra person $10. MC, V. From Haleakala Hwy., turn left on Makawao Ave., then turn right on the 5th street on the right off Makawao Ave. (Pakani Place); 2nd to the last house on the right (green house with white picket fence and water tower). *In room:* TV, hair dryer.

KULA

Lodgings in Kula are the closest options to the entrance of Haleakala National Park (about 60 min. away).

MODERATE

Malu Manu ⭐⭐ *Finds* This is one of the most romantic places to stay on Maui, with a panoramic view of the entire island from the front door. Tucked into the side of Haleakala Volcano at 4,000 feet is this old Hawaiian estate with a single-room log cabin (built as a writer's retreat in the early 1900s) and a 30-year-old family home. The writer's cabin has a full kitchen, a fireplace, and antiques galore. The two-bedroom, 2½-bathroom home also has antiques, koa walls, and beautiful eucalyptus floors. It's an ideal retreat for a romantic couple, a family, or two couples traveling together. The 7-acre property is filled with native forest, organic gardens (help yourself to lemons, avocados, and whatever else is ripe), a paddle-tennis court, and a Japanese-style out-door soaking tub. If you're a dog person, the resident golden retriever, Alohi, may come over and make your acquaintance. This is one of the closest accommodations to Haleakala; restaurants are about a 15-minute drive away.

446 Cooke Rd. (mailing address: P.O. Box 175, Kula, HI 96790). (C) 888/878-6161 or 808/878-6111. www.mauisunrise. com. 2 units. $150 double in log cabin; $185 double in 2-bedroom house. Extra person $10. 3-night minimum. MC, V. Amenities: Hot tub; paddle-tennis court; in-room massage; laundry facilities. In room: Kitchen, fridge, coffeemaker, iron.

INEXPENSIVE

In addition to the options below, also consider **Gildersleeve's Vacation Rentals,** for-merly known as Elaine's Upcountry Guest Rooms ((C) **808/878-6623;** fax 808/878-2619; papag@hawaii.rr.com). The warm and welcoming hosts rent three rooms in their spacious pole house ($70 double; 3-night minimum).

Kili's Cottage (Value (Kids If you're looking for a quiet getaway in the cool eleva-tion of Kula, this sweet cottage, situated on 2 acres, is the place. The amenities are numerous: large lanai, full kitchen, gas barbecue, washer/dryer, views, even toys for the kids. The hostess, Kili Namau'u, who is the director of a Hawaiian-language immersion school, greets each guest with royal aloha—from the flowers (picked from the garden) that fill the house to the welcome basket filled with tropical produce grown on the property.

Kula. Reservations c/o Hawaii's Best Bed & Breakfast, P.O. Box 758, Volcano, HI 96785. (C) 800/262-9912 or 808/ 985-7488. Fax 808/967-8610. www.bestbnb.com. 1 3-bedroom/2-bathroom house. $115 double. Extra person $15. 2-night minimum. No credit cards. In room: TV, kitchen, fridge, coffeemaker, washer/dryer.

Kula Cottage (Finds I can't imagine having a less-than-fantastic vacation here. Tucked away on a quiet street amid a large grove of blooming papaya and banana trees, Cecilia and Larry Gilbert's romantic honeymoon cottage is very private—it even has its own driveway and carport. The 700-square-foot cottage has a full kitchen (complete with dishwasher), and three huge closets that offer enough storage space for you to move in permanently. An outside lanai has a big gas barbecue and an umbrella-covered table and chairs. Cecilia delivers a continental breakfast daily. Groceries and a small takeout lunch counter are within walking distance. It's a 30-minute drive to the beach.

40 Puakea Place (off Lower Kula Rd.), Kula, HI 96790. (C) 808/878-2043 or 808/871-6230. Fax 808/871-9187. www.kulacottage.com. 1 cottage. $95 double. Rate includes continental breakfast. 2-night minimum. No credit cards. In room: TV, kitchen, fridge, coffeemaker, washer/dryer.

Kula Lynn Farm Bed & Bath (Kids The Coons, the same great family that runs Maui's best sailing adventure on the *Trilogy,* offer this spectacular 1,600-square-foot unit on the ground floor of a custom-built pole house. From its location on the slopes of Haleakala, the panoramic view—across Maui's central valley, with the islands of Lanai and Kahoolawe in the distance—is worth the price alone. Wall-to-wall windows and high ceilings add to the feeling of spaciousness throughout. The two bedrooms, two bathrooms, and two queen-size sofa beds in the living room make this the perfect place for a family. No expense has been spared in the European-style kitchen, with top appliances and Italian marble floors. This place should appeal to those who enjoy a quiet location and such activities as barbecuing on the lanai and watching the sun set.

P.O. Box 847, Kula, HI 96790. (C) 800/874-2666, ext. 211, or 808/878-6176. Fax 808/878-6320. captcoon@verizon. net. 1 unit. $119 double. 5-night minimum. Rate includes breakfast fixings. Extra person $20. No credit cards. In room: TV/VCR, kitchen, fridge, coffeemaker, iron.

Kula View B&B *(Finds* Hostess and gardener extraordinaire Susan Kauai has this cute private suite (with its own deck and private entrance) upstairs in her home. You are greeted on arrival by George, a big, fluffy tabby cat. The roomy studio has a huge deck with a panoramic view of Haleakala. Inside are a reading area with a comfy lounge chair and an eating area with table and chairs, toaster oven, coffeemaker, and electric teakettle. Susan serves breakfast in your suite (or will pack a picnic breakfast if you are out early) of tasty breads or muffins, fruit, juice, and tea and coffee. She has plenty of warm jackets, sweaters, and blankets you can borrow if you plan to make the trip to the top of Haleakala. Be sure to take a stroll through her magical garden.

P.O. Box 322, Kula, Hi 96790. (*C*) 808/878-6736. www.kulaview.com. 1 suite. $95 double. No credit cards. Rate includes continental breakfast. 2-night minimum. *In room:* Fridge, coffeemaker.

5 East Maui: On the Road to Hana

KUAU

MODERATE

The Inn at Mama's Fish House *★★* The fabulous location (nestled in a coconut grove on secluded Kuau Beach), duplex cottages with beautifully decorated interiors (island-style rattan furniture and works by Hawaiian artists), and extras like Weber gas barbecues, huge 27-inch TVs, and lots of beach toys make this place a gem for those seeking a centrally located vacation rental. Guests even get a discount off lunch or dinner at Mama's Fish House next door. The one-bedroom units are nestled in tropical jungle (red ginger surrounds the garden patio), while the two-bedroom units face the beach. Both have terra-cotta floors, complete kitchens (even dishwashers), sofa beds, and laundry facilities.

799 Poho Place (off the Hana Hwy. in Kuau), Paia, HI 96779. (*C*) 800/860-HULA or 808/579-9764. Fax 808/579-8594. www.mamasfishhouse.com. 9 units. $175 1-bedroom (sleeps up to 4); $475 2-bedroom (up to 6). 3-night minimum stay. AE, DC, DISC, MC, V. *In room:* A/C, TV/VCR, kitchen, fridge, coffeemaker, hair dryer, iron.

HAIKU

MODERATE

Honopou Lodge *★* *(Finds* Hidden on Maui's north shore, next door to a 750-acre ranch, is this upscale vacation retreat. The Lodge is a unique, 4,000-square-foot, architect-designed, octagonal house with native ohia posts and cedar wood. The three rooms in the house can be rented separately or you can rent the entire complex as a whole. Downstairs, two spacious octagonal studios share the deluxe, gourmet kitchen. Upstairs, a smaller studio has its own private entrance and a small kitchenette. Outside is a huge (32×16-ft.), ozone-filtered swimming pool, Jacuzzi, and satellite TV. Awe-inspiring ocean views greet you from every room, and sculptures and paintings created by the owners fill the house. Honopou Lodge is minutes from hiking trails and waterfalls.

Honopou Rd., Haiku. Reservations c/o Hawaii's Best Bed & Breakfasts, P.O. Box 758, Volcano, HI 96785. (*C*) 800/ 262-9912 or 808/962-0100. Fax 808/962-6360. www.bestbnb.com. 3 units. $125 studio double; $325 2-bedroom downstairs of house; $375 entire house (5-night minimum). Additional person $25. 3-night minimum. No credit cards. **Amenities:** Outdoor pool; Jacuzzi. *In room:* TV, kitchen (downstairs), kitchenette (upstairs), fridge, coffeemaker, hair dryer, iron.

Pilialoha B&B Cottage *★* The minute you arrive at this split-level country cottage, located on a large lot with half-century-old eucalyptus trees, you'll see owner Machiko Heyde's artistry at work. Just in front of the quaint cottage (which is great for couples but can sleep up to five) is a garden blooming with some 200 varieties of roses. You'll find more of Machiko's handiwork inside. There's a queen-size bed in the master bedroom, a twin bed in a small adjoining room, and a queen-size sofa bed in the living room. A large lanai extends from the master bedroom. There's a great movie collection for rainy days or cool country nights, and a garage. Machiko delivers breakfast daily; if you plan on an early-morning ride to the top of Haleakala, she'll make sure you go with a thermos of coffee and her homemade bread.

2512 Kaupakalua Rd. (½ mile from Kokomo intersection), Haiku, HI 96708. © 808/572-1440. Fax 808/572-4612. www.pilialoha.com. 1 cottage. $130 double. Rates include continental breakfast. Extra person $20. 3-night minimum. MC, V. **Amenities:** Complimentary use of beach paraphernalia (including snorkel equipment); complimentary use of washer/dryer. *In room:* TV, kitchenette, fridge, coffeemaker.

Wild Ginger Falls 🌟🌟 *Finds*   This cozy, romantic intimate cottage, hidden in Miliko Gulch, overlooks a stream with a waterfall, bamboo, sweet-smelling ginger, and banana trees. It's perfect for honeymooners, lovers, and fans of Hawaiiana art. The moment you step into this 400-square-foot, artistically decorated Hawaiian cottage (with additional 156-sq.-ft. screened deck), you will be delighted at the memorabilia (ukulele tile, canoe paddle, and the like) found throughout. The cottage has a full kitchen with everything you need for cooking. The comfy queen-size bed opens to the living area. The screened porch has a table, chairs, and a couch, perfect for curling up with a good book. Outside there's a barbecue, plus plenty of beach toys to borrow. Your hosts are Bob, a ceramic artist (with his creations on display throughout the cottage) and his wife, Sunny, who manages Dolphin Galleries (where she buys artwork for the cottage).

355 Kaluanui Rd., Makawao, HI 96768. ©/fax 808/573-1173. www.wildgingerfalls.com. 1 unit. $125 double. 3-night minimum. No credit cards. *In room:* TV/VCR, kitchen, fridge, coffeemaker, hair dryer, iron, washer/dryer.

INEXPENSIVE

Aloha Maui Cottages *Finds*   On 2 acres of jungle, tucked away in the Twin Falls area, is this budget-traveler accommodations. Three separate bungalows offer a back-to-nature experience. The rustic, clean, well-outfitted cabins are all landscaped to offer privacy, and offer good value for the price. The cabins range from the Mango cottage with hardwood floors, full kitchen, and big bedroom with ocean view, to the Banana Room, a small room with a kitchenette and a CD player. All rooms are stocked with coffee or tea and locally grown fruit (some comes from right outside your front door) in season. Host Ken knows all the hiking and biking trails (he will lend you his mountain bikes to go exploring) and secret waterfalls. This is the perfect place if you are on a tight budget and looking for a vacation in Maui's rainforest.

P.O. Box 790210, Paia, HI 96779. © 808/572-0298. www.alohamauicottages.com. 5 units, 2 with shared bathroom. $70–$135 double. Extra person $5. 3-night minimum. DISC, MC, V. **Amenities:** Gas barbecue. *In room:* Kitchen or kitchenette, CD player.

Maui Dream Cottages *Value*   Essentially a vacation rental, this country estate is located atop a hill overlooking the ocean. The grounds are dotted with fruit trees (bananas, papayas, and avocados, all free for the picking), and the front lawn is comfortably equipped with a double hammock, chaise longues, and table and chairs. One cottage has two bedrooms, a full kitchen, a washer/dryer, and an entertainment center. The other is basically the same but with only one bedroom (plus a sofa bed in the living room). They're both very well maintained and comfortably outfitted with furniture that's attractive but casual. The Haiku location is quiet and restful and offers the opportunity to see how real islanders live. However, you'll have to drive a good 20 to 25 minutes to restaurants in Makawao or Paia. Hookipa Beach is about a 20-minute drive, and Baldwin Beach (good swimming) is 25 minutes away.

265 W. Kuiaha Rd. (1 block from Pauwela Cafe), Haiku, HI 96708. ℭ 808/575-9079. Fax 808/575-9477. www.maui dreamcottage.com. 2 cottages (with shower only). $80 for 2. 7-night minimum. MC, V. *In room:* TV, kitchen, fridge, coffeemaker, washer/dryer.

Over Yonder Maui If you don't mind sharing a house with the host, this hidden bed-and-breakfast offers a quiet, relaxing vacation on 2 acres in Haiku. Host Nina Cahoj has the perfect eye for decorating and has created an absolutely gorgeous, comfy home. You have your own entrance into the sun room with floor-to-ceiling windows that overlook the lush tropical jungle of koa, guava, and kukui nut trees. Two rooms are available: the antiques-filled Ginger Room and the Plumeria Suite, which features a bathroom with an old Chinese sideboard converted into a sink enclosure. The entire house is decorated with wonderful antiques and one-of-a-kind art and furniture. Guests have use of the kitchen, living room, sun room, and television room. A breakfast of coffee/tea, cereal, banana bread or toast, and fruit is served every morning. Nina's two dogs, Liza and Dodger, are happy to provide canine company.

2555 Lemi Place, Haiku, HI 96708. ℭ 888/222-2466 or 808/573-5320. www.overyondermaui.com. 2 units. $90–$100 double. No credit cards. **Amenities:** TV/VCR; use of kitchen; washer/dryer.

TWIN FALLS
INEXPENSIVE
Budget travelers might consider the very affordable **Halfway to Hana House** (ℭ 808/572-1176 or 808/281-3705; www.halfwaytohana.com), an adorable studio (complete with kitchenette) nestled in the jungle, just past Twin Falls, with rates from $85 to $105 double (3-night minimum).

Also consider the off-the-beaten-path **Tea House Cottage** (ℭ 808/572-5610; www.mauiteahouse.com): You park your car and follow a fern-lined path to a secluded hideaway in the jungle, powered by alternative energy (no power poles!). Here's your chance to get away from it all while still having utilities, phone, and TV—you can even plug in your laptop. Unfortunately, the rates have crept up over the years and are now at $125 double (which I think is high for this place; perhaps owner Ann DeWeese will return to her once affordable rates).

HUELO/WAILUA
EXPENSIVE
Huelo Point Flower Farm ⊛ *(Finds* Here's a little Eden by the sea on a spectacular, remote, 300-foot sea cliff near a waterfall stream. This estate overlooking Waipio Bay has two guest cottages, a guesthouse, and a main house available for rent. The studio-size Gazebo Cottage has three glass walls that make the most of the cottage's ocean-front location, a koa-wood captain's bed, a TV, a stereo, a kitchenette, a private oceanside patio, a private hot tub, and a half bathroom with outdoor shower. The new 900-square-foot Carriage House apartment sleeps four and has glass walls facing the mountain and sea, plus a kitchen, a den, decks, and a loft bedroom. The two-bedroom main house contains an exercise room, a fireplace, a sunken Roman bath, cathedral ceilings, and other extras. On-site is a natural pool with a waterfall and an oceanfront hot tub. You're welcome to pick fruit, vegetables, and flowers from the extensive garden. Homemade scones, tree-ripened papayas, and fresh-roasted coffee start your day.

The secluded location, off the crooked road to Hana, is just a half-hour from Kahului, or about 20 minutes from Paia's shops and restaurants.

Off Hana Hwy., between mile markers 3 and 4 (P.O. Box 791808, Paia, HI 96779). ℂ 808/572-1850. www.maui flowerfarm.com. 4 units. $160 cottage double; $190 carriage house double; $350 guesthouse double; $450 main house double (sleeps 8). Extra person $20–$35. 2-night minimum for smaller houses, 5-night minimum for main house. No credit cards. **Amenities:** Outdoor pool; 3 Jacuzzis; self-serve washer/dryer. *In room:* TV, kitchenette (in cottage), kitchen (in houses), fridge, coffeemaker, hair dryer.

MODERATE

Kailua Maui Gardens *(Finds*   In the middle of nowhere lies this nearly 2-acre tropical botanical garden with four bungalows dotting the property. Just a couple of miles down the serpentine Hana Highway from Huelo, in the remote area of Kailua, is an unlikely place for accommodations (it's a 30-min. drive to the nearest beach and 1 hr. to Hana), but for those who want to get away from it all, this could be your place. The small cabanas range from one-room studios with a futon and full kitchen to compact accommodations with basic kitchenette amenities. They all face out into gorgeous gardens. In the midst of the botanical garden is a pool, with cabana and covered barbecue area, and a hot tub. The garden sits right on the Hana Highway, so ask for a unit away from the road. Unfortunately, they have a 2-night minimum. Even if you don't stay here, stop by and visit the garden—hosts Kirk and Shelley love to show people their piece of paradise.

Located between mile markers 5 and 6 on the Hana Hwy. (S.R. 1, Box 9, Haiku, HI 96708). ℂ 808/572-9726. Fax 808/572-8845. www.kailuamauigardens.com. 5 units. $125–$160 double. 2-night minimum. Extra person $10. MC, V. **Amenities:** Outdoor pool; 2 hot tubs; laundry facilities. *In room:* TV/VCR, kitchen or kitchenette, fridge, coffeemaker, CD/stereo.

INEXPENSIVE

Hale Akua Shangri-la B&B Retreat Center *(Value*   This place isn't for everyone: The hang-loose atmosphere might not be your style. Way off the beaten path, Hale Akua is a collection of eclectic buildings where, at certain times of the year, guests can choose to go "clothing optional" outdoors. The main house on the property has breathtaking ocean views and private lanais off most rooms; guests share the living room, bathroom, and kitchen (but you're not allowed to cook meat). The Cabana building, next to the 60-foot pool, is a two-story house with five separate rooms, two kitchens, and a dining area. Also on the property is a cottage with two rooms. Other on-site features include a hot tub, fountain, lily pond, hammock, sauna, and panextree maze. Yoga classes are available.

Star Rte. 1, Box 161 (off Hana Hwy., between mile markers 3 and 4), Haiku, HI 96708. ℂ 888/368-5305 or 808/ 572-9300. Fax 808/572-6666. www.haleakua.com. 18 units, some with shared bathroom. $60–$400 double. Rates include breakfast. Extra person $25 (except for the Villa). AE, DISC, MC, V. **Amenities:** Giant pool; hot tub; massage; coin-operated laundry; Internet access; use of kitchen; yoga classes.

6 At the End of the Road in East Maui: Hana

To locate the following accommodations, see the "Hana" map on p. 223.

EXPENSIVE

Hotel Hana-Maui *(✦✦✦* *(Kids*   Picture Shangri-La, Hawaiian-style: 66 acres rolling down to the sea in a remote Hawaiian village, with a wellness center, two pools, and access to one of the best beaches in Hana. This is the atmosphere, the landscape, and the culture of old Hawaii set in 21st-century accommodations. Every unit is excellent, but my favorites are the Sea Ranch Cottages (especially units 215–218 for the best views of turtles frolicking in the ocean), where individual duplex bungalows look out over the craggy shoreline to the rolling surf. You step out of the oversize, open, airy units (with floor-to-ceiling sliding doors) onto a huge lanai with views that will stay with you long after your tan has faded. These comfy units have been totally redecorated with every amenity you can think of, and you won't be nickle-and-dimed for things like coffee and water—everything they give you, from the homemade banana bread to the bottled water, is complimentary. Cathedral ceilings, a plush feather bed, a giant-size soaking tub, Hawaiian artwork, bamboo hardwood floors—this is luxury. The white-sand beach (just a 5-min. shuttle away), top-notch wellness center with some of the best massage therapists in Hawaii, and numerous activities (horseback riding, mountain biking, tennis, pitch-and-putt golf) all add up to make this one of the top resorts in the state. There's no TV in the rooms, but the Club Room has a giant-screen TV, plus a VCR and Internet access. I highly recommend this little slice of paradise.

P.O. Box 9, Hana, HI 96713. (© **800/321-HANA** or 808/248-8211. Fax 808/248-7202. www.hotelhanamaui.com. 66 units. $395–$455 Bay Cottages double; $525–$895 Sea Ranch Cottages double; $1,295 2-bedroom suite for 4; 2-bedroom Plantation Guest House from $2,500. AE, DC, DISC, MC, V. **Amenities:** Restaurant (with Hawaiian entertainment twice a week); bar (entertainment 4 times a week); in-room dining; 2 outdoor pools; complimentary use of the 3-hole practice golf courses (clubs are complimentary); complimentary tennis courts; fitness center; full-service spa; game room; concierge; activities desk; car-rental desk; business center; small shopping arcade; salon; room service; babysitting; laundry service. *In room:* Dataport, kitchenette, fridge, coffeemaker, hair dryer, iron, safe.

MODERATE

Ekena 🏵 Just one glance at the 360-degree view and you can see why hosts Robin and Gaylord gave up their careers on the mainland and moved here. This 8½-acre piece of paradise in rural Hana boasts ocean and rainforest views; the floor-to-ceiling glass doors in the spacious Hawaiian-style pole house bring the outside in. The elegant two-story home is exquisitely furnished, from the comfortable U-shaped couch that invites you to relax and take in the view to the top-of-the-line mattress on the king-size bed. The kitchen is fully equipped with every high-tech convenience you can imagine (guests have made complete holiday meals here). Only one floor (and one two-bedroom unit) is rented at any one time to ensure privacy. The grounds are impeccably groomed and dotted with tropical plants and fruit trees. Hiking trails into the rainforest start right on the property, and beaches and waterfalls are just minutes away. Robin places fresh flowers in every room and makes sure you're comfortable; after that, she's available to answer questions, but she also respects your privacy.

P.O. Box 728 (off Hana Hwy., above Hana Airport), Hana, HI 96713. (© **808/248-7047.** Fax 808/248-7853. www.ekena maui.com. 2 units. $185 for 2; $250–$350 for 4. Extra person $25. 3-night minimum. No credit cards. **Amenities:** Complimentary use of washer/dryers. *In room:* TV/DVD/VCR, kitchen, fridge, coffeemaker, iron, stereo/CD player.

Hamoa Bay Bungalow 🏵 *Finds* Down a country lane guarded by two Balinese statues stands a little bit of Indonesia in Hawaii: a carefully crafted bungalow and an Asian-inspired two-bedroom house overlooking Hamoa Bay. This enchanting retreat is just 2 miles beyond Hasegawa's general store on the way to Kipahulu. It sits on 4 verdant acres within walking distance of Hamoa Beach (which author James Michener considered one of the most beautiful in the Pacific). The 600-square-foot Balinese-style cottage is distinctly tropical, with giant elephant-bamboo furniture from Indonesia, batik prints, a king-size bed, a full kitchen, and a screened porch with hot tub and shower. Hidden from the cottage is a 1,300-square-foot home with a soaking tub and private outdoor stone shower. It offers an elephant-bamboo king-size bed in one room, a queen-size bed in another, a screened-in sleeping porch, a full kitchen, and wonderful ocean views.

P.O. Box 773, Hana, HI 96713. © 808/248-7884. Fax 808/248-7853. www.hamoabay.com. 2 units. $195 cottage (sleeps only 2); $250 house for 2; $350 house for 4. 3-night minimum. No credit cards. **Amenities:** Hot tub; complimentary use of washer/dryers. *In room:* TV/DVD/VCR, kitchen, fridge, coffeemaker, iron, stereo/CD.

Hana Hale Malamalama *(Finds)* Hana Hale Malamalama sits on a historic site with ancient fish ponds and a cave mentioned in ancient chants. Host John takes excellent care of the ponds (you're welcome to watch him feed the fish at 5pm daily) and is fiercely protective of the hidden cave ("It's not a tourist attraction, but a sacred spot"). There's access to a nearby rocky beach, which isn't good for swimming but makes a wonderful place to watch the sunset. All accommodations include fully equipped kitchens, bathrooms, bedrooms, living/dining areas, and private lanais. Next to the fish pond, the Royal Lodge, a 2600-square-foot architectural masterpiece built entirely of Philippine mahogany, has large skylights the entire length of the house and can be rented as a house or two separate units. The oceanfront Bamboo Inn contains two units (a studio and a one- or two-bedroom unit). The cottages range from the separate two-level Tree House cottage (with Jacuzzi tub for two, a Balinese bamboo bed, small kitchen/living area, and deck upstairs) to the Pond Side Bungalow (with private outdoor Jacuzzi tub and shower).

P.O. Box 374, Hana, HI 96713. © 808/248-7718. www.hanahale.com. 7 units. $135–$285 double. Extra person $15. 2-night minimum. MC, V. **Amenities:** Jacuzzi. *In room:* TV/DVD, kitchen, fridge, coffeemaker, Jacuzzi (in all but 1 unit).

Hana Kai Maui Resort Hana's only vacation condo complex, Hana Kai offers studio and one-bedroom units overlooking Hana Bay. All units have a large kitchen and private lanai. Each of the one-bedroom units has a sliding door that separates the bedroom from the living room, plus a sofa bed that sleeps two additional guests. There are no phones or TVs in the units (a pay phone is located on the property), so you can really get away from it all. Ask for a corner unit with wraparound ocean views.

1533 Uakea Rd. (P.O. Box 38), Hana, HI 96713. © 800/346-2772 or 808/248-8426. Fax 808/248-7482. www.hana kaimaui.com. 16 units. $125–$135 studio double; $145–$195 1-bedroom (sleeps up to 4). Children under 8 stay free in parent's room. AE, MC, V. *In room:* Kitchen, fridge, coffeemaker, no phone.

Hana Oceanfront *(★★)* Just across the street from Hamoa Bay, Hana's premier white-sand beach, lie these two plantation-style units, impeccably decorated in old Hawaii decor. My favorite unit is the romantic cottage, complete with a front porch where you can sit and watch the ocean; a separate bedroom (with a bamboo sleigh bed), plus a pullout sofa for extra guests; top-notch kitchen appliances; and comfy living room. The 1,000-square-foot vacation suite, located downstairs from hosts Dan and Sandi's home (but totally soundproof—you'll never hear them) has an elegant master bedroom with polished bamboo flooring, a spacious bathroom with custom hand-painted tile, and a fully appointed gourmet kitchen. Outside is a 320-square-foot lanai. The units sit on the road facing Hana's most popular beach, so there is traffic during the day. At night the traffic disappears, the stars come out, and the sound of the ocean soothes you to sleep.

P.O. Box 843, Hana, HI 96713. © 808/248-7558. Fax 808/248-8034. www.hanaoceanfrontcottages.com. 2 units. $225–$250 double. 3-night minimum. MC, V. **Amenities:** Barbecue area. *In room:* TV/VCR/DVD, full gourmet kitchen, fridge, coffeemaker, hair dryer, iron, stereo/CD.

Heavenly Hana Inn *(★★)* *(Finds)* This place on the Hana Highway, just a stone's throw from the center of Hana town, is a little bit of heaven, where no attention to detail has been spared. Each suite has a sitting room with futon and couch, polished hardwood floors, and separate bedroom with a raised platform bed (with an excellent, firm mattress). The black-marble bathrooms have huge tubs. Flowers are everywhere, ceiling fans keep the rooms cool, and the delicious gourmet breakfast—worth splurging for—is served in a setting filled with art. The grounds are done in Japanese style with a bamboo fence, tiny bridges over a meandering stream, and Japanese gardens.

P.O. Box 790, Hana, HI 96713. ©/fax 808/248-8442. www.heavenlyhanainn.com. 3 units. $200–$275 suite. Full gourmet breakfast available for $17 per person. 2-night minimum. AE, DISC, MC, V. No children under age 15 accepted. *In room:* TV, no phone.

INEXPENSIVE

Mrs. Nakamura has been renting her **Aloha Cottages** (© **808/248-8420**) since the 1970s. Located in residential areas near Hana Bay, these five budget rentals are simply but adequately furnished, varying in size from a roomy studio with kitchenette to a three-bedroom, two-bathroom unit. They're all fully equipped, clean, and fairly well kept. Rates run from $65 to $95 double. Not all units have TVs, and none have phones, but Mrs. N. is happy to take messages.

Baby Pigs Crossing Bed & Breakfast 😊 *Finds* If you're looking for a quiet, romantic little cottage, nestled away from it all in old Hawaii but close enough to Hana to drive in for dinner, this is your place. International artist Arabella Gail Ark (formerly known as Gail Bakutis) has created a lovely retreat on her 1-acre parcel of land, which is landscaped in a "fragrance" garden with Hawaii's best sweet-smelling plants carefully planted throughout the property. The separate guesthouse, with an ocean view from the lanai, is professionally decorated with comfort in mind, from the very cozy rattan furniture to the king-size sofa bed. There's a separate bedroom with a queen-size bed and a small but utilitarian kitchenette. The unique bathroom features a glass ceiling and walls (with discreet privacy curtains) and opens out to a garden area. Even if you are not staying here, stop by and see the Ark Ceramics Gallery (daily 11am–4pm).

P.O. Box 667, Hana, HI 96713. © **808/248-8890**. Fax 808/248-4865. www.mauibandb.com. 1 unit. $185–$225 double. 2 nights minimum. AE, MC, V. **Amenities:** Barbecue. *In room:* TV/VCR, kitchenette (with rice cooker, blender), fridge, coffeemaker.

Hana's Tradewinds Cottage 😊 *Value* Nestled among the ginger and heliconias on a 5-acre flower farm are two separate cottages, each with full kitchen, carport, barbecue, private hot tub, TV, ceiling fans, and sofa bed. The studio cottage sleeps up to four; a bamboo shoji blind separates the sleeping area (with queen-size bed) from the sofa bed in the living room. The Tradewinds cottage has two bedrooms (with a queen-size bed in one room and two twins in the other), one bathroom (shower only), and a huge front porch. The atmosphere is quiet and relaxing, and hostess Rebecca Buckley, who has been in business for a decade, welcomes families (she has two children, a cat, and a very sweet golden retriever). You can use the laundry facilities at no extra charge.

135 Alalele Place (the airport road), P.O. Box 385, Hana, HI 96713. © **800/327-8097** or 808/248-8980. Fax 808/ 248-7735. www.hanamaui.net. 2 cottages. $120 studio double; $145 2-bedroom double. Extra person $10. 2-night minimum. AE, DISC, MC, V. *In room:* TV, kitchen, fridge, coffeemaker, no phone.

Joe's Place *Value* This is as close to a hostel as you can get in Hana. Joe's is a large rambling house located just spitting distance from Hana Bay. Seven spartan but immaculately clean bedrooms share showers and bathroom; one has private facilities. All the guests are welcome to use the large living room with TV and adjoining communal kitchen (free coffee available all day). Other amenities include a rec room, barbecue, and owner Ed Hill himself. He'll tell you the long story about the name if you ask and can also talk about what to do and see in Hana all day if you let him.

4870 Ua'kea Rd. (Reservations: P.O. Box 746), Hana, HI 96713. ℂ **808/248-7033**. www.joesrentals.com. 8 units, 7 with shared bathroom. $45 double with shared bathroom; $55 double with private bathroom. Extra person $10. MC. V.

Kulani's Hideaway in Hana, Maui 🍀 (Value

On the road to Waianapanapa State Park is one of Hana's best deals—two one-bedroom units, each with pullout sofa beds in the living room, full kitchen, cable TV (a plus in Hana), and washer/dryer, within walking distance of a fabulous black-sand beach. Outside is a large lanai for watching the clouds go by, with a barbecue area and picnic table in the yard. Book early.

P.O. Box 483, Hana, HI 96713. ℂ/fax **808/248-8234** or 808/248-4815. kulanis@maui.net. 2 units. $80 double. Extra person $15. **Amenities:** Complimentary coffee. *In room:* TV, kitchen, fridge, coffeemaker, washer/dryer, no phone.

Waianapanapa State Park Cabins (Value

These 12 rustic cabins are the best lodging deal on Maui. Everyone knows it too—so make your reservations early (up to 6 months in advance). The cabins are warm and dry and come complete with kitchen, living room, bedroom, and bathroom with hot shower; furnishings include bedding, linen, towels, dishes, and very basic cooking and eating utensils. Don't expect luxury—this is a step above camping, albeit in a beautiful tropical jungle setting. The key attraction at this 120-acre state beach park is the unusual horseshoe-shaped black-sand beach on Pailoa Bay, popular for shore fishing, snorkeling, and swimming. There's a caretaker on-site, along with restrooms, showers, picnic tables, shoreline hiking trails, and historic sites. But bring mosquito protection—this *is* the jungle, after all.

Off Hana Hwy., c/o State Parks Division, 54 S. High St., Room 101, Wailuku, HI 96793. ℂ **808/984-8109**. 12 cabins. $45 for 4 (sleeps up to 6). Extra person $5. 5-night maximum. No credit cards. *In room:* Kitchen, fridge, coffeemaker, no phone.

6

Where to Dine

With soaring visitor statistics and a glamorous image, the Valley Isle is fertile ground for Hawaii's famous enterprising chefs (like Roy Yamaguchi from Roy's; Gerard Reversade of Gerard's; James McDonald of I'o and Pacific'o; Peter Merriman of Hula Grill; Mark Ellman of Maui Taco and Penne Pasta Cafe; D. K. Kodoma of Sansei Seafood and now, Vino; and Beverly Gannon of Haliimaile General Store and Joe's Bar and Grill), as well as an international name or two (Wolfgang Puck of Spago). Plus a few newcomers are cooking up a storm and getting a well-deserved following (Jennifer Nguyen of A Saigon Cafe, Tom Lelli of Mañana Garage, Dana Pastula of Café O'Lei restaurants, and Don Ritchey of Moana Bakery and Café). Dining on Maui has become a culinary treat able to hold its own against most major metropolitan areas.

In this dizzying scenario, some things haven't changed: You can still dine well at Lahaina's open-air waterfront watering holes, where the view counts for 50% of the experience. There are still budget eateries, but not many; Maui's old-fashioned, multigenerational mom-and-pop diners are disappearing, eclipsed by the flashy newcomers, or clinging to the edge of existence in the older neighborhoods of central Maui, such as lovable Wailuku. Although you'll have to work harder to find them in the resort areas, you won't have to go far to find creative cuisine, pleasing style, and stellar dining experiences.

In the listings below, reservations are not necessary unless otherwise noted.

1 Central Maui

KAHULUI
MODERATE
Mañana Garage ★★ (Finds LATIN AMERICAN Chef Tom Lelli, formerly of Haliimaile General Store, is serving up some incomparable fare at this central Maui hot spot. The industrial motif features table bases like hubcaps, a vertical garage door as a divider for private parties, blown-glass chandeliers, and gleaming chrome and cobalt walls with orange accents. The menu is brilliantly conceived and executed. Fried green tomatoes are done just right and served with slivered red onions. Three different kinds of ceviche perfectly balance flavors and textures: lime, cilantro, chile, coconut, and fresh fish. They even have barbecued ribs. Mañana Garage has introduced exciting new flavors to Maui's dining scene—if you are on this side of the island, don't miss this incredible experience.

33 Lono Ave., Kahului. ℂ 808/873-0220. Reservations recommended. Lunch main courses $7–$13; dinner main courses $16–$29. AE, DISC, MC, V. Mon 11am–9pm; Wed–Sat 11am–10:30pm; Sun 5–9pm.

Marco's Grill & Deli ITALIAN Located in the thick of central Maui, where the roads to upcountry, west, and South Maui converge, Marco's is popular among area residents for its homemade Italian fare and friendly informality. Everything—from the meatballs, sausages, and burgers to the sauces, salad dressings, and raviolis—is made in-house. The 35 different choices of hot and cold sandwiches and entrees are served all day, and they include vodka rigatoni with imported prosciutto; *pasta e fagioli* (a house specialty: smoked ham hock simmered for hours in tomato sauce, with red and white beans); and simple pasta with marinara sauce. This is one of those comfortable neighborhood fixtures favored by all generations. The antipasto salad, vegetarian lasagna, and roasted peppers are taste treats, but the meatballs and Italian sausage are famous in central Maui. They also have a full bar.

Dairy Center, 395 Dairy Rd., Kahului. ℂ 808/877-4446. Main courses $11–$27. AE, DC, DISC, MC, V. Daily 7:30am–10pm.

INEXPENSIVE

The **Queen Kaahumanu Center,** the structure that looks like a white *Star Wars* umbrella in the center of Kahului, at 275 Kaahumanu Ave. (5 min. from Kahului Airport on Hwy. 32), has a very popular food court. **Edo Japan** teppanyaki is a real find, its flat Benihana-like grill dispensing marvelous, flavorful mounds of grilled fresh vegetables and chicken teriyaki for $5.70. **Maui Mixed Plate** dishes out "local style" cuisine of meat with rice and macaroni salad in the $4.45-to-$7 range. **Yummy Korean B-B-Q** offers the assertive flavors of Korea ranging from $4.75 to $7.50; **Panda Express** serves tasty Chinese food; and **Sushi Go** is a great place for fast sushi. Outside of the food court but still in the shopping center are **The Coffee Store** (p. 151); **Ruby's,** dishing out hamburgers, fries, and shakes; and **Starbucks.** There's also a branch of **Maui Tacos** (p. 146). When you leave Kaahumanu Center, take a moment to gaze at the West Maui Mountains to your left from the parking lot.

Down to Earth *Value* ORGANIC HEALTH FOOD If you are looking for a healthy alternative to fast foods, here's your place. Healthful organic ingredients, 90% vegan, appear in scrumptious salads, lasagna, chili, curries, and dozens of tasty dishes, presented at hot and cold serve-yourself stations. Stools line the counters in the simple dining area, where a few tables are available for those who don't want takeout. The food is great: millet cakes, mock tofu chicken, curried tofu, and Greek salad, everything organic and tasty, with herb-tamari marinades and pleasing condiments such as currants or raisins, apples, and cashews. (The fabulous tofu curry has apples, raw cashews, and raisins.) The food is sold by the pound, but you can buy a hearty, wholesome plate for $7. Vitamin supplements, health-food products, fresh produce, and cosmetics fill the rest of the store.

305 Dairy Rd., Kahului. ℂ 808/877-2661. Self-serve hot buffet and salad bar; food sold by the pound. Average $6–$8 for a plate. AE, MC, V. Mon–Sat 7am–9pm; Sun 8am–8pm.

Ichiban *Finds* JAPANESE/SUSHI What a find: an informal neighborhood restaurant that serves inexpensive, home-cooked Japanese food *and* good sushi at realistic prices. Local residents consider Ichiban a staple for breakfast, lunch, or dinner and a haven of comforts: egg-white omelets; great saimin; combination plates of teriyaki chicken, teriyaki meat, *tonkatsu* (pork cutlet), rice, and pickled cabbage; chicken yakitori; and sushi—everything from unagi and scallop to California roll. The sushi items may not be cheap, but like the specials, such as steamed *opakapaka*, they're a good value. I love the tempura, miso soup, and spicy ahi hand roll.

Kahului Shopping Center, 47 Kaahumanu Ave., Kahului. ℂ 808/871-6977. Main courses $4.50–$5.25 breakfast, $5.95–$9.50 lunch (combination plates $8), $4.95–$28 dinner (combination dinner $12, dinner specials from $8.95).

> ### *Moments* Roselani: Maui's Best Ice Cream
>
> For the culinary experience of your trip to Maui, try **Roselani Ice Cream,** Maui's only made-from-scratch, old-fashioned ice cream. In fact, be sure to try it early in your trip so you can eat your way through this little bit of heaven at restaurants and scooping parlors, or get your own stash at grocery stores. There are more than 40 different flavors, divided into two different brands under the Roselani label: the Premium Parlour Flavors (ranging from the traditional vanilla to the unique black cherry, cappuccino chip, fresh-brewed coffee, and choco-cookie crunch) and Tropics (with delicious varieties like the best-selling haupia, made from coconut and macadamia nut, or the popular chocolate macadamia nut, Kona mud pie, mango and cream, coconut pineapple, and luau fudge pie). Each rich, creamy flavor contains 12% to 16% butter fat.
>
> For a list of hotels, restaurants, parlors, and grocery stores carrying Rose-lani, either call (808/244-7951 or check online at www.roselani.com.

AE, DC, MC, V. Mon–Fri 7am–2pm; Sat 10:30am–2pm; Mon–Sat 5–9pm. Closed 2 weeks around Christmas and New Year's.

Restaurant Matsu JAPANESE/LOCAL   Customers have come from Hana (more than 50 miles away) just for Matsu's California rolls, while regulars line up for the cold saimin (julienned cucumber, egg, Chinese-style sweet pork, and red ginger on noodles) and for the bento plates, various assemblages of chicken, teriyaki beef, fish, and rice. The nigiri sushi items are popular, especially among the don't-dally lunch crowd. The katsu pork and chicken, breaded and deep-fried, are other specialties of this casual Formica-style diner. I love the tempura udon and the saimin, steaming mounds of wide and fine noodles swimming in homemade broths and topped with condiments. The daily specials are a changing lineup of home-cooked classics: oxtail soup, roast pork with gravy, teriyaki ahi, miso butterfish, and breaded mahimahi.

Maui Mall, 161 Alamaha St., Kahului. (808/871-0822. Most items less than $6. No credit cards. Mon–Tues and Sat 10am–3pm; Wed–Fri 10am–8pm.

WAILUKU
MODERATE
Class Act 🎔 GLOBAL   Part of a program run by the distinguished Food Service Department of Maui Community College (soon to be housed in a new state-of-the-art, $15-million culinary facility), this restaurant has a following. Student chefs show their stuff with a flourish in their "classroom," where they pull out all the stops. Linen, china, servers in ties and white shirts, and a four-course lunch make this a unique value. The appetizer, soup, salad, and dessert are set, but you can choose between the regular entrees and a heart-healthy main course prepared in the culinary tradition of the week. The menu roams the globe with highlights of Italy, Mexico, Maui, Napa Valley, France, New Orleans, and other locales. The filet mignon of French week is popular, as are the New Orleans gumbo and Cajun shrimp, the sesame-crusted mahimahi on taro-leaf pasta, the polenta flan with eggplant, and the bean- and green-chile chilaquile.

Tea and soft drinks are offered—and they can get pretty fancy, with fresh fruit and spritzers—but otherwise it's BYOB.

Maui Community College, 310 Kaahumanu Ave., Wailuku. © **808/984-3480.** www.hawaii.edu/maui/mca. Reservations recommended. 4-course lunch $25. Menu and cuisine type change weekly. MC, V. Wed and Fri 11am–12:30pm. Closed May–Aug for summer vacation.

A Saigon Cafe *(Finds)* VIETNAMESE   Jennifer Nguyen has stuck to her guns and steadfastly refused to erect a sign, but diners find their way here anyway. That's how good the food is. Fans drive from all over the island for her crisped, spiced Dungeness crab, her steamed *opakapaka* with ginger and garlic, and her wok-cooked Vietnamese specials, tangy with spices, herbs, and lemon grass. There are a dozen different soups, cold and hot noodles (including the popular beef noodle soup called *pho*), and chicken and shrimp cooked in a clay pot. You can create your own Vietnamese "burritos" from a platter of tofu, noodles, and vegetables that you wrap in rice paper and dip in garlic sauce. Among my favorites are the shrimp lemon grass, savory and refreshing, and the tofu curry, swimming in herbs and vegetables straight from the garden. The Nhung Dam—a hearty spread of basil, cucumbers, mint, romaine, bean sprouts, pickled carrots, turnips, and vermicelli, wrapped in rice paper and dipped in a legendary sauce—is cooked at your table.

1792 Main St., Wailuku. © **808/243-9560.** Main courses $6.50–$17. DC, MC, V. Mon–Sat 10am–9:30pm; Sun 10am–8:30pm. Heading into Wailuku from Kahului, go over the bridge and take the 1st right onto Central Ave., then the 1st right on Nani St. At the next stop sign, look for the building with the neon sign that says OPEN.

INEXPENSIVE

AK's Café *(Value)* HEALTHY/PLATE LUNCHES   Chef Elaine Rothermel has a winner with this tiny cafe in the industrial district of Wailuku. It may be slightly off the tourist path, but it is well worth the effort to find this delicious eatery, with creative cuisine coming out of the kitchen—most dishes are healthy, and a few dishes are for those who just want to enjoy good food (forget about the calories). Prices are so eye-poppingly cheap, you might find yourself wandering back here during your vacation. Lunches feature everything from grilled chicken, garlic-crusted ono, and eggplant Parmesan to hamburger steak, beef stew, and spaghetti with meat balls. Dinner shines with blackened ona with mango-basil sauce, tofu napoleon with ginger pesto, crab cakes with papaya beurre blanc, grilled chicken, barbecued baby back ribs, and, of course, the special of the day.

1237 Lower Main St., Wailuku. © **808/244-8774.** www.akscafe.com. Plate lunches $6.75–$7.40; dinners $11–$13. MC, V. Mon–Sat 10:30am–2pm and 4:30–8:30pm.

Main Street Bistro *(Value)* AMERICAN   Formerly Who's the Boss restaurant and before that Iao Café, this popular eatery, located on the main street of Wailuku, is now owned by Chef Tom Selman, well known in culinary circles on Maui. He was formerly the *chef du cuisine* at David Paul's Lahaina Grill and also was corporate chef for the Sansei/Vino restaurants. As we went to press, the restaurant was only open for lunch, but Selman was talking about possibly creating a "pau hana pupu" menu (after-work appetizers) sometime in the future. Chef Selman calls his food "refined comfort food," with signature menu items that include onion rings with house-made smoky ketchup, roasted Chinese chicken salad (with won tons), blackened-chicken-and-shrimp pasta salad (with a creamy avocado ranch dressing), slow-cooked baby back ribs (with poha-honey-mustard glaze), and Mother's Roast Beef Sandwich (served open-faced on a French roll). The chef will happily customize any menu item for people who prefer low-calorie, low-fat, or low-carbohydrate options. Daily specials range from grilled steak to roasted eggplant terrine.

2051 Main St., Wailuku. ℭ **808/244-6816.** Entrees $9–$11; daily lunch specials $6.95–$15. No credit cards. Mon–Fri 10:30am–2:30pm.

Maui Bake Shop BAKERY/DELI   Sleepy Vineyard Street has seen many a mom-and-pop business come and go, but Maui Bake Shop is here to stay. Maui native Claire Fujii-Krall and her husband, baker José Krall (who was trained in the south of France), are turning out buttery brioches, healthful nine-grain and two-tone rye breads, focaccia, strudels, sumptuous fresh-fruit gâteaux, puff pastries, and dozens of other baked goods and confections. The breads are baked in one of Maui's oldest brick ovens, installed in 1935; a high-tech European diesel oven handles the rest. The front window displays more than 100 bakery and deli items, among them salads, a popular eggplant marinara focaccia, homemade quiches, and an inexpensive calzone filled with chicken, pesto, mushroom, and cheese. Homemade soups (clam chowder, minestrone, cream of asparagus) team up nicely with sandwiches on freshly baked bread. Save room for the Ultimate Dessert: white-chocolate macadamia-nut cheesecake.

2092 Vineyard St. (at N. Church St.), Wailuku. ℭ **808/242-0064.** Most items under $5. AE, MC, V. Mon–Fri 6am–3pm; Sat 7am–1pm.

Sam Sato's NOODLES/PLATE LUNCHES   Sam Sato's is a Maui institution, not only for its noodles (saimin, dry noodles, chow fun), but also its flaky baked *manju* (a pastry), filled with sweetened lima beans or adzuki beans. Sam opened his family eatery in 1933, and his daughter, Lynne Toma, makes the broth from scratch. The saimin and the dry noodles, with broth that comes in a separate bowl, are big sellers. One regular comes to the counter, with its wooden stools and homemade salt and pepper shakers, for his usual: two barbecued meat sticks, two scoops of rice, and three macaroni salads. The peach, apple, coconut, and pineapple turnovers fly out the door, as do takeout noodles. *Tip:* If you want them to hold the MSG, be sure to make your request early.

Millyard, 1750 Wili Pa Loop, Wailuku. ℭ **808/244-7124.** Plate lunches $5.75–$6.75. No credit cards. Mon–Sat 7am–2pm.

2 West Maui

LAHAINA

There's a **Maui Tacos** (p. 146) in Lahaina Square (ℭ **808/661-8883**). Maui's branch of the **Hard Rock Cafe** is in Lahaina at 900 Front St. (ℭ **808/667-7400**).

VERY EXPENSIVE

David Paul's Lahaina Grill 🍴 *Kids* NEW AMERICAN   Even after David Paul Johnson's departure, this Lahaina hot spot has maintained its popularity. It's still filled with chic, tanned diners in stylish aloha shirts, and there's still attitude aplenty at the entrance. The signature items remain: tequila shrimp and firecracker rice, Kona coffee–roasted rack of lamb, Maui onion–crusted seared ahi, and Kalua duck quesadilla. A special custom-designed chef's table can be arranged with 72-hour notice for larger parties. The ambience—black-and-white tile floors, pressed tin ceilings, eclectic 1890s decor—is striking, and the bar, even without an ocean view, is the busiest spot in Lahaina. The kids' menu includes spaghetti, chicken fingers, mahimahi, and more for $12.

127 Lahainaluna Rd. ℭ **808/667-5117.** Reservations required. Main courses $29–$43. AE, DC, DISC, MC, V. Daily 5:30–10pm. Bar daily 5:30pm–midnight.

Where to Dine in Lahaina & Kaanapali

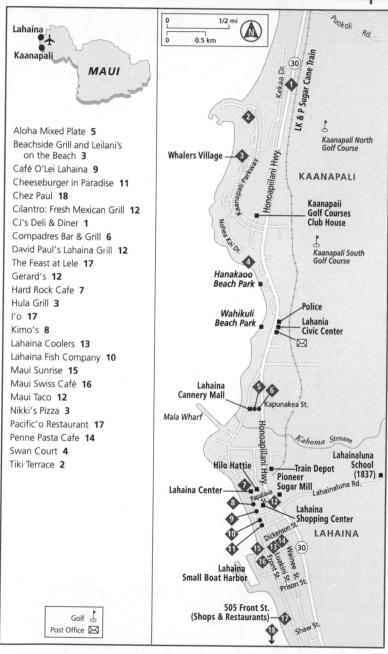

Aloha Mixed Plate **5**
Beachside Grill and Leilani's on the Beach **3**
Café O'Lei Lahaina **9**
Cheeseburger in Paradise **11**
Chez Paul **18**
Cilantro: Fresh Mexican Grill **12**
CJ's Deli & Diner **1**
Compadres Bar & Grill **6**
David Paul's Lahaina Grill **12**
The Feast at Lele **17**
Gerard's **12**
Hard Rock Cafe **7**
Hula Grill **3**
I'o **17**
Kimo's **8**
Lahaina Coolers **13**
Lahaina Fish Company **10**
Maui Sunrise **15**
Maui Swiss Café **16**
Maui Taco **12**
Nikki's Pizza **3**
Pacific'o Restaurant **17**
Penne Pasta Cafe **14**
Swan Court **4**
Tiki Terrace **2**

Lahaina
Kaanapali
MAUI

0   1/2 mi
0   0.5 km

Puokoli Rd.
Kekaa Dr.
LK & P Sugar Cane Train
Honoapiilani Hwy.
Kaanapali Parkway
Nohea Kai Dr.
Kaanapali North Golf Course
KAANAPALI
Kaanapaii Golf Courses Club House
Kaanapali South Golf Course
Whalers Village
Hanakaoo Beach Park
Wahikuli Beach Park
Police
Lahania Civic Center
Lahaina Cannery Mall
Kapunakea St.
Mala Wharf
Kahoma Stream
Lahainaluna School (1837)
Hilo Hattie
Train Depot
Pioneer Sugar Mill
Lahainaluna Rd.
Lahaina Center
Papalaua St.
Lahaina Shopping Center
LAHAINA
Dickenson St.
Wainee St.
Luakini St.
Front St.
Prison St.
Lahaina Small Boat Harbor
505 Front St. (Shops & Restaurants)
Shaw St.

Golf
Post Office

The Feast at Lele ⭐⭐ POLYNESIAN   The owners of Old Lahaina Luau (see the section "West Maui: Lahaina, Kaanapali, Kapalua," in chapter 10), have teamed up with chef James McDonald's culinary prowess (I'o and Pacific'o), placed it in a perfect outdoor oceanfront setting, and added the exquisite dancers of the Old Lahaina Luau. The result: a culinary and cultural experience that sizzles. As if the sunset weren't heady enough, dances from Hawaii, Tonga, Tahiti, and Samoa are presented, up close and personal, in full costumed splendor. Chanting, singing, drumming, dancing, the swish of ti-leaf skirts, the scent of plumeria—it's a full adventure, even for the most jaded luau aficionado. Guests sit at white-clothed, candlelit tables set on the sand (unlike the luau, where seating is en masse) and dine on entrees from each island: Kalua pig, tasty steamed moi, and savory pohole ferns and hearts of palm from Hawaii; lobster-ogo (seaweed) salad and grilled steak from Tonga; steamed chicken and taro leaf in coconut milk from Tahiti; and grilled fish in banana leaf from Samoa. Particularly mesmerizing is the evening's opening: A softly lit canoe carries three people ashore to the sound of conch shells.

505 Front St. ℂ 886/244-5353 or 808/667-5353. www.feastatlele.com. Reservations a must. Set 5-course menu $99 for adults, $69 for children 2–12; gratuity not included. AE, MC, V. Apr 1–Sept 30 daily 6–9pm; Oct 1–Mar 31 daily 5:30–8:30pm.

EXPENSIVE

Chez Paul ⭐⭐ *Finds* FRENCH   Chez Paul is located in the middle of nowhere, in Olowalu Village (a blip on the highway—if you blink you'll miss it). But it's worth the drive to this classic French restaurant, now that chef Patrick Callarec (formerly of the Ritz-Carlton's Anuenue Room) has taken over the cooking. Look forward to such delights as wild-mushroom-and-brie pastry in an aged port-wine sauce, just to get started. Or choose their signature dish of crispy duck with local fruits or fresh island fish in a champagne-and-cream sauce. Don't miss the pineapple-and-vanilla crème brûlée, served in a pineapple shell. The dress here is Maui casual, which means anything short of tank tops and shorts.

Olowalu Village, Honoapiilani Hwy., Olowalu. ℂ 808/661-3843. Reservations recommended. Main courses $28–$45. DISC, MC, V. Daily 6–8:30pm.

Gerard's ⭐⭐⭐ *Finds* FRENCH   The charm of Gerard's—soft lighting, Edith Piaf on the sound system, excellent service—is matched by a menu of uncompromising standards. After more than 2 decades in Lahaina, Gerard Reversade never runs out of creative offerings yet stays true to his French roots. A frequent winner of the *Wine Spectator* Award of Excellence, Gerard's offers roasted *opakapaka* with star anise, fennel fondue, and hints of orange and ginger, a stellar entree on a menu of winners. The Kona lobster ragout with pasta and morels promises ecstasy, and the spinach salad with scallops is among the finest I've tasted. Gerard's has an excellent appetizer menu, with shiitake and oyster mushrooms in puff pastry, fresh ahi and smoked salmon carpaccio, and a very rich, highly touted escargot ragout with burgundy butter and garlic cream.

In the Plantation Inn, 174 Lahainaluna Rd. ℂ 808/661-8939. www.gerardsmaui.com. Reservations recommended. Main courses $30–$39. AE, DC, DISC, MC, V. Daily 6–9pm.

I'o ⭐ PACIFIC RIM   I'o is a fantasy of sleek curves and etched glass, co-owned by chef James McDonald. He offers an impressive selection of appetizers (his strong suit) and some lavish Asian-Polynesian interpretations of seafood, such as stir-fried lobster with mango-Thai curry sauce. Unless you're sold on a particular entree, my advice is to go heavy on the superb appetizers, especially the silken purse, a brilliant concoction of tricolored pot stickers stuffed with roasted peppers, mushrooms, spinach, macadamia nuts, and silken tofu. Foie gras lovers take heed: The foie gras fish is topped with foie gras truffle butter over a vegetable salad. Chef McDonald also owns Pacific'o, the restaurant next door, and is the chef for the Feast at Lele, which is on the ocean side of I'o.

505 Front St. (© 808/661-8422. www.iomaui.com. Reservations recommended. Main courses $23–$59. AE, DC, MC, V. Daily 5:30–10pm.

Pacific'o Restaurant ⊀ PACIFIC RIM/CONTEMPORARY PACIFIC   You can't get any closer to the ocean than the tables here, which are literally on the beach. With good food complementing this sensational setting, foodies and aesthetes have much to enjoy. The split-level dining starts near the entrance, with a long bar (where you can also order lunch or dinner) and a few tables along the railing. Steps lead down to the outdoor tables, where the award-winning seafood dishes come to you with the backdrop of Lanai across the channel. The prawn-and-basil won tons, fresh fish over wilted arugula and bean sprouts, and ahi and ono tempura with miso and lime-basil sauce are among Pacific'o's memorable offerings. The vegetarian special, a marinated, roasted tofu steak crowned with quinoa, Maui onions, red lentils, and a heavenly dose of shiitake mushrooms, is a longtime favorite. If you like seafood, sunsets, and touches of India and Indonesia in your fresh-from-the-sea dining choices, you should be happy here.

505 Front St. (© 808/667-4341. www.pacificomaui.com. Reservations recommended. Main courses $11–$14 lunch, $26–$32 dinner. AE, DC, MC, V. Daily 11am–4pm and 5:30–10pm.

MODERATE

Café O'Lei Lahaina ⊀⊀ (Value) AMERICAN   Just over 10 years ago, restaurateurs Dana and Michael Pastula opened their first Café O'Lei in Makawao (Dana has managed such premier restaurants as Hulo'poe Court and Ihilani in Manele Bay Resort on Lanai and Pacific Grill at Four Seasons Maui, and Michael has been a chef for more than 25 years, including stints at the Swan Court in the Hyatt Regency Maui and Wailea Maui Marriott). The tiny, hidden eatery was packed from day one. The duo has brought their unique blend of island-fresh ingredients and zippy preparations to Lahaina (and also to Maalaea, Iao Valley, and Outrigger Napili Shores). The location could not be better: alfresco dining on upper and lower decks, both with an unobstructed 180-degree view of the ocean and the island of Lanai in the distance. Despite the fact that this is Front Street, Lahaina, the Pastulas still have great food and

---

(Finds **The Ultimate Cookies**

Looking for the ultimate taste treat to take to the folks back home? Try mouthwatering, delicious **Broke da Mouth Cookies,** 190 Alamaha St., Kahului (© 808/ 873-9255). They're open weekdays from 6am to 7pm and on Saturday from 7am to 5pm (get there early before locals buy everything up). These terrific cookies ($3.10 a bag) range from chocolate mac-nut, oatmeal raisin, and shortbread to almond, peanut butter, and coconut crunch. While you are there take a look at the other goodies (a chocolate-haupia pie to die for and a lilikoi cake that will make your taste buds stand up and applaud). *Warning:* These cookies are so good, you may eat half of your take-home gifts before you get home.

reasonable prices; the plate-lunch special is only $6.95. Because the view is so roman-tic, I recommend that you go here for dinner before the sun sets to take in that ocean panorama as you dine on seared ahi, sautéed mahi, macadamia-nut roast duckling, Thai coconut lobster, jumbo shrimp, or calamari.

839 Front St. Ⓒ **808/661-9491.** Reservations recommended. Main courses lunch $6.50–$11, dinner $14–$23. AE, DISC, MC, V. Daily 10:30am–9:30pm.

Compadres Bar & Grill MEXICAN   Despite its concrete floor and high industrial ceilings, Compadres exudes good cheer. And that cheer has burgeoned lately with a new open-air seating area and a takeout taqueria window for diners on the run. The food is classic Tex-Mex, beginning with huevos rancheros, egg burritos, hot cakes, and omelets (the Acapulco is heroic) for breakfast and progressing to enchiladas and appe-tizers for the margarita-happy crowd. Stay spare (vegetable enchilada in fresh spinach tortilla) or get hefty (Texas T-bone and enchiladas). This is a carefree place with a large capacity for merrymaking. Don't miss Taco Tuesdays, from 4 to 8pm, where margar-itas are just $3.

Lahaina Cannery Mall, 1221 Honoapiilani Hwy. Ⓒ **808/661-7189.** Main courses $10–$23. AE, DC, DISC, MC, V. Daily 8am–10pm.

Kimo's STEAK/SEAFOOD   Kimo's has a loyal following that keeps it from falling into the faceless morass of waterfront restaurants serving surf-and-turf with great sun-set views. It's a formula restaurant (sibling to Leilani's and Hula Grill) that works not only because of its oceanfront patio and upstairs dining room but also because, for the price, there are some satisfying choices. It's always crowded, buzzing with people on a deck offering views of Molokai, Lanai, and Kahoolawe. Burgers and sandwiches are affordable and consistent, and the fresh catch in garlic-lemon and a sweet-basil glaze is a top seller. The waistline-defying hula pie—macadamia-nut ice cream in a choco-late-wafer crust with fudge and whipped cream—originated here.

845 Front St. Ⓒ **808/661-4811.** www.kimosmaui.com. Reservations recommended for dinner. Main courses $8–$12 lunch, $17–$26 dinner. AE, DC, DISC, MC, V. Daily 11am–3:30pm and 5–10:30pm. Bar open 11am–1:30am.

Lahaina Fish Company SEAFOOD   This restaurant's open-air dining room is lit-erally over the water, with flickering torches after sunset and an affordable menu that covers the seafood-pasta basics. Head to an oceanside table and order a cheeseburger, chicken burger, fish burger, generous basket of peel-and-eat shrimp, or sashimi—lingering is highly recommended. The light lunch/grill menu offers appetizers (sashimi, seared ahi, spring rolls, and pot stickers), salads, and soups. The restaurant has spiffed up its dinner selections to include hand-carved steaks, several pasta choices, and local fare such as stir-fry dishes, teriyaki chicken, and luau-style ribs. The specialty, though, remains the fresh seafood: Four types of fresh fish are offered nightly, in three prepa-rations. Pacific Rim specials include fresh ahi, seared spicy or cooked in a sweet ginger-soy sauce.

831 Front St. Ⓒ **808/661-3472.** Main courses $10–$36. AE, MC, V. Daily 11am–11pm.

INEXPENSIVE

Aloha Mixed Plate ⚐ 𝘝𝘢𝘭𝘶𝘦 PLATE LUNCHES/BEACHSIDE GRILL   Look for the festive turquoise-and-yellow, plantation-style front with the red corrugated-iron roof and adorable bar, tiny and busy, directly across from the Lahaina Cannery Mall. Grab a picnic table at ocean's edge, in the shade of large kiawe and milo trees, where you can watch the bobbing sailboats and two islands on the near horizon. (On the upper level, there are umbrellas and plumeria trees—just as charming.) Then tuck into inexpensive mahimahi, Kalua pig and cabbage, shoyu chicken, teriyaki beef, and other local plate-lunch specials, all at budget-friendly prices, served with macaroni salad and rice. The shoyu chicken is the best I've had, fork tender and tasty, and the spicy chicken drumettes come from a fabled family recipe. (The bestsellers are the coconut prawns and Aloha Mixed Plate of shoyu chicken, teriyaki beef, and mahimahi.) I don't know of anywhere else where you can order a mai tai with a plate lunch and enjoy table service with an ocean view.

1285 Front St. ⓒ **808/661-3322**. www.alohamixedplate.com. Main courses $4.95–$9.95. MC, V. Daily 10:30am–10pm.

Cheeseburger in Paradise AMERICAN
Wildly successful, always crowded, highly visible, and very noisy, with live music in the evenings, Cheeseburger is a shrine to the American classic. This is burger country, tropical-style, with everything from tofu and garden burgers to the biggest, juiciest beef and chicken burgers, served on whole-wheat and sesame buns baked fresh daily. There are good reasons why the two-story green-and-white building next to the seawall is always packed: good value, good grinds, and a great ocean view. The Cheeseburger in Paradise—a hefty hunk with Jack and cheddar cheeses, sautéed onions, lettuce, fresh tomatoes, and Thousand Island dressing—is a paean to the basics. You can build your own burger by adding sautéed mushrooms, bacon, grilled Ortega chilies, and other condiments for an extra charge. Onion rings, chili-cheese fries, and cold beer complete the carefree fantasy.

811 Front St. ⓒ **808/661-4855**. www.cheeseburgerland.com. Burgers $7–$10. AE, DISC, MC, V. Daily 8am–10pm.

Cilantro: Fresh Mexican Grill ✸ 𝘬𝘪𝘥𝘴 𝘧𝘪𝘯𝘥𝘴 MEXICAN
This is Maui's best bet for fabulous Mexican food at frugal prices. And, believe it or not, this fast-food restaurant serves fresh, healthy food. The chef and owner is Pris Nabavi, creator of Maui's Pizza Paradiso Italian Kitchen. He wanted the "challenge of something different," so he took off to Mexico to find out how the Mexicans used to cook in "the old days." He's back on Maui with this unbelievably delicious eatery where everything is made from scratch. Even the corn tortillas are handmade daily. Signature dishes include the cit-rus-and-herb-marinated chipotle rotisserie chicken, the veggie Mariposa salad, and the popular Mother Clucker Flautas. Plus lip-smacking "al pastor"-style adobo pork. All this at budget-pleasing prices. It's a great place to take the kids; the Los Ninos menu items are under $3.75.

170 Papalaua Ave. ⓒ **808/667-5444**. www.cilantrogrill.com. Entrees $3.25–$8.95. MC, V. Mon–Thurs 11am–9:30pm; Fri–Sat 11am–10pm; Sun 11am–8pm.

Lahaina Coolers ✸ AMERICAN/INTERNATIONAL
A huge marlin hangs above the bar, epic wave shots and wall sconces made of surfboard fins line the walls, and open windows on three sides of this ultracasual indoor/outdoor restaurant take advantage of the shade trees to create a cheerful ambience. This is a great breakfast joint, with feta-cheese Mediterranean omelets, huevos rancheros, and fried jasmine rice with Kula vegetables and Portuguese sausage. There are three types of eggs Benedict: the classic, a vegetarian version (with Kula vegetables—excellent), and the Local, with Portuguese sausage and sweet bread. At lunch burgers rule and the sandwiches, from grilled por-tobellos to the classic tuna melt, are ideal for casual Lahaina. Made fresh daily, the pasta is prepared Asian-style (chicken breast in a spicy Thai peanut sauce), with pesto, or veg-etarian (in a spicy Creole sauce). Pizzas, pastas, fresh catch, steak, and enchiladas round out the entrees, and everything can be prepared vegetarian.

180 Dickensen St. (C) **808/661-7082**. Main courses $7.50–$11 lunch, $14–$25 dinner. AE, DC, DISC, MC, V. Daily 8am–2am (full menu until midnight).

Maui Sunrise Café *Value* GOURMET DELI/CAFE   If you want to know where the best breakfasts are or the most filling lunch on a budget, follow the surfers to this teeny-tiny cafe located on Front Street, next door to the library. Eat in the patio garden out back or take your lunch to the beach. You'll find huge breakfasts, delicious gourmet sandwiches, and filling lunch plates all at bargain prices. It's tough to find a parking spot nearby (and you can't park at the library), but you'll probably want a brisk walk after eating here anyway.

693A Front St., Lahaina. (C) **808/661-8558**. Breakfast under $10; lunch $6–$10. No credit cards. Daily 6am–6pm.

Maui Swiss Cafe SANDWICHES/PIZZA   Newly renovated and double its original size (which was tiny), Swiss Cafe now has five Internet stations and continues to serve excellent sandwiches and continental breakfast. Having gone from a sandwich-and-pizza shop to a European-style sidewalk Internet cafe, it still serves $5 lunch specials and two scoops of ice cream for $2.50 (and sometimes the ice cream is free with the lunch special). Top-quality breads baked fresh daily, Dijon mustard, good Swiss cheese, and keen attention to sandwich fillings and pizza toppings make this a very special sandwich shop. The Swiss owner, Dominique Martin, has imbued this corner of Lahaina with a European flavor, down to the menus printed in English and German and the Swiss breakfast of sliced ham, Emmenthal cheese, hard-boiled egg, and freshly baked croissant. *Tip:* The "signature melt" sandwiches, with imported Emmenthal cheese baked on an Italian Parmesan crust, are something to watch for, and there are excellent vegetarian and turkey sandwiches as well.

640 Front St. (C) **808/661-6776**. www.swisscafe.net. Sandwiches and 8-in. pizzas $6.50–$8.95. No credit cards. Daily 9am–8pm.

Penne Pasta Café *Finds* ITALIAN/MEDITERRANEAN   Bargain hunters don't pass up this neighborhood cafe, under the helm of chef Mark Ellman (of Maui Taco fame). It features delicious Italian and Mediterranean cuisine. You'll get a sit-down meal at takeout prices, and *mama mia*—those are big plates of pasta, pizzas, salads, and sandwiches. So, what's the catch? No wait help. You order at the counter and the manager delivers your *molto bene* linguine pesto, baked penne, olive-caper-basil-roasted pepper pizza, or whatever you ordered. Wine (less than $6 a glass) and beer are available too.

180 Dickenson St., Lahaina. (C) **808/661-6633**. Basic menu items under $10; specials up to $14. AE, DC, DISC, MC, V. Mon–Fri 11am–9:30pm; Sat–Sun 5–9:30pm.

KAANAPALI
EXPENSIVE

Swan Court CONTINENTAL   What could be better than a fantasy restaurant in a fantasy resort? It's not exactly a hideaway (this is, after all, a Hyatt), but Swan Court is wonderful in a resorty sort of way, with a dance floor, waterfalls, flamingos, and an ocean view adding to the package. Come here as a splurge or on a bottomless expense account, and enjoy Pacific lobster coconut soup, rock shrimp crab cake, Maui sugar-cane-skewered ahi, and sautéed *opakapaka* in striking surroundings. The menu sticks to the tried-and-true, making Swan Court a safe choice for those who like a respectable and well-executed selection in a romantic setting with candlelight, a Japanese garden, and swans serenely gliding by. A year-round Valentine dinner.

Chef McDonald Has a Farm, E-I-E-I-O

Here's your chance to see where those delicious greens, sweet basil, and wonderful tropical fruits that make up your dinner at **Pacific'o** and **I'o** restaurants come from. **Chef James McDonald** was the first in the state to own and operate a farm for the purpose of supplying his two restaurants.

Chef McDonald offers two farm tours: The morning tour includes hot apple cider and pastries before your culinary specialist tour guide helps you handpick items to take with you for a sampler. The cost is $25. The second, longer tour, includes the first tour plus lunch for $50. Tours start at 10:30am on Monday, Wednesday, and Friday. For more information, call © 808/667-4341.

In the Hyatt Regency Maui, 200 Nohea Kai Dr. © 808/661-1234. Reservations recommended for dinner. Main courses $30–$38. AE, DC, DISC, MC, V. Daily 6:30–11:30am (noon on Sun); Tues, Thurs, and Sat 6–10pm.

MODERATE

Beachside Grill and Leilani's on the Beach STEAK/SEAFOOD   The Beachside Grill is the informal, less-expensive room downstairs on the beach, where folks wander in off the sand for a frothy beer and a beachside burger. Leilani's is the dinner-only room, with more expensive but still not outrageously priced steak and seafood offerings. At Leilani's you can order everything from affordable spinach, cheese, and mushroom ravioli to lobster and steak. Children can get a quarter-pound hamburger for under $5 or a broiled chicken breast for a couple of dollars more—a value, for sure. Pasta, rack of lamb, filet mignon, and Alaskan king crab at market price are among the choices in the upstairs room. Although the steak-and-lobster combinations can be pricey, the good thing about Leilani's is the strong middle range of entree prices, especially the fresh fish for around $20 to $25. All of this, of course, comes with an ocean view. There's live Hawaiian music every afternoon except Friday, when the Rock 'n' Roll Aloha Friday set gets those decibels climbing. Free concerts are usually offered on a stage outside the restaurant on the last Sunday of the month.

In Whalers Village, 2435 Kaanapali Pkwy. © 808/661-4495. www.leilanis.com. Reservations suggested for dinner at both restaurants. Lunch and dinner (Beachside Grill) $6.95–$13; dinner (Leilani's) $18–$25. AE, DC, DISC, MC, V. Beachside Grill daily 11am–11pm (bar daily until 12:30am). Leilani's daily 5–10pm.

Hula Grill (ℛ (Kids) HAWAII REGIONAL/SEAFOOD   Who wouldn't want to tuck into crab-and-corn cakes, banana-glazed opah, mac-nut-roasted *opakapaka*, or crab won tons under a thatched umbrella, with palm trees at arm's length and a view of Lanai? Peter Merriman, one of the originators of Hawaii Regional Cuisine, segued seamlessly from his smallish, Big Island upcountry enclave to this large, high-volume, open-air dining room on the beach. Hula Grill offers a wide range of prices and choices; it can be expensive but doesn't have to be. The menu includes Merriman's signature firecracker mahimahi, seafood pot stickers, and several different fresh-fish preparations, including his famous ahi poke rolls—lightly sautéed rare ahi wrapped in rice paper with Maui onions. At lunch the menu is more limited, with a choice of sandwiches, entrees, pizza, appetizers, and salads. The kids' menu includes free pasta

⸢*Finds*⸥ The Tiki Terrace

Bravo to the **Kaanapali Beach Hotel** for the low-salt, employee-tested Native Hawaiian Diet served in its **Tiki Terrace,** 2525 Kaanapali Pkwy. (© **808/667-0124**). Titled Kulaiwi Cuisine, the menu features the healthy, traditional Hawaiian diet of fresh fish and taro greens, flavored with herbs and spices. Salt is kept to a minimum, but you can always add your own. The Kulaiwi menu consists of pohole fern shoots from Keanae Valley (on the way to Hana), marinated with onions and seaweed and served with ginger-tomato dressing. (With their freshness, pleasing crunch, and mild flavor, fern shoots are one of the most underused greens of Hawaii.)

Entree choices might be oven-poached chicken breast or fresh catch, served with puréed taro tops (like spinach, but better), grilled bananas, steamed sweet potato, taro, and fresh poi made on the premises. Entrees run from $17 to $37 and include chilled Hana papaya with lemon.

The use of taro greens is a noteworthy touch in the a la carte menu as well, where baked crab and taro-leaf dip, spiced up with artichoke hearts, Parmesan cheese, and homemade mayonnaise, is served with focaccia bread. The pohole ferns with smoked salmon and fresh poke with roasted kukui nut are special Hawaiian touches. The a la carte menu offers everything from steak and lobster to tiger shrimp basted in Hawaiian chili pepper and seaweed sauce, served in a laulau pouch. The dining room is old-fashioned Hawaii, not fancy, with tables on a terrace ringed with plumeria and palm trees and a nightly Hawaiian trio (6–9pm in the courtyard, with hula dancing 6:30–7:30pm).

The regular Tiki Terrace breakfast menu presents a good opportunity to sample Hawaiian food in a familiar context: taro hash browns; three-egg lomi salmon omelet with sweet-potato home fries; a fruit plate of banana baked in ti leaf with lehua honey and macadamia nuts, served with yogurt; and French toast made with taro bread. There are even Hawaiian taro pancakes, and they're wonderful. The Hawaiian Sunday Champagne Brunch ($31) features Hawaiian music to go with the Hawaiian food, along with Belgian waffles and great desserts.

At the buffet-style **Mixed Plate,** the Hawaiian Friday lunch is widely touted among residents, who voted this the best Hawaiian food in the *Maui News:* fresh poi, lomi salmon, laulau, Kalua pig, and ahi poke, for $11. Dinner includes all of the above and prime rib (early bird, $15 6–9pm). The hotel also sponsors a complimentary (for guests of the hotel) **Ohana Welcome Breakfast** at 8am Monday through Saturday, with live music, hula, breakfast (scrambled eggs, Portuguese sausage, and rice), and advice on how to save money on your Maui vacation. The slide show of Maui activities lasts about 1½ hours.

The emphasis on Hawaiian food is only one part of a pervasive spirit of aloha that distinguishes this hotel. Reservations are recommended for dining in the Tiki Terrace. American Express, Diner's Club, Discover, MasterCard, and Visa are accepted. Dinner is served daily from 6 to 9pm.

for kids under 4, cheese pizza, chicken, burgers, and more. There's happy-hour entertainment and Hawaiian music daily. For those wanting a more casual atmosphere, the Barefoot Bar, located on the beach, offers burgers, fish, pizza, and salads.

In Whalers Village, 2435 Kaanapali Pkwy. ℭ **808/667-6636**. www.hulagrill.com. Reservations recommended for dinner. Lunch and Barefoot Bar menus $8–$16; dinner main courses $16–$32. AE, DC, DISC, MC, V. Daily 11am–10:30pm.

INEXPENSIVE

Whalers Village has a food court where you can buy pizza, very good Japanese food (including tempura, soba, and other noodle dishes), Korean plates, and fast-food burgers at serve-yourself counters and courtyard tables. It's an inexpensive alternative and a quick, handy stop for shoppers and Kaanapali beachgoers.

CJ's Deli and Diner 𝒦 (Value) AMERICAN/DELI If you are staying in Kaanapali, this restaurant is within walking distance of your resort; if you're not staying in Kaanapali, it's worth the drive to sample the "comfort food" (as they call it) at this hip, happening eatery with prices so low you won't believe you're still on Maui (most items under $10). A huge billboard menu hangs from the yellow and gold textured wall, and highly polished wooden floors give the roadside eatery a homey feeling. You can eat in or take out (you can even get a "chef-to-go" to come to your accommodations and cook for you), the atmosphere is friendly, and there's even a computer with high-speed Internet connection to keep the techies humming. Huge, delicious breakfasts start at 6:30am (check out the $4.95 early-bird special of two eggs, bacon or sausage, rice, and coffee) and is served until 11am. They have a wide selection of egg dishes, plus pancakes and waffles, and don't forget the tempting delights from the bakery. Lunch ranges from deli sandwiches, burgers, and hot sandwiches to pot roast, ribs, and fish dishes. If you are on your way to Hana or up to the top of Haleakala, stop by and get a box lunch. They even have a menu for the kids.

Kaanapali Fairway Shops, 2580 Keka'a Dr. (just off the Honoapiilani Hwy.), Kaanapali Resort. ℭ **808/667-0968**. Breakfast items $1.75–$9.50; lunch $6.50–$9.95. AE, MC, V. Daily 6:30am–7:30pm.

Nikki's Pizza PIZZA Formerly Pizza Paradiso, Nikki's has a full menu of pastas, pizzas, and desserts, including smoothies, coffee, and ice cream. This is a welcome addition to the Kaanapali scene, where casual is king and good food doesn't have to be fancy. The pizza reflects a simple and effective formula that has won acclaim through the years: good crust, true-blue sauces, and toppings loyal to tradition but with just enough edge for those who want it. Create your own pizza with roasted eggplant, mushrooms, anchovies, artichoke hearts, spicy sausages, cheeses, and a slew of other toppings. Nikki's offers some heroic choices, from the Veg Wedge to the Maui Wowie (ham and Maui pineapple) and the Godfather (roasted chicken, artichoke hearts, and sun-dried tomatoes).

In Whalers Village, 2435 Kaanapali Pkwy. ℭ **808/667-0333**. Gourmet pizza $3.85–$4.65 (by the slice); whole pizzas $12–$27. MC, V. Daily 11am–10pm.

HONOKOWAI, KAHANA & NAPILI
EXPENSIVE

Roy's Kahana Bar & Grill 𝒦𝒦 EURO-ASIAN Despite the lack of dramatic view and an upstairs location in a shopping mall, Roy's remains crowded and extremely popular for one reason—fabulous food. It bustles with young, hip, impeccably trained servers delivering blackened ahi or perfectly seared lemon grass *shutome* (broadbill swordfish) to tables of satisfied customers. Roy's is known for its rack of lamb and fresh seafood (usually eight or nine choices), and for the chain's large, open kitchens that turn out everything from pizza to sake-grilled New York steak. If polenta is on the menu, don't resist: On my last visit, the polenta was rich and fabulous, with garlic, cream, spinach, and wild mushrooms. Large picture windows open up Roy's Kahana but don't quell the noise, another tireless trait long ago established by Roy's Restaurant in Honolulu, the flagship of Yamaguchi's burgeoning empire.

In the Kahana Gateway Shopping Center, 4405 Honoapiilani Hwy. ⒞ **808/669-6999. www.roysrestaurant.com.** Reservations strongly recommended. Main courses $14–$31. AE, DC, DISC, MC, V. Daily 5:30–10pm.

Sea House Restaurant ASIAN/PACIFIC   The Sea House is not glamorous, famous, or hip, but it's worth mentioning for its spectacular view of Napili Bay. The Napili Kai Beach Club, where Sea House is located, is a charming throwback to the days when hotels blended in with their surroundings and had lush tropical foliage. Dinner entrees come complete with soup or salad, vegetables, and rice or potato. The lighter appetizer menu is a delight—more than a dozen choices ranging from sautéed or blackened crab cake to crisp Pacific Rim sushi of ahi capped in nori and cooked tempura-style.

In Napili Kai Beach Resort, 5900 Honoapiilani Hwy. ⒞ **808/669-1500.** Reservations required for dinner. Main courses $18–$49; appetizer menu $5–$14. AE, DISC, MC, V. Sun–Fri 8–10:30am, noon–2pm, and 5:30–9pm. Pupu menu Sat–Thurs 2–9pm; Fri 2–9pm; Sat 5:30–9pm

MODERATE

Fish & Game Brewing Co. & Rotisserie SEAFOOD/STEAK   This restaurant consists of an oyster bar, deli counter and retail section, and tables. The small retail section sells fresh seafood, and the sit-down menu covers basic tastes: salads (Caesar, Oriental chicken with won tons), fish and chips, fresh-fish sandwiches, cheeseburgers, and beer—lots of it. At dinner count on heavier meats and the fresh catch of the day (ahi, mahimahi, ono), with rotisserie items such as grilled chicken, steaks, and duck. The late-night menu offers shrimp, cheese fries, quesadillas, and lighter fare.

In the Kahana Gateway Shopping Center, 4405 Honoapiilani Hwy. ⒞ **808/669-3474.** Reservations recommended for dinner. Main courses $7–$13 lunch, $16–$32 dinner. AE, DC, DISC, MC, V. Daily 11am–2am; late-night menu 10:30pm–1am. During football season (Sept–Jan) brunch Sat–Sun 7am–3pm.

INEXPENSIVE

Maui Tacos *Kids* MEXICAN   Mark Ellman's Maui Tacos chain has grown faster than you can say "Haleakala." Ellman put gourmet Mexican on paper plates and on the island's culinary map long before the island became known as Hawaii's center of salsa and chimichangas. Barely more than a takeout counter with a few tables, this and the six other Maui Tacos in Hawaii (four on Maui alone) are the rage of hungry surfers, discerning diners, burrito buffs, and Hollywood glitterati, like Sharon Stone, whose picture adorns a wall or two. Choices include excellent fresh-fish tacos (garlicky and flavorful), chimichangas, and mouth-breaking compositions such as the Hookipa (a personal favorite): a "surf burrito" of fresh fish, black beans, and salsa. The green-spinach burrito contains four kinds of beans, rice, and potatoes—it's a knockout, requiring a siesta afterwards. Kids' menu items start at $2.75.

In Napili Plaza, 5095 Napili Hau St. ⒞ **808/665-0222. www.mauitacos.com.** Items range $4–$7.50. AE, DC, DISC, MC, V. Daily 9am–9pm.

Pizza Paradiso Italian Caffe PIZZA/ITALIAN   Order at the counter (pastas, gourmet pizza whole or by the slice, salads, and desserts) and find a seat at one of the few tables. The pasta sauces—marinara, pescatore, Alfredo, Florentine, and pesto, with options and add-ons—are as popular as the pizzas and panini sandwiches. The Massimo, a pesto sauce with artichoke hearts, sun-dried tomatoes, and capers, comes with a choice of chicken, shrimp, or clams, and is so good it was a Taste of Lahaina winner in 1999. Whether you take out or dine in, this is a hot spot in the neighborhood, with free delivery.

In the Honokowai Marketplace, 3350 Lower Honoapiilani Rd. © 808/667-2929. www.pizzaparadiso.com. Pastas $7.95–$9.25; pizzas $13–$27. MC, V. Daily 11am–10pm.

KAPALUA
EXPENSIVE

The Banyan Tree Restaurant ✮✮✮ CONTEMPORARY AUSTRALIAN   Fasten your seat belts food fans, this is one of the hottest, most creative chefs to come to Hawaii in decades. Australian Chef Antony Scholtmeyer said his philosophy is "dining shouldn't be safe, but a sexy blend of flavors and textures to create an exciting and sensual experience." His combinations may sound like a walk on the wild side, but once you taste his "sexy" cuisine, you'll be hooked. It takes a creative mind to come up with a signature amuse bouche of foie gras ice cream (don't laugh until you've tried it) with the taste of duck a l'orange (thanks to the confit orange zest and fresh orange segments) and the creamy taste of foie gras. Another zingers is the crispy-skin moi (the Hawaiian fish of royalty), served with lentil dhal, raita, and micro cilantro. Honey roasted duck breast served with celery root risotto and pineapple jus is another winner. Save room for his warm bitter chocolate "meltaway" with sour cream sorbet, lilikoi sauce, and local berries. *Food and Wine* magazine has named him a "Chef to Watch." Word is out, so book a reservation at the Ritz-Carlton's signature restaurant before you leave home or you'll never get in.

Ritz-Carlton Kapalua Resort. © 808/669-6200. Reservations recommended for dinner. Main courses $32–$48. 4-course meal $80. AE, DISC, MC, V. Daily 11am–2pm and 5:30–9pm.

Plantation House Restaurant ✮✮ SEAFOOD/HAWAIIAN-MEDITERRANEAN   With its teak tables, fireplace, and open sides, Plantation House gets stellar marks for atmosphere. The 360-degree view from high among the resort's pine-studded hills takes in Molokai and Lanai, the ocean, the rolling fairways and greens, the northwestern flanks of the West Maui Mountains, and the daily sunset spectacular. Readers of the *Maui News* have deemed this the island's "Best Ambience"—a big honor on an island of wonderful views. It's the best place for breakfast in West Maui, hands down, and one of my top choices for dinner. The menu changes constantly but may include fresh fish prepared several ways—among them, Mediterranean (seared), Upcountry (sautéed with Maui onions and vegetable sauté), Island (pan-seared in sweet sake and macadamia nuts), and Rich Forest (with roasted wild mushrooms), the top seller. At breakfast, the Eggs Mediterranean is superb, and at lunch, sandwiches (open-faced smoked turkey, roasted vegetable, and goat-cheese wrap) and salads rule. When the sun sets, the menu expands to marvelous starters such as polenta and scampi-style shrimp, crab cakes, Kula and Mediterranean salads, and a hearty entree selection of fish, pork tenderloin, roast duck, and filet mignon with apple-smoked Maui onion.

2000 Plantation Club Dr. (at Kapalua Plantation Golf Course). © 808/669-6299. www.theplantationhouse.com. Reservations recommended. Main courses $24–$35. AE, DC, MC, V. Daily 8am–3pm and 5:30–10pm.

MODERATE

Sansei Seafood Restaurant and Sushi Bar ⭐⭐ PACIFIC RIM   Perpetual award-winner Sansei offers an extensive menu of Japanese and East-West delicacies. Part fusion, part Hawaii Regional Cuisine, Sansei is tirelessly creative, with a menu that scores higher with adventurous palates than with purists (although there are endless traditional choices as well). Maki is the mantra here. If you don't like cilantro, watch out for those complex spicy crab rolls. Other choices include panko-crusted ahi sashimi, sashimi trio, ahi carpaccio, noodle dishes, lobster, Asian rock-shrimp cakes, traditional Japanese tempura, and sauces that surprise, in creative combinations such as ginger-lime chile butter and cilantro pesto. But there's simpler fare as well, such as shrimp tempura, noodles, and wok-tossed upcountry vegetables. Desserts are not to be missed. If it's autumn, don't pass up persimmon crème brûlée made with Kula persimmons. In other seasons opt for tempura-fried ice cream with chocolate sauce. There's karaoke every night from 10pm to 1am. *Money-saving tip:* Eat early; all food is 25% off between 5:30 and 6pm.

At the Kapalua Shops, 115 Bay Dr. ⓒ 808/669-6286. Also in Kihei at the Kihei Town Center ⓒ 808/879-0004. www.sanseihawaii.com. Reservations recommended. Main courses $19–$29. AE, DISC, MC, V. Daily 5:30–10pm. Thurs–Fri pupu and bar menu with karaoke until 1am.

Vino Italian Tapas & Wine Bar ⭐⭐⭐ *Finds* ITALIAN   Two Japanese guys, D. K. Kodama (chef and owner of Sansei Seafood Restaurant and Sushi Bar, reviewed above) and Chuck Furuya (Hawaii's only master sommelier) teamed up to create this culinary adventure for foodies. Vino opened in August 2003 to big, big accolades. Probably the best Italian food on Maui is served at this exquisite restaurant, overlooking the rolling hills of the Kapalua Golf Course. Always wanting to be on the cutting edge, the duo rebranded the restaurant in December 2004 to Vino Italian Tapas & Wine Bar. The new menu features more than two dozen tapas (small plates), ranging from the signature asparagus Milanese (just $5.95) to slow butter-poached Kona lobster ($18). Plus they have retained the most popular large plate dishes, like fresh mahimahi with artichokes and grape tomatoes on capellini, Mudicca-crusted pan-fried veal stuffed with prosciutto, and *osso buco* with spinach risotto. Go to Vino early during your stay on Maui; you most likely will want to return.

Kapalua Village Course Golf Club House, Kapalua Resort. ⓒ 808/661-VINO. Reservations recommended. Tapas $5.95–$18; large plates $19–$25. AE, DISC, MC, V. Daily 11am–2pm and 6–9:30pm.

3 South Maui

KIHEI/MAALAEA

There's a **Maui Tacos** at Kamaole Beach Center in Kihei (ⓒ 808/879-5005).

EXPENSIVE

Buzz's Wharf AMERICAN   Buzz's is another formula restaurant that offers a superb view, substantial sandwiches, meaty french fries, and surf-and-turf fare—in a word, satisfying but not sensational. Still, this bright, airy dining room is a fine way station for whale-watching over a cold beer and a fresh mahimahi sandwich with fries. Some diners opt for several appetizers (stuffed mushrooms, steamer clams, clam chowder, onion soup) and a salad, then splurge on dessert. Buzz's prize-winning Tahitian Baked Papaya is a warm, fragrant melding of fresh papaya with vanilla and coconut—the pride of the house.

Maalaea Harbor, 50 Hauoli St. ⓒ 808/244-5426. Reservations recommended. Main courses $20–$33. AE, DC, DISC, MC, V. Mon–Sat 11am–9pm; Sun 10am–9pm

Buzz's Wharf **1**
Caffe Ciao **12**
Cheeseburger, Mai Tai's
  & Rock-n-Roll **8**
The Coffee Store **3**
Ferraro's at Seaside **11**
Five Palms **7**
Honolulu Coffee Co. **8**
Hula Moons **10**
Joe's Bar & Grill **9**
Joy's Place **5**
Longhi's **8**
Ma'alaea Grill **1**
Maui Tacos **6**
Nick's Fishmarket Maui **12**
Peggy Sue's **3**
Prince Court **14**
Ruth's Chris Steak House **8**
SeaWatch **13**
Shaka Sandwich & Pizza **4**
Spago **11**
Stella Blues Cafe **2**
Tommy Bahama's Tropical Cafe **8**
The Waterfront at Maalaea **1**

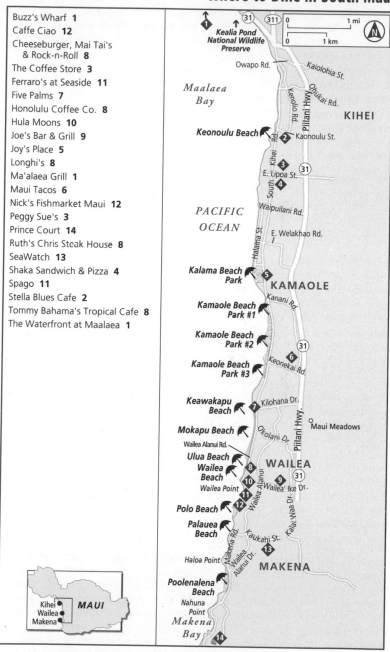

Five Palms ☆ PACIFIC RIM   This is the best lunch spot in Kihei—open-air, with tables a few feet from the beach and up-close-and-personal views of Kahoolawe and Molokini. You'll have to walk through a nondescript parking area and the modest entrance of the Mana Kai Resort to reach this unpretentious place. They feature a menu of breakfast and lunch items served from 8am to 2:30pm, so if you're jetlagged and your stomach isn't on Hawaiian time, you can get a snow-crab omelet at two in the afternoon or a juicy Angus beef hamburger at eight in the morning. At dinner, with the torches lit on the beach and the main dining room open, the ambience shifts to evening romantic but still casual. Just-caught fish is the star of the dinner menu.

In the Mana Kai Resort, 2960 S. Kihei Rd. ℂ 808/879-2607. Reservations recommended for dinner. Dinner $23–$40. AE, DC, MC, V. Daily 8am–2:30pm and 5–9pm, with pupu menu daily 2:30–6pm.

The Waterfront at Maalaea ☆☆ SEAFOOD   The family-owned Waterfront has won many prestigious awards for wine excellence, service, and seafood, but its biggest boost is word of mouth. Loyal diners rave about the friendly staff and seafood, fresh off the boat in nearby Maalaea Harbor and prepared with care. The bay and harbor view is one you'll never forget, especially at sunset. You have nine choices of preparations for the several varieties of fresh Hawaiian fish, ranging from *en papillote* (baked in buttered parchment) to Southwestern (smoked chile and cilantro butter) to Cajun spiced and island-style (sautéed, broiled, poached, or baked and paired with tiger prawns). Other choices: Kula onion soup, an excellent Caesar salad, the signature lobster chowder, and grilled eggplant layered with Maui onions, tomatoes, and spinach, served with red-pepper coulis and Big Island goat cheese. Like the seafood, it's superb.

Maalaea Harbor, 50 Hauoli St. ℂ 808/244-9028. Reservations recommended. Main courses $19–$35. AE, DC, DISC, MC, V. Opens daily at 5pm; last seating at 8:30pm

MODERATE

Ma'alaea Grill ☆ *(Finds* PACIFIC RIM   This charming eatery is another great restaurant from the people behind Café O'Lei Lahaina (reviewed earlier in this chapter) and is superbly located, overlooking the Maalaea Small Boat Harbor. There is outside seating, but the harbor is almost always windy, so if you don't want your lettuce blown across the shopping center, eat inside. Lunches include creative salads (curry chicken salad), hefty sandwiches (crab club), and reasonably priced entrees (blackened mahimahi for just $9). Dinner features appetizers so interesting you could make a meal out of them (fried-ahi-stuffed calamari, tempura potato cakes, grilled seafood tower), mouthwatering main courses (macadamia-nut roast duckling, kiawe grilled New York steak, calamari, stir-fried vegetable pad Thai), and yummy desserts.

Maalaea Harbor Village, 300 Maalaea Rd. (the triangle between Honoapiilani Hwy. and Maalaea Rd.). ℂ 808/243-2206. Reservations recommended. Lunch $7–$11; dinner $16–$21. AE, MC, V. Tues–Sun 10:30am–5pm and 5:30–9pm.

Stella Blues Cafe ☆ *(Kids* AMERICAN   Stella Blues gets going at breakfast and continues through to dinner with something for everyone—vegetarians, kids, pasta and sandwich lovers, and hefty steak eaters. Grateful Dead posters line the walls, and a covey of gleaming motorcycles is invariably parked outside. It's loud, lively, irreverent, and unpretentious. Sandwiches are the highlight, ranging from Tofu Extraordinaire to Mom's Egg Salad on a croissant to garden burgers and grilled chicken. Tofu wraps and mountain-size Cobb salads are popular, and for the reckless, there are large coffee shakes with mounds of whipped cream. Daily specials include fresh seafood, and everything's made from scratch, down to the pesto mayonnaise and herb bread. At dinner selections range from affordable full dinners to pastas and burgers.

Azeka II Shopping Center, 1279 S. Kihei Rd. ℂ 808/874-3779. Main courses $7–$23. AE, DC, DISC, MC, V. Daily 7:30am–10pm.

INEXPENSIVE

The Coffee Store COFFEEHOUSE   This simple, classic coffeehouse for caffeine connoisseurs serves two dozen different types of coffee and coffee drinks, from mochas and lattes to cappuccinos, espressos, and toddies. Breakfast items include smoothies, lox and bagels, quiches, granola, and assorted pastries. Pizza, salads, vegetarian lasagna, veggie-and-shrimp quesadillas, and sandwiches (garden burger, tuna, turkey, ham, grilled veggie panini) also move briskly from the takeout counter. The turkey-and-veggie wraps are a local legend. There are only a few small tables and they fill up fast, often with musicians and artists who've spent the previous evening entertaining at the Wailea and Kihei resorts.

In Azeka Place II, 1279 Kihei Rd. ℂ 808/875-4244. www.mauicoffee.com. All items less than $8.50. AE, MC, V. Mon–Sat 6:30am–8pm; Sun 6:30am–7pm.

Joy's Place *Value* HEALTHY DELI/SANDWICHES   If you are in Kihei and are looking for a healthy, delicious lunch at a rock-bottom price, it's worth hunting around for Joy's Place. This tiny hole in the wall has humongous sandwiches, wheat-free wraps, fresh salads, hot items (falafel burger, turkey or tuna pizza melt, and spinach quinoa burger), soups, and desserts. Most items are organic. There are a few places to sit in the deli, but the beach is just a couple minutes' walk away.

Island Surf Building, 1993 S. Kihei Rd. (entrance to the restaurant is on Auhana St.). ℂ 808/879-9258. All items under $10. No credit cards. Mon–Sat 10am–5pm.

Peggy Sue's *Kids* AMERICAN   Just for a moment, forget that diet and take a leap. It's Peggy Sue's to the rescue! This 1950s-style diner has oodles of charm and is a swell place to spring for the best chocolate malt on the island. You'll also find sodas, shakes, floats, egg creams, milkshakes, and scoops of made-on-Maui Roselani-brand gourmet ice cream—14 flavors. Old-fashioned soda-shop stools, an Elvis Presley Boulevard sign, and jukeboxes on every Formica table serve as a backdrop for the famous burgers (and garden burgers), brushed with teriyaki sauce and served with all the goodies. The fries are great, too. Kids' meals go for just $3.95.

In Azeka Place II, 1279 S. Kihei Rd. ℂ 808/875-8944. Burgers $7–$11; plate lunches $6–$12. AE, DISC, MC, V. Sun–Thurs 11am–9pm; Fri–Sat 11am–10pm.

Shaka Sandwich & Pizza PIZZA   How many "best pizzas" are there on Maui? It depends on which shore you're on, the west or the south. At this south-shore old-timer, which recently moved to a new (and much larger) location, they still are serving those award-winning pizzas, New York–style heroes and Philly cheese steaks, calzones, salads, homemade garlic bread, and homemade meatball sandwiches. Shaka uses fresh Maui produce, long-simmering sauces, and homemade Italian bread. Choose thin or Sicilian thick crust with gourmet toppings: Maui onions, spinach, anchovies, jalapeños, and a spate of other vegetables. Try the white pizza; with the perfectly balanced flavors of olive oil, garlic, and cheese, you won't even miss the tomato sauce. Clam-and-garlic pizza, spinach pizza (with olive oil, spinach, garlic, and mozzarella), and the Shaka Supreme (with at least 10 toppings) should satisfy even the biggest appetites.

1770 S. Kihei Rd. ℂ 808/874-0331. Sandwiches $4.35–$11; pizzas $13–$26. No credit cards. Daily 10:30am–9pm.

WAILEA

The Shops at Wailea, a sprawling location between the Grand Wailea Hotel and Outrigger Wailea Resort, has added a spate of new shops and restaurants to this stretch of south Maui. Five restaurants and dozens of shops, most of them upscale, are among the new tenants of this complex. **Ruth's Chris Steak House** is here, as well as **Tommy Bahama's Tropical Cafe & Emporium; Honolulu Coffee Company; Cheeseburger, Mai Tai's and Rock-n-Roll;** and **Longhi's.** Next door at the Outrigger Wailea, **Hula Moons,** the retro-Hawaiian-themed restaurant, has reopened after a $3-million renovation and moved to the upper level of the lobby building, where it serves midpriced steak and seafood with an ocean view.

VERY EXPENSIVE

Spago 𝕽𝕽𝕽 HAWAIIAN/CALIFORNIA/PACIFIC REGIONAL   California meets Hawaii in this contemporary-designed eatery featuring fresh, local Hawaii ingredients prepared under the culinary watch of master chef Wolfgang Puck. The room has a sleek, modern stone-and-wood design in an open-air setting overlooking the Pacific Ocean. The menu features traditional Hawaiian dishes with Puck's own brand of cutting-edge innovations, including an unbelievable coconut soup with local lobster, keffir, chili, and galangal. For entrees, try the whole steamed fish served with chili, ginger, and baby choy sum; the incredible Kona lobster with sweet-and-sour banana curry, coconut rice, and dry-fried green beans; or the grilled *côte de boeuf* with braised celery, armagnac, peppercorns, and *pommes aligot.* The wine and beverage list is well thought-out and extensive. Save room for the warm guanaja chocolate tart. Make reservations as soon as you land on the island (if not before); this place is popular. And bring plenty of cash, or your platinum card.

Four Seasons Resort Maui, 3900 Wailea Alanui Dr., Wailea, 96753. Ⓒ 808/879-2999. www.wolfgangpuck.com. Reservations required. Entrees $27–$48. AE, DC, DISC, MC, V. Daily 5:30–9pm.

EXPENSIVE

Ferraro's at Seaside 𝕽 ITALIAN   This was a master stroke for Four Seasons: authentic Italian fare in a casual outdoor tropical setting, with a drop-dead gorgeous view of the ocean and the West Maui Mountains. Ferraro's is not inexpensive, but the food is first-rate, including dishes such as oregano-marinated shrimp with avocado, and linguine puttanesca. Mango margaritas, generous salads such as the Maine lobster with avocado and toasted sourdough, and sandwiches and half-pound burgers cater to the poolside crowd at lunch, but at dinnertime, the choices intensify. The fish selection is noteworthy: pepper-crusted ahi, grilled sea scallops and steamed mussels with saffron risotto cake, and poached snapper with red onion–orange marmalade. It won't be easy to choose.

In the Four Seasons Resort Maui at Wailea, 3900 Wailea Alanui Dr. Ⓒ 808/874-8000. Reservations recommended. Lunch entrees $15–$22; dinner $25–$46. AE, DC, DISC, MC, V. Daily 11:30am–4pm, 4–6pm (pupu menu), and 6–9pm.

Joe's Bar & Grill 𝕽𝕽 AMERICAN GRILL   The 270-degree view spans the golf course, tennis courts, ocean, and Haleakala—a worthy setting for Beverly Gannon's style of American home cooking with a regional twist. The hearty staples include excellent mashed potatoes, fresh fish, and filet mignon, but the meatloaf upstages them all. The Tuscan white-bean soup is superb, and the tenderloin, with roasted portobellos, mashed potatoes with whole garlic, and a pinot noir demiglace, is American home cooking at its best. Daily specials could be grilled ahi with white truffle–Yukon gold mashed potatoes or sautéed mahimahi with shrimp bisque and sautéed spinach. If apple-pumpkin cheesecake is on the menu, you should definitely spring for it.

In the Wailea Tennis Club, 131 Wailea Ike Place. © 808/875-7767. Reservations recommended. Main courses $23–$33. AE, DC, DISC, MC, V. Daily 5:30–9:30pm.

Longhi's 🎝🎝 ITALIAN   This is a great alternative to the high-priced restaurants in the surrounding resorts. The open-air room, coupled with restaurateur Bob Longhi's trademark black-and-white checkered floor, provide a great way to start the day. Breakfasts here are something you want to wake up to: perfect baguettes, fresh-baked cinnamon rolls (one is enough for two people), and eggs Benedict or Florentine with hollandaise. Lunch is either an Italian banquet (ahi torino, prawns amaretto, and a wide variety of pastas) or fresh salads and sandwiches. Dinner (overlooking the water) is where Longhi shines, with a long list of fresh-made pasta dishes, seafood platters, and beef and chicken dishes (like filet mignon with béarnaise or veal sauté). Leave room for the daily dessert specials. There's live music Saturday nights until 1:30am.

The Shops at Wailea, 3750 Wailea Alanui Dr., Wailea. © 808/891-8883. www.longhi-maui.com. Reservations for dinner recommended. Main courses $18–$35. AE, DC, MC, V. Mon–Fri 8am–10pm; Sat 7:30am–1:30am; Sun 7:30am–10pm.

Nick's Fishmarket Maui 🎝🎝🎝 SEAFOOD   I do love Nick's. The ambience is spectacular, the stephanotis have grown in on the terrace, and the seafood is fresh. This is a classic seafood restaurant that sticks to the tried-and-true (in other words, *not* an overwrought menu) but stays fresh with excellent ingredients and a high degree of professionalism in service and preparation. I love the onion vichyssoise with taro swirl and a hint of *tobiko* (flying-fish roe), and the bow-tied servers with almond-scented cold towels. The Greek Maui Wowie salad gets my vote as one of the top salads in Hawaii. The blackened mahimahi has been a Nick's signature for eons, and why not— it's wonderful. Fresh opah (moonfish), salmon, scallops, Hawaiian lobster tails, and chicken, beef, and lamb choices offer ample choices for diners enjoying the fantasy setting on the south Maui shoreline. The round bar, where you can sit facing the ocean, is highlighted with dangling amber lights, giving it a warm, friendly feel.

In the Fairmont Kea Lani Hotel, 4100 Wailea Alanui. © 808/879-7224. www.tri-star-restaurants.com. Reservations recommended. Main courses $25–$50; prix-fixe dinners $55 to market price. AE, DC, DISC, MC, V. Mon–Thurs 5:30–10pm; Fri–Sat 5:30–10:30pm; bar until 11pm.

MODERATE

Caffé Ciao 🎝 ITALIAN   There are two parts to this charming trattoria: the deli, with a takeout section, and the cafe, with tables under the trees, next to the bar. Rare and wonderful wines, such as Vine Cliff, are sold in the deli, along with ultraluxe rose soaps and other bath products, assorted pastas, pizzas, roasted potatoes, vegetable panini, vegetable lasagna, abundant salads, and an appealing selection of microwavable and takeout goodies. On the terrace under the trees, the tables are cheerfully accented with Italian herbs growing in cachepots. *A fave:* the linguine pomodoro, with fresh tomatoes, spinach-tomato sauce, and a dollop of mascarpone. Unfortunately, lunch is seasonal (summer and mid-Dec to mid-Mar, when most of the tourists are around).

In the Kea Lani Hotel, 4100 Wailea Alanui. © 808/875-4100. Reservations recommended. Main courses $13–$20 lunch, $17–$36 dinner; pizzas $17–$19. AE, DC, DISC, MC, V. Lunch (seasonally) daily noon–3pm; dinner daily 5:30–10pm. Bar daily 11am–10pm.

SeaWatch ⭐ ISLAND CUISINE   Under the same ownership as Kapalua's Plantation House (reviewed earlier in this chapter), SeaWatch is one of the more affordable stops in tony Wailea. You'll dine on the terrace or in a high-ceilinged room, on a menu that carries the tee-off-to-19th-hole crowd with ease. For breakfast, try bagels and lox with Maui onions, scrambled eggs with Kalua pork and Maui onions, or crab cake Benedict with roasted-pepper hollandaise. Lunchtime sandwiches, pastas, salads, wraps, and soups are moderately priced, and you get 360-degree views to go with them. The cashew chicken wrap with mango chutney is a winner, as are the tropical-fish quesadilla and the grilled fresh-catch sandwich with Kula lime aioli. Save room for the bananas Foster.

100 Wailea Golf Club Dr. 🕐 **808/875-8080**. www.seawatchrestaurant.com. Reservations required for dinner. Main courses $4–$12 breakfast, $6.50–$15 lunch, $23–$30 dinner. AE, DC, MC, V. Daily 8am–10pm.

MAKENA
Prince Court ⭐⭐ CONTEMPORARY ISLAND   Half of the Sunday brunch experience here is the head-turning view of Makena Beach, Molokini islet, and Kahoolawe island. The other half is the fabled Sunday buffet, bountiful and sumptuous, spread over several tables: pasta, omelets, cheeses, pastries, sashimi, crab legs, smoked salmon, fresh Maui produce, and a smashing array of ethnic and Continental foods. The dinner menu changes regularly; the current winners are the steamed Manila clams scampi with roasted garlic, diced tomatoes, and fried basil; Dungeness crab and goat-cheese won ton with Maui-onion guacamole; and the Prince Court Sampler with Kona lobster cakes, Kalua duck lumpia, and sugar-cane-speared grilled prawns. New game entrees (venison, rack of lamb, breast of duck) come in highly acclaimed preparations, such as poha compote and black cherry cabernet sauce.

In the Maui Prince Hotel, 5400 Makena Alanui. 🕐 **808/874-1111**. Reservations recommended. Main courses $19–$38; kids 6 and under eat free. Fri prime rib and seafood buffet $42 ($25 children); Sun brunch $42. AE, MC, V. Sun 9am–2pm (with last seating at noon); daily 6–9:30pm (Fri buffet 2 seatings: 6–6:30pm and 8–8:30pm)

4 Upcountry Maui
HALIIMAILE (ON THE WAY TO UPCOUNTRY MAUI)
EXPENSIVE
Haliimaile General Store ⭐⭐⭐ AMERICAN   More than a decade later, Bev Gannon, one of the 12 original Hawaii Regional Cuisine chefs, is still going strong at her foodie haven in the pineapple fields. You'll dine at tables set on old wood floors under high ceilings, with works by local artists hanging on the walls. The food puts an innovative spin on Hawaii Regional Cuisine. Even the fresh-catch sandwich on the lunch menu is anything but prosaic. Sip the lilikoi lemonade and nibble the sashimi napoleon or the house salad (island greens with mandarin oranges, onions, toasted walnuts, and blue-cheese crumble)—all are notable items on a menu that bridges Hawaii with Gannon's Texas roots. Kids can enjoy "kid cocktails" like kiwi soda and a special menu featuring pizza, ribs, chicken, and spaghetti.

Haliimaile Rd., Haliimaile. 🕐 **808/572-2666**. www.haliimailegeneralstore.com. Reservations recommended for dinner. Lunch $10–$20; dinner $20–$30. AE, DC, DISC, MC, V. Mon–Fri 11am–2:30pm; daily 5:30–9:30pm.

MAKAWAO & PUKALANI
MODERATE
Casanova Italian Restaurant ⭐ ITALIAN   Look for the tiny veranda with a few stools, always full, in front of a deli at Makawao's busiest intersection—that's the most

Upcountry & East Maui Dining & Attractions

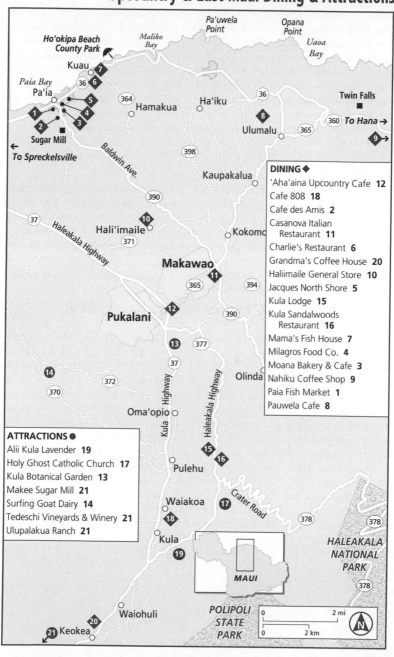

DINING ◆

'Aha'aina Upcountry Cafe **12**
Cafe 808 **18**
Cafe des Amis **2**
Casanova Italian
    Restaurant **11**
Charlie's Restaurant **6**
Grandma's Coffee House **20**
Haliimaile General Store **10**
Jacques North Shore **5**
Kula Lodge **15**
Kula Sandalwoods
    Restaurant **16**
Mama's Fish House **7**
Milagros Food Co. **4**
Moana Bakery & Cafe **3**
Nahiku Coffee Shop **9**
Paia Fish Market **1**
Pauwela Cafe **8**

ATTRACTIONS ●

Alii Kula Lavender **19**
Holy Ghost Catholic Church **17**
Kula Botanical Garden **13**
Makee Sugar Mill **21**
Surfing Goat Dairy **14**
Tedeschi Vineyards & Winery **21**
Ulupalakua Ranch **21**

visible part of the Casanova restaurant and lounge. Makawao's nightlife center contains a stage, dance floor, restaurant, and bar—and food to love and remember. This is pasta heaven: Try the spaghetti fra diavolo or the spinach gnocchi in a fresh tomato-Gorgonzola sauce. Other choices include a huge pizza selection, grilled lamb chops in an Italian mushroom marinade, lots more pasta dishes, and luscious desserts. My personal picks on a stellar menu: garlic spinach topped with Parmesan and pine nuts, polenta with radicchio (the mushroom-and-cream sauce is fabulous!), and tiramisu, the best on the island.

1188 Makawao Ave. ℂ 808/572-0220. Reservations recommended for dinner. Main courses $10–$24; 12-in. pizzas from $10. AE, DC, DISC, MC, V. Mon–Sat 11:30am–2pm; daily 5:30–9pm; dancing Wed–Sat 9:45pm–1am. Lounge daily 5:30pm–12:30am. Deli Mon–Sat 7:30am–6pm, Sun 8:30am–6pm.

INEXPENSIVE
'Aha'aina Upcountry Cafe AMERICAN/LOCAL   Pukalani's inexpensive, casual, and very popular cafe features simple, home-cooked comfort food, such as humongous hamburgers, chicken katsu, fresh-fish tacos, sesame-crusted ahi-and-chicken tortilla soup, plus home-baked bread, oven-fresh muffins, and local faves such as saimin, loco moco, and shoyu chicken. The dreamy breakfast menu features fluffy pancakes and big egg dishes.

In the Andrade Building, 7 Aewa Place (just off Haleakala Hwy.), Pukalani. ℂ 808/572-2395. Breakfast $5–$10; lunch $6–$15. MC, V. Tues–Sat 7am–2pm; Sun 7am–1pm.

KULA (AT THE BASE OF HALEAKALA NATIONAL PARK)
EXPENSIVE
Kula Lodge ⚐ HAWAII REGIONAL/AMERICAN   Don't let the dinner prices scare you: The Kula Lodge is equally enjoyable at breakfast and lunch, when the prices are lower and the views through the picture windows have an eye-popping intensity. The million-dollar vista spans the flanks of Haleakala, central Maui, the ocean, and the West Maui Mountains. The Kula Lodge has always been known for its breakfasts: fabulous eggs Benedict, including a vegetarian version with Kula onions, shiitake mushrooms, and scallions; legendary banana–mac-nut pancakes; and a highly recommended tofu scramble with green onions, Kula vegetables, and garlic chives. If possible, go for sunset cocktails and watch the colors change into deep end-of-day hues. When darkness descends, a roaring fire and lodge atmosphere add to the coziness of the room. The dinner menu features "small plates" of Thai summer rolls, seared ahi, and other starters. Top seafood dishes include sesame-seared ono, Cuban-style spicy swordfish with rum-soaked bananas, and miso salmon with wild mushrooms. There's also pasta, rack of lamb, filet mignon, and free-range chicken breast.

Haleakala Hwy. (Hwy. 377). ℂ 808/878-2517. Reservations recommended for dinner. Breakfast $7.50–$16; lunch $11–$18; dinner main courses $14–$28. AE, DC, DISC, MC, V. Daily 6:30am–9pm.

INEXPENSIVE
Cafe 808 AMERICAN/LOCAL   Despite its out-of-the-way location (or perhaps because of it), Cafe 808 has become the universal favorite among upcountry residents of all ages. The breakfast coffee group, the lunchtime crowd, and dinner regulars all know it's the place for tasty home-style cooking with no pretensions: chicken lasagna, smoked-salmon omelets, famous burgers (teriyaki, hamburger, cheeseburger, garden burger, mahimahi, taro), roast pork, smoked turkey, and a huge selection of local-style specials. Regulars rave about the chicken katsu, saimin, and beef stew. The few tables

are sprinkled around a room with linoleum-tile floors, hardwood benches, plastic patio chairs, and old-fashioned booths—rough around the edges in a pleasing way, and very camp.

Lower Kula Rd., past Holy Ghost Church, across from Morihara Store. © 808/878-6874. Burgers from $4; main courses $5.50–$9.95. No credit cards. Daily 6am–8pm.

Grandma's Coffee House ☞ COFFEEHOUSE/AMERICAN   Alfred Franco's grandmother started what is now a five-generation coffee business back in 1918, when she was 16 years old. Today this tiny wooden coffeehouse, still serving homegrown Haleakala coffee, is the quintessential roadside oasis. Grandma's offers espresso, hot and cold coffees, home-baked pastries, inexpensive pasta, sandwiches (including sensational avocado and garden burgers), homemade soups, fresh juices, and local plate-lunch specials that change daily. Rotating specials include Hawaiian beef stew, ginger chicken, saimin, chicken curry, lentil soup, and sandwiches piled high with Kula vegetables. The lemon squares and the pumpkin bread are standouts.

At the end of Hwy. 37, Keokea (about 6 miles before the Tedeschi Vineyards in Ulupalakua). © 808/878-2140. Most items less than $8.95. MC, V. Daily 7am–5pm.

Kula Sandalwoods Restaurant ☞ AMERICAN   Chef Eleanor Loui, a graduate of the Culinary Institute of America, makes hollandaise sauce every morning from fresh upcountry egg yolks, sweet butter, and Myers lemons, which her family grows in the yard above the restaurant. This is Kula cuisine, with produce from the backyard and everything made from scratch, including French toast with home-baked Portuguese sweet bread, hotcakes or Belgian waffles with fresh fruit, baguettes, open-faced country omelets, hamburgers drenched in a sharp cheddar cheese sauce, and an outstanding veggie burger. The grilled-chicken-breast sandwich is marvelous, served with the soup of the day and Kula mixed greens. Dine in the gazebo or on the terrace, with dazzling views in all directions, including, in the spring, a yard dusted with lavender jacaranda flowers and a hillside ablaze with fields of orange akulikuli blossoms.

15427 Haleakala Hwy. (Hwy. 377). © 808/878-3523. Breakfast $6.95–$9.75; lunch $7.25–$13; Sun brunch $6.95–$9.75. MC, V. Mon–Sat 6:30am–2pm; Sun 6:30am–noon.

5 East Maui: On the Road to Hana

PAIA
MODERATE

Charlie's Restaurant ☞ AMERICAN/MEXICAN   Although Charlie's (named after Charlie P. Woofer, a Great Dane) serves three meals a day, breakfast is really the time to come here. Located in downtown Paia, Charlie's is a cross between a 1960s hippie hangout, a windsurfers' power-breakfast spot, and a honky-tonk bar that gets going after dark. Before you head out to Hana, head to Charlie's for a larger-than-life breakfast (eggs, potatoes, toast, and coffee will set you back only $7). They have plenty of espresso drinks, but the regular coffee is excellent. Lunch is burgers, sandwiches, calzones, and pizza. Dinner is grilled fish and steak—hearty, but nothing to write home about. You'll see all walks of life here, from visitors on their way to Hana at 7am to buff windsurfers chowing down at noon to Willy Nelson on his way to the bar to play a tune.

142 Hana Hwy., Paia © 808/579-9453. Breakfast items around $3.75–$12; lunch items $7.95–$12; dinner main courses $10–$22. AE, DISC, MC, V. Daily 7am–10pm. Food at the bar until 12:30am.

Jacques North Shore ★★ *(Value* SEAFOOD/SUSHI   Of the numerous restaurants that have come and gone over the years at this location, this eclectic outdoor eatery is my favorite. Jacques is difficult to pin down: Some have called it a hipper, cheaper version of the upscale Mama's Fish House. The clientele tend to be trendy, hard-body windsurfers; blonde, tan surfers; and chic North Shore residents. The decor is patio dining under a big circus tent. Some might be distracted by the hostess and servers (20-something beauty queens dressed in "barely there" clothes), but the main attraction is the food. Do not miss the North Shore pumpkin fish (fish, bananas, and oranges served with a ginger pumpkin sauce and miso butter), Greek pasta (roasted bell peppers, roasted garlic, and feta cheese over orrechiette pasta), or one of the fabulous vegetarian entrees like the vegetable curry (with tofu, bananas, and oranges). The sushi bar (closed Sun–Mon) whips out a mean spicy ahi roll and a died-and-gone-to-heaven California roll.

120 Hana Hwy., Paia. ✆ **808/579-8844**. No reservations. Main courses $11–$20. AE, DC, DISC, MC, V. Daily 11:30am–3pm and 5–10pm. Sushi bar Tues–Sat 5:30–10pm.

Milagros Food Company ★ SOUTHWESTERN/SEAFOOD   Milagros has gained a following with its great home-style cooking, upbeat atmosphere, and highly touted margaritas. Sit outdoors for some great people-watching as you tuck into dishes created with a combination of Southwestern and Pacific Rim styles and flavors accompanied by fresh veggies and Kula greens. Blackened ahi taquitos, pepper-crusted ono pasta, blue shrimp tostadas, and sandwiches, salads, and combination plates are some of the offerings here. For breakfast, I recommend the Olive Oyl spinach omelet or the huevos rancheros, served with home fries. I love Paia's tie-dyes, beads, and hippie flavor, and this is the front-row seat for it all. Watch for happy hour, with cheap and fabulous margaritas.

Hana Hwy. and Baldwin Ave., Paia. ✆ **808/579-8755**. Breakfast around $7; lunch $6–$10; dinner $15–$20. AE, MC, V. Daily 8am–10pm.

Moana Bakery & Cafe ★★ LOCAL/EUROPEAN   Moana gets high marks for its stylish concrete floors, high ceilings, booths and cafe tables, and fabulous food. Don Ritchey, formerly a chef at Haliimaile General Store, has created the perfect Paia eatery, a casual bakery-cafe that highlights his stellar skills. All the bases are covered: saimin, omelets, wraps, pancakes, and fresh-baked goods in the morning; soups, sandwiches, pasta, and satisfying salads for lunch; and for dinner, varied selections with Asian and European influences and fresh island ingredients. The lemon-grass-grilled prawns with green-papaya salad are an explosion of flavors and textures, the roasted vegetable napoleon is gourmet fare, and the Thai red curry with coconut milk, served over vegetables, seafood, or tofu, comes atop jasmine rice with crisp rice noodles and fresh sprouts to cool the fire. Ritchey has a special gift with fish, especially the nori-sesame-crusted *opakapaka* with wasabi beurre blanc. There's entertainment 3 nights a week, ranging from jazz to vintage Hawaiian to Latin.

71 Baldwin Ave. ✆ **808/579-9999**. Reservations recommended for dinner. Breakfast $4.60–$9.95; lunch $5.95–$9.95; dinner main courses $7.95–$24. MC, V. Tues–Sun 8am–9pm; Mon 8am–2:30pm.

INEXPENSIVE

Cafe des Amis ★ CREPES/SALADS   This Paia newcomer has quickly become known as the place for healthy and tasty lunches that are easy on the wallet. Crepes are the star here, and they are popular: spinach with feta cheese, scallops with garlic and chipotle chile, shrimp curry with coconut milk, and dozens more choices, including breakfast crepes and dessert crepes (like banana and chocolate or caramelized apples with rum). Equally popular are the salads (including Niçoise, Greek, and Caesar) and smoothies. The crepes come with a house salad—a great deal.

42 Baldwin Ave. ✆ 808/579-6323. Crepes $6.50–$8.50. MC, V. Open daily 8:30am–8:30pm.

Paia Fish Market ☆ SEAFOOD   This really is a fish market, with fresh fish to take home and cooked seafood, salads, pastas, fajitas, and quesadillas to take out or enjoy at the few picnic tables inside the restaurant. It's an appealing and budget-friendly selection: Cajun-style fresh catch, fresh-fish specials (usually ahi or salmon), fresh-fish tacos and quesadillas, and seafood and chicken pastas. You can also order hamburgers, cheeseburgers, fish and chips (or shrimp and chips), and wonderful lunch and dinner plates, cheap and tasty. Peppering the walls are photos of the number-one sport here, windsurfing.

110 Hana Hwy. ✆ 808/579-8030. Lunch and dinner plates $6.95–$20. DISC, MC, V. Daily 11am–9:30pm.

ELSEWHERE ON THE ROAD TO HANA

Mama's Fish House ☆☆☆ SEAFOOD   If you love fish, this is the place for you. The restaurant's entrance, a cove with windsurfers, tide pools, white sand, and a canoe resting under palm trees, is a South Seas fantasy worthy of Gauguin. The interior features curved lauhala-lined ceilings, walls of split bamboo, lavish arrangements of tropical blooms, and picture windows to let in the view. With servers wearing Polynesian prints and flowers behind their ears, and the sun setting in Kuau Cove, Mama's mood is hard to beat. The fish is fresh (the fishermen are even credited by name on the menu) and prepared Hawaiian-style, with tropical fruit or baked in a macadamia-nut-and-vanilla-bean crust, or in a number of preparations involving ferns, seaweed, Maui onions, and roasted kukui nut. My favorite menu item is mahimahi laulau with luau leaves (taro greens) and Maui onions, baked in ti leaves and served with Kalua pig and Hanalei poi. You can get deep-water ahi seared with coconut and lime, or ono "caught by Keith Nakamura along the 40-fathom ledge near Hana" in Hana ginger teriyaki with mac-nuts and crisp Maui onion. Other special touches include the use of Molokai sweet potato, Hana breadfruit, organic lettuces, Haiku bananas, and fresh coconut, which evoke the mood and tastes of old Hawaii.

799 Poho Place, just off the Hana Hwy., Kuau. ✆ 808/579-8488. Reservations recommended for lunch, required for dinner. Main courses $29–$36 lunch, $32–$49 dinner. AE, DC, DISC, MC, V. Opens daily at 11am, last seating at 9pm (light menu 2:30–4:45pm).

Nahiku Coffee Shop, Smoked Fish Stand, and Ti Gallery ☆ *Finds* SMOKED KABOBS   What a delight to stumble across this trio of comforts on the long drive to Hana! The small coffee shop sells locally made baked goods, Maui-grown coffee, banana bread, organic tropical-fruit smoothies, and the Original and Best Coconut Candy made by Hana character Jungle Johnny. Next door the Ti Gallery sells locally made Hawaiian arts and crafts, such as pottery and koa-wood vessels.

The barbecue smoker is my favorite part of the operation. It puts out superb smoked and grilled fish, fresh and locally caught, sending seductive aromas out into the moist Nahiku air. These are not jerkylike smoked meats; the process keeps the kabobs moist while retaining the smoke flavor. The breadfruit—sliced, wrapped in banana leaf, and baked—can be bland and starchy (like a baked potato), but it's a stroke of genius to give visitors a taste of this important Polynesian staple. The teriyaki-based marinade, made by the owner, adds a special touch to the fish (ono, ahi, marlin). One of the biggest sellers is the Kalua pig sandwich. Also a hit are the fish, beef, and chicken tacos, served with cheese, jalapeños, and salsa. When available, fresh corn on the cob from Kipahulu is also served. There are a few roadside picnic tables, or you can take your lunch to go.

Hana Hwy., ½ mile past mile marker 28. No phone. Kabobs $3 each. No credit cards. Coffee shop daily 9am–5:30pm. Fish stand Fri–Wed 10am–5pm. Gallery daily 10am–5pm.

Pauwela Cafe *Finds* INTERNATIONAL   It's easy to get lost while searching out this wonderful cafe, but it's such a find. I never dreamed you could dine so well with such pleasing informality. The tiny cafe with a few tables indoors and out has a strong local following for many reasons. Three local boys purchased this well-loved cafe from the original owners in 2004. Brandon Shim is the chef (formerly with Tommy Bahamas in Wailea) and trained under previous owner Chris Speere at the Maui Community College Culinary Arts School. Nearly everything in this tiny cafe is made from scratch. Breakfasts feature such scrumptious items as pain perdu (French bread in orange vanilla custard), veggie frittata, and Belgian waffles. Lunch is a great collection of salads and sandwiches, where the scene-stealing Kalua turkey sandwich consists of moist, smoky shredded turkey with cheese on home-baked French bread and covered with a green-chili-and-cilantro sauce. Also available are burgers (including a vegetarian taro burger), chicken quesadillas, and veggie burritos. Dinner entrees include a range of items, from chicken quesadillas to veggie lasagna to Cajun-grilled mahi. Because this cafe is located in an industrial center of sailboard and surfboard manufacturers, you may find a surf legend dining at the next table. The cafe is a little less than 1½ miles past the Haiku turn-off and ½ mile up on the left.

375 W. Kuiaha Rd., off Hana Hwy., past Haiku Rd., Haiku. © 808/575-9242. Breakfast $4.25–$7; lunch $5.25–$7.50; dinner $6.50–$9. MC, V. Mon–Fri 7am–2:30pm; Tues–Fri 5–8pm; Sun 8am–2pm.

6 At the End of the Road in East Maui: Hana

Hana Ranch Restaurant *Overrated* AMERICAN   Part of the Hotel Hana-Maui operation, the Hana Ranch Restaurant is the informal alternative to the hotel's dining room. Dinner choices include New York steak, prawns and pasta, and Pacific Rim options like spicy shrimp won tons or the predictable fresh-fish poke. The warmly received Wednesday Pizza Night and the luncheon buffets are the most affordable prospects: baked mahimahi, pita sandwiches, chicken stir-fry, cheeseburgers, and club and fresh-catch sandwiches. It's not an inspired menu, and the service can be practically nonexistent when the tour buses descend during lunch rush. There are indoor tables as well as two outdoor pavilions that offer distant ocean views. At the adjoining takeout stand, fast-food classics prevail: teriyaki plate lunch, mahimahi sandwich, cheeseburgers, hot dogs, and ice cream.

Hana Hwy. © 808/248-8255. Reservations required Fri–Sat. Main courses $18–$33. AE, DISC, MC, V. Daily 7–10am and 11am–3pm; Wed and Fri–Sat 6–8:30pm. Takeout counter open Wed, Fri, and Sat 6am–4pm; Sun–Tues and Thurs 6am–7pm.

Hotel Hana Maui *Finds* ECLECTIC   Not even Passport Resorts' executive chef, John Cox, who is in charge of developing the daily menu changes here, can put his finger on the delicious type of cuisine served for breakfast, lunch and dinner in the open-aired, large window dining room. "I call it cuisine inspired by Eastern Maui," he said pointing to the ingredients-driven menu: the fresh fish caught by local fishermen, the produce brought in by nearby farmers, the fruits that are in season. The result is true "Hawaiian" food, grown right on the island. Breakfast features an omelet with local Maui onions and a Hana fern salad, almond-crusted French toast, or local papaya with yogurt and homemade granola. Lunch ranges from Maui Cattle Company burgers to just-caught fish sandwiches. Dinner, which changes daily, can include just-picked lettuce for salads (Kula-grown baby romaine with Gruyere crostini and sherry-thyme vinaigrette, or baby lettuces with Kula citrus, local radishes, and Kalamata olives), a range of soups (like a chilled Kula cucumber soup) and a range of entrees (seared rare Hana-caught ahi with smoked bacon, forest mushrooms, and wilted greens, or oven-roasted chicken breast with crispy polenta, Nihiku bush beans, and mole sauce). Try the 3- or 4-course tasting menu, or even better, the chef's choice custom tasting.

Hana Hwy. Ⓒ **808/248-8211**. Reservations recommended for Fri–Sat dinner. Entrees $10–$14 breakfast, $12–$16 lunch, $31–$35 dinner; tasting menu $55 for 3-courses, $65 for 4-courses, $105 for Chef's Choice. AE, DISC, MC, V. Daily 7:30–10:30am, 11:30am–2:30pm, and 6–8:30pm. Friday buffet and Hawaiian show 6-8:30pm.

7

Fun on & off the Beach

This is why you've come to Maui—the sun, the sand, and the surf. In this chapter, I'll tell you about the best beaches, from where to soak up the rays to where to plunge beneath the waves. I've covered a range of ocean activities on Maui, as well as my favorite places and outfitters for these marine adventures. Also in this chapter are things to do on dry land, including the best spots for hiking and camping and the greatest golf courses.

1 Beaches

Maui has more than 80 accessible beaches of every conceivable description, from rocky black-sand beaches to powdery golden ones; there's even a rare red-sand beach. What follows is a personal selection of the finest of Maui's beaches, carefully chosen to suit a variety of needs, tastes, and interests.

Hawaii's beaches belong to the people. All beaches (even those in front of exclusive resorts) are public property, and you are welcome to visit. Hawaii state law requires all resorts and hotels to offer public right-of-way access to the beach, along with public parking. So just because a beach fronts a hotel doesn't mean that you can't enjoy the water. Generally, hotels welcome nonguests to their facilities. They frown on nonguests using the beach chairs reserved for guests, but if a nonguest has money and wants to rent gear, buy a drink, or eat a sandwich, well, money is money, and they will gladly accept it from anyone. For beach toys and equipment, contact the **Activity Warehouse** (© **800/343-2087**; www.travelhawaii.com), which has branches in Lahaina at 578 Front St., near Prison Street (© **808/667-4000**), and in Kihei at Azeka Place II, on the mountain side of Kihei Road near Lipoa Street (© **808/875-4000**). Beach chairs rent for $2 a day, coolers (with ice) for $2 a day, and a host of toys (Frisbees, volleyballs, and more) for $1 a day.

WEST MAUI

D. T. FLEMING BEACH PARK ☆☆

This quiet, out-of-the-way beach cove, named after the man who started the commercial growing of pineapples on the Valley Isle, is a great place to take the family. The crescent-shaped beach, located north of the Ritz-Carlton Hotel, starts at the 16th hole of the Kapalua golf course (Makaluapuna Point) and rolls around to the sea cliffs at the other side. Ironwood trees provide shade on the land side. Offshore, a shallow sandbar extends to the edge of the surf. The waters are generally good for swimming and snorkeling; sometimes, off on the right side near the sea cliffs, the waves build enough for body boarders and surfers to get a few good rides in. This park has lots of facilities: restrooms, showers, picnic tables, barbecue grills, and a paved parking lot.

KAANAPALI BEACH ⭐⭐

Four-mile-long Kaanapali is one of Maui's best beaches, with grainy gold sand as far as the eye can see. The beach parallels the sea channel through most of its length, and a paved beach walk links hotels and condos, open-air restaurants, and Whalers Village shopping center. Because Kaanapali is so long, and because most hotels have adjacent swimming pools, the beach is crowded only in pockets—there's plenty of room to find seclusion. Summertime swimming is excellent.

There's fabulous snorkeling around **Black Rock,** in front of the Sheraton. The water is clear, calm, and populated with clouds of tropical fish. You might even spot a turtle or two.

Facilities include outdoor showers; you can use the restrooms at the hotel pools. Various beach-activity vendors line up in front of the hotels, offering nearly every type of water activity and equipment.

Parking is a problem, though. There are two public entrances: At the south end, turn off Honoapiilani Highway into the Kaanapali Resort, and pay for parking there, or continue on Honoapiilani Highway, turn off at the last Kaanapali exit at the stoplight near the Maui Kaanapali Villas, and park next to the beach signs indicating public access (this is a little tricky to find and limited to only a few cars, so to save time, you might want to just head to the Sheraton or Whalers Village and plunk down your money).

KAPALUA BEACH ⭐⭐⭐

The beach cove that fronts the Kapalua Bay hotel is the stuff of dreams: a golden crescent bordered by two palm-studded points. The sandy bottom slopes gently to deep water at the bay mouth; the water is so clear that you can see where the gold sands turn to green and then deep blue. Protected from strong winds and currents by the lava-rock promontories, Kapalua's calm waters are great for snorkelers and swimmers of all ages and abilities, and the bay is big enough to paddle a kayak around without getting into the more challenging channel that separates Maui from Molokai. Waves come in just right for riding. Fish hang out by the rocks, making it great for snorkeling.

The beach is accessible from the hotel on one end, which provides sun chairs with shades and a beach-activities center for its guests, and a public access way on the other. It isn't so wide that you'll burn your feet getting in or out of the water, and the inland side is edged by a shady path and cool lawns. Outdoor showers are stationed at both ends. You'll also find restrooms, lifeguards, a rental shack, and plenty of shade.

Parking is limited to about 30 spaces in a small lot off Lower Honoapiilani Road, by Napili Kai Beach Club, so arrive early.

WAHIKULI COUNTY WAYSIDE PARK

This small stretch of beach, adjacent to Honoapiilani Highway between Lahaina and Kaanapali, is one of Lahaina's most popular beach parks. It's packed on weekends, but during the week it's a great place for swimming, snorkeling, sunbathing, and picnics. Facilities include paved parking, restrooms, showers, and small covered pavilions with picnic tables and barbecue grills.

LAUNIUPOKO COUNTY WAYSIDE PARK

Families with children will love this small park off Honoapiilani Highway, just south of Lahaina. A large wading pool for kids fronts the shady park, with giant boulders protecting the wading area from the surf outside. Just to the left is a small sandy beach

Beaches & Outdoor Activities

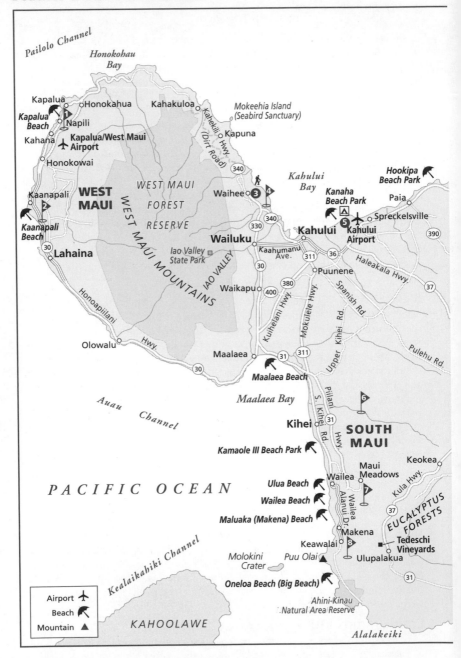

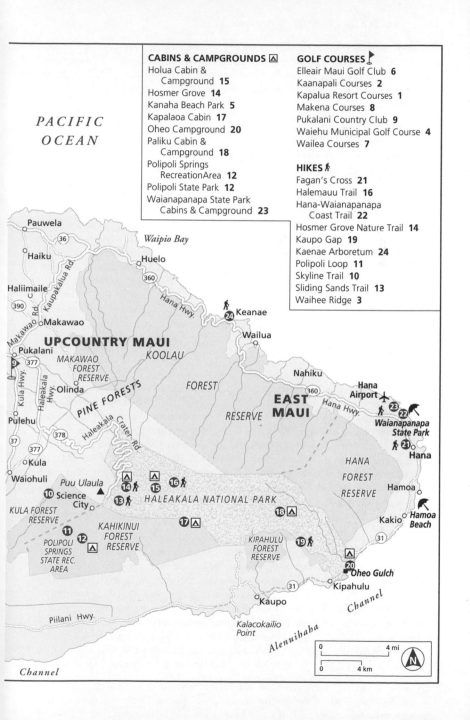

CABINS & CAMPGROUNDS ⌂
Holua Cabin & Campground **15**
Hosmer Grove **14**
Kanaha Beach Park **5**
Kapalaoa Cabin **17**
Oheo Campground **20**
Paliku Cabin & Campground **18**
Polipoli Springs RecreationArea **12**
Polipoli State Park **12**
Waianapanapa State Park Cabins & Campground **23**

GOLF COURSES
Elleair Maui Golf Club **6**
Kaanapali Courses **2**
Kapalua Resort Courses **1**
Makena Courses **8**
Pukalani Country Club **9**
Waiehu Municipal Golf Course **4**
Wailea Courses **7**

HIKES 𝄁
Fagan's Cross **21**
Halemauu Trail **16**
Hana-Waianapanapa Coast Trail **22**
Hosmer Grove Nature Trail **14**
Kaupo Gap **19**
Kaenae Arboretum **24**
Polipoli Loop **11**
Skyline Trail **10**
Sliding Sands Trail **13**
Waihee Ridge **3**

PACIFIC OCEAN

Pauwela
Haiku
Haliimaile
Makawao
Pukalani
Olinda
Pulehu
Kula
Waiohuli

UPCOUNTRY MAUI

MAKAWAO FOREST RESERVE

PINE FORESTS

KOOLAU

Waipio Bay
Huelo
Keanae
Wailua

FOREST

RESERVE

Nahiku

EAST MAUI

Hana Airport
Waianapanapa State Park
Hana
Hamoa
Kakio
Hamoa Beach

HANA FOREST RESERVE

Hana Hwy.

Puu Ulaula
Science City

HALEAKALA NATIONAL PARK

KULA FOREST RESERVE

KAHIKINUI FOREST RESERVE

POLIPOLI SPRINGS STATE REC. AREA

KIPAHULU FOREST RESERVE

Oheo Gulch
Kipahulu

Kaupo

Piilani Hwy.

Kalacokailio Point

Alenuihaha

Channel

0   4 mi
0   4 km

N

with good swimming when conditions are right. Offshore, the waves are occasionally big enough for surfing. The view from the park is one of the best: You can see the islands of Kahoolawe, Lanai, and Molokai in the distance. Facilities include a paved parking lot, restrooms, showers, picnic tables, and barbecue grills. It's crowded on weekends.

SOUTH MAUI
KAMAOLE III BEACH PARK ☆

Three beach parks—Kamaole I, II, and III—stand like golden jewels in the front yard of the funky seaside town of Kihei, which is exploding with suburban sprawl. The beaches are the best things about Kihei. All three are popular with local residents and visitors because they're easily accessible. On weekends they're jampacked with fishermen, picnickers, swimmers, and snorkelers.

The most popular is Kamaole III, or "Kam-3," as locals say. The biggest of the three beaches, with wide pockets of golden sand, it's the only one with a playground for children and a grassy lawn that meets the sand. Swimming is safe here, but scattered lava rocks are toe stubbers at the water line, and parents should watch to make sure that kids don't venture too far out, because the bottom slopes off quickly. Both the north and south shores are rocky fingers with a surge big enough to attract fish and snorkelers, and the winter waves attract bodysurfers. Kam-3 is also a wonderful place to watch the sunset. Facilities include restrooms, showers, picnic tables, barbecue grills, and lifeguards. There's also plenty of parking on South Kihei Road, across from the Maui Parkshore condos.

WAILEA BEACH ☆☆

Wailea is the best golden-sand crescent on Maui's sunbaked southwestern coast. One of five beaches within Wailea Resort, Wailea is big, wide, and protected on both sides by black lava points. It's the front yard of the Four Seasons Wailea and the Grand Wailea Resort Hotel and Spa. From the beach, the view out to sea is magnificent, framed by neighboring Kahoolawe and Lanai and the tiny crescent of Molokini, probably the most popular snorkel spot in these parts. The clear waters tumble to shore in waves just the right size for gentle riding, with or without a board. From shore, you can see Pacific humpback whales in season (Dec–Apr), and unreal sunsets nightly. Facilities include restrooms, outdoor showers, and limited free parking at the blue SHORELINE ACCESS sign, on Wailea Alanui Drive, the main drag of this resort.

ULUA BEACH ☆

One of the most popular beaches in Wailea, Ulua is a long, wide, crescent-shaped gold-sand beach between two rocky points. When the ocean is calm, Ulua offers Wailea's best snorkeling; when it's rough, the waves are excellent for bodysurfers. The ocean bottom is shallow and gently slopes down to deeper waters, making swimming generally safe. The beach is usually occupied by guests of nearby resorts; in high season (Christmas–Mar and June–Aug), it's carpeted with beach towels. Facilities include showers and restrooms. A variety of equipment is available for rent at the nearby Wailea Ocean Activity Center. To find Ulua, look for the blue SHORELINE ACCESS sign on South Kihei Road, near Stouffer Wailea Beach Resort. A tiny parking lot is nearby.

MALUAKA BEACH (MAKENA BEACH) ☆☆

On the southern end of Maui's resort coast, development falls off dramatically, leaving a wild, dry countryside of green kiawe trees. The Maui Prince sits in isolated splendor, sharing Makena Resort's 1,800 acres with only a couple of first-rate golf courses and a necklace of perfect beaches. The strand nearest the hotel is Maluaka Beach, often called Makena, notable for its beauty and its views of Molokini Crater, the offshore islet, and Kahoolawe, the so-called "target" island. It's a short, wide, palm-fringed crescent of golden, grainy sand set between two black-lava points and bounded by big sand dunes topped by a grassy knoll. Swimming in this mostly calm bay is considered the best on Makena Bay, which is bordered on the south by Puu Olai cinder cone and historic Keawala'i Congregational Church. Facilities include restrooms, showers, a landscaped park, lifeguards, and roadside parking. Along Makena Alanui, look for the SHORELINE ACCESS sign near the hotel, turn right, and head down to the shore.

ONELOA BEACH (BIG BEACH) ✪✪

Oneloa, which means "long sand" in Hawaiian, is one of the most popular beaches on Maui. Locals call it Big Beach—it's 3,300 feet long and more than 100 feet wide. Mauians come here to swim, fish, sunbathe, surf, and enjoy the view of Kahoolawe and Lanai. Snorkeling is good around the north end at the foot of Puu Olai, a 360-foot cinder cone. During storms, however, big waves lash the shore and a strong rip current sweeps the sharp drop-off, posing a danger for inexperienced open-ocean swimmers. There are no facilities except portable toilets, but there's plenty of parking. To get here, drive past the Maui Prince Hotel to the second dirt road, which leads through a kiawe thicket to the beach.

On the other side of Puu Olai is **Little Beach,** a small pocket beach where assorted nudists work on their all-over tans, to the chagrin of uptight authorities, who take a dim view of public nudity. You can get a nasty sunburn and a lewd-conduct ticket, too.

EAST MAUI
BALDWIN PARK

Located off the Hana Highway between Sprecklesville and Paia, this beach park draws lots of Maui residents, especially body-board enthusiasts. It's easy to see why this place is so popular: The surf breaks along the entire length of the white-sand beach, creating perfect conditions for body boarding. On occasion the waves get big enough for surfing. A couple of swimming areas are safe enough for children: one in the lee of the beach rocks near the large pavilion, and another at the opposite end of the beach, where beach rocks protect a small swimming area. There's a large pavilion with picnic tables and kitchen facilities, barbecue grills, additional picnic tables on the grassy area, restrooms, showers, a semipaved parking area, a baseball diamond, and a soccer field. The park is well used on weekends; weekdays are much quieter.

HOOKIPA BEACH PARK ✪

Two miles past Paia on the Hana Highway, you'll find one of the most famous wind-surfing sites in the world. Due to its constant winds and endless waves, Hookipa attracts top windsurfers and wave jumpers from around the globe. Surfers and fishermen also enjoy this small, gold-sand beach at the foot of a grassy cliff, which provides a natural amphitheater for spectators. Except when international competitions are being held, weekdays are the best time to watch the daredevils fly over the waves. When the water is flat, snorkelers and divers explore the reef. Facilities include restrooms, showers, pavilions, picnic tables, barbecue grills, and a parking lot.

Tips Safety Tip

Be sure to see the section "Health & Safety" in chapter 2 before setting out on your Maui adventures. It includes useful information on hiking, camping, and ocean safety, plus how to avoid seasickness and sunburn, and what to do should you get stung by a jellyfish.

WAIANAPANAPA STATE PARK 𝒢

Four miles before Hana, off the Hana Highway, is this beach park, which takes its name from the legend of the Waianapanapa Cave. Chief Kaakea, a jealous and cruel man, suspected his wife, Popoalaea, of having an affair. Popoalaea left her husband and hid herself in a chamber of the Waianapanapa Cave. A few days later, when Kaakea was passing by the cave, the shadow of a servant gave away Popoalaea's hiding place, and Kaakea killed her. During certain times of the year, the water in the tide pool turns red as a tribute to Popoalaea, commemorating her death. (Scientists claim, however, that the change in color is due to the presence of small red shrimp.)

Waianapanapa State Park's 120 acres have 12 cabins (see chapter 5), a caretaker's residence, a beach park, picnic tables, barbecue grills, restrooms, showers, a parking lot, a shoreline hiking trail, and a black-sand beach (it's actually small black pebbles). This is a wonderful area for both shoreline hikes (mosquitoes are plentiful, so bring insect repellent) and picnicking. Swimming is generally unsafe due to powerful rip currents and strong waves breaking offshore, which roll into the beach unchecked. Waianapanapa is crowded on weekends; weekdays are generally a better bet.

HAMOA BEACH 𝒢𝒢

This half-moon-shaped, gray-sand beach (a mix of coral and lava) in a truly tropical setting is a favorite among sunbathers seeking rest and refuge. The Hotel Hana-Maui maintains the beach and acts as though it's private, which it isn't—so just march down the lava-rock steps and grab a spot on the sand. James Michener said of Hamoa, "Paradoxically, the only beach I have ever seen that looks like the South Pacific was in the North Pacific—Hamoa Beach . . . a beach so perfectly formed that I wonder at its comparative obscurity." The 100-foot-wide beach is three football fields long and sits below 30-foot black-lava sea cliffs. Hamoa is often swept by powerful rip currents. Surf breaks offshore and rolls ashore, making this a popular surfing and bodysurfing area. The calm left side is best for snorkeling in summer. The hotel has numerous facilities for guests; there's an outdoor shower and restrooms for nonguests. Parking is limited. Look for the Hamoa Beach turnoff from Hana Highway.

2 Watersports

Activity Warehouse (© 800/343-2087; www.travelhawaii.com), which has branches in Lahaina at 578 Front St., near Prison Street (© 808/667-4000), and in Kihei at Azeka Place II, on the mountain side of Kihei Road near Lipoa Street (© 808/875-4000), rents everything from beach chairs and coolers to kayaks, boogie boards, and surfboards.

Snorkel Bob's (www.snorkelbob.com) has snorkel gear, boogie boards, and other ocean toys at four locations: 1217 Front St., Lahaina (© 808/661-4421); Napili Village, 5425-C Lower Honoapiilani Hwy., Napili (© 808/669-9603); in North Kihei at Azeka Place II, 1279 S. Kihei Rd. #310 (℃ **808/875-6188**); and in South Kihei/Wailea at the Kamaole Beach Center, 2411 S. Kihei Rd., Kihei (℃ **808/879-7449**). All locations are open daily from 8am to 5pm. If you're island hopping, you can rent from a Snorkel Bob's location on one island and return it at a branch on another.

BOATING & SAILING

To really appreciate Maui, you need to get off the land and get on the sea. Trade winds off the Lahaina Coast and the strong wind that rips through Maui's isthmus make sailing around the island exciting. Many different boats, from a three-masted schooner to spacious trimarans, offer day cruises from Maui.

Later in this section, you can find information on snorkel cruises to Molokini under "Snorkeling"; fishing charters under "Sport Fishing"; and trips that combine snorkeling with whale-watching under "Whale-Watching Cruises."

America II ✿ This U.S. contender in the 1987 America's Cup race is a true racing boat, a 65-foot sailing yacht offering 2-hour **morning sails, afternoon sails,** and **sunset sails** year-round, plus **whale-watching** in winter. These are sailing trips, so there's no snorkeling—just the thrill of racing with the wind. Complimentary bottled water, soda, and chips are available.

Lahaina Harbor, slip 5. ℃ **888/667-2133** or 808/667-2195. www.galaxymall.com/stores/americaii. Trips $33 adults, $17 children 12 and under. Whale-watching $25 adults, $13 children.

Scotch Mist Sailing Charters This 50-foot Santa Cruz sailboat offers 2-hour sailing adventures. Prices include snorkel gear, juice, fresh pineapple spears, Maui chips, beer, wine, and soda.

Lahaina Harbor, slip 2. ℃ **808/661-0386**. www.scotchmistsailingcharters.com. Sail trips $35 adults, $18 children ages 5–12, free for children under 5; sunset sail $45.

DAY CRUISES TO MOLOKAI

You can travel across the seas by ferry from Maui's Lahaina Harbor to Molokai's Kaunakakai Wharf on the *Molokai Princess* (℃ **800/275-6969** or 808/667-6165; www.mauiprincess.com). The 100-foot yacht, certified for 149 passengers, is fitted with the latest generation of gyroscopic stabilizers, making the ride smoother. The ferry makes the 90-minute journey from Lahaina to Kaunakakai daily; the cost is $85 for adults and $43 for children (ages 3–12) round-trip. Or you can choose to tour the island from two different package options: Cruise-Drive, which includes round-trip passage and a rental car for $169 for the driver, $80 per additional adult passenger, and $40 for children; or the Alii Tour, which is a guided tour in an air-conditioned van plus lunch for $169 for adults and $109 for children.

They also offer trips to the Kalaupapa Peninsula. A van takes you from the ferry landing to the head of the switchback trail down into the Kalaupapa Leprosy Settlement, then you can either fly out ($299 per person), or hike back out ($249 per person). See "The Legacy of Father Damien: Kalaupapa National Historic Park" on p. 277 for more information about the settlement.

DAY CRUISES TO LANAI

Expeditions Lahaina/Lanai Passenger Ferry *(Value* The cheapest way to Lanai is the ferry, which runs five times a day, 365 days a year. It leaves Lahaina at 6:45am, 9:15am, 12:45pm, 3:15pm, and 5:45pm; the return ferry from Lanai's Manele Bay Harbor leaves at 8am, 10:30am, 2pm, 4:30pm, and 6:45pm. The 9-mile channel crossing takes between 45 minutes and an hour, depending on sea conditions. Reservations are strongly recommended. Baggage is limited to two checked bags and one carry-on. Call **Lanai City Service** (© 800/800-4000 or 808/565-7227) to arrange a car rental or bus ride when you arrive.

Boat: Lahaina Harbor. Office: 658 Front St., Suite 127, Lahaina, HI 96761. © 800/695-2624 or 808/661-3756. www.go-lanai.com. Round-trip from Maui to Lanai $50 adults, $40 children 2–11 (free for children under 2).

Trilogy ⊛⊛⊛ *Kids*   Trilogy offers my favorite **snorkel-sail trips.** Hop aboard one of the custom-built catamarans, from 54 to 64 feet long, for a 90-mile sail from Lahaina Harbor to **Lanai's Hulopoe Beach,** a terrific marine preserve, for a fun-filled day of sailing, snorkeling, swimming, and **whale-watching** (in season). This is the only cruise that offers a personalized ground tour of the island, and the only one with rights to take you to Hulopoe Beach. The full-day trip costs $179 for adults, half-price for children ages 3 to 12. Ask about overnighters to Lanai.

Trilogy also offers snorkel-sail trips to **Molokini,** one of Hawaii's best snorkel spots. This half-day trip leaves from Maalaea Harbor and costs $110 for adults, half-price for kids ages 3 to 12, including breakfast and a barbecue lunch. There's also a late-morning half-day snorkel-sail off Kaanapali Beach for the same price.

These are the most expensive sail-snorkel cruises on Maui, but they're worth every penny. The crews are fun and knowledgeable, and the boats are comfortable and well-equipped. All trips include breakfast (homemade cinnamon buns) and a very good barbecue lunch (shipboard on the half-day trip, on land on the Lanai trip). Note, however, that you will be required to wear a flotation device no matter how good your swimming skills are; if this bothers you, go with another outfitter.

Other trips that Trilogy offers are: sailing/snorkeling from Kaanapali to Honolua Bay, with lunch, $110; a 1½-hour dolphin-watching excursion on a Zodiac for $60; a 2-hour whale-watching trip for $39; and a host of others.

© 888/MAUI-800 or 888/628-4800. www.sailtrilogy.com. Prices and departure points vary with cruise.

BODY BOARDING (BOOGIE BOARDING) & BODYSURFING

Bodysurfing—riding the waves without a board, becoming one with the rolling water—is a way of life in Hawaii. Some bodysurfers just rely on their hands to ride the waves; others use hand boards (flat, paddlelike gloves). For additional maneuverability, try a boogie board or body board (also known as belly boards or *paipo* boards). These 3-foot-long boards support the upper part of your body and are easy to carry and very maneuverable in the water. Both bodysurfing and body boarding require a pair of open-heeled swim fins to help propel you through the water.

Baldwin Beach, just outside of Paia, has great bodysurfing waves nearly year-round. In winter Maui's best bodysurfing spot is **Mokuleia Beach,** known locally as Slaughterhouse because of the cattle slaughterhouse that once stood here, not because of the waves—although they are definitely for expert bodysurfers only. To get to Mokuleia, take Honoapiilani Highway just past Kapalua Bay Resort; various hiking trails will take you down to the pocket beach. Storms from the south bring fair bodysurfing conditions and great boogie boarding to the lee side of Maui: **Oneloa (Big Beach)** in Makena, **Ulua** and **Kamaole III** in Kihei, and **Kapalua** beaches are all good choices.

OCEAN KAYAKING

Gliding silently over the water, propelled by a paddle, seeing Maui from the sea the way the early Hawaiians did—that's what ocean kayaking is all about. One of Maui's best kayak routes is along the **Kihei Coast,** where there's easy access to calm water.

Early mornings are always best, because the wind comes up around 11am, making seas choppy and paddling difficult.

The island's cheapest kayak rentals are at the **Activity Warehouse** (© **800/ 343-2087**; www.travelhawaii.com), which has branches in Lahaina at 578 Front St., near Prison Street (© **808/667-4000**), and in Kihei at Azeka Place II, on the mountain side of Kihei Road near Lipoa Street (© **808/875-4000**), where one-person kayaks are $10 a day, and two-person kayaks are $15 a day.

For the uninitiated, my favorite kayak-tour operator is **Makena Kayak Tours** ✪ (© **877/879-8426** or 808/879-8426; makenakyak@aol.com). Professional guide Dino Ventura leads a 2½-hour trip from Makena Landing and loves taking first-timers over the secluded coral reefs and into remote coves. His wonderful tour will be a highlight of your vacation. It costs $55, including refreshments and snorkel and kayak equipment.

South Pacific Kayaks, 2439 S. Kihei Rd., Kihei (© **800/776-2326** or 808/875-4848; www.mauikayak.com), is Maui's oldest kayak-tour company. Its expert guides lead ocean-kayak trips that include lessons, a guided tour, and snorkeling. Tours run from 2½ to 5 hours and range in price from $65 to $139. South Pacific also offers kayak rentals starting at $30 a day.

In Hana, **Hana-Maui Sea Sports** (© **808/248-7711**; www.hana-maui-seasports. com) runs 2-hour tours of Hana's coastline on wide, stable "no roll" kayaks, with snorkeling, for $89 per person. They also feature kayak surfing lessons for $89.

OCEAN RAFTING

If you're semiadventurous and looking for a more intimate experience with the sea, try ocean rafting. The inflatable rafts hold 6 to 24 passengers. Tours usually include snorkeling and coastal cruising. One of the best (and most reasonable) outfitters is **Hawaiian Ocean Raft** (© **888/677-RAFT** or 808/667-2191; www.hawaiioceanrafting.com), which operates out of Lahaina Harbor. The best deal is the 5-hour morning tour, which costs $70 for adults and $50 for children ages 5 to 12 (book online and save $10). It includes three snorkeling stops and time spent searching for dolphins, not to mention continental breakfast and midmorning snacks.

PARASAILING

Soar high above the crowds (at around 400 ft.) for a bird's-eye view of Maui. This ocean adventure sport, which is something of a cross between skydiving and water-skiing, involves sailing through the air, suspended under a large parachute attached by a towline to a speedboat. Keep in mind, though, that parasailing tours don't run during whale season, which is roughly December through May.

I recommend **UFO Parasail** (© **800/FLY-4-UFO** or 808/661-7-UFO; www.ufo parasail.net), which picks you up at Kaanapali Beach. UFO offers parasail rides daily from 8am to 2pm. The cost is $52 for the standard flight of 7 minutes of air time at 400 feet, $62 for a 10-minute ride at 800 feet, or $72 for 10 minutes at 1,200 feet. You can go up alone or with a friend; no experience is necessary. *Tip:* Take the early-bird special (when the light is fantastic and the price is right) at 8am for just $47 for 400 feet or $57 for 800 feet.

SCUBA DIVING

Some people come to Maui for the sole purpose of plunging into the tropical Pacific and exploring the underwater world. You can see the great variety of tropical marine life (more than 100 endemic species found nowhere else on the planet), explore sea

Tips An Expert Shares His Secrets: Maui's Best Dives

Ed Robinson, of Ed Robinson's Diving Adventures (see above), knows what makes a great dive. Here are some of his favorites on Maui:

Hawaiian Reef   This area off the Kihei-Wailea Coast is so named because it hosts a good cross section of Hawaiian topography and marine life. Diving to depths of 85 feet, you'll see everything from lava formations and coral reef to sand and rubble, plus a diverse range of both shallow- and deep-water creatures. It's clear why this area was so popular with ancient Hawaiian fishermen: Large helmet shells, a healthy garden of antler coral heads, and big schools of snapper are common.

Third Tank   Located off Makena Beach at 80 feet, this World War II tank is one of the most picturesque artificial reefs you're likely to see around Maui. It acts like a fish magnet: Because it's the only large solid object in the area, any fish or invertebrates looking for a safe home come here. Surrounding the tank is a cloak of schooling snappers and goatfish just waiting for photographers. It's fairly small, but Third Tank is loaded with more marine life per square inch than any site off Maui.

Molokini Crater   The backside of the crater is always done as a live boat-drift dive. The vertical wall plummets from more than 150 feet above sea level to around 250 feet below. Looking down to unseen depths gives you a feeling for the vastness of the open ocean. Pelagic fish and sharks are often sighted, and living coral perches on the wall, which is home to lobsters, crabs, and a number of photogenic black-coral trees at 50 feet.

There are actually two great dive sites around Molokini Crater. Named after common chub or rudderfish, **Enenue Side** gently slopes from the surface to about 60 feet, then drops rapidly to deeper waters. The shallower

caves, and swim with sea turtles and monk seals in the clear tropical waters off the island. I recommend going early in the morning. Trade winds often rough up the seas in the afternoon, so most dive operators schedule early-morning dives that end at noon, and then take the rest of the day off.

Unsure about scuba diving? Take an introductory dive: Most operators offer no-experience-necessary dives, ranging from $95 to $125. You can learn from this glimpse into the sea world whether diving is for you.

Everyone dives **Molokini,** a marine-life park and one of Hawaii's top dive spots. This crescent-shaped crater has three tiers of diving: a 35-foot plateau inside the crater basin (used by beginning divers and snorkelers), a wall sloping to 70 feet just beyond the inside plateau, and a sheer wall on the outside and backside of the crater that plunges 350 feet. This underwater park is very popular thanks to calm, clear, protected waters and an abundance of marine life, from manta rays to clouds of yellow butterfly fish.

For personalized diving, **Ed Robinson's Diving Adventures** (© 800/635-1273 or 808/879-3584; www.mauiscuba.com) is the only Maui company rated one of *Scuba Diver* magazine's top five best dive operators for 7 years straight. Ed, a widely published area is an easy dive, with lots of tame butterfly fish. It's also the home of Morgan Bentjaw, one of our friendliest moray eels. Enenue Side is often done as a live boat-drift dive to extend the range of the tour. Diving depths vary. Divers usually do a 50-foot dive, but on occasion advanced divers drop to the 130-foot level to visit the rare boarfish and the shark condos.

Almost every kind of fish found in Hawaii can be seen in the crystalline waters of **Reef's End.** It's an extension of the rim of the crater, which runs for about 600 feet underwater, barely breaking the surface. Reef's End is shallow enough for novice snorkelers and exciting enough for experienced divers. The end and outside of this shoal drop off in dramatic terraces to beyond diving range. In deeper waters there are shark ledges at varying depths and dozens of eels, some of which are tame, including moray, dragon, snowflake, and garden eels. The shallower inner side is home to Garbanzo, one of the largest and first eels to be tamed. The reef is covered with cauliflower coral; in bright sunlight it's one of the most dramatic underwater scenes in Hawaii.

La Pérouse Pinnacle   In the middle of scenic La Pérouse Bay, site of Haleakala's most recent lava flow, is a pinnacle rising from the 60-foot bottom to about 10 feet below the surface. Getting to the dive site is half the fun: The scenery above water is as exciting as that below the surface. Underwater, you'll enjoy a very diversified dive. Clouds of damselfish and triggerfish will greet you on the surface. Divers can approach even the timid bird wrasse. There are more porcupine puffers here than anywhere else, as well as schools of goatfish and fields of healthy finger coral. La Pérouse is good for snorkeling and long, shallow second dives.

underwater photographer, offers specialized charters for small groups. Two-tank dives are $120 ($135 with equipment); his dive boats depart from Kihei Boat Ramp.

If Ed is booked, call **Mike Severns Diving** (✆ **808/879-6596;** www.mikeseverns diving.com), for small (maximum 12 people, divided into two groups of six), personal diving tours on a 38-foot Munson/Hammerhead boat with freshwater shower. Mike and his wife, Pauline Fiene-Severns, are both biologists who make diving in Hawaii not only fun but also educational (they have a spectacular underwater photography book called *Molokini Island*). In their 25 years of operation, they have been accident-free. Two-tank dives are $110 (with equipment).

Stop by any location of **Maui Dive Shop** ☆ (www.mauidiveshop.com), Maui's largest diving retailer, with everything from rentals to scuba-diving instruction to dive-boat charters, for a free copy of the 24-page *Maui Dive Guide*. Inside are maps of and details on the 20 best shoreline and offshore dives and snorkel sites, each ranked for beginner, intermediate, or advanced snorkelers/divers. Maui Dive Shop has branches in Kihei at Azeka Place II Shopping Center, 1455 S. Kihei Rd. (✆ **808/879-3388**), Kamaole Shopping Center (✆ **808/879-1533**), and Shops at Wailea (✆ **808/875-9904**); in Lahaina at Lahaina Cannery Mall (© **808/661-5388**); and in the Honokowai Market Place (© **808/661-6166**). Other locations include Whalers Village, Kaanapali (© **808/661-5117**), Kaanapali Fairway Shops (© **808/551-9663**), Maalaea Village (© **808/244-5514**), and Kahana Gateway, Kahana (© **808/669-3800**).

SNORKELING

Snorkeling is the main attraction in Maui—and almost anyone can do it. All you need are a mask, a snorkel, fins, and some basic swimming skills. Floating over underwater worlds through colorful clouds of tropical fish is like a dream. In many places all you have to do is wade into the water and look down. If you've never snorkeled before, most resorts and excursion boats offer instruction, but it's plenty easy to figure it out for yourself.

Some snorkel tips: Always go with a buddy. Look up every once in a while to see where you are, how far offshore you are, and whether there's any boat traffic. Don't touch anything; not only can you damage coral, but camouflaged fish and shells with poisonous spines might surprise you. Always check with a dive shop, lifeguards, and others on the beach about the area in which you plan to snorkel: Are there any dangerous conditions you should know about? What are the current surf, tide, and weather conditions? If you're not a good swimmer, wear a life jacket or other flotation device, which you can rent at most places offering watersports gear.

Snorkel Bob's ⭐ (www.snorkelbob.com) and the **Activity Warehouse** will rent you everything you need; see the introduction to this section for locations. Also see "Scuba Diving" (above) for Maui Dive Shop's free booklet on great snorkeling sites.

When the whales aren't around, **Capt. Steve's Rafting Excursions** (© **808/667-5565;** www.captainsteves.com) offers 7-hour snorkel trips from Mala Wharf in Lahaina to the waters around **Lanai** (you don't actually land on the island). Rates of $150 for adults and $115 for children 12 and under include breakfast, lunch, snorkel gear, and wet suits.

Maui's best snorkeling beaches include **Kapalua Beach; Black Rock,** at Kaanapali Beach, in front of the Sheraton; along the Kihei coastline, especially at **Kamaole III Beach Park;** and along the Wailea coastline, particularly at **Ulua Beach.** Mornings are best because local winds don't kick in until around noon. **Olowalu** has great snorkeling around the **14-mile marker,** where there is a turtle-cleaning station about 150 to 225 feet out from shore. Turtles line up here to have cleaner wrasses pick off small parasites.

Ahihi-Kinau Natural Preserve is another terrific place. It requires more effort to reach it, but it's worth it because it's home to Maui's tropical marine life at its best. You can't miss in Ahihi Bay, a 2,000-acre state natural area reserve in the lee of Cape Kinau, on Maui's rugged south coast, where Haleakala spilled red-hot lava that ran to the sea in 1790. Fishing is strictly *kapu* (forbidden) here, and the fish know it; they're everywhere in this series of rocky coves and black-lava tide pools. The black, barren, lunarlike land stands in stark contrast to the green-blue water. After you snorkel, check out La Pérouse Bay on the south side of Cape Kinau, where the French admiral La Pérouse became the first European to set foot on Maui. A lava-rock pyramid known as Pérouse Monument marks the spot. To get here, drive south of Makena past Puu Olai to Ahihi Bay, where the road turns to gravel and sometimes seems like it'll disappear under the waves. At Cape Kinau, there are three four-wheel-drive trails that lead across the lava flow; take the shortest one, nearest La Pérouse Bay. If you have a standard car, drive as far as you can, park, and walk the remainder of the way.

If you'd like to head over to Lanai for a day of snorkeling in its pristine waters, see **"Day Cruises to Lanai"** above.

SNORKEL CRUISES TO MOLOKINI

Like a crescent moon fallen from the sky, the crater of **Molokini** 🅰 sits almost midway between Maui and the uninhabited island of Kahoolawe. Tilted so that only the thin rim of its southern side shows above water in a perfect semicircle, Molokini stands like a scoop against the tide, and it serves, on its concave side, as a natural sanctuary for tropical fish and snorkelers, who commute daily in a fleet of dive boats to this marine-life preserve. Note that in high season, Molokini can be crowded with dozens of boats, each carrying scores of snorkelers.

Maui Classic Charters 🅰🅰   Maui Classic Charters offers morning and afternoon **snorkel-sail cruises to Molokini** on *Four Winds II,* a 55-foot glass-bottom catamaran, for $79 adults ($49 children 3–12) for the morning sail and $40 adults ($30 children) in the afternoon. *Four Winds* trips include a continental breakfast; a barbecue lunch; complimentary beer, wine, and soda; complimentary snorkeling gear and instruction; and sport fishing along the way.

Those looking for speed should book a trip on the fast, state-of-the-art catamaran *Maui Magic.* The company offers a 5-hour snorkel journey to both Molokini and La Pérouse for $99 for adults and $79 for children ages 5 to 12, including a continental breakfast, barbecue lunch, drinks (beer, wine, and soda), snorkel gear, and instruction. During **whale season** (Dec–Apr) the Maui Magic Whale Watch, a 1½-hour trip with beverages, is $40 for adults and $30 for children ages 3 to 12.

Maalaea Harbor, slip 55 and slip 80. 🕾 **800/736-5740** or 808/879-8188. www.mauicharters.com. Prices vary depending on cruise.

Pacific Whale Foundation   This not-for-profit foundation supports its whale research by offering **whale-watch cruises** and **snorkel tours,** some to Molokini and Lanai. It operates a 65-foot power catamaran called *Ocean Spirit,* a 50-foot sailing catamaran called *Manute'a,* and a fleet of other boats. There are 15 daily trips to choose from, offered from December through May, out of both Lahaina and Maalaea harbors.

101 N. Kihei Rd., Kihei. 🕾 **800/942-5311** or 808/879-8811. www.pacificwhale.org. Trips from $20 adults, $15 children ages 7–12, free for ages 6 and under; snorkeling cruises from $30.

Pride of Maui   For a high-speed, action-packed snorkel-sail experience, consider the *Pride of Maui.* These 5½-hour **snorkel cruises** take in not only **Molokini** but also Turtle Bay and Makena for more snorkeling, and cost $86 for adults, $53 for children ages 3 to 12. Continental breakfast, barbecue lunch, gear, and instruction are included. They also have an afternoon Molokini cruise ($35 adults, $27 children, plus an optional lunch for an additional $5), an evening cocktail cruise ($47 adults, $20 children), and during whale season, a whale-watching cruise ($26 adults, $17 children).

Maalaea Harbor. 🕾 **877/TO-PRIDE** or 808/875-0955. www.prideofmaui.com. Prices vary; see above.

SPORT FISHING

Marlin (as big as 1,200 lb.), tuna, ono, and mahimahi await the baited hook in Maui's coastal and channel waters. No license is required; just book a sport-fishing vessel out of Lahaina or Maalaea harbors. Most charter boats that troll for big-game fish carry a maximum of six passengers. You can walk the docks, inspecting boats and talking to captains and crews, or book through an activities desk or one of the outfitters recommended below.

Shop around: Prices vary widely according to the boat, the crowd, and the captain. A shared boat for a half day of fishing starts at $100; a shared full day of fishing starts at around $140. A half-day exclusive (you get the entire boat) is around $400 to $700; a full-day exclusive can range from $500 to $1,000. Also, many boat captains tag and release marlin or keep the fish for themselves (sorry, that's Hawaii style). If you want to eat your mahimahi for dinner or have your marlin mounted, tell the captain before you go.

The best way to book a sport-fishing charter is through the experts: The best booking desk in the state is **Sportfish Hawaii** ✦ (✆ **877/388-1376** or 808/396-2607; www.sportfishhawaii.com), which not only books boats on Maui but on all the islands. These fishing vessels have been inspected and must meet rigorous criteria. Prices range from $850 to $950 for a full-day exclusive charter for up to six people; it's $599 to $750 for a half-day exclusive.

SUBMARINE DIVES

Plunging 100 feet below the surface of the sea in a state-of-the-art, high-tech submarine is a great way to experience Maui's magnificent underwater world, especially if you're not a swimmer. **Atlantis Submarines** ✦, 658 Front St., Lahaina (✆ **800/548-6262** or 808/667-2224; www.goatlantis.com), offers trips out of Lahaina Harbor every hour on the hour from 9am to 2pm at a cost of $80 for adults and $40 for children under 12 (children must be at least 3 ft. tall). Allow 2 hours for this underwater adventure. This is not a good choice if you're claustrophobic.

SURFING

The ancient Hawaiian sport of *hee nalu* (wave sliding) is probably the sport most people picture when they think of the islands. If you'd like to give it a shot, just sign up at any one of the recommended surfing schools listed below.

Tide and Kiva Rivers, two local boys (actually twins) who have been surfing since they could walk, operate **Rivers to the Sea** (✆ **808/280-8795** or 808/280-6236; www.riverstothesea.com), one of the best surfing schools on Maui. Rates are $75 each for a group of three or more, $200 for a couple, and $150 for a private lesson. All lessons are 2 hours long and include equipment and instruction. Tide, who has been surfing for 25 years, says they decide where the lesson will take place based on their client's ability and where the surf is on that day. He says he has beginners standing up in their first lesson.

Always wanted to learn to surf but didn't know whom to ask? Call the **Nancy Emerson School of Surfing,** 358 Papa Place, Suite F, Kahului (✆ **808/244-SURF** or 808/662-4445; fax 808/662-4443; www.surfclinics.com). Nancy has been surfing since 1961 and has even been a stunt performer for various movies, including *Waterworld.* She's pioneered a new instructional technique called "Learn to Surf in One Lesson"—you can, really. It's $75 per person for a 2-hour group lesson; private 2-hour classes are $160.

In Hana, **Hana-Maui Sea Sports** (✆ **808/248-7711;** www.hana-maui-seasports. com) has 2-hour long-board lessons taught by a certified ocean lifeguard for $89.

WHALE-WATCHING

Every winter pods of Pacific humpback whales make the 3,000-mile swim from the chilly waters of Alaska to bask in Maui's summery shallows, fluking, spy hopping, spouting, and having an all-around swell time.

The humpback is the star of the annual whale-watching season, which usually begins in December or January and lasts until April or sometimes May. About 1,500 to 3,000 humpback whales appear in Hawaii waters each year. Adults grow to be about 45 feet long and weigh a hefty 40 tons. Humpbacks are officially an endangered species: In 1997 some of the waters around the state were designated the Hawaiian Islands Humpback Whale National Marine Sanctuary, the country's only federal single-species sanctuary.

WHALE-WATCHING FROM SHORE

Between mid-December and April, you can just look out to sea. There's no best time of day for whale-watching, but the whales seem to appear when the sea is glassy and the wind calm. Once you see one, keep watching in the same vicinity—they might stay down for 20 minutes. Bring a book—and binoculars, if you can. You can rent binoculars for $2 a day at the **Activity Warehouse** (© **800/343-2087;** www.travelhawaii. com), which has branches in Lahaina at 578 Front St., near Prison Street (© **808/ 667-4000**), and in Kihei at Azeka Place II, on the mountain side of Kihei Road near Lipoa Street (© **808/875-4000**). Some good whale-watching points on Maui are:

McGregor Point   On the way to Lahaina, there's a scenic lookout at mile marker 9 (just before you get to the Lahaina Tunnel). It's a good viewpoint to scan for whales.

Outrigger Wailea Resort   On the Wailea coastal walk, stop at this resort to look for whales through the telescope installed as a public service by the Hawaiian Islands Humpback Whale National Marine Sanctuary.

Olowalu Reef   Along the straight part of Honoapiilani Highway, between McGregor Point and Olowalu, you'll often spot whales leaping out of the water. Sometimes their appearance brings traffic to a screeching halt: People abandon their cars and run down to the sea to watch, causing a major traffic jam. If you stop, pull off the road so that others can pass.

Puu Olai   It's a tough climb up this coastal landmark near the Maui Prince Hotel, but you're likely to be well rewarded: This is the island's best spot for offshore whale-watching. On the 360-foot cinder cone overlooking Makena Beach, you'll be at the right elevation to see Pacific humpbacks as they dodge Molokini and cruise up Alalakeiki Channel between Maui and Kahoolawe. If you don't see one, you'll at least have a whale of a view.

WHALE-WATCHING CRUISES

For a closer look, take a whale-watching cruise. The **Pacific Whale Foundation,** 101 N. Kihei Rd., Kihei (© **800/942-5311** or 808/879-8811; www.pacificwhale.org), is a nonprofit foundation in Kihei that supports its whale research by offering cruises and snorkel tours, some to Molokini and Lanai. They operate a 65-foot power catamaran called the *Ocean Spirit,* a 50-foot sailing catamaran called the *Manute'a,* and a sea kayak. They have 15 daily trips to choose from, and their rates for a 2-hour whale-watching cruise would make Captain Ahab smile (starting at $20 for adults, $15 for children). Cruises are offered from December through May, out of both Lahaina and Maalaea harbors.

If you want to combine ocean activities, then a snorkel or dive cruise to Molokini, the sunken crater off Maui's south coast, might be just the ticket. You can see whales on the way there, at no extra charge. See "Scuba Diving" and "Boating & Sailing" earlier in this section.

Tips Not So Close! They Hardly Know You

In your excitement at seeing a whale or a school of dolphins, don't get too close—both are protected under the Marine Mammals Protection Act. Swimmers, kayakers, and windsurfers must stay at least 300 feet away from all whales, dolphins, and other marine mammals. And yes, they have prosecuted visitors for swimming with dolphins! If you have any questions, call the **National Marine Fisheries Service** (© 808/541-2727) or the **Hawaiian Islands Humpback Whale National Marine Sanctuary** (© 800/831-4888).

WHALE-WATCHING BY KAYAK & RAFT

Seeing a humpback whale from an ocean kayak or raft is awesome. **Capt. Steve's Rafting Excursions** (© 808/667-5565; www.captainsteves.com) offers 2-hour whale-watching excursions out of Lahaina Harbor for $45 adults, $35 for children 12 and under. *Tip:* Save $10 by booking the "Early Bird" adventure, which leaves at 7:30am.

WINDSURFING

Maui has Hawaii's best windsurfing beaches. In winter windsurfers from around the world flock to the town of **Paia** to ride the waves. **Hookipa Beach,** known all over the globe for its brisk winds and excellent waves, is the site of several world-championship contests. **Kanaha,** west of Kahului Airport, also has dependable winds. When the winds turn northerly, **Kihei** is the spot to be: Some days you can spot whales in the distance behind the windsurfers. The northern end of Kihei is best: **Ohukai Park,** the first beach as you enter South Kiehi Road from the northern end, has not only good winds but parking, a long strip of grass to assemble your gear, and good access to the water. Experienced windsurfers here are found in front of the **Maui Sunset** condo, 1032 S. Kihei Rd., near Waipuilani Street (a block north of McDonald's), which has great windsurfing conditions but a very shallow reef (not good for beginners).

  Hawaiian Island Surf and Sport, 415 Dairy Rd., Kahului (© 800/231-6958 or 808/871-4981; www.hawaiianisland.com), offers lessons (from $79), rentals, and repairs. Other shops that offer rentals and lessons are **Hawaiian Sailboarding Techniques,** 425 Koloa St., Kahului (© 800/968-5423 or 808/871-5423; www.hstwindsurfing.com), with 2½-hour lessons from $79; and **Maui Windsurf Co.,** 22 Hana Hwy., Kahului (© 800/872-0999 or 808/877-4816; www.maui-windsurf.com), which has complete equipment rental (board, sail, rig harness, and roof rack) from $45 and lessons starting at $75.

  For daily reports on wind and surf conditions, call the **Wind and Surf Report** at © 808/877-3611.

3 Hiking & Camping

In the past 3 decades, Maui has grown from a rural island to a fast-paced resort destination, but its natural beauty largely remains; there are still many places that can be explored only on foot. Those interested in seeing the backcountry—complete with virgin waterfalls, remote wilderness trails, and quiet meditative settings—should head for Haleakala's upcountry or the tropical Hana coast.

  Camping on Maui can be extreme (inside a volcano) or benign (by the sea in Hana). It can be wet, cold, and rainy, or hot, dry, and windy—often all on the same day. If you're heading for Haleakala, remember that U.S. astronauts trained for the moon inside the volcano: Bring survival gear. Don't forget both your swimsuit and your rain gear if you're bound for Waianapanapa. Bring your own gear, as there are no places to rent camping equipment on Maui.

For more information on Maui camping and hiking trails and to obtain free maps, contact **Haleakala National Park,** P.O. Box 369, Makawao, HI 96768 (© **808/572-4400;** www.nps.gov/hale), and the **State Division of Forestry and Wildlife,** 54 S. High St., Wailuku, HI 96793 (© **808/984-8100;** www.hawaii.gov). For information on trails, hikes, and camping, and permits for state parks, contact the **Hawaii State Department of Land and Natural Resources,** State Parks Division, P.O. Box 621, Honolulu, HI 96809 (© **808/587-0300;** www.state.hi.us/dlnr); note that you can get information from the website but cannot obtain permits there. For information on Maui County Parks, contact **Maui County Parks and Recreation,** 1580-C Kaahumanu Ave., Wailuku, HI 96793 (© **808/243-7380;** www.mauimapp.com).

TIPS ON SAFE HIKING & CAMPING   Water might be everywhere in Hawaii, but it more than likely isn't safe to drink. Most stream water must be treated because cattle, pigs, and goats have probably contaminated the water upstream. The department of health continually warns campers of bacterium leptospirosis, which is found in freshwater streams throughout the state and enters the body through breaks in the skin or through the mucous membranes. It produces flulike symptoms and can be fatal. Make sure that your drinking water is safe by vigorously boiling it, or if boiling is not an option, use tablets with hydroperiodide; portable water filters will not screen out bacterium leptospirosis. Firewood isn't always available, so it's a good idea to carry a small, light backpacking stove, which you can use both to boil water and to cook meals.

Remember, the island is not crime-free: Never leave your valuables (wallet, airline ticket, and so on) unprotected. Carry a day pack if you have a campsite, and never camp alone. Some more do's and don'ts: Do bury personal waste away from streams, don't eat unknown fruit, do carry your trash out, and don't forget there is very little twilight in Maui when the sun sets—it gets dark quickly.

See "Health & Safety" in chapter 2 for more hiking and camping tips.

GUIDED HIKES   If you'd like a knowledgeable guide to accompany you on a hike, call **Maui Hiking Safaris** ✦ (© **888/445-3963** or 808/573-0168; www.mauihiking safaris.com). Owner Randy Warner takes visitors on half- and full-day hikes into valleys, rainforests, and coastal areas. Randy's been hiking around Maui for more than 15 years and is wise in the ways of Hawaiian history, native flora and fauna, and volcanology. His rates are $59 to $69 for a half day and $89 to $109 for a full day and include day packs, rain parkas, snacks, water, and, on full-day hikes, sandwiches.

Maui's oldest hiking guide company is **Hike Maui** ✦ (© **808/879-5270;** fax 808/893-2515; www.hikemaui.com), headed by Ken Schmitt, who pioneered guided hikes on the Valley Isle. Hike Maui offers five different hikes a day, ranging from an easy 1-mile, 3-hour hike to a waterfall ($65) to a strenuous, full-day hike in Haleakala Crater ($145). All prices include equipment and transportation.

Venture into the lush West Maui Mountains with an experienced guide on one of the numerous hikes offered by **Maui Eco-Adventures** (© **877/661-7720** or 808/661-7720; www.ecomaui.com). After a continental breakfast, you'll hike by streams and waterfalls, through native trees and plants, and on to breathtaking vistas. The tour includes a picnic lunch, swims in secluded pools, and memorable photo ops. The

---

(Moments   **A Different Viewpoint: Zipping Over the Forest Canopy**

For those looking for a different perspective on Haleakala, try **Skyline Eco-Adventures' Zipline Haleakala Tour** (P.O. Box 880518, Pukalani, HI 96788; (©) **808/878-8400**; www.skylinehawaii.com), which blends a short hike through a eucalyptus forest with four "zipline" crossings. During the zipline crossing, you'll be outfitted with a seat harness and connected to a cable, then launched from a 70-foot-high platform to "zip" along the cable suspended over the slopes of Haleakala. From this viewpoint, you fly over treetops, valleys, gulches, and waterfalls at 10 to 35 mph. These bird's-eye tours operate daily and take riders from ages 12 up, weighing between 80 and 300 pounds. The trip costs $79 ($67 if you book online).

6-hour excursion costs $115 per person, including meals, a fanny pack with bottled water, and rain gear if necessary. No children under 13 are allowed. An easier jaunt costs just $75.

About 1,500 years ago the verdant Kahakuloa Valley was a thriving Hawaiian village. Today only a few hundred people live in this secluded hamlet, but old Hawaii still lives on here. Explore the valley with **Ekahi Tours** ((©) **888/292-2422** or 808/877-9775; www.ekahi.com). Your guide, a Kahakuloa resident and a Hawaiiana expert, walks you through a taro farm, explains the mystical legends of the valley, and provides you with a peek into ancient Hawaii. The 7½-hour Kahakuloa Valley Tour is $80 for adults, $60 for children 11 and younger; snacks, beverages, and hotel pickup are included.

For information on hikes given by the **Hawaii Sierra Club** on Maui, call (©) **808/573-4147** (www.hi.sierraclub.org).

HALEAKALA NATIONAL PARK ⟨⟨⟨

For complete coverage of the national park, see "House of the Sun: Haleakala National Park" in chapter 8.

INTO THE WILDERNESS: SLIDING SANDS & HALEMAUU TRAILS

Hiking into Maui's dormant volcano is really the best way to see it. The terrain inside the wilderness area of the volcano, which ranges from burnt-red cinder cones to ebony-black lava flows, is simply spectacular. Inside the crater there are some 27 miles of hiking trails, two camping sites, and three cabins.

The best route takes in two trails: into the crater along **Sliding Sands Trail** ⟨⟨, which begins on the rim at 9,800 feet and descends into the belly of the beast, to the valley floor at 6,600 feet, and back out along **Halemauu Trail** ⟨⟨. Hardy hikers can consider making the 11-mile one-way descent, which takes 9 hours, and the equally long return ascent in 1 day. The rest of us will need to extend this steep but wonderful hike to 2 days. The descending and ascending trails aren't loops—you'll need to make advance transportation arrangements to get back to your car, which you'll leave at the beginning of the hike, about a 30- to 45-minute drive from where the Hale-mauu trail ends. You either arrange with someone to pick you up, hitchhike back up to your car, or hook up with other people doing the same thing and drop off one car at each trail head.

Arrange to stay at least 1 night in the park; 2 or 3 nights will allow you more time to actually explore the fascinating interior of the volcano. See below for details on the cabins and campgrounds in the wilderness area in the valley. Before you set out, stop at park headquarters to get camping and hiking updates. There is no registration for day hikers.

The trail head for Sliding Sands is well marked and the trail is easy to follow over lava flows and cinders. As you descend, look around: The view is breathtaking. In the afternoon, waves of clouds flow into the Kaupo and Koolau gaps. Vegetation is sparse to nonexistent at the top, but the closer you get to the valley floor, the more vegetation you'll see: bracken ferns, pili grass, shrubs, even flowers. On the floor the trail travels across rough lava flows, passing rare silversword plants, volcanic vents, and multicolored cinder cones.

The Halemauu Trail goes over red and black lava and past vegetation such as evening primrose as it begins its ascent up the valley wall. Occasionally, riders on horseback use this trail as an entry and exit from the park. The proper etiquette is to step aside and stand quietly next to the trail as the horses pass.

DAY HIKES FROM THE MAIN ENTRANCE

In addition to the difficult hike into the crater, the park has a few shorter and easier options. Anyone can take a ½-mile walk down the **Hosmer Grove Nature Trail** 🥾, or you can start down **Sliding Sands Trail** for a mile or two to get a hint of what lies ahead. Even this short hike can be exhausting at the high altitude. A good day hike is **Halemauu Trail** to Holua Cabin and back, an 8-mile, half-day trip. A 20-minute orientation presentation is given daily in the Summit Building at 9:30, 10:30, and 11:30am. The park rangers offer two **guided hikes.** The 2-hour, 2-mile **Cinder Desert Hike** takes place Tuesday and Friday at 10am and starts from the Sliding Sands Trailhead at the end of the Haleakala Visitor Center parking lot. The 3-hour, 3-mile **Waikamoi Cloud Forest Hike** leaves every Monday and Thursday at 9am; it starts at the Hosmer Grove, just inside the park entrance, and traverses through the Nature Conservancy's Waikamoi Preserve. *Always call in advance:* The hikes and briefing sessions may be canceled, so check first. For details, call the park at ℂ **808/ 572-4400** or visit www.nps.gov/hale.

Tips A Word of Warning About the Weather

The weather at nearly 10,000 feet can change suddenly and without warning. Come prepared for cold, high winds, rain, and even snow in winter. Temperatures can range from 77°F (25°C) down to 26°F (–3°C, and it feels even lower when you factor in the wind chill), and high winds are frequent. Rainfall varies from 40 inches a year on the west end of the crater to more than 200 inches on the eastern side. Bring boots, waterproof gear, warm clothes, extra layers, and lots of sunscreen—the sun shines very brightly up here.

CAMPING NEAR THE MAIN ENTRANCE

Most people stay at one of two tent campgrounds, unless they get lucky and win the lottery—the lottery, that is, for one of the three wilderness cabins. For more information, contact **Haleakala National Park,** P.O. Box 369, Makawao, HI 96768 (© 808/ 572-4400; www.nps.gov/hale).

CABINS   It can get really cold and windy down in the valley (see "A Word of Warning About the Weather" above), so try for a cabin. They're warm, protected from the elements, and reasonably priced. Each has 12 padded bunks (but no bedding; bring your own), a table, chairs, cooking utensils, a two-burner propane stove, and a wood-burning stove with firewood (you might also have a few cockroaches). The cabins are spaced so that each one is an easy walk from the other: Holua cabin is on the Halemauu Trail, Kapalaoa cabin on Sliding Sands Trail, and Paliku cabin on the eastern end by the Kaupo Gap. The rates are $55 a night for groups of one to six, $110 a night for groups of 7 to 12. The cabins are so popular that the National Park Service has a lottery system for reservations. Requests for cabins must be made 3 months in advance (be sure to request alternate dates). You can request all three cabins at once; you're limited to no more than 2 nights in one cabin and no more than 3 nights within the wilderness per month.

CAMPGROUNDS   If you don't win the cabin lottery, all is not lost—there are three tent-camping sites that can accommodate you: two in the wilderness, and one just outside at Hosmer Grove. There is no charge for tent camping.

Hosmer Grove, located at 6,800 feet, is a small, open grassy area surrounded by a forest. Trees protect campers from the winds, but nights still get quite cold—sometimes there's ice on the ground up here. This is the best place to spend the night in a tent if you want to see the Haleakala sunrise, and you don't have to take a long, grueling hike to get here (it's close to the road). Come up the day before, enjoy the park, take a day hike, and then turn in early. The enclosed-glass summit building opens at sunrise for those who come to greet the dawn—a welcome windbreak. Facilities include a covered pavilion with picnic tables and grills, chemical toilets, and drinking water. No permits are needed at Hosmer Grove, and there's no charge—but you can stay for only 3 nights in a 30-day period.

The two tent-camping areas inside the volcano are **Holua,** just off Halemauu at 6,920 feet; and **Paliku,** just before the Kaupo Gap at the eastern end of the valley, at 6,380 feet. Facilities at both campgrounds are limited to pit toilets and nonpotable catchment water. Water at Holua is limited, especially in summer. No open fires are allowed inside the volcano, so bring a stove if you plan to cook. Tent camping is restricted to the signed area. Camping is free but limited to 2 consecutive nights and no more than 3 nights a month inside the volcano. Permits are issued daily at park headquarters on a first-come, first-served basis. Occupancy is limited to 25 people in each campground.

THE EAST MAUI SECTION OF THE PARK AT KIPAHULU (NEAR HANA)

In the East Maui section of Haleakala National Park, you can set up at **Oheo Campground,** a first-come, first-served, drive-in campground with tent sites for 100 near the ocean, a few tables, barbecue grills, and chemical toilets. No permit is required, but there's a 3-night limit. No food or drinking water is available, so bring your own.

Bring a tent as well—it rains 75 inches a year here. Contact **Kipahulu Ranger Station,** Haleakala National Park, HI 96713 (© **808/248-7375;** www.nps.gov/hale).

HIKING FROM THE SUMMIT   If you hike from the crater rim down **Kaupo Gap** to the ocean, more than 20 miles away, you'll pass through climate zones ranging from arctic to tropical. On a clear day you can see every island except Kauai on the trip down.

APPROACHING KIPAHULU FROM HANA   If you drive to Kipahulu, you'll have to approach it from the Hana Highway—it's not accessible from the summit. Always check in at the ranger station before you begin your hike; the staff can inform you of current conditions and share their wonderful stories about the history, culture, flora, and fauna of the area. The entry fee is $10 a car, the same as for the summit atop Haleakala.

There are two hikes you can take here. The first is a short, easy .5-mile loop along the **Kaloa Point Trail** (Kaloa Point is a windy bluff overlooking **Oheo Gulch**), which leads toward the ocean along pools and waterfalls and back to the ranger station. The clearly marked path leaves the parking area and rambles along the flat, grassy peninsula. Along the way you'll see the remnants of an ancient fishing shrine, a house site, and a lauhala-thatched building depicting an earlier time. The pools are above and below the bridge; the best for swimming are usually above the bridge.

The second hike is for the more hardy. Although just a 4-mile round-trip, the trail is steep and you'll want to stop and swim in the pools, so allow 3 hours. You'll be climbing over rocks and up steep trails, so wear hiking boots. Take water, snacks, swim gear, and insect repellent. Always be on the lookout for flash-flood conditions. This walk will pass two magnificent waterfalls, the 181-foot **Makahiku Falls** and the even bigger 400-foot **Waimoku Falls** 🎔. The trail starts at the ranger station, where you'll walk uphill for .5 mile to a fence overlook at the thundering Makahiku Falls. If you're tired, you can turn around here; true adventurers should press on. Behind the lookout the well-worn trail picks up again and goes directly to a pool on the top of the Makahiku Falls. The pool is safe to swim in as long as the waters aren't rising; if they are, get out and head back to the ranger station. The rest of the trail takes you through a meadow and bamboo forest to Waimoku Falls.

GUIDED HIKES   The rangers at Kipahulu conduct a 1-mile hike to the **Bamboo Forest** 🎔 at 9am daily; .5-mile hikes or orientation talks are given at noon, 1:30, 2:30, and 3:30pm daily; and a 4-mile round-trip hike to **Waimoku Falls** takes place on Saturday at 9:30am. All programs and hikes begin at the ranger station. Again, always call in advance to make sure the hike will take place that day by contacting the **Kipahulu Ranger Station,** Haleakala National Park, HI 96713 (© **808/248-7375;** www.nps. gov/hale).

SKYLINE TRAIL, POLIPOLI SPRINGS STATE RECREATION AREA 🎔

This is some hike—strenuous but worth every step. It's 8 miles, all downhill, with a dazzling 100-mile view of the islands dotting the blue Pacific, plus the West Maui Mountains, which seem like a separate island.

The trail is located just outside Haleakala National Park at Polipoli Springs National Recreation Area; however, you access it by going through the national park to the summit. The Skyline Trail starts just beyond the Puu Ulaula summit building on the south side of Science City and follows the southwest rift zone of Haleakala from its lunarlike cinder cones to a cool redwood grove. The trail drops 3,800 feet on a 4-hour hike to the recreation area in the 12,000-acre Kahikinui Forest Reserve. If you'd rather drive, you'll need a four-wheel-drive vehicle to access the trail.

There's a **campground** at the recreation area, at 6,300 feet. No fee or reservations are required, but your stay must be limited to 5 nights. Tent camping is free, but you'll need a permit. One 10-bunk cabin is available for $45 a night for one to four guests ($5 for each additional guest); it has a cold shower, a gas stove, and no electricity. There is no drinking water available, so bring your own. To reserve, contact the **State Parks Division,** 54 S. High St., Room 101, Wailuku, HI 96793 (© **808/984-8109;** open 8am–4pm Mon–Fri; www.hawaii.gov).

POLIPOLI STATE PARK ⚑

You'll find one of the most unusual hiking experiences in the state at Polipoli State Park, part of the 21,000-acre Kula and Kahikinui Forest Reserve on the slope of Haleakala. At Polipoli it's hard to believe that you're in Hawaii. First of all, it's cold, even in summer, because the loop is up at 5,300 to 6,200 feet. Second, this former forest of native koa, ohia, and mamane trees, which was overlogged in the 1800s, was reforested in the 1930s with introduced species: pine, Monterey cypress, ash, sugi, red adler, redwood, and several varieties of eucalyptus.

The **Polipoli Loop** ⚑ is an easy, 5-mile hike that takes about 3 hours; dress warmly for it. To get here, take the Haleakala Highway (Hwy. 37) to Keokea and turn right onto Highway 337; after less than ½ mile, turn on Waipoli Road, which climbs swiftly. After 10 miles Waipoli Road ends at the Polipoli State Park campground. The well-marked trail head is next to the parking lot, near a stand of Monterey cypress; the tree-lined trail offers the best view of the island.

The Polipoli Loop is really a network of three trails: Haleakala Ridge, Plum Trail, and Redwood Trail. After .5 mile of meandering through groves of eucalyptus, black-wood, swamp mahogany, and hybrid cypress, you'll join the Haleakala Ridge Trail, which, about a mile into the trail, joins with the Plum Trail (named for the plums that ripen in June–July). It passes through massive redwoods and by an old Conservation Corps bunkhouse and a rundown cabin before joining up with the Redwood Trail, which climbs through Mexican pine, tropical ash, Port Orford cedar, and—of course—redwood.

Camping is allowed in the park with a $5-per-night permit from the **Division of State Parks,** 54 S. High St., Room 101, Wailuku, HI 96793 (© **808/984-8109;** www.hawaii.gov). There's one cabin, available by reservation.

KANAHA BEACH PARK CAMPING

One of the few Maui County camping facilities on the island is Kanaha Beach Park, located next to the Kahului Airport. The county has two separate areas for camping: 7 tent sites on the beach and an additional 10 tent sites inland. This well-used park is a favorite of windsurfers, who take advantage of the strong winds that roar across this end of the island. Facilities include a paved parking lot, portable toilets, outdoor showers, barbecue grills, and picnic tables. Camping is limited to 3 consecutive days; the permit fee is $3 per adult and 50¢ for children, per night, and can be obtained from the **Maui County Parks and Recreation Department,** 1580-C Kaahumanu Ave., Wailuku, HI 96793 (© **808/243-7389;** www.mauimapp.com). The 17 sites book up quickly; reserve your dates far in advance (the county will accept reservations a year in advance).

WAIANAPANAPA STATE PARK 𝕮𝕮

Tucked in a tropical jungle, on the outskirts of the little coastal town of Hana is Waianapanapa State Park, a black-sand beach set in an emerald forest.

HANA-WAIANAPANAPA COAST TRAIL 𝕮   This is an easy, 6-mile hike that takes you back in time. Allow 4 hours to walk along this relatively flat trail, which parallels the sea, along lava cliffs and a forest of lauhala trees. The best time of day is in either the early morning or the late evening, when the light on the lava and surf makes for great photos. Midday is the worst time; not only is it hot (lava intensifies the heat), but there's no shade or potable water available. There's no formal trail head; join the route at any point along the Waianapanapa Campground and go in either direction.

Along the trail, you'll see remains of an ancient *heiau* (temple), stands of lauhala trees, caves, a blowhole, and a remarkable plant, *naupaka,* that flourishes along the beach. Upon close inspection, you'll see that the naupaka has only half-blossoms; according to Hawaiian legend, a similar plant living in the mountains has the other half of the blossoms. One ancient explanation is that the two plants represent never-to-be-reunited lovers: As the story goes, the two lovers bickered so much that the gods, fed up with their incessant quarreling, banished one lover to the mountain and the other to the sea.

CAMPING   Waianapanapa has 12 cabins and a tent campground. Go for the cabins, as it rains torrentially here, sometimes turning the campground into something like a mud-wrestling arena. Tent-camping is $5 per night but limited to 5 nights in a 30-day period. Permits are available from the **State Parks Division,** 54 S. High St., Room 101, Wailuku, HI 96793 (© **808/984-8109;** www.hawaii.gov). Facilities include restrooms, outdoor showers, drinking water, and picnic tables.

HANA: THE HIKE TO FAGAN'S CROSS

This 3-mile hike to the cross erected in memory of Paul Fagan, the founder of Hana Ranch and Hotel Hana-Maui, offers spectacular views of the Hana Coast, particularly at sunset. The uphill trail starts across Hana Highway from the Hotel Hana-Maui. Enter the pastures at your own risk; they're often occupied by glaring bulls and cows with new calves. Watch your step as you ascend this steep hill on a jeep trail across open pastures to the cross and the breathtaking view.

KEANAE ARBORETUM 𝕮

About 47 miles from Kahului, along the Hana Highway and just after the Keanae YMCA Camp (and just before the turnoff to the Keanae Peninsula), is an easy family walk through the Keanae Arboretum, which is maintained by the State Department of Land and Natural Resources, Division of Forestry and Wildlife. The walk, which is just over 2 miles, passes through a forest with both native and introduced plants. Allow 1 to 2 hours, longer if you take time out to swim. Take rain gear and mosquito repellent.

Park at the Keanae Arboretum and pass through the turnstile. Walk along the fairly flat jeep road to the entrance. For .5 mile, you will pass by plants introduced to Hawaii (ornamental timber, pomelo, banana, papaya, hibiscus, and more), all with identifying tags. At the end of this section is a taro patch showing the different varieties that Hawaiians used as their staple crop. After the taro, a 1-mile trail leads through a Hawaiian rainforest. The trail crisscrosses a stream as it meanders through the forest. My favorite swimming hole is just to the left of the first stream crossing, at about 300 feet.

WAIHEE RIDGE ✔

This strenuous 3- to 4-mile hike, with a 1,500-foot climb, offers spectacular views of the valleys of the West Maui Mountains. Allow 3 to 4 hours for the round-trip hike. Pack a lunch, carry water, and pick a dry day, as this area is very wet. There's a picnic table at the summit with great views.

To get here from Wailuku, turn north on Market Street, which becomes the Kahekilii Highway (Hwy. 340) and passes through Waihee. Go just over 2½ miles from the Waihee Elementary School and look for the turnoff to the Boy Scouts' Camp Maluhia on the left. Turn into the camp and drive nearly a mile to the trail head on the jeep road. About ⅓ mile in, there will be another gate, marking the entrance to the West Maui Forest Reserve. A foot trail, kept in good shape by the State Department of Land and Natural Resources, begins here. The trail climbs to the top of the ridge, offering great views of the various valleys. The trail is marked by a number of switchbacks and can be extremely muddy and wet. In some areas it's so steep that you have to grab onto the trees and bushes for support. The trail takes you through a swampy area, then up to **Lanilili Peak,** where a picnic table and magnificent views await.

4 Great Golf

In some circles, Maui is synonymous with golf. The island's world-famous golf courses start at the very northern tip of the island and roll right around to Kaanapali, jumping down to Kihei and Wailea in the south. There are also some lesser-known municipal courses that offer challenging play for less than $100.

Golfers new to Maui should know that it's windy here, especially between 10am and 2pm, when winds of 10 to 15 mph are the norm. Play two to three clubs up or down to compensate for the wind factor. I also recommend bringing extra balls—the rough is thicker here and the wind will pick your ball up and drop it in very unappealing places (like water hazards).

If your heart is set on playing on a resort course, book at least a week in advance. For the ardent golfer on a tight budget: Play in the afternoon, when discounted twilight rates are in effect. There's no guarantee you'll get 18 holes in, especially in winter when it's dark by 6pm, but you'll have an opportunity to experience these world-famous courses at half the usual fee.

For last-minute and discount tee times, call **Stand-by Golf** (✆ **888/645-BOOK** or 808/874-0600; www.stand-bygolf.com) between 7am and 9pm. Stand-by offers discounted (up to 50% off greens fees), guaranteed tee times for same-day or next-day golfing.

Golf Club Rentals (✆ **808/665-0800;** www.mauiclubrentals.com) has custombuilt clubs for men, women, and juniors (both right- and left-handed), which can be delivered island-wide; the rates are just $20 to $25 a day. The company also offers lessons with pros starting at $150 for 9 holes plus greens fees.

CENTRAL MAUI

Waiehu Municipal Golf Course *Value* This public, oceanside, par-72 golf course is like playing two different courses: The first 9 holes, built in 1930, are set along the dramatic coastline, while the back 9 holes, added in 1966, head toward the mountains. It's a fun course that probably won't challenge your handicap. The only hazard here is the wind, which can rip off the ocean and play havoc with your ball. The only hole that can raise your blood pressure is the 511-yard, par-5, 4th hole, which is very narrow and very long.

Facilities include a snack bar, driving range, practice greens, golf-club rental, and clubhouse. Because this is a public course, the greens fees are low—but getting a tee time is tough.

P.O. Box 507, Wailuku, HI 96793. (C) 808/244-5934. Greens fees $25 Mon–Fri, $30 Sat–Sun and holidays. From the Kahului Airport, turn right on the Hana Hwy. (Hwy. 36), which becomes Kaahumanu Ave. (Hwy. 32). Turn right at the stoplight at the junction of Waiehu Beach Rd. (Hwy. 340). Go another 1½ miles, and you'll see the entrance on your right.

WEST MAUI

Kaanapali Courses 🏌 Both courses at Kaanapali offer a challenge to all golfers, from high handicappers to near-pros. The par-72, 6,305-yard **North Course** is a true Robert Trent Jones, Sr., design: an abundance of wide bunkers; several long, stretched-out tees; and the largest, most contoured greens on Maui. The tricky 18th hole (par 4, 435 yd.) has a water hazard on the approach to the green. The par-72, 6,250-yard **South Course** is an Arthur Jack Snyder design; although shorter than the North Course, it requires more accuracy on the narrow, hilly fairways. It also has a water hazard on its final hole, so don't tally up your score card until you sink the final putt.

Facilities include a driving range, putting course, and clubhouse with dining. You'll have a better chance of getting a tee time on weekdays.

Off Hwy. 30, Kaanapali. (C) 808/661-3691. www.kaanapali-golf.com. Greens fees: $160 (North Course), $130 (South Course); Kaanapali guests pay $130 (North), $117 (South); twilight rates $77 (North), $74 (South) for everyone. At the 1st stoplight in Kaanapali, turn onto Kaanapali Pkwy.; the 1st building on your right is the clubhouse.

Kapalua Resort Courses 🏌🏌🏌 The views from these three championship courses are worth the greens fees alone. The par-72, 6,761-yard **Bay Course** ((C) 808/669-8820) was designed by Arnold Palmer and Ed Seay. This course is a bit forgiving, with its wide fairways; the greens, however, are difficult to read. The often-photographed 5th overlooks a small ocean cove; even the pros have trouble with this rocky par-3, 205-yard hole. The par-71, 6,632-yard **Village Course** ((C) 808/669-8830), another Palmer/Seay design, is the most scenic of the three courses. The hole with the best vista is the 6th, which overlooks a lake with the ocean in the distance. But don't get distracted by the view—the tee is between two rows of Cook pines. The **Plantation Course** ((C) 808/669-8877), site of the Mercedes Championships, is a Ben Crenshaw/Bill Coore design. This 6,547-yard, par-73 course, set on a rolling hillside, is excellent for developing your low shots and precise chipping.

Facilities for all three courses include locker rooms, a driving range, and an excellent restaurant. Weekdays are your best bet for tee times.

Off Hwy. 30, Kapalua. (C) 877/KAPALUA. www.kapaluamaui.com. Greens fees: Village Course $185 ($130 for hotel guests), $85 twilight rate; Bay Course $200 ($140 for hotel guests), $90 twilight rate; Plantation Course $250 ($160 for hotel guests), $100 twilight rate.

SOUTH MAUI

Elleair Maui Golf Club (formerly Silversword Golf Club) Sitting in the foothills of Haleakala, just high enough to afford spectacular ocean vistas from every hole, this is a course for golfers who love the views as much as the fairways and greens. It's very forgiving. *Just one caveat:* Go in the morning. Not only is it cooler, but more important it's also less windy. In the afternoon the winds bluster down Haleakala with great gusto. This is a fun course to play, with some challenging holes: The par-5 2nd hole is a virtual minefield of bunkers, and the par-5 8th hole shoots over a swale and then uphill. Facilities include a clubhouse, driving range, putting green, pro shop, and lessons.

1345 Piilani Hwy. (near Lipoa St. turnoff), Kihei. © 808/874-0777. Greens fees: $100; twilight rates $80; 9-hole rates $60.

Makena Courses ⚲⚲ Here you'll find 36 holes of "Mr. Hawaii Golf"—Robert Trent Jones, Jr.—at its best. Add to that spectacular views: Molokini islet looms in the background, humpback whales gambol offshore in winter, and the tropical sunsets are spectacular. The par-72, 6,876-yard **South Course** has a couple of holes you'll never forget. The view from the par-4 15th hole, which shoots from an elevated tee 183 yards downhill to the Pacific, is magnificent. The 16th hole has a two-tiered green that's blind from the tee 383 yards away (that is, if you make it past the gully off the fairway). The par-72, 6,823-yard **North Course** is more difficult and more spectacular. The 13th hole, located partway up the mountain, has a view that makes most golfers stop and stare. The next hole is even more memorable: a 200-foot drop between tee and green.

Facilities include a clubhouse, a driving range, two putting greens, a pro shop, lockers, and lessons. Beware of weekend crowds.

On Makena Alanui Dr., just past the Maui Prince Hotel. © 808/879-3344. www.maui.net/~makena. Greens fees: North Course $170 ($95–$140 for Makena Resort guests), twilight rates $95 ($80 for guests); South Course $180 ($105–$150 for resort guests), twilight rates $105 ($90 for guests); guest rates vary seasonally, with higher rates in the winter.

Wailea Courses ⚲⚲ There are three courses to choose from at Wailea. The **Blue Course,** a par-72, 6,758-yard course designed by Arthur Jack Snyder and dotted with bunkers and water hazards, is for duffers and pros alike. The wide fairways appeal to beginners, while the undulating terrain makes it a course everyone can enjoy. A little more difficult is the par-72, 7,078-yard championship **Gold Course,** with narrow fairways, several tricky dogleg holes, and the classic Robert Trent Jones, Jr., challenges: natural hazards, like lava-rock walls. The **Emerald Course,** also designed by Robert Trent Jones, Jr., is Wailea's newest, with tropical landscaping and a player-friendly design.

With 54 holes to play, getting a tee time is slightly easier on weekends than at other resorts, but weekdays are best (the Emerald Course is usually the toughest to book). Facilities include two pro shops, restaurants, locker rooms, and a complete golf training facility.

Wailea Alanui Dr. (off Wailea Iki Dr.), Wailea. © 888/328-MAUI or 808/875-7450. www.waileagolf.com. Greens fees: Blue Course $175 ($135 resort guests), twilight rates $100 ($90 resort guests); Gold Course $185 ($145 resort guests); Emerald Course $185 ($145 resort guests).

UPCOUNTRY MAUI
Pukalani Country Club This cool, par-72, 6,962-yard course at 1,100 feet offers a break from the resorts' high greens fees, and it's really fun to play. The 3rd hole offers golfers two different options: a tough (especially into the wind) iron shot from the tee, across a gully (yuck!) to the green; or a shot down the side of the gully across a second green into sand traps below. (Most people choose to shoot down the side of the gully; it's actually easier than shooting across a ravine.) High handicappers will love this course, and more experienced players can make it more challenging by playing from the back tees. Facilities include club and shoe rentals, practice areas, lockers, a pro shop, and a restaurant.

360 Pukalani St., Pukalani. © 808/572-1314. www.pukalanigolf.com. Greens fees, including cart $60 for 18 holes before 11am; $55 11am–2pm; $45 after 2pm. 9 holes $35. Take the Hana Hwy. (Hwy. 36) to Haleakala Hwy. (Hwy. 37) to the Pukalani exit; turn right onto Pukalani St. and go 2 blocks.

5 Biking, Horseback Riding & Other Outdoor Activities
BIKING

It's not even close to dawn, but here you are, rubbing your eyes awake, riding in a van up the long, dark road to the top of Maui's sleeping volcano. It's colder than you ever thought possible for a tropical island. The air is thin. You stomp your chilly feet while you wait, sipping hot coffee. Then comes the sun, exploding over the yawning Haleakala Crater, which is big enough to swallow Manhattan whole—it's a mystical moment you won't soon forget, imprinted on a palette of dawn colors. Now you know why Hawaiians named it the House of the Sun. But there's no time to linger: Decked out in your screaming yellow parka, you mount your steed and test its most important feature, the brakes—because you're about to coast 37 miles down a 10,000-foot volcano.

Cruising down Haleakala, from the lunarlike landscape at the top, past flower farms, pineapple fields, and eucalyptus groves, is quite an experience—and you don't have to be an expert cyclist to do it. This is a safe, comfortable bicycle trip, although it requires some stamina in the colder, wetter months between November and March. Wear layers of warm clothing, because there may be a 30°F (16°C) change in temperature from the top of the mountain to the ocean. Generally, tour groups will not take riders under 12, but younger children can ride along in the van that accompanies the groups, as can pregnant women. The trip usually costs between $100 and $140, which includes hotel pickup, transport to the top, bicycle and safety equipment, and meals.

Maui's oldest downhill company is **Maui Downhill** ⚡ (© **800/535-BIKE** or 808/871-2155; www.mauidownhill.com), which offers a sunrise safari bike tour, including continental breakfast and brunch, starting at $150 (book online and save $48). If it's all booked up, try **Maui Mountain Cruisers** (© **800/232-6284** or 808/871-6014; www.mauimountaincruisers.com), which has sunrise trips at $130 (book online and save $35), or **Mountain Riders Bike Tours** (© **800/706-7700** or 808/242-9739; www.mountainriders.com), with sunrise rides for $115 (book online and save $17). All rates include hotel pickup, transport to the top, bicycle, safety equipment, and meals.

If you want to avoid the crowd and go down the mountain at your own pace, call **Haleakala Bike Company** (© **888/922-2453;** www.bikemaui.com), which will outfit you with the latest gear, take you up to the top, make sure you are secure on the bike, then let you ride down by yourself at your own pace. Trips range from $65 to $85; they also have bicycle rentals to tour other parts of Maui on your own (from $47 a day).

If you want to venture out on your own, rentals—$10 a day for cruisers and $20 a day for mountain bikes—are available from the **Activity Warehouse** (© **800/ 343-2087;** www.travelhawaii.com), which has branches in Lahaina at 602 Front St., near Prison Street (© **808/667-4000**), and in Kihei at Azeka Place II, on the mountain side of Kihei Road near Lipoa Street (© **808/875-4000**).

For information on bikeways and maps, get a copy of the *Maui County Bicycle Map,* which has information on road suitability, climate, trade winds, mileage, elevation changes, bike shops, safety tips, and various bicycling routes. The map is available for $7.50 ($6.25 for the map and $1.25 postage), bank checks or money orders only, from: Tri Isle R, C, and D Council, Attn: Bike Map Project, 200 Imi Kala St., Suite 208, Wailuku, HI 96793.

A great book for mountain bikers who want to venture out on their own is John Alford's *Mountain Biking the Hawaiian Islands,* published by Ohana Publishing (www.bikehawaii.com).

HORSEBACK RIDING

Maui offers spectacular adventure rides through rugged ranch lands, into tropical forests, and to remote swimming holes. One of our favorites is **Piiholo Ranch,** in Makawao (© **866/572-5544** or 808/357-5544; www.piiholo.com). A working cattle ranch, owned by the *kamaaina* (longtime resident) Baldwin family, this is a horseback-riding adventure with a variety of different rides to suit your ability, from the morning picnic ride, a 3½-hour ride on the ranch, with a picnic lunch, for $160 per person, to private rides, including working with the cowboys to round up the cattle, at $190 per person per hour.

If you're out in Hana, don't pass up the **Maui Stables** in Kipahulu (a mile past Oheo Gulch; © **808/248-7799;** www.mauistables.com). Not only do they offer two rides daily (9:30am and 1pm) through the mountains above Kipahulu Valley, but you also get a fantastic historical and cultural tour through the unspoiled landscape. It is an experience you will not forget. Both rides are $150.

For those horse lovers who are looking for the ultimate equine experience, check out Frank Levinson's **"Maui Horse Whisperer Experience"** (© **808/572-6211;** www.mauihorses.com), which includes a seminar on the language of the horse. It costs $200 for half-day and $300 for full-day workshops.

HALEAKALA ON HORSEBACK   If you'd like to ride down into Haleakala's crater, contact **Pony Express Tours** (© **808/667-2200** or 808/878-6698; www.pony expresstours.com), which offers a variety of rides down to the crater floor and back up, from $155 to $190 per person. Shorter 1- and 2-hour rides are also offered at Haleakala Ranch, located on the beautiful lower slopes of the volcano, for $95 and $115. If you book via the Internet, you get 10% off. Pony Express provides well-trained horses and experienced guides and accommodates all riding levels. You must be at least 10 years old, weigh no more than 230 pounds, and wear long pants and closed-toe shoes.

WAY OUT WEST ON MAUI: RANCH RIDES   I recommend riding with **Mendes Ranch & Trail Rides**, 3530 Kahekili Hwy., 4 miles past Wailuku (© **808/ 244-7320;** www.mendesranch.com). The 300-acre Mendes Ranch is a real-life working cowboy ranch that has the essential elements of an earthly paradise—rainbows, waterfalls, palm trees, coral-sand beaches, lagoons, tide pools, a rainforest, and its own volcanic peak (more than a mile high). Allan Mendes, a third-generation wrangler, will take you from the edge of the rainforest out to the sea. On the way you'll cross tree-studded meadows, where Texas longhorns sit in the shade, and pass a dusty corral where Allan's father, Ernest, a champion roper, may be breaking in a wild horse. Allan keeps close watch, turning often in his saddle to make sure everyone is happy. He points out flora and fauna and fields questions but generally just lets you soak up Maui's natural splendor in golden silence. The morning ride, which lasts 3 hours and ends with a barbecue back at the corral (the perfect ranch-style lunch after a morning in the saddle), is $130; the 2½-hour afternoon ride costs $89, including snacks.

SPELUNKING

Don't miss the opportunity to see how the Hawaiian Islands were made by exploring a million-year-old underground lava tube/cave. Chuck Thorne, of **Maui Cave Adventures** (© **808/248-7308;** www.mauicave.com), offers several tours of this unique geological feature. After more than 10 years of leading scuba tours through underwater caves around Hawaii, Chuck discovered some caves on land that he wanted to show visitors. When the land surrounding the largest cave on Maui went on the market in 1996, Chuck snapped it up and started his own tour company. The shortest (and cheapest) tour is a self-guided 30- to 45-minute tour for just $12, and kids as young as 6 years old can do it. His 75-minute walking tour ($29; no children under 6) is a fun, safe, and easy stroll through a huge, extinct lava tube with 40-foot ceilings. Chuck is a longtime student of the science of volcano-speleology and can discuss every little formation in the cave. He supplies all the equipment you'll need: lights, hard hats, gloves, and water bottles. For those looking for a longer experience, his "Wild Adventure Tours" are 2½ hours long and cost $79 (no one under 15). Wear long pants and closed shoes, and bring your camera.

If you want to combine caving with a tour of Hana, contact **Temptation Tours** (© **808/877-8888;** www.temptationtours.com). Their "Cave Quest" tour offers a 2-hour cave tour, plus an air-conditioned van tour from your hotel to Hana; the $184 cost includes continental breakfast, beachside picnic lunch, and a stop for a swim.

TENNIS

Maui has excellent public tennis courts; all are free and available from daylight to sunset (a few are even lit for night play until 10pm). The courts are available on a first-come, first-served basis; when someone's waiting, limit your play to 45 minutes. For a complete list of public courts, call **Maui County Parks and Recreation** (© **808/ 243-7230**). Because most public courts require a wait and are not conveniently located near the major resort areas, most visitors pay a fee to play at their own hotels. The exceptions to that rule are in Kihei (which has courts in Kalama Park on S. Kihei Rd. and in Waipualani Park on W. Waipualani Rd., behind the Maui Sunset Condo), in Lahaina (courts are in Malu'uou o lele Park, at Front and Shaw sts.), and in Hana (courts are in Hana Park, on the Hana Hwy.).

Private tennis courts are available at most resorts and hotels on the island. The **Kapalua Tennis Garden and Village Tennis Center,** Kapalua Resort (© **808/669-5677;** www.kapaluamaui.com), is home to the Kapalua Open, which features the largest purse in the state, on Labor Day weekend. Court rentals are $10 per person for resort guests and $12 per person for nonguests. The staff will match you up with a partner if you need one. In Wailea try the **Wailea Tennis Club,** 131 Wailea Iki Place (© **808/879-1958;** www.wailea-resort.com), with 11 Plexipave courts. Court fees are $12 per player.

8

Seeing the Sights

After a few days of just relaxing on the beach, the itch to explore the rest of Maui sets in: What's on top of Haleakala, looming in the distance? Is the road to Hana really the tropical jungle everyone raves about? What does the inside of a 19th-century whaling boat look like?

There is far more to the Valley Isle than just sun, sand, and surf. Get out and see for yourself the otherworldly interior of a 10,000-foot volcanic crater; watch endangered sea turtles make their way to nesting sites in a wildlife sanctuary; wander back in time to the days when whalers and missionaries fought for the soul of Lahaina; and feel the energy of a thundering waterfall cascade into a serene mountain pool.

1 By Air, Land & Sea: Guided Island Adventures

The adventures below aren't cheap. However, each one offers such a wonderful opportunity to see Maui from a unique perspective that, depending on your interests, you might make one of them the highlight of your trip—it'll be worth every penny.

FLYING HIGH: HELICOPTER RIDES

Only a helicopter can bring you face-to-face with remote sites like Maui's little-known Wall of Tears, near the summit of Puu Kukui in the West Maui Mountains. You'll glide through canyons etched with 1,000-foot waterfalls and over dense rainforests; you'll climb to 10,000 feet, high enough to glimpse the summit of Haleakala, and fly by the dramatic vistas at Molokai.

The first chopper pilots in Hawaii were good ol' boys on their way back from Vietnam—hard-flying, hard-drinking cowboys who cared more about the ride than the scenery. But not anymore. Today pilots, like the ones at Blue Hawaiian (see below), are an interesting hybrid: part Hawaiian historian, part DJ, part tour guide, and part amusement-ride operator. As you soar through the clouds, you'll learn about the island's flora, fauna, history, and culture.

Among the many helicopter-tour operators on Maui, the best is **Blue Hawaiian** ⚹⚹, at Kahului Airport (© **800/745-BLUE** or 808/871-8844; www.bluehawaiian.com), which not only takes you on the ride of your life but also entertains, educates, and leaves you with an experience you'll never forget. Blue Hawaiian also is the only helicopter company in the state to have the latest, high-tech, environmentally friendly (and quiet) Eco-Star helicopter, specially designed for air-tour operators. Flights vary from 30 to 100 minutes and range from $125 to $280. A keepsake video of your flight is available for $20 (so your friends at home can ooh and aah).

If Blue Hawaiian is booked, try **Sunshine Helicopters** (© **800/544-2520** or 808/871-0722; www.sunshinehelicopters.com), which offers a variety of flights from

(Kids) Especially for Kids

A Submarine Ride   **Atlantis Submarines** (© 800/548-6262) takes you down into the shallow coastal waters off Lahaina in a real sub. The kids will love seeing all the fish—maybe even a shark—and you'll stay dry the entire time. See "Going Under: Submarine Rides" below for details.

The Sugar Cane Train   This ride will appeal to small kids as well as train buffs of all ages. A steam engine pulls open passenger cars of the Lahaina/Kaanapali & Pacific Railroad on a 30-minute, 12-mile round-trip through sugar-cane fields between Lahaina and Kaanapali. The conductor sings and calls out the landmarks, and along the way you can see Molokai, Lanai, and the backside of Kaanapali. Tickets are $19 for adults, $13 for kids 3 to 12. Call © 808/661-0089 or www.sugarcanetrain.com for details.

Star Searches   The stars over Kaanapali shine big and bright because the tropical sky is almost entirely free of both pollutants and the interference of big-city lights. Amateur astronomers can probe the Milky Way, see the rings of Saturn and Jupiter's moons, and scan the Sea of Tranquillity in a 60-minute star search on the world's first recreational computer-driven telescope. This cosmic adventure takes place every night at the **Hyatt Regency Maui,** 200 Nohea Kai Dr. (© 808/661-1234), at 8, 9, and 10pm. If you are staying at the hotel, it is $20 for adults and $10 for children under 12; for nonguests it's $25 for adults and $15 for children.

Sharks, Stingrays & Starfish   Hawaii's largest aquarium, the **Maui Ocean Center** (© 808/875-1962), has a range of sea critters—from tiger sharks to tiny starfish—that are sure to fascinate kids of all ages. At this 5-acre facility in Maalaea, visitors can take a virtual walk from the beach down to the ocean depths via the three dozen tanks, countless exhibits, and 100-foot-long main oceanarium.

A Dragonfly's View   Kids will think this is too much fun to be educational. Don a face mask and get the dizzying perspective of what a dragonfly sees as it flies over a mountain stream, or watch the tiny *oopu* fish climb up a stream at the **Hawaii Nature Center** (© 808/244-6500) in beautiful Iao Valley, where you'll find some 30 hands-on, interactive exhibits and displays of Hawaii's natural history.

short hops around the West Maui Mountains to island tours. Prices range from $125 to $320.

GOING UNDER: SUBMARINE RIDES

Plunge 100 feet under the sea in a state-of-the-art, high-tech submarine and meet swarms of vibrant tropical fish up close and personal as they flutter through the deep blue waters off Lahaina. **Atlantis Submarines,** 665 Front St., Lahaina (© **800/548-6262** or 808/667-7816), offers trips out of Lahaina Harbor every hour on the hour from 9am to 1pm; tickets are $80 for adults and $40 for children under 12 (kids must be at least 3 ft. tall). Allow 2 hours for this underwater adventure.

ECOTOURS

Venture into the lush West Maui Mountains with an experienced guide on one of the numerous hikes offered by **Maui Eco-Adventures** (© 877/661-7720 or 808/661-7720; www.ecomaui.com). After a continental breakfast you'll hike by streams and waterfalls, through native trees and plants, and on to breathtaking vistas. The tour includes a stop for a picnic lunch, a swim in secluded pools, and memorable photo ops. The 6-hour excursion costs $115 per person, including meals, a fanny pack with bottled water, and rain gear if necessary. No children under 13 are allowed.

About 1,500 years ago the verdant Kahakuloa Valley was a thriving Hawaiian village. Today only a few hundred people live in this secluded hamlet, but old Hawaii still lives on here. Explore the valley with **Ekahi Tours** (© 888/292-2422 or 808/877-9775; www.ekahi.com). Your guide, a Kahakuloa resident and a Hawaiiana expert, walks you through a taro farm, explains the mystical legends of the valley, and provides you with a peek into ancient Hawaii. The 7½-hour Kahakuloa Valley Tour is $80 for adults, $60 for children under 12; snacks, beverages, and hotel pickup are included.

2 Central Maui

Central Maui isn't exactly tourist central; this is where real people live. You'll most likely land here and head directly to the beach. However, there are a few sights worth checking out if you need a respite from the sun and surf.

KAHULUI

Under the airport flight path, next to Maui's busiest intersection and across from Costco in Kahului's new business park, is the most unlikely place: **Kanaha Wildlife Sanctuary,** Haleakala Highway Extension and Hana Highway (© 808/984-8100). In the parking area off Haleakala Highway Extension (behind the mall, across the Hana Hwy. from Cutter Automotive), you'll find a 150-foot trail that meanders along the shore to a shade shelter and lookout. Watch for the sign proclaiming this the permanent home of the endangered black-neck Hawaiian stilt, whose population is now down to about 1,000 to 1,500. Naturalists say this is a good place to see endangered Hawaiian Koloa ducks, stilts, coots, and other migrating shorebirds. For a quieter, more natural-looking wildlife preserve, try the **Kealia Pond National Wildlife Preserve** in Kihei (p. 208).

PUUNENE

This town, located in the middle of the central Maui plains, is nearly gone. Once a thriving sugar-plantation town with hundreds of homes, a school, a shopping area, and a community center, today Puunene is little more than the sugar mill, a post office, and a museum. The Hawaiian Commercial & Sugar Co., owner of the land and the mill, has slowly phased out the rental plantation housing to open up more land to plant sugar.

Alexander & Baldwin Sugar Museum This former sugar-mill superintendent's home has been converted into a museum that tells the story of sugar in Hawaii. Exhibits explain how sugar is grown, harvested, and milled. An eye-opening display shows how Samuel Alexander and Henry Baldwin managed to acquire huge chunks of land from the Kingdom of Hawaii, then ruthlessly fought to gain access to water on the other side of the island, making sugar cane an economically viable crop. Allow about a half-hour to enjoy the museum.

Puunene Ave. (Hwy. 350) and Hansen Rd. © 808/871-8058. www.sugarmuseum.com. Admission $5 adults, $2 children 6–17, free for children 5 and under. Daily 9:30am–4:30pm.

WAIKAPU

Across the sugar-cane fields from Puunene, and about 3 miles south of Wailuku on the Honoapiilani Highway, lies the tiny, one-street village of Waikapu, which has two attractions that are worth a peek, especially if you're trying to kill time before your flight out.

Relive Maui's past by taking a 40-minute narrated tram ride around fields of pineapple, sugar cane, and papaya trees at **Maui Tropical Plantation,** 1670 Honoapiilani Hwy., Waikapu (© **800/451-6805** or 808/244-7643), a real working plantation (open daily 9am–5pm). A shop sells fresh and dried fruit, and a restaurant serves lunch. Admission is free; the tram tours, which start at 10am and leave about every 45 minutes, are $9.50 for adults and $3.50 for kids 3 to 12.

Marilyn Monroe and Frank Lloyd Wright meet for dinner every night (well, sort of) at the **Waikapu Golf and Country Club,** 2500 Honoapiilani Hwy. (© **808/244-2011**), one of Maui's most unusual buildings. Neither actually set foot on Maui, but these icons of glamour and architecture share a Hawaiian legacy. Wright designed this place for a Pennsylvania family in 1949, but it was never constructed. In 1957 Marilyn and husband Arthur Miller wanted it built for them in Connecticut, but they separated the following year. When Tokyo billionaire Takeshi Sekiguchi went shopping at Taliesen West for a signature building to adorn his 18-hole golf course, he found the blueprints and had Marilyn's Wright house cleverly redesigned as a clubhouse. It doesn't quite fit the setting, but it's still the best-looking building on Maui today. You can walk in and look around at Wright's architecture and the portraits of Marilyn in Monroe's, the restaurant.

WAILUKU

This historic gateway to Iao Valley (see below) is worth a visit, if only for a brief stop at the Bailey House Museum and some terrific shopping (see chapter 9).

Bailey House Museum Missionary and sugar planter Edward Bailey's 1833 home—an architectural hybrid of stones laid by Hawaiian craftsmen and timbers joined in a display of Yankee ingenuity—is a treasure trove of Hawaiiana. Inside you'll find an eclectic collection, from precontact artifacts like scary temple images, dogtooth necklaces, and a rare lei made of tree-snail shells to latter-day relics like Duke Kahanamoku's 1919 redwood surfboard and a koa-wood table given to President Ulysses S. Grant, who had to refuse it because he couldn't accept gifts from foreign countries. There's also a gallery devoted to a few of Bailey's landscapes, painted from 1866 to 1896, which capture on canvas a Maui we can only imagine today.

2375-A Main St. © 808/244-3326. www.mauimuseum.org. Admission $5 adults, $4 seniors, $1 children 7–12, free for children 6 and under. Mon–Sat 10am–4pm.

IAO VALLEY

A couple of miles north of Wailuku, past the Bailey House Museum, where the little plantation houses stop and the road climbs ever higher, Maui's true nature begins to reveal itself. The transition between suburban sprawl and raw nature is so abrupt that most people who drive up into the valley don't realize they're suddenly in a rainforest. The walls of the canyon begin to close around them, and a 2,250-foot needle pricks gray clouds scudding across the blue sky. The air is moist and cool, and the shade a welcome comfort. This is Iao Valley, a 6-acre state park whose great nature, history, and beauty have been enjoyed by millions of people from around the world for more than a century.

Iao ("Supreme Light") Valley, 10 miles long and encompassing 4,000 acres, is the eroded volcanic caldera of the West Maui Mountains. The head of the Iao Valley is a broad circular amphitheater where four major streams converge into Iao Stream. At the back of the amphitheater is rain-drenched Puu Kukui, the West Maui Mountains' highest point. No other Hawaiian valley lets you go from seacoast to rainforest so easily. This peaceful valley, full of tropical plants, rainbows, waterfalls, swimming holes, and hiking trails, is a place of solitude, reflection, and escape for residents and visitors alike.

From Wailuku, take Main Street, then turn right on Iao Valley Road to the entrance to the state park. The park is open daily from 7am to 7pm. Go early in the morning or late in the afternoon, when the sun's rays slant into the valley and create a mystical atmosphere. You can bring a picnic and spend the day, but be prepared at any time for a tropical cloudburst, which often soaks the valley and swells both waterfalls and streams.

For information, contact **Iao Valley State Park,** State Parks and Recreation, 54 S. High St., Room 101, Wailuku, HI 96793 (✆ **808/984-8109;** www.hawaii.gov). The **Hawaii Nature Center** ⚡, 875 Iao Valley Rd. (✆ **808/244-6500;** www.hawaiinature center.org), home of the Iao Valley Nature Center, features hands-on, interactive exhibits and displays relating the story of Hawaiian natural history; it's an important stop for all who want to explore Iao Valley. Hours are daily from 10am to 4pm. Admission is $6 for adults, $4 for children 4 to 12, and free for children under 4.

Two paved walkways loop into the massive green amphitheater, across the bridge of Iao Stream, and along the stream itself. The .33-mile loop on a paved trail is an easy walk—you can even take your grandmother on this one. A leisurely stroll will allow you to enjoy lovely views of the Iao Needle and the lush vegetation. Others often proceed beyond the state park border and take two trails deeper into the valley, but the trails enter private land, and NO TRESPASSING signs are posted.

The feature known as **Iao Needle** is an erosional remnant composed of basalt dikes. The phallic rock juts an impressive 2,250 feet above sea level. Youngsters play in **Iao Stream,** a peaceful brook that belies its bloody history. In 1790 King Kamehameha the Great and his men engaged in the bloody battle of Iao Valley to gain control of Maui. When the battle ended, so many bodies blocked Iao Stream that the battle site was named Kepaniwai, or "damming of the waters." An architectural heritage park of Hawaiian, Japanese, Chinese, Filipino, and New England–style houses stands in harmony by Iao Stream at **Kepaniwai Heritage Garden.** This is a good picnic spot, with plenty of picnic tables and benches. You can see ferns, banana trees, and other native and exotic plants in the **Iao Valley Botanic Garden** along the stream.

3 Lahaina & West Maui

OLOWALU

Most people drive right by Olowalu, on the Honoapiilani Highway 5 miles south of Lahaina; there's little to mark the spot but a small general store and Chez Paul (p. 138), an excellent French restaurant. Olowalu (many hills) was the scene of a bloody massacre in 1790. The Hawaiians stole a skiff from the USS *Eleanora,* took it back to shore here, and burned it for its iron parts. The captain of the ship, Simon Metcalf, was furious and tricked the Hawaiians into sailing out in their canoes to trade with the ship. As the canoes approached, he mowed them down with his cannons, killing 100 people and wounding many others.

Olowalu has great snorkeling around **mile marker 14,** where there is a turtle-cleaning station about 150 to 225 feet out from shore. Turtles line up here to have cleaner wrasses (small bony fish) pick off small parasites.

HISTORIC LAHAINA

Located between the West Maui Mountains and the deep azure ocean offshore, Lahaina stands out as one of the few places in Hawaii that has managed to preserve its 19th-century heritage while still accommodating 21st-century guests.

In ancient times, powerful chiefs and kings ruled this hot, dry, oceanside village. At the turn of the 19th century, after King Kamehameha united the Hawaiian Islands, he made Lahaina the royal capital—which it remained until 1845, when Kamehameha III moved the capital to the larger port of Honolulu.

In the 1840s the whaling industry was at its peak: Hundreds of ships called into Lahaina every year. The streets were filled with sailors 24 hours a day. Even Herman Melville, who later wrote *Moby-Dick*, visited Lahaina.

Just 20 years later the whaling industry was waning, and sugar had taken over the town. The Pioneer Sugar Mill Co., which still stands but no longer operates today, reigned over Lahaina for the next 100 years.

Today the drunken and derelict whalers who wandered through Lahaina's streets in search of bars, dance halls, and brothels have been replaced by hordes of tourists crowding into the small mile-long main section of town in search of boutiques, art galleries, and chic gourmet eateries. Lahaina's colorful past continues to have a profound influence today. This is no quiet seaside village, but a vibrant, cutting-edge kind of place, filled with a sense of history—but definitely with its mind on the future.

See chapter 7 for details on the various cruises and outfitters operating out of Lahaina.

Baldwin Home Museum 𝄞 The oldest house in Lahaina, this coral-and-rock structure was built in 1834 by Rev. Dwight Baldwin, a doctor with the fourth company of American missionaries to sail to Hawaii. Like many missionaries, he came to Hawaii to do good—and did very well for himself. After 17 years of service, Baldwin was granted 2,600 acres in Kapalua for farming and grazing. His ranch manager experimented with what Hawaiians called *hala-kahiki*, or pineapple, on a 4-acre plot. The rest is history. The house looks as if Baldwin has just stepped out for a minute to tend a sick neighbor down the street.

Next door is the **Masters' Reading Room,** Maui's oldest building. This became visiting sea captains' favorite hangout once the missionaries closed down all of Lahaina's grog shops and banned prostitution. By 1844, once hotels and bars started reopening,

---

Day Trips to Molokai

It's possible to visit Molokai's famous leper colony (officially known as Kalaupapa National Historic Park) as a day trip from Maui. You won't be able to squeeze in the exhilarating mule ride down the 1,600-foot cliffs (they start at 8am), but you didn't want to sit on your own ass all day long anyway, now did you? (Sorry, bad pun.) **Pacific Wings** (✆ 808/873-0877; www.pacificwings.com) offers daily scheduled flights to Kalaupapa from Honolulu and Kahului, Maui, for $160 round-trip. Or check out **Paragon Air** (✆ 808/244-3356; www. paragon-air.com), which offers a $279 package deal that includes round-trip airfare from Kahului Airport to Molokai's Kalaupapa airport, a 4-hour tour, lunch, and drinks. All visitors must be at least 16 years old.

Lahaina

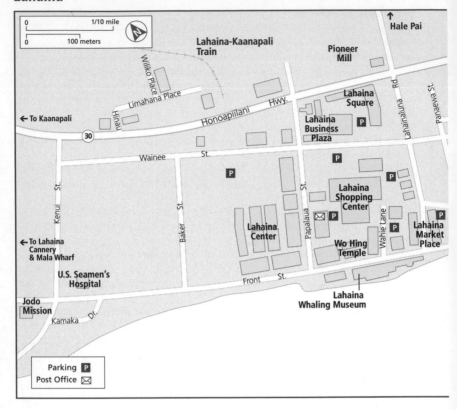

it lost its appeal. It's now the headquarters of the **Lahaina Restoration Foundation** (© **808/661-3262**), a plucky band of historians who try to keep this town alive and antique at the same time. Stop in and pick up a self-guided walking-tour map of Lahaina's most historic sites.

120 Dickenson St. (at Front St.). © **808/661-3262**. www.lahainarestoration.org. Admission $3 adults, $2 seniors, $5 families. Daily 10am–4:30pm.

Banyan Tree (Kids) Of all the banyan trees in Hawaii, this is the greatest of all—so big that you can't get it in your camera's viewfinder. It was only 8 feet tall when it was planted in 1873 by Maui sheriff William O. Smith to mark the 50th anniversary of Lahaina's first Christian mission. Now it's more than 50 feet tall, has 12 major trunks, and shades ⅔ acre in Courthouse Square.

At the Courthouse Building, 649 Wharf St.

Hale Pai When the missionaries arrived in Hawaii to spread the word of God, they found the Hawaiians had no written language. They quickly rectified the situation by converting the Hawaiian sounds into a written language. They then built the first printing press in order to print educational materials that would assist them on their mission. Hale Pai was the printing house for the Lahainaluna Seminary, the oldest

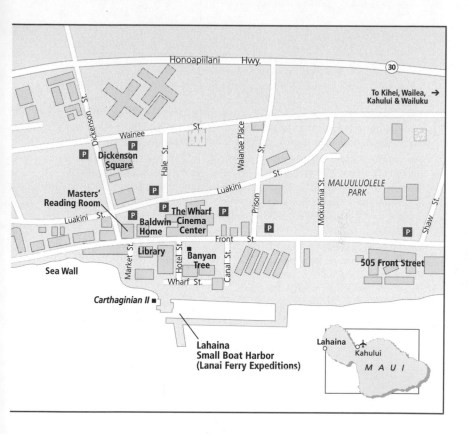

American school west of the Rockies. Today Lahainaluna is the public high school for the children of West Maui.

Lahainaluna High School Campus, 980 Lahainaluna Rd. (at the top of the mountain). © 808/661-3262. www.lahainarestoration.org/halepai. Free admission. Mon–Fri by appointment only.

Lahaina Heritage Museum   Located on the second floor of the old Lahaina Courthouse, this museum tells the story of the history and the culture of Lahaina. In addition to ever-changing exhibits, there also are videos, live demonstrations by cultural artisans, "touch and feel" displays, and interactive exhibits.

648 Wharf St., Lahaina. © 808/661-1959. www.visitlahaina.com. Free admission. Daily 9am–5pm.

Lahaina Jodo Mission   This site has long been held sacred. The Hawaiians called it Puunoa Point, which means "the hill freed from taboo." Once a small village named *Mala* (garden), this peaceful place was a haven for Japanese immigrants, who came to Hawaii in 1868 as laborers for the sugar-cane plantations. They eventually built a small wooden temple to worship here. In 1968, on the 100th anniversary of Japanese presence in Hawaii, a Great Buddha statue (some 12 ft. high and weighing 3½ tons) was brought here from Japan. The immaculate grounds also contain a replica of the original wooden temple and a 90-foot-tall pagoda.

12 Ala Moana St. (off Front St., near the Mala Wharf). © 808/661-4304. Free admission. Daily during daylight hours.

Tips   Where to Park for Free—or Next to Free—in Lahaina

Lahaina is the worst place on Maui for parking. The town was created and filled with shops, restaurants, and historic sites before the throngs of tourists (and their cars) invaded. Street parking is hit-or-miss. You can either drive around the block for hours looking for a free place to park on the street or park in one of the nearly 20 parking lots. I've divided the lots into three classes: free for customers, discount with validation, and pay.

Free for Customers: The three lots on Papalaua Street are all free for customers. The largest is the Lahaina Shopping Center lot, with 2 free hours. Next in size is the Lahaina Center, across the street (which allows 4 hr. free, but you must get validation from a store in the Lahaina Center); the smallest is the Lahaina Square lot at Wainee street, which offers 2 free hours for customers.

Discount with Validation: Customers of the Wharf Cinema Center, located on Front Street, can get a discount by parking at either of the theater's two lots—both are between Dickenson and Prison streets, but one is on Wainee Street and the other on Luakini Street.

Pay: Lahaina is filled with pay lots ranging from 50¢ for a half-hour to all-day parking for $8 to $10. Pay lots on Front Street are located between Papalaua and Lahainaluna streets, on the corner of Dickenson Street, and underground at the 505 Front St. shopping center. Pay lots on Luakini Street are located near the Prison Street intersection and near the Lahainaluna Road intersection. Lahainaluna Road has several pay lots between Wainee and Front streets. Dickenson Street has three pay lots between Wainee and Luakini streets.

Maluuluolele Park *(Kids* At first glance this Front Street park appears to be only a hot, dry, dusty softball field. But under home plate is the edge of Mokuula, where a royal compound once stood more than 100 years ago—it's now buried under tons of red dirt and sand. Here, Prince Kauikeaolui, who ascended the throne as King Kamehameha III when he was only 10, lived with the love of his life, his sister Princess Nahienaena. Missionaries took a dim view of incest, which was acceptable to Hawaiian nobles in order to preserve the royal bloodlines. Torn between love for her brother and the new Christian morality, Nahienaena grew despondent and died at the age of 21. King Kamehameha III, who reigned for 29 years—longer than any other Hawaiian monarch—presided over Hawaii as it went from kingdom to constitutional monarchy, and absolute power over the islands began to transfer from island nobles to missionaries, merchants, and sugar planters. Kamehameha died in 1854 at the age of 39. In 1918 his royal compound, containing a mausoleum and artifacts of the kingdom, was demolished and covered with dirt to create a public park. The baseball team from Lahainaluna School now plays games on the site of this royal place, still considered sacred to many Hawaiians.

Front and Shaw sts.

Wo Hing Temple *(* The Chinese were among the various immigrants brought to Hawaii to work in the sugar-cane fields. In 1909 several Chinese workers formed the

Wo Hing society, a chapter of the Chee Kun Tong society, which dates from the 17th century. In 1912 they built this social hall for the Chinese community. Completely restored, the Wo Hing Temple contains displays and artifacts on the history of the Chinese in Lahaina. Next door in the old cookhouse is a theater with movies of Hawaii taken by Thomas Edison in 1898 and 1903.

Front St. (between Wahie Lane and Papalaua St.). © 808/661-3262. Admission by donation. Daily 10am–4pm.

WALKING TOUR   HISTORIC LAHAINA

Getting There: From the Kahului Airport, take the Kuihelani Highway (Hwy. 38) to the intersection of Honoapiilani Highway (Hwy. 30), where you turn left. Follow Honoapiilani Highway to Lahaina and turn left on Lahainaluna Road. When Lahainaluna Road ends, make a left on Front Street. Dickenson Street is a block down (see the box on parking, above).

Start: Front and Dickenson streets.
Finish: Same location.
Time: About an hour.

Back when "there was no God west of the Horn," Lahaina was the capital of Hawaii and the Pacific's wildest port. Today it's a mild, mollified version of its old self—mostly a hustle-bustle of whale art, timeshares, and "Just Got Lei'd" T-shirts. I'm not sure the rowdy whalers would have been pleased. But, if you look hard, you'll still find the historic port town they loved, filled with the kind of history that inspired James Michener to write his best-selling epic novel *Hawaii.*

Members of the Lahaina Restoration Foundation have worked for 3 decades to preserve Lahaina's past. They have labeled a number of historical sites with brown-and-white markers; below, I provide explanations of the significance of each site as you walk through Lahaina's historic past.

Begin your tour at the:
❶ Masters' Reading Room
This coral-and-stone building looks just as it did in 1834, when Rev. William Richards and Rev. E. Spaulding convinced the whaling-ship captains that they needed a place for the ships' masters and captains, many of whom traveled with their families, to stay while they were ashore. The bottom floor was used as a storage area for the mission; the top floor, from which you could see the ships at anchor in the harbor, was for the visiting ships' officers.

Next door is the:
❷ Baldwin Home
Harvard-educated physician Rev. Dwight Baldwin, with his wife of just a few weeks, sailed to Hawaii from New England in 1830. Baldwin was first assigned

to a church in Waimea, on the Big Island, and then to Lahaina's Wainee Church in 1838. He and his family lived in this house until 1871. The Baldwin Home and the Masters' Reading Room are the oldest standing buildings in Lahaina, made from thick walls of coral and hand-milled timber. Baldwin also ran his medical office and his missionary activities out of this house. (See the listing for the Baldwin Home Museum, p. 197, for information on hours and admission.)

On the other side of the Baldwin Home is the former site of the:
❸ Richards House
The open field is empty today, but it represents the former home of Lahaina's first Protestant missionary, Rev. William Richards. Richards went on to become

the chaplain, teacher, and translator to Kamehameha III. He was also instrumental in drafting Hawaii's constitution and acted as the king's envoy to the United States and England, seeking recognition of Hawaii as an independent nation. After his death in 1847, he was buried in the Wainee Churchyard.

From here, cross Front Street and walk toward the ocean, with the Lahaina Public Library on your right and the green Pioneer Inn on your left, until you see the:

❹ Taro Patch

The lawn in front of the Lahaina Library was once a taro patch stretching back to the Baldwin Home. The taro plant was a staple of the Hawaiian diet: The root was used to make poi, and the leaves were used in cooking. At one time Lahaina looked like a Venice of the tropics, with streams, ponds, and waterways flooding the taro fields. As the population of the town grew, the water was siphoned off for drinking water.

Walk away from the Lahaina Harbor toward the edge of the lawn, where you'll see the:

❺ Hauola Stone

Hawaiians believed that certain stones placed in sacred places had the power to heal. *Kahuna* (priests) of medicine used stones like this to help cure illnesses.

Turn around and walk back toward the Pioneer Inn; look for the concrete depression in the ground, which is all that's left of the:

❻ Brick Palace

This structure was begun in 1798 as the first Western-style building in Hawaii. King Kamehameha I had this 20×40-foot, two-story brick structure built for his wife, Queen Kaahumanu (who is said to have preferred a grass-thatched house nearby). Inside, the walls were constructed of wood and the windows were glazed glass. Kamehameha I lived here from 1801 to 1802, when he was building his war canoe, *Peleleu,* and preparing to invade Kauai. A handmade stone seawall surrounded the palace to protect it from the surf. The building stood for 70

years. In addition to being a royal compound, it was also used as a meetinghouse, storeroom, and warehouse.

Behind you, dockside of the loading pier of the Lahaina Harbor, is the:

❼ Former site of the *Carthaginian*

This was once the site of a replica of a 19th-century brig, which carried commerce back and forth to Hawaii, and, until 2004, served as a museum and exhibit of 19th-century boating and whaling. As we went to press, the *Carthaginian,* which had been plagued with numerous maintenance problems for years, had been removed from the slip, and the Lahaina Restoration Foundation was in the process of finding a replacement ship.

Directly opposite the *Carthaginian* is the:

❽ Pioneer Inn

Lahaina's first hotel was the scene of some wild parties at the turn of the 20th century. George Freeland, of the Royal Canadian Mounted Police, tracked a criminal to Lahaina and then fell in love with the town. He built the hotel in 1901 but soon discovered that Lahaina wasn't the tourist mecca it is today. To make ends meet, Freeland built a movie theater, which was wildly successful. The Pioneer Inn remained the only hotel in all of West Maui until the 1950s. You can stay at this restored building today (p. 92).

From the Pioneer Inn, cross Hotel Street and walk along Wharf Street, which borders the harbor. On your left is the:

❾ Banyan Tree

This ancient tree has witnessed decades of luaus, dances, concerts, private chats, public rallies, and resting sojourners under its mighty boughs. It's hard to believe that this huge tree was only 8 feet tall when it was planted here.

Continue along Wharf Street; near the edge of the park is the:

❿ Courthouse

In 1858 a violent windstorm destroyed about 20 buildings in Lahaina, including

← To Kaanapali

Honoapiilani Hwy.

30

To Kihei, Wailea, →
Kahului & Wailuku

Dickenson St.

Wainee St.

Dickenson Square

Hale St.

Waianae Place

21

22 23

20

19

17

18

Luakini St.

Prison St.

Mokuhinia St.

MALUULUOLELE PARK

16

Shaw St.

24

25

The Wharf Cinema Center

Front St.

Library

1 2 3

8 9

13

15

14

505 Front Street

Sea Wall

Market St.

Hotel St.

Canal St.

6 4

10

11 12

5

Wharf St.

7

Lahaina
Small Boat Harbor
(Lanai Ferry Expeditions)

0   1/10 mile

0   100 meters

1 Masters' Reading Room	10 Courthouse	18 Waihee Cemetery
2 Baldwin Home	11 Fort	19 Hongwanji Mission
3 Richards House	12 Canal	20 David Malo's Home
4 Taro Patch	13 Government Market	21 Old Prison
5 Hauola Stone	14 Holy Innocents	22 Episcopal Cemetery
6 Brick Palace	Episcopal Church	23 Hale Aloha
7 Former *Carthaginian II* site	15 Hale Piula	24 Buddhist Church
8 Pioneer Inn	16 Maluuluolele Park	25 Luakini Street
9 Banyan Tree	17 Wainee Church	

Hale Piula, which served as the courthouse and palace of King Kamehameha III. It was rebuilt immediately, using the stones from the previous building. It served not only as courthouse, but also as custom house, post office, tax collector's office, and government offices. Upstairs on the second floor is the Lahaina Heritage Museum, with exhibits on the history and culture of Lahaina (free admission; open daily 9am–5pm).

Continue down Wharf Street to Canal Street. On the corner are the remains of the:

⓫ Fort

This structure once covered an acre and had 20-foot-high walls. In 1830 some whalers fired a few cannonballs into Lahaina in protest of Rev. William Richards's meddling in their affairs. (Richards had convinced Governor Hoapili to create a law forbidding the women of Lahaina from swimming out to greet the whaling ships.) The fort was constructed from 1831 to 1832 with coral blocks taken from the ocean where the Lahaina Harbor sits today. As a further show of strength, cannons were placed along the waterfront, where they remain today. Historical accounts seem to scoff at the "fort," saying it appeared to be more for show than for force. It was later used as a prison, until it was finally torn down in the 1850s; its stones were used for construction of the new prison, Hale Paahao (see no. 21 below).

Cross Canal Street to the:

⑫ Canal

Unlike Honolulu, with its natural deep-water harbor, Lahaina was merely a roadstead with no easy access to the shore. Whalers would anchor in deep water offshore, then board smaller boats (which they used to chase down and harpoon whales) to make the passage over the reef to shore. If the surf was up, coming ashore could be dangerous. In the 1840s the U.S. consular representative recommended digging a canal from one of the freshwater streams that ran through Lahaina and charging a fee to the whalers who wanted to obtain fresh water. In 1913 the canal was filled in to construct Canal Street.

Up Canal Street is the:

⑬ Government Market

A few years after the canal was built, the government built a thatched marketplace with stalls for Hawaiians to sell goods to the sailors. Merchants quickly took advantage of this marketplace and erected drinking establishments, grog shops, and other pastimes of interest nearby. Within a few years, this entire area became known as "Rotten Row."

Make a right onto Front Street and continue down the street, past Kamehameha III Elementary School. Across from the park is:

⑭ Holy Innocents Episcopal Church

When the Episcopal missionaries first came to Lahaina in 1862, they built a church across the street from the current structure. In 1909 the church moved to its present site, which was once a thatched house built for the daughter of King Kamehameha I. The present structure, built in 1927, features unique paintings of a Hawaiian Madonna and endemic birds and plants to Hawaii, executed by DeLos Blackmar in 1940.

Continue down Front Street, and at the next open field, look for the white stones by the ocean, marking the former site of the "iron-roofed house":

⑮ Hale Piula

In the 1830s the two-story stone building with a large surrounding courtyard was built for King Kamehameha III. However, the king preferred sleeping in a small thatched hut nearby, so the structure was never really completed. In the 1840s Kamehameha moved his capital to Honolulu and wasn't using Hale Piula, so it became the local courthouse. The windstorm of 1858, which destroyed the courthouse on Wharf Street (see no. 10 above), also destroyed the iron-roofed house. The stones from Hale Piula were used to rebuild the courthouse on Wharf Street.

Continue down Front Street; across from the 505 Front St. complex is:

⑯ Maluuluolele Park

This sacred spot to Hawaiians is now the site of a park and ball field. This used to be a village, Mokuhinia, with a sacred pond that was the home of a *moo* (a spirit in the form of a lizard), which the royal family honored as their personal guardian spirit. In the middle of the pond was a small island, Mokuula, home to Maui's top chiefs. After conquering Maui, Kamehameha I claimed this sacred spot as his own; he and his two sons, Kamehameha II and III, lived here when they were in Lahaina. In 1918, in the spirit of progress, the pond was drained and the ground leveled for a park.

Make a left onto Shaw Street and then another left onto Wainee Street; on the left side, just past the cemetery, is:

⑰ Wainee Church

This was the first stone church built in Hawaii (1828–32). At one time the church could seat some 3,000 people, albeit tightly packed together, complete with "calabash spittoons" for the tobacco-chewing Hawaiian chiefs and the ship captains. That structure didn't last long—the 1858 windstorm that destroyed several buildings in Lahaina also blew the roof off the original church, knocked over the belfry, and picked up the church's bell and deposited it 100 feet away. The structure was rebuilt, but that too was destroyed—this time by Hawaiians protesting the 1894 overthrow of the monarchy. Again the church was rebuilt, and again it was destroyed—by fire in 1947. The next incarnation of the church was destroyed by yet another windstorm in 1951. The current church has been standing since 1953. Be sure to walk around to the back of the church: The row of palm trees on the ocean side includes some of the oldest palm trees in Lahaina.

Wander next door to the first Christian cemetery in Hawaii:

⑱ Waihee Cemetery

Established in 1823, this cemetery tells a fascinating story of old Hawaii, with graves of Hawaiian chiefs, commoners, missionaries and their families (infant mortality was high then), and sailors. Enter this ground with respect because Hawaiians consider it sacred—many members of the royal family were buried here, including Queen Keopuolani, who was wife of King Kamehameha I, mother of kings Kamehameha II and III, and the first Hawaiian baptized as a Protestant. Among the other graves are Rev. William Richards (the first missionary in Lahaina) and Princess Nahienaena (sister of kings Kamehameha II and III).

Continue down Waihee Street to the corner of Luakini Street and the:

⑲ Hongwanji Mission

The temple was originally built in 1910 by members of Lahaina's Buddhist sect. The current building was constructed in 1927, housing a temple and language school. The public is welcome to attend the New Year's Eve celebration, Buddha's birthday in April (see "Maui, Molokai & Lanai Calendar of Events" in chapter 2), and O Bon Memorial Services in August.

Continue down Wainee Street. Just before the intersection with Prison Street, look for the historical marker for:

⑳ David Malo's Home

Although no longer standing, the house that once stood here was the home of Hawaii's first scholar, philosopher, and well-known author. Educated at Lahainaluna School, his book on ancient Hawaiian culture, *Hawaiian Antiquities,* is considered *the* source on Hawaiiana today. His alma mater celebrates David Malo Day every year in April in recognition of his contributions to Hawaii.

Cross Prison Street. On the corner of Prison and Waihee is the:

㉑ Old Prison

The Hawaiians called the prison Hale Paahao ("stuck in irons house"). Sailors who refused to return to their boats at sunset used to be arrested and taken to the old fort (see no. 11 above). In 1851, however, the fort physician told the government that sleeping on the ground at night made the prisoners ill, costing the government quite a bit of money to treat them—so the Kingdom of Hawaii used the prisoners to build a prison from the coral block of the old fort. Most prisoners here had terms of a year or less (those with longer terms were shipped off to Honolulu) and were convicted of crimes like deserting ship, being drunk, or working on Sunday. Today the grounds of the prison have a much more congenial atmosphere, as they are rented out to community groups for parties.

Continue down Waihee Street, just past Waianae Place, to the small:

㉒ Episcopal Cemetery

This burial ground tells another story in Hawaii's history. During the reign of King Kamehameha IV, his wife, Queen Emma, formed close ties with the British royalty. She encouraged Hawaiians to join the Anglican Church after asking the

Archbishop of Canterbury to form a church in Hawaii. This cemetery contains the burial sites of many of those early Anglicans.

Next door is:

㉓ Hale Aloha

This "house of love" was built in 1858 by Hawaiians in "commemoration of God's causing Lahaina to escape the smallpox," while it desolated Oahu in 1853, carrying off 5,000 to 6,000 of its population. The building served as a church and school until the turn of the 20th century, when it fell into disrepair.

Turn left onto Hale Street and then right onto Luakini Street to the:

㉔ Buddhist Church

This green wooden Shingon Buddhist temple is very typical of myriad Buddhist churches that sprang up all over the island when the Japanese laborers were brought to work in the sugar-cane fields. Some of the churches were little more than elaborate false "temple" fronts on existing buildings.

On the side of Village Galleries, on the corner of Luakini and Dickenson streets, is the historical marker for:

㉕ Luakini Street

"Luakini" translates as a *heiau* (temple) where the ruling chiefs prayed and where human sacrifices were made. This street received its unforgettable name after serving as the route for the funeral procession of Princess Harriet Nahienaena, sister of kings Kamehameha II and III. The princess was a victim of the rapid changes in Hawaiian culture. A convert to Protestantism, she had fallen in love with her brother at an early age. Just 20 years earlier, their relationship would have been nurtured in order to preserve the purity of the royal bloodlines. The missionaries, however, frowned on brother and sister marrying. In August 1836 the couple had a son, who only lived a few short hours. Nahienaena never recovered and died in December of that same year (the king was said to mourn her death for years, frequently visiting her grave at the Waihee Cemetery; see no. 18 above). The route of her funeral procession through the breadfruit and koa trees to the cemetery became known as "Luakini," in reference to the gods "sacrificing" the beloved princess.

Turn left on Dickenson and walk down to Front Street, where you'll be back at the starting point.

WINDING DOWN
Ready for some refreshment after your stroll? Head to **Maui Swiss Cafe**, 640 Front St. ((C) 808/661-6776), for tropical smoothies, great espresso, and affordable snacks. Sit in the somewhat funky garden area, or get your drink to go and wander over to the seawall to watch the surfers.

A WHALE OF A PLACE IN KAANAPALI

Heading north from Lahaina, the next resort area you'll come to is Kaanapali, which boasts a gorgeous stretch of beach. If you haven't seen a real whale yet, go to **Whalers Village,** 2435 Kaanapali Pkwy., a shopping center that has adopted the whale as its mascot. You can't miss it: A huge, almost life-size metal sculpture of a mother whale and two nursing calves greets you. A few more steps and you're met by the looming, bleached-white bony skeleton of a 40-foot sperm whale. It's pretty impressive.

On the second floor of the mall is the **Whale Center of the Pacific** ((C) 808/661-5992), a museum celebrating the "Golden Era of Whaling" (1825–60). Harpoons and scrimshaw are on display; the museum has even re-created the cramped quarters of a whaler's seagoing vessel. Open during mall hours, daily from 9:30am to 10pm; admission is free.

THE SCENIC ROUTE FROM WEST MAUI TO CENTRAL OR UPCOUNTRY MAUI: THE KAHEKILI HIGHWAY

The usual road from West Maui to Wailuku is the Honoapiilani Highway (Hwy. 30), which runs along the coast and then turns inland at Maalaea. But those in search of a back-to-nature driving experience should go the other way, along the **Kahekili Highway (Hwy. 340)** ℛ. (*Highway* is a bit of a euphemism for this paved but somewhat precarious narrow road; check your rental-car agreement before you head out—some don't allow cars on this road. If it is raining or has been raining, skip this road due to mud and rock slides.) It was named after the great chief Kahekili, who built houses from the skulls of his enemies.

You'll start out on the Honoapiilani Highway (Hwy. 30), which becomes the Kahekili Highway (Hwy. 340) after Honokohau, at the northernmost tip of the island. Around this point are **Honolua** ℛ and **Mokuleia** ℛ **bays,** which have been designated as Marine Life Conservation Areas (the taking of fish, shells, or anything else is prohibited).

From this point, the quality of the road deteriorates, and you may share the way with roosters, goats, cows, and dogs. The narrow road weaves along for the next 20 miles, following an ancient Hawaiian coastal footpath and showing you the true wild nature of Maui. These are photo opportunities from heaven: steep ravines, rolling pastoral hills, tumbling waterfalls, exploding blowholes, crashing surf, jagged lava coastlines, and a tiny Hawaiian village straight off a postcard.

Just before mile marker 20, look for a small turnoff on the mauka side of the road (just before the guardrail starts). Park here and walk across the road, and on your left you'll see a spouting **blowhole.** In winter this is an excellent spot to look for whales.

About 3 miles farther along the road, you'll come to a wide turnoff providing a great photo op: a view of the jagged coastline down to the crashing surf.

Less than ½ mile farther along, just before mile marker 16, look for the POHAKU KANI sign, marking the huge, 6×6-foot, bell-shaped stone. To "ring" the bell, look on the side facing Kahakuloa for the deep indentations, and strike the stone with another rock.

Along the route, nestled in a crevice between two steep hills, is the picturesque village of **Kahakuloa** ℛ ("the tall hau tree"), with a dozen weather-worn houses, a church with a red-tile roof, and vivid green taro patches. From the northern side of the village, you can look back at the great view of Kahakuloa, the dark boulder beach, and the 636-foot Kahakuloa Head rising in the background.

At various points along the drive are artists' studios, nestled into the cliffs and hills. One noteworthy stop is the **Kaukini Gallery,** which features work by more than two dozen local artists, with lots of gifts and crafts to buy in all price ranges. (You may also want to stop here to use one of the few restrooms along the drive.)

When you're approaching Wailuku, stop at the **Halekii and Pihanakalani Heiau,** which visitors rarely see. To get here from Wailuku, turn north from Main Street onto Market Street. Turn right onto Mill Street and follow it until it ends; then make a left on Lower Main Street. Follow Lower Main until it ends at Waiehu Beach Road (Hwy. 340), and turn left. Turn left on Kuhio Street and again at the first left onto Hea Place, and drive through the gates and look for the Hawaii Visitor's Bureau marker.

These two *heiau,* built in 1240 from stones carried up from the Iao Stream below, sit on a hill with a commanding view of central Maui and Haleakala. Kahekili, the last chief of Maui, lived here. After the bloody battle at Iao Stream, Kamehameha I reportedly came to the temple here to pay homage to the war god, Ku, with a human sacrifice.

Halekii (House of Images) is made of stone walls with a flat grassy top, whereas *Pihanakalani* (gathering place of supernatural beings) is a pyramid-shaped mount of stones. If you sit quietly nearby (never walk on any *heiau*—it's considered disrespectful), you'll see that the view alone explains why this spot was chosen.

4 South Maui

MAALAEA

At the bend in the Honopiilani Highway (Hwy. 30), Maalaea Bay runs along the south side of the isthmus between the West Maui Mountains and Haleakala. This is the windiest area on Maui: Trade winds blowing between the two mountains are funneled across the isthmus, and by the time they reach Maalaea, gusts of 25 to 30 mph are not uncommon.

This creates ideal conditions for **windsurfers** out in Maalaea Bay. Surfers are also seen just outside the small boat harbor in Maalaea, which has one of the fastest breaks in the state.

Maui Ocean Center ★★ *Kids*   This 5-acre facility houses the largest aquarium in Hawaii and features one of Hawaii's largest predators: the tiger shark. Exhibits are geared toward the residents of Hawaii's ocean waters. As you walk past the three dozen or so tanks and numerous exhibits, you'll slowly descend from the "beach" to the deepest part of the ocean, without ever getting wet. Start at the surge pool, where you'll see shallow-water marine life like spiny urchins and cauliflower coral, then move on to the reef tanks, turtle pool, "touch" pool (with starfish and urchins), and eagle-ray pool before reaching the star of the show: the 100-foot-long, 600,000-gallon main tank featuring tiger, gray, and white-tip sharks, as well as tuna, surgeonfish, triggerfish, and numerous other tropicals. A walkway goes right through the tank, so you'll be surrounded on three sides by marine creatures. A very cool place, and well worth the time. Some new additions are a hammerhead exhibit and the Shark Dive Maui Program—if you're a certified scuba diver, you can plunge into the aquarium with sharks, stingrays, and tropical fish while friends and family watch safely from the other side of the glass. *Helpful hint:* Buy your tickets online to avoid the long admission lines.

Maalaea Harbor Village, 192 Maalaea Rd. (the triangle between Honoapiilani Hwy. and Maalaea Rd.) ✆ 808/ 270-7000. www.mauioceancenter.com. Admission $21 adults, $18 seniors, $14 children 3–12. Daily 9am–5pm (until 6pm July–Aug).

KIHEI

Capt. George Vancouver landed at Kihei in 1778, when it was only a collection of fishermen's grass shacks on the hot, dry, dusty coast (hard to believe, eh?). A **totem pole** stands today where he's believed to have landed, across from Aston Maui Lu Resort, 575 S. Kihei Rd. Vancouver sailed on to what later became British Columbia, where a great international city and harbor now bear his name.

West of the junction of Piilani Highway (Hwy. 31) and Mokulele Highway (Hwy. 350) is **Kealia Pond National Wildlife Preserve** (✆ **808/875-1582**), a 700-acre U.S. Fish and Wildlife wetland preserve where endangered Hawaiian stilts, coots, and ducks hang out and splash. These ponds work two ways: as bird preserves and as sedimentation basins that keep the coral reefs from silting from runoff. You can take a self-guided tour along a boardwalk dotted with interpretive signs and shade shelters, through sand dunes, and around ponds to Maalaea Harbor. The boardwalk starts at the outlet of Kealia Pond on the ocean side of North Kihei Road (near mile marker 2 on Piilani Hwy.). Among the Hawaiian waterbirds seen here are the black-crowned high heron, Hawaiian coot, Hawaiian duck, and Hawaiian stilt. There are also shorebirds like sanderling, Pacific golden plover, ruddy turnstone, and wandering tattler. From July to December, the hawksbill turtle comes ashore here to lay her eggs. *Tip:* If you're bypassing Kihei, take the Piilani Highway (Hwy. 31), which parallels stripmall laden South Kihei Road, and avoid the hassle of stoplights and traffic.

WAILEA

The dividing line between arid Kihei and artificially green Wailea is distinct. Wailea once had the same kiawe-strewn, dusty landscape as Kihei until Alexander & Baldwin Inc. (of sugar-cane fame) began developing a resort here in the 1970s (after piping water from the other side of the island to the desert terrain of Wailea). Today the manicured 1,450 acres of this affluent resort stand out like an oasis along the normally dry leeward coast.

The best way to explore this golden resort coast is to rise with the sun and head for Wailea's 1.5-mile **coastal nature trail** *&*, stretching between the Kea Lani Hotel and the kiawe thicket just beyond the Renaissance Wailea. It's a great morning walk, a serpentine path that meanders uphill and down past native plants, old Hawaiian habitats, and a billion dollars' worth of luxury hotels. You can pick up the trail at any of the resorts or from clearly marked SHORELINE ACCESS points along the coast. The best times to go are early morning or sunset; by midmorning, it gets crowded with joggers and later with beachgoers. As the path crosses several bold black-lava points, it affords vistas of islands and ocean. Benches allow you to pause and contemplate the view across Alalakeiki Channel, where you might see **whales** in season.

MAKENA

A few miles south of Wailea, the manicured coast changes over to the wilderness of *Makena* (abundance). In the 1800s cattle were driven down the slope from upland ranches and loaded onto boats that waited to take them to market. Now **Makena Landing** *&* is a beach park with boat-launching facilities, showers, toilets, and picnic tables. It's great for snorkeling and for launching kayaks bound for Pérouse Bay and Ahihi-Kinau preserve.

From the landing, go south on Makena Road; on the right is **Keawali Congregational Church** *&* (*©* 808/879-5557), built in 1855 with walls 3 feet thick. Surrounded by ti leaves, which by Hawaiian custom provides protection, and built of lava rock with coral used as mortar, this Protestant church sits on its own cove with a goldsand beach. It always attracts a Sunday crowd for its 9:30am Hawaiian-language service. Take some time to wander through the cemetery; you'll see some tombstones with a ceramic picture of the deceased on them, which is an old custom.

A little farther south on the coast is **La Pérouse Monument** *&*, a pyramid of lava rocks that marks the spot where French explorer Admiral Comte de La Pérouse set foot on Maui in 1786. The first Westerner to "discover" the island, La Pérouse described the "burning climate" of the leeward coast, observed several fishing villages near Kihei, and sailed on into oblivion, never to be seen again; some believe he may have been eaten by cannibals in what is now Vanuatu. To get here, drive south past Puu Olai to Ahihi Bay, where the road turns to gravel. Go another 2 miles along the coast to La Pérouse Bay; the monument sits amid a clearing in black lava at the end of the dirt road.

The rocky coastline and sometimes rough seas contribute to the lack of appeal for water activities here; **hiking** opportunities, however, are excellent. Bring plenty of water and sun protection, and wear hiking boots that can withstand walking on lava.

From La Pérouse Bay, you can pick up the old King's Highway trail, which at one time circled the island. Walk along the sandy beach at La Pérouse and look for the trail indentation in the lava, which leads down to the lighthouse at the tip of Cape Hanamanioa, about a ¾ miles round-trip. Or you can continue on the trail as it climbs up the hill for 2 miles, then ventures back toward the ocean, where there are quite a few old Hawaiian home foundations and rocky/coral beaches.

5 House of the Sun: Haleakala National Park ⊕⊕⊕

At once forbidding and compelling, **Haleakala National Park** is Maui's main natural attraction (*Haleakala* means house of the sun). More than 1.3 million people a year ascend the 10,023-foot-high mountain to peer down into the crater of the world's largest dormant volcano. (Haleakala is officially considered to be "active, but not currently erupting," even though it has not rumbled or spewed lava since 1790.) That hole would hold Manhattan: 3,000 feet deep, 7½ miles long by 2½ miles wide, and encompassing 19 square miles.

The Hawaiians recognized the mountain as a sacred site. Ancient chants tell of Pele, the volcano goddess, and one of her siblings doing battle on the crater floor where *Kawilinau* (Bottomless Pit) now stands. Commoners in ancient Hawaii didn't spend much time here, though. The only people allowed into this sacred area were the kahunas, who took their apprentices to live for periods of time in this intensely spiritual place. Today New Agers also revere Haleakala as one of the earth's powerful energy points, and even the U.S. Air Force has a not-very-well-explained presence here.

But there's more to do here than simply stare in a big black hole: Just going up the mountain is an experience in itself. Where else on the planet can you climb from sea level to 10,000 feet in just 37 miles, or a 2-hour drive? The snaky road passes through big, puffy, cumulus clouds to offer magnificent views of the isthmus of Maui, the West Maui Mountains, and the Pacific Ocean.

Many drive up to the summit in predawn darkness to watch the **sunrise** over Haleakala. Writer Mark Twain called it "the sublimest spectacle" of his life. Others take a trail ride inside the bleak lunar landscape of the wilderness inside the crater or coast down the 37-mile road from the summit on a bicycle with special brakes (see "Biking" and "Horseback Riding" in chapter 7). Hardy adventurers hike and camp inside the crater's wilderness (see "Hiking & Camping" in chapter 7). Those bound for the interior bring their survival gear because the terrain is raw, rugged, and punishing. However you choose to experience Haleakala National Park, it will prove memorable—guaranteed.

JUST THE FACTS

Haleakala National Park extends from the summit of Mount Haleakala into the crater, down the volcano's southeast flank to Maui's eastern coast, beyond Hana. There are actually two separate and distinct destinations within the park: **Haleakala Summit** ⊕ and the **Kipahulu** ⊕ coast (see "Just Beyond Hana" later in this chapter). The summit gets all the publicity, but Kipahulu draws crowds too—it's lush, green, and tropical, and home to Oheo Gulch (also known as Seven Sacred Pools). No road links the summit and the coast; you have to approach them separately, and you need at least a day to see each place.

WHEN TO GO   At the 10,023-foot summit, weather changes fast. With wind chill, temperatures can be below freezing any time of year. Summer can be dry and warm, winters wet, windy, and cold. Before you go, get current weather conditions from the park (© **808/572-4400**) or the **National Weather Service** (© **808/871-5054**).

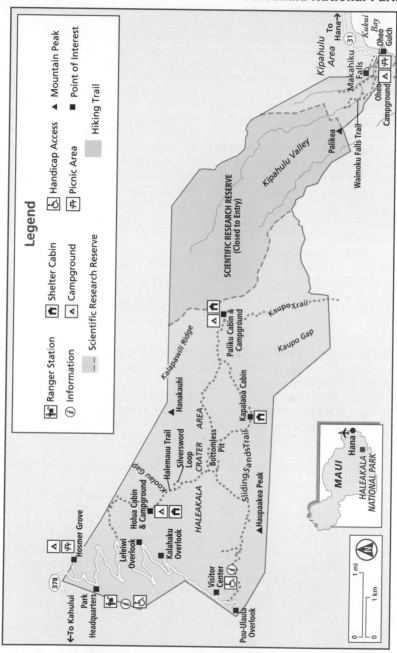

Haleakala National Park

Legend

🛖 Ranger Station	🏠 Shelter Cabin	♿ Handicap Access	▲ Mountain Peak
ⓘ Information	⛺ Campground	♨ Picnic Area	■ Point of Interest
╍╍ Scientific Research Reserve			░ Hiking Trail

MAUI

HALEAKALA NATIONAL PARK

Hana

To Kahului
Park Headquarters
378
Hosmer Grove
Leleiwi Overlook
Holua Cabin & Campground
Kalahaku Overlook
Visitor Center
Puu-Ulaula Overlook
Koolau Gap
Kalapawili Ridge
Hanakauhi
Halemauu Trail
Silversword Loop
HALEAKALA CRATER AREA
Bottomless Pit
Kapalaoa Cabin
Sliding Sands Trail
Haupaakea Peak
Paliku Cabin & Campground
Kaupo Trail
Kaupo Gap
SCIENTIFIC RESEARCH RESERVE
(Closed to Entry)
Kipahulu Valley
Kipahulu Area
To Hana
31
Kukui Bay
Oheo Gulch
Makahiku Falls
Palikea
Waimoku Falls Trail
Oheo Campground

1 mi
1 km
0

211

Impressions

There are few enough places in the world that belong entirely to themselves. The human passion to carry all things everywhere, so that every place is home, seems well on its way to homogenizing our planet, save for the odd unreachable corner. Haleakala crater is one of those corners.

—Barbara Kingsolver, the *New York Times*

From sunrise to noon, the light is weak, but the view is usually free of clouds. The best time for photos is in the afternoon, when the sun lights the crater and clouds are few. Go on full-moon nights for spectacular viewing. However, even when the forecast is promising, the weather at Haleakala can change in an instant—be prepared.

ACCESS POINTS   **Haleakala Summit** is 37 miles, or about a 2-hour drive, from Kahului. To get here, take Highway 37 to Highway 377 to Highway 378. For details on the drive, see "The Drive to the Summit" below. Pukalani is the last town for water, food, and gas.

The **Kipahulu** section of the national park is on Maui's east end near Hana, 60 miles from Kahului on Highway 36 (the Hana Hwy.). Due to traffic and rough road conditions, plan on 4 hours for the drive from Kahului (see "Driving the Road to Hana" below). Hana is the only nearby town for services, water, gas, food, and overnight lodging; some facilities may not be open after dark.

At both entrances to the park, the admission fee is $5 per person or $10 per car, good for a week of unlimited entry.

INFORMATION, VISITOR CENTERS & RANGER PROGRAMS   For information before you go, contact **Haleakala National Park,** P.O. Box 369, Makawao, HI 96768 (© **808/572-4400;** www.nps.gov/hale).

One mile from the park entrance, at 7,000 feet, is **Haleakala National Park Headquarters** (© **808/572-4400**), open daily from 7am to 4pm. You can pick up information on park programs and activities, get camping permits, and, occasionally, see a *nene* (Hawaiian goose)—one or more are often here to greet visitors. Restrooms, a pay phone, and drinking water are available.

The **Haleakala Visitor Center,** open daily from sunrise to 3pm, is near the summit, 11 miles from the park entrance. It offers a panoramic view of the volcanic landscape, with photos identifying the various features, and exhibits that explain its history, ecology, geology, and volcanology. Park staff members are often handy to answer questions. The only facilities are restrooms and water.

Rangers offer excellent, informative, and free **naturalist talks** at 9:30, 10:30, and 11:30am daily in the summit building. For information on **hiking** (including guided hikes) and **camping,** including cabins and campgrounds in the wilderness itself, see "Hiking & Camping" in chapter 7.

THE DRIVE TO THE SUMMIT

If you look on a Maui map, almost in the middle of the part that resembles a torso, there's a black wiggly line that looks like this: WWWWW. That's **Highway 378,** also known as **Haleakala Crater Road**—one of the fastest-ascending roads in the world. This grand corniche has at least 33 switchbacks; passes through numerous climate zones; goes under, in, and out of clouds; takes you past rare silversword plants and endangered Hawaiian geese sailing through the clear, thin air; and offers a view that extends for more than 100 miles.

Going to the summit takes about 2 hours from Kahului. No matter where you start out, you'll follow Highway 37 (Haleakala Hwy.) to Pukalani, where you'll pick up Highway 377 (which is also Haleakala Hwy.), which you take to Highway 378. Along the way, expect fog, rain, and wind. You might encounter stray cattle and downhill bicyclists. Fill up your gas tank before you go—the only gas available is 27 miles below the summit at Pukalani. There are no facilities beyond the ranger stations, so bring your own food and water.

Remember, you're entering a high-altitude wilderness area. Some people get dizzy due to the lack of oxygen; you might also suffer lightheadedness, shortness of breath, nausea, or worse: severe headaches, flatulence, and dehydration. People with asthma, pregnant women, heavy smokers, and those with heart conditions should be especially careful in the rarefied air. Bring water and a jacket or a blanket, especially if you go up for sunrise. Or you might want to go up to the summit for sunset, which is also spectacular.

As you go up the slopes, the temperate drops about 3°F (2°C) every 1,000 feet, so the temperature at the top can be 30°F (16°C) cooler than it was at sea level. Come prepared with sweaters, jackets, and rain gear.

At the **park entrance,** you'll pay an entrance fee of $10 per car (or $2 for a bicycle). About a mile from the entrance is **Park Headquarters,** where an endangered **nene,** or Hawaiian goose, might greet you with its unique call. With its black face, buff cheeks, and partially webbed feet, the gray-brown bird looks like a small Canada goose with zebra stripes; it brays out "nay-nay" (thus its name), doesn't migrate, and prefers lava beds to lakes. The unusual goose clings to a precarious existence on these alpine slopes. Vast populations of more than 25,000 once inhabited Hawaii, but hunters, pigs, feral cats and dogs, and mongooses preyed on the nene; coupled with habitat destruction, these predators nearly caused its extinction. By 1951 there were only 30 left. Now protected as Hawaii's state bird, the wild nene on Haleakala number fewer than 250—and the species remains endangered.

Beyond headquarters are **two scenic overlooks** on the way to the summit. Stop at Leleiwi on the way up and Kalahaku on the way back down, if only to get out, stretch,

---

⟨Fun Fact⟩ The Legend of the House of the Sun

According to ancient legend, Haleakala got its name from a very clever trick that the demigod Maui pulled on the sun. Maui's mother, the goddess Hina, complained one day that the sun sped across the sky so quickly that her tapa cloth couldn't dry.

Maui, known as a trickster, devised a plan. The next morning he went to the top of the great mountain and waited for the sun to poke its head above the horizon. Quickly, Maui lassoed the sun, bringing its path across the sky to an abrupt halt.

The sun begged Maui to let go, and Maui said he would on one condition: that the sun slow its trip across the sky to give the island more sunlight. The sun assented. In honor of this agreement, the Hawaiians call the mountain Haleakala, or "House of the Sun."

To this day, the top of Haleakala has about 15 minutes more sunlight than the communities on the coastline below.

and get accustomed to the altitude. Take a deep breath, look around, and pop your ears. If you feel dizzy or drowsy, or get a sudden headache, consider turning around and going back down.

Leleiwi Overlook ✦ is just beyond mile marker 17. From the parking area, a short trail leads you to a panoramic view of the lunarlike crater. When the clouds are low and the sun is in the right place, usually around sunset, you can experience a phenomenon known as the "Specter of the Brocken"—you can see a reflection of your shadow, ringed by a rainbow, in the clouds below. It's an optical illusion caused by a rare combination of sun, shadow, and fog that occurs in only three places on the planet: Haleakala, Scotland, and Germany.

Two miles farther along is **Kalahaku Overlook** ✦, the best place to see a rare **silversword.** You can turn into this overlook only when you are descending from the top. The silversword is the punk of the plant world, its silvery bayonets displaying tiny purple bouquets—like a spacey artichoke with attitude. This botanical wonder proved irresistible to humans, who gathered them in gunnysacks for Chinese potions, for British specimen collections, and just for the sheer thrill of having something so rare. Silverswords grow only in Hawaii, take from 4 to 50 years to bloom, and then, usually between May and October, send up a 1- to 6-foot stalk with a purple bouquet of sunflower-like blooms. They're now very rare, so don't even think about taking one home.

Continue on, and you'll quickly reach the **Haleakala Visitor Center** ✦, which offers spectacular views. You'll feel as if you're at the edge of the earth. But don't turn around here: The actual summit's a little farther on, at **Puu Ulaula Overlook** ✦ (also known as Red Hill), the volcano's highest point, where you'll find a mysterious cluster of buildings officially known as Haleakala Observatories, but unofficially called **Science City.** If you do go up for sunrise, the building at Puu Ulaula Overlook, a triangle of glass that serves as a windbreak, is the best viewing spot. After the daily miracle of sunrise—the sun seems to rise out of the vast crater (hence the name "House of the Sun")—you can see all the way across Alenuihaha Channel to the often snow-capped summit of Mauna Kea on the Big Island.

MAKING YOUR DESCENT Put your car in low gear; that way, you won't destroy your brakes by riding them the whole way down.

6 More in Upcountry Maui

Come upcountry and discover a different side of Maui: On the slopes of Haleakala, cowboys, planters, and other country people make their homes in serene, neighborly communities like **Makawao** and **Kula,** a world away from the bustling beach resorts. Even if you can't spare a day or two in the cool upcountry air, there are some sights that are worth a look on your way to or from the crater. Shoppers and gallery hoppers especially might want to make the effort; see chapter 9 for details. For a map of this area, turn to the "Upcountry & East Maui Dining & Attractions" map on p. 155.

On the slopes of Haleakala, Maui's farmers have been producing vegetables since the 1800s. In fact, during the gold rush in California, the Hawaiian farmers in Kula shipped so many potatoes that it was nicknamed Nu Kaleponi, a sort of pidgin Hawaiian pronunciation of "New California." In the late 1800s, Portuguese and Chinese immigrants, who had fulfilled their labor contracts with the sugar-cane companies, moved to this area, drawn by the rural agricultural lifestyle. That lifestyle continues today, among the fancy gentlemen's farms that have sprung up in the past 2 decades. Kula continues to grow its well-known onions, lettuce, tomatoes, carrots,

Moments Stop & Smell the Lavender

While in the upcountry Kula region, stop by the **Alii Kula Lavender**, 1100 Waipoli Rd. (© **808/878-3004;** www.aliikulalavender.com), where they grow several different varieties of lavender, so one species of lavender will always be in bloom year-round. There are a couple of great tours to take while you're there. On the **Lavender Garden Tea Tour** (10am daily), you are served lavender herb tea with a lavender scone and given a garden and studio tour. On the **Lavender Garden Culinary Tour**, you also get lunch and a demonstration of how to cook using their lavender products. Be sure to stop by the store and look over their culinary products (lavender seasonings, dressings, scones, honey, jelly, and teas), bath and body products (lotion, soaps, bubble baths, bath gel, and salve), aromatherapy (oil, candles, eye pillow), and other products (T-shirts, gift baskets, and dried lavender).

cauliflower, and cabbage. It is also a major source of cut flowers for the state: Most of Hawaii's proteas, as well as nearly all the carnations used in leis, come from Kula.

To experience a bit of the history of Kula, turn off the Kula Highway (Hwy. 37) onto Lower Kula Road. Well before the turnoff, you'll see a white octagonal building with a silver roof, the **Holy Ghost Catholic Church** (© **808/878-1091**). Hawaii's only eight-sided church, it was built between 1884 and 1897 by Portuguese immigrants. It's worth a stop to see the hand-carved altar and works of art for the stations of the cross, with inscriptions in Portuguese.

Kula Botanical Garden You can take a self-guided, informative, leisurely stroll through more than 700 native and exotic plants—including three unique collections of orchids, proteas, and bromeliads—at this 5-acre garden. It offers a good overview of Hawaii's exotic flora in one small, cool place.

Hwy. 377, south of Haleakala Crater Rd. (Hwy. 378), ½ mile from Hwy. 37. © **808/878-1715**. Admission $5 adults, $1 children 6–12. Daily 9am–4pm.

Tedeschi Vineyards and Winery On the southern shoulder of Haleakala is **Ulupalakua Ranch,** a 20,000-acre spread once owned by legendary sea captain James Makee, celebrated in the Hawaiian song and dance *Hula O Makee.* Wounded in a Honolulu waterfront brawl in 1843, Makee moved to Maui and bought Ulupalakua. He renamed it Rose Ranch, planted sugar as a cash crop, and grew rich. Still in operation, the ranch is now home to Maui's only winery, established in 1974 by Napa vintner Emil Tedeschi, who began growing California and European grapes here and producing serious still and sparkling wines, plus a silly wine made of pineapple juice. The rustic grounds are the perfect place for a picnic. Pack a basket before you go, and enjoy it with a bottle of Tedeschi wine.

Across from the winery are the remains of the three smokestacks of the **Makee Sugar Mill,** built in 1878. This is home to Maui artist Reems Mitchell, who carved the mannequins on the front porch of the Ulupalakua Ranch Store: a Filipino with his fighting cock, a cowboy, a farmhand, and a sea captain, all representing the people of Maui's history.

Off Hwy. 37 (Kula Hwy.). © **808/878-6058.** www.mauiwine.com. Daily 9am–5pm. Free tastings; tours given 10:30am–1:30pm.

7 Driving the Road to Hana ⊛⊛⊛

Top down, sunscreen on, radio tuned to a little Hawaiian music on a Maui morning: It's time to head out to Hana along the Hana Highway (Hwy. 36), a wiggle of a road that runs along Maui's northeastern shore. The drive takes at least 3 hours, but plan to take all day. Going to Hana is about the journey, not the destination.

There are wilder roads and steeper roads and even more dangerous roads, but in all of Hawaii, no road is more celebrated than this one. It winds for 50 miles past taro patches, magnificent seascapes, waterfall pools, botanical gardens, and verdant rainforests, and it ends at one of Hawaii's most beautiful tropical places.

The outside world discovered the little village of Hana in 1926, when the narrow coastal road, carved by pickax-wielding convicts, opened. The mud-and-gravel road, often subject to landslides and washouts, was paved in 1962, when tourist traffic began to increase; today more than 1,000 cars traverse the road each day, according to storekeeper Harry Hasegawa. That equals about 500,000 people a year on this road, which is way too many. Go at the wrong time and you'll be stuck in a bumper-to-bumper rental-car parade—peak traffic hours are midmorning and midafternoon year-round, especially on weekends.

In the rush to "do" Hana in a day, most visitors spin around town in 10 minutes flat and wonder what all the fuss is about. It takes time to take in Hana, play in the waterfalls, sniff the tropical flowers, hike to bamboo forests, and marvel at the spectacular scenery; stay overnight if you can.

However, if you really must do the Hana Highway in a day, go just before sunrise and return after sunset: On a full-moon night, the sea and the waterfalls glow in soft white light, with mysterious shadows appearing in the jungle. And you'll have the road almost to yourself on the way back.

Tips: Forget your mainland road manners. Practice aloha: Give way at the one-lane bridges, wave at oncoming motorists, and let the big guys in four-by-fours with pig-hunting dogs in the back have the right of way—it's just common sense, brah. If the guy behind you blinks his lights, let him pass. And don't honk your horn—in Hawaii it's considered rude.

THE JOURNEY BEGINS IN PAIA Before you even start out, fill up your gas tank. Gas in Paia is very expensive (even by Maui standards), and it's the last place for gas until you get to Hana, some 42 miles, 54 bridges, and 600 hairpin turns down the road.

The former plantation village of Paia was once a thriving sugar-mill town. The mill is still here, but the population shifted to Kahului in the 1950s when subdivisions opened there, leaving Paia to shrivel up and die. But the town refused to give up and has proven its ability to adapt to the times. Now chic eateries and trendy shops stand next door to the mom-and-pop establishments that have been serving generations of Paia customers.

Plan to be here early, around 7am, when **Charley's** ⊛, 142 Hana Hwy. (© **808/ 579-9453**), opens. Enjoy a big, hearty breakfast for a reasonable price.

After you leave Paia, just before the bend in the road, you'll pass the Kuau Mart on your left; a small general store, it's the only reminder of the once-thriving sugar plantation community of **Kuau.** The road then bends into an S-turn; in the middle of the S is the entrance to **Mama's Fish House,** marked by a restored boat with Mama's logo on the side. Just past the truck on the ocean side is the entrance to Mama's parking lot and adjacent small sandy cove in front of the restaurant. It's not good for swimming—ocean access is over very slippery rocks into strong surf—but the beach is a great place to sit and soak up some sun.

WINDSURFING MECCA A mile from Mama's, just before mile marker 9, is a place known around the world as one of the greatest windsurfing spots on the planet, **Hookipa Beach Park** ★. *Hookipa* (hospitality) is where the top-ranked windsurfers come to test themselves against the forces of nature: thunderous surf and forceful wind. World-championship contests are held here (see "Maui, Molokai & Lanai Calendar of Events" in chapter 2), but on nearly every windy afternoon (the board surfers have the waves in the morning), you can watch dozens of windsurfers twirling and dancing in the wind like colorful butterflies. To watch the windsurfers, go past the park and turn left at the entrance on the far side of the beach. You can either park on the high grassy bluff or drive down to the sandy beach and park alongside the pavilion. The park also has restrooms, a shower, picnic tables, and a barbecue area.

INTO THE COUNTRY Past Hookipa Beach the road winds down into ***Maliko* (Budding) Gulch** at mile marker 10. At the bottom of the gulch, look for the road on your right, which will take you out to **Maliko Bay.** Take the first right, which goes under the bridge and past a rodeo arena (scene of competitions by the Maliko Roping Club in summer) and on to the rocky beach. There are no facilities here except a boat-launch ramp. In the 1940s Maliko had a thriving community at the mouth of the bay, but its residents rebuilt farther inland after a strong tidal wave wiped it out. The bay may not look that special, but if the surf is up, it's a great place to watch the waves.

Back on the Hana Highway, as you leave Maliko Gulch, around mile marker 11, you'll pass through the rural area of **Haiku,** with banana patches, cane grass blowing in the wind, and forests of guava trees, avocados, kukui trees, palms, and Christmas berry. Just before mile marker 15 is the **Maui Grown Market and Deli** (**© 808/572-1693**), a good stop for drinks or snacks for the ride.

JAWS If it's winter and the waves are up (like 60 ft. or so), here's your chance to watch tow-in surfing off Pauwela Point at an area known as Jaws (because the waves will chew you up), where expert tow-in surfers battle the mammoth waves. To get there, make a small detour off the Hana Highway by turning left at Hahana Road, between mile markers 13 and 14. When the paved road ends, the dirt road is private property (Maui Land and Pine), so you may have to hike in about a mile and a half to get close to the ocean. Practice aloha, do not park in the pineapple fields, and do not pick or even touch the pineapples. Be very careful along the oceanside cliffs.

At mile marker 16, the curves begin, one right after another. Slow down and enjoy the view of bucolic rolling hills, mango trees, and vibrant ferns. After mile marker 16, the road is still called the Hana Highway, but the number changes from Highway 36 to Highway 360, and the mile markers go back to 0.

Tips **Travel Tip**

If you'd like to know exactly what you're seeing as you head down the road to Hana, I suggest renting a cassette tour, available from **Activity Warehouse** (www.travelhawaii.com), which has branches in Lahaina at 602 Front St., near Prison Street (**© 808/667-4000**), and in Kihei at Azeka Place II, on the mountain side of Kihei Road near Lipoa Street (**© 808/875-4000**), for $10 a day.

The Road to Hana

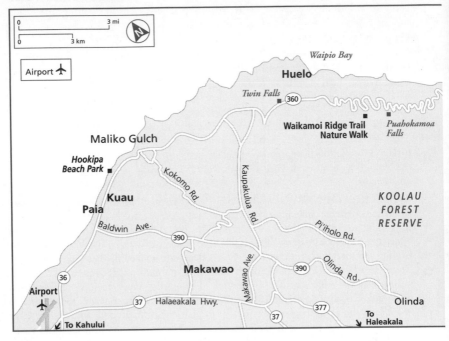

A GREAT PLUNGE ALONG THE WAY   A dip in a waterfall pool is everybody's tropical-island fantasy. A great place to stop is **Twin Falls** 🍦, at mile marker 2. Just before the wide, concrete bridge, pull over on the mountain side and park. There is a NO TRESPASSING sign on the gate. Although you will see several cars parked in the area and a steady line of people going up to the falls, be aware that this is private property and trespassing is illegal in Hawaii. If you decide that you want to "risk it," you will walk about 3 to 5 minutes to the waterfall and pool, or continue on another 10 to 15 minutes to the second, larger waterfall and pool (don't go in if it has been raining).

HIDDEN HUELO   Just before mile marker 4 on a blind curve, look for a double row of mailboxes on the left-hand side by the pay phone. Down the road lies a hidden Hawaii of an earlier time, where an indescribable sense of serenity prevails. Hemmed in by Waipo and Hoalua bays is the remote community of **Huelo** 🍦. This fertile area once supported a population of 75,000; today only a few hundred live among the scattered homes here, where a handful of B&Bs and exquisite vacation rentals cater to a trickle of travelers (see chapter 5).

The only reason Huelo is even marked is the historic 1853 **Kaulanapueo Church.** Reminiscent of New England architecture, this coral-and-cement church, topped with a plantation-green steeple and a gray tin roof, is still in use, although services are held just once or twice a month. It still has the same austere, stark interior of 1853: straight-backed benches, a no-nonsense platform for the minister, and no distractions on the walls to tempt you from paying attention to the sermon. Next to the church is a small graveyard, a personal history of this village in concrete and stone.

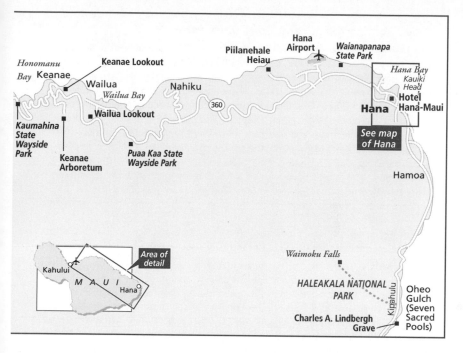

KOOLAU FOREST RESERVE

KOOLAU FOREST RESERVE After Huelo, the vegetation seems lusher, as though Mother Nature had poured Miracle-Gro on everything. This is the edge of the **Koolau Forest Reserve.** *Koolau* means "windward," and this certainly is one of the greatest examples of a lush windward area: The coastline here gets about 60 to 80 inches of rain a year, as well as runoff from the 200 to 300 inches that falls farther up the mountain. Here you'll see trees laden with guavas, as well as mangoes, java plums, and avocados the size of softballs. The spiny, long-leafed plants are *hala* trees, which the Hawaiians used for weaving baskets, mats, and even canoe sails.

From here on out, there's a waterfall (and one-lane bridge) around nearly every turn in the road, so drive slowly and be prepared to stop and yield to oncoming cars.

DANGEROUS CURVES About ½ mile after mile marker 6, there's a sharp U-curve in the road, going uphill. The road is practically one-lane here, with a brick wall on one side and virtually no maneuvering room. Sound your horn at the start of the U-curve to let approaching cars know you're coming. Take this curve, as well as the few more coming up in the next several miles, very slowly.

Just before mile marker 7 is a forest of waving **bamboo.** The sight is so spectacular that drivers are often tempted to take their eyes off the road. Be very cautious. Wait until just after mile marker 7, at the **Kaaiea Bridge** and stream below, to pull over and take a closer look at the hand-hewn stone walls. Then turn around to see the vista of bamboo.

A GREAT FAMILY HIKE At mile marker 9 there's a small state wayside area with restrooms, picnic tables, and a barbecue area. The sign says KOOLAU FOREST RESERVE, but the real attraction here is the **Waikamoi Ridge Trail** ⚐, an easy .75-mile loop.

Kids   Touring the Surfing Goat Dairy Farm

Just beyond the sugar-cane fields, on the slopes of Haleakala, lies the **Surfing Goat Dairy**, 3661 Omaopio Rd., Kula (© 808/878-2870; www.surfinggoatdairy. com). Some 140 dairy goats blissfully graze the 42 acres and contribute the milk for the 24 different cheeses, which are made every day. If you have kids in tow, they will love the 2-hour **Grand Dairy Tour,** where they can be a goat herder for a day and even try to milk a goat. They can also play with the kids—goat kids that is. Meanwhile, mom and dad can learn how to make cheese and sample the different varieties of cheese made on the premises. The admission price is $15. The Grand Dairy Tours are scheduled several times each month; call for information. If you don't have a lot of time, drop by for the 20-minute casual dairy tour (Mon–Sat 10am–4pm and Sun 10am–1pm) for just $5 a person.

The start of the trail is just behind the QUIET TREES AT WORK sign. The well-marked trail meanders through eucalyptus, ferns, and *hala* trees.

SAFETY WARNING   I used to recommend another waterfall, **Puohokamoa Falls,** at mile marker 11, but not anymore. Unfortunately, what once was a great thing has been overrun by hordes of not-so-polite tourists. You will see cars parking on the already dangerous, barely two-lane Hana Highway a half a mile before the waterfall. Slow down after the 10-mile marker. As you get close to the 11-mile marker, the road becomes a congested one-lane road due to visitors parking on this narrow highway. Don't add to the congestion by trying to park: There are plenty of other great waterfalls; just drive slowly and safely through this area.

CAN'T-MISS PHOTO OPS   Just past mile marker 12 is the **Kaumahina State Wayside Park** ⚶. This is not only a good pit stop (restrooms are available) and a wonderful place for a picnic (with tables and a barbecue area), but also a great vista point. The view of the rugged coastline makes an excellent shot—you can see all the way down to the jutting Keanae Peninsula.

Another mile and a couple of bends in the road, and you'll enter the Honomanu Valley, with its beautiful bay. To get to the **Honomanu Bay County Beach Park** ⚶, look for the turnoff on your left, just after mile marker 14, as you begin your ascent up the other side of the valley. The rutted dirt-and-cinder road takes you down to the rocky black-sand beach. There are no facilities here. Because of the strong rip currents offshore, swimming is best in the stream inland from the ocean. You'll consider the drive down worthwhile as you stand on the beach, well away from the ocean, and turn to look back on the steep cliffs covered with vegetation.

MAUI'S BOTANICAL WORLD   Farther along the winding road, between mile markers 16 and 17, is a cluster of bunkhouses composing the YMCA Camp Keanae. A ¼-mile down is the **Keanae Arboretum** ⚶⚶, where the region's botany is divided into three parts: native forest, introduced forest, and traditional Hawaiian plants, food, and medicine. You can swim in the pools of Piinaau Stream, or press on along a mile-long trail into Keanae Valley, where a lovely tropical rainforest waits at the end (see "Hiking & Camping" in chapter 7).

KEANAE PENINSULA   The old Hawaiian village of **Keanae** ⚶⚶ stands out against the Pacific like a place time forgot. Here, on an old lava flow graced by an

1860 stone church and swaying palms, is one of the last coastal enclaves of native Hawaiians. They still grow taro in patches and pound it into poi, the staple of the old Hawaiian diet. And they still pluck *opihi* (limpet) from tide pools along the jagged coast and cast throw-nets at schools of fish.

The turnoff to the Keanae Peninsula is on the left, just after the arboretum. The road passes by farms as it hugs the peninsula. Where the road bends, there's a small beach where fishermen gather to catch dinner. A ¼ mile farther is the **Kaenae Congregational Church** (© **808/248-8040**), built in 1860 of lava rocks and coral mortar, standing out in stark contrast to the green fields surrounding it. Beside the church is a small beachfront park, with false kamani trees against a backdrop of black lava and a roiling turquoise sea.

For an experience in an untouched Hawaii, follow the road until it ends. Park by the white fence and take the short, 5-minute walk along the shoreline over the black lava. Continue along the footpath through the tall California grass to the black rocky beach, separating the freshwater stream, **Pinaau,** which winds back into the Keanae Peninsula, nearly cutting it off from the rest of Maui. This is an excellent place for a picnic and a swim in the cool waters of the stream. There are no facilities here, so be sure you carry everything out with you and use restroom facilities before you arrive. As you make your way back, notice the white PVC pipes sticking out of the rocks— they're fishing-pole holders for fishermen, usually hoping to catch ulua.

ANOTHER PHOTO OP: KEANAE LOOKOUT   Just past mile marker 17 is a wide spot on the ocean side of the road, where you can see the entire Keanae Peninsula's checkerboard pattern of green taro fields and its ocean boundary etched in black lava. Keanae was the result of a postscript eruption of Haleakala, which flowed through the Koolau Gap and down Keanae Valley and added this geological punctuation to the rugged coastline.

FRUIT & FLOWER STANDS   Around mile marker 18, the road widens; you'll start to see numerous small stands selling fruit or flowers. Many of these stands work on the honor system: You leave your money in the basket and select your purchase. I recommend stopping at **Uncle Harry's,** which you'll find just after the Keanae School around mile marker 18. Native Hawaiian Harry Kunihi Mitchell, an expert in native plants and herbs, devoted his life to the Hawaiian-rights and nuclear-free movements. His family sells a variety of fruits and juices here Monday through Saturday from 9am to 4pm.

WAILUA   Just after Uncle Harry's, look for the Wailua Road off on the left. This will take you through the hamlet of homes and churches of Wailua, which also contains a shrine depicting what the community calls a "miracle." Behind the pink **St. Gabriel's Church** is the smaller, blue and white **Coral Miracle Church,** home of the **Our Lady of Fatima Shrine.** According to legend, in 1860 the men of this village were building a church by diving for coral to make the stone. But the coral offshore was in deep water and the men could only come up with a few pieces at a time, making the construction of the church an arduous project. A freak storm hit the area and deposited the coral from the deep on a nearby beach. The Hawaiians gathered what they needed and completed the church. After the church was completed, another freak storm hit the area and swept all the remaining coral on the beach back out to sea.

If you look back at Haleakala from here, on your left you can see the spectacular, near-vertical **Waikani Falls.** On the remainder of the dead-end road is an eclectic collection of old and modern homes. Turning around at the road's end is very difficult, so I suggest you just turn around at the church and head back for the Hana Highway.

Back on the Hana Highway, just before mile marker 19, is the **Wailua Valley State Wayside Park** ⚐, on the right side of the road. Climb up the stairs for a view of the Keanae Valley, waterfalls, and Wailua Peninsula. On a really clear day, you can see up the mountain to the Koolau Gap.

For a better view of the Wailua Peninsula, continue down the road about ¼ mile; on the ocean side, there will be a pull-off area with parking.

PUAA KAA STATE WAYSIDE PARK You'll hear this park long before you see it, about halfway between mile markers 22 and 23. The sound of waterfalls provides the background music for this small park area with restrooms, a phone, and a picnic area. There's a well-marked path to the falls and to a swimming hole. Ginger plants are everywhere: Pick some flowers and put them in your car so that you can travel with that sweet smell.

OLD NAHIKU Just after mile marker 25 is a narrow 3-mile road leading from the highway, at about 1,000 feet elevation, down to sea level—and to the remains of the old Hawaiian community of **Nahiku.** At one time this was a thriving village of thousands; today the population has dwindled to fewer than a hundred—including a few Hawaiian families, but mostly extremely wealthy mainland residents who jet in for a few weeks at a time to their luxurious vacation homes. At the turn of the 20th century, this site saw brief commercial activity as home of the Nahiku Rubber Co., the only commercial rubber plantation in the United States. You can still see rubber trees along the Nahiku Road. However, the amount of rainfall, coupled with the damp conditions, could not support the commercial crop; the plantation closed in 1912, and Nahiku was forgotten until the 1980s, when multimillionaires "discovered" the remote and stunningly beautiful area.

At the end of the road, you can see the remains of the old wharf from the rubber-plantation days. Local residents come down here to shoreline fish; there's a small picnic area off to the side. Dolphins are frequently seen in the bay.

HANA AIRPORT After mile marker 31, a small sign points to the Hana Airport, down Alalele Road on the left. Newly formed commuter airline **Pacific Wings** (© **888/575-4546;** www.pacificwings.com) offers three flights daily to and from Hana, with connecting flights from Kahului and traveling on to Honolulu. There is no public transportation in Hana. Car rentals are available through **Dollar Rent A Car** (© **800/800-4000** or 808/248-8237).

WAIANAPANAPA STATE PARK ⚐⚐ At mile marker 32, just on the outskirts of Hana, shiny black-sand Waianapanapa Beach appears like a vivid dream, with bright-green jungle foliage on three sides and cobalt-blue water lapping at its feet. The 120-acre park on an ancient *aa* lava flow includes sea cliffs, lava tubes, arches, and the beach, plus 12 cabins, tent camping, picnic pavilions, restrooms, showers, drinking water, and hiking trails. If you're interested in staying here, see chapter 5; also see "Beaches" and "Hiking & Camping" in chapter 7.

8 The End of the Road: Heavenly Hana ⚐⚐

Green, tropical Hana is a destination all its own, a small coastal village that's probably what you came to Maui in search of. Here you'll find a rainforest dotted with cascading waterfalls and sparkling blue pools, skirted by red- and black-sand beaches.

Beautiful Hana enjoys more than 90 inches of rain a year—more than enough to keep the scenery lush. Banyans, bamboo, breadfruit trees—everything seems larger than life in this small town, especially the flowers, such as wild ginger and plumeria.

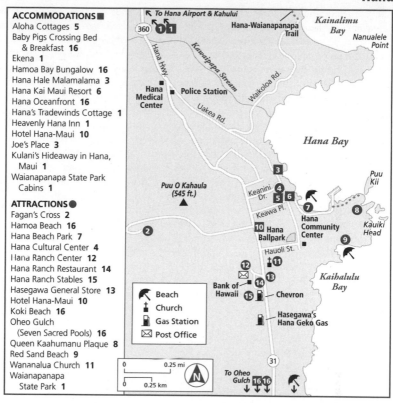

ACCOMMODATIONS ■
Aloha Cottages **5**
Baby Pigs Crossing Bed
  & Breakfast **16**
Ekena **1**
Hamoa Bay Bungalow **16**
Hana Hale Malamalama **3**
Hana Kai Maui Resort **6**
Hana Oceanfront **16**
Hana's Tradewinds Cottage **1**
Heavenly Hana Inn **1**
Hotel Hana-Maui **10**
Joe's Place **3**
Kulani's Hideaway in Hana,
  Maui **1**
Waianapanapa State Park
  Cabins **1**

ATTRACTIONS ●
Fagan's Cross **2**
Hamoa Beach **16**
Hana Beach Park **7**
Hana Cultural Center **4**
Hana Ranch Center **12**
Hana Ranch Restaurant **14**
Hana Ranch Stables **15**
Hasegawa General Store **13**
Hotel Hana-Maui **10**
Koki Beach **16**
Oheo Gulch
  (Seven Sacred Pools) **16**
Queen Kaahumanu Plaque **8**
Red Sand Beach **9**
Wananalua Church **11**
Waianapanapa
  State Park **1**

Several roadside stands offer exotic blooms for $1 a bunch. Just "put money in box." It's the Hana honor system.

A LOOK AT THE PAST

The Hana coast is rich in Hawaiian history and the scene of many turning points in Hawaiian culture. The ancient chants tell of rulers like the 15th-century **Piilani,** who united the island of Maui and built fishponds, irrigation fields, paved roads, and the massive **Piilanihale Heiau,** which still stands today. It was Piilani's sons and grandson who finished the *heiau* and built the first road to Hana from West Maui, not only along the coast, but also up the Kaupo Gap and through the Haleakala Crater.

In 1849 the cantankerous sea captain **George Wilfong** brought commerce to this isolated village when he started the first sugar plantation on some 60 acres. Because his harsh personality and set demands for plantation work did not sit well with the Hawaiians, Wilfong brought in the first Chinese immigrants to work his fields.

In 1864 two Danish brothers, **August and Oscar Unna,** contributed to the growth of the local sugar industry when they established the Hana Plantation. Four years later they brought in Japanese immigrants to labor in the fields.

By the turn of the 20th century, sugar wasn't the only crop booming in Hana (there were some six plantations in the area): Rubber was being commercially grown in Nahiku, wheat in Kaupo, pineapple in Kipahulu, and tobacco in Ulupalakua.

In the 1920s and 1930s, several self-sufficient towns lined the coast, each with its own general store, school, and churches; some had movie theaters as well. Hana has all of the above plus some 15 stores, a pool hall, and several restaurants.

One can only guess what those towns would have been like today if not for the huge tidal wave that hit the state on April 1, 1946. The damage along the Hana coast was catastrophic: The Keanae Peninsula was swept clear (only the stone church remained), Hamoa was totally wiped out, and entire villages completely disappeared.

After World War II the labor movement became a powerful force in Hawaii. **C. Brewer,** owner of the largest sugar plantation in Hana, decided to shut down his operation instead of fighting the labor union. The closure of the plantation meant not only the loss of thousands of jobs but also the loss of plantation-supplied homes and the entire plantation lifestyle. Thankfully, **Paul I. Fagan,** an entrepreneur from San Francisco who had purchased the Hana Sugar Co. from the Unna Brothers in the 1930s, became the town's guardian angel.

Fagan wanted to retire here, so he focused his business acumen on the tiny town with big problems. Recognizing that sugar was no longer economically feasible, he looked at the community and saw other opportunities. He bought 14,000 acres of land in Hana, stripped it of sugar cane, planted grass, and shipped in cattle from his ranch on Molokai.

Next he did something that was years ahead of his time: He thought tourism might have a future in Hana, so he established an inn in 1946 that later became the **Hotel Hana-Maui.** Fagan also pulled off a public-relations coup: He brought the entire San Francisco Seals baseball team (which he happened to own) to Hana for spring training, and, more important, he brought out the sportswriters as well. The writers loved Hana and wrote glowing reports about the town; one even gave the town a nickname that stuck: "Heavenly Hana."

In 1962 the state paved the Hana Highway. By the 1970s, tourists had not only "discovered" Maui, but they also were willing to make the long trek out to Hana.

The biggest change to the local lifestyle came in December 1977, when television finally arrived—after a local cable operator spent 6 months laying cable over cinder cones, mountain streams, and cavernous gulches from one side of the island to the other. Some 125 homes tuned in to the tube—and the rural Hawaiian community was never the same. Today Hana is inhabited by 2,500 people, many part Hawaiian.

SEEING THE SIGHTS

Most visitors will zip through Hana, perhaps taking a quick look out their car windows at a few sights before buzzing on down the road. They might think they've "seen" Hana, but they definitely haven't "experienced" Hana. Allow at least 2 or 3 days to really let this land of legends show you its beauty and serenity.

Another recommendation: See Hana's attractions, especially the pools, ponds, waterfalls, and hikes, early in the day. You'll have them all to yourself. The day-tourists arrive in Hana around 11 and stay until about 4pm; that's when the area is overrun with hundreds and hundreds of people in a hurry and wanting to see everything in just a few hours.

As you enter Hana, the road splits about ½ mile past mile marker 33, at the police station. Both roads will take you to Hana, but the lower road, Uakea Road, is more scenic. Just before you get to Hana Bay, you'll see the old wood-frame **Hana District Police Station and Courthouse.** Next door is the **Hana Cultural Center and Museum** ⚓, on Uakea Road (✆ 808/248-8622; http://hookele.com/hccm), usually open daily from 10am to 4pm. This small building has an excellent collection of Hawaiian quilts, artifacts, books, and photos. Also on the grounds are Kauhala O Hana, composed of four *hale* (houses) for living, meeting, cooking, and canoe building or canoe storage.

Cater-corner from the cultural center is the entrance to **Hana Bay** ⚓. You can drive right down to the pier and park. There are restrooms, showers, picnic tables, barbecue areas, and even a snack bar here. The 386-foot, red-faced cinder cone beside the bay is **Kauiki Hill,** the scene of numerous fierce battles in ancient Hawaii and the birthplace of Queen Kaahumanu in 1768. A short, 5-minute walk will take you to the spot. Look for the trail along the hill on the wharf side, and follow the path through the ironwood trees; the lighthouse on the point will come into view, and you'll see pocket beaches of red cinder below. Grab onto the ironwood trees for support because the trail has eroded in some areas. This is a perfect place for a secluded picnic, or you can continue on the path out to the lighthouse. To get to the lighthouse, which sits on a small island, watch the water for about 10 minutes to get a sense of how often and from which direction the waves are coming. Between wave sets, either swim or wade in the shallow, sandy bottom channel or hop across the rocks to the island.

To get to the center of town, leave Hana Bay, cross Uakea Road, and drive up Keawa Place; turn left on Hana Highway, and on the corner will be the **Hotel Hana-Maui,** the once-luxurious hotel established by Paul Fagan in 1946. It has been neglected of late, but new management has taken over, and I'm hoping this historic hotel gets the care and maintenance it deserves. On the green hills above Hotel Hana-Maui stands a 30-foot-high white cross made of lava rock. Citizens erected the cross in memory of Paul Fagan, who founded the Hana Ranch as well as the hotel and helped keep the town alive. The hike up to **Fagan's Cross** provides a gorgeous view of the Hana coast, especially at sunset, when Fagan himself liked to climb this hill (see p. 185 for details).

Back on the Hana Highway, just past Hauoli Road, is the majestic **Wananalua Congregation Church.** It's on the National Historic Register not only because of its age (it was built in 1838–42 from coral stones) but also because of its location, atop an old Hawaiian *heiau.*

Just past the church, on the right side of the Hana Highway, is the turnoff to the **Hana Ranch Center,** the commercial center for Hana, with a post office, bank, general store, the Hana Ranch Stables, and a restaurant and snack bar (see chapter 6). But the real shopping experience is across the Hana Highway at the **Hasegawa General Store** ⚓, a Maui institution (see chapter 9), which carries oodles of merchandise from soda and fine French wines to fishing line to name-brand clothing, plus everything you need for a picnic or a gourmet meal. This is also the place to find out what's going on in Hana: The bulletin board at the entrance has fliers and handwritten notes advertising everything from fundraising activities to classes to community-wide events. Don't miss this unique store.

If you need gas before heading back, fill up at the **Chevron Service Station** on the right side of the Hana Highway as you leave town. *Warning:* The price of gas here will take your breath away.

OUTDOOR ACTIVITIES

Hana is one of the best areas on Maui for ocean activities, and also boasts a wealth of nature hikes, remote places to explore on horseback, waterfalls to discover, and even lava tube caves to investigate.

For more information on the lava tubes, see **Maui Cave Adventures** (📞 808/248-7308) on p. 190; for details on horseback riding, see **Maui Stables** (📞 808/248-7799) on p. 190. If you're a tennis player, you can take advantage of the free public courts located next to the Hotel Hana-Maui, available on a first-come, first-served basis.

BEACHES & OCEAN ACTIVITIES

Hana's beaches come in numerous varieties—white, black, gray, or red sand; perfectly shaped coves, crescents, or long stretches—and they're excellent for just about every kind of ocean activity you can think of. Call **Hana-Maui Sea Sports** (© **808/248-7711;** www.hana-maui-seasports.com) if you'd like to snorkel or kayak, or venture out on your own at one of my favorite beaches:

HANA   The waters in the Hana Bay are calm most of the time and great for swimming. There's excellent snorkeling and diving by the lighthouse. Strong currents can run through here, so don't venture farther than the lighthouse. See Hana Bay, above, for more details on the facilities and hikes here.

RED SAND BEACH   The Hawaiian name for this beach is *Kaihalulu* (roaring sea) Beach. It's truly a sight to see. The beach is on the ocean side of Kauiki Hill, just south of Hana Bay, in a wild, natural setting on a pocket cove, where the volcanic cinder cone lost its seaward wall to erosion and spilled red cinders everywhere to create the red sands. Before you put on your bathing suit, there are three things to know about this beach: You have to trespass to get here (which is against the law); due to recent heavy rains, there have been several serious injuries on the muddy, slippery terrain (enter at your own risk, it can be extremely dangerous); and nudity (also illegal in Hawaii—arrests have been made) is common here.

If you are determined to go, ask for permission at the Hotel Hana-Maui. And ask about conditions on the trail (which drops several stories down to the ocean rocks). To reach the beach, put on solid walking shoes (no flip-flops) and walk south on Uakea Road, past Haoli Street and the Hotel Hana-Maui, to the parking lot for the hotel's Sea Ranch Cottages. Turn left and cross the open field next to the Hana Community Center. Look for the dirt trail and follow it to the huge ironwood tree, where you turn right (do not go ahead to the old Japanese cemetery). Use the ironwood trees to maintain your balance as you follow the ever-eroding cinder footpath a short distance along the shoreline, down the narrow cliff trail (do not attempt this if it's wet). The trail suddenly turns the corner, and into view comes the burnt-red beach, set off by the turquoise waters, black lava, and vivid green ironwood trees.

The lava outcropping protects the bay and makes it safe for swimming. Snorkeling is excellent, and there's a natural whirlpool area on the Hana Bay side of the cove. Stay away from the surge area where the ocean enters the cove.

KOKI BEACH ⋆   One of the best surfing and boogie-boarding beaches on the Hana Coast lies just a couple of miles from the Hasegawa General Store in the Oheo Gulch direction. There is a very strong rip current here, so unless it is dead calm and you are a strong swimmer, do not attempt swimming here. However, it's a great place to sit on the white sand and watch the surfers. The only facility is a big parking area. To get here, drive toward Oheo Gulch from Hana, where Highway 36 changes to Highway 31. About 1½ miles outside of Hana, turn left at Haneoo Road.

HAMOA BEACH ⋆⋆   For one of Hana's best beaches—great for swimming, boogie boarding, and sunbathing—continue another ½ mile down the Haneoo Road loop to Hamoa Beach. There is easy access from the road down to the sandy beach, and facilities include a small restroom and an outdoor shower. The large pavilion and beach accessories are for Hotel Hana-Maui guests.

WAIOKA POND   Locally, this swimming hole in a series of waterfalls and pools is called Venus Pool, and the rumor is that in ancient Hawaii, only royalty were allowed to use this exquisite site. The freshwater swimming area used to be a great place to spend a secluded day. Unfortunately, it has become overrun with impolite tourists who park on the narrow highway, tear down the fence, and aren't very considerate about cleaning up their trash. The land owner, Hana Ranch, has put up NO TRESPASSING signs and is enforcing trespassing laws. (Getting arrested is not a great way to spend your vacation.) I recommend you skip this pond and keep driving to Haleakala National Park down the road. Not only does the park have adequate parking but also restrooms. If you hike just 10 to 15 minutes upstream from the national park's parking lot, you will find much better pools and most likely have them to yourself.

HIKING

Hana is woven with hiking trails along the shoreline, through the rainforest, and up in the mountains. See "Hiking & Camping" in chapter 7 for a discussion of hiking in Waianapanapa and up to Fagan's Cross.

Another excellent hike that takes you back in time is through Kahanu Gardens and to **Piilanihale Heiau** 𝒦𝒦, one of the largest ancient Hawaiian temples in the state. Turn toward the ocean on Ulaino Road, by mile marker 31. Drive down the paved road (which turns into a dirt road but is still drivable) to the first stream (about 1½ miles). If the stream is flooded, turn around and go back. If you can forge the stream, cross it and park on the right side of the road by the huge breadfruit trees. The trees are part of the 122-acre **Kahanu Garden** 𝒦𝒦 (𝒞 **808/248-8912**), owned and operated by the National Tropical Botanical Garden (www.ntbg.org), which also has two gardens on Kauai. Open Monday through Friday from 10am to 2pm, admission is $10 for self-guided tours. Allow at least an hour and a half to explore the gardens and *heiau.*

The 122 acres encompass plant collections from the Pacific Islands, concentrating on plants of value to the people of Polynesia, Micronesia, and Melanesia. Kahanu Garden contains the largest known collection of breadfruit cultivars from more than 17 Pacific Island groups and Indonesia, the Philippines, and the Seychelles.

The real draw here is the *Piilanihale Heiau* (**House of Piilani,** one of Maui's greatest chiefs—see "A Look at the Past" earlier in this section). Believed to be the largest in the state, it measures 340 feet by 415 feet, and it was built in a unique terrace design not seen anywhere else in Hawaii. The walls are some 50 feet tall and 8 to 10 feet thick. Historians believe that Piilani's two sons and his grandson built the mammoth temple, which was dedicated to war, sometime in the 1500s.

JUST BEYOND HANA
TROPICAL HALEAKALA: OHEO GULCH AT KIPAHULU 𝒦𝒦

If you're thinking about heading out to the so-called Seven Sacred Pools, out past Hana at the Kipahulu end of Haleakala National Park, let's clear this up right now: There are more than seven pools—about 24, actually—and *all* water in Hawaii is considered sacred. It's all a PR scam that has spun out of control into contemporary myth. Folks here call the attraction by its rightful name, **Oheo Gulch,** and visitors sometimes refer to it as Kipahulu, which is actually the name of the area where Oheo Gulch is located. No matter what you call it, it's a beautiful sight. The dazzling series of waterfall pools and cataracts cascading into the sea is so popular that it now has its own roadside parking lot.

Even though Oheo is part of Haleakala National Park, you cannot drive here from the summit. Even hiking from Haleakala to Oheo is tricky: The access trail out of Haleakala is down Kaupo Gap, which ends at the ocean, a good 6 miles down the coast from Oheo. To drive to Oheo, head for Hana, some 60 miles from Kahului on the Hana Highway (Hwy. 36). Oheo is about 30 to 50 minutes beyond Hana, along Highway 31. The Highway 31 bridge passes over pools near the ocean; the other pools, plus magnificent 400-foot Waimoku falls, are reachable via an often-muddy, but rewarding, hour-long uphill hike (see "Hiking & Camping" in chapter 7). Expect showers on the Kipahulu coast. The admission fee is $5 per person or $10 per car.

The **Kipahulu Ranger Station** (✆ **808/248-7375**) is staffed from 9am to 5pm daily. Restrooms are available, but there's no drinking water. Kipahulu rangers offer safety information, exhibits, books, and a variety of walks and hikes year-round; check at the station for current activities.

There are a number of hikes in the park, and tent camping is allowed. See "Hiking & Camping" in chapter 7 for details.

Check with the Haleakala Park rangers before hiking up to or swimming in the pools, and always keep one eye on the water in the streams; the sky can be sunny near the coast, but floodwaters from Kipahulu Valley can cause the pools to rise 4 feet in less than 10 minutes.

LINDBERGH'S GRAVE

A mile past Oheo Gulch on the ocean side of the road is **Lindbergh's Grave.** First to fly across the Atlantic Ocean, Charles A. Lindbergh (1902–74) found peace in the Pacific; he settled in Hana, where he died of cancer in 1974. The famous aviator is buried under river stones in a seaside graveyard behind the 1857 **Palapala Hoomau Congregational Church,** where his tombstone is engraved with his favorite words from the 139th Psalm: "If I take the wings of the morning and dwell in the uttermost parts of the sea . . ."

EVEN FARTHER AROUND THE BEND

About 2½ miles past Oheo Gulch, Kaupo Road, or Old Piilani Highway (Hwy. 31), turns rough and unpaved in parts, often full of potholes and ruts. In the spring this is a beautiful drive. But if it has rained recently, this narrow, winding road washes out and becomes treacherous. Many car-rental companies forbid you from taking their cars on this road (not because they're worried about your safety, but because they don't want to send their tow trucks all the way out here); check your rental agreement before setting out. Ask around about road conditions, or call the **Maui Public Works Department** (✆ **808/248-8254**) or the **Police Department** (✆ **808/248-8311**). Note that Kaupo Road links back to upcountry Maui, not South Maui. If you're heading back to the beaches after your visit to Hana, you're better off retracing your route on the Hana Highway.

The road is unpaved all the way to the fishing village of **Kaupo,** one lane at times, wandering in and out of valleys with sharp rock walls and blind bends hugging the ocean cliffs. You may encounter wild pigs and stray cows. About 6 miles and about 60 minutes from Oheo Gulch, you'll see the restored **Huialoha Congregationalist "Circuit" Church,** originally constructed in 1859. Across from the church and down the road a bit is the **Kaupo Store** (✆ **808/248-8054**), which marks the center of the ranching community of Kaupo. Store hours are officially Monday through Friday from 7:30am to 4:30pm, but in this arid cattle country, posted store hours often prove meaningless. The Kaupo Store is the last of the Soon family stores, which at one time stretched from Kaupo to Keanae.

From the Kaupo Store, the landscape turns into barren, dry desert. In the lee of Haleakala, this area gets little rain. There are no phones or services until you reach **Ulupalakua Ranch** (p. 215), where there's a winery, general store, and gas station, which is likely to be closed.

Between mile markers 29 and 30, look for the ancient lava flow that created an arch as it rolled down Haleakala. Keep an eye peeled for cattle, because this is open range country. Eventually the road will wind uphill, and suddenly the forest and greenery of Ulupalakua come into sight. From here, you're about 45 minutes from Kahului.

9

Shops & Galleries

Maui is a shopaholic's dream as well as an arts center, with a large number of resident artists who show their works in dozens of galleries and countless gift shops. Maui is also the queen of specialty products, an agricultural cornucopia that includes Kula onions, upcountry protea, Kaanapali coffee, world-renowned potato chips, and many other tasty treats that are shipped worldwide.

As with any popular visitor destination, you'll have to wade through bad art and mountains of trinkets, particularly in Lahaina and Kihei, where touristy boutiques line the streets between rare pockets of treasures. If you shop in South or West Maui, expect to pay resort prices, clear down to a bottle of Evian or sunscreen.

With a well-heeled flourish, **The Shops at Wailea,** an upscale shopping-and-restaurant complex, opened in South Maui in 2001. The 16-acre complex features more than 50 shops and five restaurants, including Louis Vuitton, Tiffany, Gap, Banana Republic, and the

ever-popular local retailers Martin & MacArthur and Ki'i Gallery. This is resort shopping much in the vein of Whalers Village in Kaanapali, where shopping and restaurant activity is concentrated in a single oceanfront complex. The Shops at Wailea signal a repositioning of the resort as a place of heightened commercial activity.

Don't ignore central Maui, home to some first-rate boutiques. Watch Wailuku, which is poised for a resurgence. The town has its own antiques alleys, the new Sig Zane Designs has brought a delightful infusion of creative and cultural energy, and a major promenade on Main Street is in the works. The Kaahumanu Center, in neighboring Kahului, is becoming more fashionable by the month.

Upcountry, Makawao's boutiques are worth seeking out, despite some attitude and high prices. The charm of shopping on Maui has always rested in the small, independent shops and galleries that crop up in surprising places.

1 Central Maui

KAHULUI

Kahului's best shopping is concentrated in two places. Almost all of the shops listed below are at one of the following centers:

The once rough-around-the-edges **Maui Mall,** 70 E. Kaahumanu Ave. (© 808/877-7559), is the talk of Kahului. Newly renovated, it's now bigger and better and has retained some of my favorite stores while adding a 12-screen movie megaplex that features current releases as well as art-house films. The mall is still a place of everyday good things, from **Long's Drugs** to **Star Market** to **Tasaka Guri Guri,** the decades-old purveyor of inimitable icy treats, neither ice cream nor shave ice but something in between.

Queen Kaahumanu Center, 275 Kaahumanu Ave. (© 808/877-3369), 5 minutes from the Kahului Airport on Highway 32, offers more than 100 shops, restaurants, and theaters. Its second-floor Plantation District offers home furnishings and accessories, and gift and accessories shops. Kaahumanu covers all the bases, from arts and crafts to a **Foodland Supermarket** and everything in between: a thriving food court; the island's best beauty supply, **Lisa's Beauty Supply & Salon** (© 808/877-6463), and its sister store for cosmetics, **Madison Avenue Day Spa and Boutique** (© 808/873-0880); mall standards like **Sunglass Hut, Radio Shack,** and **Local Motion** (surf and beach wear); and standard department stores like **Macy's** and **Sears** and great specialty shops like **Sharper Image.**

Apricot Rose   The former Caswell-Massey has changed its name but still offers the same selection of products for beauty and home: unique Maui-made soaps and bath products that use tropical fragrances and botanicals. Caswell-Massey is America's oldest perfume company, established in 1752. The company triple-mills all of its soaps (so they last longer) and scents them with natural oils. Choose from hundreds of specialty products, from decadent bath salts with 23-karat gold flakes to Damask rose shampoo and bath gels, body lotions, sachets, candles, perfume bottles, potpourris, room mists, and more. You can also get handsome, custom-designed baskets at no extra charge. In the Kaahumanu Center. © 808/877-7761.

Cost Less Imports   Natural fibers are ubiquitous in this newly expanded corner of the Maui Mall, which is three times larger than before. Household accessories include lauhala, bamboo blinds, grassy floor and window coverings, shoji-style lamps, burlap yardage, baskets, Balinese cushions, Asian imports, *noreng* (Japanese folk curtains), and top-of-the-line, made-on-Maui soaps and handicrafts. A good source of tropical and Asian home decor. In the Maui Mall. © 808/877-0300.

Lightning Bolt Maui Inc.   Here's an excellent selection of women's board shorts, aloha shirts, swimwear, sandals and shoes, and all the necessary accoutrements for fun in the sun. Quality labels such as Patagonia and high-tech, state-of-the-art outdoor gear attract adventurers heading for the chilly hinterlands as well as the sun-drenched shores. 55 Kaahumanu Ave. © 808/877-3484.

Maui County Store   Attention T-shirt collectors: Here's your chance to get official Maui County Police and Fire logo T-shirts and other Maui County logo shirts, plus logo wear from the University of Hawaii and other made-in-Maui items. This fundraising store (it helps the police and fire departments) is staffed by students from Maui Community College learning retail sales. Prices are great, money goes to a good cause, the students get to learn a trade, and you get to take home excellent souvenirs from your Maui vacation. Maui Mall, 70 Kaahumanu Ave., Kahului. © 808/877-6669. www.mauicountystore.com.

Maui Swap Meet   The Maui Swap Meet is a large and popular event. After Thanksgiving and throughout December, the activity reaches fever pitch. The colorful Maui specialties include vegetables from Kula and Keanae, fresh taro, plants, proteas, crafts, household items, homemade ethnic foods, and baked goods, including some fabulous fruit breads. Every Saturday from 7am to noon, vendors spread out their wares in booths and under tarps, in a festival-like atmosphere. Between the cheap Balinese imports and New Age crystals and incense, you may find some vintage John Kelly prints and 1930s collectibles. Admission is 50¢, and if you go early while the vendors are setting up, no one will turn you away. As we went to press, the Maui Swap Meet owners were in negotiations to stay in their longtime location on Puunene

Avenue, but they may be forced to move. Please contact them first to make sure they are still there. S. Puunene Ave. (next to the Kahului Post Office). ℂ **808/877-3100.**

Summerhouse   Sleek and chic, tiny Summerhouse is big on style: casual and party dresses, separates by Russ Berens, FLAX, and Kiko, and Tencel jeans by Signatur—the best. During the holiday season the selection gets dressy and sassy, but it's a fun browse year-round. I adore the hats, accessories, easy-care clothing, and up-to-the-minute evening dresses that Summerhouse carries in abundance. The high-quality T-shirts are always a cut above. The casual selection is well suited to the island lifestyle. In the Dairy Center, 395 Dairy Rd. ℂ **808/871-1320.** Also on the west side at 4405 Honoapiilani Hwy. ℂ **808/ 669-6616.**

EDIBLES

The **Star Market** and **Long's Drugs** in the Maui Mall, **Foodland** in the Kaahumanu Center, and **Safeway** at 170 E. Kamehameha Ave. will satisfy your ordinary grocery needs. On Saturday you may want to check out the **Maui Swap Meet** (see above).

Down to Earth Natural Foods, 305 Dairy Rd. (ℂ **808/877-2661**), a health-food staple for many years, has fresh organic produce, a bountiful salad bar, sandwiches and smoothies, vitamins and supplements, fresh-baked goods, snacks, whole grains, and several packed aisles of vegetarian and health foods.

Maui's produce has long been a source of pride for islanders, and **Ohana Farmers Market,** in the Kahului Shopping Center (ℂ **808/871-8347**), is the place to find a fresh, inexpensive selection of Maui-grown fruit, vegetables, flowers, and plants. Crafts and gourmet foods add to the event, and the large monkeypod trees provide welcome shade.

WAILUKU

Located at the gateway to Iao Valley, Wailuku is the county seat, the part of Maui where people live and work. Wailuku's attractive vintage architecture, smattering of antiques shops, and mom-and-pop eateries imbue the town with a down-home charm noticeably absent in Maui's resort areas. The community spirit fuels festivals throughout the year and is slowly attracting new businesses, but Wailuku is still a work in progress. It's a mixed bag—of course, there's junk, but a stroll along Main and Market streets usually turns up a treasure or two.

Bailey House Gift Shop   For made-in-Hawaii items, Bailey House is a must-stop. It offers a thoroughly enjoyable browse through authentic Hawaiiana, in a museum that's one of the finest examples of missionary architecture, dating from 1833. Gracious gardens, rare paintings of early Maui, wonderful programs in Hawaiian arts and culture, and a restored hand-hewn koa canoe await visitors. The small shop packs a wallop with its selection of remarkable gift items, from Hawaiian music to exquisite woods; traditional Hawaiian games to pareus and books. Prints by the legendary Hawaii artist Madge Tennent, lauhala hats hanging in midair, hand-sewn pheasant hatbands, jams and jellies, Maui cookbooks, and an occasional Hawaiian quilt are some of the treasures to be found here. Bailey House Museum Shop, 2375-A Main St. ℂ **808/244-3326.**

Bird of Paradise Unique Antiques   Owner Joe Myhand loves furniture, old Matson liner menus, blue willow china, kimonos for children, and anything nostalgic that happens to be Hawaiian. The furniture ranges from 1940s rattan to wicker and old koa—those items tailor-made for informal island living and leisurely moments on the lanai. Myhand also collects bottles, and mails his license plates all over the world. The collection ebbs and flows with his finds, keeping buyers waiting in the wings for his Depression glass, California pottery from the 1930s and 1940s, old dinnerware, perfume bottles, vintage aloha shirts, and vintage Hawaiian music on cassettes. 56 N. Market St. © 808/242-7699.

Brown-Kobayashi   Graceful living is the theme here. Prices range from a few dollars to the thousands in this 750-square-foot treasure trove. The owners have added a fabulous selection of antique stone garden pieces that mingle quietly with Asian antiques and old and new French, European, and Hawaiian objects. Although the collection is eclectic, there's a cohesive aesthetic that sets Brown-Kobayashi apart from other Maui antiques stores. Japanese kimonos and obi, Bakelite and Peking glass beads, breathtaking Japanese lacquerware, cricket carriers, and cloisonné are among the delights here. Exotic and precious Chinese woods glow discreetly from quiet corners, and an occasional monarchy-style lidded milo bowl comes in and flies out. 160-A N. Market St. © 808/242-0804.

Gottling Ltd.   Karl Gottling's shop specializes in Asian antique furniture, but you can also find smaller carvings, precious stones, jewelry, netsuke, opium weights, and finds in all sizes. I saw a cabinet with 350-year-old doors, and a 17th-century Buddha lending an air of serenity next to a 150-year-old Chinese cabinet. Ming dynasty ceramics, carved wooden apples for $15, and a Persian rug for $65,000 give you an idea of the range of possibilities here. 34 N. Market St. © 808/244-7779.

Old Daze   Nineteenth-century Americana and Hawaiian collectibles are nicely wedded in this charming shop. The collection features a modest furniture selection, Hawaiian pictures, 1960s ashtrays, Depression glass, old washboards, and souvenir plates from county fairs. Choices range from hokey to rustic to pleasantly nostalgic, with many items for the kitchen. Some recent finds: an 1850s German sideboard, a Don Blanding teapot, Royal Worcester china, an antique kimono, and framed vintage music sheets. Owner Geni Dowling's love of nostalgia fills every corner of this tiny shop. 7 North Market St. (close to Main St.). © 808/249-0014.

Sig Zane Designs   As we went to press, designer Sig Zane was considering moving his Wailuku store to Kahului, so be sure to call first if you plan to stop by. Here is a designer with a graphic sense and personal integrity that never wanes. Whether it's a T-shirt, golf shirt, pareu, duffel bag, aloha shirt, or muumuu, a Sig Zane design has depth and sizzle. Zane and co-owner Punawai Rice have redefined Hawaiian wear by creating an inimitable style in clothing, textiles, furnishings, bedding, and lifestyle accessories, and this, their Maui store, has proven enormously successful. Zane's strong, graphic fabrics are made into aloha shirts and women's wear and used in interiors and furnishings that evoke the gracious Hawaii of an earlier time. The staff is helpful and willing to share the background of each design, so you can learn much about the culture, botany, mythology, and beauty of the islands. 53 Market St. © 808/249-8997.

EDIBLES

Located in the northern section of Wailuku, **Takamiya Market,** 359 N. Market St. (© **808/244-3404**), is much loved by local folks and visitors with adventurous palates, who often drive all the way from Kihei to stock up on picnic fare and mouthwatering ethnic foods for sunset gatherings. Unpretentious home-cooked foods from East and West are prepared daily and served on plastic-foam plates. From the chilled-fish counter come fresh sashimi and poke, and in the renowned assortment of prepared foods are mounds of shoyu chicken, tender fried squid, roast pork, Kalua pork, laulau, Chinese noodles, fiddlehead ferns, and Western comfort foods, such as corn bread and potato salad. Fresh produce and paper products are also available, but it's the prepared foods and fresh-fish counter that have made Takamiya's a household name in central Maui.

2 West Maui

LAHAINA

Lahaina's merchants and art galleries go all out from 7 to 9pm on Friday, when **Art Night** brings an extra measure of hospitality and community spirit. The Art Night openings are usually marked with live entertainment, refreshments, and a livelier-than-usual street scene.

If you're in Lahaina on the second or last Thursday of the month, stroll by the front lawn of the **Baldwin Home,** 120 Dickenson St. (at Front St.), for a splendid look at lei making and an opportunity to meet the gregarious seniors of Lahaina. In a program sponsored by AARP, they gather from 10am to 4pm to demonstrate lei making, to sell their floral creations, and, equally important, to socialize.

What was formerly a big, belching pineapple cannery is now a maze of shops and restaurants at the northern end of Lahaina town, known as the **Lahaina Cannery Mall,** 1221 Honoapiilani Hwy. (© **808/661-5304**). Find your way through the T-shirt and sportswear shops to coffee at **Sir Wilfred's Coffee House,** where you can unwind with espresso and croissants, or head for **Compadres Bar & Grill** (p. 140), where the margaritas flow freely and the Mexican food is tasty. For film, water, aspirin, groceries, sunscreen, and other things you can't live without, nothing beats **Long's Drugs** and **Safeway,** two old standbys. **Roland's** may surprise you with its selection of footwear, everything from Cole-Haan sophisticates to inexpensive sandals. At the recently expanded food court, the new **Compadres Taquería** sells Mexican food to go, while **L & L Drive-Inn** sells plate lunches near Greek, pizza, Vietnamese, and Japanese food booths.

The **Lahaina Center,** 900 Front St. (© **808/667-9216**), is still a work in progress. It's located north of Lahaina's most congested strip, where Front Street begins. Across the street from the center, the seawall is a much-sought-after front-row seat to the sunset. There's plenty of free validated parking and easy access to more than 30 shops, a salon, restaurants, a nightclub, and a four-plex movie-theater complex. **Ruth's Chris Steak House** has opened its doors in Lahaina Center, and **Maui Brews** serves lunch and dinner and offers nighttime live music on weekdays. Among the shopping stops: **Banana Republic,** the **Hilo Hattie Fashion Center** (a dizzying emporium of aloha wear), **ABC Discount Store,** and a dozen other recreational, dining, and entertainment options.

The conversion of 10,000 square feet of parking space into the re-creation of a traditional Hawaiian village is a welcome touch of Hawaiiana at Lahaina Center. With the commercialization of modern Lahaina, it's easy to forget that it was once the capital of the Hawaiian kingdom and a significant historic site. The village, called **Hale Kahiko** (www.lahainacenter.com/hale_kahiko.html), features three main houses, called *hale:* a sleeping house, the men's dining house, and the crafts house, where women pounded *hala* (pandanus) strips to weave into mats and baskets. Construction of the houses consumed 10,000 square feet of ohia wood from the island, 20 tons of pili grass, and more than 4 miles of hand-woven coconut sennit for the lashings. Artifacts, weapons, a canoe, and indigenous trees are among the authentic touches in this village, which can be toured privately or with a guide.

David Lee Galleries   This gallery is devoted to the works of David Lee, who uses natural powder colors to paint on silk. The pigments and technique create a luminous, ethereal quality. 712 Front St. ℭ 808/667-7740.

Lahaina Arts Society Galleries   With its membership of more than 185 Maui artists, the nonprofit Lahaina Arts Society is an excellent community resource. Changing monthly exhibits in the Banyan Tree and Old Jail galleries offer a good look at the island's artistic well: two-dimensional art, fiber art, ceramics, sculpture, prints, jewelry, and more. In the shade of the humongous banyan tree in the square across from Pioneer Inn, "Art in the Park" fairs are offered every second and fourth weekend of the month. 648 Wharf St. ℭ 808/661-3228.

Lei Spa Maui   Expanded to include two massage rooms and shower facilities, this day spa offers facials and other therapies. About 95% of the beauty and bath products sold here are made on Maui, and that includes Hawaiian Botanical Pikake shower gel; kukui and macadamia-nut oils; Hawaiian potpourris; mud masks with Hawaiian seaweed; and a spate of rejuvenating, cleansing, skin-soothing potions for hair and skin. Aromatherapy body oils and perfumes are popular, as are the handmade soaps and fragrances of torch ginger, plumeria, coconut, tuberose, and sandalwood. Scented candles in coconut shells, inexpensive and fragrant, make great gifts. 505 Front St. ℭ **808/661-1178.**

Maggie Coulombe *(finds*   Imagine a high-fashion store with the unique designs of Maggie Coulombe in the midst of Lahaina. Maggie's latest couture, jersey, linen, pareo, and shoes, plus accessories, jewelry, purses, and a few surprises, are available here. 505 Front St. ℭ **808/662-0696.** www.maggiecoulombe.com.

Martin Lawrence Galleries   The front is garish, with pop art, kinetic sculptures, and bright, carnivalesque glass objects. Toward the back of the gallery, however, there's a sizable inventory of two-dimensional art and some plausible choices for collectors of Keith Haring, Andy Warhol, and other pop artists. The originals, limited-edition graphics, and sculptures also include works by Marc Chagall, Pablo Picasso, Joan Miró, Roy Lichtenstein, and other noted artists. The focus is pop art and national and international artists. In Lahaina Market Place, 126 Lahainaluna Rd. ℭ **808/661-1788.**

Na Mea Hawaii   The best of Hawaii can be found here, if not in the striking Tutuvi silk-screened dresses and shirts, then in the delicately patterned shawls and scarves of Maile Andrade that depict Hawaiian scenes and traditions on velvet. Arts, crafts, gifts, and clothing, all made by Hawaii artists, fill this cozy niche of Lahaina in the historic Baldwin House on Front Street. You might find a beautifully made lauhala bag, a colorful muumuu, a Hawaii-themed book, or a pheasant hat lei made by master feather lei makers Mary Lou Kekuewa and Paulette Kahalepuna. The shop is tiny, filled with the colors, fibers, and spirit of Hawaii. Lahaina Cannery Mall, 1221 Honoapiilani Hwy. ℭ **808/667-5345.**

The Old Lahaina Book Emporium   What a bookstore! Chockablock with used books in stacks, shelves, counters, and aisles, this bookstore is a browser's dream. More than 25,000 quality used books are lovingly housed in this shop, where owner JoAnn Carroll treats books and customers well. The store is 95% used books and 100% delight. Specialties include Hawaiiana, fiction, mystery, sci-fi, and military history, with substantial selections in cookbooks, children's books, and philosophy/religion. You could pay as little as $2 for a quality read, or a whole lot more for that rare first edition. Books on tape, videos, the classics, and old guitar magazines are among the treasures of this two-story emporium. 834 Front St. ℭ **808/661-1399.**

Totally Hawaiian Gift Gallery   This gallery makes a good browse for its selection of Niihau shell jewelry, excellent Hawaiian CDs, Norfolk pine bowls, and Hawaiian quilt kits. Hawaiian quilt patterns sewn in Asia (at least they're honest about it) are labor-intensive, less expensive, and attractive, although not totally Hawaiian. Hawaiian-quilt-patterned gift-wraps and tiles, perfumes and soaps, handcrafted dolls, and koa accessories are of good quality, and the artists, such as Kelly Dunn (Norfolk wood bowls), Jerry Kermode (wood), and Pat Coito (wood), are among the tops in their fields. In the Lahaina Cannery Mall, 1221 Honoapiilani Hwy. (C) 808/667-2558.

Trouvaille   Hidden in the Pioneer Inn Museum and Marketplace is this gem of a boutique, owned by Carol Wilson and Joan McKelvey, who have traveled the globe looking for the unusual and the unique, especially Asian and Pacific art (*trouvaille* translates as "finding something special"). Here you will find everything from a Borneo ceremonial sword to a story board from Palau, a flute from Nepal, baskets/purses from Laos, and an interesting array of jewelry. Pioneer Inn Museum & Marketplace, Shops 3–4, Hotel St. (C) 808/661-6885.

Village Galleries in Lahaina   The nearly 30-year-old Village Galleries is the oldest continuously running gallery on Maui, and it's highly esteemed as one of the few galleries with consistently high standards. Art collectors know this as a respectable showcase for regional artists; the selection of mostly original two- and three-dimensional art offers a good look at the quality of work originating on the island. The newer contemporary gallery offers colorful gift items and jewelry. 120 and 180 Dickenson St. (C) 808/661-4402 or 808/661-5559. Also at the Ritz-Carlton Kapalua, 1 Ritz-Carlton Dr. (C) 808/669-1800.

KAANAPALI

On a recent trip I was somewhat disappointed with upscale **Whalers Village,** 2435 Kaanapali Pkwy. ((C) 808/661-4567). Although it offers everything from whale blubber to Prada and Ferragamo, it is short on local shops, and parking at the nearby lot is expensive. The complex is home to the Whalers Village Museum, with interactive exhibits and a 40-foot sperm-whale skeleton, but shoppers come for the designer thrills and beachfront dining. You can find most of the items featured here in the shops in Lahaina and can avoid the parking hassle and the high prices by skipping Whalers Village.

If you do decide to check it out, don't miss my favorite shoe store, **Sandal Tree** (with two other locations, one at Hyatt Regency Maui and the other at Grand Wailea Resort in Wailea). **Martin & MacArthur,** a mainstay of the village, offers a dizzying array of Hawaii crafts: Hawaiian-quilt cushion covers, jewelry, soaps, books, and a stunning selection of woodworks. The always wonderful **Lahaina Printsellers** has a selection of antique prints, maps, paintings, and engravings, including 18th- to 20th-century cartography, all of which offer great browsing and gift potential. You can find award-winning **Kimo Bean** coffee at a kiosk, an expanded **Reyn's** for aloha wear, and **Cinnamon Girl,** a hit in Honolulu for its matching mother-daughter clothing. The return of **Waldenbooks** makes it that much easier to pick up the latest bestseller on the way to the beach. Once you've stood under the authentic whale skeleton at the **Whale Center of the Pacific** (see chapter 8), you can blow a bundle at **Tiffany, Prada, Chanel, Ferragamo, Vuitton, Coach, Dolphin Galleries, The Body Shop,** or any of the more than 60 shops and restaurants that have sprouted up in this open-air shopping center. Despite obvious efforts to offer more of a balance between island-made and designer goods, the chain luxury stores still dominate.

Other mainstays: The **Eyecatcher** has an extensive selection of sunglasses; it's located just across from the busiest **ABC** store in the state. **Pizza Paradiso** has taken over the former **Maui Yogurt Company** and sells ice cream and smoothies in a food court of other dine-and-dash goodies. Whalers Village is open daily from 9:30am to 10pm.

Ki'i Gallery   Some of the works are large and lavish, such as the Toland Sand prisms for just under $5,000 and the John Stokes handblown glass. Those who love glass in all forms, from handblown vessels to jewelry, will love a browse through Ki'i. I found Pat Kazi's work in porcelain and found objects, such as the mermaid in a teacup, inspired by fairy tales and mythology, both fantastic and compelling. The gallery is devoted to glass and original paintings and drawings; roughly half of the artists are from Hawaii. In the Hyatt Regency Maui, 200 Nohea Kai Dr. ℂ 808/661-4456. Also at the Grand Wailea Resort, ℂ 808/874-3059, and the Shops at Wailea, ℂ 808/874-1181.

Paul Ropp *(Finds)*   The Bali fashion designer's only store outside of Indonesia is found on the ground level at Whalers Village. The renowned Rupp sees fashion as a medium, and he calls his creations "sexual clothes." Stop by and check out his sense of fashion (lively and colorful) and eccentric style of dressing, which is perfect for Maui's tropical climate. In Whalers Village, 2435 Kaanapali Pkwy. ℂ 808/661-8000.

Sandal Tree   It's unusual for a resort shop to draw local customers on a regular basis, but the Sandal Tree attracts a flock of footwear fanatics who come here from throughout the islands for rubber thongs and Top-Siders, sandals and dressy pumps, athletic shoes and hats, designer footwear, and much more. Sandal Tree also carries a generous selection of Mephisto and Arche comfort sandals, Donald Pliner, Anne Klein, Charles Jourdan, and beachwear and casual footwear for all tastes. Accessories range from fashionable knapsacks to avant-garde geometrical handbags—for town and country, day and evening, kids, women, and men. Prices are realistic too. In Whalers Village, 2435 Kaanapali Pkwy. ℂ 808/667-5330. Also in Grand Wailea Resort, 3850 Wailea Alanui Dr., Wailea (ℂ 808/874-9006); and in the Hyatt Regency Maui, 200 Nohea Kai Dr. (ℂ 808/661-3495).

KAHANA/NAPILI/HONOKOWAI

Those driving north of Kaanapali toward Kapalua will notice the **Honokowai Marketplace** on Lower Honoapiilani Road, only minutes before the Kapalua Airport. There are restaurants and coffee shops, a dry cleaner, the flagship **Star Market, Hula Scoops** for ice cream, a gas station, a copy shop, a few clothing stores, and the sprawling **Hawaiian Interiorz.**

Nearby **Kahana Gateway** is an unimpressive mall built to serve the condominium community that has sprawled along the coastline between Honokowai and Kapalua. If you need women's swimsuits, however, **Rainbow Beach Swimwear** is a find. It carries a selection of suits for all shapes, at lower-than-resort prices, slashed even further during the frequent sales. **Hutton's Fine Jewelry** offers high-end jewelry from designers around the country (lots of platinum and diamonds), reflecting discerning taste for those who can afford it. Tahitian black pearls and jade are among Hutton's specialties.

KAPALUA

Honolua Store   Walk on the old wood floors peppered with holes from golf shoes and find your everyday essentials: bottled water, stationery, mailing tape, jackets, chips, wine, soft drinks, paper products, fresh fruit and produce, and aisles of notions and necessities. With picnic tables on the veranda and a takeout counter offering deli items—more than a dozen types of sandwiches, salads, and budget-friendly

A Creative Way to Spend the Day

Make a bowl from clay or paint a premade one, then fire it and take it home. The **Art School at Kapalua** (© 808/665-0007; www.kapaluamaui.com), in a charming 1920s plantation building that was part of an old cannery operation, features local and visiting instructors and is open daily for people of all ages and skill levels. Projects, classes, and workshops at this not-for-profit organization highlight creativity in all forms, including photography, figure drawing, ceramics, landscape painting, painting on silk, and the performing arts (ballet, yoga, creative movement, Pilates). Classes are inexpensive. Call the school to see what's scheduled while you're on Maui.

breakfasts—there are always long lines of customers. Golfers and surfers love to come here for the morning paper and coffee. 502 Office Rd. (next to the Ritz-Carlton Kapalua). © 808/669-6128.

Kapalua Shops   Shops have come and gone in this small, exclusive, and once-chic shopping center, now much quieter than in days past. The closing of elegant Mandalay is a big loss. The **Elizabeth Dole Gallery** has loads of Dale Chihuly studio glass, fabulous and expensive, a dramatic counterpoint to **South Seas Trading Post** and its exotic artifacts such as New Guinea masks, Balinese beads, tribal jewelry, lizard-skin drums, and coconut-shell carvings with mother-of-pearl inlay. Otherwise, it's slim pickings for shoppers in Kapalua. In the Kapalua Bay Hotel and Villas. © 808/669-1029.

Village Galleries   Maui's finest exhibit their works here and in the other two Village Galleries in Lahaina. Take heart, art lovers: There's no clichéd marine art here. Translucent, delicately turned bowls of Norfolk pine gleam in the light, and George Allan, Betty Hay Freeland, Fred KenKnight, and Pamela Andelin are included in the pantheon of respected artists represented in the tiny gallery. Watercolors, oils, sculptures, handblown glass, Niihau shell leis, jewelry, and other media are represented. The Ritz-Carlton's monthly Artist-in-Residence program features gallery artists in demonstrations and special hands-on workshops—free, including materials. In the Ritz-Carlton Kapalua, 1 Ritz-Carlton Dr. © 808/669-1800.

3 South Maui

KIHEI

Kihei is one long stretch of strip malls. Most of the shopping here is concentrated in the **Azeka Place Shopping Center** on South Kihei Road. Fast foods abound at Azeka, as do tourist-oriented clothing shops like **Crazy Shirts.** Across the street **Azeka Place II** houses several prominent attractions, including **General Nutrition Center,** the **Coffee Store,** and a cluster of specialty shops with everything from children's clothes to shoes, sunglasses, beauty services, and swimwear. Also on South Kihei Road is the **Kukui Mall,** with movie theaters, **Waldenbooks,** and **Whaler's General Store.**

Hawaiian Moons Natural Foods   Hawaiian Moons is an exceptional health-food store, as well as a minisupermarket with one of the best selections of Maui products on the island. The tortillas are made on Maui (and good!), and much of the produce here, such as organic vine-ripened tomatoes and organic onions, is grown in the fertile upcountry soil of Kula. There's also locally grown organic coffee, gourmet salsas,

Maui shiitake mushrooms, organic lemon grass and okra, Maui Crunch bread, free-range Big Island turkeys and chickens (no antibiotics or artificial nasties), and fresh Maui juices. Cosmetics are top-of-the-line: a staggering selection of sunblocks, fragrant floral oils, kukui-nut oil from Waialua on Oahu, and Island Essence made-on-Maui mango-coconut and vanilla-papaya lotions, the ultimate in body pampering. The salad bar is one of the most popular food stops on the coast. 2411 S. Kihei Rd. ℂ 808/875-4356. Also on the west side at 3636 Lower Honoapiilani Rd. ℂ 808/665-1339.

Tuna Luna   There are treasures to be found in this small cluster of tables and booths where Maui artists display their work. Ceramics, raku, sculpture, glass, koa-wood books and photo albums, jewelry, soaps, handmade paper, and fiber-art accessories make great gifts to go. Something to watch for: Maui Metal handcrafted journals, aluminum books with designs of hula girls, palms, fish, and sea horses. Tuna Luna also has a new booth in the back pavilion. In Kihei Kalama Village, 1941 S. Kihei Rd. ℂ 808/874-9482.

WAILEA

CY Maui   Women who like washable, flowing clothing in silks, rayons, and natural fibers will love this shop, formerly the popular Manikin in Kahului. If you don't find what you want on the racks of simple bias-cut designs, you can have it made from the bolts of stupendous fabrics lining the shop. Except for a few hand-painted silks, everything in the shop is washable. In The Shops at Wailea, 3750 Wailea Alanui Dr, A-30. ℂ 808/891-0782.

Grand Wailea Shops   The sprawling Grand Wailea Resort is known for its long arcade of shops and galleries tailored to hefty pocketbooks. However, gift items in all price ranges can be found at Lahaina Printsellers (for old maps and prints), Dolphin Galleries, H. F. Wichman, Sandal Tree, and Napua Gallery, which houses the private collection of the resort owner. Ki'i Gallery is luminous with studio glass and exquisitely turned woods, and **Sandal Tree** (p. 236) raises the footwear bar. At Grand Wailea Resort, 3850 Wailea Alanui Dr. ℂ 808/875-1234.

Nell   This chic boutique in the Fairmont Kea Lani stands out due to the careful eye of buyer Barbara Cipro, who has an excellent sense of fashion and accessories. Here you will find labels like Michael Stars and Custo Barcelona T-shirts, Michael Simon and Matisse sandals, Gretchen Scott bags, Brent Black hats and a range of clothing by Citron, Nicole Miller, Harari, Sigrid Olsen, and Betsy Johnson. It's definitely worth your time to browse this airy and well-lit shop, with a truly helpful staff. Fairmont Kea Lani Hotel. ℂ 808/875-4100, ext. 390.

The Shops at Wailea   This is the big shopping boost that resort goers have been awaiting for years. Chains still rule **(Gap, Louis Vuitton, Banana Republic, Tiffany, Crazy Shirts, Honolua Surf Co.),** but there is still fertile ground for the inveterate shopper in the nearly 60 shops in the complex. **Martin & MacArthur** (furniture and gift gallery) has landed in Wailea as part of a retail mix that is similar to Whalers Village. The high-end resort shops sell expensive souvenirs, gifts, clothing, and accessories for a life of perpetual vacations. 3750 Wailea Alanui. ℂ 808/891-6770.

4 Upcountry Maui

MAKAWAO

Besides being a shopper's paradise, Makawao is the home of the island's most prominent arts organization, the **Hui No'eau Visual Arts Center,** 2841 Baldwin Ave. (ℂ 808/572-6560; www.huinoeau.com). Designed in 1917 by C. W. Dickey, one of

Hawaii's most prominent architects, the two-story, Mediterranean-style stucco home that houses the center is located on a sprawling 9-acre estate called Kaluanui. A legacy of Maui's prominent *kamaaina* (old-timers) Harry and Ethel Baldwin, the estate became an arts center in 1976. Visiting artists offer lectures, classes, and demonstrations, all at reasonable prices, in basketry, jewelry making, ceramics, painting, and other media. Classes on Hawaiian art, culture, and history are also available. Call ahead for schedules and details. The exhibits here are drawn from a wide range of disciplines and multicultural sources, and include both contemporary and traditional art from established and emerging artists. The gift shop, featuring many one-of-a-kind works by local artists and artisans, is worth a stop. Hours are Monday through Saturday from 10am to 4pm.

Altitude   This tiny shop, run by Jeannine de Roode, is a treasure trove of interesting fashions found nowhere else on Maui, like custom jewelry by Monies (abalone shells, mother-of-pearl, and bone used to create big, big earrings, bracelets, and necklaces) and Hobo bags (Italian leather lined with contrasting fabric). She carries a range of clothing labels like Juicy Couture, James Perse, David Dart, Mica, and Sazah Arizona. 3660 Baldwin Ave. (C) **808/573-4733.**

Collections   This longtime Makawao attraction is showing renewed vigor after more than 2 decades on Baldwin Avenue. It's one of my favorite Makawao stops, full of gift items and spirited clothing reflecting the ease and color of island living. Its selection of sportswear, soaps, jewelry, candles, and tasteful, marvelous miscellany reflects good sense and style. Dresses (including up-to-the-moment Citron in cross-cultural and vintage-looking prints), separates, home and bath accessories, sweaters, and a shop full of good things make this a Makawao must. 3677 Baldwin Ave. (C) **808/572-0781.**

Cuckoo for Coconuts   The owner's quirky sense of humor pervades every inch of this tiny shop, which is brimming with vintage collectibles, gag gifts, silly coconuts, 1960s and 1970s aloha wear, tutus, sequined dresses, vintage wedding gowns, and all sorts of oddities. Things I've seen there: an Elvira wig, very convincing; a raffia hat looking suspiciously like a nest, with blue eggs on top; and some vintage aloha shirts that would make a collector drool. New items include crazy sunglasses, colored wigs, tie-dyes, and party hats. Vintage aloha wear comes and goes, and gets grabbed up fast. Services like singing telegrams, balloon deliveries, costumes, makeup, and gag gifts keep the laughs coming. 1158 Makawao Ave. (C) **808/573-6887.**

Gallery Maui   Follow the sign down the charming shaded pathway to a cozy gallery of top-notch art and crafts. Most of the works here are by Maui artists, and the quality is outstanding. About 30 artists are represented: Wayne Omura and his Norfolk pine bowls, Pamela Hayes's watercolors, Martha Vockrodt and her wonderful paintings, a stunning Steve Hynson dresser of curly koa and ebony. The two- and three-dimensional original works reflect the high standards of gallery owners Deborah and Robert Zaleski (a painter), who have just added to their roster the talented ceramic artist David Stabley, a two-time American Craft Council juror. 3643-A Baldwin Ave. (C) **808/572-8092.**

Gecko Trading Co. Boutique   The selection in this tiny boutique is eclectic and always changing: One day it's St. John's Wort body lotion and mesh T-shirts in a dragon motif, the next it's Provence soaps and antique lapis jewelry. I've seen everything from hair scrunchies to handmade crocheted bags from New York, clothing from Spain and France, collectible bottles, toys, shawls, and Mexican hammered-tin candleholders. The prices are reasonable, the service is friendly, and it's more homey than glam and not as self-conscious as some of the other local boutiques. 3621 Baldwin Ave. (C) **808/572-0249.**

Holiday & Co. Attractive women's clothing in natural fibers hangs from racks, while jewelry to go with it beckons from the counter. Recent finds include elegant fiber evening bags, luxurious bath gels, easygoing dresses and separates, Dansko clogs, shawls, shoes, soaps, aloha shirts, books, picture frames, and jewelry. 3681 Baldwin Ave. ℭ **808/572-1470.**

Hot Island Glassblowing Studio & Gallery You can watch the artist transform molten glass into works of art and utility in this studio in Makawao's Courtyard, where an award-winning family of glassblowers built its own furnaces. It's fascinating to watch the shapes emerge from glass melted at 2,300°F (1,260°C). The colorful works range from small paperweights to large vessels. Four to five artists participate in the demonstrations, which begin when the furnace is heated, about half an hour before the studio opens at 9am. 3620 Baldwin Ave. ℭ **808/572-4527.**

Hurricane This boutique carries clothing, gifts, accessories, and books that are two steps ahead of the competition. Tommy Bahama aloha shirts and aloha print dresses; Sigrid Olsen's knitted shells, cardigans, and extraordinary silk tank dresses; hats; art by local artists; a notable selection of fragrances for men and women; and hard-to-find, eccentric books and home accessories are part of the Hurricane appeal. 3639 Baldwin Ave. ℭ **808/572-5076.**

Maui Hands Maui hands have made 90% of the items in this shop/gallery. Because it's a consignment shop, you'll find Hawaii-made handicrafts and prices that aren't inflated. The selection includes paintings, prints, jewelry, glass marbles, native-wood bowls, and tchotchkes for every budget. This is an ideal stop for made-on-Maui products and crafts of good quality. The original Maui Hands is in Makawao at the Courtyard, 3620 Baldwin Ave. ℭ **808/572-5194.** Another Maui Hands can be found in Paia at 84 Hana Hwy. ℭ **808/579-9245.**

The Mercantile The jewelry, home accessories (especially the Tiffany-style glass-and-shell lamps), dinnerware, Italian linens, plantation-style furniture, and clothing here are a salute to the good life. The exquisite bedding, rugs, and furniture include hand-carved armoires, down-filled furniture and slipcovers, and a large selection of Kiehl's products. The clothing—comfortable cottons and upscale European linens— is for men and women, as are the soaps, which include Maui Herbal Soap products and some unusual finds from France. Maui-made jams, honey, soaps, and ceramics, and Jurlique organic facial and body products are among the new winners. 3673 Baldwin Ave. ℭ **808/572-1407.**

Sherri Reeve Gallery and Gifts If you want to take a little bit of the beauty of Maui home with you, stop by this open-air gallery. Artist Sherri Reeve grew up in Hawaii (the local phone book featured her art on the cover one year), and she has captured the vibrant color and feel of the islands. You can find everything here from inexpensive cards, hand-painted tiles, and T-shirts to original works and limited editions. 3669 Baldwin Ave. ℭ **808/572-8931.** www.sreeve.com.

Tropo Tropo is a magnet for stylish, sensitive, *and* rugged men searching for tasteful aloha wear and comfortable basics. Books, clothing, Tilley hats, and Crabtree & Evelyn products are among the finds here. Men can shop for Tommy Bahama trousers and shorts, tasteful T-shirts, stylish winter wovens by Toes on the Nose, and aloha shirts by Reyn Spooner, Tori Richards, Que, and Kahala. 3643 Baldwin Ave. ℭ **808/573-0356.**

Viewpoints Gallery Maui's only fine-arts cooperative showcases the work of 20 established artists in an airy, attractive gallery located in a restored theater with a courtyard, glassblowing studio, and restaurants. The gallery features two-dimensional art, jewelry, fiber art, stained glass, paper, sculpture, and other media. This is a fine example of what can happen in a collectively supportive artistic environment. 3620 Baldwin Ave. ℂ **808/572-5979.**

EDIBLES

Working folks in Makawao pick up spaghetti, lasagna, sandwiches, salads, and wide-ranging specials from the **Rodeo General Store,** 3661 Baldwin Ave. (ℂ **808/572-7841**). At the far end of the store is the oenophile's bonanza, a superior wine selection housed in its own temperature-controlled cave.

Down to Earth Natural Foods, 1169 Makawao Ave. (ℂ **808/572-1488**), always has fresh salads and sandwiches, a full section of organic produce (Kula onions, strawberry papayas, mangos, and litchis in season), bulk grains, beauty aids, herbs, juices, snacks, tofu, seaweed, soy products, and aisles of vegetarian and health foods. Whether it's a smoothie or a salad, Down to Earth has fresh, healthy, vegetarian offerings.

In the more than 6 decades that the **T. Komoda Store and Bakery,** 3674 Baldwin Ave. (ℂ **808/572-7261**), has spent in this spot, untold numbers have creaked over the wooden floors to pick up Komoda's famous cream puffs. Old-timers know to come early, before they're sold out. Then the cinnamon rolls, doughnuts, pies, and chocolate cake take over. Pastries are just the beginning: Poi, macadamia-nut candies and cookies, and small bunches of local fruit keep the customers coming.

FRESH FLOWERS IN KULA

Like anthuriums on the Big Island, proteas are a Maui trademark and an abundant crop on Haleakala's rich volcanic slopes. They also travel well, dry beautifully, and can be shipped with ease worldwide. Among Maui's most prominent sources is **Sunrise Protea** (ℂ **808/876-0200;** www.sunriseprotea.com), in Kula. It offers a walk-through garden and gift shops, friendly service, and a larger-than-usual selection. Freshly cut flowers arrive from the fields on Tuesday and Friday afternoons. You can order individual blooms, baskets, arrangements, or wreaths for shipping all over the world. (Next door, the Sunrise Country Market offers fresh local fruits, snacks, and sandwiches, with picnic tables for lingering.)

Proteas of Hawaii (ℂ **808/878-2533;** www.proteasofhawaii.com), another reliable source, offers regular walking tours of the University of Hawaii Extension Service gardens across the street in Kula.

5 East Maui

ON THE ROAD TO HANA: PAIA

Biasa Rose Boutique   You'll find unusual gift items and clothing with a tropical flair: capri pants in bark cloth, floating plumeria candles, retro fabrics, dinnerware, handbags and accessories, and stylish vintage-inspired clothes for kids. If the aloha shirts don't get you, the candles and handbags will. You can also custom-order clothing from a selection of washable rayons. 104 Hana Hwy. ℂ **808/579-8602.**

Hemp House   Clothing and accessories made of hemp, a sturdy, ecofriendly, and sensible fiber, are finally making their way into the mainstream. The Hemp House has as complete a selection as you can expect to see in Hawaii, with "denim" hemp jeans, lightweight linenlike trousers, dresses, shirts, and a full range of sensible, easy-care wear. 16 Baldwin Ave. ℂ **808/579-8880.**

Maui Crafts Guild   The old wooden storefront at the gateway to Paia houses crafts of high quality and in all price ranges, from pit-fired raku to bowls of Norfolk pine and other Maui woods, fashioned by Maui hands. Artist-owned and -operated, the guild claims 25 members who live and work on Maui. Basketry, hand-painted fabrics, jewelry, beadwork, traditional Hawaiian stone work, pressed flowers, fused glass, stained glass, copper sculpture, banana bark paintings, pottery of all styles, and hundreds of items are displayed in the two-story gift gallery. Upstairs, sculptor Arthur Dennis Williams displays his breathtaking work in wood, bronze, and stone. Everything can be shipped. **Aloha Bead Co.** (© 808/579-9709), in the back of the gallery, is a treasure trove for beadworkers. 43 Hana Hwy. © 808/579-9697.

Moonbow Tropics   If you're looking for a tasteful aloha shirt, go to Moonbow. The selection consists of a few carefully culled racks of the top labels in aloha wear, in fabrics ranging from the finest silks and linens to Egyptian cotton and spun rayons. Some of the finds: aloha shirts by Tori Richard, Reyn Spooner, Kamehameha, Paradise Found, Kahala, Tommy Bahama, and other top brands. Silk pants, silk shorts, vintage-print neckwear, and an upgraded women's selection hang on neat, colorful racks. The jewelry pieces, ranging from tanzanite to topaz, rubies, and moonstones, are mounted in unique settings made on-site. 36 Baldwin Ave. © 808/579-8592.

HANA

Hana Coast Gallery   This gallery is a good reason to go to Hana: It's an aesthetic and cultural experience that informs as it enlightens. Tucked away in the posh hideaway hotel, the gallery is known for its high level of curatorship and commitment to the cultural art of Hawaii. There are no jumping whales or dolphins here—and except for a section of European and Asian masters (Renoir, Japanese woodblock prints), the 3,000-square-foot gallery is devoted entirely to Hawaii artists. Dozens of well-established local artists display their sculptures, paintings, prints, feather work, stonework, and carvings in displays that are so natural they could well exist in someone's home. In response to the ongoing revival of the American Crafts Movement, director-curator Patrick Robinson (of impeccable artistic integrity) has expanded the selection of koa-wood furniture with a Hawaiian/Japanese influence. Stellar artists Tai Lake from the Big Island and Randall Watkins from Maui are among those represented.

Connoisseurs of hand-turned bowls will find the crème de la crème of the genre here: J. Kelly Dunn, Ron Kent, Todd Campbell, Ed Perrira, and Gary Stevens. You won't find a better selection anywhere under one roof. The award-winning gallery has won accolades from the top travel and arts magazines in the country and has steered clear of trendiness and unfortunate tastes. In the Hotel Hana-Maui. © 808/248-8636.

Hasegawa General Store   Established in 1910, immortalized in song since 1961, burned to the ground in 1990, and back in business in 1991, this legendary store is indefatigable and more colorful than ever in its fourth generation in business. The aisles are choked with merchandise: coffee specially roasted and blended for the store, Ono Farms organic dried fruit, fishing equipment, every tape and CD that mentions Hana, the best books on Hana to be found, T-shirts, beach and garden essentials, baseball caps, film, baby food, napkins, and other necessities. Hana Hwy., in Hana. © 808/248-8231.

10

Maui After Dark

Centered in the $32-million **Maui Arts and Cultural Center** in Kahului (℃ **808/ 242-7469;** www.mauiarts.org), the performing arts are alive and well on this island. The MACC remains the island's most prestigious entertainment venue, a first-class center for the visual and performing arts. Bonnie Raitt has performed here, as have Hiroshima, Pearl Jam, Ziggy Marley, Tony Bennett, the American Indian Dance Theatre, the Maui Symphony Orchestra, and Jonny Lang, not to mention the finest in local and Hawaiian talent. The center is as precious to Maui as the Met is to New York, with a visual-arts gallery, an outdoor amphitheater, offices, rehearsal space, a 300-seat theater for experimental performances, and a 1,200-seat main theater. The center's activities are well publicized locally, so check the *Maui News* or ask your hotel concierge what's going on during your visit.

People are still agog over **'Ulalena,** an extraordinary production that tells the story of Hawaii in chant, song, original music, acrobatics, and dance, using state-of-the-art technology and some of the most creative staging to be seen in Hawaii. There's nothing else like it in the state. A local and international cast performs this $9.5-million production at the comfy **Maui Myth and Magic Theatre** in Lahaina (see section 1 below). Recently opened at the **Kaanapali Beach Hotel** is a wonderful show that is perfect for the entire family, called *Kupanaha.*

IN SEARCH OF HAWAIIAN, JAWAIIAN & MORE

Nightlife options on this island are limited. Revelers generally head for **Casanova** in Makawao and **Maui Brews** in Lahaina. Because they are in different parts of this spread-out island, you'll either have to drive a great distance to these clubs or explore what's happening in the major hotels near you. The hotels generally have lobby lounges offering Hawaiian music, soft jazz, or hula shows beginning at sunset.

If **Hapa, Willie K., Amy Gilliom,** or the soloist **Keali'i Reichel** are playing anywhere on their native island, don't miss them; they're among the finest Hawaiian musicians around today. Most clubs with dance floors play a combination of Hawaiian and reggae, called Jawaiian, with a heated-up rhythm that young dancers love.

HAWAIIAN MUSIC The best of Hawaiian music can be heard every Tuesday night at the indoor amphitheater at the Ritz-Carlton Kapalua with the **Masters of Hawaiian Slack Key Guitar Series** (℃ 808/669-3858; www.slackkey.com). The weekly shows presents a side of Hawaii that few visitors ever get to see. Host George Kahumoku, Jr., introduces a new slack-key master every week. Not only is there incredible Hawaiian music and singing, but George and his guest "talk story" about old Hawaii, music, and Hawaiian culture. Not to be missed. Tickets are $40.

AT THE MOVIES

The 12-screen movie megaplex at the **Maui Mall,** 70 E. Kaahumanu Ave. (℃ **808/ 249-2222**), in Kahului, comes complete with comfortable reclining seats. The megaplex features current releases. The **Maui Film Festival** presents "Academy House" films for the avant-garde, ultrahip movie buff Wednesday nights at the **Maui Art and Cultural Center,** 1 Cameron Way (just off Kahului Beach Rd.), Kahului (℃ **808/572-3456;** www.mauifilmfestival.com), usually followed by live music and poetry readings. In May or June the Maui Film Festival also puts on nights of cinema under the stars in Wailea.

Film buffs can check the local newspapers to see what's playing at the other theaters around the island (or go to www.mauigateway.com/~rw/movie): the **Kaahumanu Theatres,** in the Kaahumanu Center in Kahului (℃ **808/873-3133**); the **Kukui Mall Theatre,** 1819 S. Kihei Rd., in Kihei (℃ **808/875-4533**); the Wallace Theatres in Lahaina at the **Wharf Cinema Center,** 658 Front St. (℃ **808/249-2222**); and the **Front Street Theatres** at the Lahaina Center, 900 Front St.

AT THE THEATER

It's not Broadway, but Maui does have live community theater at the **Iao Theater,** 68 N. Market St., in Wailuku (℃ **808/244-8680** or 808/242-6969 for the box office and program information; www.mauionstage.com). Shows range from locally written productions to well-known plays to musicals.

1 West Maui: Lahaina, Kaanapali & Kapalua

Maui Brews, 900 Front St. (℃ **808/667-7794**), draws the late-night crowd to its corner of the Lahaina Center with swing, salsa, reggae, and jams—either live or with a DJ every night. The restaurant serves breakfast, lunch, and dinner beginning at 7:30am, and happy hour extends from 3 to 7pm, with $1 drafts and $1 wells. The nightclub opens at 9pm and closes at 2am. Depending on the entertainment, sometimes there's a cover charge after 9pm; generally if there is one, it's $5. For recorded information on entertainment (which changes, so it's a good idea to check), call ℃ **808/669-2739.**

At **Longhi's** (℃ **808/667-2288**) live music spills out into the streets from 9:30pm on weekends (with a cover charge of $5). It's usually salsa or jazz, but call ahead to confirm. Other special gigs can be expected if rock-'n'-rollers or jazz musicians who are friends of the owner happen to be passing through.

The **Hard Rock Cafe,** 900 Front St. (℃ **808/667-7400**), occasionally offers live music, so it wouldn't hurt to call them to see if something's up. Usually they feature mainland bands, normally on weekends after 10pm. Cover ranges from $3 to $5.

You won't have to ask what's going on at **Cheeseburger in Paradise** (℃ **808/ 661-4855**), the two-story green-and-white building at the corner of Front and Lahainaluna streets. Just go outside and you'll hear it. Loud, live tropical rock blasts into the streets and out to sea nightly from 4:30 to 11pm (no cover charge).

Other venues for music in West Maui include the following:

- **B.J.'s Chicago Pizzeria,** 730 Front St. (℃ **808/661-0700**), offers live music from 7:30 to 10pm every night.
- **Compadres Bar & Grill,** Lahaina Cannery Mall (℃ **808/661-7189**), features Salsa Night on Saturday starting at 10pm and local jam sessions on Wednesday (call for times).

- **Fish & Game Brewing Co.,** Kahana Gateway Center (© **808/669-3474**), has live music every night from 6:30 to 9:30pm (6–9pm in summer).
- **Hula Grill,** Whalers Village (© **808/667-6636**), has live music (usually Hawaiian) from 3 to 5pm and again from 6:30 to 9pm nightly.
- **Kimo's,** 845 Front St. (© **808/661-4811**), has live musicians at various times; call for details.
- **Kobe Japanese Steak House,** Whalers Village (© **808/667-5555**), has entertainment from 9pm to closing Thursday through Saturday (live music Thurs, karaoke Fri–Sat).
- **Leilani's on the Beach,** Whalers Village (© **808/661-4495**), has live music from 4 to 6pm Wednesday through Sunday. The style ranges from contemporary Hawaiian to rock.
- **Moose McGillycuddy's,** 844 Front St. (© **808/667-7758**), offers a DJ some nights (the schedule varies; call for details) from 5:30 to 8:30pm.
- **Pacific'O,** 505 Front St. (© **808/667-4341**), offers live jazz Friday and Saturday from 9pm to midnight.
- **Pancho & Lefty's,** Wharf Cinema Center (© **808/661-4666**), features live music from 9pm to midnight on Friday and from 6 to 9pm on Saturday and Sunday.
- **Paradise Bluz,** 744 Front St. (© **808/667-5299**), has live blues, live jazz, and other live music from 9pm to 2am; call for details.
- **Pioneer Inn,** 658 Wharf St. (© **808/661-3636**), offers a variety of live music every night starting at 6pm.
- **Sansei,** Shops at Kapalua (© **808/669-6286**), has karaoke on Friday and Saturday from 10pm to 1am.
- **Sea Horse Restaurant,** Napili Kai Beach Resort (© **808/669-1500**), has live music from 7 to 9pm Wednesday through Monday and a Polynesian dinner show on Tuesday.
- **Tropica,** Westin Maui (© **808/667-2525**), offers nightly music (call for times).

A NIGHT TO REMEMBER: LUAU, MAUI STYLE

Most of the larger hotels in Maui's major resorts offer luaus on a regular basis. You'll pay about $75 to attend one. To protect yourself from disappointment, don't expect it to be a homegrown affair prepared in the traditional Hawaiian way. There are, however, commercial luaus that capture the romance and spirit of the luau with quality food and entertainment in outdoor settings.

Maui's best luau is indisputably the nightly **Old Lahaina Luau** (© **800/248-5828** or 808/667-1998; www.oldlahainaluau.com). On its 1-acre site just ocean-side of the Lahaina Cannery at 1251 Front St., the Old Lahaina Luau maintains its high standards in food and entertainment in a peerless setting. Local craftspeople display their wares only a few feet from the ocean. Seating is provided on lauhala mats for those who wish to dine as the traditional Hawaiians did, but there are tables for everyone else. There's no fire dancing in the program, but you won't miss it (for that, go to **The Feast at Lele;** p. 138). This luau offers a healthy balance of entertainment, showmanship, authentic high-quality food, educational value, and sheer romantic beauty. (No watered-down mai tais, either—these are the real thing.)

The luau begins at sunset and features Tahitian and Hawaiian entertainment, including ancient hula, hula from the missionary era, modern hula, and an intelligent narrative on the dance's rocky course of survival into modern times. The entertainment

Moments It Begins with Sunset . . .

Nightlife in Maui begins at sunset, when all eyes turn westward to see how the day will end. And what better way to take it all in than over cocktails? With its view of Molokai to the northwest and Lanai to the west, Kaanapali and West Maui boast panoramic vistas unique to this island. In South Maui's resort areas of Wailea and Makena, tiny Kahoolawe and the crescent-shaped Molokini islet are visible on the horizon, and the West Maui Mountains look like an entirely separate island. No matter what your vantage point, you are likely to be treated to an astonishing view.

In Kaanapali, park in Whalers Village and head for **Leilani's** (© 808/661-4495) or **Hula Grill** (© 808/667-6636), next to each other on the beach. Both have busy, upbeat bars and tables bordering the sand. These are happy places for great people-watching, gazing at the lump of Lanai that looks to be a stone's throw away, and enjoying end-of-day rituals like mai tais and margaritas. Hula Grill's Barefoot Bar appetizer menu is a cut above. Leilani's has live music daily from 3:30 to 6pm, while at Hula Grill the happy hour starts at 3pm, live music at 6pm, and hula at 8pm.

Now, Lahaina: It's a sunset-lover's nirvana, lined with restaurants that have elevated mai tais to an art form. If you love loud rock, head for **Cheeseburger in Paradise** (© 808/661-4855). A few doors away the **Lahaina Fish Company** (© 808/661-3472), **Café O'Lei Lahaina** (© 808/661-9492), and **Kimo's** (© 808/661-4811) are magnets all day long and especially at sunset, when their open decks fill up with revelers. For the most part, you can expect great seafood appetizers at these oceanfront haunts. These four restaurants occupy the section of Front Street between Lahainaluna Road and Papalaua Street.

At the southern end of Lahaina, in the 505 Front St. complex, **Pacific'o** (© 808/667-4341) is a solid hit, with a raised bar, seating on the ocean, and a backdrop of Lanai across the channel. They've also won many awards for their seafood. A few steps away from Pacific'o, sister restaurant **I'o** shares the same vista, with an appetizer menu and a techno-curved bar that will wow you as much as the drop-dead-gorgeous view.

is riveting, even for jaded locals. The food, served from an open-air thatched structure, is as much Pacific Rim as authentically Hawaiian: imu-roasted Kalua pig, baked mahimahi in Maui-onion cream sauce, guava chicken, teriyaki sirloin steak, lomi salmon, poi, dried fish, poke, Hawaiian sweet potato, sautéed vegetables, seafood salad, and the ultimate taste treat, taro leaves with coconut milk. The cost is $85 for adults, $55 for children 12 and under.

'ULALENA: HULA, MYTH & MODERN DANCE

The highly polished **'Ulalena,** staged in the Maui Myth and Magic Theatre, 878 Front St. (© 877/688-4800 or 808/661-9913; www.ulalena.com), is a riveting

Moving south toward Wailea, the harbor stop called Maalaea is famous for its whale sightings during the winter months. Year-round, **Buzz's Wharf** (© 808/244-5426) offers a superb ocean view and continuous service between lunch and dinner. Add an ice-cold beer or mai tai, elegant fresh sashimi, or a steaming order of fish and chips, and the sunset package is complete.

In Wailea the restaurants at the new Shops at Wailea, including the highly successful **Tommy Bahama** (© 808/875-9983) and **Longhi's** (© 808/891-8883), are a noteworthy addition to the beachfront retail-and-dining scene. **Ferraro's** and **Pacific Grill** (© 808/874-8000), both at the neighboring Four Seasons Resort Wailea, have great sunset views to go with their Italian and Pacific Rim menus. Farther south, in Makena, you can't beat the Maui Prince's **Molokini Lounge** (© 808/874-1111), with its casual elegance and unequaled view of Molokini islet on the ocean side and, on the mauka side, a graceful, serene courtyard with ponds, rock gardens, and lush foliage. Adding to the setting is the appetizer menu, which comes from the esteemed Prince Court kitchen. From 5 to 9:30pm nightly the pupu menu features an exceptional Prince Court sampler platter: Kona lobster cakes, steamed clams, Kalua duck lumpia, Pacific oysters on the half shell, grilled tiger prawns, and grilled teriyaki steak poke. Live Hawaiian entertainment runs nightly from 6 to 10:30pm, beginning with a mini–hula show from 6pm on Monday, Wednesday, and Friday and the contemporary Hawaiian melodies of Mele Ohana or Ron Kuala'au until 10:30pm. Ron Kuala'au plays Monday, Tuesday, Thursday, and Saturday; Mele Ohana plays Monday through Saturday.

Don't forget the upcountry view, a perfect way to end the day if you don't mind the drive. **Kula Lodge** (© 808/878-2517) has a phenomenal view that takes in central Maui, the West Maui Mountains (looking like Shangri-La in the distance), and the coastline. From 3:30 to 5pm, the appetizer-only menu includes everything from Maui onion soup to a host of gourmet salads (the farmers are a stone's throw away), plus pot stickers, summer rolls, seared ahi, and crab cakes. Dinner begins at 5pm, so you can take in the sunset over steamed clams, rack of lamb, Cajun ahi, New York steak, and other country-comfort fare.

production that weaves Hawaiian mythology with drama, dance, and state-of-the-art multimedia capabilities in a brand-new, multimillion-dollar theater.

A local and international cast performs Polynesian dance, original music, acrobatics, and chant to create an experience that often leaves the audience speechless. It's interactive, with dancers coming down the aisles, drummers and musicians in surprising corners, and mind-boggling stage and lighting effects that draw the audience in. Some special moments: the goddess dancing on the moon, the white sail signaling the arrival of the first Europeans, the wrath of the volcano goddess, Pele (the stage effects depicting lava are brilliant), and the despairing labors of the field-worker immigrants. The effects of the modern choreography and traditional hula, a fusion of genres, are surprisingly evocative and emotional. The story unfolds seamlessly, and at the end you'll be shocked to realize that not a single word of dialogue has been spoken. Performances are Tuesday through Saturday at 6:30pm. Tickets are $48 to $68 for adults and $28 to $48 for children ages 12 and under.

HAWAIIAN CULTURE

Not many visitors get to experience the art of Hawaiian storytelling, but the Ritz-Carlton Kapalua has a play called *The Legend of Kaulula'au,* every Sunday at 4 and 6:30pm, that is not to be missed. In old Hawaii, legends and family history would be passed down from generation to generation orally. *Mo'olelo,* or the art of storytelling, would captivate the listeners, and the best storytellers would receive the same attention a movie star gets today. In the one-man play *The Legend of Kaulula'au,* Hawaiian actor Moses Goods gives a spellbinding performance as he acts out the legend of Kaulula'au, a mischievous child who was banished to the island of Lanai. According to legend, Lanai was once inhabited by ghosts. Kaulula'au not only defeats the ghosts but he goes on to become the chief of Lanai and Maui. Tickets for this hour-long performance are $30 and are available by calling © **888/808-1055.**

MAGIC—MAUI STYLE

A very different type of live entertainment is **Warren & Annabelle's,** 900 Front St., Lahaina (© **808/667-6244;** www.warrenandannabelles.com), a magic/comedy cocktail show with illusionist Warren Gibson and "Annabelle," a ghost from the 1800s who plays the grand piano as Warren dazzles you with his sleight-of-hand magic. Appetizers, desserts, and cocktails are available. Check-in is at 5pm, and the show-only price is $45. You must be 21 years old to attend, although they occasionally have a 4pm family show (minimum age 6) without food or cocktails; call for details.

The **Kaanapali Beach Hotel** has a wonderful show called **Kupanaha** that is perfect for the entire family. It features the renowned magicians Jody and Kathleen Baran and their entire family, including child prodigy magicians Katrina and Crystal. The dinner show features magic, illusions, and the story of the Hawaii fire goddess, Pele, presented through hula and chant performed by the children of the Kano'eau Dance Academy. The shows are Tuesday through Saturday from 5 to 8pm; tickets are $69 to $79 for adults, $49 for teens, and $29 for children ages 6 to 12 (free for children 5 and under). Included in the ticket price is dinner (entree choices include island fish, roasted stuffed chicken, steak and shrimp, or a vegetarian dish, with a *keiki* [children's] menu available). For reservations and tickets, call © **808/661-0011** or visit www.kbhmaui.com.

2 Kihei-Wailea

The Kihei area in South Maui also features music in a variety of locations:

- **Bocalino,** 1279 S. Kihei Rd. (© **808/874-9299**), has live music Monday through Saturday starting at 10pm.
- **Hapa's Night Club,** 41 E. Lipoa St. (© **808/879-9001**), has nightly music, generally Hawaiian; call for details.
- **Henry's Bar and Grill,** 41 E. Lipoa (© **808/87-2949**), offers live music Thursday through Saturday from 9pm to midnight.
- **Kahale's Beach Club,** 36 Keala Place (© **808/875-7711**), offers a potpourri of live music nightly; call for details.
- **Life's a Beach,** 1913 S. Kihei Rd. (© **808/891-8010**), has nightly live music; call for times.

Hana Nightlife

Nightlife in Hana is pretty sparse. The only exception is the **Hotel Hana-Maui** (© **808/248-8211**), which features Hawaiian music in the Paniolo Lounge Thursday through Sunday from 6:30 to 9:30pm, and has a hula show every Thursday and Sunday from 7:30 to 8:15pm in the Main Dining Room.

- **Lobby Lounge,** Four Seasons Wailea (© **808/874-8000**), features nightly live music from 8:30 to 11:30pm.
- **Lulu's,** 1945 S. Kihei Rd. (© **808/879-9944**), offers entertainment starting at 8pm; karaoke on Wednesday, live music Thursday through Sunday.
- **Mulligan's on the Blue,** 100 Kaukahi St., Wailea (© **808/874-1131**), has live music starting at 9pm Friday and Saturday.
- **Sansei,** Kihei Town Center (© **808/879-0004**), features karaoke Thursday through Saturday from 10pm to 1am.
- **Sports Page Bar,** 2411 S. Kihei Rd. (© **808/879-0602**), has live music Monday through Saturday starting at 9pm.
- **Tsunami Nightclub,** Grand Wailea Beach Hotel (© **808/875-1234**), offers dancing to a DJ's selection on Friday and Saturday from 9:30pm to 2am.
- **Yorman's by the Sea,** 760 S. Kihei Rd. (© **808/874-8385**), has live jazz from 6:30pm Wednesday through Sunday. Call for details.

3 Upcountry Maui

Upcountry in Makawao, the party never ends at **Casanova,** 1188 Makawao Ave. (© **808/572-0220**), the popular Italian ristorante where the good times roll. If a big-name mainland band is resting up on Maui following a sold-out concert on Oahu, you may find its members setting up for an impromptu night here. DJs take over on Wednesday (ladies' night) and, on Thursday, Friday, and Saturday, live entertainment draws fun-lovers from even the most remote reaches of the island. Entertainment starts at 9:45pm and continues to 1:30am. Expect good blues, rock 'n' roll, reggae, jazz, Hawaiian, and the top names in local and visiting entertainment. Elvin Bishop, the local duo Hapa, Los Lobos, and many others have filled Casanova's stage. The cover is usually $5. Come Sunday afternoons from 3 to 6pm for excellent live jazz.

Another place for live music in the upcountry area is the **Stopwatch Sports Bar,** 1127 Makawao Ave. (© **808/572-1380**), which has live music from 9pm on Friday and Saturday.

4 Paia & Central Maui

In the unlikely location of Paia, **Moanai Bakery & Café,** at 71 Baldwin Ave. (© **808/579-9999**), not only has some of the best and most innovative cuisine around, but recently it has added live music: vintage Hawaiian from 6:30 to 9pm on Wednesday; smooth jazz and hot blues from 6:30 to 9pm on Friday; and flamingo guitar and gypsy violin from 6 to 9pm on Sunday. There's no cover; just come and enjoy. Also in Paia, **Charley's Restaurant,** 142 Hana Hwy. (© **808/579-9453**), features an eclectic selection of music from country and western (Willie Nelson has been seen sitting in) to fusion/reggae to rip-roaring rock 'n' roll; call for details. Other venues for live music in Paia include **Jacque's,** 120 Hana Hwy. (© **808/579-8844**), and **Sand Bar and Grill,** 89 Hana Hwy. (© **808/579-8742**).

In central Maui the **Kahului Ale House,** 355 E. Kamehameha Ave. (© **808/877-9001**), features karaoke on Sunday, Monday, and Wednesday from 10pm to 2am, live music on Thursday and Friday (call for times), and a DJ on Saturday from 10pm.

Other locations for live music include: **Mañana Garage,** 33 Lono Ave., in Kahului (© **808/873-0220**), which has live music Wednesday through Saturday nights from 6:30pm on, and **Sushi Go,** in the Queen Kaahumanu Shopping Center, 275 Kaahumanu Ave., in Kahului (© **808/877-8744**), which also features live music on Friday and Saturday nights from 6:30 to 8:30pm.

11

Molokai: The Most Hawaiian Isle

Born of volcanic eruptions 1.5 million years ago, Molokai remains a time capsule on the dawn of the 21st century. It has no deluxe resorts, no stoplights, and no buildings taller than a coconut tree. Molokai is the least developed, most "Hawaiian" of all the islands, making it especially attractive to adventure travelers and peace seekers.

Molokai lives up to its reputation as the most Hawaiian place chiefly through its lineage: More people here are of Hawaiian blood than anywhere else. This slipper-shaped island was the cradle of Hawaiian dance (the hula was born here) and the ancient science of aquaculture. An aura of ancient mysticism clings to the land here, and the old ways still govern life. The residents survive by taking fish from the sea and hunting wild pigs and axis deer on the range. Some folks still catch fish for dinner by throwing nets and trolling the reef.

Modern Hawaii's high-rise hotels, shopping centers, and other trappings of tourism haven't been able to gain a foothold here. The lone low-rise resort on the island, Kaluakoi—a now-closed, empty hotel built 30 years ago—was Molokai's token attempt at contemporary tourism. The only "new" developments since Kaluakoi are the Molokai Ranch's ecotourism project of upscale "camping" in semipermanent "tentalows" (a combination of a bungalow and a tent) and an upscale 22-room lodge on the 53,000-acre ranch. The focus of both is on outdoor recreation and adventure, with all the comforts of home.

Not everyone will love Molokai. The slow-paced, simple life of the people and the absence of contemporary landmarks attract those in search of the "real" Hawaii. We got a letter from a New York City resident who claimed that any "big city resident" would "blanche" at the lack of "sophistication." But that is exactly the charm of the "Friendly Isle." This is a place where Mother Nature is wild and uninhibited, with very little intrusion by man. Forget sophistication, this is one of the few spots on the planet where one can stand in awe of the island's diverse natural wonders: Hawaii's highest waterfall and greatest collection of fishponds; the world's tallest sea cliffs; sand dunes, coral reefs, rainforests, and hidden coves; and gloriously empty beaches.

EXPLORING THE "MOST HA-WAIIAN" ISLE Only 38 miles from end to end and just 10 miles wide, Molokai stands like a big green wedge in the blue Pacific. It has an east side, a west side, a backside, and a topside. This long, narrow island is like yin and yang: One side is a flat, austere, arid desert; the other is a lush, green, steepled tropical Eden. Three volcanic eruptions formed Molokai; the last produced the island's "thumb"—a peninsula jutting out of the steep cliffs of the north shore, like a punctuation mark on the island's geological story.

On the red-dirt southern plain, where most of the island's 6,000 residents live, the rustic village of **Kaunakakai** 𝄐 looks like the set of an old Hollywood Western, with sun-faded clapboard houses and horses tethered on the side of the road. Mile marker 0, in the center of town, divides the island into east and west; an arid cactus desert lies on one side and a lush coco-palm jungle on the other.

Eastbound, along the **coastal highway** 🐎🐎🐎 named for King Kamehameha V, are Gauguin-like, palm-shaded cottages set on small coves or near fishponds; spectacular vistas that take in Maui, Lanai, and Kahoolawe; and a fringing coral reef visible through the crystal-clear waves.

Out on the sun-scorched West End, overlooking a gold-sand beach with water usually too rough to swim in, is the island's lone destination resort, **Kaluakoi** (where the hotel is currently closed). The old hilltop plantation town of **Maunaloa** has been razed and rebuilt as a gentrified plantation community, complete with an expensive country lodge with a pricey dining room. Cowboys still ride the range on **Molokai Ranch,** a 53,000-acre spread, while adventure travelers and outdoor-recreation buffs stay at the tentalows on the ranch property and spend their days mountain biking, kayaking, horseback riding, sailing, hiking, snorkeling, and just vegetating on the endless white-sand beaches.

Elsewhere around the island, in hamlets like **Kualapuu,** old farmhouses with pickup trucks in the yards and sleepy dogs under the shade trees stand amid row crops of papaya, coffee, and corn— just like farm towns in Anywhere, USA.

But that's not all there is. The "backside" of Molokai is a rugged wilderness of spectacular beauty. On the outskirts of **Kaunakakai,** the land rises gradually from sea-level fishponds to cool uplands and the Molokai Forest, long ago stripped of sandalwood for the China trade. All that remains is an indentation in the earth that natives shaped like a ship's hull, a crude matrix that gave them a rough idea of when they'd cut enough sandalwood to

fill a ship (it's identified on good maps as *Luanamokuiliahi,* or Sandalwood Boat).

The land inclines sharply to the lofty mountains and the nearly mile-high summit of Mount Kamakou, then ends abruptly with emerald-green cliffs, which plunge into a lurid aquamarine sea dotted with tiny deserted islets. These breathtaking 3,250-foot **sea cliffs** 🐎🐎, the highest in the world, stretch 14 majestic miles along Molokai's north shore, laced by waterfalls and creased by five valleys— Halawa, Papalaua, Wailau, Pelekunu, and Waikolu—once occupied by early Hawaiians who built stone terraces and used waterfalls to irrigate taro patches.

Long after the sea cliffs were formed, a tiny volcano erupted out of the sea at their feet and spread lava into a flat, leaflike peninsula called **Kalaupapa** 🐎🐎🐎—the 1860s leper exile where Father Damien de Veuster of Belgium devoted his life to care for the afflicted. A few people remain in the remote colony by choice, keeping it tidy for the daily company that arrives on mules and by small planes.

WHAT A VISIT TO MOLOKAI IS *REALLY* LIKE There's plenty of aloha on Molokai, but the so-called "friendly island" remains ambivalent about vacationers. One of the least visited Hawaiian islands, Molokai welcomes about 70,000 visitors annually on its own take-it-or-leave-it terms and makes few concessions beyond that of gracious host; it never wants to attract too big of a crowd anyway. A sign at the airport offers the first clue: SLOW DOWN, YOU ON MOLOKAI NOW—wisdom to heed on this island, where life proceeds at its own pace.

Rugged, red-dirt Molokai isn't for everyone, but those who like to explore remote places and seek their own adventures should love it. The best of the island can be seen only on foot, bicycle, mule, horseback, kayak, or boat. The sea cliffs are accessible only by sea in summer, when the Pacific is calm, or via a 10-mile

Molokai

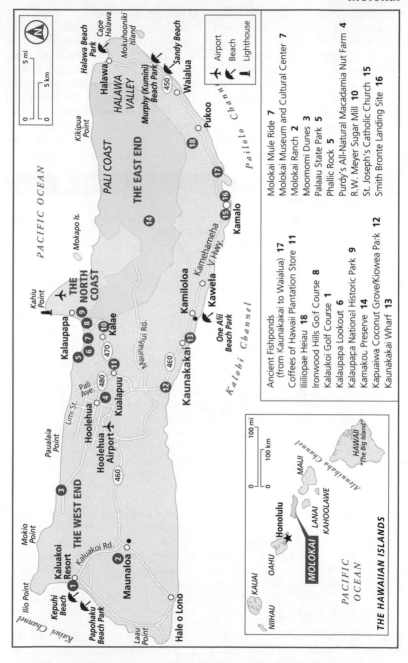

Map legend / list of locations:

Ancient Fishponds (from Kaunakakai to Waialua) **17**
Coffees of Hawaii Plantation Store **11**
Iliiliopae Heiau **18**
Ironwood Hills Golf Course **8**
Kalaukoi Golf Course **1**
Kalaupapa Lookout **6**
Kalaupapa National Historic Park **9**
Kamakou Preserve **14**
Kapuaiwa Coconut Grove/Kiowea Park **12**
Kaunakakai Wharf **13**

Molokai Mule Ride **7**
Molokai Museum and Cultural Center **7**
Molokai Ranch **2**
Moomomi Dunes **3**
Palaau State Park **5**
Phallic Rock **5**
Purdy's All-Natural Macadamia Nut Farm **4**
R.W. Meyer Sugar Mill **10**
St. Joseph's Catholic Church **15**
Smith Bronte Landing Site **16**

trek through the Wailau Valley—an adventure only a handful of hardy hikers attempt each year. The great Kamakou Preserve is open just once a month, by special arrangement with the Nature Conservancy. Even Moomomi, which holds bony relics of prehistoric flightless birds and other creatures, requires a guide to divulge the secrets of the dunes.

Those in search of nightlife have come to the wrong place: Molokai shuts down after sunset. The only public diversions are softball games under the lights of Mitchell Pauole Field, movies at Maunaloa, and the few restaurants that stay open after dark, often serving local brews and pizza.

The "friendly" island may enchant you as the "real" Hawaii of your dreams. On the other hand, you may leave shaking your head, never to return. Regardless of how you approach Molokai, remember my advice: Take it slow.

1 Orientation

ARRIVING

BY PLANE   Molokai has two airports, but you'll most likely fly into **Hoolehua Airport,** which everyone calls "the Molokai Airport." It's on a dusty plain about 6 miles from Kaunakakai town. Twin-engine planes offer daily service, **Island Air** (© 800/323-3345 from the mainland or 800/652-6541 interisland; www.islandair. com), with seven direct flights a day from Honolulu and two direct flights from Maui. **Molokai Air Shuttle** (© 808/545-4988) has four to five flights a day from Honolulu in small planes. **Pacific Wings** (© 888/575-4546 from the mainland or 808/873-0877 from Maui; www.pacificwings.com) has one daily flight from Honolulu to the Kalaupapa Peninsula (see p. 277 for tours of Kalaupapa).

BY BOAT   You can travel across the seas by ferry from Maui's Lahaina Harbor to Molokai's Kaunakakai Wharf on the *Molokai Princess* (© 800/275-6969 or 808/667-6165; www.mauiprincess.com). The 100-foot yacht, certified for 149 passengers, is fitted with the latest generation of gyroscopic stabilizers, making the ride smoother. The ferry makes the 90-minute journey from Lahaina to Kaunakakai daily; the round-trip cost is $85 for adults and $43 for children ages 3 to 12. Or you can choose to tour the island from two different package options: Cruise-Drive, which includes round-trip passage and a rental car for $169 for the driver, $80 per additional adult passenger, and $40 for children; or the Alii Tour, which is a guided tour in an air-conditioned van plus lunch for $169 for adults and $109 for children.

VISITOR INFORMATION

The **Molokai Visitors Association,** P.O. Box 960, Kaunakakai, HI 96748 (© 800/800-6367 from the U.S. mainland and Canada, 800/553-0404 interisland, or 808/553-3876; www.molokai-hawaii.com), can give you all the information you need on what to see and do while you're on Molokai. If you want to drop by and see them when you are on the island, they are located in the Moore Center, 2 Kamoi Ave., Suite 200, in beautiful downtown Kaunakakai.

THE ISLAND IN BRIEF

Kaunakakai ✸
Dusty vehicles—mostly pickup trucks—are parked diagonally along Ala Malama Street. It could be any small town, except it's Kaunakakai, the closest thing Molokai has to a business district. Friendly Isle Realty and Friendly Isle Travel offer islanders dream homes

and vacations; Rabang's Filipino Food posts bad checks in the window; deerhead trophies guard the grocery aisles at Misaki's Market; and Kanemitsu's, the town's legendary bakery, churns out fresh loaves of onion-cheese bread daily.

Once an ancient canoe landing, Kaunakakai was the royal summer residence of King Kamehameha V. The port town bustled when pineapple and sugar were king, but those days, too, are gone. With its Old West–style storefronts laid out in a 3-block grid on a flat, dusty plain, Kaunakakai is a town from the past. At the end of Wharf Road is Molokai Wharf, a picturesque place to fish, photograph, and just hang out.

Kaunakakai is the dividing point between the lush, green East End and the dry, arid West End. On the west side of town stands a cactus and on the east side of town, there's thick, green vegetation.

The North Coast 🌟🌟

Upland from Kaunakakai the land tilts skyward and turns green, with scented plumeria in yards and glossy coffee trees all in a row, until it blooms into a true forest—and then abruptly ends at a great precipice, falling 3,250 feet to the sea. The green sea cliffs are creased with five V-shaped crevices so deep that light is seldom seen (to paraphrase a Hawaii poet). The north coast is a remote, forbidding place, with a solitary peninsula—**Kalaupapa** 🌟🌟🌟—that was once the home for exiled lepers (it's now a National Historical Park). This region is easy on the eyes but difficult to visit. It lies at a cool elevation, and frequent rain squalls blow in from the ocean. In summer the ocean is calm, providing great opportunities for kayaking, fishing, and swimming, but during the rest of the year, giant waves come rolling onto the shores.

The West End 🌟

This end of the island, home to **Molokai Ranch,** is miles of stark desert terrain bordered by the most beautiful white-sand beaches in Hawaii. The rugged rolling land slopes down to Molokai's only destination resort, **Kaluakoi,** a cul-de-sac of condos clustered around a 3-decades-old seafront hotel (which closed in 2001 and was still closed when we went to press) near 3-mile-long Papohaku, the island's biggest beach. On the way to Kaluakoi, you'll find **Maunaloa,** a 1920s-era pineapple-plantation town that's in the midst of being transformed into a master-planned community, Maunaloa Village, with an upscale lodge, triplex theater, restaurants, and shops. The West End is dry, dry, dry. It hardly ever rains, but when it does (usually in the winter), expect a downpour and lots of red mud.

The East End 🌟🌟🌟

The area east of Kaunakakai becomes lush, green, and tropical, with golden pocket beaches and a handful of cottages and condos that are popular with thrifty travelers. With this voluptuous landscape comes rain. However, most storms are brief (15-min.) affairs that blow in, dry up, and disappear. Winter is Hawaii's rainy season, so expect more rain from January to March, but even then, the storms usually are brief and the sun comes back out.

Beyond Kaunakakai the two-lane road curves along the coast past piggeries, palm groves, and a 20-mile string of fishponds as well as an ancient *heiau* (temple), Damien-built churches, and a few contemporary condos by the sea. The road ends in the glorious **Halawa Valley** 🌟, one of Hawaii's most beautiful valleys.

FAST FACTS

Molokai and Lanai are both part of Maui County. For **local emergencies,** call ✆ 911. For nonemergencies, call the **police** at ✆ 808/553-5355, the **fire department** at ✆ 808/553-5601, or **Molokai General Hospital,** in Kaunakakai, at ✆ 808/553-5331.

Downtown Kaunakakai has a **post office** (✆ 808/553-5845) and several banks, including the **Bank of Hawaii** (✆ 808/553-3273), which has a 24-hour ATM.

2 Getting Around

Getting around Molokai isn't easy if you don't have a rental car, and rental cars are often hard to find here. On holiday weekends—and remember, Hawaii celebrates different holidays than the rest of the United States (see "When to Go" in chapter 2)—car-rental agencies simply run out of cars. Book before you go. There's no municipal transit or shuttle service, but a 24-hour taxi service is available (see below).

CAR-RENTAL AGENCIES   Rental cars are available from **Budget** (✆ 808/567-6877) and **Dollar** (✆ 808/567-6156); both agencies are located at the Molokai Airport. Nonchain operators include **Molokai Outdoors** (✆ 877/553-4477 or 808/553-4477; www.molokai-outdoors.com), whose prices range from $25 a day for a compact to $65 a day for a 4×4 jeep. We also recommend **Island Kine** (✆ 808/553-5242; www.molokai-car-rental.com)—not only are the cars cheaper, but Barbara Shonely and her son, Steve, also give personalized service. They'll meet you at the Molokai Airport, take you to their office in Kaunakakai, and recommend specific outfitters for your activities. The used cars are in excellent condition (to quote Barbara: "I would drive every one of them with my grandkids") and are air-conditioned. Vans and pickup trucks are also available. You won't need a four-wheel-drive vehicle unless you're planning some specialized hiking, but if that's the case, Island Kine has what you're looking for.

TAXI & TOUR SERVICES   Molokai Off-Road Tours & Taxi (✆ 808/553-3369; www.molokai.com/offroad) offers regular taxi service, an airport shuttle ($8 per person one-way to Molokai Ranch Lodge; $8.50 per person one-way to Kaunakakai), and island tours (the Molokai highlights tour is $49 per person).

3 Where to Stay

Molokai is Hawaii's most affordable island, especially for hotels. And because the island's restaurants are few, most hotel rooms and condo units come with kitchens, which can save you a bundle on dining costs.

There aren't a ton of accommodations options on Molokai—mostly B&Bs, condos, a few quaint oceanfront vacation rentals, an aging resort, and a very expensive lodge. For camping on Molokai, you have two options: the upscale tentalows offered by the Beach Village at Molokai Ranch, or, for hardy souls, camping with your own tent at the beach or in the cool upland forest (see "Hiking & Camping" later in this chapter). I've listed my top picks below; for additional options, contact **Molokai Visitors Association** (see "Visitor Information" under "Orientation," above).

Note: Taxes of 11.42% will be added to your hotel bill. Parking is free.

KAUNAKAKAI

MODERATE

Marc Molokai Shores *Kids*   Basic units with kitchens and large lanais face a small gold-sand beach in this quiet complex of three-story Polynesian-style buildings, less

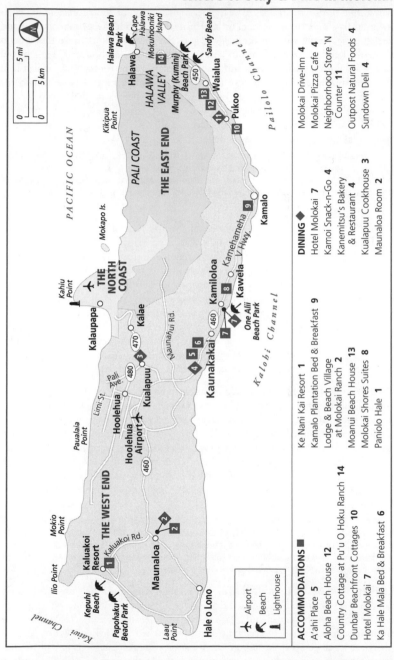

Where to Stay & Dine in Molokai

PACIFIC OCEAN

Kaiwi Channel

Ilio Point

Mokio Point

Kepuhi Beach

Papohaku Beach Park

Kaluakoi Resort **1**

Kaluakoi Rd.

Laau Point

Hale o Lono

Maunaloa

THE WEST END

460

Hoolehua Airport

480

470

Pali Ave.

Limi St.

460

Hoolehua

Kualapuu

Pualaia Point

Kalaupapa

Kahiu Point

THE NORTH COAST

Kalae

Mokapo Is.

Kikipua Point

Naunahui Rd.

PALI COAST

THE EAST END

Halawa Beach Park

Halawa

Cape Halawa

Mokuhooniki Island

HALAWA VALLEY **14**

Sandy Beach

Murphy (Kumini) Beach Park

450

Waialua **13**

12

Pukoo **11**

10

Pailolo Channel

Kamalo

Kamehameha V Hwy.

9

Kawela

8

7 **1**

One Alii Beach Park

Kamiloloa

460

Kaunakakai

5 **6**

4

3 **2**

2

Kalohi Channel

✈ Airport

🏖 Beach

🚩 Lighthouse

ACCOMMODATIONS ■

A'ahi Place **5**
Aloha Beach House **12**
Country Cottage at Pu'u O Hoku Ranch **14**
Dunbar Beachfront Cottages **10**
Hotel Molokai **7**
Ka Hale Mala Bed & Breakfast **6**
Ke Nani Kai Resort **1**
Kamalo Plantation Bed & Breakfast **9**
Lodge & Beach Village at Molokai Ranch **2**
Moanui Beach House **13**
Molokai Shores Suites **8**
Paniolo Hale **1**

DINING ◆

Hotel Molokai **7**
Kamoi Snack-n-Go **4**
Kanemitsu's Bakery & Restaurant **4**
Kualapuu Cookhouse **3**
Maunaloa Room **2**
Molokai Drive-Inn **4**
Molokai Pizza Cafe **4**
Neighborhood Store 'N Counter **11**
Outpost Natural Foods **4**
Sundown Deli **4**

than a mile from Kaunakakai. Alas, the beach is mostly for show (offshore, it's shallow mud flats underfoot), fishing, or launching kayaks, but the swimming pool and barbecue area come with an ocean view, and the spacious units make this a good choice for families. Well-tended gardens, spreading lawns, and palms frame a restful view of fishponds, offshore reefs, and neighbor islands. The central location can be a plus, minimizing driving time from the airport or town, and it's convenient to the mule ride, as well as the lush East End countryside. There's no daily maid service. Check the website for Internet-only discounts. We have gotten some letters complaining about the lack of maintenance and cleanliness; the management swears that they are taking steps to correct these deficiencies.

Kamehameha V Hwy. (P.O. Box 1037), Kaunakakai, HI 96748. © 800/535-0085 or 808/553-5954. Fax 808/553-3241. www.marcresorts.com. 102 units. $169 1-bedroom apt (sleeps up to 4); $250 2-bedroom apt (up to 6). Discounted rates for weekly and extended stays, plus corporate, military, and senior discounts. AE, DC, MC, V. **Amenities:** Putting green; salon; coin-op washer/dryers. *In room:* TV, kitchen, fridge, coffeemaker, iron.

INEXPENSIVE

A'ahi Place (Value)   Just outside of the main town of Kaunakakai and up a small hill lies this dream vacation cottage, complete with a wicker-filled sitting area, a kitchen, and two full-size beds in the bedroom. Two lanais make great places to just sit and enjoy the stars at night. The entire property is surrounded by tropical plants, flowers, and fruit trees. You can choose to forgo breakfast or for $10 more per night (for two) get all the fixings for a continental breakfast (home-grown Molokai coffee, fresh-baked goods, and fruit from the property) placed in the kitchen, so you can enjoy it at your leisure. For those who seek a quiet vacation, with no phone or TV to distract you, this is the place. And for those who wish to explore Molokai, the central location is perfect.

P.O. Box 2006, Kaunakakai, HI 96748. © 808/553-8033. www.molokai.com/aahi. 1 unit. $75 double. Continental breakfast $10 extra. Extra person $20. 3-night minimum. No credit cards. *In room:* Kitchen, fridge, coffeemaker, no phone.

Hotel Molokai ⭐   This nostalgic Hawaiian motel complex is composed of a series of modified A-frame units, nestled under coco palms along a gray-sand beach with a great view of Lanai. The Travel Advantage Network purchased this property a couple of years ago and immediately spent $270,000 upgrading the rooms with new phones, televisions, decorations, and roof coverings. The rooms are basic (be sure to ask for one with a ceiling fan), with a lanai. The mattresses are on the soft side, the sheets thin, and the bath towels rough, but you're on Molokai—and this is the only hotel in Kaunakakai. The kitchenettes, with coffeemaker, toaster, pots, and two-burner stove, can save you money on eating out.

Kamehameha V Hwy. (P.O. Box 1020), Kaunakakai, HI 96748. © 800/367-5004 on the mainland, 800/272-5275 in Hawaii, or 808/553-5347. Fax 800/477-2329. www.hotelmolokai.com. 45 units. $90–$175 double. Extra bed/crib $17. AE, DC, DISC, MC, V. **Amenities:** Fairly good and reasonably priced restaurant with bar; outdoor pool; watersports equipment rentals; bike rentals; activities desk; babysitting; coin-op washer/dryers. *In room:* A/C, TV, dataport, kitchenette (in some units), fridge, coffeemaker, hair dryer, iron, safe.

Ka Hale Mala Bed & Breakfast (Value)   In a subdivision just outside town (off Kamehameha V Hwy., before mile marker 5) is this large four-room unit, with a private entrance through the garden and a Jacuzzi just outside. Inside, you'll find white rattan furnishings, room enough to sleep four, and a full kitchen. The helpful owners, Jack and Cheryl, meet all guests at the airport like long-lost relatives. They'll happily share their homegrown, organic produce; we recommend paying the extra $5 each for breakfast here. The owners can also supply a couple of bikes and snorkel and picnic gear.

7 Kamakana Place (P.O. Box 1582), Kaunakakai, HI 96748. ℭ/fax **808/553-9009**. www.molokai-bnb.com. 1 unit. $70 double without breakfast; $80 double with breakfast. Extra person $10. No credit cards. **Amenities:** Jacuzzi. *In room:* TV, kitchen, fridge, coffeemaker.

THE WEST END
VERY EXPENSIVE
The Lodge at Molokai Ranch   This quaint 22-room inn in Maunaloa is back in the hands of the Molokai Ranch and under the new management (which is a member of the Small Luxury Hotels of the World—Hotel Hana-Maui is the only other Hawaii hotel in this group). The attractive, two-story lodge sits on 8 nicely landscaped acres located 6 miles and a 20- to 25-minute shuttle ride to the nearest beach. Designed to resemble a 1930s-style Hawaii ranch owner's private home, The Lodge features a giant fireplace, huge wooden beam construction, panoramic views, and lots of details (cuffed cowboy boots beside the door, old books lining the shelves) to make it look and feel like a real ranch. Guests step back in time to a Hawaii of yesteryear.

The guest rooms, each with individual country decor, are of two types: deluxe ($398) and luxury ($478). Be sure to check out their money-saving package deals on the website or call for the latest pricing. The luxury rooms are spacious corner units that feature either greenhouse-type skylights or a cozy king-size daybed nestled in a comfy alcove. My luxury room was wonderful, with a free-standing four-poster bed, 270-degree view, and a TV that hydraulically lifted out of a credenza, then magically disappeared again.

Other amenities include a dining room (p. 263), the option of dining at buffets at the beach pavilion, a small but practical spa (with massage treatments, men and women's sauna, and locker facilities), outdoor heated swimming pool, and access to a host of activities. The Lodge, along with the Beach Village at Molokai Ranch (p. 284), sits on the 53,000-acre Molokai Ranch and is geared toward outdoorsy types, with lots of activities available (horseback riding, mountain biking, hiking, kayaking, snorkeling, beach activities, and more, ranging in price from $25–$350). There's also wonderful local entertainment in the Great Room in the evening; even if you don't stay here, come for the free entertainment.

P.O. Box 259, Maunaloa, HI 96770. ℭ **888/627-8082** or 808/660-2824. Fax 808/552-2773. www.molokairanch.com. 22 units. $398–$478 double, plus $15 per day resort fee for transportation to beach, use of facilities at The Lodge, and use of beach equipment at the beach camp. Extra person $50. Children 12 and under stay and eat free with adult. Check for money-saving packages. AE, DC, DISC, MC, V. **Amenities:** Restaurant (see Maunaloa Dining Room, p. 265); bar with entertainment Tues–Sat evenings; gorgeous heated outdoor "infinity" pool; workout room; small spa with massage room; bike rentals; game room; concierge; activities desk; car-rental desk; shopping arcade; massage; laundry service. *In room:* A/C, TV, dataport, fridge, coffeemaker, hair dryer, iron, safe.

MODERATE
Ke Nani Kai Resort 🏖 *Kids*   This place is great for families, who will appreciate the space. The large apartments are set up for full-time living with real kitchens, washer/dryers, VCRs, attractive furnishings, and breezy lanais. There's a huge pool, a volleyball court, tennis courts, and golf on the neighboring Kaluakoi course. These condos are farther from the sea than other local accommodations but are still just a brief walk from the beach. The two-story buildings are surrounded by parking and garden areas. The only downside: Maid service is only every third day.

In the Kaluakoi Resort development, Kaluakoi Rd., off Hwy. 460 (P.O. Box 289), Maunaloa, HI 96770. Reservations c/o Molokai Vacation Rentals, P.O. Box 1979, Kaunakakai, HI 96748. ℭ **800/367-2984** or 808/553-8334. Fax 808/553-3783. www.molokai-vacation-rental.com. 100 units. $95–$105 1-bedroom apt (sleeps up to 4); $120–$135 2-bedroom apt (up to 6). AE, DC, DISC, MC, V. **Amenities:** Outdoor pool; golf course; 2 tennis courts; Jacuzzi. *In room:* TV, kitchen, fridge, coffeemaker; washer/dryers.

Believe It or Not: High-Priced Camping

This was a great idea: a unique eco-adventure that combines camping and outdoor activities with the amenities of a resort. The **Beach Village at Molokai Ranch** (✆ **888/627-8082** or 808/660-2824; fax 808/552-2773; www.molokai ranch.com) features camping on an exclusive private beach, with very upscale "camping" accommodations. The Beach Village offers "tentalows" (safari-type tents mounted on wooden platforms). This is yuppie camping—with queen-size or twin beds, ceiling fans, solar-powered lights, private bathrooms with composting toilets, and solar hot-water showers, plus big decks with lounge chairs, personal hammocks for two, and picnic tables. There's even daily maid service! A big pavilion down at the beach has all-you-can-eat buffet meals three times a day, plus nightly entertainment under the stars.

When the ranch first opened these camps in 1997, the price included airport pickup, meals, and a large menu of outdoor activities (horseback riding, mountain biking, hiking, sailing, snorkeling, kayaking, and other adventures). It was all-inclusive and quite a deal at $185 per person.

Today the prices have risen to an astounding $268 for garden tentalows, $308 (near the beach) to $358 (directly on the beach) double or single occupancy (plus the ubiquitous "resort fee" of $15 a day), and meals and activities are no longer included. Children 17 and under do stay free (with an adult), and children 12 and under also eat free when accompanied by an adult. Meal prices are $15 for breakfast, $15 for lunch, and $31 for dinner. It starts to add up: Two adults staying in the least expensive room will spend $315 a day—including tax and $15 daily resort fee—just on the room! With meals and tax (before any tipping), add another $127 a day, it comes out to $442 a day for two—and that's not including any activities you may want to do. That's pretty expensive "camping."

Now that the ranch has taken over the reins again, the new management promises many changes (including money-saving package deals). We hope they return to the all-inclusive policy, priced closer to camping than to luxury accommodations.

Paniolo Hale 🖈 *Finds*   Tucked into a verdant garden on the dry West End, this condo complex has the advantage of being next door to a white-sand beach and a golf course. The two-story, old Hawaii ranch-house design is airy and homey, with oak floors and walls of folding-glass doors that open to huge screened verandas, doubling your living space. The one- and two-bedroom units come with two bathrooms and accommodate three or four easily. Some units have hot tubs on the lanai. All are spacious, comfortably furnished, and well equipped, with full kitchens and washer/dryers.

The whole place overlooks the Kaluakoi Golf Course (recently reopened), a green barrier that separates these condos from the rest of Kaluakoi Resort. Out front, Kepuhi Beach is a scenic place for walkers and beachcombers, but the seas are too hazardous for most swimmers. A pool, paddle tennis, and barbecue facilities are on the property, which adjoins open grassland countryside.

As with most condominiums in a rental pool, the quality and upkeep of the individually owned units can vary widely. When booking, spend some time talking with the friendly people at Molokai Vacation Rentals so that you can get a top-quality condo that has been renovated recently.

Lio Place (next door to Kaluakoi Resort), Kaluakoi, HI 96770. Reservations c/o Molokai Vacation Rentals, P.O. Box 1979, Kaunakakai, 96748. ℂ 800/367-2984 or 808/553-8334. Fax 808/553-3783. www.molokai-vacation-rental. com. 77 units. $105–$145 double studio; $130–$195 1-bedroom apt (sleeps up to 4); $225 2-bedroom apt (up to 6). 3-night minimum; 1-week minimum Dec 20–Jan 5. AE, MC, V. **Amenities:** Outdoor pool; nearby golf course. *In room:* TV, kitchen, fridge, coffeemaker, washer/dryers.

THE EAST END
MODERATE
Aloha Beach House ★★ *(Finds)*   This is a great place to stay on Molokai. This Hawaiian-style beach house sits right on the white-sand beach of Waialua on the lush East End. Perfect for families, this impeccably decorated, two-bedroom, 1,600-square-foot beach house has a huge open living/dining/kitchen area that opens out to an old-fashioned porch for meals or just sitting in the comfy chairs and watching the clouds roll by. It's fully equipped, from the complete kitchen (including a dishwasher), to a VCR (plus a library of videos), to all the beach toys you can think of. It's located close to the Neighborhood Store (p. 284).

Located just after mile marker 19. Reservations c/o The Rietows, P.O. Box 79, Kilauea, Hi 96754. ℂ 888/828-1008 or 808/828-1100. Fax 808/828-2199. www.molokaivacation.com. 1 2-bedroom house (sleeps up to 5). $220 (for up to 5) plus $95 cleaning fee. 3-night minimum. No credit cards. *In room:* TV, kitchen, fridge, coffeemaker, washer/dryer.

Dunbar Beachfront Cottages ★★ *(Kids)*   This is one of the most peaceful, comfortable, and elegant properties on Molokai's East End, and the setting is simply stunning. Each of these two green-and-white plantation-style cottages sits on its own secluded beach (good for swimming)—you'll feel like you're on your own private island. The Puunana Cottage has a king-size bed and two twins, while the Pauwalu has a queen-size and two twins—great for families. Each has a full kitchen, VCR, ceiling fans, comfortable tropical furniture, a large furnished deck (perfect for whale-watching in winter), and views of Maui, Lanai, and Kahoolawe across the channel.

Kamehameha V Hwy., past mile marker 18. Reservations c/o Kip and Leslie Dunbar, HC01 Box 901, Kaunakakai, HI 96748. ℂ 800/673-0520 or 808/558-8153. Fax 808/558-8153. www.molokai-beachfront-cottages.com. 2 2-bedroom cottages (each sleeps up to 4). $170 cottage, plus 1-time $75 cleaning charge. 3-night minimum. No credit cards. *In room:* TV, kitchen, fridge, coffeemaker, washer/dryer.

Moanui Beach House ★ *(Kids)*   If you're looking for a quiet, remote beach house, this is it. The genial Glenn and Akiko Foster (no relation to the author), who have lived in the islands for many years, run the popular Kamalo Plantation Bed & Breakfast (see below). They recently purchased and renovated this two-bedroom beach house, right across the street from a secluded white-sand cove beach. The A-frame has a shaded lanai facing the ocean, a screened-in lanai on the side of the house, a full kitchen, plenty of room for families, and an ocean view that's worth the price alone. The Fosters leave a "starter supply" of breakfast foods for guests (fruit basket, home-baked bread, tropical fruit juices, tea, and coffee).

Kamehameha V Hwy., at mile marker 20. Reservations c/o Glenn and Akiko Foster, HC01, Box 300, Kaunakakai, HI 96748. ℂ/fax 808/558-8236. www.molokai.com/kamalo. 1 2-bedroom unit. $140 double. Extra person $20. 3-night minimum. No credit cards. *In room:* TV, kitchen, fridge, coffeemaker, hair dryer, iron, washer/dryer.

INEXPENSIVE

Country Cottage at Pu'u O Hoku Ranch 𝔯 *Kids* *Pu'u o Hoku* ("Star Hill") Ranch, which spreads across 14,000 acres of pasture and forests, is the last place to stay before Halawa Valley—it's at least an hour's drive from Kaunakakai along the shoreline. Two acres of tropically landscaped property circle the ranch's rustic cottage, which boasts breathtaking views of rolling hills and the Pacific Ocean. The wooden cottage features comfortable country furniture, a full kitchen, two bedrooms (one with a double bed, one with two twins), two bathrooms, and a separate dining room on the enclosed lanai. TVs and VCRs are available on request. We recommend stargazing at night, watching the sunrise in the morning, and hiking, swimming, or a game of croquet in the afternoon. Kids will have plenty of room to run and play. For larger parties, there's a four-bedroom, three-bathroom house (sleeps up to eight) on the property. Horseback riding is available at the ranch; see "Horseback Riding" under "Golf & Other Outdoor Activities," later in this chapter.

Kamehameha V Hwy., at mile marker 25. Reservations: P.O. Box 1889, Kaunakakai, HI 96748. © **808/558-8109.** Fax 808/558-8100. www.puuohoku.com. 1 unit. $140 double for 2-bedroom cottage. Extra person $20. 2-night minimum. MC, V. **Amenities:** Swimming pool. *In room:* TV/VCR available on request, kitchen, fridge, coffeemaker.

Kamalo Plantation Bed & Breakfast 𝔯 *Value* The Foster's 5-acre spread includes an ancient *heiau* ruin in the front yard, plus leafy tropical gardens and a working fruit orchard. Their Eden-like property is easy to find: It's right across the East End road from Father Damien's historic St. Joseph church. The plantation-style cottage is tucked under flowering trees and surrounded by swaying palms and tropical foliage. It has its own lanai, a big living room with a queen-size sofa bed, and a separate bedroom with a king-size bed, so it can sleep four comfortably. The kitchen is fully equipped (it even has spices), and there's a barbecue outside. A breakfast of fruit and freshly baked bread is served every morning. There's no TV reception, but the cottage does have a VCR, a radio, and a CD and cassette player.

Kamehameha V Hwy., just past mile marker 10 (HC01, Box 300), Kaunakakai, HI 96748. ©/fax **808/558-8236.** www.molokai.com/kamalo. 1 unit. $85 cottage. Rate includes continental breakfast. Extra person $10. 2-night minimum. No credit cards. *In room:* Kitchen, fridge, coffeemaker, hair dryer.

4 Where to Dine

Molokai is strong on adventure, the outdoors, and the get-away-from-it-all feeling. No traffic lights and honking horns here, nor long lines at overbooked, self-important restaurants. But when it comes to dining, Molokai is not nirvana. Even with the first upscale hotel and dining room open in Maunaloa, Molokai's culinary offerings are spare.

A lot of people like it that way and acknowledge that the island's character is unchangeably rugged and natural. But a few years ago, when the renovated Hotel Molokai unveiled a tropical fantasy of an oceanfront dining room, the islanders thought this was the height of culinary pleasure. And it quickly became the island's busiest restaurant.

In 1999, when the Molokai Ranch opened The Lodge, it introduced the concept of Molokai having its own gourmet culinary cuisine, using local ingredients in not only traditional Molokai preparations but also in other ethnic styles of cooking.

Even with these new developments, Molokai has retained its glacial pace of change. The culinary offerings of the island are dominated by mom-and-pop eateries, nothing fancy, most of them fast-food or takeout places and many of them with a home-cooked touch. Lovers of the fast lane might consider this aspect of the island's personality a con rather than a pro, but they wouldn't choose to come here anyway. Molokai is for those who want to get away from it all, who consider the lack of high-rises and traffic lights a welcome change from the urban chaos that keeps nibbling at the edges of the more popular and populated islands. Sybarites, foodies, and pampered oenophiles had best lower their expectations upon arrival, or turn around and leave the island's natural beauty to nature lovers.

Personally, I like the unpretentiousness of the island; it's an oasis in a state where plastic aloha abounds. Most Molokai residents fish, collect seaweed, grow potatoes and tomatoes, and prepare for backyard luaus. Unlike Lanai (see chapter 12), which is small and rural but offers sophisticated dining in the two classy hotels, Molokai provides no such mix of innocence and erudition. Molokai doesn't pretend to be anything more than a combination of old ways and an informal lifestyle that's closer to the land than to a chef's toque.

You'll even find a certain defiant stance against the trappings of modernity. Although some of the best produce in Hawaii is grown on this island, you're not likely to find much of it served in its restaurants, other than in the takeout items at Outpost Natural Foods, or at the Molokai Pizza Cafe (one of the most pleasing eateries on the island), and the Hotel Molokai. The rest of the time, content yourself with ethnic or diner fare—or by cooking for yourself. The many visitors who stay in condos find that it doesn't take long to sniff out the best sources of produce, groceries, and fresh fish to fire up at home when the island's other dining options are exhausted. The "Edibles" sections in "Shopping" (later in this chapter) will point you to the places where you can pick up foodstuffs for your own island-style feast.

Molokai's restaurants are inexpensive or moderately priced, and several of them do not accept credit cards. Regardless of where you eat, you certainly won't have to dress up. In most cases, I've listed just the town rather than the street address because, as you'll see, street addresses are as meaningless on this island as fancy cars and sequins. Reservations are not accepted unless otherwise noted.

Note: You'll find the restaurants reviewed in this chapter on the "Where to Stay & Dine in Molokai" map on p. 257.

KAUNAKAKAI

Hotel Molokai ☆ AMERICAN/ISLAND   On the ocean, with a view of Lanai, torches flickering under palm trees, and tiny fairy lights lining the room and the neighboring pool area, the Hotel Molokai's dining room evokes the romance of a South Seas fantasy. It's a casual room, and since its 1999 reopening, provides the only nightlife in Kaunakakai (see "Molokai After Dark" later in this chapter) and the most pleasing ambience on the island. Lunch choices consist of the basics; most promising are salads (Big Island organic greens) and sandwiches, from roast beef to grilled mahimahi. As the sun sets and the torches are lit for dinner, the menu turns to heavier meats, ribs, fish, and pasta. Try the fresh catch, Korean kalbi ribs, barbecued pork ribs, New York steak, coconut shrimp, or garlic chicken. Temper your expectations of culinary excellence, and you're sure to enjoy a pleasing dinner in an atmosphere that's unequaled on the island.

On Kamehameha V Hwy. © 808/553-5347. Reservations recommended for dinner. Main courses $7–$8 lunch, $12–$19 dinner. AE, DC, MC, V. Daily 7–10am, 11am–2pm, and 6–9pm; bar until 10:30pm.

Kamoi Snack-N-Go ICE CREAM/SNACKS   The Kamoi specialty: sweets and icy treats. Ice cream made by Dave's on Oahu comes in flavors such as green tea, lychee sherbet, *ube* (a brilliant purple color, made from Okinawan sweet potato), haupia, mango, and many other tropical—and traditional—flavors. Young and old alike line up for the cones, shakes, sundaes, and popular Icee floats served at this tiny snack shop. If the ice cream doesn't tempt you, maybe something in the aisles full of candies will. It's takeout only, no tables.

In Kamoi Professional Center. ℂ 808/553-3742. Ice cream $1.65–$3.40. MC, V. Mon–Sat 9am–9pm; Sun noon–9pm.

Kanemitsu's Bakery & Restaurant ⚲ BAKERY/DELI   Morning, noon, and night, this local legend fills the Kaunakakai air with the sweet smells of baking. Taro lavosh is the hot seller, joining Molokai bread—developed in 1935 in a cast-iron, kiawe-fired oven—as a Kanemitsu signature. Flavors range from apricot-pineapple to mango (in season), but the classics remain the regular white, wheat, cheese, sweet, and onion-cheese breads. For those who like their bread warm, the bread mixes offer a way to take Molokai home. In the adjoining coffee shop/deli, all sandwiches come on their own freshly baked buns and breads. The hamburgers, egg-salad sandwiches, mahi burgers, and honey-dipped fried chicken are popular and cheap.

Kanemitsu's has a life after dark, too. Whenever anyone on Molokai mentions "hot bread," he's talking about the nightly **hot-bread run** at Kanemitsu's, the surreal late-night ritual for die-hard bread lovers. Those in the know line up at the bakery's back door beginning at 10:30pm, when the bread is whisked hot out of the oven and into waiting hands. You can order your fresh bread with butter, jelly, cinnamon, or cream cheese, and the bakers will cut the hot loaves down the middle and slather on the works so it melts in the bread. The cream cheese and jelly bread makes a fine substitute for dessert.

79 Ala Malama St. ℂ 808/553-5855. Most items less than $5.50. No credit cards. Restaurant Wed–Mon 5:30–11:30am; bakery Wed–Mon 5:30am–6:30pm.

Molokai Drive-Inn AMERICAN/TAKEOUT   It is a greasy spoon, but it's one of the rare drive-up places with fresh *akule* (mackerel) and ahi (when available), plus fried saimin, at budget-friendly prices. The honey-dipped fried chicken is a favorite among residents, who also come here for the floats, shakes, and other artery-clogging choices. But don't expect much in terms of ambience: This is a fast-food takeout counter that smells like fried food—and it doesn't pretend to be otherwise.

Kaunakakai. ℂ 808/553-5655. Most items less than $7.75. No credit cards. Mon–Thurs 5:30am–10pm; Fri–Sun 6am–10:30pm.

Molokai Pizza Cafe ⚲ PIZZA   This gathering place serves excellent pizzas and sandwiches that have made it a Kaunakakai staple as well as one of our favorite eateries on the island. The best-selling pies are the Molokai (pepperoni and cheese), the Big Island (pepperoni, ham, mushroom, Italian sausage, bacon, and vegetables), and the Molokini (plain cheese slices). Pasta, sandwiches, and specials round out the menu. Our personal fave is the vegetarian Maui pizza, but others tout the fresh-baked submarine and pocket sandwiches and the gyro pocket with spinach pie. Sunday is prime-rib day, Wednesday is Mexican, and Hawaiian plates are sold on Thursday. Coin-operated cars and a toy airplane follow the children's theme, but adults should feel equally at home with the very popular barbecued-baby-back-rib plate and the fresh-fish dinners. Children's art and letters in the tiled dining room add an entertaining and charming touch. Free delivery to Hotel Molokai is a welcome development.

In Kahua Center, on the old Wharf Rd. ℂ 808/553-3288. Large pizzas $13–$23. No credit cards. Sun 11am–10pm; Mon–Thurs 10am–10pm; Fri–Sat 10am–11pm.

Outpost Natural Foods 🦆 VEGETARIAN   The healthiest and freshest food on the island is served at the lunch counter of this health-food store, around the corner from the main drag on the ocean side of Kaunakakai town. The tiny store abounds in Molokai papayas, bananas, herbs, potatoes, watermelon, and other local produce, complementing its selection of vitamins, cosmetics, and health aids, as well as bulk and shelf items. But the real star is the closet-size lunch counter. The salads, burritos, tempeh sandwiches, vegetarian potpie, tofu-spinach lasagna, and mock chicken, turkey, and meatloaf (made from oats, sprouts, seeds, and seasonings) are testament to the fact that vegetarian food need not be boring. A must for health-conscious diners and shoppers.

70 Makaena Place. 📞 808/553-3377. Most items less than $5. AE, DISC, MC, V. Sun–Fri 10am–3pm.

Sundown Deli 🦆 DELI   From "gourmet saimin" to spinach pie, Sundown's offerings are home-cooked and healthful, with daily specials that include vegetarian quiche, vegetarian lasagna, and club sandwiches. The sandwiches (like smoked turkey and chicken salad) and several salads (Caesar, Oriental, stuffed tomato) are served daily, with a soup that changes by the day (clam chowder, Portuguese bean, cream of broccoli). Vitamins, T-shirts, and snacks are sold in this tiny cafe, but most of the business is takeout.

145 Puali St. (across the street from Veteran's Memorial Park). 📞 808/553-3713. Sandwiches, soups, and salads $3.95–$7.50. AE, MC, V. Mon–Fri 7am–4pm; Sat 10:30am–2pm.

EN ROUTE TO THE NORTH COAST
Kualapuu Cook House 🦆 AMERICAN   An old wagon in front of a former plantation house marks this down-home eatery, now takeout only. Local residents flock here, not only for the family atmosphere, but for the oversize servings. Breakfasts feature giant omelets, homemade corned beef hash, and, for those who dare, The Works—buttermilk pancakes, eggs, and home fries (you'll either be fueled for the day or ready to take a nap). Lunch can either be a burger or sandwich or one of their humongous plate lunches of pork katsu or chicken, served up with rice, of course.

Farrington Hwy., 1 block west of Hwy. 470, Kalapuu. 📞 808/567-9655. Most items under $15. No credit cards. Mon 7am–2pm; Tues–Sat 7am–8pm.

THE WEST END
Maunaloa Dining Room 🦆 MOLOKAI REGIONAL   Molokai has never had anything resembling fine dining, but this restaurant changes the picture. It's in the island's first upscale hotel, The Lodge at Molokai Ranch, a 22-room lodge fashioned after a ranch owner's private home in the cool hills of Maunaloa, where you can see Oahu past the rolling ranchlands and the ocean. Fresh Molokai ingredients come in cross-cultural preparations. Breakfast features banana-stuffed Molokai sweetbread French toast or eggs with taro hash. The dinner menu includes entrees such as fresh fish prepared with ling hing mui chutney; Hawaiian snapper with tropical-fruit salsa and ginger lime butter; grilled Korean kal bi ribs with kim chee; New York steak with garlic butter; even vegetarian dishes like fried tofu in peanut oil with sweet chili sauce. Sunday night is Wok's Cooking with an all-you-can-eat buffet featuring a wok station with stir-fried vegetables, chicken, shrimp, and beef. The room's rustic, lodgelike ambience fits the *paniolo* (cowboy/Western) surroundings, and Hawaiian proverbs stenciled on the walls are a nice cultural touch.

The Lodge at Molokai Ranch, Maunaloa. 📞 888/627-8082 or 808/660-2824. Reservations recommended for dinner. Breakfast entrees $7.50–$16; dinner main courses $19–$29. AE, DC, DISC, MC, V. Daily 7–10am; Mon–Sat 6–9pm; Sun 5–9pm buffet ($20, kids under 12 $10). Lunch served 10am–4pm in the bar; most sandwiches under $10.

THE EAST END

Neighborhood Store 'N Counter *✿* AMERICAN   The Neighborhood Store is nothing fancy, and that's what we love about it. This store/lunch counter appears like a mirage near mile marker 16 in the Pukoo area en route to the East End. Picnic tables under a royal poinciana tree are a wonderful sight, and the food does not disappoint. The place serves omelets, Portuguese sausage, and other breakfast specials (brunch is very popular), then segues into sandwiches, salads, mahimahi plates, and varied over-the-counter lunch offerings. Favorites include the mahimahi plate lunch, the chicken katsu, and the Mexican plate, each one with a tried-and-true home-cooked flavor. There are daily specials, ethnic dishes, and some vegetarian options, as well as burgers (including a killer veggie burger), saimin, and legendary desserts. Made-on-Maui Roselani ice cream is a featured attraction, and customers rave over the Portuguese doughnut dessert, a deep-fried doughnut filled with ice cream. A Molokai treasure, the Neighborhood Store is also the only grocery store on the East End (see "Shopping" later in this chapter).

Pukoo. © 808/558-8498. Most items less than $6.95; bento $7.30. No credit cards. Daily 8am–6pm.

5 Beaches

With imposing sea cliffs on one side and lazy fishponds on the other, Molokai has little room for beaches along its 106-mile coast. Still, a big gold-sand beach flourishes on the West End, and you'll find tiny pocket beaches on the East End. The emptiness of Molokai's beaches is both a blessing and a curse: The seclusion means no lifeguards on any of the beaches.

See the "Molokai" map on p. 253 for locations of these beaches.

KAUNAKAKAI

ONE ALII BEACH PARK

This thin strip of sand, once reserved for the *alii* (chiefs), is the oldest public beach park on Molokai. You'll find One Alii Beach Park (*One* is pronounced *o*-nay, not *won*) by a coconut grove on the outskirts of Kaunakakai. Safe for swimmers of all ages and abilities, it's often crowded with families on weekends, but it can be all yours on weekdays. Facilities include outdoor showers, restrooms, and free parking.

THE WEST END

PAPOHAKU BEACH *✿✿*

Nearly 3 miles long and 300 feet wide, gold-sand Papohaku Beach is one of the biggest in Hawaii (17-mile-long Polihale Beach on Kauai is the biggest). It's great for walking, beachcombing, picnics, and sunset watching year-round. The big surf and rip tides make swimming risky except in summer, when the waters are calmer. Go early in the day when the tropic sun is less fierce and the winds are calm. The beach is so big that you may never see another soul except at sunset, when a few people gather on the shore in hopes of spotting the elusive green flash, a natural wonder that takes place when the horizon is cloud-free. Facilities include outdoor showers, restrooms, picnic grounds, and free parking.

KEPUHI BEACH

Golfers see this picturesque golden strand in front of the Kaluakoi Resort and Golf Course as just another sand trap, but sunbathers like the semiprivate grassy dunes; they're seldom, if ever, crowded. Beachcombers often find what they're looking for here, but swimmers have to dodge lava rocks and risk rip tides. Oh, yes—look out for errant golf balls. There are no facilities or lifeguards, but cold drinks and restrooms are handy at the resort.

THE EAST END
SANDY BEACH 𝒢
Molokai's most popular swimming beach—ideal for families with small kids—is a roadside pocket of gold sand protected by a reef, with a great view of Maui and Lanai. You'll find it off the King Kamehameha V Highway (Hwy. 450) at mile marker 20. There are no facilities—just you, the sun, the sand, and the surf.

MURPHY BEACH PARK (KUMIMI BEACH PARK)
In 1970 the Molokai Jaycees wanted to create a sandy beach park with a good swimming area for the children of the East End. They chose a section known as Kumimi Beach, which was owned by the Puu o Hoku Ranch. The beach was a dump, literally. The ranch owner, George Murphy, gave his permission to use the site as a park, and the Jaycees cleaned it up and built three small pavilions, plus picnic tables and barbecue grills. Officially, the park is called the George Murphy Beach Park (shortened to Murphy Beach Park over the years), but some old-timers still call it Kumimi Beach, and, just to make things really confusing, some people call it Jaycees Park.

No matter what you call it, this small park is shaded by ironwood trees that line a white-sand beach. It's generally a very safe swimming area. On calm days snorkeling and diving are great outside the reef. Fishermen are also frequently spotted here looking for papio and other island fish.

HALAWA BEACH PARK 𝒢
At the foot of scenic Halawa Valley is this beautiful black-sand beach with a palm-fringed lagoon, a wave-lashed island offshore, and a distant view of the West Maui Mountains across the Pailolo Channel. The swimming is safe in the shallows close to shore, but where the waterfall stream meets the sea, the ocean is often murky and unnerving. A winter swell creases the mouth of Halawa Valley on the north side of the bay and attracts a crowd of local surfers. Facilities are minimal; bring your own water. To get here, take King Kamehameha V Highway (Hwy. 450) east to the end.

6 Watersports

The best place to rent beach toys (snorkels, boogie boards, beach chairs, fishing poles, and more) is **Molokai Outdoors Activities,** in the lobby of Hotel Molokai, just outside Kaunakakai (✆ **877/553-4477** or 808/553-4477; www.molokai-outdoors.com). They have everything you'll need for a day at the beach and can also give you advice on where to find a great swimming beach or where the waves are breaking. Another good place to check out is **Molokai Fish & Dive,** Kaunakakai (✆ **808/553-5926;** www.molokaifishanddive.com), a mind-boggling store filled with outdoor gear. You can rent snorkels, fishing gear, even ice chests here. This is also a hot spot for fishing news and tips on what's running where.

For general advice on the activities listed below, see "The Active Vacation Planner," in chapter 2.

BODY BOARDING (BOOGIE BOARDING) & BODYSURFING
Molokai has only three beaches that offer ridable waves for body boarding and bodysurfing: Papohaku, Kepuhi, and Halawa. Even these beaches are only for experienced

bodysurfers, due to the strength of the rip currents and undertows. You can rent boogie boards with fins for just $5 a day or $19 a week at **Molokai Outdoors Activities,** in the lobby of Hotel Molokai, just outside Kaunakakai (© **877/553-4477** or 808/553-4477; www.molokai-outdoors.com).

OCEAN KAYAKING

During the summer months, when the waters on the north shore are calm, Molokai offers some of the most spectacular kayaking in Hawaii. You can paddle from remote valley to remote valley, spending a week or more exploring the exotic terrain. However, most of Molokai is for the experienced kayaker only. You must be adept in paddling through open ocean swells and rough waves.

Molokai Outdoors Activities, in the lobby of Hotel Molokai, just outside Kaunakakai (© **877/553-4477** or 808/553-4477; www.molokai-outdoors.com), has sunset tours ($47 per person) of the ancient Hawaii fishponds and a coastline tour ($61 per person). They also rent kayaks; rates start at $12 an hour and $26 a day.

On the West End, **The Lodge at Molokai Ranch** (© **888/627-8082** or 808/ 660-2824; www.molokairanch.com) offers a range of ocean-kayaking trips with snorkeling from $75 to $85.

SAILING

Molokai Charters ⚓ (© **808/553-5852**) offers a variety of sailing trips on *Satan's Doll,* a 42-foot sloop: 2-hour sunset sails for $40 per person, half a day of sailing and whale-watching for $50 (mid-Dec to mid-Mar), and a full-day sail to Lanai with swimming and snorkeling for $90 (which includes lunch, cold drinks, snacks, and all equipment). Owners Richard and Doris Reed have been sailing visitors around Molokai's waters since 1975.

SCUBA DIVING

Want to see turtles or manta rays up close? How about sharks? Molokai resident Bill Kapuni has been diving the waters around the island his entire life. He'll be happy to show you whatever you're brave enough to encounter. **Bill Kapuni's Snorkel and Dive,** Kaunakakai (© **808/553-9867**), can provide gear, a boat, and even instruction. Two-tank dives in his 22-foot Boston whaler cost $125 and include Bill's voluminous knowledge of the legends and lore of Hawaii. You can also just rent tanks for $11 a day.

On the West End, **The Lodge at Molokai Ranch** (© **888/627-8082** or 808/660-2824; www.molokairanch.com) offers scuba-diving trips from $125 to $275.

SNORKELING

When the waters are calm, Molokai offers excellent snorkeling: You'll see a wide range of butterfly fish, tangs, and angelfish. Good snorkeling can be found—when conditions are right—at many of Molokai's beaches (see the box titled "Molokai's Best Snorkel Spots," below). **Molokai Outdoors Activities** (© **877/553-4477** or 808/553-4477; www.molokai-outdoors.com) offers the least-expensive snorkel gear for rent ($9 a day for fins, mask, and snorkel, or $37 a week). Molokai Outdoors also offers snorkel/kayak tours for $130 per person.

For snorkeling tours on a boat, contact **Bill Kapuni's Snorkel & Dive,** Kaunakakai (© **808/553-9867**), which charges $65 for a 2½-hour trip. Walter Naki of **Molokai Action Adventures** (© **808/558-8184**) offers leisurely snorkeling, diving, and swimming trips in his 21-foot Boston whaler for $100 per person for a 4- to 6-hour custom tour.

Molokai's Best Snorkel Spots

Most Molokai beaches are too dangerous for snorkeling in winter, when big waves and strong currents are generated by storms that sweep down from Alaska. From mid-September to April, stick to Murphy Beach Park (also known as Kumimi Beach Park) on the East End. In summer, roughly May to mid-September, when the Pacific Ocean takes a holiday and turns into a flat lake, the whole west coast of Molokai opens up for snorkeling. Mike Holmes, of Molokai Ranch & Fun Hogs Hawaii, says the best spots are as follows:

Kawaikiunui, Ilio Point, and **Pohaku Moiliili** (West End)   These are all special places seldom seen by even those who live on Molokai. You can reach Kawaikiunui and Pohaku Moiliili on foot after a long, hot, dusty ride in a four-wheel-drive vehicle, but it's much easier and quicker to go by sea. See above for places to rent a kayak and get advice. It's about 2 miles as the crow flies from Pohaku Moiliili to Ilio Point.

Kapukahehu (Dixie Maru) Beach (West End)   This gold-sand family beach is well protected, and the reef is close and shallow. The name Dixie Maru comes from a 1920s Japanese fishing boat stranded off the rocky shore. One of the Molokai Ranch cowboys hung the wrecked boat's nameplate on a gate by Kapukahehu Beach, and the name Dixie Maru stuck. To get here, take Kaluakoi Road to the end of the pavement, and then take the footpath 300 feet to the beach.

Murphy (Kumimi) Beach Park ✎ (East End)   This beach is located between mile markers 20 and 21, off Kamehameha V Highway. The reef here is easily reachable, and the waters are calm year-round.

SPORT FISHING

Molokai's waters can provide prime sporting opportunities, whether you're looking for big-game sport fishing or bottom fishing. When customers are scarce, Capt. Joe Reich, who has been fishing the waters around Molokai for decades, goes commercial fishing, so he always knows where the fish are biting. He runs **Alyce C Sportfishing** out of Kaunakakai Harbor (© 808/558-8377; www.alycecsportfishing.com). A full day of fishing for up to six people is $400, three-fourths of a day is $350, and half a day is $300. You can usually persuade him to do a whale-watching cruise during the winter months.

For fly-fishing or light-tackle reef-fish trolling, contact Walter Naki at **Molokai Action Adventures** (© 808/558-8184). Walter's been fishing his entire life and loves to share his secret spots with visiting fishermen—he knows *the* place for bonefishing on the flats. A full-day trip in his 21-foot Boston whaler, for up to four people, is $300.

For deep-sea fishing, contact **Fun Hogs Hawaii** (© 808/567-6789). Fun Hogs has fishing excursions on a 27-foot, fully equipped sportfishing vessel. Prices are $365 for six passengers for 4 hours, $417 for 6 hours, and $550 for 8 hours.

If you just want to try your luck casting along the shoreline, **Molokai Outdoors Activities,** in the lobby of Hotel Molokai, just outside Kaunakakai (© 877/553-4477 or 808/553-4477; www.molokai-outdoors.com), offers the least expensive fishing poles for rent ($5 a day or $24 for the week), and can tell you where they're biting.

SURFING

Depending on the time of year and the wave conditions, Molokai can offer some great surfing for the beginner, as well as the expert. **Molokai Outdoors Activities,** in the lobby of Hotel Molokai, just outside Kaunakakai (© **877/553-4477** or 808/553-4477; www.molokai-outdoors.com), not only will know where the waves are, but they also rent gear: soft surfboards ($13 a day), short surfboards ($20 a day), and long boards ($24 a day). Good surfing spots include Kaunakakai Wharf in town, Hale O Lono Beach and Papohaku Beach on the West End, and Halawa Beach on the East End.

7 Hiking & Camping

HIKING MOLOKAI'S PEPEOPAE TRAIL

Molokai's most awesome hike is the **Pepeopae Trail** *🌟🌟*, which takes you back a few million years. On the cloud-draped trail (actually a boardwalk across the bog), you'll see mosses, sedges, native violets, knee-high ancient ohias, and lichens that evolved in total isolation over eons. Eerie intermittent mists blowing in and out will give you an idea of this island at its creation.

The narrow boardwalk, built by volunteers, protects the bog and keeps you out of the primal ooze. Don't venture off it; you could damage this fragile environment or get lost. The 3-mile round-trip takes about 90 minutes to hike—but first you have to drive about 20 miles from Kaunakakai, deep into the Molokai Forest Preserve on a four-wheel-drive road. *Warning:* Don't try this with a regular rental car. Plan a full day for this outing. Better yet, go on a guided nature hike with the **Nature Conservancy of Hawaii,** which guards this unusual ecosystem. For information, write to the Nature Conservancy at 1116 Smith St., Suite 201, Honolulu, HI 96817. No permit is required for this easy hike. Call ahead (© **808/537-4508** or 808/553-5236) to check on the condition of the ungraded, four-wheel-drive, red-dirt road that leads to the trail head and to let people know that you'll be up there.

To get here, take Highway 460 west from Kaunakakai for 3½ miles and turn right before the Maunawainui Bridge onto the unmarked Molokai Forest Reserve Road (sorry, there aren't any road signs). The pavement ends at the cemetery; continue on the dirt road. After about 2 to 2½ miles, you'll see a sign telling you that you are now in the Molokai Forest Reserve. At the Waikolu Lookout and picnic area, which is just over 9 miles on the Molokai Forest Reserve Road, sign in at the box near the entrance. Continue on the road for another 5 miles to a fork in the road with the sign PUU KOLEKOLE pointing to the right side of the fork. Do not turn right; instead, continue straight at the fork, which will lead to the clearly marked trail head. The drive will take about 45 minutes.

HIKING TO KALAUPAPA *🌟🌟*

This hike to the site of Molokai's famous leper colony is like going down a switchback staircase with what seems like a million steps. You don't always see the breathtaking view because you're too busy watching your step. It's easier going down (surprise!)—in about an hour, you'll go 2½ miles, from 2,000 feet to sea level. The trip up sometimes takes twice as long. The trail head starts on the *mauka* (inland) side of Highway 470, just past the Mule Barn (you can't miss it). Check in here at 7:30am, get a permit, and go before the mule train departs. You must be 16 or older (it's an old state law that kept kids out of the leper colony) and should be in good shape. Wear good hiking boots or sneakers; you won't make it past the first turn in sandals.

A Tip for the Adventurous

If it's action you crave, call **Molokai Action Adventures** (© 808/558-8184). Island guide Walter Naki will take you skin diving, reef trolling, kayaking, hunting, or hiking into Molokai's remote hidden valleys. Hiking tours are $50 per person for 4 hours; the number of participants is limited to no more than four. Not only does Walter know Molokai like the back of his hand, but he also loves being outdoors and talking story with visitors. He'll tell you about the island, the people, the politics, the myths, and anything else you want to know.

HIKING THE WEST END

Molokai's entire West End, some 53,000 acres, is open to hike tours through **The Lodge at Molokai Ranch** (© 888/627-8082 or 808/660-2824; www.molokairanch.com), which offers a range of hikes to fit different abilities. Prices range from $45 for an easy 2- to 3-hour hike to $85 for advanced hikes along the sea cliff coast.

Molokai Outdoors Activities, in the lobby of Hotel Molokai, just outside Kaunakakai (© 877/553-4477 or 808/553-4477; www.molokai-outdoors.com), has a range of hikes from a Halawa Cultural hike at $75 to an East End Cultural tour and waterfall hike for $180.

CAMPING

Bring your own camping equipment, as none is available for rent on the island.

AT THE BEACH

One of the best year-round places to camp on Molokai is **Papohaku Beach Park** 🏖, on the island's West End. This drive-up seaside site makes a great getaway. Facilities include restrooms, drinking water, outdoor showers, barbecue grills, and picnic tables. Groceries and gas are available in Maunaloa, 6 miles away. Kaluakoi Resort is a mile away. Get camping permits by contacting **Maui County Parks Department,** P.O. Box 526, Kaunakakai, HI 96748 (© 808/553-3204). Camping is limited to 3 days, but if nobody else has applied, the time limit is waived. The cost is $3 a person per night.

IN AN IRONWOOD FOREST

At the end of Highway 470 is the 234-acre piney woods known as **Palaau State Park** 🏖🏖, home to the Kalaupapa Lookout (the best vantage point for seeing the historic leper colony if you're not hiking or riding a mule in). It's airy and cool in the park's ironwood forest, where many love to camp at the designated state campground. Camping is free, but you'll need a permit from the **State Division of Parks** (© 808/567-6618). For more on the park, see p. 276.

8 Golf & Other Outdoor Activities

GOLF

Golf is one of Molokai's best-kept secrets: It's challenging and fun, tee times are open, and the rates are lower than your score will be. After being closed for a number of years, the **Kaluakoi Golf Course** (© 808/552-0255) is open again. After extensive renovation (repairs to irrigation, new grass planted, redesigned bunkers, and narrower fairways), all 18 holes are again in play. Most of the work was cosmetic, and the Ted Robinson–designed course is still as challenging as ever. Using the natural terrain and

Frommer's Favorite Molokai Experiences

Riding a Mule into a Leper Colony. Don't pass up the opportunity to see this hauntingly beautiful peninsula. Buzzy Sproat's mules go up and down the 3-mile Kalaupapa Trail (with 26 switchbacks) to Molokai's famous leper colony. The views are breathtaking: You'll see the world's highest sea cliffs (over 300 stories tall) and waterfalls plunging thousands of feet into the ocean. If you're afraid of heights, catch the views from the Kalaupapa Lookout.

Venturing into the Garden of Eden. Drive the 30 miles along Molokai's East End. Take your time. Stop to smell the flowers and pick guavas by the side of the road. Pull over for a swim. Wave at every car you pass and every person you see. At the end of the road, stand on the beach at Halawa Valley and see Hawaii as it must have looked in A.D. 650, when the first people arrived in the islands.

Celebrating the Ancient Hula. Hula is the heartbeat of Hawaiian culture, and Molokai is its birthplace. Although most visitors to Hawaii never get to see the real thing, it's possible to see it here—once a year, on the third Saturday in May, when Molokai celebrates the birth of the hula at its **Ka Hula Piko Festival.** The daylong affair includes dance, music, food, and crafts; see the "Maui, Molokai & Lanai Calendar of Events," in chapter 2 for details.

Strolling the Sands at Papohaku. Go early, when the tropical sun isn't so fierce, and stroll this 3-mile stretch of unspoiled golden sand on Molokai's West End. It's one of the longest beaches in Hawaii. The big surf and rip tides make swimming somewhat risky, but Papohaku is perfect for walking, beachcombing, and, in the evening, sunset watching.

Traveling Back in Time on the Pepeopae Trail. This awesome hike takes you through the Molokai Forest Reserve and back a few million years in time. Along the misty trail (actually a boardwalk across the bog), expect close encounters of the botanical kind: mosses, sedges, violets, lichens, and knee-high ancient ohias.

Soaking in the Warm Waters off Sandy Beach. On the East End, about 20 miles outside Kaunakakai—just before the road starts to climb to Halawa Valley—lies a small pocket of white sand known as Sandy Beach. Submerging yourself here in the warm, calm waters (an outer reef protects the cove) is a sensuous experience par excellence.

narrow fairways, there are some tough bunkers and water hazards to maneuver around. The first 9 holes are at sea level with panoramic views over the isolated 3-mile white-sand Papohaku Beach, the island of Oahu in the distance. A stiff wind is often present—this course provides a scenic and challenging experience. The back 9 holes play up along lush green hillsides, over a tropical gulch and back down to the shore. Kaluakoi offers a golf range, a practice area, and three sets of tees, making this course

Snorkeling Among Clouds of Butterfly Fish. The calm waters off Murphy (Kumimi) Beach, on the East End, are perfect for snorkelers. Just don your gear and head to the reef, where you'll find lots of exotic tropical fish, including long-nosed butterfly fish, saddle wrasses, and convict tangs.

Kayaking Along the North Shore. This is the Hawaii of your dreams: water-falls thundering down sheer cliffs, remote sand beaches, miles of tropical vegetation, and the sounds of the sea splashing on your kayak and the wind whispering in your ear. The best times to go are late March and early April, or in summer, especially August to September, when the normally galloping ocean lies down flat.

Watching the Sunset from a Coconut Grove. Kapuaiwa Coconut Beach Park, off Maunaloa Highway (Hwy. 460), is a perfect place to watch the sunset. The sky behind the coconut trees fills with a kaleidoscope of colors as the sun sinks into the Pacific. Be careful where you sit, though: Falling coconuts could have you seeing stars well before dusk.

Sampling the Local Brew. Saunter up to the Espresso Bar at the Coffees of Hawaii Plantation Store in Kualapuu for a fresh cup of java made from beans that were grown, processed, and packed on this 450-acre plantation. While you sip, survey the vast collection of native crafts.

Tasting Aloha at a Macadamia Nut Farm. It could be the owner, Tuddie Purdy, and his friendly disposition that make the macadamia nuts here taste so good. Or it could be his years of practice in growing, harvesting, and shelling them on his 1½-acre farm. Either way, Purdy produces a perfect crop. See how he does it on a short, free tour of Purdy's All-Natural Macadamia Nut Farm in Hoolehua, just a nut's throw from the airport.

Talking Story with the Locals. The number-one favorite pastime of most islanders is "talking story," or exchanging experiences and knowledge. It's an old Hawaiian custom that brings people, and generations, closer together. You can probably find residents more than willing to share their wisdom with you while fishing from the wharf at Kaunakakai, hanging out at Molokai Fish & Dive, or having coffee at any of the island's restaurants.

Posting a Nut. Why send a picturesque postcard to your friends and family back home when you can send a fresh coconut? The Hoolelua Post Office will supply the free coconuts, if you'll supply the $3.95 postage fee.

playable for all levels of golfers. Greens fees are $70 with cart. If you didn't bring your clubs, you can rent them from **Molokai Rentals and Tours,** Kaunakakai (© 808/553-5663; www.molokai-rentals.com). Prices start at $6 a day ($24 for the week).

The real find is the **Ironwood Hills Golf Course,** off Kalae Highway (© 808/567-6000). It's located just before the Molokai Mule Ride Mule Barn, on the road to the Lookout. One of the oldest courses in the state, Ironwood Hills (named after the two predominant features of the course, ironwood trees and hills) was built in 1929 by Del Monte Plantation for its executives. This unusual course, which sits in the cool air at 1,200 feet, delights with its rich foliage, open fairways, and spectacular views of the rest of the island. If you play here, use a trick developed by the local residents: After teeing off on the 6th hole, just take whatever clubs you need to finish playing the hole and a driver for the 7th hole, and park your bag under a tree. The climb to the 7th hole is steep—you'll be glad that you're only carrying a few clubs. Greens fees are $15 for 9 holes or $20 for 18 holes. Cart fees are $7 for 9 holes or $14 for 18. You can also rent a hand cart for just $2.50. Club rentals are $7 for 9 holes and $12 for 18.

BICYCLING

Molokai is a great place to see by bicycle. The roads are not very busy, and there are great places to pull off the road and take a quick dip.

Molokai Outdoors Activities, in the lobby of Hotel Molokai, just outside Kaunakakai (© **877/553-4477** or 808/553-4477; www.molokai-outdoors.com), offers a bike/kayak tour of the East End of Molokai, with snorkeling. All gear, lunch, guide, and transportation is $140. Bike rentals are $13 an hour, $26 a day, or $113 a week and include a complimentary bicycle rack for your rental.

The best mountain biking in the state is on the trails of **The Lodge at Molokai Ranch** (© **888/627-8082** or 808/660-2824; www.molokairanch.com). Imagine 53,000 acres with inter-crossing trails that weave up and down the West End to the beach—simply spectacular. Guided tours range from $45 for 2 to 3 hours, and bike rentals are $35 a day.

HORSEBACK RIDING

One of the most scenic places to go riding on Molokai is **Pu'u O Hoku Ranch** (© **808/558-8109;** www.puuohoku.com), about 25 miles outside Kaunakakai on the East End. Guided trail rides pass through green pasture on one of the largest working ranches on Molokai, then head up into the high mountain forest. Don't forget your camera: There are plenty of scenic views of waterfalls, the Pacific Ocean, and the islands of Maui and Lanai in the distance. Rates are $55 for an hour-long ride, $75 for a 2-hour ride, and $120 for a beach adventure.

For those looking for a little more than just a horseback ride, **The Lodge at Molokai Ranch** (© **888/627-8082** or 808/660-2824; www.molokairanch.com) offers a "Paniolo Roundup." You can learn horsemanship from the ranch's working cowboys and compete in traditional rodeo games; the half-day adventure is $85. Two-hour trail rides also are $85.

TENNIS

The only two tennis courts on Molokai are located at the **Mitchell Pauole Center** in Kaunakakai (© **808/553-5141**). Both are lit for night play and are available free on a first-come, first-served basis, with a 45-minute time limit if someone is waiting. You can rent a racket for just $4 a day ($16 a week) from **Molokai Rentals and Tours,** HC01 Box 28, Kaunakakai (© **808/553-5663;** www.molokai-rentals.com). You can also rent tennis rackets and balls from **Molokai Outdoors Activities,** in the lobby of Hotel Molokai, just outside Kaunakakai (© **877/553-4477** or 808/553-4477; www.molokai-outdoors.com).

9 Seeing the Sights

Note: You'll find the following attractions on the "Molokai" map on p. 253.

IN & AROUND KAUNAKAKAI

Kapuaiwa Coconut Grove/Kiowea Park ⭐ *(Kids)* This royal grove—1,000 coconut trees on 10 acres planted in 1863 by the island's high chief Kapua'iwa (later, King Kamehameha V)—is a major roadside attraction. The shoreline park is a favorite subject of sunset photographers and visitors who delight in a hand-lettered sign that warns: DANGER: FALLING COCONUTS. In its backyard, across the highway, stands Church Row: seven churches, each a different denomination—clear evidence of the missionary impact on Hawaii.

Along Maunaloa Hwy. (Hwy. 460), 2 miles west of Kaunakakai.

Post-A-Nut ⭐ Postmaster Margaret Keahi-Leary will help you say "Aloha" with a dried Molokai coconut. Just write a message on the coconut with a felt-tip pen, and she'll send it via U.S. mail. Coconuts are free, but postage starts at $3.95 for a mainland-bound coconut.

Hoolehua Post Office, Puu Peelua Ave. (Hwy. 480), near Maunaloa Hwy. (Hwy. 460). (C) **808/567-6144.** Mon–Fri 7:30–11:30am and 12:30–4:30pm.

Purdy's All-Natural Macadamia Nut Farm (Na Hua O'Ka Aina) ⭐ *(Finds)* The Purdys have made macadamia-nut buying an entertainment event, offering tours of the homestead and giving lively demonstrations of nutshell-cracking in the shade of their towering trees. The tour of the 70-year-old nut farm explains the growth, bearing, harvesting, and shelling processes, so that by the time you bite into the luxurious macadamia nut, you'll have more than a passing knowledge of its entire life cycle.

Lihi Pali Ave. (behind Molokai High School), Hoolehua. (C) **808/567-6601.** www.visitmolokai.com. Free admission. Mon–Fri 9:30am–3:30pm; Sat 10am–2pm. Closed holidays.

THE NORTH COAST

Even if you don't get a chance to see Hawaii's most dramatic coast in its entirety—not many people do—you shouldn't miss the opportunity to glimpse it from the **Kalaupapa Lookout** at Palauu State Park. On the way, there are a few diversions (arranged here in geographical order).

EN ROUTE TO THE NORTH COAST

Coffees of Hawaii Plantation Store The defunct Del Monte pineapple town of Kualapuu is rising again—only this time coffee is the catch, not pineapples. Located in the cool foothills, Coffees of Hawaii has planted coffee beans on 600 acres of former pineapple land. The plantation is irrigating the plants with a high-tech, continuous water and fertilizer drip system. You can see it all on the walking tour; call 24 hours in advance to set it up. The Plantation Store sells arts and crafts from Molokai. Stop by the Espresso Bar for a Mocha Mama (Molokai coffee, ice, chocolate ice cream, chocolate syrup, whipped cream, and chocolate shavings on top). It'll keep you going all day—maybe even all night.

Hwy. 480 (near the junction of Hwy. 470). (C) **800/709-BEAN** or 808/567-9241. www.molokaicoffee.com. Walking tour $7 adults, $3.50 children 5–12. Tours Mon–Fri 9:30 and 11:30am. Store open Mon–Fri 9am–4pm; Sat 8am–4pm; Sun 10am–4pm.

(Kids Especially for Kids

Flying a Kite (p. 284)   Not only can you get a guaranteed-to-fly kite at the **Big Wind Kite Factory** (© 808/552-2634) in Maunaloa, but kite designer Jonathan Socher offers free kite-flying classes to kids, who'll learn how to make their kites soar, swoop, and, most important, stay in the air for more than 5 minutes.

Spending the Day at Murphy (Kumimi) Beach Park (p. 267)   Just beyond Wailua on the East End is this small wayside park that's perfect for kids. You'll find safe swimming conditions, plenty of shade from the ironwood trees, and small pavilions with picnic tables and barbecue grills.

Watching Whales (p. 268)   From mid-December to mid-March, kids of all ages can go whale-watching on Molokai Charters' 42-foot sloop, *Satan's Doll*.

Renting Gear   You don't have to schlep your car seat, jogging stroller, regular stroller, or portable crib to Molokai. **Molokai Outdoors Activities,** in the lobby of Hotel Molokai, just outside Kaunakakai (© 877/553-4477 or 808/553-4477; www.molokai-outdoors.com), has all that equipment for rent at very reasonable prices (daily and weekly rates).

Molokai Museum and Cultural Center   En route to the California Gold Rush in 1849, Rudolph W. Meyer (a German professor) came to Molokai, married the high chieftess Kalama, and began to operate a small sugar plantation near his home. Now on the National Register of Historic Places, this restored 1878 sugar mill, with its century-old steam engine, mule-driven cane crusher, copper clarifiers, and redwood evaporating pan (all in working order), is the last of its kind in Hawaii. The mill also houses a museum that traces the history of sugar growing on Molokai and features special events, such as wine tastings every 2 months, taro festivals, an annual music festival, and occasional classes in ukulele making, loom weaving, and sewing. Call for a schedule.

Meyer Sugar Mill, Hwy. 470 (just after the turnoff for the Ironwood Hills Golf Course and 2 miles below Kalaupapa Overlook), Kalae. © 808/567-6436. Admission $2.50 adults, $1 students. Mon–Sat 10am–2pm.

Palaau State Park 🏕   This 234-acre piney-woods park, 8 miles out of Kaunakakai, doesn't look like much until you get out of the car and take a hike, which literally puts you between a rock and a hard place. Go right and you end up on the edge of Molokai's magnificent sea cliffs, with its panoramic view of the well-known Kalaupapa leper colony; go left and you come face to face with a stone phallus.

If you have no plans to scale the cliffs by mule or on foot (see "Hiking & Camping," earlier in this chapter), the **Kalaupapa Lookout** 🏕🏕🏕 is the only place from which to see the former place of exile. The trail is marked, and historic photos and interpretive signs will explain what you're seeing.

It's airy and cool in the ironwood forest, where camping is free at the designated state campground. You'll need a permit from the **State Division of Parks** (© 808/567-6618). Not many people seem to camp here, probably because of the legend associated with the **Phallic Rock** 🏕. Six feet high, pointed at an angle that means business, Molokai's famous Phallic Rock is a legendary fertility tool—according to

Hawaiian legend, a woman who wishes to become pregnant need only spend the night near the rock and, *voilà!* It's probably just a coincidence, of course, but Molokai does have a growing number of young, pregnant women.

Phallic Rock is at the end of a well-worn uphill path that passes an ironwood grove and several other rocks that vaguely resemble sexual body parts. No mistaking the big guy, though. Supposedly, it belonged to Nanahoa, a demigod who quarreled with his wife, Kawahuna, over a pretty girl. In the tussle, Kawahuna was thrown over the cliff, and both husband and wife were turned to stone. Of all the phallic rocks in Hawaii and the Pacific, this is the one to see. It's featured on a postcard with a tiny, awestruck Japanese woman standing next to it.

At the end of Hwy. 470.

THE LEGACY OF FATHER DAMIEN: KALAUPAPA NATIONAL HISTORIC PARK 🐦🐦🐦

Kalaupapa, an old tongue of lava that sticks out to form a peninsula, became infamous because of man's inhumanity to victims of a formerly incurable contagious disease.

King Kamehameha V sent the first lepers—nine men and three women—into exile on this lonely shore, at the base of ramparts that rise like temples against the Pacific, on January 6, 1866. By 1874, more than 11,000 lepers had been dispatched to die in one of the world's most beautiful—and lonely—places. They called Kalaupapa "The Place of the Living Dead."

Leprosy is actually one of the world's least contagious diseases, transmitted only by direct, repetitive contact over a long period of time. It's caused by a germ, *Mycobacterium leprae,* that attacks the nerves, skin, and eyes and is found mainly, but not exclusively, in tropical regions. American scientists found a cure for the disease in the 1940s.

Before science intervened, there was Father Damien. Born to wealth in Belgium, Joseph de Veuster traded a life of excess for exile among lepers; he devoted himself to caring for the afflicted at Kalaupapa. Horrified by the conditions in the leper colony, Father Damien worked at Kalaupapa for 11 years, building houses, schools, and churches, and giving hope to his patients. He died on April 15, 1889, in Kalaupapa, of leprosy. He was 49.

A hero nominated for Catholic sainthood, Father Damien is buried not in his tomb next to Molokai's St. Philomena Church but in his native Belgium. Well, most of him anyway. His hand was recently returned to Molokai, and was reinterred at Kalaupapa as a relic of his martyrdom.

This small peninsula is probably the final resting place of more than 11,000 souls. The sand dunes are littered with grave markers, sorted by the religious affiliation— Catholic, Protestant, Buddhist—of those who died here. But so many are buried in unmarked graves that no accurate census of the dead exists.

Kalaupapa is now a National Historic Park (© **808/567-6802;** www.nps.gov/kala) and one of Hawaii's richest archaeological preserves, with sites that date from A.D. 1000. About 60 former patients chose to remain in the tidy village of whitewashed houses with statues of angels in their yards. The original name for their former affliction, leprosy, was officially banned in Hawaii by the state legislature in 1981. The name used now is "Hansen's disease," for Dr. Gerhard Hansen of Norway, who discovered the germ in 1873. The few remaining residents of Kalaupapa still call the disease leprosy, although none are too keen on being called lepers.

Kalaupapa welcomes visitors who arrive on foot, by mule, or by small plane. Father Damien's St. Philomena church, built in 1872, is open to visitors, who can see it from a yellow school bus driven by resident tour guide Richard Marks, an ex-seaman and sheriff who survived the disease. You won't be able to roam freely, and you'll be allowed to enter only the museum, the crafts shop, and the church.

MULE RIDES TO KALAUPAPA   The first turn's a gasp, and it's all downhill from there. You can close your eyes and hold on for dear life, or slip the reins over the pommel and sit back, letting the mule do the walking down the precipitous path to Kalaupapa National Historic Park.

Even if you have only 1 day to spend on Molokai, spend it on a mule. This is a once-in-a-lifetime ride. The cliffs are taller than a 300-story skyscraper, but Buzzy Sproat's mules go safely up and down the narrow 3-mile trail daily, rain or shine. Starting at the top of the nearly perpendicular ridge (1,600 ft. high), the surefooted mules step down the muddy trail, pausing often on the 26 switchbacks to calculate their next move—and always, it seems to us, veering a little too close to the edge. Each switchback is numbered; by the time you get to number four, you'll catch your breath, put the mule on cruise control, and begin to enjoy Hawaii's most awesome trail ride.

The mule tours are offered once daily starting at 8am, and they last until about 3:30pm. It costs $165 per person for the all-day adventure, which includes the round-trip mule ride, a guided tour of the settlement, a visit to Father Damien's church and grave, lunch at Kalawao, and souvenirs. To go, you must be at least 16 years old and physically fit. Contact **Molokai Mule Ride** ★★★, 100 Kalae Highway, Suite 104, on Highway 470, 5 miles north of Highway 460 (© **800/567-7550,** or 808/567-6088 between 8 and 10pm; www.muleride.com). Advance reservations (at least 2 weeks ahead) are required.

SEEING KALAUPAPA BY PLANE   The fastest and easiest way to get to Kalaupapa is by hopping on a plane and zipping to Kalaupapa airport. From here, you can pick up the same Kalaupapa tour that the mule riders and hikers take. **Molokai Mule Ride** ★★★, 100 Kalae Hwy., Suite 104, on Highway 470, 5 miles north of Highway 460 (© **800/567-7550,** or 808/567-6088 between 8 and 10pm; www.muleride.com) will pick you up at the Kalaupapa airport and take you to some of the area's most scenic spots, including Kalawao, where Father Damien's church still stands, and the town of Kalaupapa. Packages include a round-trip flight to Kalaupapa, entry permits, historical park tour with Damien Tours, and a light picnic lunch and cost $299 from Honolulu. All visitors must be at least 16 years old.

SEEING KALAUPAPA BY FERRY/HIKING   From Maui, take the *Molokai Princess* ferry to Molokai (© **800/275-6969** or 808/667-6165; www.mauiprincess. com), where you are met and transported by van to the top of the 1,700-foot sea cliffs. Here you hike down the 3-mile trail to the Kalaupapa National Historic Park; at the park you are met by Damien tours and given a van tour of the peninsula, during which you'll visit Father Damien's St. Philomena Church, see his early gravesite, and hear the stories of struggle and courage of the residents of Kalaupapa. The only catch is you have to hike back up the 1,700-foot cliffs, where you are picked up by the van and returned to the ferry dock for the trip back to Maui. This fabulous experience really should be undertaken only by the physically fit (it will take about an hour hiking down and another 1½ hr. to hike back up). Cost for ferry, transportation, tour, and lunch is $249 (participants must be 16 or older). If you would like to hike in, tour, then fly back to Maui, the fee is $299.

THE WEST END
MAUNALOA
In the first and only urban renewal on Molokai, the 1920s-era pineapple-plantation town of Maunaloa is being reinvented. Streets are getting widened and paved, and curbs and sidewalks are being added to serve a new tract of houses. Historic Maunaloa is becoming Maunaloa Village—there's already a town center with a park, a small restaurant, a triplex movie theater, a gas station, a KFC, and an upscale lodge.

This master-planned village will also have a museum and artisans' studios—uptown stuff for Molokai. The downside is the constant clouds of red dust raised by construction crews.

ON THE NORTHWEST SHORE: MOOMOMI DUNES
Undisturbed for centuries, the Moomomi Dunes, on Molokai's northwest shore, are a unique treasure chest of great scientific value. The area may look like just a pile of sand as you fly over on the final approach to Hoolehua Airport, but Moomomi Dunes is much more than that. Archaeologists have found adz quarries, ancient Hawaiian burial sites, and shelter caves; botanists have identified five endangered plant species; and marine biologists are finding evidence that endangered green sea turtles are coming out from the waters once again to lay eggs here. The greatest discovery, however, belongs to Smithsonian Institute ornithologists, who have found bones of prehistoric birds—some of them flightless—that existed nowhere else on earth.

Accessible by jeep trails that thread downhill to the shore, this wild coast is buffeted by strong afternoon breezes. It's hot, dry, and windy, so take water, sunscreen, and a windbreaker.

At Kawaaloa Bay, a 20-minute walk to the west, there's a broad golden beach that you can have all to yourself. *Warning: Due to the rough seas, stay out of the water.* Within the dunes there's a 920-acre preserve accessible via monthly guided nature tours led by the **Nature Conservancy of Hawaii;** call ✆ **808/553-5236** or 808/524-0779 for an exact schedule and details.

To get here, take Highway 460 (Maunaloa Hwy.) from Kaunakakai; turn right onto Highway 470, and follow it to Kualapuu. At Kualapuu, turn left on Highway 480 and go through Hoolehua Village; it's 3 miles to the bay.

THE EAST END
The East End is a cool and inviting green place that's worth a drive to the end of King Kamehameha V Highway (Hwy. 450). Unfortunately, the trail that leads into the area's greatest natural attraction, Halawa Valley, is now off-limits.

A HORSEBACK RIDE TO ILIILIOPAE HEIAU
On horseback (where the elevated view is magnificent), you bump along a dirt trail through an incredible mango grove, bound for an ancient temple of human sacrifice. This temple of doom—right out of *Indiana Jones*—is Iliiliopae, a huge rectangle of stone made of 90 million rocks, overlooking the once-important village of Mapulehu and four ancient fishponds. The horses trek under the perfumed mangoes, then head uphill through a kiawe forest filled with Java plums to the *heiau* (temple), which stands across a dry stream bed under cloud-spiked Kaunolu, the 4,970-foot island summit.

Hawaii's most powerful *heiau* attracted *kahuna* (priests) from all over the islands. They came to learn the rules of human sacrifice at this university of sacred rites. Contrary to Hollywood's version, historians say that the victims here were always men, not young virgins, and that they were strangled, not thrown into a volcano, while priests sat on lauhala mats watching silently. Spooky, eh?

This is the biggest, oldest, and most famous *heiau* on Molokai. The massive 22-foot-high stone altar is dedicated to Lono, the Hawaiian god of fertility. The *heiau* resonates with *mana* (power) strong enough to lean on. Legend says Iliiliopae was built in a single night by a thousand men who passed rocks hand over hand through the Wailau Valley from the other side of the island; in exchange for the rock *(ili'ili)*, each received a shrimp *('opae)*. Others say it was built by *menehune,* mythic elves who accomplished Herculean feats.

After the visit to the temple, your horse takes you back to the mango grove. Contact **Molokai Wagon Rides,** King Kamehameha V Highway (Hwy. 450), at mile marker 15, Kaunakakai, HI 96748 ((**808/558-8380**). The tour and horseback ride costs $50 per person. The hour-long ride goes up to the *heiau,* then beyond it to the top of the mountain for those breathtaking views, and finally back down to the beach.

KAMAKOU PRESERVE

It's hard to believe, but close to the nearly mile-high summit here, it rains more than 80 inches a year—enough to qualify as a rainforest. The Molokai Forest, as it was historically known, is the source of 60% of Molokai's water. Nearly 3,000 acres, from the summit to the lowland forests of eucalyptus and pine, are now held by the Nature Conservancy, which has identified 219 Hawaiian plants that grow here exclusively. The preserve is also the last stand of the endangered Molokai thrush *(olomao)* and Molokai creeper *(kawawahie).*

To get to the preserve, take the Forest Reserve road from Kaunakakai. It's a 45-minute, four-wheel-drive trip on a dirt trail to Waikolu Lookout Campground; from here, you can venture into the wilderness preserve on foot across a boardwalk on a 1½-hour hike (see "Hiking Molokai's Pepeopae Trail," earlier in this chapter). For more information, contact the **Nature Conservancy** ((**808/553-5236**).

EN ROUTE TO HALAWA VALLEY

No visit to Molokai is complete without at least a passing glance at the island's **ancient fishponds,** a singular achievement in Pacific aquaculture. With their hunger for fresh fish and lack of ice or refrigeration, Hawaiians perfected aquaculture in A.D. 1400, before Christopher Columbus "discovered" America. They built gated, U-shaped stone and coral walls on the shore to catch fish on the incoming tide, then would raise them in captivity. The result: a constant, ready supply of fresh fish.

The ponds, which stretch for 20 miles along Molokai's south shore and are visible from Kamehameha V Highway (Hwy. 450), offer insight into the island's ancient population. It took something like a thousand people to tend a single fishpond, and more than 60 ponds once existed on this coast. All the fishponds are named; a few are privately owned. Some are silted in by red-dirt runoff from south coast gulches; others have been revived by folks who raise fish and seaweed.

The largest, 54-acre **Keawa Nui Pond,** is surrounded by a 3-foot-high, 2,000-foot-long stone wall. **Alii Fish Pond,** reserved for kings, is visible through the coconut groves at One Alii Beach Park (p. 266). From the road, you can see **Kalokoeli Pond,** 6 miles east of Kaunakakai on the highway.

Our Lady of Sorrows Catholic Church, one of five built by Father Damien on Molokai and the first outside Kalaupapa, sits across the highway from a fishpond. Park in the church lot (except on Sun) for a closer look.

Moments **Halawa Valley: A Hike Back in History**

"There are things on Molokai, sacred things, that you may not be able to see or may not hear, but they are there," said Pilipo Solotario, who was born and raised in Halawa Valley, and survived the 1946 tsunami that barreled into the ancient valley. "As Hawaiians, we respect these things."

If people are going to "like Molokai," Solotario feels it is important that they learn about the history and culture; that is part of the secret of appreciating the island.

"I see my role, and I'm 67 years old, as educating people, outsiders on our culture, our history," he said at the beginning of his cultural hike into his family property in Halawa Valley. "To really appreciate Molokai, you need to understand and know things so that you are pono, you are right with the land and don't disrespect the culture. Then, then you see the real Molokai."

Solotario and his family, who own the land in the valley, are the only people allowed to hike into Halawa. They lead daily tours that begin at the County Park pavilion with a history of the valley, a discussion of Hawaiian culture, and a display of the fruits, trees, and other flora you will be seeing in the valley. As you hike through the valley, Solotario stops to point out historical and cultural aspects, including chanting in Hawaiian before entering a sacred heiau. At the falls, after another brief chant, visitors can swim in the brisk waters of the waterfall. Cost for the 4-hour tour is $75. Contact **The Lodge at Molokai Ranch** (© **888/627-8082** or 808/660-2824) for more information. There's also information online at www.molokai-aloha.com/hikes. Bring insect repellent, water, a snack, and a swimsuit. And don't forget your camera.

Note that if you venture away from the County Park into the valley on your own, you are trespassing and can be prosecuted.

St. Joseph's Catholic Church   The afternoon sun strikes St. Joseph's Church with such a bold ray of light that it looks as if God is about to perform a miracle. This little 1876 wood-frame church is one of four Father Damien built "topside" on Molokai. Restored in 1971, the church stands beside a seaside cemetery, where feral cats play under the gaze of a Damien statue amid gravestones decorated with flower leis.

King Kamehameha V Hwy. (Hwy. 450), just after mile marker 10.

Smith Bronte Landing Site   In 1927 Charles Lindbergh soloed the Atlantic Ocean in a plane called *The Spirit of St. Louis* and became an American hero. That same year, Ernie Smith and Emory B. Bronte took off from Oakland, California, on July 14, in a single-engine Travelair aircraft named *The City of Oakland,* and headed across the Pacific Ocean for Honolulu, 2,397 miles away. The next day, after running out of fuel, they crash-landed upside-down in a kiawe thicket on Molokai, but emerged unhurt to become the first civilians to fly to Hawaii from the U.S. mainland. The 25-hour, 2-minute flight landed Smith and Bronte a place in aviation history—and on a roadside marker on Molokai.

King Kamehameha V Hwy. (Hwy. 450), at mile marker 11, on the *makai* (ocean) side.

HALAWA VALLEY 🖈

Of the five great valleys of Molokai, only Halawa, with its two waterfalls, golden beach, sleepy lagoon, great surf, and offshore island, is easily accessible. Unfortunately, the trail through fertile Halawa Valley, which was inhabited for centuries, and on to the 250-foot Moaula Falls has been closed for some time. One operator conducts hikes to the falls (see box below).

You can spend a day at the county beach park (described under "Beaches," earlier in this chapter), but do not venture into the valley on your own. In a kind of 21st-century *kapu,* the private landowners in the valley, worried about slip-and-fall lawsuits, have posted NO TRESPASSING signs on their property.

To get to Halawa Valley, drive north from Kaunakakai on Highway 450 for 30 miles along the coast to the end of the road, which descends into the valley past Jersalema Hou Church. If you'd just like a glimpse of the valley on your way to the beach, there's a scenic overlook along the road: After Puuo Hoku Ranch at mile marker 25, the narrow two-lane road widens at a hairpin curve, and you'll find the overlook on your right; it's 2 miles more to the valley floor.

10 Shopping

KAUNAKAKAI

Molokai Surf, Molokai Island Creations, and **Lourdes** are clothing and gift shops in close proximity to one another in downtown Kaunakakai, where most of the retail shops sell T-shirts, muumuus, surf wear, and informal apparel. For food shopping, there are several good options. Because many visitors stay in condos, knowing the grocery stores is especially important. Other than that, serious shoppers will be disappointed, unless they love kites or native-wood vessels. The following are Kaunakakai's notable stores.

Imamura Store   Wilfred Imamura, whose mother founded this store, recalls the old railroad track that stretched from the pier to a spot across the street. "We brought our household things from the pier on a hand-pumped vehicle," he recalls. His store, appropriately, is a leap into the past, a marvelous amalgam of precious old-fashioned things. Rubber boots, Hawaiian-print tablecloths, Japanese tea plates, ukulele cases, plastic slippers, and even coconut bikini tops line the shelves. But it's not all nostalgia: The Molokai T-shirts, jeans, and palaka shorts are of good quality and inexpensive, and the pareu fabrics are a find. In Kaunakakai. ✆ 808/553-5615.

Molokai Drugs   David Mikami, whose father-in-law founded this pharmacy in 1935, has made this more than a drugstore. It's a gleaming, friendly stop full of life's basic necessities, with generous amenities such as a phone and a restroom for passersby. Here you'll find the best selection of guidebooks, books about Molokai, and maps, as well as greeting cards, paperbacks, cassette players, flip-flops, and every imaginable essential. The Mikamis are a household name on the island not only because of their pharmacy, but also because the family has shown exceptional kindness to the often economically strapped Molokaians. In Kamoi Professional Center. ✆ 808/553-5790.

Molokai Fish & Dive   Here you'll find the island's largest selection of T-shirts and souvenirs, crammed in among fishing, snorkeling, and outdoor gear that you can rent or buy. Find your way among the fish nets, boogie boards, diving equipment, bamboo rakes, beach towels, postcards, juices and soft drinks, disposable cameras, and staggering miscellany of this chockablock store. One entire wall is lined with T-shirts, and the selection of Molokai books and souvenirs is extensive. The staff is happy to point out the best snorkeling spots of the day. In Kaunakakai. (C) **808/553-5926.**

Molokai Surf This brand-new wooden building now houses Molokai Surf and its selection of skateboards, surf shorts, sweatshirts, sunglasses, T-shirts, footwear, boogie boards, backpacks, and a broad range of clothing and accessories for life in the surf and sun. In Kaunakakai. 130 Kamehameha V Hwy. (C) **808/553-5093.**

Take's Variety Store If you need luggage tags, buzz saws, toys, candy, cloth dolls, canned goods, canteens, camping equipment, hardware, batteries, candles, pipe fittings, fishing supplies—whew!—and other products for work and play, this 54-year-old variety store is the answer. You may suffer from claustrophobia in the crowded, dusty aisles, but Take's carries everything. In Kaunakakai. (C) **808/553-5442.**

EDIBLES

For fresh-baked goods, see the review of Kanemitsu's Bakery & Restaurant on p. 264.

Friendly Market Center You can't miss this salmon-colored wooden storefront on the main drag of "downtown" Kaunakakai, where people of all generations can be found just talking story in the Molokai way. Friendly's has an especially good selection of produce and healthy foods—from local poi to Glenlivet. Blue-corn tortilla chips, soy milk, organic brown rice, a good selection of pasta sauces, and Kumu Farms macadamia-nut pesto, the island's stellar gourmet food, are among the items that surpass standard grocery-store fare. In Kaunakakai. (C) **808/553-5595.**

Misaki's Grocery and Dry Goods Established in 1922, this third-generation local legend is one of Kaunakakai's two grocery stores. Some of its notable items: chopped garlic from Gilroy, California, fresh luau leaves (taro greens), fresh okra, Boca Burgers, large Korean chestnuts in season, gorgeous bananas, and an ATM. The fish section includes akule and ahi, fresh and dried, but the stock consists mostly of meats, produce, baking products, and a humongous array of soft drinks. Liquor, stationery, candies, and paper products round out the selection of this full-service grocery. In Kaunakakai. (C) **808/553-5505.**

Molokai Wines & Spirits This is your best bet on the island for a decent bottle of wine. The shop offers 200 labels, including Caymus, Silver Oak, Joseph Phelps, Heitz, Bonny Doon, and a carefully culled European selection. *Wine Spectator* reviews are tacked to some of the selections, which always helps, and the snack options include imported gourmet cheeses, salami, and Carr's biscuits. In Kaunakakai. (C) **808/553-5009.**

EN ROUTE TO THE NORTH COAST

Coffees of Hawaii Plantation Store and Espresso Bar This is a fairly slick—for Molokai—combination coffee bar, store, and gallery for more than 30 artists and craftspeople from Molokai, Maui, and the Big Island. Sold here are the Malulani Estate and Muleskinner coffees that are grown, processed, and packed on the 500-acre plantation surrounding the shop, as well as Hawaii-grown flavored coffees. See p. 275 for details on plantation tours. You may find better prices on coffee at other retail outlets, but the gift items are worth a look: pikake and plumeria soaps from Kauai, perfumes and pure beeswax candles from Maui, koa bookmarks and hair sticks, pottery, woods, and baskets. Hwy. 480 (near the junction of Hwy. 470), Kualapuu. (C) **800/709-BEAN** or 808/567-9023.

Molokai Museum Gift Shop The restored 1878 sugar mill sits 1,500 feet above the town of Kualapuu. It's a considerable drive from town but a good cause for those who'd like to support the museum and the handful of local artisans who sell their crafts, fabrics, cookbooks, quilt sets, and other gift items in the tiny shop. There's also a modest selection of cards, T-shirts, coloring books, and, at Christmastime, handmade ornaments made of lauhala and koa. Meyer Sugar Mill, Hwy. 470 (just after the turnoff for the Ironwood Hills Golf Course, and 2 miles below Kalaupapa Overlook), Kalae. (C) 808/567-6436.

EDIBLES
Kualapuu Market   This market, in its third generation, is a stone's throw from the Coffees of Hawaii store. It's a scaled-down, one-stop shop with wine, food, and necessities—and a surprisingly presentable, albeit small, assortment of produce, from Molokai sweet potatoes to Ka'u navel oranges in season. The shelves are filled with canned goods, propane, rope, hoses, paper products, and baking goods, reflecting the uncomplicated, rural lifestyle of the area. In Kualapuu. (C) 808/567-6243.

THE WEST END
Big Wind Kite Factory & the Plantation Gallery   Jonathan and Daphne Socher, kite designers and inveterate Bali-philes, have combined their interests in a kite factory/import shop that dominates the commercial landscape of Maunaloa, the reconstituted plantation town. Maunaloa's naturally windy conditions make it ideal for kite-flying classes, which are offered free when conditions are right. The adjoining Plantation Gallery features local handicrafts such as milo-wood bowls, locally made T-shirts, Hawaii-themed sandblasted glassware, baskets of lauhala and other fibers, and Hawaiian-music CDs. Many Balinese handicrafts, from jewelry to clothing and fabrics, are also for sale. In Maunaloa. (C) 808/552-2364.

Lodge & Beach Village at Molokai Ranch Logo Shop   Located between the front desk check-in and the bike rentals in a recently renovated wooden building, this shop can outfit you for life's great adventures. Heavy-duty sweatshirts, Bullfrog sunscreens, sandals, swimwear, T-shirts, walking sticks, and fashionable dresses line the shelves. The food items and souvenirs are also diverse: mugs, magnets, CDs and cassettes, Molokai jams and jellies, mobiles, toys, plastic buckets, lidded koa boxes, fine wines, cold beer, Muleskinner coffees, coconut-shell soap dishes, picture frames, and other attractive gifts to go. In Maunaloa. (C) 808/552-2791.

Maunaloa General Store   Maunaloa's only general store sells everything from paper products to batteries, dairy products, frozen and fresh meats, wine, canned goods, and a cross section of necessities. In Maunaloa. (C) 808/552-2346.

A Touch of Molokai   Even though the Kalaukoi Hotel is closed, this fabulous shop remains open. It is well worth the drive. The surf shorts and aloha shirts sold here are better than the norm, with attractive, up-to-date choices by Jams, Quiksilver, and other name brands. Tencel dresses, South Pacific shell necklaces (up to $400), and a magnificent, hand-turned milo bowl also caught our attention. Most impressive are the wiliwili, kamani, and soap-berry leis and a handsome array of lauhala bags, all made on Molokai. At Kaluakoi Hotel & Golf Club. (C) 808/552-0133.

THE EAST END
EDIBLES
The Neighborhood Store 'N Counter   The Neighborhood Store, the only grocery on the East End, sells batteries, film, aspirin, cookies, beer, Molokai produce, candies, paper products, and other sundries. There's good food pouring out of the kitchen for the breakfast and lunch counter too. See "Where to Dine," earlier in this chapter, for a restaurant review. In Pukoo. (C) 808/558-8498.

11 Molokai After Dark

Hotel Molokai, in Kaunakakai (© **808/553-5347**), offers live entertainment from local musicians poolside and in the dining room on Friday from 4 to 11pm. With its South Seas ambience and poolside setting, it's become the island's premier venue for local and visiting entertainers.

Molokai musicians to watch for include **Pound for Pound,** a powerful group of artists, each over 250 pounds. The members are lead vocalist Jack Stone, Shane Dudoit, Danny Reyes, John Pele, and Alika Lani. As popular off-island as on, they perform Hawaiian, reggae, country, and contemporary Hawaiian numbers, many of them originals. Their CD, *100% Molokai,* has become a local legend.

Darryl Labrado is a teen phenomenon and the island's rising star. He sings and plays the ukulele to a huge local following. And **Pa'a Pono,** with its contemporary Hawaiian and reggae sounds, is a familiar name on the local nightlife circuit. *Molokai Now,* a CD anthology of original music from Molokai, is a terrific memento for those who love the island and its music.

Movie buffs, too, finally have a place to call their own on Molokai. **Maunaloa Cinemas** (© **808/552-2707**) is a triplex theater that shows first-run movies in the middle of Maunaloa town—four screenings a day at each of the three theaters.

Also in Maunaloa, the lounge at **The Lodge at Molokai Ranch** (© **888/627-8082** or 808/660-2824) offers live music Friday and Saturday from 7 to 9pm, ranging from Hawaiian songs to keiki hula.

12

Lanai: A Different Kind of Paradise

An old shield volcano in the rain shadow of Maui, Lanai (pronounced lah-*nigh*-ee) is the nation's biggest defunct pineapple patch—and now claims to be one of the world's top tropical destinations. It's a bold claim because so little is here. There are no direct flights from the mainland, and there's nary a stoplight on the island's mere 30 miles of paved road. It's almost as if this quiet, gentle oasis—known, paradoxically, for both its small-town feel and its celebrity appeal—demands that its visitors go to great lengths to get here in order to ensure that they will appreciate it.

As soon as you arrive on Lanai, you'll feel the small-town coziness. People wave to every car; residents stop to "talk story" with their friends; fishing and working in the garden are considered priorities in life; and leaving the keys in the car's ignition is standard practice. Don't expect a lot of dining or accommodations choices (Lanai has even fewer than Molokai). This almost virgin island is unspoiled by what passes for progress, except for a tiny 1920s-era plantation village—and, of course, the village's fancy new arrivals: two first-class luxury hotels where room rates start at $400 a night and go up from there.

For generations, Lanai was little more than a small village, owned and operated by the pineapple company, surrounded by acres of pineapple fields. The few visitors to the island were either relatives of the mainly Filipino residents or occasional weekend hunters. Life in the 1960s was pretty much the same as in the 1930s. But all that changed in 1990, when The Lodge at Koele, a 102-room hotel resembling an opulent English Tudor mansion, opened its doors, followed a year later by the 250-room Manele Bay Hotel, a Mediterranean-style luxury resort overlooking Hulopoe Bay. Overnight, the isolated island was transformed: Corporate jets streamed into tiny Lanai Airport, former plantation workers were retrained in the art of serving gourmet meals, and the population of 2,500 swelled with transient visitors and outsiders coming to work in the island's new hospitality industry. Microsoft billionaire Bill Gates chose the island for his lavish wedding, buying up all of its hotel rooms to fend off the press—and uncomplicated Lanai went on the map as a vacation spot for the rich and powerful.

But this island is also a place where people come looking for dramatic beauty, quiet, solitude, and to experience nature away from the bright lights of Waikiki, the publicity of Maui, and the hoopla surrounding most resorts. The sojourners who find their way to Lanai come seeking the dramatic views, the tropical fusion of stars at night, and the chance to be alone with the elements.

They also come for the wealth of activities: snorkeling and swimming in the marine preserve known as Hulopoe Bay;

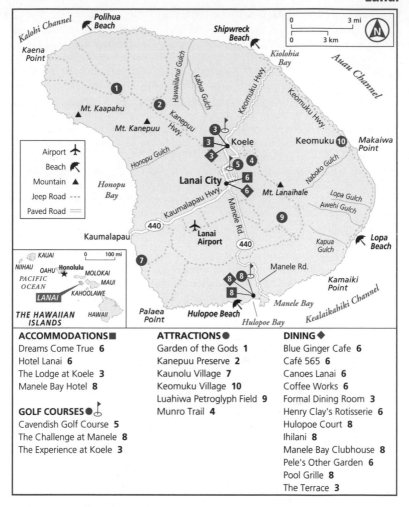

Lanai

ACCOMMODATIONS ■
Dreams Come True **6**
Hotel Lanai **6**
The Lodge at Koele **3**
Manele Bay Hotel **8**

GOLF COURSES ●
Cavendish Golf Course **5**
The Challenge at Manele **8**
The Experience at Koele **3**

ATTRACTIONS ●
Garden of the Gods **1**
Kanepuu Preserve **2**
Kaunolu Village **7**
Keomuku Village **10**
Luahiwa Petroglyph Field **9**
Munro Trail **4**

DINING ◆
Blue Ginger Cafe **6**
Café 565 **6**
Canoes Lanai **6**
Coffee Works **6**
Formal Dining Room **3**
Henry Clay's Rotisserie **6**
Hulopoe Court **8**
Ihilani **8**
Manele Bay Clubhouse **8**
Pele's Other Garden **6**
Pool Grille **8**
The Terrace **3**

hiking on 100 miles of remote trails; talking story with the friendly locals; and beachcombing and whale-watching along stretches of otherwise deserted sand. For the adventurous, there's horseback riding in the forest, scuba diving in caves, playing golf on courses with stunning ocean views, or renting a four-wheel-drive vehicle for the day and discovering wild plains where spotted deer run free.

In a single decade, a plain red-dirt pineapple patch has become one of Hawaii's top fantasy destinations. But the real Lanai is a multifaceted place that's so much more than a luxury resort—and it's the traveler who comes to discover the island's natural wonders, local lifestyle, and other inherent joys who's bound to have the most genuine island experience.

THE PINEAPPLE ISLAND'S UNUSUAL PAST

This old shield volcano in the rain shadow of Maui has a history of resisting change in a big way. Early Polynesians, fierce Hawaiian kings, European explorers, 20th-century farmers—the island has seen them all and sent most of them packing, empty-handed and broken. The ancient Hawaiians believed that the island was haunted by spirits so wily and vicious that no human could survive here. People didn't settle here until around A.D. 1400.

But those spirits never really went away, it seems. In 1778 the king of the Big Island, Kalaniopuu, invaded Lanai in what was called "the war of loose bowels." His men slaughtered every warrior, cut down trees, and set fire to all that was left except a bitter fern whose roots gave them all dysentery.

In 1802 Wu Tsin made the first attempt to harvest a crop on the island, but he ultimately abandoned his cane fields and went away. Charles Gay acquired 600 acres at public auction to experiment with pineapple as a crop, but a 3-year drought left him bankrupt. Others tried in vain to grow cotton, sisal, and sugar beets; they started a dairy and a piggery and raised sheep for wool. But all enterprises failed, mostly for lack of water.

Harry Baldwin, a missionary's grandson, was the first to succeed on Lanai. He bought Lanai for $588,000 in 1917, developed a 20-mile water pipeline between Koele and Manele, and sold the island 5 years later to Jim Dole for $1.1 million.

Dole planted and irrigated 18,000 acres of pineapple, built Lanai City, blasted out a harbor, and turned the island into a fancy fruit plantation. For a half century, he enjoyed great success. Even Dole was ultimately vanquished, however; cheaper pineapple production in Asia brought an end to Lanai's heyday.

The island still resembles old photographs taken in the glory days of Dole. Any minute now you half expect to look up and see old Jim Dole himself rattling up the road in a Model-T truck with a load of fresh-picked pineapples. Only now, there's a new lord of the manor, and his name is David Murdock.

Of all who have looked at Lanai with a gleam in their eye, nobody has succeeded quite like Murdock, a self-made billionaire who acquired the island in a merger more than a decade ago. About 97% of it is now his private holding.

Murdock spent $400 million to build two grand hotels on the island: The Lodge at Koele, which resembles an English country retreat, and the Manele Bay Hotel, a green tile-roofed Mediterranean palazzo by the sea. Murdock recycled the former field hands into waitstaff, even summoning a London butler to school the natives in the fine art of service, and carved a pair of daunting golf courses, one in the island's interior and the other along the wave-lashed coast. He then set out to attract tourists by touting Lanai as "the private island."

Murdock is now trying to make all this pay for itself by selling vacation homes and condos next door to the two resorts. They cost from $500,000 to upwards of $3 million.

The redevelopment of this tiny rock should have been a pushover for the big-time tycoon, but island-style politics have continually thwarted his schemes. GO SLOW, a sun-faded sign at Dole's old maintenance shed once said. Murdock might have heeded the warning, because his grandiose plans are taking twice as long to accomplish as he had expected. Lanai is under the political thumb of many who believe that the island's precious water supply shouldn't all be diverted to championship golf courses and

Jacuzzis, and there remains opposition from Lanaians for Sensible Growth, who advocate affordable housing, alternative water systems, and civic improvements that benefit residents.

Lanai residents might have lived in a rural setting, but they certainly haven't been isolated. Having watched the other islands in Hawaii attempt the balancing act of economic growth and the maintenance of an island lifestyle, the residents of Lanai are cautiously welcoming visitors, but at a pace that is still easy for this former plantation community to digest.

1 Orientation

ARRIVING

BY PLANE   No matter where you're coming from, you'll have to make a connection in Honolulu or Kahului (on Maui), where you can easily catch a small plane for the 25-minute flight to Lanai's airport. Twin-engine planes are the only air service to Lanai. **Island Air** (© 800/652-6541 or 808/565-6744; www.islandair.com) offers seven flights a day from Honolulu. For more details on these airlines—including details on how to get the cheapest fares—see "Getting There" and "Money-Saving Package Deals" in chapter 2.

You'll touch down in Puuwai Basin, once the world's largest pineapple plantation; it's about 10 minutes by car to Lanai City and 25 minutes to Manele Bay.

BY BOAT   A round-trip on **Expeditions Lahaina/Lanai Passenger Ferry** (© 808/661-3756) takes you between Maui and Lanai for $50. The ferry service runs five times a day, 365 days a year, between Lahaina and Lanai's Manele Bay harbor. The ferry leaves Lahaina at 6:45 and 9:15am and at 12:45, 3:15, and 5:45pm; the return ferry from Lanai's Manele Bay Harbor leaves at 8 and 10:30am, and at 2, 4:30, and 6:45pm. The 9-mile channel crossing takes 45 minutes to an hour, depending on sea conditions. Reservations are strongly recommended. Baggage is limited to two checked bags and one carry-on.

VISITOR INFORMATION

Lanai Visitors Bureau, P.O. Box 631436, Lanai City, HI 96763, or 431 Seventh St., Suite A, Lanai City (© 800/947-4774 or 808/565-7600; fax 808/565-9316; www.visitlanai.net), and the **Hawaii Visitors and Convention Bureau** (© 800/GO-HAWAII or 808/923-1811; www.gohawaii.com) will both provide brochures, maps, and island guides. For a free *Road and Site Map* of hikes, archaeological sites, and other sights, contact the **Castle and Cooke Resorts,** P.O. Box 310, Lanai City, HI 96763 (© 808/565-3000; www.lanai-resorts.com).

THE ISLAND IN BRIEF

Inhabited Lanai is divided into three parts—Lanai City, Koele, and Manele—and two distinct climate zones: hot and dry, and cool and misty.

Lanai City (pop. 3,000) sits at the heart of the island at 1,645 feet above sea level. It's the only place on the island where you'll find services. Built in 1924, this plantation village is a tidy grid of quaint tin-roofed cottages in bright pastels, with roosters penned in tropical gardens of banana, lilikoi, and papaya. Many of the residents are Filipino immigrants who worked the pineapple fields and imported the art, culture, language, food, and lifestyle of the Philippines. Their clapboard homes, now worth

$175,000 or more, are excellent examples of historic preservation. The whole town looks like it's been kept under a bell jar.

Around Dole Park Square, a charming village square lined with towering Norfolk and Cook Island pines, plantation buildings house general stores with basic necessities as well as a U.S. Post Office (where people stop to chat), two banks, four restaurants, an art gallery, an art center, a whimsical shop full of life's non-necessities, even a coffee shop that outshines any Starbucks. A victim of "progress" was the local, one-room police station with a jail that consists of three blue-and-white wooden outhouse-size cells with padlocks. It's now a block from the square with "modern facilities," including regulation-size jail cells.

In the nearby cool upland district of **Koele** is The Lodge at Koele, standing alone on a knoll overlooking pastures and the sea at the edge of a pine forest, like a grand European manor. The other bastion of indulgence, the Manele Bay Hotel, is on the sunny southwestern tip of the island at **Manele.** You'll get more of what you expect from Hawaii here—beaches, swaying palms, mai tais, and the like.

FAST FACTS

Lanai is part of Maui County. In case of an **emergency,** call the police, fire department, or ambulance services at ℂ 911, or the **Poison Control Center** at ℂ 800/362-3585. For nonemergencies, call the **police** (ℂ 808/565-6428).

For emergency dental care, call **Dr. James Sagawa** (ℂ 808/565-6418). If you need a doctor, contact the **Lanai Family Health Center** (ℂ 808/565-6423) or the **Lanai Community Hospital** (ℂ 808/565-6411).

For a weather report, call the **National Weather Service** at ℂ 808/565-6033.

2 Getting Around

With so few paved roads here, you'll need a four-wheel-drive vehicle if you plan on exploring the island's remote shores, its interior, or the summit of Mount Lanaihale. Even if you have only 1 day on Lanai, rent one and see the island. Both cars and four-wheel-drive vehicles are available at the **Dollar Rent-A-Car** desk at **Lanai City Service/Lanai Plantation Store,** 1036 Lanai Ave. (ℂ **800/588-7808** for Dollar reservations, or **808/565-7227** for Lanai City Service). Expect to pay about $60 a day for the least expensive car available, a Nissan Sentra, and up to $129 a day for a four-wheel-drive jeep.

Warning: Gas is expensive on Lanai and those four-wheel-drive vehicles get terrible gas mileage. Because everything in Lanai City is within walking distance, it makes sense to rent a jeep only for the days you want to explore the island.

Though it's fun to rent a car and explore the island, it's possible to stay here and get to the beach without one. The two big resort hotels run shuttle vans around the island, but only for their guests. If you are staying at The Lodge at Koele or Hotel Lanai, the shuttles to Manele Bay Hotel run every hour. From the Manele Bay Hotel, you walk over to Hulopoe Beach. When you want to return, you just catch the hourly shuttle (it may run on the half-hour from Manele Bay Hotel) back to Lanai City.

If you're staying elsewhere, you can walk to everything in Lanai City and take a taxi to the beach. **Lanai Plantation Store** (ℂ **808/565-7227**) will provide transportation from Lanai City to Hulopoe Beach for $10 per person one-way (you can arrange with them when you want to be picked up, or you can walk over to the Manele Bay Hotel and phone them to come and get you—or you can most likely get a ride back up to

Lanai City with a local). Whether or not you rent a car, sooner or later you'll find yourself at Lanai City Service/Lanai Plantation Store. This all-in-one grocery store, gas station, rental-car agency, and souvenir shop serves as the island's Grand Central Station; here you can pick up information, directions, maps, and all the local gossip.

3 Where to Stay

The majority of the accommodations are located "in the village," as residents call Lanai City. Above the village is the luxurious The Lodge at Koele, while down the hill at Hulopoe Bay are two options: the equally luxurious Manele Bay Hotel or tent camping under the stars at the park.

In addition to the choices listed below, also consider the B&B accommodations offered by **Delores Fabrao** (© **808/565-6134;** dmfabrao@hotmail.com), who has two guest rooms in her home: a double with a shared bathroom and a family room that sleeps up to six ($55 double, $100 for four) with a private bathroom. She doesn't provide breakfast, but you'll have the run of the entire house, including the kitchen. At **Hale Moe** (© **808/565-9520;** www.staylanai.com), host and Lanai native Momi Suzuki makes three bedrooms in her Lanai City home available to guests; all have private bathrooms ($80–$90 double). Guests are welcome to use the entertainment center, large deck, and Momi's two bicycles. She also has a vacation rental house for $300. **Hale O Lanai,** in Lanai City (© **808/247-3637;** www.hibeach.com), has a fully equipped, two-bedroom vacation rental that sleeps up to six; rates range from $115 to $135.

A great resource for vacation rentals is Julie Archambeau at **Lanai Homes and Rentals** (© **808/565-9200** or 808/559-0133).

Don't forget to add 11.42% in taxes to all accommodation bills. Parking is free.

Note: You'll find the hotels reviewed in this chapter on the map on p. 287.

VERY EXPENSIVE

The Lodge at Koele 🌴🌴🌴   Step back into history in the cool mist of the mountains. Most guests here are looking for relaxation: sitting on the rattan lawn chairs on the porch, reading, watching the turkeys mosey across the manicured lawns, strolling through the Japanese hillside garden, or watching the sun sink into the Pacific. The Lodge, as folks here call it, stands in a 21-acre grove of Norfolk Island pines at 1,700 feet above sea level, 8 miles inland from any beach. The atmosphere is informal during the day and more formal after sunset (jackets are required in the main dining room; see review on p. 293).

The 102-room resort resembles a grand English country estate. Inside, heavy timbers, beamed ceilings, and the two huge stone fireplaces of the Great Hall complete the look. Overstuffed furniture sits invitingly around the fireplaces, richly patterned rugs adorn the floor, and museum-quality art hangs on the walls. The guest rooms continue the English theme with four-poster beds, sitting areas (complete with window seats), flowery wallpaper, formal writing desks, and luxury bathrooms with oversize tubs. There are plenty of activities here and at the sister resort down the hill, Manele Bay, so you'll get the best of both hotels. Other pluses include: complimentary shuttle to the golf courses, beach, and Manele Bay Hotel; complimentary coffee and tea in the lobby; formal afternoon tea; twice-daily maid service; and some rooms with butler service. Additional activities include croquet lawns, horse-riding stables, hiking trails, and garden walks.

As we went to press, Castle and Cooke Resorts, owners of The Lodge, were "still in negotiations" (it's been over a year now) with Four Seasons Hotels and Resort for a possible management change.

P.O. Box 630310, Lanai City, HI 96793. ℂ 800/321-4666 or 808/565-7300. Fax 808/565-3868. www.islandoflanai. com. 102 units. $400–$575 double; from $725 suite. Extra person $75. Children under 17 stay free in parent's room. Numerous packages (such as 5th night free, adventure, golf, and wedding) available. AE, DC, MC, V. Airport shuttle $25 round-trip. **Amenities:** 2 restaurants; bar (with quiet live music, hula, and occasional talks by celebrities); outdoor pool; golf at The Experience at Koele, an 18-hole championship Greg Norman/Ted Robinson–designed course, and executive putting green; tennis courts; fitness room; Jacuzzi; watersports equipment rentals at sister hotel Manele Bay Hotel; bike rentals; children's program; game room; concierge; activities desk; car-rental desk; business center; shopping arcade; room service; massage; babysitting; laundry service; dry cleaning. In room: A/C (suites only), TV, dataport, minibar, fridge, coffeemaker, hair dryer, iron, safe.

Manele Bay Hotel ⊙⊙⊙   Located on a sun-washed southern bluff overlooking Hulopoe Beach, one of Hawaii's best stretches of golden sand, this U-shaped hotel steps down the hillside to the pool and the beach, then fans out in oceanfront wings separated by gardens with lush flora, man-made waterfalls, lotus ponds, and streams. On the other side it's bordered by golf greens. The place is a real oasis against the dry Arizona-like heat of Lanai's south coast.

Designed as a traditional luxury beachfront hotel, the Manele Bay features open, airy rooms, each with a peek of the big blue Pacific. Murals depicting scenes from Hawaiian history, sea charts, potted palms, soft camel-hued club chairs, and hand-woven kilim rugs fill the lobby. The oversize guest rooms are done in the style of an English country house: sunny chintz fabrics, mahogany furniture, Audubon prints, huge marble bathrooms, and semiprivate lanais. This resort is much less formal than The Lodge up the hill and attracts more families.

The 10-year-old small spa's six treatment rooms were redesigned in 2002. In addition to a variety of massages, facials, wraps, and scrubs (don't miss the signature Ali'i banana-coconut scrub), the spa also has a separate fitness area with cardiovascular equipment, free weights, and a multistation gym.

As we went to press, Castle and Cooke Resorts, owners of the Manele Bay Hotel, were "still in negotiations" (it's been over a year now) with Four Seasons Hotels and Resort for a possible management change.

P.O. Box 630310, Lanai City, HI 96793. ℂ 800/321-4666 or 808/565-7700. Fax 808/565-2483. www.islandoflanai. com. 250 units. $400–$800 double; $1,200–$3,500 suite. Additional person $75. Numerous packages (such as 5th night free, adventure, golf, and wedding) available. AE, DC, MC, V. Airport shuttle $25 round-trip. **Amenities:** 3 restaurants (the Ihilani, p. 294; the Hulopoe Court, p. 294; and the Pool Grille, p. 295); bar with breathtaking views; large outdoor pool; golf at the Jack Nicklaus–designed The Challenge at Manele; tennis courts; fitness room; small spa; Jacuzzi; watersports equipment rentals; children's program; game room; concierge; activities desk; business center; shopping arcade; salon; room service; massage; babysitting; laundry service; dry cleaning. In room: A/C, TV, dataport, minibar, hair dryer, iron, safe.

MODERATE

Hotel Lanai ⊙ ⅅⅈⅆⓈ   This hotel lacks the facilities of the two resorts described above, but it's perfect for families and other vacationers who can't afford to spend $400 (and up) a night. In fact, if you are looking for the old-fashioned aloha that Lanai City is famous for, this is the place to stay. Built in the 1920s for VIP plantation guests, this clapboard plantation-era relic has retained its quaint character and lives on as a country inn. A well-known chef from Maui, Henry Clay Richardson, is the inn's owner and the dining room's executive chef (see review on p. 294).

In 2005 the entire hotel underwent renovations—repainting, remodeling, and a general sprucing up. The guest rooms, although extremely small, are clean and newly decorated with Hawaiian quilts, wood furniture, and ceiling fans (but no air-conditioning or televisions). The most popular are the lanai units, which feature a shared lanai with the room next door. All rooms have ceiling fans and private, shower-only bathrooms. The small, one-bedroom cottage, with a TV and bathtub, is perfect for a small family.

The hotel serves as a down-home crossroads where total strangers meet local folks on the lanai to drink beer and talk story or play the ukulele and sing into the dark, tropical night. Often, a curious visitor in search of an authentic experience will join the party and discover Lanai's very Hawaiian heart. Guests have the use of the complimentary shuttle to The Lodge at Koele, the Manele Bay Hotel, the golf courses (at which they get the same lower rates given to guests at the two resorts), and the beach.

828 Lanai Ave. (P.O. Box 630520), Lanai City, HI 96763. ℂ 800/795-7211 or 808/565-7211. Fax 808/565-6450. www.hotellanai.com. 11 units. $105–$135 double; $175 cottage double. Rates include continental breakfast. Extra person $10. AE, MC, V. Airport shuttle $25 round-trip. **Amenities:** Excellent restaurant; intimate bar; access to 2 resort courses on the island and the 9-hole golf course in town; nearby tennis courts; complimentary snorkeling equipment.

INEXPENSIVE

Dreams Come True ⭐ *Finds* This quaint plantation house is tucked away among papaya, banana, lemon, and avocado trees in the heart of Lanai City, at 1,620 feet. Hosts Susan and Michael Hunter have filled their house with Southeast Asian antiques collected on their travels. Both are jewelers, and they operate a working studio on the premises. Two of the four bedrooms feature a four-poster canopied bed, with an additional single bed (perfect for a small family), while the other rooms have just one queen-size bed. The common area looks out on the garden and is equipped with both TV and VCR. Breakfast usually consists of freshly baked bread with homemade jellies and jams, tropical fruit, eggs, toast, juice, and coffee.

547 12th St. (P.O. Box 525), Lanai City, HI 96763. ℂ 800/566-6961 or 808/565-6961. Fax 808/565-7056. www. dreamscometruelanai.com. 4 units. $99 double. Rates include full breakfast. Extra person $25. Entire house $380. AE, DISC, MC, V. *In room:* No phone.

4 Where to Dine

Lanai is a curious mix of innocence and sophistication, with strong cross-cultural elements that liven up its culinary offerings. You can dine like a sultan on this island, but be prepared for high prices. The tony hotel restaurants require deep pockets and there are only a handful of other options.

Note: You'll find the restaurants reviewed in this chapter on the map on p. 287.

VERY EXPENSIVE

Formal Dining Room ⭐⭐ RUSTIC AMERICAN/UPCOUNTRY HAWAIIAN The setting: a roaring fire, bountiful sprays of orchids, sienna-colored walls, and well-dressed women in pearls sitting across from men in jackets, with wine buckets tableside. The menu highlights American favorites with intense flavors. Foie gras has a strong presence on the seasonally changing menu, as do venison, local seafood, wild mushrooms, rack of lamb, and the vaunted threadfish. During fall and winter months, expect to see pumpkins, beans, ragouts, and braised items offered in creative seasonal preparations. The Dining Room is known for its use of fresh herbs, vegetables, and fruit grown on the island, harvested just minutes away. Extremely pricey.

In The Lodge at Koele. ℂ 808/565-4580. Reservations required. Jackets requested for men. Entrees $42–$46. AE, DC, MC, V. Daily 6–9:30pm.

Ihilani ⭐⭐ MEDITERRANEAN   A number of top Hawaii chefs (such as Phillippe Padovani and Edwin Goto) have each added their style of melding Mediterranean with island cuisine during their tenure here. The result is Lanai's top gourmet restaurant in a formal atmosphere (jackets for men) with inspiring food at eye-popping prices. Standouts include appetizers like homemade goat cheese and spinach ravioli with roasted eggplant and asparagus salad in a sun-dried-tomato cilantro sauce ($13), or terrine of foie gras with pear d'anjou, Madeira wine gelee, and warm toasted black truffle brioche ($23). Entrees include baked onaga and citrus in a sea-salt crust ($38) and lavender-honey-glazed duck breast ($34). The prix-fixe menu is very complete and comes with selected wines.

In the Manele Bay Hotel. ℂ 808/565-2296. Reservations strongly recommended. Resort attire recommended. Main courses $23–$40; set menu $85 without wine, $135 with wine. AE, DC, MC, V. Tues–Sat 6–9:30pm.

EXPENSIVE

Hulopoe Court ⭐⭐ HAWAII REGIONAL   Hulopoe is casual compared to the hotel's fine dining room, Ihilani, but more formal than the Pool Grille, the hotel's lunchtime spot. The 17th-century palanquin in the adjoining lower lobby, the Asian accents, the tropical murals by gifted Lanai artists, and the high vaulted ceilings add up to an eclectic ambience. The new menu showcases local ingredients such as Maui asparagus, hearts of palm, locally caught fresh fish, and gourmet breakfasts, including an impressive buffet. The crab-coconut soup and mahimahi on poblano mashed potatoes are both good bets.

In the Manele Bay Hotel. ℂ 808/565-2290. Reservations recommended. Collared shirt required for men. Breakfast entrees $12–$25; dinner main courses $28–$35. AE, DC, MC, V. Daily 7–11am and 6–9:30pm.

The Terrace ⭐⭐ AMERICAN   Located next to the Formal Dining Room in The Lodge at Koele, between the 35-foot-high Great Hall and a wall of glass looking out over prim English gardens, the Terrace is far from your typical hotel dining room. The menu may be fancy for comfort food, but it does, indeed, comfort. Hearty breakfasts of waffles and cereals, fresh pineapple from the nearby Palawai Basin, frittata, and Kauai Shrimp Benedict (sautéed Kauai shrimp, grilled taro bread, and wilted spinach with poached eggs and blue crab hollandaise) are a grand start to the day. Dinner choices include seared New York strip loin with sweet corn-blue cheese potatoes and braised chard, grilled fresh catch with corn cake and roasted tomato, and pan-roasted chicken with forest mushrooms served with a spicy pecan wild rice and asparagus.

In The Lodge at Koele. ℂ 808/565-4580. Reservations recommended. Breakfast courses $12–$16; dinner entrees $28–$42. AE, DC, MC, V. Daily 6am–9:30pm.

MODERATE

Henry Clay's Rotisserie ⭐⭐ COUNTRY CUISINE   Henry Clay Richardson, a New Orleans native, has made some welcome changes to Lanai's dining landscape with his rustic inn in the middle of Lanai City. It's very popular and always full. Maybe that's because it's the only option on Lanai that occupies the vast gap between deli-diner and upscale-luxe.

The menu focuses on French country fare: fresh meats, seafood, and local produce in assertive preparations. Appetizers and entrees reflect Cajun, regional, and international influences, particularly the Rajun Cajun Clay's shrimp, a fiery concoction of hefty shrimp in a spiced tomato broth, or the "Almost Grandma's Gumbo," straight from his New Orleans roots. The meats, which could be rabbit, duck, quail, venison, *osso buco*, beef, or chicken, are spit-roasted on the rotisserie. Gourmet pizzas and salads occupy the lighter end of the spectrum. Diners rave about the fresh catch in lemon butter caper sauce; we loved the eggplant Creole, presented with perfect sugar snap peas on a bed of herbed angel-hair pasta. Don't leave without a piece of the New Orleans–style pecan pie. The decor consists of plates on the pine-paneled walls, chintz curtains, peach tablecloths and hunter-green napkins, and fireplaces in both rooms.

In the Hotel Lanai. 828 Lanai Ave., Lanai City. © 808/565-7211. www.hotellanai.com. Main courses $19–$33. MC, V. Daily 5:30–9pm.

Manele Bay Clubhouse ℛ PACIFIC RIM   The view from the alfresco tables here may be the best on the island, encompassing Kahoolawe, Haleakala on Maui, and, on an especially clear day, the peaks of Mauna Kea and Mauna Loa on the Big Island. Lighter fare prevails at lunch: salads and sandwiches, burgers, Caesar salad with chicken, herbed chicken sandwich on sourdough, fish and chips, and excellent shrimp spring rolls and fresh catch of the day on sourdough bread. The clubhouse is casual, the view of the ocean is awe-inspiring, and it's a great gathering place to rehash your day on the course.

In the Challenge at Manele Clubhouse. © 808/565-2230. Reservations recommended. Lunch entrees $10–$22; dinner entrees $25-$38. AE, DC, MC, V. Lunch daily 10:30am–3:30pm; pupu appetizer menu daily 3:30–5:30pm; dinner Thurs–Mon 5:30–9pm.

Pool Grille ℛ ECLECTIC   At this, the most casual of the hotel's restaurants, you'll dine poolside under beach umbrellas, feasting on huge hamburgers (homemade buns, of course) and gourmet salads. Salad choices include spicy chicken, grilled tiger prawn, and Cobb. Lanai venison pastrami and grilled Hawaiian taro burger are among the popular sandwich choices. This is one of only two restaurants on the beach open for lunch, so nonguests eat here too.

In the Manele Bay Hotel. © 808/565-7700. Main courses $11–$16. AE, DC, MC, V. Daily 11am–5pm.

INEXPENSIVE

Blue Ginger Cafe COFFEE SHOP   Famous for its mahimahi sandwiches and inexpensive omelets, Blue Ginger is a very local, very casual, and inexpensive alternative to Lanai's fancy hotel restaurants. The four tables on the front porch face the cool Norfolk pines of Dole Park and are always filled with locals who talk story from morning to night. The tiny cafe is often jammed from 6 to 7am with construction workers on their way to work. The offerings are solid, no-nonsense, everyday fare: fried saimin (no MSG), very popular hamburgers on homemade buns, and mahimahi with capers in a white-wine sauce. Blue Ginger also serves a tasty French toast made with homemade bread, vegetable lumpia (the Filipino version of a spring roll), and Mexican specials. The stir-fried vegetables—a heaping platter of fresh, perfectly cooked veggies, including summer squash and fresh mushrooms—are a hit.

409 Seventh St. (at Lilima St), Lanai City. © 808/565-6363. Breakfast and lunch items under $7.50; dinner under $15. No credit cards. Daily 6am–8pm.

Café 565 PIZZA/SUB SANDWICHES   This colorful pizzeria, with hot and cold sub sandwiches, spills out of the old house and into the umbrella tables in the front yard. Named after Lanai's phone prefix, 565, the pizzas here are the real thing, baked in pizza ovens, and the sub sandwich rolls are baked fresh every day. The sub sandwiches range from hot (like Philly cheese steak) to cold (Genoa salami, capicollo, mortadella, and Provolone). Daily plate-lunch specials and great salads complete the menu. In the works are plans to add a children's menu, calzones, thick-crust pizza, and sushi.

408 Eighth St. (at Ilima St.), Lanai City. © **808/565-6622**. Sub sandwiches $5–$10; pizza $13–$20. No credit cards. Mon–Fri 10am–3pm and 5–8pm.

Canoes Lanai LOCAL   Formerly Tanigawa's, this ma-and-pa eatery may have changed its name, but it still remains the landmark that it's been since the 1920s. In those days the tiny storefront sold canned goods and cigarettes; the 10 tables, hamburgers, and Filipino food came later. This hole-in-the-wall is a local institution, with a reputation for serving local-style breakfasts. The fare—fried rice, omelets, short stack, and simple ham and eggs—is more greasy spoon than gourmet, but it's friendly to the pocketbook.

419 Seventh St., Lanai City. © **808/565-6537**. Reservations not accepted. Breakfast less than $8.50; lunch sandwiches $2.50–$8.50; burgers $2–$5. No credit cards. Thurs–Tues 6:30am–1pm.

Coffee Works 🎭 COFFEEHOUSE   Oahu's popular Ward Warehouse coffeehouse has opened a new branch in Lanai City with a menu of espresso coffees and drinks, ice cream (from gelatos to local brands like Lapperts and Roselani), and a small selection of pastries. It's Lanai City's new gathering place, a tiny cafe with tables and benches on a pleasing wooden deck surrounded by tall pines and a stone's throw from Dole Park. Formerly a plantation house, the structure fits in with the surrounding plantation homes in the heart of Lanai City. There are some nice gift items available, including T-shirts, tea infusers, Chai, teapots, cookies, and gourmet coffees.

604 Ilima, Lanai City (across from Post Office). © **808/565-6962**. Most items under $5. AE, DC, DISC, MC, V. Mon–Sat 6am–4pm.

Pele's Other Garden 🎭🎭 DELI/BISTRO   This popular Lanai City eatery has added a patio with umbrella tables outside and expanded the kitchen in the back, so there's a lot more seating than there used to be—and a fuller menu to match. Owners Mark and Barbara have turned Pele's Other Garden from a small sandwich shop to a full-scale deli and bistro. Daily soup and menu specials, excellent pizza, fresh organic produce, fresh juices, and special items such as top-quality black-bean burritos, roasted red peppers, and stuffed grape leaves are some of the features that make Pele's Other Garden a Lanai City must. At lunch the pizzas and sandwiches are still top-drawer and popular. Sandwiches are made with wraps or whole-wheat, rye, sourdough, or French bread, all baked on the island and delivered fresh daily; the turkey is free-range. In the evening you dine on china at cloth-covered tables, and the menu expands to include pastas (bow-tie pasta with butterfly garlic shrimp, fettuccine with smoked salmon), pizza, and salads. The bright-yellow building is easy to spot along tree-shaded Dole Park.

Dole Park, 811 Houston St., Lanai City. © **808/565-9628**. Most lunch items less than $7; dinner items $17–$20. AE, DISC, MC, V. Mon–Fri 10am–2:30pm; Mon–Sat 5–8pm.

5 Beaches

If you like big, wide, empty, gold-sand beaches and crystal-clear, cobalt-blue water full of bright tropical fish—and who doesn't?—go to Lanai. With 18 miles of sandy shoreline, Lanai has some of Hawaii's least crowded and most interesting beaches. One spot in particular is perfect for swimming, snorkeling, and watching spinner dolphins play: Hulopoe Beach, Lanai's best.

HULOPOE BEACH ☆☆☆

In 1997 Dr. Stephen Leatherman of the University of Maryland (a professional beach surveyor who's also known as "Dr. Beach") ranked Hulopoe the best beach in the United States. It's easy to see why. This palm-fringed, gold-sand beach is bordered by black-lava fingers, protecting swimmers from the serious ocean currents that sweep around Lanai. In summer Hulopoe is perfect for swimming, snorkeling, or just lolling about; the water temperature is usually in the mid-70s (20s Celsius). Swimming is usually safe, except when swells kick up in winter. The bay at the foot of the Manele Bay Hotel is a protected marine preserve, and the schools of colorful fish know it. So do the spinner dolphins that come here to play, as well as the humpback whales that cruise by in winter. Hulopoe is also Lanai's premier beach park, with a grassy lawn, picnic tables, barbecue grills, restrooms, showers, and ample parking. You can camp here, too.

HULOPOE'S TIDE POOLS   Some of the best lava-rock tide pools in Hawaii are found along the south shore of Hulopoe Bay. These miniature Sea Worlds are full of strange creatures: asteroids (sea stars) and holothurians (sea cucumbers), not to

---

Moments Frommer's Favorite Lanai Experiences

Snorkeling Hulopoe Beach. Crystal-clear waters teem with brilliant tropical fish off one of Hawaii's best beaches. There are tide pools to explore, waves to play in, and other surprises—like a pod of spinner dolphins that often makes a splashy entrance.

Exploring the Garden of the Gods. Eroded by wind, rain, and time, these geologic badlands are worth visiting at sunrise or sunset, when the low light plays tricks on the land—and your mind.

Hiking the Munro Trail. The 11-mile Munro Trail is a lofty, rigorous hike along the rim of an old volcano. You'll get great views of the nearby islands. Take a four-wheel-drive vehicle if you want to spend more time on top of the island.

Four-Wheeling It. Four-wheeling is a way of life on Lanai because there are only 30 miles of pavement. Plenty of rugged trails lead to deserted beaches, abandoned villages, and valleys filled with wild game. No other island offers off-road adventures like this one.

Camping Under the Stars. The campsites at Hulopoe Beach Park are about as close to the heavens as you can get. The sound of the crashing surf will lull you to sleep at night, while the chirping of the birds will wake you in the morning. If you're into roughing it, this is a great way to experience Lanai.

Watching the Whales at Polihua Beach. Located on the north shore, this beach—which gets its name from the turtles that nest here—is a great place to spend the day scanning the ocean for whales during the winter months.

mention spaghetti worms, Barber Pole shrimp, and Hawaii's favorite local delicacy, the opihi, a tasty morsel also known as the limpet. Youngsters enjoy swimming in the enlarged tide pool at the eastern edge of the bay. When you explore tide pools, do so at low tide. Never turn your back on the waves. Wear tennis shoes or reef walkers, as wet rocks are slippery. Collecting specimens in this marine preserve is forbidden, so don't take any souvenirs home.

SHIPWRECK BEACH 🞰

This 8-mile-long windswept strand on Lanai's northeastern shore—named for the rusty ship *Liberty* stuck on the coral reef—is a sailor's nightmare and a beachcomber's dream. The strong currents yield all sorts of flotsam, from Japanese handblown-glass fish floats and rare pelagic paper nautilus shells to lots of junk. This is also a great place to spot whales from December to April, when the Pacific humpbacks cruise in from Alaska to winter in these calm offshore waters. The road to the beach is paved most of the way, but you really need a four-wheel-drive to get down here.

POLIHUA BEACH 🞰

So many sea turtles once hauled themselves out of the water to lay their eggs in the sunbaked sand on Lanai's northwestern shore that Hawaiians named the beach here *Polihua,* or "egg nest." Although the endangered green sea turtles are making a comeback, they're seldom seen here now. You're more likely to spot an offshore whale (in season) or the perennial litter that washes up onto this deserted beach at the end of Polihua Road, a 4-mile jeep trail. Known for its expanses of white sand, Polihua is one of Hawaii's more photographed beaches. This strand is ideal for beachcombing (those little green-glass Japanese fishing-net floats often show up here), fishing, or just being alone. Beware of the strong wind and currents, which make the water unsafe for swimming. There are no facilities except fishermen's huts and driftwood shelters. Bring water and sunscreen.

6 Watersports

Lanai has Hawaii's best water clarity because it lacks major development, has low rainfall and runoff, and because its coast is washed clean daily by the sea current known as "The Way to Tahiti." But the strong sea currents pose a threat to swimmers, and there are few good surf breaks. Most of the aquatic adventures—swimming, snorkeling, scuba diving—are centered on the somewhat protected south shore, around Hulopoe Bay.

The only outfitter for watersports on the island is **Trilogy Lanai Ocean Sports** 🞰 (© **888/MAUI-800** or 808/565-9303; www.visitlanai.com), which has also built a well-deserved reputation as the leader in sailing/snorkeling cruises in Hawaii.

OCEAN KAYAKING

Discover the thrill of kayaking with **Trilogy**'s guided trips into Lanai's complex ecosystems and unique flora and fauna (see contact information above). You'll either paddle along Lanai's magnificent south shore to explore the water and sea caves at Kahekili Ho'e, where thousand-foot sea cliffs still hide the bones of ancient Hawaiians; or you'll travel along the north shore at Shipwreck Beach, one of the longest barrier reefs in Hawaii, where you can explore the shipwreck and paddle your kayak amongst the numerous turtles who frequent the reef. Both trips offer lunch, sodas and snacks, single and double kayaks, and snorkeling gear. The cost is $125 (half price for children 3–15), $75 for nonpaddlers who join the tour and enjoy a guided hike along the coast.

SAILING/SNORKELING

Trilogy Lanai Ocean Sports 𝒜 (see contact information above) has an acclaimed morning **snorkel/sailing trip** on Monday, Wednesday, and Friday from 8:45am to 1pm and on Saturday from 10am to 2:30pm onboard their luxury custom sailing catamarans. The trips along Lanai's protected coastline include sailing past hundreds of spinner dolphins and into some of the best snorkeling sites in the world. The $110 price (half price for children 3–15) includes breakfast, lunch, sodas, snacks, snorkel gear, and instruction. In the evening Trilogy offers a **sunset sail** for $59 per person (half-price for children ages 3–5).

SCUBA DIVING

Two of Hawaii's best-known dive spots are found in Lanai's clear waters, just off the south shore: **Cathedrals I** and **II,** so named because the sun lights up an underwater grotto like a magnificent church. **Trilogy Lanai Ocean Sports** 𝒜 (see above for contact information) offers several different kinds of sailing, diving, and snorkeling trips on catamarans and from their new 32-foot, high-tech, jet-drive ocean raft. At the crack of dawn (6:30–8am) on Tuesday, Thursday, and Saturday, Trilogy has its own version of "sunrise services" at the Cathedrals. Not only is this the best time of day to dive this incredible area, but there are virtually no other dive boats in the water at this time. Cost is $95.

For those wanting to sleep in, **Trilogy** offers an afternoon dive (3–6pm) on Monday, Wednesday, and Friday for the serious diver looking for a two-tank dive in the areas that have made Lanai famous. Cost is $130 and includes sodas, snacks, scuba gear, and a dive master. Noncertified divers can check out Trilogy's Discover Scuba (Mon–Fri 10am) for $169; certified divers can join in for $159 from the boat and $95 for noncertified and $85 for certified divers from the beach.

SNORKELING

Hulopoe is Lanai's best snorkeling spot. Fish are abundant in the marine-life conservation area. Try the lava-rock points at either end of the beach and around the lava pools. Newcomers can get lessons from **Triology's Beach Snorkeling Class** (Mon–Fri 10am); after the lessons there's a 30-minute guided reef tour. The cost is $30 ($15 for children under 15), including all equipment.

SPORT FISHING

Jeff Menze will take you out on the 28-foot Omega boat *Spinning Dolphin* (℃ 808/ 565-6613). His fishing charters cost $400 for six people for 4 hours, or $600 for six people for 8 hours. He also offers exclusive 3-hour whale-watching trips in season, which cost $300 for six passengers.

WHALE-WATCHING

Year-round, **Trilogy** offers 1½-hour adventures on a 32-foot, 26-passenger, rigid-hulled inflatable boat. From late December through April, they are on the lookout for whales, but the remainder of the year, schools of spinner dolphins are featured on this Blue Water Marine Mammal Watch. The cost is $75 (half-price for children 3–15).

7 Hiking & Camping

HIKING

A LEISURELY MORNING HIKE

The 3-hour self-guided **Koele Nature Hike** starts by the reflecting pool in the backyard of The Lodge at Koele and takes you on a 5-mile loop through a cathedral of Norfolk Island pines, into Hulopoe Valley, past wild ginger, and up to Koloiki Ridge, with its panoramic view of Maunalei Valley and Molokai and Maui in the distance. You're welcome to take the hike even if you're not a guest at The Lodge. The trail head isn't obvious—just keep going mauka (inland) toward the trees—and the path isn't clearly marked, but the concierge will give you a free map. We suggest doing this hike in the morning; by afternoon the clouds usually roll in, marring visibility at the top and increasing your chance of being caught in a downpour.

THE CHALLENGING MUNRO TRAIL

This tough, 11-mile (round-trip) uphill climb through the groves of Norfolk pines is a lung-buster, but if you reach the top, you'll be rewarded with a breathtaking view of Molokai, Maui, Kahoolawe, the peaks of the Big Island, and—on a really clear day—Oahu in the distance. Figure on 7 hours. The trail begins at Lanai Cemetery along Keomoku Road (Hwy. 44) and follows Lanai's ancient caldera rim, ending up at the island's highest point, Lanaihale. Go in the morning for the best visibility. After 4 miles you'll get a view of Lanai City. The weary retrace their steps from here, while the more determined go the last 1.25 miles to the top. Diehards head down Lanai's steep south-crater rim to join the highway to Manele Bay. For more details on the Munro Trail—including information on four-wheel-driving it to the top—see "Five Islands at a Single Glance: The Munro Trail" under "Seeing the Sights," later in this chapter.

A SELF-GUIDED NATURE TRAIL

This self-guided nature trail in the Kanepuu Preserve is about a 10- to 15-minute walk through eight stations, with interpretive signs explaining the natural or cultural significance of what you're seeing. The trail head is clearly marked on the Polihua Road on the way to the Garden of the Gods. Kanepuu is one of the last remaining examples of the type of forest that once covered the dry lowlands throughout the state. There are some 49 plant species here that are found only in Hawaii. The **Nature Conservancy** (© 808/565-7430) conducts guided hikes every month; call for details.

GUIDED HIKES

The Lodge at Koele (© 808/5657300; www.lanai-resorts.com) has a 2½-hour Koloiki Ridge Nature hike through 5 miles of the upland forests of Koele at 11am daily. The fee is $15.

The **Manele Bay Hotel** (© 808/565-7700; www.lanai-resorts.com) has a 1½-hour fitness hike along an old fisherman's trail at 9am Tuesday and Friday, led by Joe West, wildlife and outdoor photographer extraordinaire. Bring your camera and ask Joe for photographing tips. The fee is $15.

CAMPING AT HULOPOE BEACH PARK

There is only one legal place to camp on Lanai: Hulopoe Beach Park, which is owned by Castle and Cooke Resorts. To camp in this exquisite beach park, with its crescent-shaped, white-sand beach bordered by kiawe trees, contact **Wendell Sarme–Park Manager,** Castle and Cooke Resorts, P.O. Box 630310, Lanai City, HI 96763

(© **808/565-2970**; www.lanai-resorts.com). There's a $5 registration fee, plus a charge of $5 per person per night. Hulopoe has six campsites; each can accommodate up to six people. Facilities include restrooms, running water, showers, barbecue areas, and picnic tables.

8 Golf & Other Outdoor Activities

GOLF

Cavendish Golf Course *Finds* This quirky par-36, 9-hole public course not only has no clubhouse or club pros but also no tee times, score cards, or club rentals. To play, just show up, put a donation into the little wooden box next to the first tee ($5–$10 would be nice), and hit away. The 3,071-yard, E. B. Cavendish–designed course was built by the Dole plantation in 1947 for its employees. The greens are a bit bumpy, but the views of Lanai are great, and the temperatures usually quite mild.

Next to The Lodge at Koele in Lanai City. No phone.

The Challenge at Manele ★★ This target-style, desert-links course, designed by Jack Nicklaus, is one of the most challenging courses in the state. Check out the local rules: "No retrieving golf balls from the 150-foot cliffs on the ocean holes 12, 13, or 17," and "All whales, axis deer, and other wild animals are considered immovable obstructions." That's just a hint of the uniqueness of this course, which is routed among lava outcroppings, archaeological sites, kiawe groves, and ilima trees. The five sets of staggered tees pose a challenge to everyone from the casual golfer to the pro. Facilities include a clubhouse, a pro shop, rentals, a practice area, lockers, and showers.

Next to the Manele Bay Hotel in Hulopoe Bay. © **800/321-4666** or 808/565-2222. Greens fees: $225 ($185 for guests).

The Experience at Koele ★★ This traditional par-72 course, designed by Greg Norman with fairway architecture by Ted Robinson, has very different front and back 9 holes. Mother Nature reigns throughout: You'll see Cook Island and Norfolk pines, indigenous plants, and water—lots of water, including seven lakes, flowing streams, cascading waterfalls, and one green (the 17th) completely surrounded by a lake. All goes well until you hit the signature hole, number 8, where you tee off from a 250-foot elevated tee to a fairway bordered by a lake on the right and trees and dense shrubs on the left. After that, the back 9 holes drop dramatically through ravines filled with pine, koa, and eucalyptus trees. The grand finale, the par-five 18th, features a green rimmed by waterfalls that flow into a lake on the left side. To level the playing field, there are four different sets of tees. Facilities include a clubhouse, a pro shop, rentals, a practice area, lockers, and showers.

Next to The Lodge at Koele in Lanai City. © **800/321-4666** or 808/565-4653. Greens fees: $225 ($185 for guests).

BICYCLING

The Lodge at Koele (© **808/565-7300**) has mountain bikes to rent for $8 an hour, $35 for 4 hours, and $40 to $55 for 8 hours. For general information about bike trails, check out **www.bikehawaii.com**.

HORSEBACK RIDING

Horses can take you to many places in Lanai's unique landscape that are otherwise unreachable even in a four-wheel-drive vehicle. The **Stables at Koele** (© **808/565-4424**) offers various rides, including group rides that are a slow, gentle walk, starting at $65 for a 1½-hour trip. We recommend the 2-hour **Paniolo Trail Ride,** which takes you into the hills surrounding Koele. You'll meander through guava groves and patches of ironwood trees; catch glimpses of axis deer, quail, wild turkeys, and Santa Getrudis cattle; and end with panoramic views of Maui and Lanai. The cost is $75. Private rides (where you can canter, gallop, and trot) are $90 per person for 1 hour and $150 per person for 2 hours. Long pants and shoes are required; safety helmets are provided. Bring a jacket: The weather is chilly and rain is frequent. Children must be at least 9 years old and 4 feet tall, and riders cannot weigh more than 250 pounds.

TENNIS

Public courts, lit for night play, are available in Lanai City at no charge; call ⊘ **808/ 565-6979** for reservations. Guests staying at The Lodge at Koele or the Manele Bay Hotel have tennis privileges at either the Tennis Center at Manele, with its six Plexi-pave courts, a fully equipped pro shop, and tournament facilities; or at the courts at Koele. Instruction is available for $25 for a clinic, $65 for a private 1-hour lesson. Courts are complimentary for hotel guests. For more information, call ⊘ **808/565-2072.**

9 Seeing the Sights

You'll need a four-wheel-drive vehicle to reach all the sights listed below. Renting a jeep is an expensive proposition on Lanai—from $129 to $179 a day—so we suggest that you rent one just for the day (or days) you plan on sightseeing; otherwise, it's easy enough to get to the beach and around Lanai City without your own wheels. For details on vehicle rentals, see "Getting Around," earlier in this chapter.

Note: You'll find the following attractions on the map on p. 287.

GARDEN OF THE GODS ⚔

A desolate, windswept place, dotted by lunarlike rock formations of awesome shapes and colors, the so-called Garden of the Gods lives up to its name. According to island legend, the strange rocks and boulders on the island's north shore were dropped from the sky by the gods tending their gardens. Scientists dismiss this supernatural explanation—calling the area an "ongoing posterosional event" or just "plain and simple badlands." Still, it's impossible to ignore the mystery of the place—the rock's brilliant reds, oranges, ochers, and yellows set against a rugged and barren backdrop. Go early in the morning or just before sunset, when the light casts eerie shadows on the beautiful lava formations.

About 7 miles north of Lanai City, the Garden of the Gods is approached by a four-wheel-drive ride through the now-uncultivated pineapple fields, past the Kanepuu Preserve (a dry-land forest preserve teeming with rare plant and animal life). Drive west from the Lodge on Polihua Road; in about 2 miles you'll see a hand-painted sign that'll point you in the right direction, left down a one-lane, red-dirt road through a kiawe forest and past sisal and scrub to the site.

FIVE ISLANDS AT A SINGLE GLANCE: THE MUNRO TRAIL ⚔

In the first golden rays of dawn, when lone owls swoop over abandoned pineapple fields, hop into a 4×4 and head out on the two-lane blacktop toward Mount Lanai-hale, the 3,370-foot summit of Lanai. Your destination is the Munro Trail, the narrow, winding ridge trail that runs across Lanai's razorback spine to the summit. From here, you may get a rare Hawaii treat: On a clear day, you can see all of the main islands in the Hawaiian chain except Kauai.

Kids Especially for Kids

Exploring Hulopoe Tide Pools (p. 297)   An entire world of marine life lives in the tide pools on the eastern side of Hulopoe Bay. Everything in the water, including the tiny fish, is small—kid-size. After examining the wonders of the tide pool, check out the larger swimming holes in the lava rock, perfect for children.

Hunting for Petroglyphs (p. 303)   The Luahiwa Petroglyphs Field, located just outside Lanai City, is spread out over a 3-acre site. Make it a game: Whoever finds the most petroglyphs gets ice cream from the Pine Isle Market.

Listening to Storytellers   Check with the Lanai Library, Fraser Avenue near Fifth Street, Lanai City (© **808/565-6996**), to see if any storytelling or other children's activities are scheduled. The events are usually free and open to everyone.

When it rains the Munro Trail becomes slick and boggy with major washouts. Rainy-day excursions often end with a rental jeep on the hook of the island's lone tow truck—and a $250 tow charge. You could even slide off into a major gulch and never be found, so don't try it. But in late August and September, when trade winds stop and the air over the islands stalls in what's called a *kona* condition, Mount Lanaihale's suddenly visible peak becomes an irresistible attraction.

When you're on Lanai, look to the summit. If it's clear in the morning, get a four-wheel-drive vehicle and take the Munro Trail to the top. Look for a red-dirt road off Manele Road (Hwy. 440), about 5 miles south of Lanai City; turn left and head up the ridge line. No sign marks the peak, so you'll have to keep an eye out. Look for a wide spot in the road and a clearing that falls sharply to the sea.

From here you can see Kahoolawe, Maui, the Big Island of Hawaii, and Molokini's tiny crescent. Even the summits show. You can also see the silver domes of Space City on Haleakala in Maui; Puu Moaulanui, the tongue-twisting summit of Kahoolawe; and, looming above the clouds, Mauna Kea on the Big Island. At another clearing farther along the thickly forested ridge, all of Molokai, including the 4,961-foot summit of Kamakou, and the faint outline of Oahu (more than 30 miles across the sea) are visible. You actually can't see all five in a single glance anymore because a thriving pine forest blocks the view. For details on hiking the trail, see "Hiking & Camping," earlier in this chapter.

LUAHIWA PETROGLYPH FIELD

With more than 450 known petroglyphs in Hawaii at 23 sites, Lanai is second only to the Big Island in its wealth of prehistoric rock art, but you'll have to search a little to find it. Some of the best examples are on the outskirts of Lanai City, on a hillside site known as Luahiwa Petroglyph Field. The characters you'll see incised on 13 boulders in this grassy 3-acre knoll include a running man, a deer, a turtle, a bird, a goat, and even a rare, curly-tailed Polynesian dog (a latter-day wag has put a leash on him—some joke).

Perfect for a Rainy Day: Lanai Art Program

A perfect activity for a rainy day in Lanai City is the **Lanai Arts Program,** 333 Seventh St., located in the heart of the small town. Top artists from across Hawaii frequently visit this homegrown art program and teach a variety of classes ranging from raku (Japanese pottery), silk printing, silk screening, pareo making (creating your own design on this islanders' wrap), gyotaku (printing a real fish on your own T-shirt), and watercolor drawing to a variety of other island crafts. The cost is usually around $25 for the 2- to 3-hour classes, plus the cost for materials. For more information, call (C) **808/565-7503.**

To get here, take the road to Hulopoe Beach. About 2 miles out of Lanai City, look to the left, up on the slopes of the crater, for a cluster of reddish-tan boulders (believed to form a rain *heiau,* or shrine, where people called up the gods Ku and Hina to nourish their crops). A cluster of spiky century plants marks the spot. Look for the Norfolk pines on the left side of the highway, turn left on the dirt road that veers across the abandoned pineapple fields, and after about 1 mile, take a sharp left by the water tanks. Drive for another ½ mile and then veer to the right at the V in the road. Stay on this upper road for about ¼ mile; you'll come to a large cluster of boulders on the right side. It's just a short walk up the cliffs (wear walking or hiking shoes) to the petroglyphs. Exit the same way you came. Go between 3pm and sunset for ideal viewing and photo ops.

KAUNOLU VILLAGE

Out on Lanai's nearly vertical, Gibraltar-like sea cliffs is an old royal compound and fishing village. Now a National Historic Landmark and one of Hawaii's most treasured ruins, it's believed to have been inhabited by King Kamehameha the Great and hundreds of his closest followers about 200 years ago. It's a hot, dry, dusty, slow-going, 3-mile 4×4 drive from Lanai City to Kaunolu, but the miniexpedition is worth it. Take plenty of water, don a hat for protection against the sun, and wear sturdy shoes.

Ruins of 86 house platforms and 35 stone shelters have been identified on both sides of Kaunolu Gulch. The residential complex also includes the Halulu Heiau temple, named after a mythical man-eating bird. The king's royal retreat is thought to have stood on the eastern edge of Kaunolu Gulch, overlooking the rocky shore facing Kahekili's Leap, a 62-foot-high bluff named for the mighty Maui chief who leaped off cliffs as a show of bravado. Nearby are burial caves, a fishing shrine, a lookout tower, and many warrior-like stick figures carved on boulders. Just offshore stands the telltale fin of little Shark Island, a popular dive spot that teems with bright tropical fish and, frequently, sharks.

Excavations are underway to discover more about how ancient Hawaiians lived, worked, and worshipped on Lanai's leeward coast. Who knows? The royal fishing village may yet yield the bones of King Kamehameha. His burial site, according to legend, is known only to the moon and the stars.

KANEPUU PRESERVE

Don't expect giant sequoias big enough to drive a car through; this ancient forest on the island's western plateau is so fragile you can only visit once a month, and even then, only on a guided hike. Kanepuu, which has 48 species of plants unique to Hawaii, survives under the Nature Conservancy's protective wing. Botanists say the

590-acre forest is the last dry lowland forest in Hawaii; the others have all vanished, trashed by axis deer, agriculture, or "progress." Among the botanical marvels of this dry forest are the remains of *olopua* (native olive), *lama* (native ebony), *mau hau hele* (a native hibiscus), and the rare *'aiea* trees, which were used for canoe parts.

Due to the forest's fragile nature, guided hikes are led only 12 times a year, on a monthly, reservations-only basis. Contact the **Nature Conservancy Oahu Land Preserve** manager at 1116 Smith St., Suite 201, Honolulu, HI 96817 (© **808/537-4508**), to reserve.

OFF THE TOURIST TRAIL: KEOMOKU VILLAGE

If you're sunburned lobster red, have read all the books you packed, and are starting to get island fever, take a little drive to Keomoku Village, on Lanai's east coast. You'll really be off the tourist trail. All that's in Keomoku, a ghost town since the mid-1950s, is a 1903 clapboard church in disrepair, an overgrown graveyard, an excellent view across the 9-mile Auau Channel to Maui's crowded Kaanapali Beach, and some very empty beaches that are perfect for a picnic or a snorkel. This former ranching and fishing village of 2,000 was the first non-Hawaiian settlement on Lanai, but it dried up after droughts killed off the Maunalei Sugar Company. The village, such as it is, is a great little escape from Lanai City. Follow Keomoku Road for 8 miles to the coast, turn right on the sandy road, and keep going for 5¾ miles.

10 Shopping

Central Bakery *(Finds)* This is the mother lode of the island's baked delights, the bakery that is, well, central to Lanai's dining pleasure. If you've noshed on the fantastic sandwiches at The Lodge at Koele's Terrace or any of the stellar desserts at its Formal Dining Room or at Manele Bay Hotel, you've enjoyed goodies from Central Bakery. The bakery supplies all breads, all breakfast pastries, specialty ice creams and sorbets, all banquet desserts, and restaurant desserts on the island. Although it's not your standard retail outlet, you can call in advance, place your order, and pick it up. They prefer as much notice as possible (preferably 48 hr.), but in a pinch will take a 24-hour order. Breads range from walnut onion ($4.50) to roasted potato bacon ($4.50) to olive onion ($4.50). They also have cookies (chocolate chip, oatmeal, coconut, all for 50¢), brownies (50¢), muffins, croissants (including chocolate croissants), Danish, and scones, plus an assortment of breakfast pastries (pineapple turnover, hazelnut roll, mascarpone apricot Danish, pistachio chocolate roll, and others). 1311 Fraser Ave., Lanai City. © **808/565-3920.**

Dis 'N Dat *(Finds)* Dis (Barry) and Dat (Susie) visited Lanai from Florida to look at buying a retirement home. They found their home and moved to Lanai to retire. That did not last. A few years later, outgoing Barry and his wife started searching for unusual, finely crafted teak and exotic wood sculptures and carvings. Along the way they took a shine to mobiles and wind chimes, the more outrageous, the better. Then they started collecting handmade jewelry, stained glass, and unique garden ornaments and home decor. All this lead to this eclectic store, which you have to see to believe. Meeting Barry is worth the trip alone. This is also the biggest collection of Hawaiian slipper necklaces, earrings, anklets, and bracelets. You'll also find T-shirts, pottery, ceramics, batik scarves, hula lamps and whimsical dragon-fly lamps, woven baskets, and even waterfalls. You can't miss this vivid green shop with hanging chimes and mobiles leading the way to the front door. 418 Eighth Ave. (at Kilele St.), Lanai City. © **866/DISNDAT** or 808/565-9170.

Gifts with Aloha ⚛ Phoenix and Kimberly Dupree's store of treasures has blossomed since they moved to a larger location on the other side of Dole Park. They are now shipping minigardens and lamps to the mainland and are selling fabulously stylish hats and hatbands, locally made clothing, T-shirts, swimwear, quilts, Jams World dresses, children's clothes, books and toys, Hawaii-themed CDs, DVDs, music, books, pareos, candles, aloha shirts, picture frames, handbags, ceramics, dolls, and art by local artists (including some of the most beautiful jewelry in the islands). The sumptuous white lehua honey from the Big Island is available here, as are jams and jellies by Lanai's Fabrao House. The made-on-Maui soaps and bath products—in gardenia, pikake, and plumeria fragrances—make great gifts to go. On our last trip they were featuring ukuleles and locally made cards for every occasion. Dole Park, 363 Seventh St. (at Ilima St.), Lanai City. ✆ 808/565-6589.

Heart of Lanai Gallery Denise Hennig, the resident artist at Hotel Lanai, displays her own photographs and watercolors of landscapes, people, and the lifestyle of Lanai's plantation past, as well as the work of other local Lanai artists at her afternoon teas, Tuesday through Saturday from 2:30 to 4:30pm. You can drop by and enjoy a cup of tea with her as she shows you the art she's displaying that week. Her home/gallery is located behind the hospital in a bright yellow house. 758 Queens St., Lanai City. ✆ 808/565-7815. www.lanaionline.com/Merchants/heart_of_lanai.htm.

High Lights Located one block off Seventh Street, across the street from Coffee Works, is this island-style beauty salon and supply store. Owner Katharina Oriol has been working in beauty salons since 1975 and offers a full-service salon with hair cuts, styling, highlighting, manicures, pedicures, waxing, and so on. Plus, she carries a wide selection of beauty products for hair and skin, and cosmetics. Katharina welcomes walk-ins. 617 Ilima Ave., Lanai City. ✆ 808/565-7207.

International Food & Clothing This store sells the basics: groceries, housewares, T-shirts, hunting and fishing supplies, over-the-counter drugs, wine and liquor, paper goods, hardware, and even offers a takeout lunch counter. We were pleasantly surprised by the extraordinary candy and bubble-gum section, the beautiful local bananas in the small produce section, the surprisingly extensive selection of yuppie soft drinks (Sobe, Snapple, and others), and the best knife-sharpener we've seen—handy for the Lanai lifestyle. 833 Ilima Ave., Lanai City. ✆ 808/565-6433.

Lanai Art Center ⚛ *Finds* This wonderful center was organized in 1989 to provide a place where both residents and visitors can come to create art. The center offers classes and studio time in ceramics, painting and drawing, calligraphy, woodworking, photography, silk and textile painting, watercolor, and glass. Plus, the center has an impressive schedule of visiting instructors from writers to folk artists (quilting, lei making, and instrument making) to oil painters. Check out their reasonably priced classes (generally in the $25 range) or browse in the gallery for excellent deals on works by Lanai residents. 333 Seventh St., Lanai City. ✆ 808/565-7503.

Lanai Marketplace Everyone on Lanai, it seems, is a backyard farmer. From 7 to 11am or noon on Saturday, they all head to this shady square to sell their dewy-fresh produce, home-baked breads, plate lunches, and handicrafts. This is Lanai's version of the green market: petite in scale (like the island) but charming, and growing.

Dolores Fabrao's jams and jellies, under the **Fabrao House** label (✆ **808/565-6134** for special orders), are a big seller at the market and at resort gift shops. Flavors include pineapple-coconut, pineapple-mango, papaya, guaivi (strawberry guava), poha (gooseberry), passion fruit, Surinam cherry, and the very tart karamay jelly. All fruits are grown on the island. Dole Sq., Lanai City.

The Local Gentry 🖈🖈 *Finds*   Open since December 1999, Jenna Gentry's wonderful boutique is the first of its kind on the island, featuring clothing and accessories that are not the standard resort-shop fare. (Visiting and local women alike make a beeline for this store.) You'll find fabulous silk aloha shirts by Iolani; mahogany wood lamps; mermaids and hula girls; Putumayo separates (perfect for Hawaii) in easy-care fabrics; a fabulous line of silk aloha shirts by Tiki; top-quality hemp-linen camp shirts; inexpensive sarongs; fabulous socks; and the Tommy Bahama line for men and women. There are also great T-shirts, swimwear, jewelry, bath products, picture frames, jeans, chic sunglasses, and offbeat sandals. Their most recent additions are wonderful children's clothes. 363 Seventh St. (behind Gifs with Aloha, facing Ilima St.), Lanai City. (C) **808/565-9130.**

Mike Carroll Gallery   If he's on the island, you'll find Mike Carroll at work on his original oil paintings, which generally depict Lanai's landscape. After a successful 22-year career as a professional artist in Chicago, Carroll moved to Lanai and has been painting the beauty and the lifestyle of the island ever since. You'll find an extensive selection of his original work, some limited editions, prints and note cards, plus that of a dozen or so of Maui and Lanai's top artists and even some locally made, one-of-a-kind jewelry. 443 Seventh St., Lanai City. (C) **808/565-7122.** www.mikecarrollgallery.com.

Pine Isle Market   A local landmark for two generations, Pine Isle specializes in locally caught fresh fish, but you can also find fresh herbs and spices, canned goods, electronic games, ice cream, toys, zoris, diapers, paint, cigars, and other basic essentials of work and play. The fishing section is outstanding, with every lure imaginable. 356 Eighth St., Lanai City. (C) **808/565-6488.**

Richard's Shopping Center   The Tamashiros' family business has been on the square since 1946; not much has changed over the years. This "shopping center" is, in fact, a general store with a grocery section, paper products, ethnic foods, meats (mostly frozen), liquor, toys, film, cosmetics, fishing gear, sunscreens, clothing, kitchen utensils, T-shirts, and other miscellany. Half a wall is lined with an extraordinary selection of fish hooks and anglers' needs. Aloha shirts, aloha-print zoris, inexpensive brocade-covered writing tablets, fold-up lauhala mats, and gourmet breads from the Central Bakery (see above) are among the countless good things to be found at Richard's. 434 Eighth St., Lanai City. (C) **808/565-6047.**

11 Lanai After Dark

The only regular nightlife venues on the island are the Lanai Playhouse, at the corner of Seventh and Lanai avenues in Lanai City, and the two resorts, The Lodge at Koele and Manele Bay Hotel.

The **Lanai Playhouse** ((C) **808/565-7500**) is a historic 1920s building that has won awards for its renovations. When it opened in 1993, the 150-seat venue stunned residents by offering first-run movies with Dolby sound—quite contemporary for anachronistic Lanai. Lanai Playhouse usually, but not always, shows two movies each evening from Friday to Tuesday (to Wed in summer), at 6:30 and 8:30pm, with occasional Sunday and Monday matinees; if a 3-hour movie is on, it's shown at 7:30pm. Tickets are $7 for adults and $4.50 for kids and seniors. The playhouse is also the venue for occasional special events.

The Lodge at Koele has stepped up its live entertainment. In The Lodge's **Great Hall,** in front of its manorial fireplaces, local artists bring contemporary Hawaiian, classical, and other genres to listeners who sip port and fine liqueurs while sinking into plush chairs. The special programs are on weekends, but throughout the week some form of nightly entertainment takes place from 7 to 10pm.

Special events will occasionally bring in a few more nightlife options. During the annual **Pineapple Festival,** generally the first weekend in July, some of Hawaii's best musicians arrive to show their support for Lanai (see "Maui, Molokai & Lanai Calendar of Events" in chapter 2). Other special events include the **Aloha Festival** (www. alohafestivals.com), which takes place either at the end of September or the first week in October, and the **Christmas Festival,** the first Saturday in December (contact **Lanai Visitors Bureau,** P.O. Box 631436, Lanai City, HI 96763, or 431 Seventh St., Suite A, Lanai City © **800/947-4774** or 808/565-7600; fax 808/565-9316; www. visitlanai.net for more information).

Appendix:
Maui in Depth

Maui is the only island in the Hawaiian chain named after a god—well, actually a demigod (half man, half god). Hawaiian legends are filled with the escapades of Maui, who had a reputation as a trickster. In one story Maui is credited with causing the birth of the Hawaiian Islands when he threw his "magic" fishhook down to the ocean floor and pulled the islands up from the bottom of the sea. Another legend tells how Maui lassoed the sun to make it travel more slowly across the sky—so that his mother could more easily dry her clothes. Maui's status as the only island to carry the name of a deity seems fitting, considering its reputation as the perfect tropical paradise, or as Hawaiians say, *Maui no ka oi* ("Maui is the best").

1 History 101

IN THE BEGINNING Paddling outrigger canoes, the first ancestors of today's Hawaiians followed the stars and birds across the sea to Hawaii, which they called "the land of raging fire." Those first settlers were part of the great Polynesian migration that settled the vast triangle of islands stretching between New Zealand, Easter Island, and Hawaii. No one is sure when they arrived in Hawaii from Tahiti and the Marquesas Islands, some 2,500 miles to the south, but a dog-bone fish hook found at the southernmost tip of the Big Island has been carbon-dated to A.D. 700. Some recent archaeological digs at the Maluuluolele Park in Lahaina even predate that.

All we have today are some archaeological finds, some scientific data, and ancient chants to tell the story of Hawaii's past. The chants, especially the *Kumulipo,* which is the chant of creation and the litany of genealogy of the *alii* (high-ranking chiefs) who ruled the islands, talk about comings and goings between Hawaii and the islands of the south, presumed to be Tahiti. In fact, the channel between Maui, Kahoolawe, and Lanai is called *Kealaikahiki* or "the pathway to Tahiti."

Around 1300, the transoceanic voyages stopped for some reason, and Hawaii began to develop its own culture in earnest. The settlers built temples, fishponds, and aqueducts to irrigate taro plantations. Sailors became farmers and fishermen. Each island was a separate kingdom. The *alii* created a caste system and established taboos. Violators were strangled. High priests asked the gods Lono and Ku for divine guidance. Ritual human sacrifices were common.

Maui's history, like the rest of Hawaii, was one of wars and conquests, with one king taking over another king's land. The rugged terrain of Maui and the water separating Maui, Molokai, Lanai, and Kahoolawe made for natural boundaries of kingdoms. In the early years there were three kingdoms on Maui: Hana, Waikulu, and Lahaina. The chants are not just strict listings of family histories. Some describe how a ruler's pride and arrogance can destroy a community. For example, according to the chants, Hana's King Hua killed a priest in the 12th century, and as a result the gods sent a severe drought to Hana as a punishment.

Three centuries later another ruler came out of Hana who was to change the course of Maui's history: Piilani was the first ruler to unite all of Maui. His rule was a time of not only peace, but Piilani also built fishponds and irrigation fields and began creating a paved road some 4 to 6 feet wide around the entire island. Piilani's sons and his grandson continued these projects and completed the *Alalou*, the royal road that circled the united island. They also completed Hawaii's largest *heiau* (temple) to the god of war, Piilanihale; it still stands today.

Maui was a part of a pivotal change in Hawaii's history: Kamehameha uniting all of the islands. It started in 1759, when yet another battle over land was going on. This time Kalaniopuu, a chief from the Big Island, had captured Hana from the powerful Maui chief Kahikili. Kahikili was busy overtaking Molokai when the Big Island chief stole Hana from him. The Molokai chief escaped and fled with his wife to Hana, where the Big Island chief welcomed him. A few years later, the Molokai chief and his wife had a baby girl in Hana, named Kaahumanu, who later married Kamehameha and during her lifetime would make major changes in Hawaii's culture, like breaking the taboo of women eating with men and converting to Christianity, which lead the way for thousands of Hawaiians to adopt the religion of their queen.

THE "FATAL CATASTROPHE"   No ancient Hawaiian ever imagined a *haole* (a white person; literally, one with "no breath") would ever appear on one of these "floating islands." But then one day in 1778, just such a person sailed into Waimea Bay on Kauai, where he was welcomed as the god Lono.

The man was 50-year-old Captain James Cook, already famous in Britain for "discovering" much of the South Pacific. Now on his third great voyage of exploration, Cook had set sail from Tahiti

northward across uncharted waters to find the mythical Northwest Passage that was said to link the Pacific and Atlantic oceans. On his way Cook stumbled upon the Hawaiian Islands quite by chance. He named them the Sandwich Islands, for the Earl of Sandwich, first lord of the admiralty, who had bankrolled the expedition.

Overnight, Stone Age Hawaii entered the age of iron. Nails were traded for freshwater, pigs, and the affections of Hawaiian women. The sailors brought syphilis, measles, and other diseases to which the Hawaiians had no natural immunity, thereby unwittingly wreaking havoc on the native population.

After his unsuccessful attempt to find the Northwest Passage, Cook returned to Kealakekua Bay on the Big Island, where a fight broke out over an alleged theft, and the great navigator was killed by a blow to the head. After this "fatal catastrophe," the British survivors sailed home. But Hawaii was now on the sea charts, and traders on the fur route between Canada and China anchored in Hawaii to get fresh water. More trade— and more disastrous liaisons—ensued.

The foreigners also had something the Hawaiians had never seen before: cannons and guns. Kamehameha, at the time a rising chief on the Big Island, was able to get his hands on these weapons, and his use of them would change the course of history: Kamehameha was the first ruler to unite all of the Hawaiian islands.

Kamehameha used the weapons in 1790 while battling the warriors of Maui's chief Kahekili at Iao. His troops followed up with a bloody battle in Iao where the Maui warriors were slaughtered. After finally conquering Maui 5 years later, Kamehameha made Lahaina the capitol of his new united kingdom, stopping there in 1801 with his fleet of Pelehu war canoes on his way to do battle on Oahu and Kauai. Kamehameha stayed in Lahaina for a year, constructing the

"Brick Palace," Hawaii's first Western-style structure. Queen Kaahumanu would have nothing to do with it and slept in a grass hut nearby.

WHALERS & MISSIONARIES On a bright, sunny day in 1819, the first whaling ship dropped anchor in Lahaina. Sailors on the *Bellina* were looking for freshwater and supplies, but they found beautiful women, mind-numbing grog, and a tropical paradise. A few years later, in 1823, the whalers were to meet rivals for this hedonistic playground: the missionaries. The God-fearing missionaries arrived from New England bent on converting the pagans. They chose Lahaina because it was the capital of Hawaii.

Intent on instilling their brand of rock-ribbed Christianity in the islands, the missionaries clothed the natives, banned them from dancing the hula, and nearly dismantled their ancient culture. They tried to keep the whalers and sailors out of the bawdy houses, where a flood of whiskey quenched fleet-size thirsts and where the virtue of native women was never safe.

The missionaries taught reading and writing, created the 12-letter Hawaiian alphabet, started a printing press in Lahaina, and began writing the islands' history, until then only an oral account in half-remembered chants. They also started the first school in Lahaina, which still exists today: Lahainaluna High School.

In Lahaina's heyday some 500 whaling ships a year dropped anchor in the Lahaina Roadstead. In 1845 King Kamehameha III moved the capital of Hawaii from Lahaina to Honolulu, where more commerce could be accommodated in the natural harbor there. Some whaling ships starting skipping Lahaina for the larger port of Honolulu. Fifteen years later the depletion of whales and the emergence of petroleum as a more suitable oil signaled the beginning of the end of the whaling industry.

KING SUGAR EMERGES When the capital of Hawaii was moved to Honolulu, Maui might have taken a back seat to Hawaii's history had it not been for the beginning of a new industry—sugar. In 1849 George Wilfong, a cantankerous sea captain, built a mill in Hana and planted some 60 acres of sugar cane, creating Hawaii's first sugar plantation. The gold rush was on in California, and sugar prices were wildly inflated. Wilfong's harsh personality and the demands he placed on plantation workers did not sit well with the Hawaiians. In 1852 he imported Chinese immigrants to work in his fields. By the end of the 1850s the gold rush had begun to diminish, and the inflated sugar prices dropped. When Wilfong's mill burned down, he finally called it quits.

Sugar production continued in Hana, however. In 1864 two Danish brothers, August and Oscar Unna, started the Hana Plantation. Four years later they imported Japanese immigrants to work the fields.

Some 40 miles away, in Haiku, two sons of missionaries, Samuel Alexander and Henry Baldwin, planted 12 acres of this new crop. The next year Alexander and Baldwin added some 5,000 acres in Maui's central plains and started Hawaii's largest sugar company. They quickly discovered that without the copious amounts of rainfall found in Hana, they would need to get water to their crop, or it would fail. In 1876 they constructed an elaborate ditch system that took water from rainy Haiku some 17 miles away to the dry plains of Wailuku, a move that cemented the future of sugar in Hawaii.

Around the same time, another sugar pioneer, Claus Spreckels, bought up land in the arid desert of Puunene from the Hawaiians who sold him the "cursed" lands at a very cheap price. The Hawaiians were sure they had gotten the better part of the deal because they believed that the lands were haunted.

Spreckels was betting that these "cursed" lands could be very productive if he could get water rights up in the rainy hills and bring that water to Puunene, just as Alexander and Baldwin had done. But first he needed that water. Thus began a series of late-night poker games with the then-king Kalakaua. Spreckels's gamble paid off: Not only did he beat the king at poker (some say he cheated), but he built the elaborate 30-mile Haiku Ditch system, which transported 50 million gallons of water a day from rainy Haiku to dry Puunene.

The big boost to sugar not only on Maui but across the entire state came in 1876 when King Kalakaua negotiated the Sugar Reciprocity Treaty with the United States, giving the Hawaiian sugar industry a "sweet" deal on prices and tariffs.

In 1891 King Kalakaua visited chilly San Francisco, caught a cold, and died in the royal suite of the Sheraton Palace. His sister, Queen Liliuokalani, assumed the throne.

A SAD FAREWELL On January 17, 1893, a group of American sugar planters and missionary descendants, with the support of U.S. Marines, imprisoned Queen Liliuokalani in her own palace in Honolulu; later she penned the sad lyric *"Aloha Oe,"* Hawaii's song of farewell. The monarchy was dead.

A new republic was established, controlled by Sanford Dole, a powerful sugar-cane planter. In 1898 Hawaii became an American territory ruled by Dole and his fellow sugar-cane planters and the Big Five, a cartel that controlled banking, shipping, hardware, and every other facet of economic life in the islands.

Planters imported more contract laborers from Puerto Rico (in 1900), Korea (in 1903), and the Philippines (1907–31). Most of the new immigrants stayed on to establish families and become a part of the islands. Meanwhile, the native Hawaiians became a landless minority in their homeland.

For nearly 75 years, sugar was king, generously subsidized by the U.S. federal government. The sugar planters dominated the territory's economy, shaped its social fabric, and kept the islands in a colonial plantation era with bosses and field hands.

BOMBS AWAY On December 7, 1941, Japanese Zeros came out of the rising sun to bomb American warships based at Pearl Harbor. It was the "day of infamy" that plunged the United States into World War II and gave the nation its revenge-laced battle cry, "Remember Pearl Harbor!"

The aftermath of the attack brought immediate changes to the islands. Martial law was declared, thus stripping the Big Five cartels of their absolute power in a single day. Feared to be spies, Japanese-Americans were interned in Hawaii as well as in California. Hawaii was "blacked out" at night, Waikiki Beach was strung with barbed wire, and Aloha Tower was painted in camouflage. Only young men bound for the Pacific came to Hawaii during the war years. Some came back to graves in a cemetery called The Punchbowl.

During the postwar years the men of Hawaii returned after seeing another, bigger world outside of plantation life and rebelled. Throwing off the mantle of plantation life, the workers struck for higher wages and improved working conditions. Within a few short years after the war, the white, Republican leaders who had ruled since the overthrow of the monarchy were voted out of office, and labor leaders in the Democratic Party were suddenly in power.

TOURISM & STATEHOOD In 1959 Hawaii became the last star on the Stars and Stripes, the 50th state of the union. But that year also saw the arrival of the first jet airliners, which brought 250,000 tourists to the fledgling state.

Tourism had already started on Maui shortly after World War II when Paul I. Fagan, an entrepreneur from San Francisco who had bought the Hana Sugar Co., became the town's angel.

Fagan wanted to retire to Hana, so he focused his business acumen on this tiny town with big problems. Years ahead of his time, he thought tourism might have a future in Hana, so he built a small six-room inn, called Kauiki Inn, which later became the **Hotel Hana-Maui.** When he opened it in October 1946, he said it was for first-class, wealthy travelers (just like his friends). Not only did his friends come, but he pulled off a public relations coup that is still talked about today. Fagan also owned a baseball team, the San Francisco Seals. He figured they needed a spring training area, so why not use Hana? He brought out the entire team to train in Hana, and, more important, he brought out the sports writers. The sports writers penned glowing reports about the town, and one writer gave the town a name that stuck: "Heavenly Hana."

However, it would be another 3 decades before Maui became a popular visitor destination in Hawaii. Waikiki was king in the tourism industry, seeing some 16,000 visitors a year by the end of the 1960s, and some four million a year by the end of the 1970s. In 1960 Amfac, owner of Pioneer Sugar Company, looked at the area outside of Lahaina that was being used to dump sugar-cane refuse and saw another use for the beachfront land. The company decided to build a manicured, planned luxury resort in the Kaanapali area. They built it, and people came.

A decade later, Alexander & Baldwin, now the state's largest sugar company, looked at the arid land they owned south of Kihei and also saw possibilities: The resort destination of Wailea was born.

By the mid-1970s some one million visitors a year were coming to Maui. Ten years later the number was up to two million.

At the close of the 20th century, the visitor industry has replaced agriculture as Maui's number-one industry. Maui is the second-largest visitors' destination in Hawaii. For 10 years in a row, the readers of *Condé Nast Traveller* and *Travel and Leisure* magazines have voted Maui the "Best Island in the World."

2 Maui Today

Since the 1970s Maui has seen a rapid increase in the number of visitors to this sleepy, agrarian community, which found itself suddenly designated the "in" place to visit. The islanders spent the 1970s trying to adjust not only to this sudden influx of visitors but also to the fact that the visitors liked what they saw and wanted to stay. Seemingly overnight a massive building campaign began, with condominiums mushrooming along the coastline.

By the 1980s the furious pace of building had slowed, but the new visitors to the island were no longer content to just sit on the beach. They wanted snorkeling and sailing trips, bike rides down Haleakala, and guided tours to Hana. A new industry developed to serve these action-oriented vacationers.

In the 1990s Hawaii's state economy went into a tailspin following a series of events: First, the Gulf War severely curtailed air travel to the island; then, Hurricane Iniki slammed into Kauai, crippling its infrastructure; and finally, sugar-cane companies across the state began shutting down, laying off thousands of workers.

Maui, however, seemed to be able to weather this turbulent economic storm. As the rest of the state struggled with the stormy economy, the outlook remained sunny and clear on Maui.

What did Maui have that the other islands didn't? According to experts, the farsightedness to build up the island's name recognition in the fickle tourism industry, coupled with a diversified economy. Not only had Maui started planning "destination resort areas" in the 1960s, with Kaanapali the first planned resort area outside of Waikiki, but the island's tourism industry also knew that a reputation for the ability to deliver was the key to success. Or as one expert put it: "Maui has been unbelievably successful at name recognition. You'd be hard-pressed to find someone in the U.S. or Canada over 20 years old who has not heard of Maui."

In addition, Maui did not put all its eggs into the visitor-industry basket. Island leaders continued to nurture Maui's agricultural roots, but instead of wooing giant agribusiness, they courted small-niche farming: organic farmers, the flower industry, and herb growers. The island also branched out into various high-tech fields, including the Internet industry. It's no coincidence that just as the World Wide Web was starting to become a household word, Maui's visitor industry—from tiny, two-bedroom B&Bs to megaresorts—had one of the highest rates of websites per capita in the United States.

Maui has seen centuries of change since Captain Cook first cruised by. The island, once populated only by Hawaiians, is today home to a diverse mix of Asians, Pacific Islanders, Caucasians, and African Americans. L.A.-style traffic jams and strip malls have arrived, but the island still maintains its natural beauty, with golden beaches, tropical waterfalls, and misty upcountry hills. The population continues to learn lessons in balance: how to nurture the visitor industry without destroying the very product that visitors come to see.

3 Life & Language

Plantations brought so many different people to Hawaii that the state is now a rainbow of ethnic groups: Living here are Caucasians, African Americans, American Indians, Eskimos, Japanese, Chinese, Filipinos, Koreans, Tahitians, Vietnamese, Hawaiians, Samoans, Tongans, and other Asian and Pacific islanders. Add a few Canadians, Dutch, English, French, Germans, Irish, Italians, Portuguese, Scottish, Puerto Ricans, and Spaniards. Everyone's a minority here.

In combination, it's a remarkable potpourri. Many retain an element of the traditions of their homeland. Some Japanese Americans in Hawaii, generations removed from the homeland, are more traditional than the Japanese of Tokyo. And the same is true of many Chinese, Korean, Filipinos, and others, making Hawaii a kind of living museum of various Asian and Pacific cultures.

THE HAWAIIAN LANGUAGE
Almost everyone here speaks English. But many folks in Hawaii now speak Hawaiian as well. All visitors will hear the words *aloha* and *mahalo* (thank you). If you've just arrived, you're a *malihini*. Someone who's been here a long time is a *kamaaina*. When you finish a job or your meal, you are *pau* (finished). On Friday it's *pau hana*, work finished. You eat *pupu* (Hawaii's version of hors d'oeuvres) when you go *pau hana*.

The Hawaiian alphabet, created by the New England missionaries, has only 12 letters: the five regular vowels (a, e, i, o, and u) and seven consonants (h, k, l, m, n, p, and w). The vowels are pronounced in the Roman fashion, that is, *ah, ay, ee, oh,* and *oo* (as in "too")—not *ay, ee, eye, oh,* and *you,* as in English. For example, *huhu* is pronounced *who-who.* Most vowels are sounded separately, though some are pronounced together, as in Kalakaua: *Kah-lah-cow-ah.*

WHAT *HAOLE* MEANS When Hawaiians first saw Western visitors, they called the pale-skinned, frail men *haole* because they looked so out of breath. In Hawaiian, *ha* means *breath,* and *ole* means an absence of what precedes it. Today the term *haole* is generally a synonym for Caucasian or foreigner and is used without any intended disrespect. If uttered by an angry stranger who adds certain adjectives (like "stupid"), the term can be construed as a racial slur.

SOME HAWAIIAN WORDS Here are some basic Hawaiian words that you'll often hear in Hawaii and see throughout this book. For a more complete list of Hawaiian words, point your Web browser to www.geocities.com/~olelo/hl tableofcontents.html or www.hisurf.com/hawaiian/dictionary.html.

alii Hawaiian royalty

aloha greeting or farewell

halau school

hale house or building

heiau Hawaiian temple or place of worship

kahuna priest or expert

kamaaina old-timer

kapa tapa, bark cloth

kapu taboo, forbidden

keiki child

lanai porch or veranda

lomilomi massage

mahalo thank you

makai a direction, toward the sea

mana spirit power

mauka a direction, toward the mountains

muumuu loose-fitting gown or dress

ono delicious

pali cliff

paniolo Hawaiian cowboy(s)

wiki quick

PIDGIN: 'EH FO'REAL, BRAH

If you venture beyond the tourist areas, you might hear another local tongue: pidgin English, a conglomeration of slang and words from the Hawaiian language. "Broke da mouth" (tastes really good) is the favorite pidgin phrase and one you might hear; "'Eh fo'real, brah" means "It's true, brother." You could be invited to hear an elder "talk story" (relating myths and memories). But because pidgin is really the province of the locals, your visit to Hawaii is likely to pass without your hearing much pidgin at all.

4 A Taste of Maui

On Maui a great lunch or dinner can lure a foodie halfway across the island. Whether it's haute cuisine, local-style diners, small mom-and-pops, or sunset appetizers in Kaanapali and Wailea, dining matters a lot on this island made for sybarites. Although Maui's restaurant kitchens are at the leading edge of Hawaii's maturing regional cuisine, the small-town charms remain, and countless gastronomic discoveries await the adventurous.

THE NEW GUARD: HAWAII REGIONAL CUISINE

Since the mid-1980s, when Hawaii Regional Cuisine (HRC) ignited a culinary revolution, Hawaii has elevated its standing on the global epicurean map to bona fide star status. Fresh ideas and sophisticated menus have made the islands a culinary destination, applauded and emulated nationwide. (In a tip of the toque to island tradition, *ahi*—a word ubiquitous in Hawaii—has replaced *tuna* on many chic New York menus.)

Waves of new Asian residents have planted the food traditions of their homelands in the fertile soil of Hawaii, resulting in unforgettable taste treats true to their Thai, Vietnamese, Japanese, Chinese, and Indo-Pacific roots. Traditions are mixed and matched—and when combined with the fresh harvests from sea and land for which Hawaii is known, these ethnic and culinary traditions take on renewed vigor and a cross-cultural, yet uniquely Hawaiian, quality.

This is good news for the eager palate. From the five-star restaurant to the informal neighborhood gathering place, from the totally eclectic to the purely Japanese, dining in Hawaii is one great culinary joy ride.

While on Maui, you'll encounter many labels that embrace the fundamentals of HRC and the sophistication, informality, and nostalgia it encompasses. Euro-Asian, Pacific Rim, Indo-Pacific, Euro-Pacific, fusion cuisine—by whatever name, Hawaii Regional Cuisine has evolved as Hawaii's singular cooking style. It highlights the fresh seafood and produce of Hawaii's rich waters and volcanic soil, the cultural traditions of Hawaii's ethnic groups, and the skills of well-trained chefs, who broke ranks with their European predecessors to forge new ground in the 50th state.

Fresh ingredients are foremost here. Farmers and fishermen work together to provide steady supplies of just-harvested seafood, seaweed, fern shoots, vine-ripened tomatoes, goat cheese, lamb, herbs, taro, gourmet lettuces, and countless harvests from land and sea. These ingredients wind up in myriad forms on ever-changing menus, prepared in Asian and Western culinary styles. Exotic fruits introduced by recent Southeast Asian emigrants—such as sapodilla, soursop, and rambutan—are beginning to appear regularly in Chinatown markets. Aquacultured

seafood, from seaweed to salmon to lobster, is a staple on many menus. Additionally, fresh-fruit sauces (mango, litchi, papaya, pineapple, guava), ginger-sesame-wasabi flavorings, corn cakes with sake sauces, tamarind and fish sauces, coconut-chile accents, tropical-fruit vinaigrettes, and other local and newly arrived seasonings from Southeast Asia and the Pacific impart unique qualities to the preparations.

Here's a sampling of what you can expect to find on a Hawaii Regional menu: seared Hawaiian fish with lilikoi shrimp butter; taro-crab cakes; Pahoa corn cakes; Molokai sweet-potato or breadfruit vichyssoise; Ka'u orange sauce and Kahua Ranch lamb; fern shoots from Waipio Valley; Maui onion soup and Hawaiian bouillabaisse, with fresh snapper, Kona crab, and fresh aquacultured shrimp; blackened ahi summer rolls; herb-crusted onaga; and gourmet Waimanalo greens, picked that day. You may also encounter locally made cheeses, squash and taro risottos, Polynesian imu-baked foods, and guava-smoked meats. If there's pasta or risotto or rack of lamb on the menu, it could be nori (red algae) linguine with *opihi* (limpet) sauce, or risotto with local seafood served in taro cups, or rack of lamb in cabernet and hoisin sauce (fermented soybean, garlic, and spices). Watch for ponzu sauce too: It's lemony and zesty, much more flavorful than the soy sauce it resembles.

PLATE LUNCHES & MORE: LOCAL FOOD

At the other end of the spectrum is the vast and endearing world of "local food." By that I mean plate lunches and poke, shave ice and saimin, bento lunches and *manapua*—cultural hybrids all.

Reflecting a polyglot population of many styles and ethnicities, Hawaii's idiosyncratic dining scene is eminently inclusive. Consider Surfer Chic: Barefoot in the sand, in a swimsuit, you chow down on a **plate lunch** ordered from a lunch wagon, consisting of fried mahimahi, "two scoops rice," macaroni salad, and a few leaves of green, typically julienned cabbage. (Generally, teriyaki beef and shoyu chicken are options.) Heavy gravy is often the condiment of choice, accompanied by a soft drink in a paper cup or straight out of the can. Like **saimin**—the local version of noodles in broth topped with scrambled eggs, green onions, and sometimes pork—the plate lunch is Hawaii's version of high camp.

But it was only a matter of time before the humble plate lunch became a culinary icon in Hawaii. These days even the most chichi restaurant has a version of this modest island symbol (not at plate-lunch prices, of course), while vendors selling the real thing—carb-driven meals served from wagons—have queues that never end.

Because this is Hawaii, at least a few licks of poi—cooked, pounded taro (the traditional Hawaiian staple crop)—are a must. Other **native foods** include those from before and after Western contact, such as *laulau* (pork, chicken, or fish steamed in ti leaves), *Kalua* pork (pork cooked in a Polynesian underground oven known here as an imu), *lomi* salmon (salted salmon with tomatoes and green onions), squid luau (cooked in coconut milk and taro tops), *poke* (cubed raw fish seasoned with onions and seaweed and the occasional sprinkling of roasted kukui nuts), *haupia* (creamy coconut pudding), and *kulolo* (steamed pudding of coconut, brown sugar, and taro).

Bento, another popular quick meal available throughout Hawaii, is a compact, boxed assortment of picnic fare usually consisting of neatly arranged sections of rice, pickled vegetables, and fried chicken, beef, or pork. Increasingly, however, the bento is becoming more health-conscious, as in macrobiotic or vegetarian brown-rice bentos. A derivative of the modest lunch box for Japanese immigrants who once labored in the sugar and

pineapple fields, bentos are dispensed everywhere, from department stores to corner delis and supermarkets.

Also from the plantations come **manapua,** a bready, doughy sphere filled with tasty fillings of sweetened pork or sweet beans. In the old days the Chinese "manapua man" would make his rounds with bamboo containers balanced on a rod over his shoulders. Today you'll find white or whole-wheat manapua containing chicken, vegetables, curry, and other savory fillings.

The daintier Chinese delicacy **dim sum** is made of translucent wrappers filled with fresh seafood, pork hash, and vegetables, served for breakfast and lunch in Chinatown restaurants. The Hong Kong–style dumplings are ordered fresh and hot from bamboo steamers rolled on carts from table to table. Much like hailing a taxi in Manhattan, you have to be quick and loud for dim sum.

For dessert or a snack, particularly on Oahu's north shore, the prevailing choice is **shave ice,** the island version of a snow cone. Particularly on hot, humid days, long lines of shave-ice lovers gather for heaps of finely shaved ice topped with sweet tropical syrups. (The sweet-sour *li hing mui* flavor is a current favorite.) The fast-melting mounds, which require prompt, efficient consumption, are quite the local summer ritual for sweet tooths. Aficionados order shave ice with ice cream and sweetened adzuki beans plopped in the middle.

PINEAPPLES, PAPAYAS & OTHER ISLAND FRUITS

Lanai isn't growing pineapples commercially anymore, but low-acid, white-fleshed, wondrously sweet Hawaiian Sugar Loaf pineapples are being commercially grown, on a small scale, on Kauai as well as the Big Island. That's just one of the developments in the rapidly changing agricultural landscape in Hawaii. The litchilike Southeast Asian rambutan;

longan (Chinese dragon's-eye litchis); 80-pound Indian jackfruits; the star fruit; the custardy mangosteen; and the usual mangoes, papayas, guava, and *lilikoi* (passion fruit) make up the dazzling parade of fresh island fruits that come and go with the seasons.

Papayas, bananas, and **pineapples** grow year-round, but pineapples are always sweetest, juiciest, and most yellow in the summer. Although new papaya hybrids are making their way into the marketplace, the classic bests include the fleshy, firm-textured Kahuku papayas, the queen of them all; the Big Island's sweet Kapoho and Puna papayas; and the fragile, juicy, and reddish-orange Sunrise papayas from Kauai. Sunrise fans claim they're sweeter, juicier, and more elegant than all others. Apple bananas are smaller, firmer, and tarter than the standard, and they are a local specialty that flourish throughout the islands.

Litchis and **mangoes** are long-awaited summer fruit. Mangoes begin appearing in late spring or early summer and can be found at roadside fruit stands, markets, and health-food stores (where the high prices may shock you). My favorite is the white pirie—rare and resinous, fiberless, and so sweet and juicy it makes the high-profile Hayden seem prosaic. A popular newcomer is the Rapoza mango, a fiberless, 2-pound fruit fairly new to the islands, yet already earning raves for its sweetness and resilience.

Watermelons are a summer hit and a signature of Molokai and Oahu. In Hawaii, more watermelons are consumed per capita than in any other state. Kahuku watermelons, available in the summer months, give the popular Molokai variety a run for its money. Juicy, fleshy, and sweet, Kahuku watermelons are now grown primarily in Waialua on Oahu's north shore, while production of the Molokai variety has expanded to central Oahu. Most markets sell these bulging orbs of refreshment throughout summer and early fall.

In the competitive world of **oranges,** the Kau Gold navel oranges from the southern Big Island put Sunkist to shame. Grown in the volcanic soil and sunny conditions of the South Point region (the southernmost point in the United States), the "Ugly Orange" is brown, rough, and anything but pretty. But the browner and uglier they look, the sweeter and juicier they taste. Because the thin-skinned oranges are tree-ripened, they're fleshy and heavy with liquid, and they will spoil you for life. Although these oranges have traditionally been a winter fruit, they're appearing more abundantly year-round.

AHI, ONO & OPAKAPAKA: A HAWAIIAN SEAFOOD PRIMER

The seafood in Hawaii has been described as the best in the world. And why not? Without a doubt, the islands' surrounding waters, including the waters of the remote northwestern Hawaiian Islands, and a growing aquaculture industry contribute to the high quality of the seafood here.

The reputable restaurants in Hawaii buy fresh fish daily at predawn auctions or from local fishermen. Some chefs even catch their ingredients themselves. "Still wiggling" or "just off the hook" are the ultimate terms for freshness in Hawaii.

Although some menus include the Western description for the fresh fish used, most often the local nomenclature is listed, turning dinner for the uninitiated into a confusing, quasi-foreign experience. To help familiarize you with the menu language of Hawaii, here's a basic glossary of island fish:

ahi yellowfin or big-eye tuna, important for its use in sashimi and poke at sushi bars and in Hawaii Regional Cuisine

aku   skipjack tuna, heavily used by local families in home cooking and poke

ehu   red snapper, delicate and sumptuous, yet lesser known than *opakapaka*

hapuupuu   grouper, a sea bass whose use is expanding

hebi   spearfish, mildly flavored, and frequently featured as the "catch of the day" in upscale restaurants

kajiki   Pacific blue marlin, also called *au*, with a firm flesh and high fat content that make it a plausible substitute for tuna

kumu   goatfish, a luxury item on Chinese and upscale menus, served *en papillote* or steamed whole, Oriental-style, with scallions, ginger, and garlic

mahimahi   dolphin fish (the game fish, not the mammal) or dorado, a classic sweet, white-fleshed fish requiring vigilance among purists because it's often disguised as fresh when it's actually "fresh-frozen"—a big difference

monchong   bigscale or sickle pomfret, an exotic, tasty fish, scarce but gaining a higher profile on Hawaiian Island menus

nairagi   striped marlin, also called *au*; good as sashimi and in poke, and often substituted for ahi in raw-fish products

onaga   ruby snapper, a luxury fish, versatile, moist, and flaky

ono   wahoo, firmer and drier than the snappers, often served grilled and in sandwiches

opah   moonfish, rich and fatty, and versatile—cooked, raw, smoked, and broiled

opakapaka   pink snapper, light, flaky, and luxurious, suited for sashimi, poaching, sautéing, and baking; the best-known upscale fish

papio   jack trevally, light, firm, and flavorful and favored in island cookery

shutome   broadbill swordfish, with beeflike texture and rich flavor

tombo   albacore tuna, with a high fat content, suitable for grilling

uhu   parrotfish, most often encountered steamed, Chinese-style

uku   gray snapper of clear, pale-pink flesh, delicately flavored and moist

ulua   large jack trevally, firm-fleshed and versatile

5 The Natural World: An Environmental Guide to Maui

Born of violent volcanic eruptions from deep beneath the ocean's surface, the first Hawaiian islands emerged about 70 million years ago—more than 200 million years after the major continental land masses formed. Two thousand miles from the nearest continent, Mother Nature's fury began to carve beauty from barren rock. Untiring volcanoes spewed forth curtains of fire that cooled into stone, while severe tropical storms, some with hurricane-force winds, battered and blasted the cooling lava rock into a series of shapes. Ferocious earthquakes flattened, shattered, and reshaped the islands into precipitous valleys, jagged cliffs, and recumbent flatlands. Monstrous surf and gigantic tidal waves rearranged and polished the lands above and below the reaches of the tide.

It took millions upon millions of years for nature to chisel the familiar form of Maui's majestic Haleakala peak, to create the waterfalls on Molokai's northern side, to shape the reefs of Hulopoe Bay on Lanai, and to establish the lush rainforests of the Hana coastline. The result is an island-chain-within-a-chain like no other on the planet—rich in unique flora and fauna, surrounded by a vibrant underwater world that will haunt you forever.

THE FLORA OF MAUI

Maui radiates with the sweet smell of flowers, lush vegetation, and exotic plant life.

AFRICAN TULIP TREES   Even from afar, you can see the flaming red flowers on these large trees, which can grow to be more than 50 feet tall. The buds hold water, and Hawaiian children use the flowers as water pistols.

ANGEL'S TRUMPETS   These small trees can grow up to 20 feet tall, with an abundance of large (up to 10 in. diameter) pendants—white or pink flowers that resemble, well, trumpets. The Hawaiians call them *nana-honua,* which means "earth gazing." The flowers, which bloom continually from early spring to late fall, have a musky scent. *Warning:* All parts of the plant are poisonous and contain a strong narcotic.

ANTHURIUMS   Anthuriums originally came from the tropical Americas and the Caribbean islands. There are more than 550 species, but the most popular are the heart-shaped red, orange, pink, white, and purple flowers with tail-like spathes. Look for the heart-shaped green leaves in shaded areas. These exotic plants have no scent but will last several weeks as cut flowers. Anthuriums are particularly prevalent on the Big Island.

BANANA TREES   Edible bananas are among the oldest of the world's food crops. By the time Europeans arrived in the islands, the Hawaiians had planted more than 40 types of bananas. Most banana plants have long green leaves hanging from the tree, with the flowers giving way to fruit in clusters.

BANYAN TREES   Among the world's largest trees, banyans have branches that grow out and away from the trunk, forming descending roots that grow down to the ground to feed and form additional trunks, making the tree very stable during tropical storms. The banyan in the courtyard next to the old Court House in Lahaina, Maui, is an excellent example of a spreading banyan—it covers ⅔ acres.

BIRDS OF PARADISE   These natives of Africa have become something of a trademark of Hawaii. They're easily recognizable by the orange-and-blue flowers nestled in gray-green bracts, looking somewhat like birds in flight.

BOUGAINVILLEA   Originally from Brazil, these vines feature colorful, tissue-thin bracts, ranging in color from majestic purple to fiery orange, that hide tiny white flowers. A good place to spot them is on the Big Island, along the Queen Kaahumanu Highway stretching from Kona Airport to Kailua-Kona.

BREADFRUIT TREES   A large tree—more than 60 feet tall—with broad, sculpted, dark-green leaves, the famous breadfruit produces a round, head-size green fruit that's a staple in the diets of all Polynesians. When roasted or baked, the whitish-yellow meat tastes somewhat like a sweet potato.

BROMELIADS   There are more than 1,400 species of bromeliads, of which the pineapple plant is the best known. "Bromes," as they're affectionately called, are generally spiky plants ranging in size from a few inches to several feet in diameter. They're popular not only for their unusual foliage but also for their strange and wonderful flowers. Used widely in landscaping and interior decoration, especially in resort areas, bromeliads are found on every island.

COFFEE   Hawaii is the only state that produces coffee commercially. Coffee is an evergreen shrub with shiny, waxy, dark-green, pointed leaves. The flower is a small, fragrant white blossom that develops into ½-inch berries that turn bright red when ripe. Look for coffee at elevations above 1,500 feet on the Kona

Marijuana

This not-so-rare-and-unusual plant—called *pakalolo,* or "crazy weed," in Hawaiian—is grown throughout the islands, despite years of police efforts to eradicate the plant. You probably won't see it as you drive along the roads, but if you go hiking, you may glimpse the feathery green leaves with tight clusters of buds. Don't be tempted to pick a few buds: The captains of this nefarious industry don't take kindly to poaching.

---

side of the Big Island and on large coffee plantations on Kauai, Molokai, Oahu, and Maui.

GINGER   White-and-yellow ginger flowers are perhaps the most fragrant in Hawaii. Usually found in clumps growing 4 to 7 feet tall in areas blessed by rain, these sweet-smelling, 3-inch-wide flowers are composed of three dainty petal-like stamens and three long, thin petals. Ginger was introduced to Hawaii in the 19th century from the Indonesia-Malaysia area. Look for white-and-yellow ginger from late spring to fall. If you see ginger on the side of the road, stop and pick a few blossoms—your car will be filled with a divine fragrance for the rest of the day.

Other members of the ginger family frequently seen in Hawaii include red, shell, and torch ginger. Red ginger consists of tall, green stalks with foot-long red "flower heads." The red "petals" are actually bracts, which protect the 1-inch-long white flowers. Red ginger, which does not share the heavenly smell of white ginger, lasts a week or longer when cut. Look for red ginger from spring through late fall. Shell ginger, which originated in India and Burma, thrives in cool, wet mountain forests. These plants, with their pearly white, clamshell-like blossoms, bloom from spring to fall.

Perhaps the most exotic ginger is the red or pink torch ginger. Cultivated in Malaysia as seasoning, torch ginger rises directly out of the ground. The flower stalks, which are about 5 to 8 inches in length, resemble the fire of a lighted torch. This is one of the few types of ginger that can bloom year-round.

HELICONIA   Some 80 species of the colorful heliconia family came to Hawaii from the Caribbean and Central and South America. The bright yellow, red, green, and orange bracts overlap and appear to unfold like origami birds. The most obvious heliconia to spot is the lobster claw, which resembles a string of boiled crustacean pincers. Another prolific heliconia is the parrot's beak: Growing to about hip height, it's composed of bright-orange flower bracts with black tips. Look for parrot's beaks in spring and summer.

HIBISCUS   The 4- to 6-inch hibiscus flowers bloom year-round and come in a range of colors, from lily white to lipstick red. The flowers resemble crepe paper, with stamens and pistils protruding spire-like from the center. Hibiscus hedges can grow up to 15 feet tall. The yellow hibiscus is Hawaii's official state flower.

JACARANDA   Beginning around March and sometimes lasting until early May, these huge, lacy-leaved trees metamorphose into large clusters of spectacular lavender-blue sprays. The bell-shaped flowers drop quickly, leaving a majestic purple carpet beneath the tree.

LITCHI   This evergreen tree, which can grow to well over 30 feet across, originated in China. Small flowers grow into panicles about a foot long in June and July. The round, red-skinned fruit appears shortly afterward.

MACADAMIA   A transplant from Australia, macadamia nuts have become a commercial crop in recent decades in Hawaii, especially on the Big Island and Maui. The large trees—up to 60 feet tall—bear a hard-shelled nut encased in a leathery husk, which splits open and dries when the nut is ripe.

MANGO   From Indonesia and Malaysia comes the delicious mango, a fruit with peachlike flesh. Mango season usually begins in the spring and lasts through the summer, depending on the variety. The trees can grow to more than 100 feet tall. The tiny reddish flowers give way to a green fruit that turns red-yellow when ripe. Note that mango sap can cause a skin rash on some people.

MONKEYPOD TREES   The monkeypod is one of Hawaii's most majestic trees; it grows to more than 80 feet tall and 100 feet across. Seen near older homes and in parks, the leaves of the monkeypod drop in February and March. Its wood is a favorite of woodworking artisans.

NIGHT-BLOOMING CEREUS   Look along rock walls for this spectacular night-blooming flower. Originally from Central America, this vinelike member of the cactus family has green scalloped edges and produces foot-long white flowers that open as darkness falls and wither as the sun rises. The plant also bears an edible red fruit.

ORCHIDS   To many minds, nothing says Hawaii more than orchids. The orchid family is the largest in the entire plant kingdom. The most widely grown variety—and the major source of flowers for leis and garnish for tropical libations—is the vanda orchid. The vandas used in Hawaii's commercial flower industry are generally lavender or white, but they grow in a rainbow of colors, shapes, and sizes. The orchids used for corsages are the large, delicate cattleya; the ones used in floral arrangements—you'll probably see them in your hotel lobby—are usually dendrobiums.

PAPAYA   One of the sweetest of all tropical fruits, the pear-shaped papaya turns yellow or reddish pink when ripe. They are found at the base of the large, scalloped-shaped leaves on a pedestal-like, nonbranched tree whose trunk is hollow. Papayas ripen year-round.

PLUMERIA   Also known as frangipani, this sweet-smelling, five-petal flower, found in clusters on trees, is the most popular choice of lei makers. The Singapore plumeria has five creamy-white petals, with a touch of yellow in the center. Another popular variety, ruba—with flowers from soft pink to flaming red—is also used in leis. When picking plumeria, be careful of the sap from the flower—it's poisonous and can stain clothes.

PROTEA   Originally from South Africa, this unusual oversize shrub comes in more than 40 different varieties. The flowers of one species resemble pincushions; those of another look like a bouquet of feathers. Once dried, proteas will last for years.

SILVERSWORD   This very uncommon and unusual plant is seen only on the Big Island and in the Haleakala Crater on Maui. This rare relative of the sunflower family blooms between July and September. The silversword in bloom is a fountain of red-petaled, daisylike flowers that turn silver soon after blooming.

TARO   Around pools, near streams, and in neatly planted fields, you'll see these green heart-shaped leaves, whose dense roots are a Polynesian staple. The ancient Hawaiians pounded the roots into poi. Originally from Sri Lanka, taro is not only a food crop but is also grown for ornamental reasons.

THE FAUNA OF MAUI

When the first Polynesians arrived in Hawaii between A.D. 500 and 800, scientists say they found some 67 varieties of endemic Hawaiian birds, a third of which are now believed to be extinct. They did not find any reptiles, amphibians, mosquitoes, lice, fleas, or even a cockroach.

There were only two endemic mammals: the hoary bat and the monk seal. The **hoary bat** must have accidentally blown to Hawaii at some point, from either North or South America. It can still be seen during its early-evening forays, especially around the Kilauea Crater on the Big Island.

The **Hawaiian monk seal,** a relative of warm-water seals found in the Caribbean and the Mediterranean, was nearly slaughtered into extinction for its skin and oil during the 19th century. These seals have recently experienced a minor population explosion; sometimes they even turn up at various beaches throughout the state. They're protected under federal law by the Marine Mammals Protection Act. If you're fortunate enough to see a monk seal, just look—don't disturb one of Hawaii's living treasures.

The first Polynesians brought a few animals from home: dogs, pigs, and chickens (all were for eating), as well as rats (stowaways). All four species are still found in the Hawaiian wild today.

BIRDS

More species of native birds have become extinct in Hawaii in the past 200 years than anywhere else on the planet. Of the 67 native species, 23 are extinct and 30 are endangered. Even the Hawaiian crow, **alala,** is threatened.

The **aeo,** or Hawaiian stilt, a 16-inch-long bird with a black head, a black coat, a white underside, and long pink legs, can be found in protected wetlands like the Kanaha Wildlife Sanctuary (where it shares its natural habitat with the Hawaiian coot) and the Kealia Pond.

Endemic to the islands, the **nene** is Hawaii's state bird. It's currently being brought back from the brink of extinction through captive breeding and by strenuous protection laws. A relative of the Canada goose, the nene stands about 2 feet high and has a black head and yellow cheek, a buff neck with deep furrows, a grayish-brown body, and clawed feet. It gets its name from its two-syllable, high nasal call: "nay-nay." The approximately 500 nenes in existence can be seen at Haleakala National Park.

The Hawaiian short-eared owl, **pueo,** which grows to between 12 and 17 inches in size, can be seen at dawn and dusk, when the black-billed, brown-and-white bird goes hunting for rodents. Pueos are highly regarded by Hawaiians; according to legend, spotting a pueo is a good omen.

SEA LIFE

Approximately 680 species of fish are known to inhabit the waters around the Hawaiian Islands. Of those, approximately 450 species stay close to the reef and inshore areas.

CORAL   The reefs surrounding Hawaii are made up of various coral and algae. The living coral grows through sunlight

---

Leapin' Lizards!

Geckos are harmless, soft-skinned, insect-eating lizards that come equipped with suction pads on their feet, enabling them to climb walls and windows to reach tasty insects like mosquitoes and cockroaches. You'll see these little guys on windows outside a lighted room at night or hear their cheerful chirp.

that feeds a specialized algae, which in turn allows the development of the coral's calcareous skeleton. The reef, which takes thousands of years to develop, attracts and supports fish and crustaceans, which use it for food and habitat. Mother Nature can batter the reef with a strong storm, but humans have proven far more destructive.

The corals most frequently seen in Hawaii are hard, rocklike formations named for their familiar shapes: antler, cauliflower, finger, plate, and razor coral. Some coral appears soft, such as tube coral; it can be found in the ceilings of caves. Black coral, which resembles winter-bare trees or shrubs, is found at depths of more than 100 feet.

REEF FISH Of the approximately 450 types of reef fish here, about 27% are native to Hawaii and are found nowhere else in the world. During the millions of years it took for the islands to sprout up from the sea, ocean currents—mainly from Southeast Asia—carried thousands of marine animals and plants to Hawaii's reef; of those, approximately 100 species adapted and thrived. You're likely to spot one or more of the following fish while underwater:

Angelfish can be distinguished by the spine, located low on the gill plate. These fish are very shy; several species live in colonies close to coral.

Blennies are small, elongated fish, ranging from 2 to 10 inches long, with the majority in the 3- to 4-inch range. Blennies are so small that they can live in tide pools; you might have a hard time spotting one.

Butterfly fish, among the most colorful of the reef fish, are usually seen in pairs (scientists believe they mate for life) and appear to spend most of their day feeding. There are 22 species of butterfly fish, of which three (bluestripe, lemon or milletseed, and multiband or pebbled butterfly fish) are endemic. Most butterfly

fish have a dark band through the eye and a spot near the tail resembling an eye, meant to confuse their predators (moray eels love to lunch on them).

Moray and **conger eels** are the most common eels seen in Hawaii. Morays are usually docile except when provoked or when there's food around. Unfortunately, some morays have been fed by divers and now associate divers with food; thus, they can become aggressive. But most morays like to keep to themselves. While morays may look menacing, conger eels look downright happy, with big lips and pectoral fins (situated so that they look like big ears) that give them the appearance of a perpetually smiling face. Conger eels have crushing teeth so they can feed on crustaceans; because they're sloppy eaters, they usually live with shrimp and crabs that feed off the crumbs they leave.

Parrotfish, one of the largest and most colorful of the reef fish, can grow up to 40 inches long. They're easy to spot— their front teeth are fused together, protruding like buck teeth that allow them to feed by scraping algae from rocks and coral. The rocks and coral pass through the parrotfish's system, resulting in fine sand. In fact, most of the white sand found in Hawaii is parrotfish waste; one large parrotfish can produce a ton of sand a year. Native parrotfish species include yellowbar, regal, and spectacled.

Scorpion fish are what scientists call "ambush predators": They hide under camouflaged exteriors and ambush their prey. Several kinds sport a venomous dorsal spine. These fish don't have a gas bladder, so when they stop swimming, they sink—that's why you usually find them "resting" on ledges and on the ocean bottom. They're not aggressive, but be very careful where you put your hands and feet in the water so as to avoid those venomous spines.

Surgeonfish, sometimes called *tang,* get their name from the scalpel-like spines located on each side of the body near the base of the tail. Several surgeonfish, such as the brightly colored yellow tang, are boldly colored; others are adorned in more conservative shades of gray, brown, or black. The only endemic surgeonfish—and the most abundant in Hawaiian waters—is the convict tang, a pale white fish with vertical black stripes (like a convict's uniform).

Wrasses are a very diverse family of fish, ranging in length from 2 to 15 inches. Wrasses can change gender from female to male. Some have brilliant coloration that changes as they age. Several types of wrasse are endemic to Hawaii: Hawaiian cleaner, shortnose, belted, and gray (or old woman).

GAME FISH   Hawaii is known around the globe as *the* place for big-game fish—marlin, swordfish, and tuna. Six kinds of **billfish** are found in the offshore waters around the islands: Pacific blue marlin, black marlin, sailfish, broadbill swordfish, striped marlin, and shortbill spearfish. Hawaii billfish range in size from the 20-pound shortbill spearfish and striped marlin to the 1,805-pound Pacific blue marlin, the largest marlin ever caught with rod and reel in the world.

Tuna ranges in size from small (1 lb. or less) mackerel tuna used as bait (Hawaiians call them *oioi*) to 250-pound yellowfin ahi tuna. Other local species of tuna are big-eye, albacore, kawakawa, and skipjack.

Other types of fish, also excellent for eating, include **mahimahi** (also known as dolphin fish or dorado), in the 20- to 70-pound range; **rainbow runner,** from 15 to 30 pounds; and **wahoo** (ono), from 15 to 80 pounds. Shoreline fishermen are always on the lookout for **trevally** (the state record for a giant trevally is 191 lb.), **bonefish, ladyfish, threadfin, leatherfish,** and **goatfish.** Bottom fishermen pursue a range of **snapper**—red, pink, gray, and others—as well as **sea bass** (the state record is a whopping 563 lb.) and **amberjack** (which weigh up to 100 lb.).

WHALES   Humpback whales are popular visitors who come to Hawaii to mate and calve every year, beginning in November and staying until spring (Apr or so), when they return to Alaska. On every island, you can take winter whale-watching cruises that will let you observe these magnificent leviathans up close. You can also spot them from shore—humpbacks grow to up to 45 feet long, so when one breaches (jumps out of the water), you can see it for miles.

Humpbacks are among the biggest whales found in Hawaiian waters, but other whales—such as pilot, sperm, false killer, melon-headed, pygmy killer, and beaked—can be seen year-round, especially in the calm waters off the Big Island's Kona Coast.

SHARKS   Yes, there *are* sharks in Hawaii, but you more than likely won't see one unless you're specifically looking. About 40 different species of sharks inhabit the waters surrounding Hawaii, ranging from the totally harmless whale shark (at 60 ft., the world's largest fish), which has no teeth and is so docile that it frequently lets divers ride on its back, to the not-so-docile, extremely uncommon great white shark. The most common sharks seen in Hawaii are white-tip or gray reef sharks (about 5 ft. long), and black-tip reef sharks (about 6 ft. long).

Index

See also Accommodations and Restaurant indexes, below.

RESTAURANTS

THE NEW TRAVELOCITY GUARANTEE

EVERYTHING YOU BOOK WILL BE RIGHT, OR WE'LL WORK WITH OUR TRAVEL PARTNERS TO MAKE IT RIGHT, RIGHT AWAY.

To drive home the point, we're going to use the word "right" in every single sentence.

Let's get right to it. Right to the meat! Only Travelocity guarantees everything about your booking will be right, or we'll work with our travel partners to make it right, right away. Right on!

Here's a picture taken smack dab right in the middle of Antigua, where the guarantee also covers you.

The guarantee covers all but one of the items pictured to the right.

Now, you may be thinking, "Yeah, right, I'm so sure." That's OK; you have the right to remain skeptical. That is until we mention help is always right around the corner. Call us right off the bat, knowing that our customer service reps are there for you 24/7. Righting wrongs. Left and right.

For example, what if the ocean view you booked actually looks out at a downright ugly parking lot? You'd be right to call – we're there for you. And no one in their right mind would be pleased to learn the rental car place has closed and left them stranded. Call Travelocity and we'll help get you back on the right track.

Now if you're guessing there are some things we can't control, like the weather, well you're right. But we can help you with most things – to get all the details in righting,* visit **travelocity.com/guarantee**.

*Sorry, spelling things right is one of the few things not covered under the guarantee.

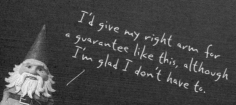

I'd give my right arm for a guarantee like this, although I'm glad I don't have to.

travelocity
You'll never rnam alone.